Reader's Digest

1001 computer hints & tips

Reader's Digest

1001
computer

hints&tips

Published by The Reader's Digest Association Limited

LONDON ■ NEW YORK ■ SYDNEY ■ MONTREAL

Contents

Contents ■

About this book

Whether you're a novice or already familiar with certain aspects of your PC – perhaps you regularly type letters, send e-mail or browse the Net – this comprehensive book will help you to get more from your home computer. It's packed with practical information to expand your knowledge and develop your skills.

The four main parts

The information in *1001 Computer Hints & Tips* is conveniently divided into four parts: Hardware, Windows, Software and The Internet. These parts are colour coded (as shown right) so that you can instantly tell where you are. Within each part, the subjects are arranged in chapters and sections so that you can easily locate the hints and tips on different topics.

Hardware

USB, WiFi, ADSL – a computer can seem a daunting set of initials and acronyms. This section demystifies all the jargon and tells you what you need to know to get your PC running reliably.

Windows

Learn about the world's most popular operating system and how to keep it running smoothly to make the most of your PC's power. Find out how the latest version, Windows XP, can give your computer added stability as well as help you out if you encounter problems.

Software

Discover quick tips and little known features of a wide range of practical programs, both familiar and new. Use the hints and tips to improve your efficiency working with standard software such as Microsoft Word and Excel.

The Internet

This section guides you through the often bewildering world of the Internet straight to the best Websites, and explores the various features that are available. Learn here how to use e-mail to keep in touch with friends, and the best ways to set up your web browser. Whether you're interested in history or travel, music or politics, you'll be amazed by what the web has to offer.

Hardware
Get physical with the building blocks of your PC. Learn to tell your modem from your MIDI, your palmtop from your printer, and find out what they can do for you.

Windows
Open up the world's most popular operating system, and discover what makes your PC tick. Learn how to keep it running like clockwork, and make the most of your PC's power.

Software
Discover the tricks of the trade with everything from Access to Zip files. Master mail merge, menus and macros; design newsletters and cards; create your own images, and conquer spreadsheets.

The Internet
Join the information revolution and learn to surf with confidence. Speed up your Internet access, brush up on your online etiquette, and come to grips with the biggest data bank on the planet.

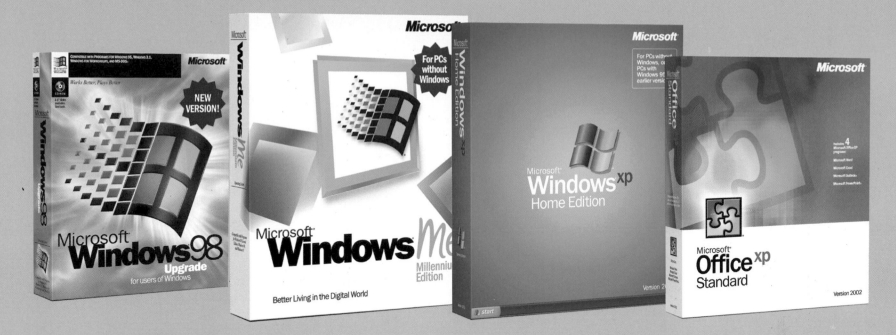

If you don't have a program featured in the book, it is often possible to download a free trial version from the Internet so you can try out the software before buying it

Which software?

This book assumes that you're using a PC running the latest edition of the Windows operating system – Windows XP (Home Edition). However, you will find the majority of the book relevant if you run earlier versions of Windows for home users, such as 98, 98(SE) or Me. You will also need a office program suite, such as Microsoft Office or Works. To create the pages in the book, the latest versions available have been used (Office XP and Works 2002), but most of the features and facilities covered are available in older versions, too. The Internet section assumes that you have an up to date web browser, such as Microsoft Internet Explorer 6, and an e-mail program such as Microsoft Outlook Express.

Glossary

For clear, concise definitions of the computer terms and common jargon used in the book – including instructions on navigating menus, dialogue boxes and Toolbars, and using your mouse – turn to the Glossary on pages 336–41.

JavaScript A programming language that allows designers to create websites with greatly enhanced interactivity.
JPEG Joint Photographic Experts Group. A file format (.jpg or .jpeg extension) used for storing images that have been compressed.
◆ See also **Compressed files**.

What's on a spread?

Chapter Title

Section headings break each chapter into smaller chunks. The sections are, in turn, split into a number of parts separated by coloured heading bars. Each part contains several hints and tips.

Information boxes highlight important extra information and useful Web addresses (see below)

'See also' links at the end of a section take you to other related articles in the book that you may find helpful.

The first few words of each tip are picked out in bold type to help you find the information you need at a glance.

Headers show where you are in the book, giving you the chapter title and section heading.

How-to features give you step-by-step guidelines to help you achieve key tasks on your PC (see opposite).

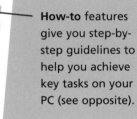

Information boxes

The centre of text operations.

This Toolbar appears when you create a text box with the Text Box tool on the Drawing Toolbar or by going to **Insert → Text Box**.

Use the **Create Text Box Link** tool (far left) to make text automatically flow from one text box to the next. To stop text flowing beyond a selected box, click the **Break Forward Link** button (above right). The links before and after will remain intact.

Click the **Previous** and **Next Text Box** buttons, in Page Layout view, to move quickly between a series of linked text boxes in your document.

Each time you press the **Change Text Direction** button, the rows of text inside the text box you have selected turn in the direction chosen.

You will find information boxes throughout the book. Some provide instructions or extra tips, such as introductions to programs, explanations of terms and tools, and helpful keyboard shortcuts, often illustrated with the buttons and screen elements that you need to look for.

Other boxes list Websites, as often as possible based in the United Kingdom, where you can find up-to-date information on many topics, or those that allow you to download useful software that is often free. Each text panel is has a border that is colour coded to match the section that it sits in.

THE NATION'S PAST ONLINE
Start your exploration of UK histories with these resources.

BBC HISTORY (www.bbc.co.uk/history)
The BBC's History zone has dozens of links to information about many excellent programmes, including A History of Britain, Great Britons and What the Romans, Tudors, Stuarts and Victorians Did For Us!

THE BRITISH LIBRARY (www.bl.uk)
This virtual bookshelf of the world's knowledge is the national library of the United Kingdom.

QUESTIA (www.questia.com)
Research UK history and locate information at the world's largest online library.

HISTORY.UK.COM (www.history.uk.com)
Hundreds of British history links, articles and timelines for tourists, teachers, educators, and history enthusiasts.

BRITAIN EXPRESS (www.britainexpress.com)
A heritage guide to British history and culture, with some great features on the folktales, myths and legends of Britain.

SUITE101.COM (www.suite101.com/ welcome.cfm/british_history)
A well-resourced site with many articles and links that cover modern British histories.

BRITANNIA (www.britannia.com/history)
Although a US site, Britannia's Britain is great for researching the chequered histories of Scotland, Wales and England.

BBC YOUR HISTORY (www.bbc.co.uk/history/your_history)
The BBC's Your History site enables you to explore the history of your family, home and community.

Special features

Interspersed within the pages that make up the main body of the book are 36 feature spreads covering topics of special interest in greater depth. You'll discover more about choosing and using scanners, backing up data on your PC, desktop publishing and Web page creation, as well as shopping and banking and the Internet. Discover the fun side of computing through the features on games and graphics, and how to keep your PC problem-free.

Each feature is colour-coded so you can tell which section of the book it comes from.

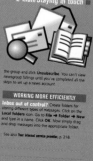

Outlook Express

E-mail/Staying in touch

Optimising performance

Information panels on the feature pages explain how to use particular aspects of the software under discussion or list Websites that contain related information.

For experienced users/Taking charge

Words in bold text linked by arrows (➜) indicate actions to carry out immediately after each other, and often refer to options you will find in on-screen menus.

'How to' step-by-step instructions

Easy-to-follow steps lead you through many of the tasks mentioned in the main entries, such as creating a business card in Word, recovering a deleted file or adding creative effects to a photograph. You are guided through each exercise by snapshots of the PC screen showing what you should be seeing on your own computer monitor as you work. Often more than one picture will be shown for each step.

Bold text is used to highlight the exact text of commands and actions that you should click on screen. An arrow (➜) indicates a series of commands to follow.

How to: Create a letterhead image

1 Open a new document. Go to **View ➜ Header and Footer**. Position your cursor in the header where you want the graphic to appear. Go to **Insert ➜ Picture** and select your graphic in the **Clip Art** or **From File** options. The graphic will be inserted.

2 Click on the image and, using the mouse pointer, drag the corners of the box to resize it. Justifying the image to the left of the screen will also justify the text, so to move your picture independently it needs to be formatted.

3 Right-click on the graphic and select **Format Picture**. Choose the **Layout** tab, choose how to arrange your graphic around the text. Experiment with this, then click **OK** to reposition the image.

Hardware

Get physical with the building blocks of your PC.
Learn to tell your modem from your MIDI, your palmtop
from your printer, and find out what they can do for you.

Your computer

First steps

A safe and comfortable working environment will boost your energy and help you to avoid fatigue.

■ **Ergonomics is the study of workspace design.** If your working area is well designed, you'll be able to work comfortably and efficiently in one position with no adverse side effects to your long-term health. It's all too easy to lose track of time when you are busy, and end up spending hours working at your computer. So, before you get started, make sure you pay particular attention to the way your work station is set up.

■ **Choose the right chair for you.** If you spend a lot of time in front of your computer screen, then a well-designed chair will help you to avoid back aches and tiredness. Back support – particularly in the lumbar region – and height-adjustment features will let you adopt an upright posture while remaining properly supported. You might even consider a knee chair if you suffer

from chronic back problems. For a fully featured chair, try a specialist office supply store. Don't settle for the cheapest chair available. Good ones are often available second-hand.

■ **Sit directly facing your monitor and keyboard.** To avoid back strain, try to sit in an upright position, with your arms roughly horizontal and your eyes level with the top of the monitor's screen. Body joints should be at right angles to each other and your feet placed firmly on the floor.

■ **Make sure you have unobstructed access** to your keyboard, monitor and mouse. To avoid Repetitive Strain Injury (RSI) in your wrists work with a computer desk that provides space for the keyboard and mouse, and a shelf that keeps your monitor at eye level (see p. 18).

■ **Don't rest the heels of your hands on the desk** while typing. Instead, keep the hands parallel with the desk surface. Although a wrist support may look useful, if it's positioned incorrectly it can actually increase strain.

■ **A good-quality monitor will reduce eye strain** and help you to avoid headaches. There are many factors that affect the impact a monitor can have on your health and well-being. These include the amount of ambient light in the room, your monitor's refresh rate (which determines the amount your screen flickers), glare from the screen's surface, reflectiveness, and dot pitch (the distance between identically coloured dots on the monitor). The lower the dot pitch, the clearer the image.

■ **Avoid sitting with your back to a window** or other light source, because your eyes' ability to read the screen is hampered by reflections. Reduce eye strain further by maintaining a distance of 50 mm or more between your eyes and your monitor.

■ **There are several keyboard shapes and layouts** to make typing easier. A contoured keyboard, for instance, provides a

Contoured keyboard

more natural position for your hands. If your desk is cluttered, try a wireless keyboard. This uses a built-in radio transmitter to send signals to a receiver plugged into your PC. Whatever keyboard you use, keep it perpendicular to your body, with the rear edge of the keyboard slightly raised.

■ **Give yourself a break from your PC** every 20 minutes or so. This reduces wear and tear on both body and mind. Keep yourself fresh by stretching, walking around and drinking water. If you're a workaholic, you can get software that prompts you to take a break and suggests anti-RSI exercises – try Ergosense by Omniquad (www.omniquad.com).

Abbreviated as PnP, Plug-and-Play was developed by Microsoft and Intel to allow Windows to set up hardware resources automatically.

■ **If you're buying second-hand** make sure any graphics adaptor, sound card or other hardware you chose is PnP compatible. You may find that it will not work under Windows XP or that you have to configure it by hand – using tiny switches or jumpers on the card, or by using special configuration software. It is also more difficult for Windows to actively manage non-Plug-and-Play hardware.

■ **Each time Windows starts,** it looks for new devices and should detect any new Plug-and-Play hardware attached. However, this sometimes goes wrong. If so, use the 'How to' on p. 15 to locate the device.

If your computer keeps crashing, or the Windows Desktop appears in only 16 colours and the icons are large, right-click on **My Computer** and choose **Properties**. Look in the **Device Manager** for yellow exclamation marks, indicating a device with a 'hardware conflict'. If you still have problems, use Help's useful **Hardware Troubleshooter**, selecting **I need to resolve a hardware conflict on my computer** to run through a series of possible solutions. If this fails, make sure you have the latest drivers for all your hardware. Take a look at the manufacturers' Websites and make sure you get the latest driver for your version of Windows.

ASK THE EXPERTS

Sometimes – no matter how much you know about computers – it's useful to call a helpline when you come across a problem.

■ **Before you call a helpline,** dig out all the relevant information you can about your computer. The person on the other end will want

to know precisely which version of the software you are having a problem with, and which version of Windows you are using. Your helper will also want details about your PC, such as the type of CPU, amount of RAM and hard drive space.

■ **Try to call the hotline number** while in front of your PC. It's likely that you can quickly work through the problem in a few simple steps as the helpline assistant talks you through. Make sure your computer is only running essential programs so nothing slows it down, and – if appropriate – is set up to re-create the problem. Using a mobile phone allows you to connect to the Internet if necessary.

■ **Note the exact text of any error messages** that constantly recur. Make sure you have the precise version number of your software, and details of your operating system and hardware.

■ **Most software and hardware manufacturers** should have Websites that

deal with common problems. New hardware drivers and versions of software are often available for free download. If you can't locate a specific troubleshooting part of a site, look for a Frequently Asked Questions (FAQ) page – it could save you a call to a helpline.

How to: Search for PnP and non-PnP devices

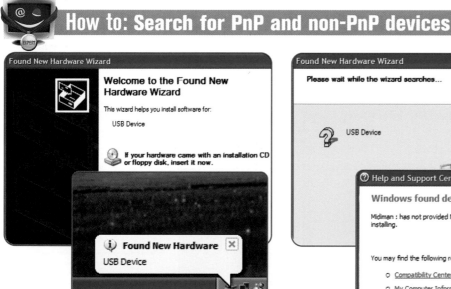

1 Attach your new piece of hardware to your computer via a USB socket (it is safe to do this for USB devices while your computer is still switched on). Windows XP will notify that it has found a new piece of hardware and launch the **Found New Hardware Wizard**.

2 If you have the installation CD that came with the device, insert it and then click Next. If you don't have the disk, click next anyway. Windows XP will search for a suitable driver for your hardware, both on your hard disk and on Microsoft's Website.

3 If nothing is found on the Microsoft Website, the best place to turn is the manufacturer's Website. Download suitable software, if available, and install it following the manufacturer's guidelines – most likely by relaunching the Found New Hardware Wizard.

UNDERSTANDING DEVICE DRIVERS

Device drivers are essential for keeping your computer hardware up-to-date and running smoothly.

■ **Device drivers are small programs** that allow pieces of hardware, such as printers, keyboards and disk drives, to run correctly on the PC. The ones you need for your computer's original configuration will be pre-installed, but if you add new hardware, you will have to install its driver before it will work. Updating device drivers can optimise your computer's performance.

■ **Download the latest drivers for free.** The company that made your hardware will usually post the latest drivers on a Website. Check the site to see if there have been any updates. Other sites such as DriversHQ (www.drivershq.com) and Mister Driver (www.mrdriver.com) list hundreds of driver types. Keep a note of the device's model type and number and make sure you download the correct version. (To update or replace a device driver, see the 'How to', below.)

■ **Beware of beta versions of drivers.** If your PC is working well already, don't rush to download beta versions, which are a pre-release version of the program. As such, they are often not fully tested and can contain glitches and errors. The frustration caused when one crashes in your system far outweighs any possible benefits. Only get new drivers if you really need them, after a system upgrade, for example.

■ **Don't change your mind during installation.** Always let a new driver finish downloading completely without interruption. Stopping an installation halfway through can sometimes badly damage the system files and put your PC out of action until it can be repaired. You may even need to call in professional help, although System Restore should be able to sort out most problems.

■ **To eliminate any installation doubts,** make use of the free software available on the Internet to help you. Microsoft have a library of common drivers approved for Windows XP, or you could try the Driver Detective, available on PC DriversHQ (www.drivershq.com). The site has its own driver database.

PROTECTING AGAINST POWER SURGES

Learn how to use a surge protector to help prevent computer damage.

■ **Surge protectors are adaptors** which fit between your PC and an electrical outlet. Some come with a guarantee against problems caused by surges. Always turn off all devices before plugging and unplugging connections.

■ **A large percentage of data loss** and computer hardware failures are the result of power problems. Even a single surge protector between your computer and the electrical outlet will provide you with protection against voltage fluctuations and surges in your power supply.

■ **Because an electrical surge** can also affect your PC through connected drives – such as the monitor, printer, modem or telephone connections – try to get a surge

Telephone surge protector

 How to: Update or replace a device driver

1 Right-click on **My Computer** in the **Start** menu. Click on **Properties**, then the **Hardware** tab and finally **Device Manager**. Find the description of the hardware you want to update or replace. Click on the + next to the name to show the associated devices.

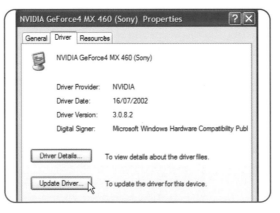

2 Double-click on the icon of the hardware whose driver you want to update, for example, the videocard. A dialogue box shows a description of drivers for the device. Select the Driver tab and click the **Update Driver** button. The Hardware Update Wizard appears.

3 The easiest way to proceed is to choose the 'Install the software automatically' option. Your PC will then connect to the Internet if you have not already done so and search Microsoft's database to see if a more up-to-date driver is available for the chosen device.

protector with several outlets, as well as telephone cable sockets. Plug all your computer devices and peripherals into it, and connect the phone line. The multi-socket version will protect against surges that can damage your PC through the monitor, serial or USB connections.

■ Live in a lightning-prone area?
Lightning strikes are thankfully rare in most areas of the UK, but a direct hit can be disastrous for any electronic equipment in the vicinity. Cheaper surge protectors will not necessarily shield your equipment from an extreme event, so you will need to install something more robust if you live in a lightning-prone area. A variety of protective devices are available, including protected wall sockets and switchboard surge diverters.

IF THE POWER FAILS

Careful planning, in addition to software and hardware tools, will help you to survive an electrical blackout.

■ Surge protectors are the most basic line of defence
in protecting your computer from power fluctuations. High-voltage spikes are not uncommon with domestic electricity, and they can cause irreparable damage to your computer, as well as other equipment, such as modems. A surge protector (see p. 16) maintains a constant flow of electricity into your computer. If there is a power interruption, Windows XP and Windows Me include a System Restore program that lets you return your computer to its original state, as it was before the problem occurred.

■ Your best insurance against data loss
in the event of a failure or 'spike' in your electrical supply, is to back up regularly. If you do that, then whatever happens, even if your computer is completely destroyed, you will not have lost all your work.

■ Uninterruptible Power Supplies,
known as UPS's, provide a more extensive form of protection. In the case of a blackout they not only incorporate surge and spike protectors but they also contain batteries that will power your computer and connected peripherals for a short period. This allows your PC to keep going long enough for you to save your work and shut down correctly.

■ Some UPS's come with software
that lets your computer respond to a power failure by automatically saving your work and shutting down. This solution is popular for computers used as file servers in office networks.

■ Use Windows ScanDisk
to restore your computer after a power failure if you use Windows 98. Users of Windows XP or ME should use the system restore feature. If files were being written to your hard disk when the power failed, the hard disk may have become corrupted. The ScanDisk program in Windows 98 (see p. 32), will fix some problems. ScanDisk automatically runs when Windows starts up if it has detected that Windows was not shut down properly.

■ Alternatively, run a repair utility,
such as Norton SystemWorks (for details see www.symantec.com) or McAfee Utilities (www.mcafee.com). Like ScanDisk, these programs scan your hard drive looking for errors, and will make repairs where possible. Although these utilities cannot replace lost data, they can often fix a damaged drive.

■ Many applications have an AutoSave
or AutoRecover option that automatically saves open documents at specified intervals. You can usually set the time in the program's Preferences dialogue box. In Microsoft Word, for example, go to **Tools ➜ Options** and click on the Save tab. Set AutoRecover to save every 10 minutes. Now, no matter what happens to your power supply, you'll never lose more than 10 minutes of work. The same option is available, and switched on by default, in the other components that make up the Microsoft Office suite: Excel, Outlook and Powerpoint.

■ If you are running a laptop
computer from your main electrical supply, it will switch to its rechargeable battery automatically if a power failure occurs. Because laptops, like PCs, can be damaged by power surges, always connect them to the electrical supply via a surge protector. Although the power supply is generally reliable in the UK, surge protectors are particularly important if you take your portable to parts of the world where blackouts and spike damage are a regular occurrence. There are a number of compact surge protectors on the market, and the best will provide protection for both phone line sockets as well as power sockets. Consider, for example, the APC SurgeArrest (www.apcc.com), which protects both the power connection and the equally vulnerable modem phone socket.

■ Take preventative action
by making regular backups of your hard drive – a back up utility is included on your Windows CD, although it is not installed by default. While hardware is replaceable, your data is probably not, so backup to a removable device like a Zip disk or a recordable CD. Store the backups somewhere safe, away from your computer, preferably in another location altogether.

▶ See also **Hard drive housekeeping,** p. 32.

AVOIDING REPETITIVE STRAIN INJURY

Learn to change the way you work to reduce the chances of getting this hand-disabling condition.

Repetitive strain injury (RSI) occurs when a particular tendon or muscle is overused while being forced into an unnatural position. It is not only due to computer use; writer's cramp and tennis elbow are also types of RSI. But if you use a keyboard and mouse regularly, it's a good idea to minimise the risk of this painful condition; it is easier to prevent RSI than to cure it.

■ **Adopt a good posture when you work.** It is not just the way you use your hands and arms that causes problems, but anything that creates awkward angles in the body. Sit up straight with your feet flat on the floor slightly in front of your knees. Your chair and keyboard should be set at a height where both your thighs and forearms are parallel with the floor.

■ **If Windows is configured to display small fonts** on-screen, you may find yourself hunched forward to see them clearly, increasing your chances of suffering from RSI. To avoid this, configure Windows to display larger fonts. Larger fonts can be displayed by right-clicking any empty area of the Desktop. In the pop-up menu select **Properties ➔ Settings**. Next click on the **Advanced** button and choose **Large Fonts** from the drop-down menu in the Font Size section. Click **OK** to apply. You can also choose to view larger fonts on Web pages by going to the **View** menu in Internet Explorer and choosing **Text Size**.

Windows and buttons:
Windows XP style
Color scheme:
Default (blue)
Font size:
Normal
Normal
Large Fonts
Extra Large Fonts

■ **Don't rest your wrists on your desk** while typing. Rather than resting your wrists in front of the keyboard and stretching your hands to reach the keys, use your arms to position your hands over the keyboard. Your wrists and hands should lie in a straight line with your arms. Make sure that you don't twist the wrists at an awkward angle.

■ **Learn to use both hands,** even if you have no ambition to become a touch typist. Two-finger typing can be surprisingly efficient once you learn where the keys are. When pressing combinations of keys, use both hands rather than twisting one hand into an awkward position to cover the required keys.

■ **Be gentle.** Computer keyboards, unlike the typewriters that preceded them, do not need pressure or velocity to be applied to the keys. Gentle pressure is all that is necessary. Similarly, when using a mouse, hold it gently

RSI DO's & DON'Ts

Increase your chances of avoiding repetitive strain injury.

- **Do** sit up straight with your feet on the floor and your legs uncrossed.
- **Do** ensure your seat is at the right height (forearms and thighs parallel to the floor) and that your lower back is supported.
- **Do** make sure you have enough elbow room around you.
- **Do** take frequent breaks for stretching.
- **Do** pay attention to your body. If your wrists or neck aches, get up and stretch.
- **Do** use keyboard shortcuts.
- **Do** investigate voice-recognition software, particularly if you tend to get RSI.
- **Don't** crane your neck forward or to one side to view your monitor.
- **Don't** work in inadequate lighting or poorly ventilated rooms.
- **Don't** work for prolonged periods in the same position.
- **Don't** hammer on the keyboard.

and apply light pressure to the buttons. If your mouse has become difficult to control, dirt and fluff may have collected on the rollers. If so, remove the ball and clean off the dirt. Better still, get one of the new breed of optical mice, with no moving parts.

▶ See also **Working comfortably,** p. 14; and **Making the most of your mouse,** p. 25.

WHEN TO USE THE RESET BUTTON

The reset button isn't always the best solution to a crash or freeze.

■ **Don't use the reset button** unless you are sure that your computer has stopped responding. If a program has crashed, or your computer does not respond, you may be able to recover from the situation without a 'hard reset'.

■ **Before you push the reset button,** try the Ctrl+Alt+Delete key combination in Windows. You'll be prompted to terminate a program or perform a 'soft reset'. However, this does not reinitialise your computer's hardware – which may be necessary with a serious crash.

■ **Do use the reset button** as an alternative to switching the computer on and off with the power switch. The advantage of the reset button is that it resets the computer's hardware without putting physical and electrical strains on the components. The reset button is also faster than using the power switch.

■ **Remember – as soon as the reset button is pressed,** any unsaved work will be lost. After a reset, Windows will also need to perform a scan of your hard drive to check for errors. For this reason, the button is often recessed to prevent it from being pressed accidentally.

TRACKING DOWN THE PROBLEM

Even the most reliable PCs can have operating problems from time to time. Here are some helpful tips to solve common computer glitches.

■ **Some hardware problems are easily solved** by simply checking the connections. If a message tells you that the printer is not connected, for example, then check that the cable from your PC to your printer is secure. Also check that the power cord is firmly connected to your printer and plugged into the wall socket, and that it is switched on.

■ **Before or after?** Many hardware devices require you to install the driver software that runs them on your PC before you connect the device to your computer. But other devices may need connecting before the drivers are installed. You may find that if you've installed items in the wrong order, your computer will not recognise the new device. Check the manual before you start.

■ **If you've installed new hardware,** it may cause conflicts with existing devices. Right-click on **My Computer** and select **Properties**. Click on the **Device Manager** button in the **Hardware** tab. If there are any devices causing problems, they will either have a yellow question mark next to them, meaning the system is having

problems resolving the function of the device, or a red cross, meaning that the device is actively tagged as being disruptive to the system.

■ **Having hardware problems?** Click on **Help and Support** in the **Start** menu. In the Help and Support window, type 'hardware' in the Search panel and click on **Go**. When the search results appear, click on the **Hardware Troubleshooter** link. In the right-hand panel a series of questions will help locate the problem and take you through the repair step by step.

■ **Printing problems** can be caused by your printer software. The first step is to make sure that your computer recognises your printer. Go to **Start ➜ Control Panel ➜ Printers and Other Hardware ➜ Printers and Faxes**. All the printers and fax modems you have installed should appear. Select the printer you want to use by clicking the appropriate icon in the box. If you have more than one printer installed, make one the printer you normally use by going to **File ➜ Set as Default**.

■ **Is your hard disk causing the problem?** Errors do occur on your hard disk, and they happen for a variety of reasons. Windows XP and ME let you return your PC to a stable state using System Restore. In Windows 98, running the ScanDisk program will sort them out. Go to **Start ➜ Programs ➜ Accessories ➜ System Tools ➜ ScanDisk**. Select the hard drive, click on **Thorough** in the Type of Test section, and make sure there's a check mark in the **Automatically Fix Errors** box. Click **Start**. You'll need to be patient, since it is likely to take a little while to scan and repair the whole disk.

■ **Does your PC freeze** whenever you run a specific program? If so, it will be either a problem of some sort with the program itself, or a conflict with another program you are running at the same time. When your computer freezes, press the Ctrl+Alt+Delete keys together. The **Close Program** window shows all the programs currently running, and highlights the program with the problem. To close the program, click the **End Task** button.

How to: Reinstall your printer software

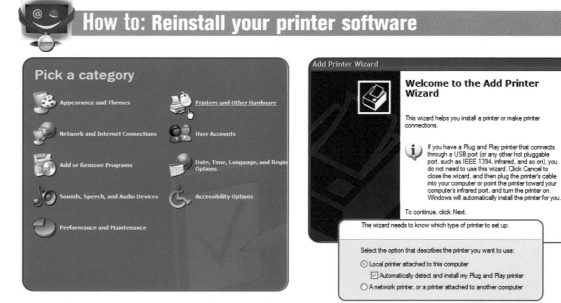

1 **To remove your printer from the Windows setup, go to the Start menu and select Control Panel, then Printers and other hardware. Click on View installed printers or fax printers. In the Printers window, click on your printer and then press the Delete key.**

2 **Double-click on Add a printer. In the Wizard, click Next, then select Local Printer, click Next again and select your printer from the Manufacturers and Printers lists. Then click Have Disk, and follow the on-screen instructions to reinstall your printer.**

Inside the box

Every PC motherboard has several slots and bays to let you upgrade or add components at any time.

■ There are two types of PC expansion slots.
Industry Standard Architecture (ISA) connections have been in use since 1984 and are found in older PCs. A newer type of connection – Peripheral Component

HINTS FOR INSTALLING HARDWARE

Find out how to become an expansion slot expert.

Open sesame
If you're purchasing a new PC, buy one with a hinged side panel on the system unit for easy access to your expansion slots.

Divide and rule
If you often play games on your PC, consider partitioning your hard disk to create two sections using the PartitionMagic software (www.powerquest.com), and dedicating one part solely to games.

Down to earth
During installation, be careful to avoid static discharge from the computer's components. Do not use magnetic screwdrivers, and wear an anti-static wrist strap attached to a grounded metal object.

AGP or PCI?
AGP (Accelerated Graphics Port) cards are faster than PCI cards. For details visit Intel (http://developer.intel.com/technology/agp).

Interconnect (PCI) is found in newer machines. ISA doesn't support Plug and Play devices, which are pieces of hardware you can simply connect to your PC and start using without complicated installation procedures.

■ Upgrading your hardware?
Check that the items are compatible with PCI expansion slots. Most modern PCs are built with these.

■ A PC usually has four to six expansion slots inside.
These are parallel sockets on the motherboard, corresponding to removable panels in the rear of the PC case. You can attach a wide range of devices to these, such as modems and video capture cards. To do this,

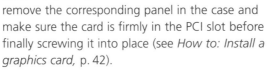

remove the corresponding panel in the case and make sure the card is firmly in the PCI slot before finally screwing it into place (see *How to: Install a graphics card,* p. 42).

■ You can attach up to four IDE devices.
IDE stands for Intelligent (or Integrated) Drive Electronics. Normally, your motherboard will have two IDE interfaces, to each of which you can attach two mass storage devices (such as your hard disk or CD-ROM) – one known as a 'master', the other the 'slave'. The cables each have a mid-connector and an end-connector. Follow the instructions to set each device as either the master or slave during installation, using jumpers (metal bridges that complete electrical circuits) on the back.

■ Add more hard disks to expand your storage.
If you have one hard disk and one CD-ROM, your computer case usually has internal space for one or more extra hard disks. You can insert them beside the existing hard disk slot. Adding an extra hard disk gives you space to keep large graphics, video or music files, or you can keep your data separate from your Windows system files. If you are installing an extra drive yourself, make sure you set the jumpers on the back before you slide it in; it's difficult to see

them once in place. Also, check that the power and IDE cables are seated properly in their sockets to make sure that a proper connection is made.

▶ See also **Choosing a monitor,** p. 28.

Upgrading your hardware can breathe new life into an older PC, and delay the expense of having to buy a new computer.

■ Expanding your computer's RAM
from 64 MB or 128 MB to 256 MB or 512 MB can dramatically improve your computer's performance, especially if you want to run more than one application at a time. Windows XP needs at least 128 MB of RAM to run correctly, and if you run graphics and video editing applications, or complex games you should consider 256 MB or more of RAM.

■ Recent graphics cards have more built-in memory
than many new PCs had only a few years ago. If your display updates slowly, you won't be able to play 3D-accelerated games or achieve the resolution or colour depth

you need. You will have to install a more recent graphics card. Make sure it is capable of displaying 3D graphics and has at least 64 MB of RAM.

■ Modern sound cards
can not only reproduce 3D sound, but also have wavetable synthesisers built in, allowing you to make your own music and play the latest computer games with surround sound. Installing a new sound card can be as simple as sliding the hardware into place on the motherboard and restarting your PC.

■ Whether you can upgrade your processor
to a higher speed depends on the processor socket on your motherboard. You can almost certainly increase the speed just by slotting in a new processor. However, if your PC is old, or if you want the fastest type of processor, you'd be

Computer crossover. Many USB devices will work on PCs and Apple Macs. If you have both types of computer in the house, you will be able to share devices, such as printers, Zip drives and CD-R writers between them.

A PC usually has several USB ports, but if you have lots of USB devices, you may still find that you run out of sockets to connect them. Get round this with a USB hub, which lets four or more devices share one USB socket on your PC. Hubs are unobtrusive and inexpensive, and require no installation. You can even connect hubs together and have up to 127 USB devices connected at one time.

If your PC doesn't have USB ports, you can buy a USB card that fits into a spare slot inside your PC. You can also get a USB port adaptor that fits into the card slot on a laptop. Installation is easy, and once installed the connection will operate just as well as a standard USB port. Before you buy, check that you have a spare PCI slot on your motherboard – these are the white blocks.

MAKING THE MOST OF COMPUTER MEMORY

Decide how much memory you need and assign or add more.

Don't confuse memory with hard drive space. Hard drive space is where your programs and files are stored all the time, while RAM memory is where your PC works with programs and data.

If anything is certain about computer memory, it is that no matter how much memory your computer already has, there never seems to be enough once you really start exploring your PC's capabilities.

The amount of memory you need depends on the kinds of tasks you are performing and the sort of software you are using. A spreadsheet program would be comfortable with 32 MB, but remember that the Windows program

itself requires plenty of memory. You need to choose memory that matches the speed of your PC's motherboard. This is difficult to tell from inspection, so it's best to ask your PC supplier. Many applications – especially those handling graphics – require at least 128 MB, but are happier with 256 MB. Consider adding memory if you have less than 256 MB and regularly work with graphics or use multimedia software.

Think you need more memory? If your PC is slow – and you are constantly closing programs to keep working – then you could probably use more memory. First, you need to know the type of memory you require. There are many different types, which come in a variety of configurations. The latest machines use DDR (Double Data Rate) SDRAM (Synchronous Dynamic Random Access Memory) in a Dual In-line Memory Module (DIMM). Older PCs use other types of DIMMs or even Single In-line Memory Modules (SIMMs), a slower form of memory. Many memory vendors' Websites will tell you the type of memory you need if you enter the type of machine that you have.

Make sure you remember to save data as you work. Anything that is in RAM memory when your PC freezes or crashes will be lost. However, the data saved on the hard drive will still be safe.

Some software can impair a PC's performance by causing a 'memory leak'. This means that the program gradually uses up its allotted amount of memory until none is left to work with, and the program crashes. Windows XP is less affected by this sort of bug than earlier versions of Windows.

To find a leaking program in Windows XP launch the Task Manager by holding down the **Ctrl** and **Alt** keys and pressing **Delete**. Click on the **Performance** tab. Under Physical Memory, note the amount of available memory. Now start a program, use it normally, then close it and check the figure again. If the available memory is not close to the original value, the program you just closed is probably the culprit – check the software maker's Website for updates.

better off buying a new PC altogether, because otherwise you would also have to buy a new motherboard, memory and other components at the same time.

Speed up your CD access and data transfer. Changing your CD-ROM for a newer, faster mechanism can speed up your data access times considerably. Alternatively, keep your old drive and add a CD burner so you can back up important data and create MP3 CDs. Because CD writing is always much slower than reading, aim for at least a 16x burner. How fast the burner can read a CD depends on the quality of the CD-ROM drive you are using and the performance of your PC. However, as a general rule, look for a read speed of at least 40x.

UNDERSTANDING USB CONNECTIONS

Most modern PCs come with USB (Universal Serial Bus) ports, often on the front for convenience.

The need for speed. USB connections can carry data at much faster rates than other serial or parallel connectors, especially the USB 2.0 sockets found on the latest PCs. This makes them ideal for connecting digital cameras, scanners and other peripherals.

Beyond the basics

AUTOMATE YOUR HOME

With home control devices attached to your PC, you can use it to control your lights, heating, TV, video and many other household items.

■ **You can start controlling your home** with a simple kit that includes a module that you plug into your computer, and smaller satellite units that plug into electrical outlets. You then plug each item you want to control into a wall socket anywhere in the house.

PROTOCOLS

Computer protocols enable machines to communicate across networks.

After installing networking hardware you need to make sure each Windows PC knows how to communicate with the others. The different languages used are called protocols. There are three common network protocols that you need to be aware of:

IPX/SPX
The fastest of the three common protocols, used for many networkable games.

NetBEUI
An IBM protocol that is easy to set up. It is very fast when used on small local area networks, and is ideal for a home situation.

TCP/IP
The Internet protocol, available on a variety of networks. It is fast becoming the protocol of home LANs, because modern messaging software and many online games require an assigned IP address to operate.

■ **Home control is modular,** so you can buy a command unit and build up additional equipment as you need it. Start off by using it to operate a few features, perhaps lighting and curtains. Then add equipment so you can use your PC to monitor other aspects of your home.

■ **Home control systems** are more popular in the USA than elsewhere, so it is useful to check American Websites for an overview of the current range of equipment on offer. Try Home Controls (www.homecontrols.com), for example, who sell a wide range of equipment.

■ **Security is often a worry,** especially when you're away from home. Add some Closed Circuit TV cameras (CCTV) to your security system, and with PC-based home control you can see what's happening in and around your house from any Internet-connected PC. Many manufacturers supply video surveillance cameras of this kind as part of their home security systems.

■ **If you already have some home automation,** you could also try voice control with HAL2000 speech recognition software (www.automatedliving.com). You can call your computer and say 'lights on', so the house looks occupied.

■ **Some control systems have a complex user interface** that makes you feel as though you're a NASA scientist if you've even managed to turn the lights on without any problems! To avoid this situation, spend some time looking for a model with a friendly, Windows-style interface.

HOME NETWORKS

For any home with more than one PC, a home network is a great idea.

■ **For older equipment** a home network can mean a whole new lease of life. If you have a computer without a CD-ROM drive, for instance,

it's hard to install new software easily. With a home network, you can log on to the PC that does have a CD-ROM drive and use that. In fact, you can share most other devices in a similar fashion, such as scanners, CD burners and a variety of data storage drives.

■ **Printer sharing** is one of the great benefits of setting up a network. If you have two PCs, plus a laser and a colour printer, a network will allow you to send pages to either printer without the nuisance of constantly moving hardware from place to place around the house as it is needed.

■ **Be patient!** Don't expect to have your new home network up and running in an hour or so. Networks can be frustrating to set up, simply because there is so much to learn, and so much that can go wrong. Difficulties are almost always due to compatibility problems, and these can take time to sort out.

It helps to have a knowledgeable expert on tap so you can get advice when it all becomes too much.

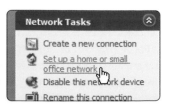

■ Each computer on the network

needs a network card. These are rarely included on cheaper home PCs. You need to open your computer up to install one, or enlist the help of an expert to do so. Some network cards are quite cheap, although you will pay more for better performance and features.

■ Networking introduces a new range of jargon

into the world of home computers. A home network is known as a LAN, which means Local Area Network. If you connect two or more PCs together – and share files and peripherals – it's called a peer-to-peer network.

■ Offices usually have a client-server network,

which uses one or more big, fast computers called servers – for keeping files, handling printing, e-mail and so on – while the client machines are where people sit and work.

■ Network cards are available in different speeds:

10 Mbps, 100 Mbps or 1000 Mbps (called gigabit ethernet). The best cards work at more than one speed.

■ WiFi networking means fewer cables.

The neatest way to set up a home network is to use WiFi (a standard officially called IEEE 802.11b). Cards in each of your PCs communicate via radio waves to a base station, which can in turn connect to the Internet. With a WiFi network you can use a laptop PC to surf the Web from anywhere in your home – or even the garden.

Wireless networking kit

■ If you have more than two computers

to network, plug all the cables into a device called a switch or a hub. These boxes allow several computers to communicate with each other and share a single connection to another network, such as broadband connection to the Internet. They also have the advantage that a problem with one computer or network card will not mean that the other computers on the network cannot connect with each other.

▶ See also **Linking computers to one another,** p. 84.

HOME CONTROL SITES

Here are some useful Websites of manufacturers and suppliers.

www.rslsteeper.com
A supplier of equipment that uses home automation techniques to help disabled people to live fuller lives.

www.letsautomate.com
A home automation supplier with a wide range of equipment from manufacturers such as X-10.

www.automatedhome.co.uk
News, reviews and how-to articles from people who have set up home automation systems in the UK.

www.habitek.co.uk
Another online home automation retailer.

How to: Share a single Internet connection

1 Any PC on your home network can access the Internet through a shared PC with direct Internet access. On the PC with the Internet connection, go to the **Control Panel,** click on **Network and Internet Connections,** then on **Network connections** in the next window.

2 Click once on the connection you want to share to select it. In the **Network Tasks** panel at the left hand side of the window, click on **Change settings of the connection.** The **Properties** dialogue box will open. Click on the **Advanced** tab.

3 In the Internet Connection Sharing panel click in the check box next to **Allow other network users to connect through this computer's Internet connection.** You can also select options to let other users control the Internet connection from their PCs.

The basic components

Talking to your computer

WHY NOT UPGRADE YOUR KEYBOARD?

More options than you might think possible are available with the humble keyboard.

■ **Often the keyboard supplied with your PC** is a budget model, but upgrading to a good-quality version is an inexpensive and worthwhile investment. Check out the dozen or more replacement models in computer stores to find one you like.

■ **Don't forget to prop your keyboard up!** Keyboards usually have two folding legs at the back or underneath, which places the keys in the optimum position for your hands. It's surprising how often this stand goes unused.

■ **Do you dribble your double-decaf?** Try a spill-proof keyboard, or cover your existing keyboard with an inexpensive plastic membrane, available from your local PC dealer. A much better idea altogether, though, would be to make the area around your computer a 'No Drinks' and 'No Food' zone.

■ **Some models have extra buttons** that you can assign to a variety of everyday tasks, such as checking e-mail, viewing a Web page or switching users. You don't have to use the keyboard maker's defaults for these extra buttons – they are often useful for controlling features in specialist software.

■ **Do you hate all the wires** snaking round your desk? Then use a wireless keyboard. Many different versions are available, most of which use very low energy radio waves. Wireless keyboards are useful in situations where you want to be at a distance from the computer, although you still have to be able to see the screen.

■ **Pressing the Print Screen key** makes a copy of whatever is open on-screen to the Windows Clipboard. To use it or print it out, open a graphics-capable program, such as Paint or Paint Shop Pro, and click on **Edit → Paste.**

■ **When you add words to previous sentences,** do you find that you end up typing over existing text instead of just inserting them? This means that you have accidentally pressed the Insert key. To correct this, simply press the **Insert** key again, but this time make sure that the letters 'OVR' at the bottom in your word-processing software are no longer in bold.

■ **If you allow your children to use your PC,** then a cheap 'emergency' keyboard is a great idea. In the event of an accident or spillage, the spare keyboard could save you from a keyboard-less 'holiday' period – and maybe a couple of missed deadlines as well.

■ **Try a Microsoft Natural keyboard.** This type of keyboard is fitted with the traditional QWERTY key layout (originally designed to slow down typists so old-fashioned typewriters could cope), but splits the area that's covered by your left and right hands into two, so that your fingers are allowed to fall more naturally on the keys. The keyboard has no special requirements – you just have to get used to using the new layout.

■ **Do away with your mouse!** Instead, look for a keyboard that incorporates a touchpad or rollerball, like the ones found on laptops. If the keyboard is also wireless, then it will make hiding all the clutter much easier. Models are available from Microsoft (www.microsoft.com/uk) and Logitech (www.logitech.com). Many cordless mice also have useful features like extra buttons.

NEWS AND REVIEWS
Keep up with what's hot and what's not in the world of computer accessories.

ZDNET (www.zdnet.co.uk)
This Website offers reviews of the latest PC products and its own guide to the best PC sites around. Users can also subscribe to a weekly magazine, ZDNet Week.

MAXIMUM PC (www.maximumpc.com)
News and reviews on a wide variety of PC equipment, products and services.

PC PRO (www.pcpro.com)
A host of great PC reference material plus buyer's guides, discussion forums and invaluable tips and tricks.

T3 (www.t3.co.uk)
A great site for computer tips and tricks as well as reviews of the latest technology.

MAKING THE MOST OF YOUR MOUSE

This small device is the link between you and your computer.

■ **If you're always getting your mouse-tail tangled,** consider a cordless option. A radio signal between the mouse and a base unit provides the connection, transmitting your commands. These models are, however, more expensive than conventional mice.

■ **If you don't have a lot of room** on your desk to manoeuvre your mouse, try using a model with a scroll wheel. This will allow you to work your way up and down a document while keeping the mouse stationary. Similarly, a trackball mouse – with a large ball on top spun by your fingertip – eliminates the need to move your mouse around. Some of the most advanced mice even have extra buttons on the side that allow you to navigate your way quickly back and forth between Web pages.

■ **If you need to adjust the way your mouse works,** go to **Start ➜ Control Panel ➜ Printers and other hardware** and click the Mouse icon. Use the Buttons, Pointer and Pointer

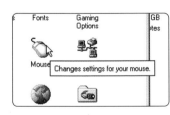

Options tabs to alter the mouse functions to suit you. If you're left-handed, you can also swap the two mouse buttons.

■ **It's a good idea to clean your mouse** about once a month to ensure smooth operation. With a conventional mouse, turn the device upside down and wipe over the base with a clean cloth. Now twist the cover off the base of the mouse (usually anticlockwise) so that the ball falls out into your hand. Clean the ball with the cloth. Sticky tape is also good for carefully removing dust or dirt. Use a cotton bud to clean the mouse ball socket (especially the rollers), and then replace the ball and cover.

▶ See also **Scroll Bar shortcuts,** p. 109.

SITES FOR JOYSTICK MANUFACTURERS

Here's a selection of the best-selling joysticks on the market.

GRAVIS (www.gravis.com)
Check out the Xterminator, Eliminator and Destroyer joysticks and gamepads, all listed at this site.

LOGITECH (www.logitech.com)
Lists many different controllers, including Logitech's WingMan joysticks.

QUICKSHOT (www.quickshot.com)
Offers a wide range of game controllers for you to browse through.

SIDEWINDER (www.microsoft.com)
Microsoft claims SideWinder devices will take your favourite flight, combat and action games to another level. Take a look at the Sidewinder news page in the Products/hardware section of the site.

JOYSTICKS ARE FOR FUN

The keyboard – usually with more than 100 keys – and a delicate mouse can take some fun out of action games, so a joystick is the perfect alternative.

■ **If a cheap and cheerful joystick** came with your PC, consider buying a new one with the latest features, which will work better with your games.

■ **For real fun, try a force-feedback joystick.** Imagine a pilot landing a real aircraft on a bumpy runway without feeling the pull and tug of the controls! That's the kind of lifeless response you get with a normal joystick. A force-feedback joystick simulates bumps and cornering forces for a more life-like experience.

■ **To make your joystick work more effectively,** go to **Start ➜ Control Panel ➜ Printers and other hardware** and click on the Gaming Controllers icon. Click on the joystick you want to adjust and select **Calibrate**. Follow the on-screen prompts to set up the joystick correctly. If you use your joystick every day, it's best to calibrate it every few months.

■ **Some joysticks use motion-sensing technology.** This

means that you only have to move your hand in the air, while holding onto the gamepad-like joystick, for the roll-and-pitch commands to take effect. With this kind of joystick you become more physically involved in the action of the game.

■ **Voice control for games is possible** using Microsoft's Game Voice controller. You can run your favourite games by telling your PC what you want to do, while also using the control to chat to other players over a network or Internet connection.

■ **If you are serious about being a computer pilot,** replace your joystick with a yoke. These are designed to look and feel as if you are at the controls of a real aircraft, from a Cessna 152 to a Boeing 747. You can also add foot pedals, used to operate the rudder and the nosewheel steering in most light aircraft.

■ **More interested in cars than planes?** If so, you too can enjoy a more realistic experience when playing your favourite racing game by fitting your computer with a steering wheel and pedals. The most expensive ones have Formula 1-style gear-changing paddles.

■ **If you have one of the simpler games** that doesn't call for the sophistication of a joystick, consider buying a paddle instead. These also plug into the games port.

▶ See also **Games,** p. 184.

Printers

Probably the most important piece of additional equipment for your computer is a printer, and many models are available. Assess your needs before making your choice, for example, do your print-outs need to be photo quality? Always try out the printers in the store before you buy.

TYPES OF PRINTERS

Colour inkjet printers are by far the most common printers for the home. They are good for printing photographs and Web pages, as well as letters and other text. These printers work by pushing tiny droplets of ink onto the page. Inkjet printers can be quite slow at times, and are often relatively noisy, especially when compared to laser printers. Ink cartridge prices vary a lot between manufacturers, and they can be costly if you do a lot of printing.

How many cartridges? When buying a colour inkjet printer you may face a choice between a one, two, four or even seven-cartridge system. Beware of a printer that has only one cartridge; you will have to constantly swap colour and black cartridges while printing, and the cartridge must be thrown away as soon as the black runs out, however much colour ink is left. Two-cartridge printers cost very little more and include one black and one

colour cartridge. Four-cartridge printers are best. They produce the highest quality colours, and are most economical with ink over long term use.

Laser printers are ideal for high-quality printing. They use LEDs or a laser to mark out each page as a positive electrical charge on a rotating drum. Negatively charged toner (the ink) is put onto the drum and placed on the paper. A heated roller ensures that the toner sticks to the paper. Laser printers are fast and produce sharply detailed output. Although they can be cheaper to run than inkjets, they are more expensive to buy.

A toner cartridge on a laser printer lasts a long time, but a replacement can be expensive. Compare the prices and life expectancy of replacement cartridges before you buy a printer.

Portable printers are powered by an internal battery and can be carried around with a laptop. However, compared with desk-bound printers, they are expensive.

Other types of printers are available. Photo printers use special photographic paper, and are excellent for printing from digital cameras. Multi-function devices can fax, scan, photocopy and print, and are useful if you spend time working from home or have relatively little space.

Don't forget your cable! Most printers don't come with a cable to connect them to your PC, so be prepared to pay an additional £10 or so for one. Remember to buy a longer cable if the printer is positioned at a distance from your PC. USB versions are the most versatile but parallel port cables give a more secure connection.

PRINTER PROBLEMS

If your printer does not seem to be connected, or it isn't printing, go to **Start ➔ Control Panel ➔ Printers and Other Hardware.** Look in Printers and Faxes to see if the printer icon is displayed. If it isn't, check that all your printer cables are plugged in. If you are using a USB printer, try unplugging then reconnecting it to the computer. Restart the computer. If Windows still doesn't recognise the printer, you may have faulty hardware. If the printer itself seems in working order, the cable may need replacing. Alternatively, you may need to reinstall your printer driver software (see *Understanding device drivers*, p. 16).

PRINTER PLACES
Most printer manufacturers have an established online presence.

BROTHER (www.brother.co.uk)
Features an ample array of printers.

CANON (www.canon.co.uk)
Provides printers for all sorts of jobs and tasks for the home and office.

EPSON (www.epson.co.uk)
Supplies a wide range of models for the demanding home computer market.

HEWLETT PACKARD (www.hp.co.uk)
Pick and purchase a printer online.

LEXMARK (www.lexmark.co.uk)
Details of the full range of Lexmark printers available in in the UK.

SAMSUNG (www.samsungelectronics.co.uk)
Fast laser printers ideal for a home office.

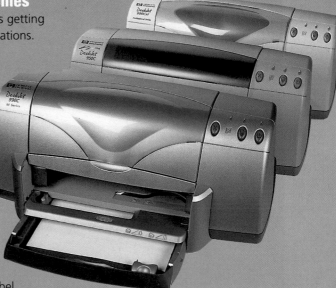

If text prints in the wrong place on a page, you may need to change the paper size or margins. Your printer software might have paper size options, but check your PC software as well. For example, in Microsoft Word 2000, go to **File ➔ Page Setup** to change the document's paper size or margin settings, and other features.

Many modern printers issue a warning when the ink cartridge gets low, and they also often have an ink status gauge that shows how full a cartridge is. You can usually continue using a cartridge for a while after the printer warns you to replace it – just have a new one to hand.

One common printer problem is a paper feed error, where a sheet gets stuck in the printer's rollers. If this happens, you should see an on-screen warning, telling you what to do. Usually it is just a matter of removing the paper, but do this slowly to·avoid tearing.

If your printer's software becomes out-of-date, you could have problems getting the printer to work with the latest applications. All the main printer manufacturers have Websites (see box, p. 26) with updated drivers available for downloading free, so keep a regular check on your manufacturer's Website.

SPECIAL PRINTING

Most printers can print labels on standard A4 sheets, and there are dozens of label sizes available to choose from. Always print a test sheet on plain paper before using the labels to check the positioning. Also make sure you use the correct type of label for your printer – laser printers should only use laser-compatible labels.

Use your printer's manual feed for tasks such as printing on special paper or card, labels, a letterhead or acetate. Many printers also have a slot for envelopes.

Use the right paper for the job. Items such as greeting cards, look much better printed on heavy photo-quality paper.

See also **Faster label printing**, p. 28; and **A label for everything**, p. 163.

How to: Set up the printer

1 Following the manufacturer's instructions provided with your computer, connect it to your printer's communications port using the cable recommended. Depending on the printer, this may be a parallel port (requiring a 1284 bi-directional cable) or a USB cable port.

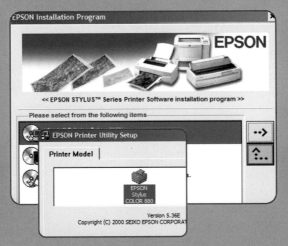

2 Install the printer drivers – the software that came with your printer. With most modern printers this is simple – Windows will notice you have connected a printer and will prompt you to insert the CD that came with it and install the necessary software.

3 If you have updated to Windows XP, or bought a new computer, you may not have an up-to-date driver. In this case, connect to the Internet and follow the instructions in the Add Hardware Wizard – most often the drivers are available on Microsoft's Website.

Putting it on paper

FASTER LABEL PRINTING

A dedicated second printer speeds up the label-making process.

■ **Special label printers are ideal** for printing multiple sets of labels. Label printers operate alongside your existing printer and they are connected to your computer via a data cable. You can print labels in quantity for business packages or for large mailings, and you can also use a label printer to print labels for envelopes, disks, CDs and 35 mm slides.

■ **Most dedicated label printers** use thermal technology and require a special thermal paper that reacts to heat to produce a black-and-white output. With this advanced thermal technology, label printers can print out a label in just a few seconds, and you won't ever need to purchase ink or toner again.

■ **There are two different types of thermal printers:** direct thermal printers and thermal transfer printers. Direct thermal printers use a paper that turns black with heat, while thermal transfer printers take untreated paper, but need a thermal transfer ribbon to operate. Thermal transfer printers are designed to print at a lower temperature than that reached by direct thermal printers, and their print heads have a longer life as a result.

■ **Working in Microsoft Word** makes printing onto sheets of ready-made labels a practical proposition. The software is already configured to work with a wide range of popular label brands and styles – such as those from the extensive Avery range – but you can also enter in the dimensions of

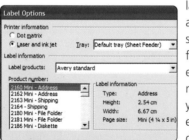

other brands of labels that you might want to use. Alternatively, you can print on labels of your own design.

■ **Use a shortcut in Word** to print an address on a label. To do this, simply highlight the address in Word and click on **Tools ➜ Envelopes and Labels**. From Labels, click on **Options** to get a list of label products. Alternatively, you can create your own label just by clicking on the **Details** button and entering in the relevant measurements.

▶ See also **Printers**, p. 26; and **A label for everything**, p. 163.

LABEL PRINTER SITES
Here's some information about where to buy your label printer.

BROTHER (www.brother.co.uk)
Information and specifications for the extensive range of Brother label printers, which range from hand-held devices to models with built-in keyboards.

CITIZEN (www.citizen.co.uk)
Manufacturer of a wide range of label and barcode printers, with both thermal and thermal transfer models.

DYNASCAN (www.dynascan.com/ label_printers.htm)
Offers links to major manufacturers for printers and label design software.

BEECHMAN & CO. (www.beechman.co.uk)
Suppliers of many manufacturers labelling hardware and software.

SEIKO SMART STORE (www.seikosmart.com)
Information and specifications on Seiko's Smart label printers, including where to buy, and all about buying labels online.

Getting the picture

CHOOSING A MONITOR

Buying the right monitor is vital to enhancing your comfort, enjoyment and the efficient use of your PC.

■ **The first consideration** when choosing a monitor is the screen size. This is measured in inches – across the diagonal – like a TV screen. Some of the screen is hidden behind the casing, so stating the actual screen size would be misleading. Manufacturers are required to quote the visible screen size, and this is the measurement to look for. A typical viewable screen size is 14 inches, but 17, 19 and 21-inch screens are available. The largest ones will almost display a full-size sheet of A3 paper. But size comes at a cost – a few extra inches can push the price up considerably. If you're going to be using several graphics programs, or multiple applications at once, however, a larger screen is worth considering, and can sometimes be a necessity for fine work. You can also buy widescreen monitors ideal for video editing.

■ **Resolution indicates the number of 'pixels'** or dots that make up the screen image. The higher the number, the better the image. Most of today's monitors can display at least 1024 x 768 pixels, and this is the minimum that you should consider buying for a monitor intended for everyday use.

■ **The refresh rate** tells you how many times the screen is redrawn every second. Poorer quality monitors often have a low refresh rate at higher resolutions, causing the screen to flicker as it redraws itself. To avoid headaches, look for a refresh rate of at least 72 Hz.

■ **The flatter the better.** Many modern screens are completely flat over their entire viewing area. This makes them less tiring to use, and also more accurate for use with applications where the shape and size of objects on the screen is important – with design software, for example.

If you want to hook up two monitors, you need to find out what type of slot is available in your machine before you go ahead and buy a second graphics card and monitor (see 'How to', below). Most modern PCs have their first graphics card in the AGP slot, and the second must be a PCI card to fit in a PCI slot. Ask your PC supplier if you are not sure which one to buy.

FLAT PANEL SCREENS

See the difference a flat panel screen provides, and enjoy the sharper resolution and a clearer on-screen image.

■ **For the best resolution and clarity** on a flat panel display, choose a Thin Film Transistor (TFT), or active matrix, screen. Each pixel is controlled by transistors within the screen, that produce a bright and clear light. Often, the surface is non-reflective as well as flat. TFT screens can help you to avoid eye strain, and they emit virtually no radiation. However, they are currently

considerably more expensive than a standard general-purpose monitor.

■ **A passive matrix screen is cheaper** and uses less power than a TFT flat panel. However, you have to sit square-on to the screen to see it properly – the display will not be

as bright or clear from an angle. These screens are useful to have when you can't recharge your battery frequently, but they can be tiring on the eyes during long periods of use.

■ **Look out for a plasma display.** This new, flat-screen technology gives a 160° viewing angle that is bright and clear. But a plasma display is very expensive, uses more power and is heavier than active or passive matrix screens. Plasma displays work very well as flat television screens, so they are good for combining TV and computer functions on one screen.

■ **Handle with care!** Laptop screens and flat panel screens in general are more easily damaged than conventional monitors. While it is normal for one or two pixels to be dark, even on a new TFT screen, you should check the guarantee if more than that many pixels stop working. Try not to touch the surface of the screen with your fingers, and remember to dust it regularly with a clean, dry cloth.

▶ See also **Laptop computers**, p. 50.

How to: Use two monitors at the same time

1 Before buying a second graphics card and monitor, you need to find out what type of slot is available. The graphics card on most standard PCs is fitted in the AGP slot. If you buy a second card, then it must be a PCI card to fit into a PCI slot.

2 Switch off the PC, open it up and plug in the second graphics card. Connect your second monitor and then switch on the second monitor and your PC. Windows will detect the new device. Begin the Installation Wizard to install your new graphics card.

3 You may only need one graphics card to drive two displays. Many modern cards include a second composite video output that you can direct to a TV or video recorder. Use the Display Properties dialogue box to set the size and pixel depth of the second display.

Storing your information

FINE TUNING YOUR DISK DRIVES

Maximise the performance of your disk drives to give faster access to your hard drive, floppies and CDs.

■ **If you often use one particular drive,** place a shortcut to it on your Desktop so that you will always have quick and easy access. Open **My Computer** and drag the icon of the desired drive onto your Desktop. Because you cannot copy a drive to the desktop, a shortcut to it will be created instead.

■ **Find out how much space is available** for storage on your hard disk in XP by double-clicking on **My Computer** in the Start menu and then clicking on the hard disk icon. Leave the mouse pointer over the icon and a dialogue will pop up showing how much space is available on the drive.

THE FAITHFUL FLOPPY

Floppy disks have been around for a long time. They're cheap, and they're still a great way to transfer small files from one PC to another.

■ **Use a compression program, such as WinZip** (www.winzip.com), to get more

onto a floppy disk. Word processor or spreadsheet files will give you the best rate of compression, at around 85 per cent. Graphics files and executable files (.exe) that you find on the Internet are already compressed and you won't be able to squash them much more.

■ **Compress several files into one.** If you select a group of files all at the same time you can compress them into a single file to save space on your floppy. This works well if you are creating back-ups.

■ **If a file is too big for one floppy,** even when compressed using WinZip, you can split the file up over several floppies. The data can then be recombined on another PC, as long as it also has WinZip installed. This method is called 'spanning', because one file spans several disks. Just make sure you have enough blank floppy disks ready at hand before you start on the operation, and also be sure to number them carefully, since you will have to insert them in the correct order when uncompressing the file at its destination.

■ **Keep floppy disks in a cool, dry place,** preferably in a special floppy disk box. Since floppy disks are magnetic media, exposure to magnetism is particularly damaging. Keep them away from loudspeakers, magnetic tools and even fridge magnets. Unfortunately, although

DISK DRIVES
Get to know your PC's drives – these are the most common types.

HARD DISK DRIVE
Often called the 'hard drive', it reads and writes onto your PC's main storage area. It's usually labelled as the C drive, with any secondary hard disks labelled D or E.

FLOPPY DISK DRIVE
Normally labelled A, this drive is used to read and write data onto a 3.5-inch magnetic media disk, holding up to 1.44 MB of data.

CD DRIVE
This drive is used only to read data from music CDs and CD-ROMs, which can store 650 MB of data. The CD drive is generally labelled D.

CD-R DRIVE
The 'R' denotes a drive that can read and record up to 650 MB of data onto compact discs. Usually, it's installed instead of a CD drive so will probably be labelled D.

ZIP DRIVE
This is a special drive that allows you to use Zip disks with your PC. Zip disks are ideal for storing back-up versions of important files. They can hold up to 250 MB of data – the equivalent to almost 150 floppy disks. Once installed, this drive will appear on your PC as the next available letter in the alphabet.

JAZ DRIVE
This is similar to a Zip drive, but packs an even bigger punch. Jaz disks can hold up to 2 GB of data. That's more than 1300 floppy disks' worth of information!

DVD DRIVE
The DVD drive plays 'digital versatile discs', also known as 'digital video discs'. If it replaces a CD drive, it's normally labelled D. Otherwise, it will take the next available letter. It holds at least 4.7 GB of data – enough to store a feature-length film.

generally reliable, all magnetic media will deteriorate over a period of a few years. Exactly how long depends on how well it is stored.

■ If you get a disk error in Windows 98 and Me when reading a floppy, you can run ScanDisk to find and repair file errors. Go to **Start ➜ Programs ➜ Accessories ➜ System Tools ➜ ScanDisk**. If the scan of the A: drive is successful, copy the data to a new disk as an extra precaution. If you find that nothing can be done to rescue the disk, throw it away – a disk that has failed once cannot be trusted again.

■ Take care of your disks. Never pull back the guard and touch the disk surface because any dirt or dust can cause the data to be misread. Don't bend a floppy disk, or put it in your pocket where it can get distorted – this will almost certainly destroy the data. If you want to send a disk though the mail, wrap it in aluminium foil and use a cardboard envelope. Make duplicate copies of disks containing valuable files.

STORE MORE ON A ZIP

Zip drives are a simple and economical way to store data. You can get a parallel or USB port version, or install one internally.

■ Zip drives come in 100, 250, or 750 MB versions. The disks are barely larger than a standard floppy disk and the external drive unit is compact. The transfer of data is a great deal faster than copying data onto a floppy, especially in the USB format. Larger capacity Zip drives are 'backwards compatible', which means that they can read data from older, smaller capacity disks.

■ You can unplug a USB drive and plug it into another computer, even an Apple Macintosh, without turning either off, so long as a Zip driver is installed on both machines.

Windows recognises the Zip drive and loads the necessary drivers automatically.

■ If you need to send information to an Apple Mac, use IBM-formatted Zip disks. These work in both machines, while Mac-formatted disks are only compatible with Macs.

■ Zip drives include software for backing up data. You can set up a scheduled backup, select specific files and folders to be backed up, and determine how frequently the backups should occur. For the sake of convenience, set the automatic back up for a time when you're not using your PC. Many people schedule their back up routines to run during the night, when the machine is idle.

■ If you want to speed up data transfer buy a Zip drive with either a firewire or USB 2.0 connection. Both of these technologies transfer data at much higher rates. Some drives also use the USB or FireWire connection to supply power, making them the ideal backup to use with laptop computers.

How to: Install a Zip drive

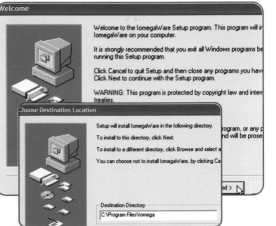

1 To install a USB Zip drive, insert the installation CD into the computer's CD-ROM drive. The program should run automatically. Follow the on-screen instructions to install the software. Choose a destination directory for the program files.

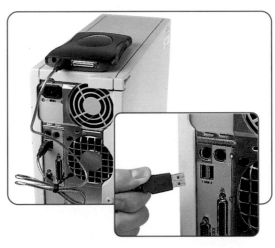

2 Use the USB cable supplied with the drive to connect it to your PC. Each end is different, so it is easy to insert them correctly. If the plug doesn't fit, try it the other way round: USB plugs only fit one way.

3 Connect the power supply to the Zip drive (unless the drive gets its power from the USB cable) and insert a disk. The Zip icon, showing that it is installed, will appear in My Computer and Windows Explorer as an extra drive.

Hard drive housekeeping

Windows XP and Me do a fantastic job of keeping your PC running smoothly and efficiently behind the scenes. But taking preventative measures, and regularly setting aside time to clean up your hard drive, can make a huge difference to your PC's speed and reliability.

A HEALTHY HARD DRIVE

Each time you boot up, Windows XP and Me take a 'snapshot' of your system, including all installed software and the hardware setup. If something goes wrong, you can roll back in time to a point prior to the problem. Coupled with the extensive System Tools and Task Scheduler, which automatically run hard drive diagnostics for you, the latest versions of Windows help to maintain your PC much better than earlier ones.

FORMATTING CHECKLIST

Make sure you have the following before reformatting your hard drive.

- A WINDOWS ME STARTUP FLOPPY DISK from which to boot your computer. To create a disk, go to **Start → Settings → Control Panel** and double-click on the **Add/Remove Programs** icon. Select the **Startup Disk** tab and click **Create Disk**. (See Your computer's insurance policy, p. 82.)

- ALL YOUR ORIGINAL SOFTWARE **CD-ROM**s or installation disks, including the registration keys (product codes).

- ANY DISKS OR **CD-ROM**s THAT CAME WITH YOUR PC for the graphics card, sound card and modem.

- A BACKUP OF ALL YOUR DATA, including templates, e-mails, addresses, Favorites and ISP connection details.

Windows needs a certain amount of free disk space to manage its swap file, also known as 'virtual memory'. The size of the file is managed automatically. However, if there is insufficient free disk space, and you have limited RAM, you will experience a noticeable reduction in speed and increased hard drive activity. Check the amount of hard drive space used by clicking on the My Computer icon.

SYSTEM TOOLS

Many tasks that will help to organise your PC automatically are found in **Start → All Programs → Accessories → System Tools**. Here you'll find Disk Defragmenter and Disk Cleanup, along with Scheduled Tasks, which allows you to set times for performing tasks.

Tidy up! When Windows saves data to your hard disk, it doesn't always put a file or piece of data all in one place. Over time, all the data, both files and programs, becomes fragmented. To reorganise the data to keep files together, run Disk Defragmenter – found under System Tools – regularly. The defragmentation process speeds up your computer by making it easier to find all the pieces of an application or file and reduces the chances of data disruption.

Error checking can repair data. Each section of data, no matter how small, occupies a 32 KB 'slot' on your hard disk. These slots are called clusters, and each one has a unique 32-bit address. Sometimes clusters get 'lost' when the operating system marks empty clusters as used, or sections of the disk get damaged and become unusable. Run error checking on a disk by going to **My Computer**, right-clicking on the disk, and selecting **Properties**. Click on **Tools** then on **Check Now** in the Error checking panel. You can choose options to have Windows automatically fix file errors as it finds them, and repair bad sectors it encounters on the disk.

Windows Me and XP have a clever feature called System Restore that stores information about your computer's setup, software and hardware each time you turn on your machine, or every 10 hours after a short period of inactivity. If you strike a major problem after installing a program, for example, you can ask the computer to restore itself to the way it was before.

The usual suspects? If you think some recently installed software or hardware has impeded your PC's performance, or caused it to crash, use System Restore. Go to **Start ➔ All Programs ➔ Accessories ➔ System Tools ➔ System Restore**. Check the box next to 'Restore my computer to an earlier time', and click **Next** to enter in the date or time.

If your PC crashes during work, or something goes wrong with an installation, temporary files (those with the .tmp suffix) may have been left on your hard disk. These are created while you work and during some software installation processes. Normally, these files are deleted when no longer needed. To check your drive and delete unnecessary temporary files, select **Disk Cleanup** in **System Tools**.

MANAGING PROGRAMS AND FILES

If you want to get rid of a software program, make sure you uninstall it carefully. Correct removal of programs ensures that Registry entries (information stored by Windows about your PC settings) referring to the program are deleted, and program groups and menu entries are erased. If you simply delete the program files, you risk leaving associated files that will clutter up your hard drive and slow loading times, and performance. To remove a program correctly, go to **Start ➔ Control Panel** and select **Add or Remove Programs** (see 'How to', p. 85).

To check the size of a file or folder, right-click on it and choose **Properties**. To find the largest files on your PC, do a search. Go to **Start ➔ Search ➔ All Files and Folders**. You can search for files greater or smaller than certain preset sizes, or specify a size to search for.

Look for files of at least 20,000 KB (20 MB). Sort the results by size by clicking at the top of the Size column. Delete any files you find with a .tmp suffix.

MAKE THE MOST OF YOUR PC

If you only have 64 MB or 32 MB of RAM in your PC and are running Windows Me, your hard disk is working overtime. It has to swap some data normally in RAM to and from spare hard disk space to let Windows function as if it has more memory than it actually has.

Upgrading your PC's memory improves its speed and makes for less wear and tear since the hard drive heads have to move back and forth less. With programs' high demands on memory, and since you probably run several programs at the same time, upgrading to 128 MB or even 256 MB of RAM will make a huge difference.

Some PC experts frequently reformat and reinstall Windows. This is usually because a large number of programs and extra hardware have been installed and uninstalled, and the PC has slowed down considerably. Sometimes it may crash too frequently. Reformatting the hard disk and reinstalling Windows and all software should

be safe so long as a few precautions are taken (see box p. 32). But reinstallation can fail halfway through, so leave it to the experts if that is at all possible.

See also **Making the most of computer memory**, p. 21; **Fine tuning your disk drives**, p. 30; and **Checking hard disk space**, p. 35.

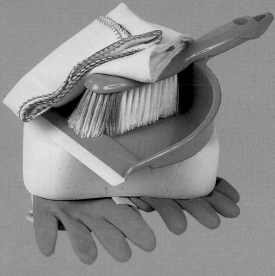

How to: Keep your hard disk healthy

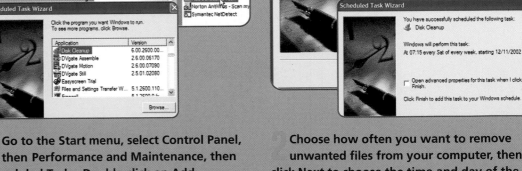

1 Go to the Start menu, select Control Panel, then Performance and Maintenance, then Scheduled Tasks. Double-click on Add Scheduled Task. The Scheduled Task Wizard will open. Click on Next then scroll down the list of Applications to Disk Cleanup. Click on it and then click Next.

2 Choose how often you want to remove unwanted files from your computer, then click Next to choose the time and day of the week that you want the process to run. Click Next and enter your password if you use one. Click Next again and then Finish to add this process to your scheduled tasks.

You can access huge amounts of information on these handy high-capacity discs.

■ Create a library of information.

CD-ROMs have become much less expensive in recent years and have opened up a massive number of channels for information storage and retrieval. Good choices for a CD-ROM library include reference titles, such as encyclopedias, and special interest titles, about music, wildlife or history.

■ Do you really need that CD-ROM?

Whether you need to purchase a CD-ROM depends on the amount of use you will get from it. For example, if you need to find out the capital

cities of all the countries in the world, a quick Internet search will give you that information. If you need more detail, buying an atlas on CD-ROM (or DVD-ROM) may be the answer.

How to: Install a CD burner

1 Push out the front panel on the PC casing to reveal the empty slot for your CD burner. Set the jumpers on the back of the burner to 'master', if connecting to a free IDE socket, or to 'slave', if connecting to a cable with another device attached. Slide the burner into the slot.

2 Now attach the power and IDE cables, but make sure you do so correctly. The red edge of the IDE cable goes next to the power socket. Screw the device in securely, then close the case and restart your machine.

Creating your own CDs at home can save you time, money and space.

■ Choose the writable CD disc

that's right for you. There are two types of disc, commonly referred to as the CD-R (CD-Recordable) and the CD-RW (CD-ReWritable). CD-R discs can only be written to or 'burned' once – their contents are then permanent. CD-RW discs can be written to and erased many times over. CD-R discs are cheaper and more reliable for audio recordings than CD-RWs.

■ Decide whether you need CD technology.

If you use a lot of floppy or even Zip disks to back up or archive your data, then a CD burner may be a good investment. A recordable CD holds about 640 MB of data, or 75 minutes of audio. That is approximately 444 floppy disks of 1.44 MB each, or more than six 100 MB Zip disks. The recordable discs themselves cost very little.

■ Create your own original audio CDs.

Once you've installed your CD burner, you can use it for more than just storage. To burn your favourite music onto a CD, all you need is a standard CD-ROM drive, as well as a CD burner attached to the PC. The software you need should come with the burner. Note, however, that most commercial discs are protected by copyright, and therefore cannot be legally duplicated.

Join the sound and vision revolution with DVD technology.

■ DVD stands for Digital Video Disc

or Digital Versatile Disc. A DVD has up to 28 times the storage capacity of a CD. With a film on DVD, you can look forward to crystal-clear digital sound and images, extras such as freeze-frame options, and special content, such as 'the making of' documentaries.

■ **DVD technology will transform** your home computer into a multimedia station. DVD software includes more and much better detailed graphics than ordinary CD-ROMs. DVD-ROMs allow you to load and run complex programs and games from a single disc, rather than having to juggle a set of several CD-ROMs. You can also watch DVD movies on your PC screen, often with access to subtitles, allowing you to watch the film in the language of your choice. A DVD-enabled laptop allows you to watch movies on the go!

■ **Don't throw away your old CD-ROMs.** DVD drives are backward compatible, which means you can play all your existing CDs on the drive, as well as any new DVDs.

■ **Videos on DVD are encoded** to prevent buyers in the UK obtaining cheap copies of DVD movies from, say, the US or China. DVDs encoded for one region will not work on players intended for another region. The regions are North America (1), Western Europe and Japan (2), South-east Asia (3), Australasia and South America (4), Eastern Europe and Russia (5) and China (6). Software DVDs are not currently encoded for regions.

CHECKING HARD DISK SPACE

Check your PC's hard disk space to see how much memory is available.

■ **Use the My Computer window to check hard disk space.** Go to **Start ➜ My Computer** and click on your hard drive (usually C:). The Details panel in the left hand column shows information about the drive, including the amount of free space on it, the total amount of space and the way it is formatted. You can find similar information for any other drives shown in the My Computer window.

■ **Check hard disk space from Windows Explorer.** Go to **Start ➜ All Programs ➜ Accessories ➜ Windows Explorer**, and navigate to My Computer using the column on the left, which shows how the files are organised on your hard disk. To see details, go to the View menu and click on **Status Bar**. Select your hard disk and its details will appear at the bottom of the window. For more information, right-click the disk icon and select **Properties** to see a pie chart of disk space usage.

DVD HARDWARE AND DISC SITES
Discover how to be versatile with your video discs.

DVD TIMES (www.dvdtimes.co.uk)
Film reviews and news, competitions, discussions, hardware news and gaming information, all on one site.

DVD REVIEWER (www.dvd.reviewer.co.uk)
Forums, technical know-how and extensive hardware reviews.

BLACKSTAR (www.blackstar.co.uk)
Online DVD store with sections on new releases and upcoming attractions.

MOVIETRAK (www.movietrak.com)
Internet DVD rental store that has a much wider range of titles than the average High Street rental shop.

How to: Make a customised audio CD

1 Use Windows Media Player to copy favourite tracks from your CD collection. Insert an audio CD and choose **Copy from CD** in Windows Media Player. Select the tracks you want to copy to your hard drive.

2 Click on **Media Library** then **New Playlist**. Type in a name for the new playlist and then click on the songs you want in the Media Library. Keeping the mouse button pressed down, drag them onto the CD. Then click on **Copy to CD or Device**. Insert a blank CD-R.

3 Click on **Copy Music**. Windows Media Player will first convert the files on your hard drive into a format suitable for use in an audio CD player, then will burn them onto your CD-R. The time taken to create your new CD depends on the speed of your CD burner.

Optional extras

The world of sound

CHOOSING A MICROPHONE

Here are some tips on selecting and using a microphone.

■ **Microphones are often bundled** with sound cards or computer packages, and more interesting and useful programs to make the most of them are becoming available. For example, you can record spoken comments as a sound file and embed the file into a spreadsheet. You can also use your PC as an answering machine. Conferencing software can enable two people to contact each other through their PCs, talking, sharing data and seeing video images. If you use instant messaging programs – such as Windows Messenger or AOL Instant Messenger – you can send voice messages as well as text.

■ **When buying a microphone** to use with your computer make sure that you buy one with the correct impedance (measured in ohms). Virtually all computers need a low-impedance microphone (less than 600 ohms). If all you have is a high-impedance microphone (50,000 ohms or more) then you will suffer from a weak input signal. If signals from your microphone sound distorted, it may be that the microphone output is too high, or you may be talking too loudly. An attenuator will lower the microphone output, while a softer voice will fix the other problem.

■ **There are programs that enable voice interaction** with your computer. One of the most exciting is speech recognition, which allows for dictation into any Windows application, such as WordPerfect or Microsoft Word. Find out about Dragon Naturally Speaking at (www.scansoft.com) or IBM Via Voice at (www.ibm.co.uk) online. You'll never have to type again!

GET ON SPEAKING TERMS WITH YOUR PC

Speech is a fast and natural way to interact with a computer or manipulate a mouse. Whether you are looking to increase or dictate documents instead of type, there is a Dragon product that can meet your needs.

What type of solution are you looking for?

Dragon NaturallySpeaking® Products

■ **Use a PC headset to add a microphone** and earphones to your computer. A headset plugs into the speaker and the microphone jacks in the back of the PC card. The connectors are marked with icons that match the icons on the PC sockets. Make sure your headset cord is long enough for you to work comfortably, even if the system unit is under your desk.

■ **Microsoft NetMeeting** – included with Windows – enables users to communicate by voice over the Internet. Internet games that previously used text chat windows for contact, now allow players to talk to each other in real time, just as if they were in the same room.

■ **Windows' Sound Recorder** can make recordings. Go to **Start → All Programs → Accessories → Entertainment → Sound Recorder**. Click the button with the red circle to start recording, and the button with the black square to stop.

▶ See also **Record that tune**, p. 206; and **Talking to your computer**, p. 208.

▶ See also **Record that tune**, p. 206; and **Talking to your computer**, p. 208.

How to: Convert a music CD into a WMA file

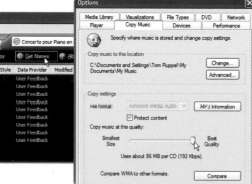

1 Insert the CD into your CD drive (if you have two drives, choose the one with the highest reading speed, as this could make the conversion quicker). Launch Windows Media Player if it has not automatically started. Click on Copy from CD in the left-hand column.

2 Get track and artist details by connecting to the Internet then clicking on Get Names. Set the quality of your converted files by going to Tools then Options and clicking on the Copy Music tab. Remember, higher quality means larger files.

3 Once you have the track names and have chosen the file quality, click on Copy Music. Depending on the speed of your CD-ROM drive, you can convert an entire CD to WMA format in just a few minutes.

DIGITAL MUSIC PLAYERS

If you love music on the move, try a portable MP3 or WMA player. You can select tracks in an instant, re-record as often as you like, and all with no moving parts.

■ **Buy a player that connects via USB.** All digital music players link to a PC in one way or another to transfer the music files. However, the data will be transferred much faster using a USB port rather than a serial communications or COM port. A USB connection also means that you can plug the player in while Windows is running on your computer; the player will be instantly detected and the correct driver loaded. Even faster data rates are possible with players that use USB 2.0 or Firewire connections, although only the most recent PCs have these ports as standard. USB 2.0 devices will work with USB ports on older machines, but won't deliver the highest transfer rates.

■ **Transferring files is as simple as copying** from one folder to another on your PC. In Windows Explorer, drag and drop your recorded music files onto the icon for your connected player, which should appear as an extra disk in **My Computer**.

■ **When buying a music player** you have a choice of solid state memory (like your computer's RAM) or a built-in hard disk drive (just like the hard disk in your PC). A player's RAM can often be added to with a removable memory card. Players with built-in disk drives are more expensive, but can store hundreds of times more music – often enough space for your entire music collection in a hand-held device.

■ **Choose which file format to use** for your music files. Windows Media Player, installed with Windows XP, creates files in WMA format, while other programs such as RealPlayer (download from www.real.com) will convert your music CDs to MP3 files. MP3 is the more universal standard, although a growing number of players are able to play both MP3 and WMA files. It is also possible to download an inexpensive plug-in for Windows Media Player that allows it to encode music as MP3s. All of these programs will encode each track on a CD as a separate WMA or MP3 file, and most allow you to download track and artist names from the Internet.

■ **Choose the rate** at which you want your MP3 tracks recorded. In Media Player go to **Tools → Options**, and click the **CD Audio** tab. The

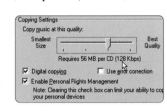

adjustment is in the Copying Settings section. The data rates can range from 48 Kbps to 192 Kbps. A 192 Kbps rate records at the highest quality, but the resulting MP3 files will be four times the size of those recorded at 48 Kbps because there will be four times the amount of data converted.

■ **Experiment with the rate settings** to get the balance between quality and file size that is best for you. If a typical CD takes up 44 MB of disk space at medium quality, it will easily fit onto a 64 MB memory card. However, at a higher setting of around 90 MB per CD, you will need more memory to fit the whole album onto your MP3 player, and may not notice the added quality if you listen to your MP3s somewhere noisy, like a train.

■ **If your PC has a CD burner installed,** burn your MP3 files onto recordable CDs. That way you keep your hard drive free from hundreds of MP3 files, and your data will be safe if the PC breaks down. Some CD players can now decode MP3 files directly – giving you some 6–8 hours of play on a single CD. Keep track of your MP3 files by labelling your CDs carefully and keeping all your original MP3 tracks in clearly labelled folders on your computer's hard drive.

■ **Each CD can store around 650 MB of data,** so you can store as much as ten albums of MP3 music on one CD. Although recordable CDs are fairly robust, you should handle them with care, like any other CDs, to avoid scratches.

▶ See also **MP3: The new face of music,** p. 203; and **Explore the world of MP3,** p. 285.

PORTABLE MP3 PLAYERS
Investigate the huge range of portable music players that are available.

DIAMOND (www.diamondmm.com)
Makers of the Rio, one of the original MP3 players. Newer, curvy models can play WMA files as well as MP3.

EXPANSYS (www.expansys.com)
Search this site for the iPAQ Personal Audio Player. It supports MP3 and other formats.

CREATIVE (www.nomadworld.com)
Creative are manufacturers of the Nomad range of MP3 players.

APPLE (www.apple.com/uk)
Makers of the iPod, available with capacities up to 20 GB, and now PC compatible too.

SONY (www.sony.co.uk)
Tiny and stylish digital music players from the makers of the original Walkman.

GOOD LOUDSPEAKERS MAKE A DIFFERENCE

With the right speakers, you can listen to five channels of Dolby Digital surround sound while playing a movie or game.

■ **Although most modern PC sound systems** are compatible with current software, it is best to stick with equipment from one of the well-known and trusted manufacturers. Not only does this ensure that you'll get high-quality sound from games and multimedia software, but, if there is a problem, help will be readily available and you can download driver updates easily from the manufacturer's Website.

■ **Using a good quality sound card** will let you play back surround sound through four speakers. Yet, this will only emulate the effect of 3D sound. To get full Dolby Digital surround sound from your PC, you will need a sound card with digital output through a coaxial

(S/PDIF) or optical connector. You will also need a decoder/amplifier, like those that come with high-quality home cinema systems, to turn the digital signal into five discrete channels of sound: two at the front, two at the back and a central channel for speech.

■ **Complete systems,** with speakers and stands included, are available from many manufacturers, such as Creative Labs. The speakers are relatively small, but powerful and of high quality. It is a good idea to inspect a few different speaker systems in the store before you buy, because sound quality is really a matter of personal taste.

■ **If you have a home sound system** situated near your PC, you don't necessarily need to have separate speakers for your computer. The PC's sound can be re-routed into a spare input on your stereo system – an auxiliary input, for example – to play back the sounds. The drawback here is that your sound system will need to be on all the time if you want to hear the Windows system and Office alert sounds while you work.

■ **A subwoofer speaker** does not need a separate sound channel. A special filter separates the lowest frequency sounds – those that cannot be adequately reproduced by small speakers – and plays them back through a much larger subwoofer speaker, which is usually placed on the floor. The subwoofer doesn't need to be positioned as carefully as the other speakers because the human ear is less sensitive to the direction of low-frequency sounds.

▶ See also **Computer games,** p. 184.

CONNECT YOUR INSTRUMENTS WITH MIDI

Musical Instrument Digital Interface (MIDI) lets your computer work as a musical instrument.

■ **MIDI lets you connect** electronic musical instruments to your PC. Use a MIDI keyboard to 'play' the synthesiser chip that's built into your PC's sound card, or use software to controls sounds on external devices. You are not limited to the sounds on your sound card – modern computers are fast enough to be able to mathematically mimic the complex mechanics of real instruments, letting you play convincing emulations of organs and pianos.

 How to: Add Dolby Digital surround sound

1 To be able to listen to Dolby Digital sound from your PC, you need a sound card that has a digital output. After installing the sound card, connect the digital output to the input of the Dolby Digital decoder box.

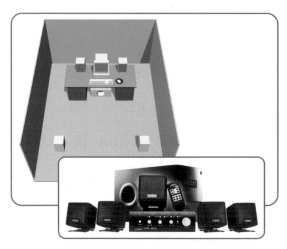

2 Position all speakers away from the walls. Place the two front speakers equidistant in front of you, with the speech speaker in the middle. Place the rear speakers behind you. Put the subwoofer on the floor, between the front two speakers, and plug in the cables.

■ **Many piano-style keyboards** that have their own built-in sounds can be controlled by a computer via MIDI. These keyboards vary in price from hundreds to thousands of pounds, depending on their features. A full-sized keyboard consists of 88 keys, weighted to feel like a real piano, but less expensive versions with fewer, lightly weighted keys are also available.

■ **There are two main types** of MIDI software you can buy. One of these is a notation program, which is designed to help musicians to print out their finished work in manuscript form. The other type of program is sequencing software, which enables the aspiring composer to mix different segments of music together. Many sequencing programs are available that allow you to record audio tracks to your hard disk as well as the signals from a MIDI keyboard.

cakewalk   Products   Purchase   Download

■ **Cakewalk produces a range of exciting programs** to help you to compose any kind of music, from the simplest pop tune to

more ambitious pieces of classical music. You can create audio for CDs, film or video soundtracks, multimedia games, live stage sound and Internet music delivery. To find out more about the service and to download trial versions of software, visit their site (www.cakewalk.com).

■ **If you have a keyboard** with its own sounds, consider how compatible those sounds are with those of other keyboards currently in use. There is a standard set of sounds, known as General MIDI, which many home computers use. If your computer uses General MIDI, you will be able to share your MIDI files with a number of other musicians from all over the world, as well as download files from the Internet and other sources and hear them correctly.

■ **Your sound card is the key.** The quality of music varies greatly between the various sound cards that are available. Although any sound card can recognise a MIDI file, each will play it slightly differently – rather like different musicians interpreting the same music in their own way. Make sure you try before you buy.

▶ See also **Music to suit every taste,** p. 282.

▶ See also **Music to suit every taste,** p. 282.

MIDI MUSIC SITES
Explore some of the vast range of MIDI resources the Web has to offer.

ABOUT.COM (www.mindspring.com/ ~s-allen/picks.htm)
Extensive information on MIDI, plus a huge MIDI archive to browse through. You can even upload your own work.

HARMONY CENTRAL (www.harmony-central.com/MIDI)
Valuable source of MIDI information for users on any platform.

SYNTHZONE (www.synthzone.com)
All you want to know about synthesisers and electronic music production.

ULTIMATE MIDI PAGE (www.ultimatemidi.com)
Extensive listing of MIDI resources, with links to dozens of related sites.

How to: Add a MIDI keyboard to your PC

1 **You can add an inexpensive MIDI controller keyboard to your computer very easily.** When you press the keys, MIDI signals are sent to your PC, and you can hear the notes coming from the PC's speakers.

2 **Depending on your keyboard, you'll attach it to your PC by a USB cable or one of** several different types of MIDI interface. Many PC sound cards have joystick ports that, with the right software and adaptors, can be used for MIDI connections.

3 **Once you have connected the keyboard, install the software that came with it.** Many music programs also allow you to record audio along with MIDI files, by attaching a microphone to your sound card.

Scanners and scanning

Several years ago, scanners were an expensive computer add-on, but they are now substantially lower in price and, as a result, have become a very popular computer purchase. With a scanner by your side, you can send photos to friends and family around the world via e-mail.

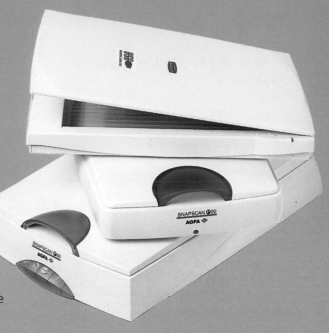

TYPES OF SCANNERS

Flatbed scanners are the most common type. They can scan a single sheet at a time, but are large. Even slim, streamlined models take up a fair amount of desk space. Although many can't cope with items any larger than a sheet of A4 paper, this type of scanner is well suited to personal use in the home.

Business card scanners are small and have optical character recognition (text-interpreting) software built in. They are expensive but can send information direct to your personal organiser software so you don't have to type it in.

High-resolution flatbed scanners with a transparency attachment are ideal for designers and photographers who want to scan slides or negatives for use in their work. Smaller versions, which can handle originals up to 100 x 125 mm (4 x 5 in), are considerably less expensive than full size models.

Handheld scanners are good for use on the move, but do not give the most accurate results.

If your PC has a USB port, get a scanner with a USB connector to take advantage of the speed it offers. Even faster speeds are

 How to: **Scan an image**

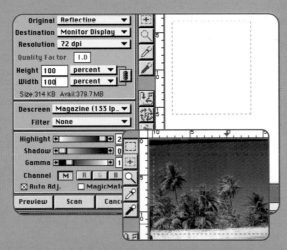

Place the original image you want to scan on the bed of the scanner and close the lid. Start the scanner's software (many scanners have a simple one-touch button to do this) and the image will start to scan.

You may get a previewed image first. If you are not happy with the image, change the image resolution and any other settings. You may be able to alter the colours scanned, the actual size of scan, the crop of the image, or apply filters to sharpen or blur the image.

Get a second preview with your new settings. When you are satisfied with the preview, complete the scan. You can then use photo-editing software for the final touches to produce an image. You might want to change the size of the picture, or edit the colours.

A wide range of Websites provide information on every type of scanner, either for use in the home or the more demanding environment of an office.

CANON (www.canon.co.uk)
Information about the full range of Canon scanners available in the UK. Also visit the Canon USA site (www.usa.canon.com), where you can download help for any of Canon's range of specialist scanners.

UMAX (www.umax.com)
First stop for drivers to accompany the scanners from this popular German company. This site offers a range of professional, business and home scanners, as well as digital cameras and printers.

DATEC (www.datecsys.co.uk)
Online IT superstore, selling leading brands.

DABS (www.dabs.com)
Internet retailer with a wide range of all computer equipment including scanners.

EPSON (www.epson.co.uk)
Purchase scanners – as well as a range of printers and digital cameras – online from this site. There are also free software downloads (including drivers), reviews and an extensive selection of useful Web links.

A software bundle is supplied with almost every scanner. Often, simplified 'lite' versions of full-priced software are included, and these are adequate for general use. Look for image-editing, image-organising and filing software, as well as for an optical character recognition (OCR) program. You may also get graphics software, such as greetings cards or e-card creation tools.

Use optical character recognition
software to turn text on a printed page into text you can edit on your computer. This is useful if you have print-outs of documents you no longer have on disk, or if you want to get text into your PC for easy searching. Or you may need to edit a document someone has sent you.

If you intend to e-mail a scanned
image, keep the image file as small as possible. A low image resolution helps, but so does

reducing the actual area being scanned. If your scanner software does not allow you to do this, use a graphics editing application, such as Paint Shop Pro, to crop off uninteresting parts of the image.

See also **The world of graphics,** p. 154; and **Editing photographs,** p. 196.

possible with USB 2.0 devices, which also work with slower USB 1.1 sockets. Other high-speed scanners use FireWire connections (also known as iLink or IEEE 1394), although only a few PCs have these sockets as standard.

TERMINOLOGY AND SPECIFICATIONS

Image resolution is often quoted as a key feature, so it is worth understanding what this means. The abbreviation used to describe image resolution is dpi, which stands for dots per inch. In an image scanned at 300dpi, every square inch is made up of 90,000 dots.

Some scanners quote an interpolated resolution as well as an optical one. The optical resolution is the true resolution at which a scanner scans. Interpolated resolution is a higher resolution, achieved by software producing more dots in an image than were actually scanned. Use the optical resolution as a buying guide.

Is more better? Most people do not need images scanned at the highest resolution of which some scanners are capable. The high quality that 1200 x 1200 dpi delivers is great if your printer is up to it, but it means your files are very large.

Files scanned at high resolution can be very large, so your friends might not appreciate you e-mailing them such bulky attachments, as they may be difficult to download. For general computer use, 300 dpi is good enough. If an image is only going to appear on screen (on a Website, for example) 72 dpi is sufficient and will speed download times.

All scanners quote their colour capability in bits. A 24-bit scanner can scan about 16.7 million different colours in an image. Scanners can pick out more colours than this, but in reality this is the highest number that most people are ever likely to need.

USING SCANNER SOFTWARE

Get to know your software. Scanner software offers a range of settings, depending

on the kind of image you want to scan – colour or black and white photos, or printed material. Also consider what you want to do with the image – print it, place it on a Website or send it as a fax.

The world of images

Upgrading your PC's graphics card can dramatically improve screen display and 3D game play.

■ **PCs are fitted with graphics cards,** also called adaptors, capable of displaying millions of colours at a variety of screen resolutions, measured in pixels. If you work with graphics or have a digital camera, you will need a good adaptor to get the best from your pictures. Also, a good graphics card can generate higher refresh rates, which reduces screen flicker.

■ **Choose the right graphics card for your games.** Special graphics cards are required to play 3D-accelerated games. Three main standards of card are available: Glide (3Dfx), OpenGL and Direct3D. Most cards will be able to play games that use any of these standards.

■ **From PCI to AGP.** In early PCs, graphics cards were plugged into the Peripheral Component Interconnect (PCI) slot inside the PC, also used for sound cards and modems. The Accelerated Graphics Port (AGP) was later developed to cope with the huge amounts of data processed in modern 3D games. Not all PCs have an AGP port, so check your motherboard's manual to see whether you have the right slot.

■ **The final conflict!** Having problems in a certain game or graphics program? There may be

a conflict between that software and your graphics adaptor. A patch – a piece of bug-fixing computer code to insert or 'patch' into a program – can often be downloaded from the relevant adaptor manufacturer's Website. Or you may get a message saying you need to update your graphics adaptor. Update it using the Hardware Update Wizard – you will need to connect to the Internet first.

Replace your mouse with a faster pen-and-pad alternative.

■ **Speed up your work.** Drawing pads or tablets use a digital pen and touch sensitive pad to create items on your Desktop. In certain situations, such as on-screen design, you may find it faster and more accurate to use them than the standard mouse.

■ **Mouse and pad in perfect harmony.** Some graphics tablets, including the Graphire pad made by Wacom (www.wacom. com) come with both a stylus and a mouse, allowing you to swap between the different types of input device according to the work that you are doing.

 ## How to: Install a graphics card

1 Disconnect the monitor and power cables, open the case and remove the old graphics card. If your new card is AGP compatible, locate the AGP slot – usually a single brown slot next to the row of white PCI slots. See your PC manual if you are unsure about this.

2 Gently, but firmly, press in the new adaptor. Close the case and reattach the monitor and power cables. Turn on your PC. Windows will detect the new hardware and prompt you to insert the graphics card disk and install the driver from it. Now restart your PC.

3 When the PC restarts, readjust the colour-depth, resolution and refresh rate to your personal choices. Most graphics cards come with extra software to allow you to fine tune the settings. Check the manuals for help on how to optimise the card and game play.

■ **Using a digital pen for long periods** may give you writer's cramp, just as a normal pen might, and a mouse can sometimes cause repetitive strain injury. So, remember to take regular breaks and practise stretching exercises at your workstation.

■ **A graphics tablet costs more** than a standard mouse so before you buy, weigh up how much you will use it and ask to try one in your local computer store.

■ **If you have ever tried to draw a detailed picture** or artwork using a standard mouse, you know just how frustrating the process can really be. Some pad manufacturers, such as Wacom, offer pressure-sensitive software bundles to accompany their standard mouse, making the process far easier and more intuitive.

CAPTURING VIDEO WITH A PC

You can edit video on your PC by importing digital video from a DV camera or converting analogue data to digital information using a capture card.

■ **Digital Video (DV) camcorders** record and store moving images as digital information – with no need for a video capture card on your PC. However, DV recordings contain enormous amounts of data that need to be processed extremely quickly, so only the latest computers with fast processors (at least a Pentium 4 1.6 GHz or equivalent), large hard drives and good video cards (ideally with a TV output so you can see what your edited work looks like on a real screen) are suitable for the task. A PC for video editing also needs a FireWire port (also called iLink or IEEE 1394) to connect to the camcorder – if you don't have one you can add it on a PCI card. Once you have edited your video, you can export it back to the camera along the firewire cable.

■ **A video capture card** fits into a PCI slot inside your PC and has connections for your camera or VCR outputs. You can even get a USB version of the card if you don't have any PCI slots

left, or if you don't want to open your PC case. You'll need a reasonably fast PC to get the best results, because converting full screen video to digital data is a processor-intensive process. Try a lower resolution if the frame rate is erratic.

■ **Video takes up considerable hard drive space** and will require a lot of memory to run. If you are thinking of editing your videos on your PC, consider increasing the amount of RAM in it to at least 512 MB, and adding a large (and fast) second hard drive, with a capacity of greater than 60 GB, just to store your video data.

WATCH TV ON YOUR PC

View your favourite television shows on your PC by installing a TV tuner card.

■ **A TV tuner card** is hardware that converts the digital signal of your PC into a television signal and vice versa, letting you watch TV on your computer, or use your TV screen as a

monitor. Make sure that the monitor and TV display are the same number of pixels in size and have the same colour settings. Go to **Start ➜ Control Panel ➜ Appearance and Themes** and click the **Display** icon. From the **Settings** tab, adjust the **Screen resolution** and **Color quality** and then click OK.

■ **Many tuner cards come with software** that allows you to record TV shows directly to your hard disk, then compress your recordings into MPEG files. MPEG stands for Motion Picture Experts Group, a group that devises standards for efficiently compressing video into relatively small files. Even so, you will need a lot of free disk space to store your recordings, and ideally should invest in a second high-capacity hard drive purely for video.

■ **Receive analogue and digital TV channels.** All tuner cards can receive analogue TV broadcasts. More sophisticated models can also receive digital broadcasts either from satellite or digital terrestrial services. One manufacturer is Hauppauge (www.hauppauge.co.uk).

How to: Connect your TV tuner card

1 **Turn off the PC and remove the cover. Plug the tuner card into a free PCI slot on your motherboard – it is a long connector (usually white) into which your tuner card will fit neatly. Replace the cover.**

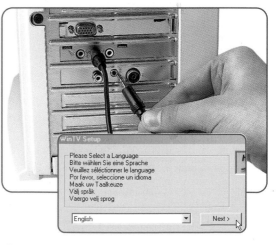

2 **To get sound, connect the audio loop-back cord from the Audio Jack-Out socket on the tuner card to the Audio Jack-In socket on your sound card. Restart your PC. Insert the installation CD and follow the sequence of instructions that appears.**

Most people already have a traditional camera that uses film, so why invest in a digital camera too?

■ **Digital photography has many advantages** over the traditional kind, including editable pictures and almost instant results, that make it an appealing option.

■ **You can get instant prints** with a digital camera. It enables you to print an image as soon as you get back to your computer. With traditional photography the film has to be developed by a lab or mail-order firm. But this can take time and it might be weeks before you finish a roll of film. Going digital means you can also e-mail images direct to friends.

■ **Most digital cameras allow you to view an image** immediately and retake the

shot if it isn't right. With the right software you can edit images on your computer, creating artistic or humorous effects. The downside of using a digital camera is that it tends to use a considerable amount of battery power.

■ **All the features of a traditional camera** are also available on a digital camera, such as a flash unit, red-eye reduction capability (to avoid those red eye-centres sometimes caused by flash light) and a self-timer, so that you can get yourself in the shot. You might find a digital camera that also offers sound-recording features, so that you can add a commentary or voice note to an image, and date and time stamping onto the picture itself. Some digital cameras can even be used for video conferencing.

■ **Taking moving pictures.** Some of the most sophisticated digital cameras can capture short movies. Imagine, for example, shooting a short sequence of a grandchild blowing out the candles on a birthday cake. You can then send it to friends and family all over the world via the

Internet on the same day. Some cameras even contain microphones so you don't have to shoot a silent movie.

■ **Most digital cameras can vary image resolution.** The image resolution is a measure of the number of dots (called pixels) that are used to make up a photograph. The more dots in an image, the sharper it will be, but it will also require more space to store it digitally. Image resolution is presented either as the number of dots on both the horizontal and vertical lines, or as a total. So an image taken at 1280 x 960 pixels (or 1.3 megapixels) will be less clear than one taken at 1800 x 1200 pixels (or 2.3 megapixels).

If you intend to print an image, use the highest resolution your camera can manage. If you just want to put an image on the Web, the lowest resolution your camera supports will usually be fine (see 'How to', left). Remember that the higher the resolution, the larger the file, and the longer it will take to download on your Web page or as an e-mail attachment.

■ **Most digital cameras support removable storage media** of some sort, though some budget models only have built-in memory. The larger the capacity of the storage media, the more pictures you can store. Some digital cameras support CompactFlash cards,

How to: Share your pictures on the web

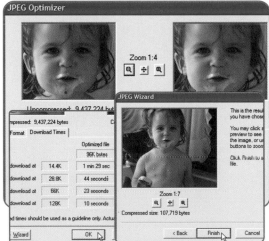

1 Digital images downloaded straight from your camera are normally too large to put on the Web or send as e-mail attachments. Use a program such as Paint Shop Pro to compress them into JPEG format first. Go to the File menu, select Export, then JPEG Optimizer.

2 The left-hand window shows the original, and the right-hand window the compressed image. Choose the amount of compression, then click the Download Times tab to see how long the compressed image will take to e-mail. The JPEG Wizard can also help.

which can come in very high capacities. When one memory card is full, you can simply take it out of the camera, replace it with an empty memory card and carry on shooting.

■ Most modern digital cameras come with a USB cable for transferring

images onto your computer. It is far quicker than the older serial cable method, and makes transferring images relatively fast. If you use digital cameras a great deal, it may be worth while investing in a memory card reader. For a few pounds you can have a reader that is permanently plugged into your computer. When you want to transfer data, take the memory card from your camera and put it into the reader. You can also plug some digital cameras directly into a printer, or even into your TV for a slide show.

■ Because digital cameras don't use film, but storage media, you can use the same

storage device over and over again. However, you have to empty it before you can reuse it, and you will need a system for storing and organising your

digital images. One method is to download the images to your computer and from there onto a storage device, such as Zip disk or a recordable CD-ROM. This allows you to carry your photographic collection around to show pictures to others, and it keeps photos secure and separate from your PC. It also means you will always know where to go to find a picture, no matter how long ago you took it.

■ When buying a digital camera you

will notice all the extra features the camera includes are usually accessed through buttons on a panel next to the LCD (liquid crystal display), but sometimes they are located elsewhere. Make sure these buttons are easy to operate and that their functions are clear. On some digital cameras you have to go through a long sequence of button pressing to gain access to some features. This can be tedious and the sequences can be difficult to remember, making the camera unnecessarily complicated to use.

▶ See also **Editing photographs,** p. 196.

DIGITAL CAMERA SITES

Before you buy, you can learn a lot from these Websites about the capabilities and limitations of the various brands of cameras.

CANON (www.canon.co.uk)
CASIO (www.casio.com)
EPSON (www.epson.co.uk)
FUJI (www.fujifilm.co.uk)
HEWLETT PACKARD (www.hp.com/uk)
KODAK (www.kodak.co.uk)
KONICA (www.konica.co.uk)
MINOLTA (www.minolta.co.uk)
OLYMPUS (www.olympus.co.uk)
PENTAX (www.pentax.co.uk)
RICOH (www.ricoh.co.uk)
SANYO (www.sanyo.co.uk)
SONY (www.sony.co.uk)
TOSHIBA (www.toshiba.co.uk)

How to: Download digital photos onto your PC

1 Linking a camera with a USB connection to a PC running Windows XP can be as easy as plugging in the USB cable. Windows will recognise most cameras instantly without extra software and will treat the camera as an extra hard drive.

2 Use the Scanner and Camera Wizard built-in to Windows XP to download images. You will see thumbnails of all the images stored on your camera. Select the ones that you want to download by clicking in the checkbox at the corner of each thumbnail image.

3 Click Next to begin the transfer – the screen will show you how many images are left to be copied. Once all the images you selected have been copied, you can choose to publish them to a Website, order prints of them or simply view them as a slideshow.

Staying in touch

PROBLEMS WITH YOUR TELEPHONE CONNECTION

Make the most of your modem and get the ultimate Internet connection for your particular device.

■ **Problems with your Internet connection?** Make sure that the dial-in telephone number for your Internet Service Provider is correct. Start Internet Explorer and click on **Tools ➔ Internet Options**. Select the **Connections** tab and then click the **Settings** button in the Dial-up settings panel. In the next dialogue box, click on **Properties.** Check the Internet Service Provider's dial-in number and area code, and adjust it if necessary. If you are unsure of the number, you may need to confirm it by phoning your Internet Service Provider's helpline.

■ **Not sure whether you are actually connected** to the Internet? Even if you are not connected, you may still see your homepage if it has been cached (stored on your hard

disk). So try loading another Web page and take a look at the System Tray in the bottom right-hand corner of your Desktop for the Dial-up icon – two green computers. Watch them for a few seconds – if the small screens flash, your computer is receiving data from the Internet.

■ **You still can't get connected?** Check that the telephone cable is securely attached to your modem. If you share a phone line with other telephones in your home, make sure that no one else is on the line and that all handsets are properly replaced, otherwise they will cause your connection to fail.

■ **How good is your connection?** A poor quality telephone line can seriously affect your Internet surfing. If you can hear crackling when you are on the phone, and you use the same line for your Internet connection, the noise can be enough to cause your connection to falter or fail completely. You may need to replace a cable or contact your telephone provider.

■ **Connection charges vary,** depending on your Internet Service Provider and the level of service you pay for. Your ISP's Website will provide you with information about the quality and cost of the full range of Internet connection services they are able to supply.

■ **Avoid missing phone calls when you are online.** Many modern modems – both internal and external – are capable of notifying you when a phone call is trying to get through while you're surfing the Net – some even act as answering machines with a message playback facility. To use such modems in this way, however, you must subscribe to your phone company's 'call waiting' services.

■ **DSL (Digital Subscriber Line) broadband** is the fastest Internet connection medium currently available at an affordable price. An ADSL (Asymmetric Digital Subscriber Line) can transmit data as much as 20 times faster than a normal modem, although uploads from your computer will be slower. You need your phone company to set up your phone line for ADSL, and you will also need a special modem-type device to

connect to your PC. With ADSL you can use the same line for voice calls and broadband Internet, and use both services at the same time.

■ **DSL does have its drawbacks.** The quality of your connection can depend on the number of people using the

DSL line through your local exchange. The length of the phone lines between you and the exchange also has an effect – beyond a certain length you may not be able to use the service.

▶ See also **Fast Net access using DSL,** p. 216.

CHOOSING A MODEM

The term 'modem' comes from two words: MOdulator-DEModulator, which describe exactly what a modem does.

■ **A modem transforms digital data** from your PC into analogue format so that it can be sent down a normal phone line, where it is then converted back into digital data by a modem at the other end.

■ **The speed of a modem** is measured in bits per second (bps) and refers to the number of bits (digital data that makes up, for example, a Web page) that it can pass down a phone line in one second. The faster the speed, the quicker you can send and receive data. Most home PCs now come equipped with modems that work at up to 56 Kbps (56,000 bits per second), which is the minimum you should consider buying.

■ **'Traffic jams' on the Internet** can slightly slow down your connection speed, as can blips on your telephone line. You can't receive data any more quickly than it is being sent, but in order to use the Internet efficiently your modem should run at a speed of at least 33 Kbps. To see your connection speed, hover your mouse

pointer over the dial-in icon in the System Tray on your Windows Taskbar.

■ Internal modems come in the form of a small circuit board

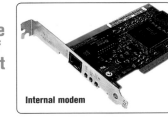

Internal modem

that fits into an expansion slot in your PC's main unit, like a sound or graphics card. The advantage of this type of modem is that they don't take up valuable desk space, although you lose a slot inside your computer that you may need later.

■ External modems are small boxes

that plug into your computer via a serial or USB port. An external modem has the advantage of portability – you can disconnect it easily from one PC to use on another, but it takes up more space and adds to your cord tangles. External modems have indicator lights to tell you that they are working properly, which many people prefer, and some can work as fax receivers without your PC needing to be switched on.

■ Voice modems contain a speaker

and microphone, allowing you to use your PC as a phone very easily. With cheap international calls now available on the Internet, this could save you money on your phone bill. You can even set up your modem to act as an answering machine, to take calls in your absence.

CONNECTING TO THE FUTURE

Slow Internet access will eventually become a thing of the past when cable modem technology comes into its own.

■ What is a cable modem?
Instead of sending and receiving data across a standard telephone line, a cable modem connects to your PC through the same cable used for your cable TV service. Contact your cable provider to see if they offer an Internet service – generally there is a set fee for unlimited Internet access, although broadband cable is not available everywhere.

■ Cable modems receive data many times faster
than an average phone modem. Speed varies according to the service, but typically, cable Internet is about ten times faster. However, the speed drops as more local people subscribe. Also, receiving speed is greater than sending speed, so don't expect the same speed when uploading files.

■ Ask what your cable company can do for you.
Have a good look at the various packages offered by your cable company. Like many Internet Service Providers, your cable company will probably offer a choice of user names, e-mail addresses and free Web space.

■ Check cable modem coverage in your area.
Not every part of the UK has a cable TV service, and not all the areas with one can receive broadband Internet via a cable modem. Check the cable companies' Websites for more information: NTL (www.ntl.co.uk) or Telewest (www.telewest.co.uk).

■ Make sure your PC is powerful enough.
Although you do not have to have an extremely fast computer to use basic broadband Internet services, things like multi-user games played over the Net and streaming video content will work much better on a recent model running a modern version of Windows. However, the speed of a broadband Internet connection is still very slow when compared with the rate at which data can be read from a hard disk, for example. This means that even older computers are able to take advantage of its benefits.

▶ See also **Fast Net access using DSL,** p. 216.

BROADBAND CONNECTION SERVICES

The following companies are just a few of the ones offering broadband services via either cable or ADSL in the UK.

NTL (www.ntl.co.uk)
One of the two UK cable companies, offering broadband services via cable modem in some areas. Look for combined TV, telephone and broadband deals.

BLUEYONDER (www.blueyonder.co.uk)
The broadband arm of Telewest, the other UK cable TV provider. Services as fast as 1 Mbps are available – as with NTL look for packages combining Internet, TV and phone.

BT OPENWORLD (www.bt.com)
The UK's biggest telephone service provider offers broadband connections suitable for homes and offices. Other companies may offer cheaper services, but many will require that you have a BT phone line.

AOL (www.aol.co.uk/broadband)
AOL now offers a broadband service in the UK giving faster access to their exclusive member content areas.

Handheld computers

Personal digital assistants, or PDAs, are handheld computers with the processing power of the desktop models of only a few years ago. You can use your PDA as a simple diary, address book and memo pad, although the latest models can also play videos, run games, store a library's worth of reading matter and even take pictures.

MAKING YOUR CHOICE

Handheld computers, also known as PDAs, fall into two broad groups, divided by the operating system that they run. PocketPC handhelds run a system closely related to Windows and generally offer colour screens, handwriting recognition and the ability to play multimedia files such as film clips. Other handhelds run the Palm operating system (OS). These machines generally cost less and may have monochrome screens rather than colour, and more restricted multimedia abilities. Both types of handheld can synchronise with your PC, so that addresses, diaries and memos remain coordinated on both desktop and handheld.

Horses for courses. Palmtops and PocketPCs have different capabilities, so your choice will depend on the sorts of tasks you want the machine to perform. Palmtops running the PocketPC operating system typically have processors running at 200-400 MHz, 64 MB of RAM, and larger screens. Palm OS machines generally have 33-120 MHz processors, a maximum of 16 MB of RAM, and lower resolution screens. Both types of machine offer handwriting recognition systems.

Battery life is another vital factor to consider when buying a handheld computer. While a monochrome palmtop may last up to 3 months on one charge, or one set of batteries, a model with a colour display may only last for 6 to 10 hours of continuous use before the batteries need recharging.

Connecting all PDAs to Windows is straightforward. Almost all PDAs come with software that needs to be installed on your PC to allow it to communicate with the handheld device. This software handles data back-ups, synchronisation and file conversion to and from the PDA and PC. Most units come with a cradle that is plugged permanently into the PC's serial port or USB port. The USB connection is the quickest, and the increased speed is noticeable when you have to copy and transfer volumes of data, especially large files, such as MP3 music files, graphic images and photographs.

If you want to record sounds, play MPEG videos and MP3 music files, as well as view images in full colour, you need a PocketPC or Palm operating system PC. PocketPC models include the Windows Media Player, which you can also download from Microsoft (www.microsoft.com/windows/windowsmedia/en/download). It can play back MP3s through stereo headphones, even while you are using other functions on the PDA. You can play graphics-based games on both Palm OS and PocketPC handhelds, although you cannot expect the same quality of graphics that you would get on a laptop or desktop model.

MP3s, MPEGs and high resolution images use a lot of memory. Although most modern Palm OS PCs have 16MB of RAM, this is also used for software and all your data. For more

memory, you can plug in memory cards to certain handhelds – available in 64, 128 and 192 MB versions. Sony's Clié supports the Memory Stick, Palm PDAs use the Secure digital card, and the Handspring Visors range use the Flash Springboard module. If you are using them to store music, keep in mind that you'll need at least 64 MB to store an MP3 album.

Transferring files to your PDA can be a lengthy process, especially via your PC's serial port. If you have a PocketPC, it's quicker to get a USB card reader and plug your CompactFlash card into that. The icon appears in My Computer and Windows Explorer as another drive to which you can drag files.

SOFTWARE UPDATES

If you already have a PDA, check the Internet regularly for additional software. You can download utilities that greatly enhance your PDA's

functionality. Some add-ins allow you to store e-books, dictionaries, and create presentation flip charts. Some are complete applications, such as spreadsheets and even global positioning system software. All programs are first downloaded onto your PC from Websites such as Handango (www.handango.com) and Tucows (www.tucows.com) for the Palm OS models. You then install them using the PDA's software.

Some PDAs will run third party software capable of translating handwriting into text. Only a few systems can read cursive handwriting – CalliGrapher for the PocketPC platform is one of them. This speeds up data entry, since you write normally on the screen and every word is turned into text as it is completed.

If you have a compatible mobile phone, you may be able to use it as a modem to connect your PDA to the Internet. Check with your PDA's manufacturer about which phones work with your device – the latest PDAs and phones can connect wirelessly via Bluetooth.

How to: Download and install a Palm spreadsheet program

1 Make sure your Palm Desktop software is installed on your PC. Log on to the Internet and go to a software download Website such as Handango (www.handango.com). Use the links to find spreadsheet programs that will run on your type of PDA.

2 Read the descriptions and choose the program that best fits your needs. To find out whether it does what you need, click on trial. This will download a free version of the program that will work for a few days while you evaluate it.

3 Depending on the program you choose, you may have to set up your PDA synchronisation software to install the program files. Many programs have installers that place files in the right folders, so that all you have to do is synchronise your PDA to install the software.

Beyond the computer

Computers on the move

LAPTOP COMPUTERS

Technological advances have made laptop computers (also known as notebooks) as powerful as desktops, yet small enough to fit comfortably inside the average briefcase or shoulder bag.

■ **Need a computer on the go?** Displays that were previously tiny and unclear are now razor sharp and capable of rendering 3D accelerated graphics in 32-bit colour. Some models have screens that double as input devices, so you can use them like a real notebook. There is also a huge range of peripherals designed to make the laptop as versatile and functional as its bigger desktop brother. You can put together a multimedia presentation with video and sound, connect to the Internet using a wireless link to your mobile phone or just sit and watch a DVD

movie wherever and whenever you like. You can also Pick up your e-mails anywhere there's a phone connection, and take your holiday photographs along with you on trips to show relatives and friends, then let them choose and print which ones they would like copies of.

■ **Making the right connections.** For  ease of connecting peripheral devices, make sure any laptop you consider has at least one USB (Universal Serial Bus) port and one Type II PC card slot, as well as a serial and a parallel port. Without these you won't be able to expand your laptop with extra card devices, or easily connect it to networks, external drives and printers. USB gives you fast access to peripheral devices, such as external CD drives, printers and scanners. A card slot allows you to insert or connect miniaturised versions of hardware that you would normally install inside a desktop, such as a network card and additional hard drive storage.

■ **Greater battery capacity** makes today's laptops better travellers than earlier models, although they don't like to be away from a charger for too long. Since most batteries can only be charged from the mains, battery life can be an important consideration if you can't spend some hours near a mains outlet at regular intervals.

■ **Buying a laptop can be confusing.** There is a wide selection of configurations and options available. The choice depends on what you intend using your laptop for. Modern screens can easily display a Word document or spreadsheet, and a 1 GHz processor with 128 MB of RAM and a 20 GB hard drive is adequate for everyday use. However, if you want to create multimedia presentations, play games that require 3D acceleration, or run several applications at one time, you'll need a large TFT (Thin Film Transfer) screen, a faster processor, at least 256 MB of RAM and a 3D accelerated graphics adaptor.

■ **Construction quality is crucial in a laptop** because all the components are so highly engineered. Unlike a desktop, most of the hardware on a laptop is built into the system and therefore can't be easily replaced if it fails. It is best to avoid unnecessary extra features because each one brings with it an increased chance of something going wrong.

■ **Handle with care.** A laptop requires more care than a standard desktop PC. The screen is especially fragile and should be closed gently and slowly. Always hold the unit firmly, plug in devices carefully, and never bump, drop or handle a laptop roughly. Keep your laptop away from heat sources, keep it out of the sun and, for security, don't leave it in the boot of your car.

ADDITIONAL SUPPORT FOR YOUR LAPTOP
Extras you can get for your laptop.

• External USB or PC Card CD-ROM for laptops without built-in CD-ROM drives.

• A hard carrying case, with extra storage for the power cord and adaptor.

• An external mouse: some people find the touch pad or 'wiggle stick' included with laptops awkward to use. Before you buy a mouse check what type of connector your laptop has, either PS2 or USB.

• A wireless network card, coupled with a matching transceiver in your computer, allowing you to connect your machine anywhere, without cables.

• If you have more than one USB device and only one slot, you can purchase a USB hub. It allows you to attach several USB devices at one time, which is more convenient.

■ **Graphics cards for laptops** can't match the power of those in desktop machines, so you may find that you cannot play the latest 3D games. However, many laptops now include a DVD drive and DVD decoder chips so you can watch a DVD movie wherever you are.

■ **If you're planning to use your laptop on the road,** there are adjustments you can make to maximise battery life. Windows lets you adjust the power options settings to reduce consumption while the PC is idle. To access these settings, go to **Start ➔ Control Panel ➔ Performance and Maintenance** and select **Power Options**.

When I press the power button on
Hibernate
When I press the sleep button on
Stand by

Choose the **Advanced** tab and then select either **Hibernate** or **Stand By**. Hibernation shuts down the computer, but keeps a record of everything you have open, so that when you press a key your Desktop is restored with it all intact. Stand By is a basic power-saving mode where your hard drive and monitor are shut down. Set separate Hibernation and Stand By times.

■ **Set up your dial-up accounts** so that you can use them when you're at home or away. Include the dial-out digit from hotels and offices (often 9) so that you don't have to modify your ISP's access number when you leave home. If you stay in accommodation with no access to telephone sockets, you can use an infra-red or Bluetooth wireless link to a mobile phone – as long as it's compatible with your system.

■ **You will need to install the correct drivers** and software to be able to use your laptop with a mobile phone, so that, in effect, Windows will see it as a modem. Drivers are usually downloadable from the phone manufacturer's Website. Data transfer speeds may vary, depending on the mobile service that you subscribe to, although it should be adequate for e-mailing. 3G mobile services should offer connection speeds comparable to broadband connections in the near future. Be aware that you may be charged for the amount of data you transfer rather than your time online.

■ **You can transfer data from your laptop** to your primary computer in many different ways. Many laptops still include floppy disk drives, perfect for small files. For larger transfers there are other options – a USB Zip drive or CD burner. Some laptops now even have DVD-burners built-in.

■ **Windows also allows a PC to PC** connection without having a home network. To do this, you need a serial or parallel cable to connect the PCs. In Windows XP, go to **Start ➔ Control Panel ➔ Network and Internet Connections ➔ Network Connections.** Click on **Create a new connection**. In the New Connection Wizard click **Next**, **Set up an advanced connection** and then **Connect directly to another computer** and follow the directions. Note that a direct connection is much slower than one via ethernet so you may have to wait for files to copy across.

Welcome to the Network Setup Wizard

This wizard will help you set up this computer to run on your network. With a network you can:

- Share an Internet connection
- Set up Internet Connection Firewall
- Share files and folders
- Share a printer

■ **If you need to regularly move data** back and forth between your laptop and desktop, a network adaptor card will allow you to connect both machines to a small home network. Copying or moving files is then a simple matter of dragging and dropping the files using Windows Explorer. If you buy a wireless network card, you don't even need to plug cables in to make a connection.

■ **A Windows Briefcase** can keep files on your laptop and desktop computers synchronised. To make a briefcase, select a location, click on the **File** menu, then **New Briefcase**. Drag the files you want into the Briefcase and copy it to your laptop. When you've worked on the files, click on the **Update** button on the Briefcase toolbar to synchronise the files.

■ **If you have an older laptop** without a built-in CD-ROM drive, your Windows installation files will be stored on your hard drive. When you install a new device, you won't need to insert the Windows CD. However, this can be a disadvantage if you want to upgrade Windows or create an emergency startup floppy disk (see *Your computer's insurance policy*, p. 82). In order to do either job, you'll need to attach an external CD-ROM drive to access the Windows operating system files.

▶ See also **Understanding USB connections**, p. 21; **Home networks**, p. 22; and **Batteries for portables**, p. 52.

LAPTOP CHOICES
Try these Websites for help with choosing the best laptop or notebook computer for your pocket and purpose.

ACTIVE BUYER'S GUIDE (www.activebuyersguide.com)
Click on the notebook computer links to receive help in deciding which laptop features are really important to you.

KELKOO (www.kelkoo.co.uk)
Comparison shopping site that looks for the best price on a chosen laptop from a large range of online retailers in the UK.

PCPLUS (www.pcplus.co.uk)
Part of Futurenet, this site has up to date reviews of PC hardware and software available in the UK.

NOTEBOOK REVIEW (www.notebookreview.com)
News, reviews and information on notebooks, together with software downloads and links to other useful sites.

ZDNET NOTEBOOK SUPERCENTER (www.zdnet.com/special/ filters/sc/notebooks/)
Comparisons, prices, reviews and articles on the full range of notebook computers, including the latest tablet models.

Make the most of your portable PC's power pack when you're out and on the go.

■ **Do you have the best battery for the job?** Many laptops come prepackaged with a battery, but that does not mean that you have to keep it for the life of the machine. Technology is constantly improving, so watch the computer press to see if a better product becomes available. While the latest battery design may be expensive, it could be worth it for the extra time you gain between charges.

■ **Be a conservationist.** Optimise the settings on your portable PC when it is idle. This will conserve power and give you more time when you really need it. If you go to **Start ➔ Control Panel ➔ Power Options** you can adjust the amount of time the

Settings for Portable/Laptop power scheme	
Turn off monitor:	After 15 mins
Turn off hard disks:	After 30 mins
System standby:	After 20 mins
System hibernates:	After 3 hours

computer spends idle before it shuts down non-essential functions, such as the screen. Not only do you save valuable power, but you can also keep work in memory, allowing you to pick up where you left off each time.

■ **There are three main types of battery** for laptop PCs: nickel-cadmium (nicad), lithium and nickel metal hydride. The nicad battery was the first to be produced and is the cheapest. A lithium battery is the longest lasting of all three options. It is more expensive as a result, but can normally provide around 4 to 5 hours of laptop computing time, as opposed to the 2 to 3 hours for other types. The nickel metal hydride battery usually lasts around 2 to 3 hours when fully charged. It is less toxic than the nicad, and is reputed to be less prone to the 'memory effect' (needing to be fully discharged before it is capable of being fully recharged again).

■ **Save your work before shutting down.** Although laptop batteries are highly reliable, you should always save your current work before switching over to Stand By. When the machine goes into Stand By, the data you have entered into the computer's memory is not saved

How to: Stay organised with a Palm Desktop

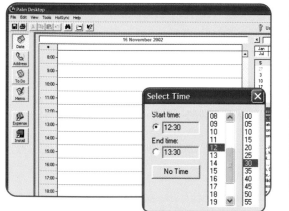

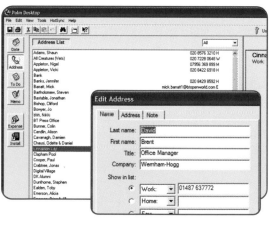

1 Click the Date button to see your diary. Clicking dates on monthly calendars will show events for those days. Click the **New Event** button to enter data. Click the **Repeat** tab to schedule appointments on several days.

2 Click the **Address** button to view your Contacts list, and click the **New Address** button to enter a contact. The memo facility allows you to record reminder notes. Click Memo, then New Memo to enter information.

3 Click the **To Do** button to see your current list of tasks, arranged by priority. Click **New To Do** to enter new tasks. The HotSync facility allows you to synchronise your desktop and palmtop computers with one another.

to the hard disk. If the power supply is cut off for any reason – you drop the PC accidentally and briefly dislodge the battery, for example – you may find that you've lost all your work when you restart your laptop again.

■ If you need to save power only

occasionally, you can set your laptop to Stand By manually in a few easy steps. The simplest way is to go to **Start ➔ Turn Off Computer ➔ Stand By**. This powers the PC down, and it will restart when you press the power key again. Alternatively, you can go to **Control Panel ➔ Performance and Maintenance ➔ Power Options ➔ Advanced**. There will be a number of options available, depending on the laptop model. These include the ability to switch to Stand By when you close the computer's lid.

■ Your laptop will have a power meter or battery scope, which you can

configure to appear on the Taskbar as you work. This feature allows you to keep an eye on the

amount of working time available before you run out of power. It can be customised to sound an alarm when power is low. If your notebook PC doesn't show a power meter, bring up the Power Options window from the Control Panel, and use the Power Meter tab to switch it on.

A COMPUTER IN THE PALM OF YOUR HAND

A palmtop is a small computer, usually without its own keyboard, that sits comfortably in the palm of your hand.

■ If you want a simple-to-use, yet

powerful device with long battery life, try out one of the Palm OS series of palmtop computers. They offer an intuitive interface, powerful performance and a compact size, although at the cost of a little sophistication.

■ Palmtops link to your PC by a cradle

attached to either a serial or a USB port. Most models also let you use an infra-red link. All allow you to backup and synchronise the palmtop with files on your PC at the touch of a button.

■ Graffiti is a type of handwriting

that Palm OS handhelds use to enter text and numbers. You write one character at a time, on a special area at the bottom of the screen. Some of the characters, especially those that normally require you to lift your pen – such as T and F – look a little different. Although this might seem unnatural at first, the technique soon becomes second nature.

■ Need to enter large amounts of

data? Get an add-on keyboard for your palmtop. Most are lightweight and fold up to a compact, easy-to-carry size, although you can also get non-folding models with the solid feel of a full-size keyboard. Just make sure it is compatible with your brand and model of palmtop. Try Palm (www.palm.com), or Handspring (www.handspring.com).

■ Need to get hundreds of

addresses onto your palmtop? No problem. All palmtops coordinate with your desk PC through a program called Palm Desktop, which you install on your PC. Palm Desktop is a calendar/address book/to-do program (see 'How to', p. 52). When you synchronise your palmtop with your desk PC, all the new information on each one is copied onto the other. If you use the Outlook or Lotus Organizer manager, you can set your palmtop to synchronise with it.

■ Many extra programs for your

handheld are available on the Web. The range includes spreadsheets (see 'How to', p. 49), communications and games. Try Palm's own Website (www.palm.com), or software sites like Tucows (www.tucows.com) or Handango (www.handango.com).

Windows

Open up the world's most popular operating system, and discover what makes your PC tick. Learn how to keep it running like clockwork, and make the most of your PC's power.

Windows 95 to XP

An operating system is an essential part of any computer and Microsoft has been producing operating systems for many years. On these pages, discover the various types available, find out about upgrading your system and get some handy tips on how to resolve compatibility problems.

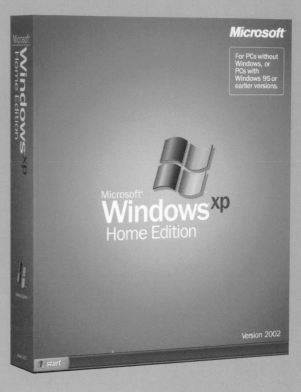

WHAT'S AN OPERATING SYSTEM?

An operating system (OS) is a collection of software that controls how your computer works. It saves you having to use – or write – programs to do every little task. For example, the operating system makes sure your printer is installed correctly and can be accessed by different programs; that your Internet connection is correctly set up and accessible by different programs; and that your programs themselves are able to talk to each other and share data if they need to. As hardware and software continues to develop apace, operating systems also have to advance, so that they can handle the latest, most complex equipment and programs.

Changes in the way computers are used means operating systems also need to change. Ten years ago hardly anyone thought of using computers to access the World Wide Web, five years ago creating and listening to music using a computer was not popular, and as recently as two or three years ago, using computers to network at home was a rarity.

Operating systems need to cater for these changing patterns of computer use, as well as being able to handle future developments.

SMOOTH OPERATORS

The Microsoft range. The release of Windows XP in late 2001 was a major milestone for Microsoft. Previously there had been two main types of Windows Operating system – those for home use, such as Windows 95, 98 and Me, and those for professional and server systems, such as Windows NT and 2000. The home versions were good at recognising a wide range of hardware and supported games and other forms of multimedia well. The professional systems had the advantage of being much more stable and easy to network, although they lacked support for many peripherals common in home setups. Windows XP represents a leap forward because it combines the stability of the earlier professional versions with the excellent Plug and Play support and multimedia features of 98 and Me, as well as integrating the Internet completely into the way it works.

Microsoft doesn't have a monopoly on operating systems. Macs (made by The Apple Corporation) have their own MAC OS, and there are other PC operating systems, such as Linux. Most PC users, however, find it easiest to stick with a Microsoft operating system, because the alternatives can be rather technical.

Updates and new editions of its operating systems are often issued by Microsoft. Windows 95 and 98 both had second edition (SE) versions. These added support for new hardware such as USB and improved networking. At the time of printing, Windows XP has not been updated by a second edition. However, Windows XP Service Pack 1, a collection of updates and bug-fixes, was released in 2002.

Besides completely new editions, there are also 'plus packs' that add new software and utilities to your operating system. Windows XP's Microsoft Plus! allows you to customise the look of your system and extends the digital media and games features of your PC.

SYSTEM REQUIREMENTS

Like all other software, operating systems have a certain set of minimum system requirements. Check that your computer meets them before installing an upgrade.

VERSION	PROCESSOR	RAM	HARD DRIVE SPACE
Windows 98	Intel 486DX/66*	24 MB	Up to 400 MB
Windows Me	Intel Pentium 150*	32 MB	Up to 645 MB
Windows XP	Intel Pentium 300*	64 MB (128 MB	Up to 1.5 GB
	*Or equivalent.	is better)	

TO UPGRADE OR NOT TO UPGRADE?

Microsoft issues different versions of its operating systems, depending on what you are upgrading from initially. If you buy the correct version, then upgrading should be a simple matter of following the instructions on your screen. However, it is always advisable, whenever you make any major changes to your computer, to back up all data that you consider valuable before you begin the installation.

You don't have to upgrade if you don't want to. Microsoft still supports Windows 95, 98 and Me through its Website. All previous systems have their own home pages on Microsoft's Website (www.microsoft.com) from which you can obtain software updates, advice on using the software and information on supported hardware.

The cost of upgrading to a newer Windows version depends on which version of the operating system you are currently running.

Check the Websites of reputable online sellers, or look in your local computer stores to track down the most competitive prices.

Sometimes it's best to leave it alone!

In certain cases you'd be well advised to continue with your current operating system rather than upgrading it. If your PC doesn't have enough system resources to run the new OS, if you don't use any of the new hardware or software that a newer OS supports, and if you've never had any problems with your current setup, then why upgrade? Instead, wait until you find that some new software you need will only work with the latest OS, and then upgrade.

Unsure about your computer's specifications?

If you want to check on your PC's processor or, perhaps, the amount of memory it has, it's easy to find out. In Windows 95 to Me, go to **Start → Settings → Control Panel**. Then double-click the System icon. The window that opens gives you at-a-glance information about the current version of your operating system and how much RAM (Random Access Memory) is in your computer. If you want to find out how much space is available on your

hard drive, click the **My Computer** icon on your Desktop, right-click **C:** and choose **Properties**. The new window will show you how much space has already been used on your hard drive and similarly, how much you still have available to store new material.

WHAT'S NEW?

Need to install new features? If your computer came with Windows XP or an earlier operating system already installed, or if you have upgraded the OS and chosen a 'typical' installation, then all the extra features of the software may not be installed. To add features in Windows XP, go to **Start → Control Panel → Add or Remove Programs → Add/ Remove Windows Components**. The Windows Components

Wizard will launch, listing the components available, and whether they have already been installed on your machine. Select and add new elements, such as Fax services, and click **Next**.

 ## How to: Set up a home network using Windows XP

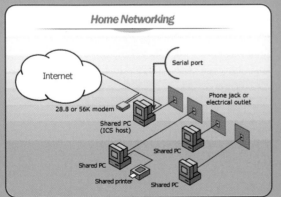

1 First, determine what hardware you need. Every computer on the network will require a network adaptor – probably in the form of a card to be installed internally in each machine. You may also need some cables unless you are using a wireless network.

2 Click on **Start → Control Panel → Network and Internet Connections**, then on **Set up or change your home or small office network**. You will be asked a series of questions about the sort of network you are setting up.

3 Once you have answered all the questions, Windows XP will set up the network for you and check that all the connections needed are present. If everything is working you will be told that the network is ready to use – you may need to restart your PC first.

Windows XP includes tutorials to help get you started with the operating system. The tutorials are a good place to pick up the basics of using your computer, and should help you understand more about the features that are built into Windows, including its many different programs. Along with screens of information for you to read through, there are illustrated tours with animated sequences to help you understand the new operating system more clearly.

XP GAMES

Windows XP has many of the traditional games included on previous operating systems and new Internet games too.

To see the list of games in Windows XP, go to **Start ➔ All Programs ➔ Games**, then click the desired game icon.

Hearts is just one of Windows' popular card games. You can play against the computer or other players on your network.

Minesweeper requires you to find hidden mines by clicking on cells in a grid. To make things tough, you play against the clock.

3D Pinball is a fast and furious game of virtual pinball – to remind you of the arcade classic.

Backgammon, Spades and Checkers are just some of the new games that can be played against opponents over the Internet.

If you're using Windows 98 as your operating system, and want to understand more about how it works, you can use the Help feature. Go to **Start ➔ Help** and select from the Help topics listed. Besides providing information on the use of various Windows 98 components, the Help section has several troubleshooters that cover a variety of technical problems.

If your computer runs Windows 95, you may not have enough system resources to upgrade to Windows XP. If this is the case, you could consider upgrading to the Second Edition of Windows 98 instead. This has a number of advantages over Windows 95. For example, it has support for USB built in, so you can use the many devices that now connect to your PC that way. USB is faster than serial connections and is also easier to set up and use, but you must make sure your PC has USB ports – or that you can fit them – before upgrading. Windows 98 also has later versions of software such as Internet Explorer.

Windows XP is based on professional versions of Windows, so it isn't possible to do incremental upgrades to bring a previous home system like Windows Me up to its level of stability. XP has higher demands of a system than earlier versions – to run it well you should have at least a 500 MHz Pentium 2 processor and 128 MB of RAM – so you will probably need to upgrade other components in your computer when you upgrade to the new operating system. The cost of buying new components, together with a Windows upgrade, may well turn out be near that of buying a completely new computer, so research your options carefully first.

Most of your software should work with XP, as all of the programs that work with Windows 98 should also work with Me. But to be on the safe side, it's a good idea to check the packaging of new programs, and to be wary of software that states it works only with later versions of Windows, if you are using an older version. You may have more problems with hardware – some older components do not have officially approved drivers for Windows XP.

Look before you leap. Although compatibility shouldn't be a problem when upgrading to XP, it is wise to take precautions. Don't dispose of your old Windows files before you have had a chance to thoroughly check all your software. If there are problems it may be cheaper to keep an old copy of expensive software for the time being, and forgo the new operating system instead.

What's so different about XP? For an experienced user of a PC, Windows XP is by turns familiar then frustrating. It retains most of the useful features and ways of working present in Me and 98, but because it is based on the core of Windows 2000 – Microsoft's professional operating system – there are significant changes. Many of the changes are cosmetic. The Desktop has a new curvier and friendlier look. Icons are larger, and the colouring used throughout the

system is less oppressively grey. Other differences are more significant. The Start menu has been greatly expanded and contains many items that would previously have been found on the Desktop. Control Panels have been organised into categories to make them less intimidating to use, and many core services like networking and Internet connectivity have been made easier to set up and use.

XP is also set up to deal automatically with many common peripherals. It's quite possible to connect a USB printer, scanner or digital camera to a PC running XP and have the new device working in seconds without needing to load any extra drivers. And XP deals intelligently with common types of files, offering to store photos in a folder called My Pictures and music files in My Music. Files in My Pictures can be displayed in a slide show, and XP makes it simple to send them to a Website or even order prints online. But the biggest difference with the older home operating systems is due to XP's roots in Windows NT, from which it inherits great stability, making program crashes truly rare events.

Whatever OS you are using, you may find it useful to keep yourself up-to-date with new developments, such as the publication of software updates. Check the Windows pages on the Microsoft Website (www.microsoft.com) regularly for the latest information. This will help to ensure that your current operating system can cope with the most up-to-date hardware and software available on the market.

Don't be too hard on your operating system.
When you start up your PC, your operating system must read millions of lines of program code and work out how to get all your PC's components working, both individually and together. It is then designed to present the results in a user-friendly fashion that you can understand. So it's not surprising if sometimes things don't go quite according to plan.

The Big Freeze.
Although Windows XP is much less prone to crashes than earlier versions,

you may have the occasional problem. So, rather than reaching for the power button to solve this problem, simply press **Ctrl+Alt+Delete** on your keyboard to show the Windows Task Manager. Click the **Applications** tab to view the programs that are running – the problematic one will most likely be marked as 'Not responding'. Click on the program to select it, then click on **End Task**. You will almost certainly be able to carry on using the other programs that are open, although it is good idea to restart Windows after any crash.

Manage your devices.
All versions of Windows come with a Device Manager to help to solve your compatibility problems. Use it to

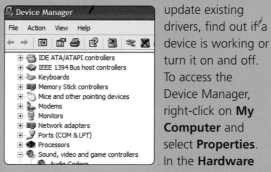

update existing drivers, find out if a device is working or turn it on and off. To access the Device Manager, right-click on **My Computer** and select **Properties**. In the **Hardware** tab (Windows XP), click **Device Manager**, and double-click on a problematic device.

When hardware causes heartache!
Sometimes a device – such as a printer – will fail to work, or work erratically with Windows. Or a peripheral that has been working perfectly under an earlier operating system will fail to work under an updated one. This is usually because one of the device drivers – software that tells the hardware how to operate – is incompatible with your computer's latest operating system. To avoid this annoyance, check your hardware's compatibility at the Windows Hardware Compatibility List Website (www.microsoft.com/hcl/default.asp).

If in doubt,
use the drivers that came with the OS, rather than the hardware – just in case the drivers are already out of date. If you have trouble with a laser printer, choose the **HP Laserjet Series II** printer in the Add Printer Wizard. This works for most laser printers

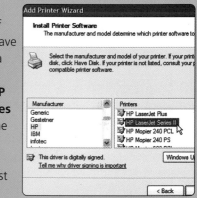

because they understand a standard language created by Hewlett-Packard (HP) for passing data from a PC to a laser printer.

How to: Use Windows Media Player

1 Windows Media Player comes packaged with XP. To access it, go to Start ➔ All Programs then select Media Player. Check it by inserting a music CD in the CD drive, click on Now Playing, and you should be able to hear the music.

2 Make your own music compilation by creating a playlist. Click the Media Library button and then choose New Playlist from the options. Now you can add new items as you choose, to create your perfect playlist for any occasion.

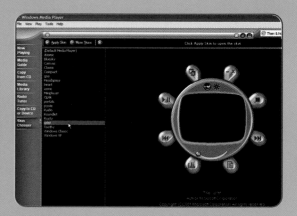

3 Media Player also supports 'skins', or different looks. To choose a new look for your player, click the Skin Chooser on the left-hand menu and browse through the skins by clicking them. When you find one you like, click on Apply Skin to cover your player.

Taking charge

Basic features of the Desktop

The secret of making the most of your PC rests with learning to manage your Desktop efficiently. No task should be more than a mouse click or two away.

The Desktop is a full-screen

display – or user interface – where all Windows activity takes place. It represents – in computer terms – a real desk, where everything that you are currently working on is at hand. Using your Desktop Toolbars, Taskbar, menus and shortcut icons, you can access any item on your PC, but if you prefer to work from the Desktop you can customise it to show the icons you wish. However, if you notice that your Desktop is becoming overcrowded, save space by creating folders to store important files so you can access them quickly. Creating shortcuts to launch your favourite programs is also a good idea, but it is best to arrange them in a logical order so that you can locate the relevant icon without confusion, and operate more efficiently.

At the foot of the Desktop is the

Taskbar. Furthest left is the Start button (see below). Next to it is the Quick Launch Toolbar, where you can click on program icons that you frequently use. Whenever you start up a program, or a new window in a program, you will see a button appear in the Taskbar in the centre of the screen, indicating that the program is running. The Taskbar can be moved or resized on the Desktop – but you may have to unlock it first.

Clicking on the Start button, located

in the bottom left-hand corner of the Desktop,

will access the Start Menu. In Windows XP this is the heart of the Desktop. The menu is split into two columns. On the left are your most often-used programs as well as a link to a listing of all the programs installed on your computer. The right-hand column contains links to useful folders such as My Documents and My Computer, as well as the Control Panel, Help and My Network Places. The new design for the Start menu aims to make it easier to use, but if you are used to the layout found in Windows 98 and Me, it's easy to switch to the 'Classic' view.

The My Computer icon is one of the

regular icons found in the Start menu in Windows XP, or on the Desktop of earlier systems. If you double-click on it, you will open a folder containing a selection of other icons for the PC's main functions and components, such as the hard disk and any floppy drives. The left-hand column lists useful tasks that you may want to perform as well as other useful places on your computer.

The My Documents icon is a

folder that provides you with a central, convenient, easy-to-back up place to store documents, pictures and music files you create. When you save a file, the My Documents folder, or one of its sub-folders, is

the default location for the saved file unless you specify another folder instead.

One Desktop icon that is slightly

different from the rest is the Recycle Bin, where you throw away unwanted files, folders and shortcut icons. Click and drag the item you want to delete to the Recycle Bin and it will be deleted when you right-click on the bin icon and select **Empty Recycle Bin**. If you accidentally throw away a file that you wanted to keep and haven't emptied the bin, just double-click on the bin icon and right-click on the item you want to rescue. Choose **Restore** from the drop-down menu, and the item will reappear in its original location.

ICONOGRAPHY
A guide to icons found in the Start menu or on your Desktop.

MY COMPUTER
Gives access to your hard disk, floppy disk and the CD-ROM drive.

INTERNET EXPLORER
This icon gains entry to the World Wide Web.

RECYCLE BIN
The computer's wastebasket for throwing away files and folders.

MY DOCUMENTS
A storage folder for your files, pictures and work documents.

OUTLOOK EXPRESS
Double-click this icon to open the standard Windows e-mail program.

MY NETWORK PLACES
Gives access to, and information on files on networked computers.

■ Net results. The other icon generally present in your Start menu is the one for Microsoft's Web browser, Internet Explorer. Once you're connected to your Internet Service Provider (ISP), click on this icon to gain access to the online riches of the World Wide Web. Internet Explorer has an address bar, where you type in the URL of the Website that you want to visit.

■ Change the way your Desktop looks by right-clicking in any empty space on the screen. In the pop-up menu, scroll to **Properties**. The Display Properties dialogue box appears, with a range of options for changing the appearance of the Desktop and the icons that appear on it.

■ Arrange your Desktop icons in groups to keep your work in order and to avoid throwing away useful files by mistake. A good location for the Recycle Bin is in the bottom right corner of the Desktop, away from your other icons. To move icons, right-click on the Desktop, select **Arrange Icons** and untick **Auto Arrange**. Then put the My Documents, My Computer and Internet Explorer icons, if you have created them, in the top left corner. Organising the Desktop helps you to find folders easily, and is useful when you have lots of software and downloads. You can always change the arrangement as you start to establish your own individual pattern of work.

■ If the number of icons on your Desktop starts to obscure the background image, and you have to search hard to find items, then it is time to create some folders to store your programs in. To do this, right-click on an empty space on the Desktop. When the pop-up menu appears, go to **New ➜ Folder**, and a new folder will appear on the Desktop. Now name the folder and then press the Enter key.

■ So much to do and so little time? If you are the kind of person who has too much to do and too little time, organise your icons into an easy-to-find format in two steps. Right-click on the Desktop, then in the pop-up menu click **Arrange Icons By** to view your options. You can sort your icons by name, size, type or date. If you scroll down and click **Auto Arrange**, the icons will be placed down the left side of the screen; then, if you try to relocate an icon, it automatically reverts to the left-hand side until you switch Auto Arrange off.

■ Adding an icon to the Quick Start Taskbar is a simple process, and it makes it easy for you to launch applications that you use on a regular basis. To do this, first go to **Start ➜ All Programs**. Scroll through the programs and click on the one you want to place on the Taskbar. Once you've located it, click and drag the icon to the Quick Launch Taskbar, then release it. The icon now appears on the Taskbar. Simply click on the icon to start the program.

■ If you want to resize the Taskbar, then place the mouse pointer by the taskbar's uppermost edge. When the cursor changes to a double-headed arrow, click and drag the edge in towards the centre of the Desktop. If you want to keep the Taskbar small, you can still access all the icons on it by clicking the double arrow at the edge of the Taskbar. A small menu appears and reveals the hidden icons.

▶ See also **Customise your Taskbar,** p. 64; **Getting rid of unwanted files,** p. 66; **Organising your Start menu,** p. 67; **Shortcuts save time,** p. 76; **Bringing the Web to your Desktop,** p. 78; and **Redecorate your Desktop,** p. 79.

How to: Create a shortcut on the desktop

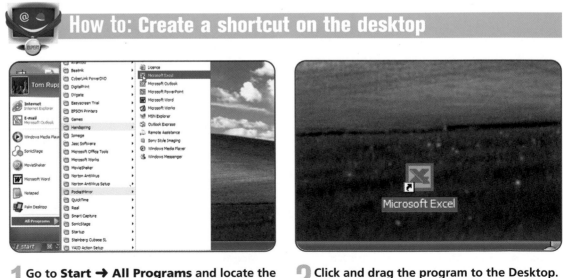

1 Go to **Start ➜ All Programs** and locate the program you want to place on the Desktop as a shortcut – in this case, Microsoft Excel.

2 Click and drag the program to the Desktop. When you release the mouse button, a shortcut icon appears, denoted by the small arrow in the bottom left corner.

WORKING WITH WINDOWS

Ensure quick and easy access to all areas of your computer.

■ **Arrange open windows** in a manageable way by right-clicking the Taskbar and selecting **Cascade Windows**, **Tile Windows Horizontally** or **Tile Windows Vertically**. Minimised windows will not be included.

■ **Resize a window.** Hold the mouse pointer over the edge of the window until it turns into a double-headed arrow. Now click and drag the edge of the window in or out as required. Clicking and dragging the corner of a window will allow you to resize both the horizontal and vertical edges of the window at the same time. Maximised windows cannot be resized manually.

■ **If navigating folders through a single window** is inconvenient, set each folder you access to open in a separate

window. To do this, go to **Start → Control Panel → Appearance and Themes** and click the **Folder Options** icon. Click on the **General** tab. Here you will see a number of options for controlling your folders. Select the option to open each folder in its own window, and click **OK**. To reverse this procedure, simply return to the Control Panel and select the option to open each folder in the same window.

■ **If you want the file icons** within a window to be arranged differently, click on the **Views** button to the right-hand side of the Toolbar. Select one of the options – 'Tiles' are larger icons, while 'List' and 'Details' arrange the files vertically to use less space. Thumbnails are large icons that show miniature representations of picture files. Some folders have special views available. My Pictures, for example, lets you view files as a Filmstrip.

■ **Are you the creative type?** Windows offers an interesting and colourful alternative to drab Desktops. For a truly original look, you can customise all your folders, except My Documents. Open the folder in question and click **View**, then **Customize This Folder**. This takes you to the

Customize tab in the Folder Properties dialogue box. Choose how you want the folder's contents to be displayed – there are a number of specialised options for music and picture folders. You can also choose a thumbnail image to appear on the folder, reminding you of its contents, or even change the icon that represents the folder.

How to: Use the Windows Magnifier

1 If you find it hard to read items of small text on screen, Windows comes with a handy program, the Magnifier, to make working with your PC easier. Go to **Start → All Programs → Accessories → Accessibility → Magnifier**.

2 Choose the settings you want from the Magnifier's display options. For instance, you can set the Magnifier to follow your mouse-pointer, keyboard, or text-editing activity. You can also invert the colour settings, which will help to improve the legibility of text.

3 When you are happy with the Magnifier settings, minimise the dialogue box and work as usual. The Magnifier will now run at the top of your screen automatically, although you can drag and resize it to suit the way you work on-screen.

■ **If you find text difficult to read,** use the Magnifier, which launches an extra window on your Desktop. The new window shows an enlarged version of the screen area around the cursor, so you can look at something in greater detail simply by moving your mouse over it. By default the Magnifier window appears at the top of the screen, but you can drag it to the position that suits you.

▶ See also **Compensating for disabilities,** p. 83; and **Hiding files from snoopers,** p. 89.

SWITCHING BETWEEN PROGRAMS

When two or more applications are running at the same time, your screen can seem a confusing mass of windows, but there are ways to bring order to the scene.

■ **To quickly change** between several active program windows, hold down the **Alt** key and press the **Tab** key. A small dialogue box appears showing program icons for the applications you have running. Keep the **Alt** key held down and press **Tab** to move from one icon to the next until you reach the program you want. To go through the icons in reverse order, hold down the **Shift** key at the same time. When you release the **Alt** key the program window selected is brought to the front.

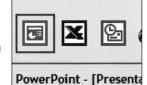

■ **If you need to see more than one** program window on your Desktop simultaneously you can change how your windows are displayed. Right-click on the Taskbar, and in the pop-up menu click on **Cascade Windows**. Now all the title bars of your windows will be visible at once, neatly stacked on your Desktop.

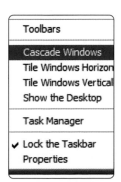

■ **To reduce screen clutter,** minimise an unused program window to the Taskbar. Just click on the **Minimize** button – the first of the three buttons at the top right of the window. Click once on a minimised Taskbar program to get it back to its previous size (see below).

THE MAXIMIZE/MINIMIZE BUTTONS

Minimise and maximise the windows on your Desktop to create a more manageable working environment.

■ **The buttons in the top right-hand corner** of a Desktop window can be used to minimise, maximise or close that particular window. If you can't remember which is which, you can easily determine what each icon does by resting your mouse over each one until a box appears to reveal its function.

■ **If you are using two monitors,** you can move your windows between the two by clicking on the **Restore Down** button (the Maximize button becomes the Restore Down button once a window is maximised) and dragging them into your chosen monitor.

■ **Minimise all open windows at once** by right-clicking the Taskbar and selecting **Show the Desktop**. Right-click the Taskbar and select **Undo Minimize All** to restore the windows to their original position.

■ **Need to hide a window in a hurry,** perhaps to keep work private from an unexpected visitor? You can minimise all the open windows instantly by pressing the **Windows** key and the letter **M** together. To return your windows to their original state when you want to start work again, press **Windows**, **Shift** and **M**.

■ **Maximisation gone mad?** If your Desktop has too many screens maximised at the same time, scroll through all of the maximised windows one at a time by holding down the **Alt** key and pressing **Tab**.

■ **Open to order.** Almost any program can be set to open as a minimised or maximised window when you first launch it. To do this, create a shortcut to the application in question, then right-click it and select **Properties**. Click the **Shortcut** tab, and select from **Normal window**, **Minimized** or **Maximized**, in the drop-down Run menu. Finally, click **OK**.

■ **If you use a particular program every time** you turn on your PC, you can save a lot of time by instructing your computer to launch the application in a minimised window at Startup. Then it will always be on the Taskbar ready for use. Go to **Start ➜ All Programs** and locate the program you want to launch at Startup. Right-click it and select **Copy**. Now right-click on the **Start** button, select **Open** and then double-click on **Programs**, then **Startup**. Right-click in

the open window and select **Paste** to place a shortcut to the program. The program will now launch every time your PC is turned on. To start this program in a minimised window, right-click the shortcut and select **Properties**. Click the **Shortcut** tab and, next to **Run**, select **Minimized** from the drop-down menu. Click **OK** to finish.

KEYBOARD SHORTCUTS
Navigate around your Desktop easily with these quick keyboard commands.

Windows key Opens the Start menu.

Alt+Tab keys Press **Alt** and a tab bar appears representing your open windows. To move around the tab bar press the **Tab** key.

Arrow keys Click on **My Computer** on the Desktop and move between folders using the arrow keys. Press **Enter** to open a folder.

CUSTOMISE YOUR TASKBAR

The Taskbar keeps the programs and files you are currently using within easy reach. You can modify it to suit the way you work.

■ **Keep your most frequently used programs** as shortcuts on the Taskbar in the Quick Launch Toolbar. To switch on the Quick Launch Toolbar right-click on an empty area of the Taskbar, go to **Toolbars** and make sure **Quick Launch** is selected. Now create a shortcut (see *Shortcuts save time,* p. 76) and simply drag it onto the Quick Launch part of the Taskbar.

■ **Regularly clean up the Quick Launch Toolbar** to prevent it from getting overcrowded with programs you no longer need on a regular basis. Drag less frequently used shortcuts to the Recycle Bin. They are quick and easy to create if you need to reinstate them again some time in the future.

■ **To clear your screen instantly** by reducing all open windows and dialogue boxes click on the **Show Desktop** icon in the Quick Launch Toolbar to hide the windows. When you

want to restore any of them to their original size, simply click on it again.

■ **You do not have to position the Taskbar at the bottom** of the screen – you can put it on either side, or even at the top. Just click in an empty area of the Taskbar and drag the whole panel to the side or top, releasing the button when it's in a position you like. You may first need to unlock the taskbar – right-click in an empty area on it and make sure **Lock the Taskbar** is not checked.

■ **If you want to close a program** which has been minimised to the Taskbar, you can do so without having to go to all the trouble of reactivating the program window, and then closing it down again. All you need to do is right-

click on the minimised program panel where it is on the Taskbar, and then click on **Close** in the pop-up menu that appears.

■ **To delete unwanted Toolbars,** which are sometimes added when you install extra services like language packs, right-click on an empty area of the Taskbar, select **Toolbars** from the menu, and uncheck the unwanted Toolbar. You can also add items and menus to your Toolbar by selecting them from the menu.

■ **Get easy access to Websites** by having a 'floating' bar on your Desktop that you

can type Web addresses into. Right-click on an empty area of the Taskbar and select **Toolbars →** **Address**. Drag the Address bar that appears onto your Desktop – again you may need to unlock the Taskbar before you do this.

How to: Add a folder to the Taskbar as a Toolbar

1 Placing a folder on the Taskbar as a new Toolbar enables quick access to the files within the folder. Right-click on an empty area of the Taskbar, select **Toolbars** from the pop-up menu, and click the **New Toolbar** option.

2 Locate the folder you want, for example, the My Pictures folder. Click the + next to any main folders to view other folders that may be inside them. Select the appropriate folder – its name appears in the Folder box at the bottom of the window – and click **OK**.

3 The chosen folder then appears as a Toolbar on the Taskbar, with its contents available for immediate use. Click on the double-headed arrow at the right of the Toolbar to display the files (and folders) not currently shown, then click on a file to open it.

USING WINDOWS EXPLORER

Windows Explorer lists all the drives, files and folders on your PC. It's like a virtual filing cabinet.

■ **To open Windows Explorer,** right-click on any folder or disk on the Desktop and select **Explore**. If you prefer to use keyboard shortcuts instead, then press **Windows+E**.

■ **Control the way the files on your PC appear in Windows Explorer.**
Double-click on a folder to open it. Click **View**, and choose how you want the information displayed. For example, you can set your folder contents to display as thumbnails. Once you have a folder view you like, you can apply the same design to every folder on your hard drive if you wish to do so. Open Windows Explorer and select the appropriate folder. Click **Tools → Folder Options**, then select the **View** tab and click the **Apply to All Folders** button.

■ **Select various Toolbar options for Explorer** by going to **View → Toolbars** and clicking on **Customize**. A dialogue box opens, which lets you select the buttons you want to see on your Toolbar. Choose a button in the left-hand panel and click **Add** or **Remove** as desired. Simply click the **Reset** button to restore the Toolbar to its original state.

■ **When you point to an option on a menu,** the status bar at the bottom of the window displays a description of what that option does and how much space it takes up. If the status bar is not visible, go to **View → Status Bar**.

▶ See also **Organising your Start Menu,** p. 67; **Folders help to organise your work,** p. 90; and **How to find files,** p. 91.

UNDERSTANDING DIALOGUE BOXES

Every time you use your computer, you will come across dialogue boxes, whether it's to save a file or shut down your PC.

■ **Dialogue boxes appear on your screen** to request information about a certain task, prompting a dialogue between you and the program. If you want to print, a dialogue box will appear with your options. When you've made your selection, you simply click **OK**.

■ **You can get help with some dialogue boxes** in the same way as with other features. With the dialogue box open, click the question mark near the upper right-hand corner of the box. Click the item or button that you want to know more about.

■ **A dialogue box will appear** if you click on a command with an ellipsis (...) after it. In Word, for example, if you go to the **Insert** menu and select **Date and Time...** or **Field...** a dialogue box will pop up with your options.

■ **Changed your mind?** A quick way to close a dialogue box is to press the **Esc** key. You can also close any dialogue box by pressing **Alt** and **F4** together, or by clicking on the cross in the upper right-hand corner of the box.

■ **You can move forward through the dialogue box options** by pressing the **Tab** key. Pressing the **Shift** key together with **Tab** will move you backwards through the options.

■ **If you're 'saving as' or opening a file,** there's an easy way to move up through the folder hierarchy. From within the dialogue box, select a folder and press the **Backspace** key. The next folder up will appear.

▶ See also **Make the most of menus,** p. 111.

 OUTLOOK EXPRESS Check your e-mail with ease.

 INTERNET EXPLORER One-click access to the Internet.

 VOLUME CONTROL Adjust your multimedia volume.

 MSN MESSENGER Chat in real time online with friends and colleagues.

 PRINTER This icon appears when your printer is printing.

 MEDIA PLAYER Play audio, video or animation files.

CLOCK Check the time, adjust it or change the display format.

GETTING RID OF UNWANTED FILES

The Recycle Bin is the Windows holding bay for rubbish. It keeps hold of the files you've deleted – in case you change your mind.

Recycle Bin

■ The amount of space set aside for the Recycle Bin can be adjusted. The default is 10 per cent of your hard drive capacity, which is probably much more space than you need on drives over 10 GB in size. If you want to free up disk space, you can reduce the size of the Recycle Bin by right-clicking on its icon and selecting **Properties**. Simply drag the slider bar to adjust the setting for the space allocated to the Bin.

■ If you have multiple hard drives, you can define the Recycle Bin space available for each drive. To do so, right-click on the Recycle Bin, select **Properties** from the menu then choose **Configure drives independently** in the **Global** tab to activate this. Each drive will have a separate tab with its own slider setting.

■ 'Are you sure?' messages pop up whenever you delete a file, but you can turn off the prompt by unchecking the **Display delete confirmation dialogue box** option in the Recycle Bin Properties window. You will still be asked for confirmation whenever you empty the Recycle Bin, because this is an irreversible action which permanently erases its contents.

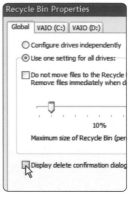

■ Floppy disks and other removable storage media cannot access the Recycle Bin. If you need to recover items deleted from these drives, maintenance programs, such as Norton Utilities, may be able to help (see *Keep your PC healthy with Norton*, p. 206).

■ To delete a file permanently, hold down the **Shift** key at the same time as you press **Delete**, or drag the file to the Recycle Bin. You'll be asked to confirm the deletion and, if you do so, the file will be erased rather than placed in

the Recycle Bin. If you don't want any of your deleted files to be put in the Recycle Bin, check the '**Do not move files to the Recycle Bin. Remove files immediately when deleted**' option in the Recycle Bin Properties dialogue box.

■ Empty the Recycle Bin regularly.
Deleted files continue to take up hard drive space until they're removed from the Recycle Bin. The quickest way to empty the Bin is to right-click on the **Recycle Bin** icon and select **Empty Recycle Bin**. This will permanently delete all the files currently held by the Bin, so be sure there's nothing in there that you might want again.

■ If you want to restore a deleted file to a location other than its original folder, right-click on the **Recycle Bin** icon and select **Explore** from the pop-up menu. This opens a standard Explorer window that allows you to drag and drop files to and from the Recycle Bin.

How to: Recover a deleted file

1 To recover a deleted file, double-click on the Recycle Bin icon on your Desktop. A window will appear displaying all the files you have deleted since you last emptied the Bin. If necessary, you can check the date you deleted the files by going to **View → Details**.

2 Highlight the file you want to retrieve. Alternatively, hold down the Ctrl key while you click on several file names to select multiple files. Click the Restore option in the panel on the left to return the files to their original folders.

LAUNCHING PROGRAMS AT STARTUP

Placing program or file shortcuts in the StartUp folder launches the programs and files automatically when you turn on your PC.

■ Resist the temptation to set lots of programs to launch when you start your computer, since too many will give you a cluttered and confusing Desktop. A packed StartUp folder also eats up system resources, as well as causing your PC to take longer to start. To delete shortcuts in your StartUp folder, click **Start → All Programs → StartUp**, right-click on a shortcut and select **Delete** from the pop-up menu.

■ To put a program or file in the StartUp folder, drag the file or program from your Desktop to the **Start** button, wait for the menu to pop up, then go to **All Programs → StartUp**, and drop the file in the StartUp

submenu. A shortcut version of the file is created there, and the next time you switch on the power to your computer the program or file will run automatically. You can also drag programs directly into the StartUp folder from the Programs menu.

■ Put shortcuts to files you use
daily in your StartUp folder to get instant access to them. Your contacts database may be a good file to store as a Shortcut.

■ If you perform variations on the same
theme on your PC most of the time – writing regular updates for a family newsletter that you have designed, for example – put a shortcut to the file template in the StartUp folder. Both the file template and the program will then be ready for use as soon as your PC starts up.

■ If you use a program often, but not
every day, it's a good idea to put a shortcut to it on the Taskbar, rather than in the StartUp folder. You'll still be able to launch it quickly and easily, no matter how many windows are open.

▶ See also **Customise your Taskbar**, p. 64; and **Shortcuts save time**, p. 76.

THE START MENU IN WINDOWS XP

The Start menu is the launch pad for much of what you do on your PC. Personalise and streamline this menu to speed up your computing.

■ One of the biggest changes in
Windows XP compared to older versions of Windows is the new Start menu. It is larger than before and arranged in two columns – one for programs, the other for useful items like the Control Panel, and Help and Support.

■ Your most often-used programs
automatically appear in the Start menu. By default the top six programs appear, but you can alter

this quantity in the Start menu properties. Right-click on **Start**, choose **Properties** and then adjust the number of programs to be shown.

■ Your Web Browser and e-mail
programs appear at the top of the left-hand column by default. You can choose which Web applications to show here in the Start menu Properties dialogue box. You can also choose not to have the programs shown at all.

■ Want a program to appear in the
Start menu permanently? Go to **Start ➜ All Programs**, right-click on the program icon and choose **Pin to Start Menu**. The program will appear in the upper left-hand portion of the Start menu. If you want to remove it, right-click on the icon and choose **Unpin from Start Menu**.

■ Don't want to learn new ways?
If you are used to earlier version of Windows, you can make Windows XP display the Start menu as a single column, with items arranged the same way as they are in Windows 98 and Me.

■ Save space by making the Control Panel
appear as a menu attached to the Start menu. Right-click on the **Start** button and select **Properties**. Click on **Customize**, then select the **Advanced** tab. Under Start menu items, choose **Display as a menu** under Control Panel. You can select a similar option for the other folders that appear on the Start menu.

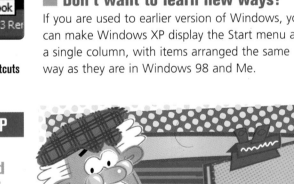

■ You can search the Internet from
the Start menu. Go to **Start ➜ Search**, then select **Search the Internet**. Type in a search term or question then press the **Enter** key. Windows connects to the Net and displays your results.

■ If you often work on the same file
on your PC – modifying data in a spreadsheet or Word document, for example – you can put a shortcut to the file in the Start menu. Drag the file's icon to the Start button, wait for the menu to pop up, and drop it in place.

USING THE CLIPBOARD

This handy feature enables you to move data between documents.

■ Every time you copy or cut
something from a document, the text, image or file is kept on the Windows Clipboard until you decide where you want to paste it. Use it to transfer a piece of text between Word and Excel, for example.

■ The Windows Clipboard helps you
to take pictures of the screen. To capture an active window only, press **Alt+Print Screen**. Press **Print Screen** by itself to capture everything on the screen. Either action sends the captured image to the Clipboard. You can then launch Paint (go to **Start ➜ All Programs ➜ Accessories ➜ Paint**) and choose **Edit ➜ Paste** to view the image.

Customising your computer

CHANGING THE WAY YOUR COMPUTER WORKS

Is there something you want to change about the way your PC works? Try the Control Panel.

■ **You can access the Control Panel in two ways.** Either go to **Start ➜ Control Panel**, or double-click on **My Computer** in the Start menu and select **Control Panel** in the Other Places panel on the left.

■ **Adjust your audio functions** so that they are exactly the way you want them. Go to **Start ➜ Control Panel ➜ Sounds, Speech and Audio Devices ➜ Sounds and Audio Devices** to reveal the Sound and Audio Devices Properties dialogue box. From here you can set the audio devices you want to use for playback and recording. You can also select a preset sound scheme, such as the ones that are used by Windows Themes.

■ **Adjust the stand-by times** for your desktop PC. For advanced power management features, go to **Start ➜ Control Panel ➜ Performance and Maintenance ➜ Power Options**. You can set different functions, such as when your monitor and hard drive will go into stand-by after inactivity. If this is set for 10 minutes, you may find it constantly interrupts your work, so try 30 minutes instead.

■ **If your PC is set to stand-by** or 'hibernate', you can set it to return to the Windows welcome screen when you wake it up again. You will need to enter your password if you have one. You can turn this off by going to the Power Options Properties dialogue box as above. Choose the **Advanced** tab and uncheck the box next to **Prompt for password when computer resumes from standby**.

■ **Keep an eye on your mouse.** Go to **Start ➜ Control Panel ➜ Printers and Other Hardware ➜ Mouse**. Select the **Pointer Options** tab. Check the **Display pointer trails** box to initiate mouse trails that are left behind when you move the pointer. Set how much of a trail to leave by adjusting the slider.

■ **You can add new programs,** or remove any old ones that you no longer use. Go to Control Panel and click **Add or Remove Programs**. You can add new software, install additional components from your Windows installation CD, and set default programs for certain activities, such as Web browsing and listening to music.

▸ See also **Organising your Start menu**, p. 67.

MANAGING PRINTER SETTINGS

The Printers folder can be found in the Control Panel. It contains all the options you need to manage your printer settings.

■ **To access your printer properties,** go to **Start ➜ Control Panel ➜ Printers and Other Hardware ➜ Printers and Faxes**. When the folder opens, right-click on your printer's icon and select **Properties**. The options included here will vary, depending on which printer drivers are installed on your computer at any particular time. Explore the tabs to see what is among the range of features that are available to you.

■ **All for one and one for all.** If you are working on a computer network, any printer settings you change in the Printer folder will be applied globally, to all of the networked computers. If you want to adjust the settings for a single job only, you must access the printer properties from within the application program you are using to print. For example, to change the printer settings for a Word document, open the

document, go to **File ➜ Print**, and click the **Properties** button.

■ **The printer icon appears on your Taskbar** whenever you begin a print job. Double-click this icon to view a list of the jobs in progress, and to cancel one if necessary.

■ **Handling that rush job.** If you need a document printed out in a hurry, but there is a queue of other print jobs ahead of it, you can change the order of the print jobs in your list. Simply drag the urgently needed job to the top of the list and drop it into its new position. However, if the printer is on a network, you'll only be able to do this for your own documents.

CONTROL PANEL ICONS
There are numerous Control Panel functions. Here are just a few of them.

 PRINTERS AND OTHER HARDWARE For adding and adjusting printers, modems and games controllers.

 APPEARANCE AND THEMES Change your computer's theme, desktop background and screensaver.

INTERNET OPTIONS Great for taking care of your History folders and temporary Internet files. It also adjusts your security settings and ISP connections, and specifies which programs Windows uses for each Internet service.

 USER ACCOUNTS Create accounts and passwords for every person that uses your computer.

 SOUNDS AND AUDIO DEVICES You can use this to assign sounds and sound controls to various Windows tasks and actions, such as startup, shutdown and alerts or warning messages.

WORKING IN OTHER LANGUAGES

Change some settings and plug in a new spell-check dictionary, and you are ready to go in Spanish, French or scores of other languages.

■ **Windows XP supports many languages** without your needing to do any additional installations. Many languages and character sets, with some exceptions, are installed by default, so you'll be able to view Websites created in Hebrew, Greek or Russian. If you don't have the right language installed you will see little squares or random characters in place of letters.

■ **Most foreign languages** should appear without any problem in documents, apart from those with complex script and those written right-to-left. To install the character sets for these, go to **Start ➜ Control Panel ➜ Date, Time, Language and Regional Options ➜ Regional and Language Options**. Choose the **Languages** tab. Check the correct box in the **Supplemental Language Support** section and click **OK**.

■ **Your software programs** may provide additional language support options. In the case of Office XP, first make sure your program CD is in your CD drive. Then go to **Start ➜ All Programs ➜ Microsoft Office Tools ➜ Microsoft Office XP Language Settings**, and select the language you need. You can then view and edit your documents in your chosen language. Office XP installs a number of languages by default, including all the major European ones.

■ **To produce documents in other languages,** you will need to 'remap' your keyboard. Go to **Start ➜ Control Panel ➜ Date, Time, Language and Regional Options ➜ Add other Languages**, and click on the **Languages** tab, then **Details** and the **Add**

button. Choose the languages you need and click **OK**. Have your Windows CD ready, if you have one, because your system may need it to install the new keyboard files.

■ **If you still can't find support** for the languages you need, search online. Windows and language updates are available from the Windows Update page on www.microsoft.com.

■ **The Language bar shows the** languages that you have installed on your PC. To switch between them click on the language bar and choose the language that you want to work in. Unlike previous version of Windows, there is no need to reboot when you do this in XP.

■ **To change the current language** while working in Word, double-click on the Language icon in the Taskbar, and choose the option you want from the menu. Alternatively you can use keyboard shortcuts to switch between languages. Pressing the left-hand **Alt** key at the same time as **Shift** switches between your installed languages. You can create other shortcuts to switch between particular pairs in the **Advanced Key Settings** feature in the Text Services and Input Languages dialogue box.

▶ See also **How to display foreign languages**, p. 250.

GETTING A CLEARER VIEW

Use the screen resolution settings on your computer to get the clearest, sharpest display possible.

■ **Screen resolution** refers to the number of dots per inch (or pixels) that make up the entire display area. The more pixels, the sharper the image on the screen. Selecting a screen resolution of 640 x 480 will tell your monitor to display 640 dots across 480 lines: 307,200 individual pixels in total. At the top end of the scale, a screen resolution of 1024 x 768 yields a million pixels.

■ **Some screens can't display every resolution.** If you have an LCD screen, you may find that your options are more limited than with a conventional Cathode Ray Tube display. This is because the LCD is made up of a fixed number of pixels (say 1024 x 768), and gives its sharpest results only at that setting. You may be able to display lower resolutions, but you may notice blurring because the display has to spread pixels over more than one of its own elements.

■ **If the text on your screen is too small** for easy reading you can always make the font size bigger. Go to **Start ➜Control Panel ➜ Appearance and Themes ➜ Change the screen resolution**. Select the **Settings** tab. Click on **Advanced**, then the **General** tab and choose from the options under **DPI setting**, in the Display section. You will need to restart your PC for the change in font size to take effect.

■ **Monitor size matters** when choosing your screen resolution. A high resolution (more pixels) on a small monitor could make the screen images too small to see. Some monitors have a widescreen format, and need to be driven at the correct resolution or shapes will appear distorted.

■ What's the ideal setting?

17 in computer monitors work well with a 1024 x 768 setting. For a smaller monitor, of 15 in or less, try 800 x 600 or even 640 x 480.

■ **Website pages** are usually designed to be viewed at a resolution of 800 x 600 pixels or higher, because this produces the best results. If you are having problems viewing a Web page, try changing your resolution and clicking the **Refresh** button.

■ To apply new colour settings

without having to restart your PC, go to **Start ➔ Control Panel ➔ Appearances and Themes ➔ Display** and select the **Settings** tab. Click **Advanced**, the **General** tab, and then select one of the options shown under Compatibility.

COLOUR SETTINGS

These are colour settings options you are likely to see on most computers.

256 Colours Uses 256 different shades of colour in the visual display. You may need this mode for some older games.

Hi Colour (16-bit) Uses more than 32,000 colours. A good setting for most home PCs.

True Colour (24-bit) Uses 16 million colours. More than the human eye can distinguish.

True Colour (32-bit) Theoretically capable of showing more than 16 million colours. In practice, this is identical in appearance to 24-bit, although it can be useful if you use your PC for photo manipulation.

CHOOSING THE BEST COLOUR SETTING

You can adjust the speed and performance of your computer by selecting different colour settings for the monitor to display.

■ **If your computer is a bit slow,** you can increase the speed by decreasing the 'colour depth' of your display monitor. This means reducing the range of colours that are used to make up the picture on the screen. However, just bear in mind that in doing so you will be sacrificing some screen detail.

■ **To access the colour depth settings** for your display, right-click on the Desktop, select **Properties**, then select the **Settings** tab. Click the small black arrow inside the **Color Quality** section to reveal a pop-up menu of your options. To decrease your colour depth select a lower number of colours than you currently have (see panel on left).

How to: Get a sharper screen image

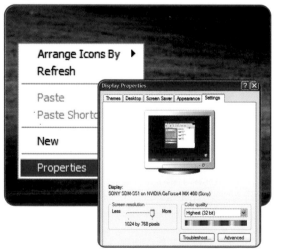

1 Open the Display Properties box by right-clicking with your mouse on a blank area of your Desktop and selecting **Properties** from the pop-up menu. When the dialogue box appears, click on the **Settings** tab.

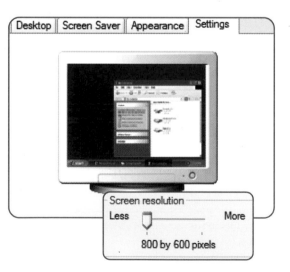

2 Adjust the screen area using the sliding bar. Moving the bar to the left will reduce the value of the screen resolution, giving you a larger screen area, but with fewer pixels and therefore a poorer quality image.

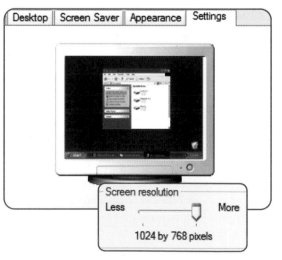

3 Slide the bar to the right for a higher resolution. Images will be sharper, but your screen area will be smaller – the display above the bar shows you how it will look. Click **OK** when you're happy with the setting.

■ **Some modern graphics cards** have extra features that enable you to optimise the colour settings of your monitor. To access them, open the **Display Properties** dialogue box, select the **Settings** tab, and then click **Advanced**.

■ **For clearer, crisper, more realistic looking images,** you should use a large number of colours. The colour depth you choose is described as a number of bits – 16 bit, 24 bit or 32 bit. This refers to how many binary numbers are used to describe each shade. A 32 bit number is made up of 32 1s and 0s, giving more than 4 billion different combinations that can be used to describe colours on screen.

■ **Some PCs require you to restart** before new colour depth settings are put into effect. Make sure that you save any work and close any programs that are open before selecting **OK** to make the adjustment. Other PCs will make the adjustment without the need for a restart, although you may need to restart any programs or applications you were using.

numerals. Alternatively, select the hour and minute numerals and use the up and down buttons to change the time. Click **OK.**

■ **Need to know the exact day and date** your retirement takes place, or when in 1986 you started that job? The Date and Time Properties calendar can tell you days and dates as far back as 1980 and as far ahead as 2099. Just use the up and down buttons to change the month and year – but don't forget to click the **Cancel** button so that your PC reverts to the current date again afterwards!

■ **Make sure your system updates itself** when the clocks go forward or back an hour, at the start and end of daylight saving time. Double-click on the time display in the Taskbar, select the **Time Zone** tab and check the box **Automatically adjust clock for daylight saving changes**.

■ **Get a super-accurate time display** on your computer by synchronising with the National Institute of Standards and Technology in the United States. Visit the World Time Server (www.worldtimeserver.com) and download

Atomic Clock Sync 2.0 for free. The program can synchronise your computer clock every day.

■ **World time users beware.** If you plan to use the world time service above you need to know that the program uses the time zone setting on your PC. Note that Windows does not always get daylight saving time correct.

KEEPING GOOD TIME

You can easily change your PC's time settings when you travel to a different time zone, or if your clock starts to run fast or slow.

■ **The current time is displayed** in the Taskbar on your computer's Desktop, (usually at the far right), in a special area called the System Tray. Icons for programs and utilities that easily alter your settings, such as the sound volume and time setting, are stored here.

■ **To reset the time,** right-click on the clock in the Taskbar and then select **Adjust Date/Time**. In the Date and Time Properties dialogue box, click in the digital time display below the analogue clock, and type over the

TAKE TIME OUT ON THE INTERNET
Set your PC to atomic time or check out the history of timepieces.

TIME AND DATE (www.timeanddate.com.)
Gives local times for places all over the world, along with other useful information such as sunrise and sunset times for each location.

THE UK HYDROGRAPHIC OFFICE (www.ukho.gov.uk)
Tide times and heights predicted for locations all around the world.

HOROLOGY (www.horology.com)
A comprehensive index with crosslinked information on horology – the science of

time and timepieces. You can find out where to have an antique clock repaired or how to set your computer time precisely over the Web.

HOW STUFF WORKS (www.howstuffworks.com)
Contains a guide to atomic clocks and how they measure time so accurately.

WORLD TIME SERVER (www.worldtimeserver.com)
Provides atomic clock synchronisation for your PC, as well as management software for your appointments calendar.

WIRED FOR SOUND

Learn how to manipulate and alter the sounds on your computer to get your machine truly wired for sound.

■ **Enjoy the sound of silence** and get rid of event sounds on your computer. Go to **Start ➜ Control Panel ➜ Sounds, Speech and Audio Devices ➜ Change the sound scheme**. Click on the down arrow beside Scheme and, from the drop-down list that appears, select **No Sounds**. System events will now take place without any accompanying sound. Simply reverse the process to reactivate a sound at a later date if you want to.

■ **Alter system event sounds** in the Sounds tab of the Sounds and Audio Devices Properties box – accessible by going to **Start ➜ Control Panel ➜ Sounds, Speech and Audio Devices ➜ Change the sound scheme**. Then save your choices as a Windows Scheme so that you can recall the configuration later. Once you've made your Sound choices, press **Save As**, type an appropriate name you will remember in the Save Scheme As dialogue box, and then click **OK**.

■ **If you prefer a visual alert,** use SoundSentry to provide you with a warning that you can see whenever a particular sound event is generated. You can choose from a variety of settings that flash different parts of your screen, depending on how you view files. Go to **Start ➜ Control Panel ➜ Accessibility Options ➜**

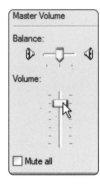

Accessibility Options, and click the **Sound** tab. Check the box next to **Use SoundSentry**, then click **Settings**. Now use the drop-down menu to select the kind of warning you want to appear.

ADJUSTING THE VOLUME

The Volume Control icon gives you quick control over all aspects of sound on your computer.

■ **If the phone rings** when you are playing pumping rock music using your computer's CD drive, you need to be able to turn it down fast. So double-click on the Volume Control icon on the Taskbar, a loudspeaker, and check the **Mute**

All box at the bottom left. The result is instant silence. Uncheck the box to get back to your music after you hang up.

■ **Not getting any sounds at all** through your speakers? Open the Volume Control through the Taskbar and make sure that you haven't checked the **Mute All** box in the master Volume Control Panel. If that isn't the problem, then check that the volume level has not been set to minimum.

■ **Before altering any of the other sound options** in Volume Control, set the master Volume Control slider on the left-hand side to between 55 and 75 per cent of maximum. This will increase or decrease the overall sound and give you a wide range of audio levels for programs.

■ **If you can't see the loudspeaker in the Taskbar,** go to **Start ➜ Control Panel ➜ Sounds, Speech and Audio Devices** then click on **Change the speaker Settings**. Select the **Volume** tab of the Sounds and Audio Devices Properties box and check the box next to **Place volume icon in the taskbar**. Click **OK** and the loudspeaker icon will then appear on the right-hand side of the Taskbar.

■ **Experiment with the Volume Control settings** to find the overall levels that suit your circumstances and the particular kind of music you like to play.

■ **Can't get the right balance** between the music you play and Windows sound effects? In the Master Volume dialogue box, reduce the Wave volume to the second or third mark on the mixer panel and raise the Line-In volume to around three-quarters of the maximum. Use the Master Volume slider to set the overall volume.

■ **Can't see the volume slider** for the function you want in the Master Volume panel? Click on **Options**, then **Properties** and choose the controls you want to see.

How to: Change your start sound

1 Go to **Start ➜ Control Panel ➜ Sounds, Speech, and Audio Devices.** Click on the **Sounds and Audio Devices** icon and then on the **Sounds** tab.

2 Windows Default events that have a sound are denoted by a loudspeaker icon. Scroll down and select **Start Windows**. Choose a new sound from the Sounds drop-down menu and save your choice as a new Sound Scheme.

MUSIC WHILE YOU WORK

Play music while you work with Windows Media Player.

■ **Use your CD-ROM drive to listen to music** while you work. It can be a great way to keep you alert and increase productivity, especially if you are only working on a routine task. Insert your favourite CD into your PC's CD-ROM drive and, as long as you have speakers or – for added privacy – a set of stereo headphones, you can hear your favourite music play automatically.

■ **When you insert an audio CD** into your computer's CD-ROM drive, Windows Media Player automatically pops up and starts playing straight away. To stop this happening, go to **Start → Control Panel → Performance and Maintenance**, select **File Types** in the left-hand menu. Select the **File Types** tab, then **Audio CD** and click the **Advanced** button. In the Actions box, click on **Play** then on **Remove**. Confirm your choice then click **OK**.

■ **You can play your CDs** in either random or continuous modes. Go to **Start → All Programs → Accessories → Entertainment → Windows Media Player**. Go to the Play menu and click **Shuffle** or **Repeat**. To hear only the first few seconds of music on each track, use **Ctrl+F** to skip from one to the next, or **Ctrl+B** to skip backward through the tracks on the CD.

■ **Almost all CDs have a serial number** that identifies artist, title and tracks. These details are stored on the Compact Disk Database (CDDB), which is accessible over the Internet. When you insert a disk, Media Player looks up its details and displays them on screen.

■ **Media Player downloads the track titles** of many CD albums automatically from the CDDB, but if it doesn't, you can add them manually by clicking on **View → Now Playing Tools → Show Playlist**. In a panel to the right, you'll see tracks listed. Right-click on each track and select **Edit**, then simply type in the name of the track. Click anywhere outside the Playlist panel to deselect the track then right-click on

the next track and work your way through the list. Media Player will then remember all the track titles you have entered and be ready to display them the next time you want to play the CD.

■ **To switch between tracks** while a CD is playing, click the **Next** button (a right-facing arrow with a vertical bar) at the base of the Media Player window. Alternatively, double-click on the track you want in the Playlist panel.

■ **Don't like the Media Player?** There are plenty of other CD players on the Internet.

Many shareware and commercial products, like Winamp, have equally advanced features. You can locate and download them from a site like Tucows (www.tucows.com).

▶ See also **Windows 95 to Me,** p. 56; **How to download files,** p. 240; and **The shareware alternative,** p. 304.

How to: Download and install the Winamp CD player

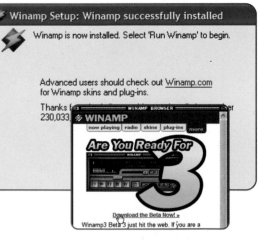

1 Go to a shareware site, such as Tucows (www.tucows.com), and search for Winamp. Follow the on-screen instructions to download the installer program. When the download is complete, double-click the icon of the installation program.

2 In the Installation Directory window ensure the program will be installed in a suitable folder, such as C:\Program Files\Winamp. When you click Next the files will be installed. Click **Next** in the Settings window, and add your details in the User information window.

3 Winamp then sends the details to its Website. When this is done, click on **Run Winamp** to start the program. The interface is split into four elements – Main Window, Playlist Editor, Equalizer and Minibrowser. You can close each without affecting the rest.

Backing up

Your PC is a great business tool, fantastic for browsing the Internet, sending e-mails and matching the best consoles for game play. But make sure things don't go wrong – to avoid losing important files, back up your system using a floppy disk, Zip drive or hard drive.

WHAT IS A BACK-UP?

A back-up can be just one file that you've copied to a floppy disk, or it can be a compressed copy of the entire contents of your hard drive. If you only have a few important files, it may not seem necessary to go to the trouble of backing up other data. However, if your hard drive fails, your Word preferences, e-mail settings and all your e-mails and Internet Favorites will be lost – not to mention programs you may have previously installed and any Windows settings.

Don't forget your back-up.
Although modern hard drives are superbly engineered, all your precious documents and files will be lost forever if something goes drastically wrong – unless you've backed up your data. Performing a back-up is a task that can be almost completely automated. Windows provides a Back up Wizard to help you, but with XP it must be installed from the program disk (see 'How to', p. 75).

DATA STORAGE OPTIONS

If you only intend copying a few files onto a floppy disk, use a file-compression program to squeeze more data onto the disk. WinZip or WinRar will compress an Excel spreadsheet or Word document by as much as 85 per cent without losing any data. Although images can't be compressed as much as text-based files, this is still a great way to maximise the number of documents you can fit onto a disk. Even if you're using a larger storage medium, compression gives you a more efficient use of space. You can download a free trial version of WinZip from the Internet at www.winzip.com.

When the number of files you want to back up exceeds the capacity of a floppy disk, there are better options available. If you want to store up to 750 MB of data, an Iomega Zip drive is one option. A Zip drive comes with simple-to-use software that helps you set up the device and establish an automatic back up schedule. It's a good idea to choose a drive with a USB 2.0 or FireWire connection. Both interfaces give high connection speeds and can be plugged in while Windows is running.

To back up several gigabytes of data, use a tape streamer – a device that backs up data very quickly onto a digital tape. There are several formats available from your local PC store. A popular one is DAT (digital audio tape), and this process normally runs overnight – despite the high speed, compressing and copying large amounts of data is time consuming.

How regularly you back up data comes down to how often you update it. If you only use your PC to type an occasional letter, then once a month is adequate. However, if you record your personal expenses daily in Excel, or use your PC for a small business, then once a week or at the end of each working day is better. You can manually copy files or set up an automatic back-up using one of several programs available, such as the Back up Wizard in Windows XP. Others are available from PC stores. The program you choose

will depend on what you want to do – some programs such as Power Quest's Drive Image 5 are good at making exact copies of your entire hard drive, others are good at noting what files have changed since the last back-up and making copies of them.

ARCHIVE OR BACK UP?

Archiving is when the data is to be kept intact rather than overwritten each time a back-up is performed. This is ideal if you are working on a long document or large spreadsheet, and might need to start again from a point you had reached a few days or weeks ago. Recordable CDs are the perfect medium for this sort of back-up, especially CD-RWs, which can be erased and used again. Programs are available that are dedicated to making it easy to back up on CD – one example is Back up Now! from New Tech Info Systems (www.ntius.com). The latest version of this software also supports backing up onto recordable DVDs.

automated back-ups, it's a great way to store your data where it can't be affected by local conditions or accessed easily by others.

LOOK IN THE MIRROR

When the data on your hard drive is virtually irreplaceable, the solution is to install a second hard drive to 'mirror' your main drive. This means whenever you write data to a drive, it is also written to a second hard drive, creating an exact copy in the event of failure. Of course, this provides no recourse if your computer is struck by a virus, because it will simultaneously infect both drives. Another option is to use software such as Norton Ghost, which creates an exact compressed copy of your primary drive on the second drive. If the first drive fails, the compressed files can be restored.

To create a back-up of your Word settings, use the Windows search utility to find a file called 'normal.dot'. This is the default Word template containing all your preferences. Make a

note of its location and copy the file to a floppy disk. Another important set of files are your Outlook Express e-mail folders. Search for '*.dbx' –. you will find a series of files representing your e-mail folders called 'inbox.dbx', 'outbox.dbx', and so on. These are large files, so you'll need to compress them. Note their folder name, and copy them to a suitable location. Make a note of your e-mail and Dial Up Networking settings.

Use System Restore rather than a back-up to return your computer back to stability if you have a problem after you've added some hardware or software. System Restore is a utility built into Windows XP that monitors your computer and notes when you make changes to its configuration. It's like having an archive of your hard drive, allowing you to go back to a point when your system worked well. But, unlike a back-up of a drive, System Restore retains new items like documents, e-mails and your Explorer History and Favorites lists. To use the program, go to **Start → All Programs → Accessories → System Tools → System Restore**.

STORAGE ON THE WEB

With a fast Internet connection, you can store data for free on the Internet. Dedicated sites provide space for use as an Internet hard drive, and they're very secure – some will even appear in your Windows Explorer window as an extra hard drive, letting you drag and drop files to and from the server. While it's not suitable for

---

How to: Install and use the Windows Back up Wizard

1 With your Windows XP CD in the CD drive, browse to the NTBackup folder. Double-click on 'NTBACKUP.MSI' to install the program. Click on **Start → Programs → Accessories → System Tools → Back up**. The Back up or Restore Wizard will launch.

2 Click **Next**, then choose **Back up files and settings** and click **Next** again. The next screens let you choose which files to back up and where you want to store the back-up copy. When you reach the final screen, click **Finish** to run the back-up immediately.

3 Alternatively, click on **Advanced** to schedule your back-up. You can choose whether to repeat the task daily, weekly or monthly and also set the time at which it will start. Remember to allow Back up to wake the computer from sleep if necessary.

The next step

It's the little extras and add-ons you discover that make Windows such fun to use.

■ **You can download sounds,** such as favourite lines from films, and assign them to events, such as starting or closing programs. Sounds need to be in .wav format. Check out SoundAmerica (www.soundamerica.com), which has almost 30,000 sounds to download. Click on a sound file to play it in Windows Media Player. To download a sound file, right-click on it and select **Save Target As**. Find a location in your computer to save it to and in the Save as type box, select **Wave Sound**. Click **Close** in the following dialogue box once the download is complete. Next, go to **Start ➜ Control Panel ➜ Sounds, Speech, and Audio Devices ➜ Change the sound scheme**. In the Program events section, scroll down and select an event,

clicking on it to highlight it. Click **Browse**, and locate your saved audio clip. Click on the clip to select it and click **OK**. You can preview the clip in the Sounds and Audio Devices Properties box by clicking on the play button with the arrow icon next to the Browse button. Once you are happy with your choice, click **Apply**, then click **OK**. The next time your computer performs the chosen function your downloaded audio clip will play.

■ **Brighten up Media Player** with help from the Web. If you're bored with the standard Media Player interface, click on **Skin Chooser** in the Player's menu and choose from a range of fun alternatives. Simply click Apply Skin to see how each one looks on your Player. If you want more skins to try out, go to the Media Player Website (www.windowsmedia.com/mediaguide/Gallery/Skins.asp), where you can download even more great designs.

■ **Find new wallpaper on the Web** to brighten up your Desktop. Do some surfing for an image. Once you've found one that you'd like to use, right-click on it, and choose **Set as Desktop background** from the pop-up menu.

The image will now be displayed as your Desktop's background pattern. To change the background to the way it was originally, right-click on the Desktop, select **Properties**, then the **Desktop** tab and then scroll through the options under Background to find your original design. Select it and click **OK**.

▶ See also **Use icons to add a personal touch,** p. 80; and **Where to find free graphics,** p. 305.

How to: Create a shortcut through Explorer

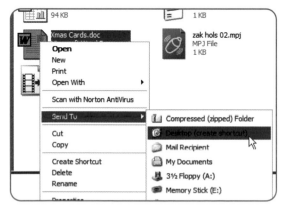

1 Using Windows Explorer, navigate to the folder where the file or program file to which you want to create a Shortcut is stored – this can be any file or program. To create the Shortcut, right-click on the file and select **Create Shortcut** from the pop-up menu.

2 The Shortcut to the file appears in the same folder, but you may drag and drop it to another location if you wish to. If you would prefer your Shortcut to appear on the Desktop, just select **Send to ➜ Desktop (create shortcut)** from the pop-up menu instead.

SHORTCUTS SAVE TIME

Shortcuts are handy icons that allow you to access programs or files directly from your Desktop. They're quick and easy to create and delete.

■ **If you don't like the look of your current Shortcut icon,** you may be able to customise it. Some programs allow you to easily give it a new look – just right-click on the icon, select **Properties** and then choose the **Shortcut** tab. Click on **Change Icon** and select a fresh icon from those displayed. You may need to browse a long way into your hard drive to find alternatives unless you have downloaded one from the Web.

You can create Shortcuts within folders as well as on the Desktop. This is handy if you often use a file or program while working in a given folder – for example, using the household expenses spreadsheet when you're in a bank letters folder. In Windows Explorer, navigate to the folder where you want to place the Shortcut and go to **File ➜ New ➜ Shortcut**. In the Create Shortcut box that

appears, click **Browse** and then navigate to the file to which you want to create the Shortcut. Double-click on the file and its path will appear in the Create Shortcut window. Click **Next** and, providing the name given to the file is the correct one, click **Finish**.

Desktop Cleanup gets rid of clutter. To sweep your Desktop clear of unused icons, launch the Desktop Cleanup Wizard. Right-click on a free area on the Desktop, select **Properties** then click on the **Desktop** tab. In the

Desktop Cleanup box, click on **Clean Desktop Now**. The Wizard will place the desktop icons you use the least into a folder called Unused Desktop Shortcuts. Check the contents of this folder, and if you don't need the icons any longer, place the entire folder in the Recycle Bin. Remember that deleting a shortcut has no effect on the program it leads to.

Change the type of window a program or file will open in to suit the design and layout of your Desktop, and the way in which you wish to work. First, right-click on the **Shortcut** icon, select **Properties** from the pop-up menu, and then the **Shortcut** tab. Now use the drop-down menu beside **Run** to select a Normal, Minimized, or Maximized window when the program or file opens.

Remember that you don't usually need a Shortcut to both a document file and the associated program in which it was created. Double-clicking on the file Shortcut will automatically open it in its associated program, so keep just the file shortcut on your Desktop.

USER ACCOUNTS IN WINDOWS XP

Imagine having a different PC for each member of the family. User Accounts in Windows XP let you treat a single computer as lots of different ones.

Each user can personalise their desktop and the way files display. Users also get personalised Favorites and History lists in Internet Explorer and a personal 'My Documents' folder, which can be set so that other users cannot access its contents.

There are two types of user account: Administrator and Limited. Administrators can change other users' account names, passwords and pictures, and can install software and hardware. Your PC needs at least one Administrator, but there can be more. A Limited user cannot install new software and hardware, cannot change to an Administrator account and cannot change account names.

How to: Set up a new user account

1 Log into an administrator account on your PC – only administrators are able to create new accounts. **Go to Start ➜ Control Panel ➜ User Accounts ➜ Create a new account**.

2 Choose a name for the new account and type it into the field, then click on **Next**. In the next screen, choose the type of account you want to set up. Roll over the buttons to see a description of the different account types. Finally click on **Create Account**.

3 The account is now set up. Customise it by clicking on the icon or name. Click on **Change the picture** and choose from the Windows set of User pictures, or browse your files for a picture of your own. Windows will automatically resize the picture to fit.

■ **If you have upgraded from an earlier version of Windows**, you may need to change your file system to take advantage of the new privacy features. Go to **My Computer**, right-click on your hard drive and choose **Properties**. If it says NTFS, next to file system, you can go ahead and set up user accounts. If It says FAT32 you will need to change it. Windows can reformat your file system without losing data. However, do not do this if you have another operating system on the same drive.

■ **Protect your account and personal files with a password.** Go to **Start ➔ Control Panel ➔ User Accounts** and click on your account. Click on **Create a password**, and in the boxes type in your chosen password, confirm it and then type a hint to prompt you if you ever forget your password.

■ **Switching between users is easy.** Your open programs and settings will be preserved while the other user is working on the PC, allowing you to quickly pick up where you left off when you log on again. To change users, go to **Start ➔ Log Off ➔ Switch User**. Click on the new user's name and enter a password if needed. The new user's Desktop will appear. To switch back, follow the same steps as before and click on your user name.

THE WEB ON YOUR DESKTOP

Using Windows Active Desktop means your computer is truly integrated with the Web.

■ **Your Windows Desktop can be made to look** and work like a Web page so you can display Web content directly on your Desktop and get the most from your Internet connection. Content is updated automatically.

■ **Many popular portal sites** feature pages that registered users can customise. Select one as your Active Desktop page, and have the latest information right there on your Desktop.

■ **Built your own Website?** Now you can create your own 'personal admin' page, hide it behind publicly accessible pages and even password-protect it. You can also make it your Active Desktop page and set up links to the files you want access to – Word or Excel documents, contacts and so on – stored on your Web server. That way you can make any PC your own by setting this page as your Active Desktop.

■ **You can include all sorts of elements** as part of the HTML code when you use your own Web page as the Windows background. Try text in different fonts, colours and sizes; use tables, pictures and links to Web pages, even often-used files on your hard drive, or locations – like an Excel spreadsheet – within those files.

◗ See also **Understanding HTML**, p. 220; and **Creating a Website,** p. 228.

SCREENSAVERS ARE FUN

Screensavers were developed to protect old-fashioned monitors from screen burn, but today they're used mostly for fun.

■ **Windows comes with its own collection of screensavers,** and you can change between them easily by right-clicking on the Desktop and selecting **Properties**. The Screen Saver tab lists all the screensavers currently installed on your PC and allows you to preview them before you make a final choice.

■ **Your screensaver appears** when your keyboard and mouse have been inactive for a specified period of time – between 1 and 60 minutes. Set how long your PC waits before launching your screensaver on the **Screen Saver** tab of the **Display Properties** dialogue box. About five minutes is a reasonable time to set.

■ **Always check out the Settings options** for your screensaver. You'll be able to customise your screensaver to your personal taste. The 3D Flying Objects screensaver, for example,

includes an option to add your own image as a texture when the Textured Flag style is selected. Another personalised option is to add your own text to the Scrolling Marquee screensaver.

Some system tools work better

if you turn off your screensaver when you're running them, particularly if you have an older PC. This is because the screensaver program interrupts other computer activity to check whether it should turn itself on or off. For instance, Disk Defragmenter clashes with some screensavers, and modem communications may be stalled if a screensaver kicks in. To disable your screensaver, choose **None** from the drop-down list on the **Screen Saver** tab of the Display Properties dialogue box.

When you download a screensaver

from the Internet it will be in one of two formats. Copy any files with the extension .scr into the directory C:\Windows on your computer. If your screensaver has the extension .exe, simply double-click on it to load it.

Use your screensaver as a Desktop security tool.

Check the box next to **On resume, display Welcome screen** on the Screen Saver tab in the Display Properties dialogue box. This means that when you use your PC again after the screensaver has appeared, you will need to enter a password to use any accounts that are protected. This is a good reason to insist that everyone who uses your computer has a password for his or her account.

Virus alert!

There are lots of screensavers available for free download from the Internet, but remember that many are executable files and can easily hide viruses. Be sure to only download files from reputable sites, and check all files with an up-to-date virus scanner. If you are at all in doubt, delete the file.

Create a unique screensaver

of one of your own pictures or photographs, and add music or your own sound to accompany it. Use a screensaver program, such as Screen Saver Studio (www.screensaverstudio.com).

REDECORATE YOUR DESKTOP

The patterns or images you can use as a Desktop wallpaper are unlimited. Select from Windows' own range, or create your own.

Redecorate.

To change your wallpaper, right-click in a clear space on your Desktop and select **Properties**. In the Display Properties box, select the **Desktop** tab. You can choose a background from one of the images listed, or if you have an image elsewhere on your PC that you'd like to use, click **Browse** and go through the folders to locate that image. You can choose to 'stretch' the background image to fill the screen, 'center' it on your Desktop, or 'tile' it, so that the image is repeated across your monitor. When you're happy with the effect, click **OK**.

If you are using a re-sizeable image as wallpaper,

do not tile it. Instead, use the Center command to position the image exactly in the middle of the Desktop, and make it fill the screen using the Stretch command.

Search the Web for images of your favourite star.

For example, go to a search engine and type in 'GeorgeClooney.jpg'. Now you will get pages containing .jpg files, the most widely used format for quality Web images.

Found a Web page with a really great image?

Even Web pages can easily be turned into Desktop wallpaper with a few clicks of your mouse (see p. 76 for details).

Wallpaper saved using the Set As Wallpaper command

will be replaced the next time you use that command. If you want to save this image rather than risk overwriting it, don't use the Set As Wallpaper option. Instead, right-click on the image, select **Save Picture As** and name it.

To fill the screen

with an image from a specialised wallpaper Website, download it at the maximum resolution offered, which is normally 1024 x 768 pixels.

Give yourself a laugh.

Download humorous wallpaper from JokeWallpaper (www. jokewallpaper.com).

Manage extensive wallpaper collections

with a free downloadable utility, such as WallMaster (www.tropicalwares.com). These small programs let you manage wallpaper files and schedule automatic changes.

WEB ADDRESSES FOR WALLPAPER

Make a start on your redecorating project at these Websites.

DESKTOP-FX (www.desktop-fx.com)
More than 1000 free wallpaper images available for download, with subjects ranging from landscapes to fantasy.

TONY HOWELL (www.tonyhowell.co.uk/ wallpaper.htm)
A selection of images taken by a commercial photographer, with a selection of images of plantlife and the English countryside.

EASTENDERS (www.bbc.co.uk/eastenders/wallpaper)
Free images from the popular soap opera – if Eastenders isn't your favourite, many other TV programmes also provide freebies.

USE ICONS TO ADD A PERSONAL TOUCH

Download icons from the Web and create your own designer Desktop.

■ Why are icons used on the Desktop?
The icons that you can place on your Desktop and in your hard disk represent programs, folders and files. They save you time – instead of typing in the file name to open it, you can double-click on the icon instead.

■ To change an existing Desktop
icon, right-click on the icon and select **Properties** from the pop-up menu that appears. Click the **Shortcut** tab then click the **Change Icon** button. In the box that appears, select a new icon and click **OK**. Click **OK** again on the Display Properties box to display the new icon on your Desktop.

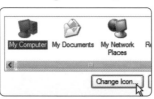

■ Search the Internet for icons.
There are hundreds of Websites where icons can be downloaded. Use a search engine such as Google UK (www.google.co.uk) to track them down. If you specify phrases such as 'free icons', 'free clip art', or 'free graphics' in your search, you'll be given plenty to choose from. Top Icons (www.topicons.com) and Icon Bazaar (www.iconbazaar.com) are just two sites your search may find.

■ Check the icon file is authentic.
Although a Website can use just about any graphic file as an icon, a PC needs to use an authentic icon file. Most icon files have the suffix .ico at the end of the file name, but some may have a .bmp suffix.

■ Many downloadable icons come in sets.
These usually comprise 10 to 20 different icons, all based around a central theme, such as animals or cartoon characters, and stored as a Zip file. Download the complete set and unzip the file into a folder for easy access. Make sure you give the folder a name you will recognise.

ICON SITES

There are thousands of amazing icons that you can download from the Internet. These sites offer some of the best designs around.

COOLARCHIVE (www.coolarchive.com/icons.cfm)
4000 icons in 125 categories, plus loads of graphics and clip art.

FREE GRAPHICS.COM (www.free-graphics.com)
Choose from over 5000 graphics images, plus links to other graphics sites and the option to download a trial version of an icon creator.

ICONSPLUS (www.iconsplus.com)
Here you'll find entertainment icons, plus a selection of comic book, science-fiction, TV, movie and pop culture icons to download.

ABSOLUTLEY FREE ICON LIBRARY (www.free-icons.com)
This Website includes 20 pages of icons, plus dozens of different links to other graphics, clip art and icon pages.

CLIP ART WAREHOUSE (www.clipart.co.uk)
Click on Desktop Icons to see a wide range of images prepared in formats suitable for use as replacement icons in Windows.

LEO'S ICON ARCHIVE (www.iconarchive.com)
Free popular comic strip icons, plus a .gif to .ico file converter program to download.

■ Do-it-yourself icons!
There are many icon-creation packages available for download from the Net. Bear in mind that Web versions may be shareware. This means that they only last a few weeks before you need to register and pay for them. This usually allows you enough time to create several

icons and decide whether or not you want to buy. Remember that different versions of Windows can use different types of icon. The icons used in Windows XP contain many more colours than those in Windows 95, for example.

■ Convert graphic files into icon images.
With an icon creator you can not only design your own icons from scratch, but you also have the ability to convert other graphic files, such as JPEG and BMP formats, into .ico images.

■ Keep it simple.
If you're familiar with using a particular graphics package, such as Paintshop Pro, you can draw your icons in that package. Save the icon as a bitmap (.bmp) file and you can use it as is. Make sure to stick to icons of 32 x 32 pixels. For the best clarity, create images without too much fiddly detail and with uncluttered backgrounds. The golden rule to bear

in mind when creating icons is always: 'keep it small and simple.'

■ **Check which formats** the graphics package can save in before you start creating icons. Some may be limited in the selection available. Otherwise, you may find your work is wasted – having found an ideal image, you discover that you can't save it in a useable format.

▶ See also **Organising your Desktop,** p. 60; **Working with Zip files,** p. 236; and **How to download files,** p. 240.

EXPERIMENTING WITH TYPEFACES

There's more to creativity than Times New Roman. Liven up your letters with interesting new fonts.

■ **The Web is a fantastic place for free fonts,** and there are thousands upon thousands to choose from. However, you will need to be discriminating, since many free fonts are not worth the effort of downloading them. To search for some additions to your collection, visit one of the many font Websites (see panel, above right). In most cases, you can simply click on the font of your choice to start the download process. The font will probably arrive on your Desktop as a Zip file, so you'll need to unzip it before you can use it (see *Working with Zip files*, p. 236).

■ **Install your new font.** You've just downloaded a font onto your Desktop, but to use it you need to install it properly. This is what you have to do: go to **Start ➤ Control Panel ➤ Appearance and Themes** and click on **Fonts** in the left-hand column. In the File menu, choose **Install New Font**. The Add Fonts dialogue box will now appear. Browse through your folders until you locate your new font. Click on it to highlight it and click **OK**. Your font is now ready for you to use.

FONT SHAREWARE SITES
Find great fonts and font creation software on the Web.

BLUE VINYL (http://reflectdesign.com/bvfonts)
Free fonts, and links to other free sites for all kinds of downloadable treats.

DOWNLOAD 32 (www.download32.com)
Liven up your letters with 3D shareware fonts – they're compatible with MS Word.

THE DINGBAT PAGES (www.dingbatpages.com)
A fascinating collection of unusual symbols.

PCFONTS.COM (www.pcfonts.com)
A comprehensive collection of links to major font sites, all given a star rating.

JUMBO! (www.jumbo.com)
Fonts, games, screensavers and MP3 files.

FONTS AND THINGS (www.fontsandthings.com)
A wide range of free fonts including retro 70s lettering and special festive sets.

ZDNET DOWNLOADS (www.zdnet.com/downloads/desktop.html)
Links to numerous font and font utility sites.

1001 FREEFONTS (www.1001freefonts.com)
An amazing array of fonts, screensavers, ClipArt and other freebies.

TYWORLD.COM (max.tyworld.com/download)
Choose from a good selection of over 500 free fonts, all arranged conveniently in alphabetical order.

■ **Want to see what a font looks like?** Go to the **Start** menu then select **Control Panel ➤ Appearance and Themes** and click on **Fonts**. Double-click on any of the fonts listed to see all the letters of the font in a range of different sizes. To see what the font looks like printed on a page, click on the **Print** button to print out a copy of the window.

■ **Spring clean your fonts folder.** Of the thousands of fonts available, you may have downloaded and stored several in your folder that are practically identical. It's a good idea to go through them periodically and have a thorough spring clean, throwing away the ones you're least likely to use again. Just right-click on the fonts you wish to discard and select **Delete** from the pop-up menu.

■ **Create your own fonts.** You can download shareware programs from the Web to do this. Font Creator (www.high-logic.com) is an easy-to-use program that enables you to create

everything from symbols to signatures. Although creating a unique font from scratch can be quite an involved process, it's great fun to do and the results can be extremely satisfying. Alternatively, you can edit fonts you already possess to achieve a similar result. Type Tool (www.fontlab.com) is a useful and affordable font editing program aimed at the home computer user.

■ **If you are serious about fonts,** create your own type book. Popular type utilities, such as Suitcase and Adobe Type Manager, allow you to print out a standard sheet showing all the characters available in any particular font, with blocks of type in various point sizes.

■ **Fonts aren't just for letters and numbers.** Many specialist fonts exist for creating special characters like bullet points, arrows and even keyboard symbols. Symbol, Webdings and Wingdings are examples of this type of font, and are installed with Windows XP. You can find other symbol fonts on the Web.

For experienced users

Create a startup disk to back up your essential applications in case of an emergency.

■ **If you use a version of Windows earlier than XP,** take out an insurance policy for your PC by creating a startup disk. This floppy disk should contain the few vital files you need to start your computer in the event of a serious system crash. It can also help to diagnose what caused the crash in the first place, and reset your system to a healthier state.

■ **Use the startup disk to restart your PC** if there's a serious problem and Windows fails to load. First make sure the computer is switched off. Put the disk in the

floppy drive and then switch on the computer. The computer will sense the disk in your floppy drive and will boot up from it. Follow the on-screen instructions to restore your machine.

■ **Don't wait until something goes wrong** before creating a startup disk – this is a

job that must be done when the system is stable. Once you have experienced a serious system crash, it will be too late.

■ **Keep your startup disk in a disk box** in a safe location, away from excessive heat and out of direct sunlight. Also print out the Readme file on your startup disk and keep it safely folded up with the disk – it contains important information.

■ **Windows XP users need their Windows Installer CD,** or their PC manufacturer's recovery CD, to restart their machine if there are major problems. XP is designed for computers that contain a bootable CD drive – one that can be used to start the computer instead of booting from the hard drive.

■ **If you do not have a bootable CD drive** on a machine running Windows XP, you can download a program that creates a set of start-up floppy disks. These disks enable the computer to read from the CD drive once it has started up, so you will also need a Windows XP installation CD to complete the recovery.

How to: Create a DOS startup disk

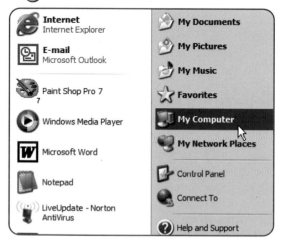

1 Although you cannot create a rescue floppy disk in Windows XP, you can create an MS-DOS startup disk, which can be useful for setting up network cards. Insert a blank floppy then go to **Start → My Computer**.

2 Right-click on the floppy disk icon. Scroll down and select **Format**. In the Dialogue box, click in the box next to **Create an MS-DOS startup disk**, then on **Start**. A warning will appear – click **OK** to start the format.

3 The process takes about 30 seconds, then you will be told the format is complete. You can now use the disk you have created to start your computer in DOS, which can be useful to support technicians.

RUNNING DOS PROGRAMS

By accessing DOS through Windows you can run older DOS programs.

■ **DOS (Disk Operating System)** is a predecessor to Windows that is still accessible through Windows **(Start → All Programs → Accessories → Command Prompt)**. Although now almost obsolete, it is still used to run DOS-based programs and games (see 'How to', below). It's also used to alter the file system, but don't attempt this unless you know what you're doing!

■ **Access DOS easily through Windows.** If you want to run a DOS program occasionally, you can create a shortcut to DOS on your Desktop. Right-click in the top right corner of the Desktop area. Select **New → Shortcut** and type 'c:\command.com' (just 'cmd' will do in Windows XP) in the Command line text window. Click **Next**, then **Finish**, and the Shortcut icon will appear on your Desktop.

■ **Windows XP is not based on DOS** unlike earlier versions of the operating system. It still can run DOS programs and games, but they may not run properly. DOS in XP is 'emulated' – software makes a program think that it is running on an old DOS-based PC – but the emulation is not perfect. There are many Websites dealing with the problems that you may encounter, for instance with strange sound and video behaviour.

COMPENSATING FOR DISABILITIES

Using a PC straight out of the box won't work for everyone, especially if you have a disability.

■ **Windows can help** if your vision, hearing or mobility is less than perfect. Windows Accessibility Options include HighContrast and Magnifier to aid readability. FilterKeys screens out inadvertent repeated keystrokes, and StickyKeys lets you press key combinations one key at a time. For further help, see the Microsoft Accessibility Website (www.microsoft.com/enable).

■ **Have trouble manoeuvring a mouse?** Go to **Start → Control Panel → Accessibility Options → Accessibility Options**. Click on the **Mouse** tab and tick the **Use MouseKeys** box. You can adjust the settings by clicking on **Settings**, or just click **OK**. Now you can use the numeric key pad numbers to move your mouse pointer around the screen.

■ **Take a Shortcut to turn Mouse Keys on and off.** Check the **Use Shortcut** box in the Settings dialogue box to switch Mouse Keys on and off by holding down your **left Shift key** and **left Alt key**, and pressing **Num Lock**.

■ **Hard of hearing?** Use SoundSentry to add visual cues to the audio warnings your PC makes. Open the Accessibility Options Control Panel, click on the **Sound** tab and check the **Use SoundSentry** box.

■ **Eyes not what they were?** Check the **Use High Contrast** box in the **Display** tab of Accessibility Options to improve the contrast between type and the screen background.

INSTALLING THE ACCESSIBILITY OPTIONS

The Accessibility Options aren't always loaded as standard in some versions of Windows prior to XP.

1. To see if you have Accessibility Options installed, click on **Start → All Programs → Accessories**. Look for an Accessibility choice on the drop-down Accessories menu.

2. If you don't see it, install it by choosing **Start → Settings → Control Panel** and selecting **Add/Remove Programs**, then the **Setup** tab. Select **Accessibility**, choose **Details**, and check both the **Accessibility** and **Accessibility Tools** options.

3. Click **OK**, then **OK** again to confirm. Windows then asks you to put the Windows CD in your disc drive and will install the Accessibility Options feature automatically.

How to: Find and launch a program in DOS

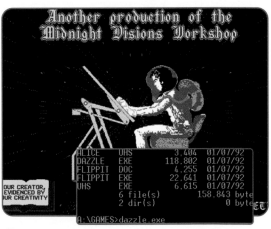

1 Click **Start → All Programs → Accessories → Command Prompt**. Type the letter of the drive with your program, then a colon, and press Return. Type 'dir' and press Return to list the disk's folders. To change folder, type 'cd', a space, the directory name, and press Return.

2 Type 'dir' then Return in the new directory and look for files with an .exe suffix. These are the executable files that run programs. Type the name of the file you want to run, followed by a Return. The program will now run. To leave DOS, type 'exit' and press Return.

LINKING COMPUTERS TOGETHER

Connecting several computers via a network allows you to share files and accessories with others.

■ Set up your home network. In
Windows XP, setting up a home network has become easier than ever. Whether you want to simply share files and a printer between two PCs or make full use of a broadband internet connection, the tools to create the network are built in to the operating system.

■ All you need is an ethernet port on
each computer. Many new computers have network connectors built in to their motherboards, otherwise network cards are cheap and easy to install. If you are only connecting two machines together, the only other equipment you'll need is an ethernet crossover cable. To connect more machines, you'll need a device called a hub as well. The hub connects the PCs on the network together in a star formation, and acts as a traffic policeman for the flow of information between them, making sure that all the data reaches the correct machine.

NETWORK KNOW-HOW

Need some help with your network? Take a look at these useful Websites.

HOMENETHELP (www.homenethelp.com)
A useful collection of articles, how-to guides, tutorials, diagrams and forums designed to help beginners and intermediate users master the basics of setting up home networks.

PRACTICALLY NETWORKED
(www.practicallynetworked.com)
This site provides a wealth of information and advice on setting up home networks.

■ One of the best uses for a
network is sharing an Internet connection. For example, one machine on the network can connect to the Internet via its modem, and then share its connection with the other PCs. Alternatively, if you have a broadband connection, you can use a device called a router that combines the roles of modem and network hub in just one box.

■ Let other PCs see your files by
enabling sharing. In Windows XP, it's best only to enable sharing on the Shared Documents folder. This means that everything else on your hard disk is safely inaccessible to the network. Go to **My Computer**, right-click on **Shared Documents** and choose **Sharing and Security** from the pop-up menu. Under 'Network sharing and security', check **Share this folder on the network**. If you only want people to be able to view the files in the folder make sure that **Allow network users to change my files** is unchecked.

■ To set up your network, make sure all
the necessary cables and equipment are in place then go to **Start ➜ Control Panel ➜ Network and Internet Connections ➜ Set up or change your home or small office network**. The Network Setup Wizard will launch. Follow the steps carefully and supply the information required about how your computer connects to the Internet. Give your computer a network name, and chose a name for your Workgroup – the computers connected to the network. Large networks can contain several Workgroups, but most home setups only need one.

■ Let the Wizard create a network
setup disk when it has finished. Windows will write a floppy disk for you with network settings on it. You can use this to configure the other PCs in your work group, as long as they are running Windows 98 or a more recent version.

◆ See also **Home networks,** p. 22.

ADDING AND REMOVING PROGRAMS

The longer you have your computer, the more software you're likely to install on it. Use the Add or Remove Programs control panel to upgrade.

■ To access the Add or Remove
Programs function, just go to **Start ➜ Control Panel ➜ Add or Remove Programs**. The Add or Remove Programs Control Panel opens. Click on **Change or Remove Programs**, scroll through the programs in the main panel, select the one you want to remove, and then click either the **Change** or **Remove** button below it (some programs have only a **Change/Remove** button to click).

■ Some software may not be as
useful as you thought and you may want to remove it to save hard disk space. Just deleting a program's folder from the Windows Explorer folder will leave traces of the program behind. Using the **Add or Remove Programs Control Panel** ensures that most significant traces of a program will be removed from your computer, usually by running a special uninstall application.

If you have upgraded to Windows XP,

you may be able to Uninstall the new operating system and revert to your old one, depending on whether you chose to back up your old system when you installed XP, and also on whether you changed the file system used on your hard drive or repartitioned it. Go to **Start ➜ Control Panel ➜ Add or Remove Programs** and scroll down the list of programs until you reach **Uninstall Windows XP.** Click on it and follow the steps shown on-screen.

When you upgrade to XP, you may

find that some of the hardware and peripherals you have don't work with your new system. In most cases Windows XP makes a very good job of analysing your system and locating new drivers for the hardware it contains. However, you may have to visit manufacturers' Websites to get the latest drivers if XP is unable to locate them

automatically. Some outdated hardware may not be able to function within Windows XP at all, in which case your only option is to buy a replacement component. Similarly, you may find that some of your programs do not work well under the new operating system. Use the Add or Remove Programs Control Panel to remove a troublesome program, then try reinstalling it. If you still have problems, check the software manufacturer's Website to see if upgrades are available. Answers to problems often appear in a Website's Frequently Asked Questions (FAQ) files. This is why it is good idea to backup your old system when you upgrade to Windows XP. Even if you need the disk space, don't throw the old files away for a week or so, until you are happy that everything is running smoothly.

You may not see an option to uninstall Windows XP

in your Add or Remove Programs icon. Often this is because you chose to use the NTFS file system for your hard drive when you installed. NTFS is incompatible with Me and earlier versions of Windows.

Even if a program that you have installed

on your PC has its own uninstall routine, it's always best to use Add or Remove Programs to make sure that no traces are left behind on your PC.

Take care when using the Add or Remove Programs Control Panel.

Don't remove a program simply because you don't recognise it. You may remove a small but vital program – such as software for your video card – and adversely affect the way your computer works.

To add or remove Windows features,

click on **Add/Remove Windows Components**. You can add items that are not installed by default, such as Fax services and specialist Networking services. Sometimes the files you need are already on your hard drive but need activating. If not you'll need to copy them from your Windows installation CD.

How to: Remove a program

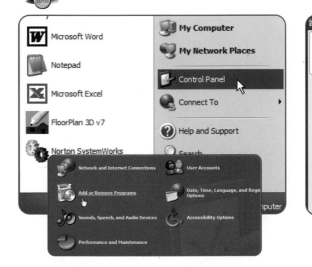

1 Open the Add or Remove Programs Control Panel. Go to **Start ➜ Control Panel**, and click on **Add or Remove Programs**. The Control Panel will open. Click on **Change or Remove Programs** in the left-hand column.

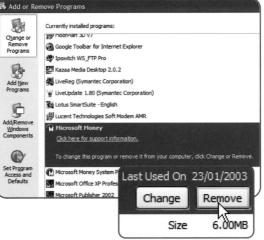

2 The window lists all the programs on your PC that the Control Panel can remove (some programs, such as games, may not appear). Click on the one you want to delete. Click on the **Remove** button (or for some programs the **Change/Remove** button).

3 What you see now will depend on the program selected. You may be asked to confirm your choice, then a series of progress bars will show your PC removing the files originally installed for the chosen program.

Optimising performance

Over time, you may notice that your PC starts to run slower. As you install more software and hardware, Windows can lose track of everything on your machine, which is why optimising and maintaining your PC is worthwhile – it may sound boring but you'll reap the rewards.

MEMORY CONSIDERATIONS

One of the most significant factors in the performance of your PC is its RAM (Random Access Memory). All versions of Windows will benefit if you give them plenty of memory to operate in.

SYSTEM INFORMATION

Use the System Information command in System Tools to access useful features.

DIRECTX DIAGNOSTIC TOOL

If there's a problem with a video or sound component, it will show up under DirectX. Click on the **Display** or **Sound** tab, then click the **Test** button to check your system.

DR. WATSON

Dr. Watson keeps an eye on your system and logs any errors. This information can be useful if you need to contact a software manufacturer about repeated errors.

REGISTRY CHECKER

The Registry is a list of all hardware and software, plus thousands of personal and global settings. Use the Registry Checker to run a diagnostic test on the Registry and back it up, if necessary.

SYSTEM RESTORE

If something goes wrong after a program installation, System Restore returns your PC to the state it was in before.

Memory is cheap. Even if you have an older machine with a Pentium 2 or 3 processor, you'll still notice considerable gains in responsiveness if you upgrade from 32 MB to 128 MB. Memory prices change rapidly, but typically an upgrade like this can cost less than twenty pounds.

Disk space is important as well.

Windows uses part of your hard disk as Virtual memory. In Windows Me you need to make sure that at least 250 MB of disk space is free for Windows' paging file (how Virtual Memory is sometimes referred to). For Windows XP it pays to have at least 512 MB of disk space available. Windows uses this disk space to store information that can't fit into memory. If there isn't enough space left on your hard disk, Windows will slow down and may even start to freeze up.

If you're low on memory, only run one program at a time. This will let your PC focus on the task in hand and minimise swapping of data from RAM to virtual memory. Programs like Outlook require a large amount of memory to run. If you are using Outlook mostly for e-mail, consider downgrading to Outlook Express instead.

If you want to try out new software, you may need to make more space available.

You may have accumulated programs that load when you start Windows, and some may be seen as icons in the System Tray (the icons in the Taskbar next to the clock). These programs may take up valuable memory, so only keep the ones you need. Go to **Start → All Programs → Startup** and remove aliases of any programs that you do not use.

A BETTER DISPLAY

The more colours and the higher the resolution you choose, the more work your PC and graphics card are going to have to do to update the screen. If you have a graphics card with less than 4 MB built-in RAM, you may see the screen redrawing slowly from top to bottom. There are two solutions: either upgrade your graphics adaptor to one with 16 MB of RAM or more, or reduce the number of colours and the resolution you use onscreen. To do this, right-click on an empty area of the desktop and choose **Properties**. Select the **Settings** tab and move the **Color Quality** slider to a lower setting.

If you opt to upgrade your graphics card
and your motherboard has an AGP (Accelerated Graphics Port) slot, choose a 3D-accelerated AGP card. The AGP system is dedicated to graphics and provides a faster connection than older PCI cards can achieve.

New graphics cards
will have 64 or 128 MB of memory – enough for high resolutions and excellent 3D performance. But make sure your monitor is up to the task before choosing a fast refresh rate – 85 Hz is ideal for avoiding flicker.

HARDWARE AND SOFTWARE

Check the Internet regularly
for driver updates for all your hardware. The most important devices are your graphics and sound cards, modem and BIOS. Each new release fixes earlier problems and upgrades performance.

SYSTEM CHECKS

Windows comes with a System Information utility
to provide in-depth information about your system, hardware and hardware resources. To access it, go to **Start →
All Programs → Accessories → System Tools** and select **System Information**. A collection of useful tools (see box, p. 86) helps to optimise your computer's performance.

Run regular disk diagnostics
(on the System Tools menu) to keep your PC healthy.

Running Disk Defragmenter at least once a month keeps your hard drive in good order. Special disk-maintenance software, like Norton Utilities, will locate errors and problems, and monitor your system while you work. It also contains a more thorough disk optimising program.

A BIOS upgrade,
often made available over the Internet, may resolve irritating glitches and speed up your PC. BIOS (Basic Input Output System) is the set of operating instructions built into your PC. Only use the correct version for your specific BIOS and motherboard – do not attempt this job if you are an inexperienced PC user.

♦ See also **Hard drive housekeeping**, p. 32.

How to: Run Disk Defragmenter

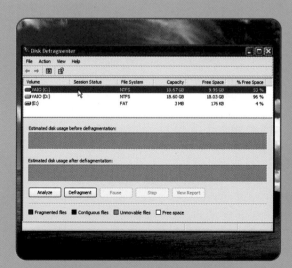

1 To run Disk Defragmenter in Windows go to **Start → All Programs → Accessories → Systems Tools**, and then click on **Disk Defragmenter**. The program will open and list the drives or disk partitions present on your PC that it can optimise.

2 Choose the drive that you wish to defragment – for example, the hard drive, C. Clicking **Analyze** makes the program check how bad the defragmentation of your chosen disk is. Clicking **Defragment** will start the optimisation process straight away.

3 Two striped bars will appear in the program window representing the degree of fragmentation on the disk before and after the process has run. You can click on **Pause** or **Stop** to either interrupt or abort the process at any time without damaging your system.

Getting organised

Handling files and folders

A file's format determines the way in which the information in it is stored on your computer. Here are some hints on choosing formats.

■ **The format of a file** is indicated by the three or four-letter extension following the file name. For example, when you save a spreadsheet in Microsoft Excel, the program always gives it the extension .xls. Files with the extension .doc are Word documents.

■ **If you send a Word document** to a person whose version of Word is older than yours – or someone who doesn't have Word at all – they will probably not be able to open your file. The solution is to save the file in a different format. Select **File ➔ Save As**, and choose **Rich Text Format (*.rtf)** in the **Save as type** box. This is a commonly supported file format that virtually every PC is able to view.

■ **If someone e-mails you a file** simply called 'greatpicture', it is difficult to view because there's no extension identifying the file's format. Windows will give it a generic file icon, and when

you double-click on it, it will ask you to choose a program to open it or use the Web to find one. If you know that the program is a picture, try opening it in Paint, which can handle many common file types. For safety you should scan the file for viruses first – sometimes the best thing to do with a file that you are unsure of is simply to delete it.

■ **When saving graphics for use on a Web page,** the file format is very important. Always save photographs as jpeg (also known as .jpg). This keeps the files small and fast to load. The .gif format is generally better for simple graphics with only a few colours. Convert files from one format to another using a graphics program like Paint (go to **Start ➔ All Programs ➔ Accessories**), or more advanced ones such as Adobe Photoshop and Jasc Paintshop Pro.

ONLINE FILE FORMAT SUPPORT

Discover the format of unidentified files and convert files to a different format.

FILEXT (www.filext.com)
This site lists many thousands of different extensions. As well as telling you the program that created a file with a given extension, the site gives you a link to the manufacturer's Website to find out more.

ICONV (www.iconv.com)
This site lets you convert a graphics file to another format online. You don't have to download or install any software.

FCODER (www.fcodersoft.com)
If you frequently convert graphics files from one format to another, you'll appreciate the power and ease-of-use of ImageConvertor Plus. Download and try out a demo of the program before you buy it.

GOHTM (www.gohtm.com)
As you might guess from the name, this site specialises in converting all kinds of documents (including .pdf, .rtf, .txt, .doc, .xls, and .ppt files) to HTML format.

WOTSIT (www.wotsit.org)
Anyone with a more technical interest in file formats will love Wotsit's Format, which contains in-depth information on precisely how file formats work.

Spend a little time working out a file-naming system so that your files are easy to locate and open.

■ **Always give your files names that describe their contents.** If you name a series of picture files image1, image2, image3, and so on, chances are you'll never be able to find the picture you want when you try to later.

■ **Windows sorts files and folders alphabetically,** with numerals at the top of the list. While this might be ideal for someone compiling a dictionary, it is not always the most practical order. If you want to view the progress of a project over time, for example, consider putting six-digit dates at the beginning of the file names.

> painter 1 letter.doc
> painter 1 quote.doc
> painter 1 refusal.doc
> painter 2 acceptance.doc

■ **When you save a file** in one of the Microsoft Office programs, it is placed in your My Documents folder. If you want to change the default folder for Word documents, open the program and click on **Tools ➔ Options** and select the **File Locations** tab. Select **Documents** in the File types list on the left, then press the **Modify** button and select a new default folder.

■ **You can sort your files by name, type, size or date** in Windows Explorer, whether you choose Icon or Display view. To arrange files by name, go to **View ➔ Arrange Icons by ➔ Name**.

■ **Sometimes, you can't see all the text in your file names,** especially if you select **Details** from a folder's **View** menu. This can be a nuisance when the file suffix is important. However, if you move the mouse to the right of the 'Name' button above the column of file names, you can drag the divider to the right to make more space for the text to be displayed. Resize other columns the same way.

■ **Search out Word files with similar file names,** using file properties. In Word, go to **File ➜ Open**, click on the **Tools** button on the Toolbar and select **Search**. You can look for a word or phrase in files on your computer, or click on the Advanced tab to make a more focused search with a number of parameters to match.

■ **If you can't remember where you put a file,** but you know all or part of the file's name, you can use Windows' search facility to look for it. Go to **Start ➜ Search** and click on the appropriate button in the left-hand column.

HIDING FILES FROM SNOOPERS

You can choose which files you wish to be displayed, and which files you want to keep hidden.

Attributes: ☐ Read-only ☑ Hidden [Advanced...]

■ **Want to keep a secret?** You can hide selected files and folders from view in Windows Explorer. Right-click on the file you want to hide, and choose **Properties** from the pop-up menu. In the box that appears, go to the Attributes section at the bottom and put a check beside **Hidden**.

■ **Hiding files completely.** You might find that files you have set to be hidden are still visible in Windows Explorer and are only greyed out. To make these hidden files completely invisible, go to the **Tools** menu in an open folder window and select **Folder Options**. Click the **View** tab and select **Do not show hidden files and folders**. Click on **OK** to confirm the change.

■ **Don't hide files to keep secrets.** This function in Windows is intended to remove clutter and make it easier to find important files. It is not a good way to prevent other users from viewing personal documents. All hidden files can be revealed again by returning to the **Folder Options** window from the **Tools** menu, clicking on the **View** tab, and selecting the **Show hidden files and folders** option under Advanced settings. If you really want to protect personal files, use a password with your account and make your My Documents folder private.

PROTECTING YOUR FILES

Making files read-only is the conventional way to protect them from being accidentally overwritten or amended.

You can check a file's read-only status by right-clicking on the file icon and selecting **Properties**. If the **Read-only** box is checked the file can be opened and viewed but not saved with the same name.

Windows needs to be able to change the contents of a variety of key files – for instance, those in the Windows folder and any system files – so beware of making files read-only if you don't know what they are. If you do so, you might cause your PC to crash, and the source of the problem will be difficult to find.

■ **Making a file read-only doesn't prevent** the file from being damaged, deleted or even from being changed and saved with a new name, so it's not an alternative to proper security and backup procedures. If a file is important enough for you to change its attribute to read-only, make sure it's also securely backed up and not available to all users (see p. 105).

How to: Convert image files on the net

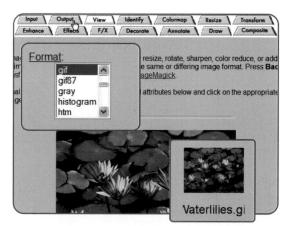

iConv, Inc

The File Format Conversion Site

Commonly used file format conversions at your fingertips - anywhere, anytime. No installation nee...

MagickStudio

net4tv

Filename:
C:\Documents and Settings\All Users\Documents\My [Browse...]
URL:
http://

Input | **Output** | **View** | **Identify** | **Colormap** | **Resize** | **Transform**
Enhance | **Effects** | **F/X** | **Decorate** | **Annotate** | **Draw** | **Composite**

Format:
gif
gif87
gray
histogram
htm

Vaterlilies.gi

1 **Navigate your way to the IConv Website** (www.iconv.com). Click on the type of conversion you want to perform, and when the MagickStudio page appears, click **Browse** to select your image, or enter its URL. Click the **view** button when you are ready.

2 **Your image appears on the Web browser, together with a set of tabs showing the range of operations you can perform.** Click the appropriate tab, and wait for the relevant Web page to download. Make your choices and click **Output** to view the converted file.

Protect master copies, forms and final drafts of documents with read-only status. This will keep your master copy clean and prevent anyone else who has access to your files from changing your documents without your knowing.

Read-only status may not prevent files from being infected by computer viruses, so use a good antivirus program rather than relying on file attribute changes to protect your files.

Files copied from a CD-ROM are usually already set to read-only, since CD-ROMs are read-only media anyway. So, if you need to edit a file from a CD, check the attribute properties before you make any changes or be prepared to save the file with a different name.

If you try to save a read-only file after making changes to it, you will get an error message. Simply give the file a different name, and you will be able to save it. The new file will not have read-only status.

FOLDERS HELP TO ORGANISE YOUR WORK

Use a filing system made up of folders to keep your work organised and easy to find.

Create new folders in Windows. In an open folder, either click on **Make a new folder** in the left-hand menu, select **File ➜ New ➜ Folder** from the menu bar, or right-click in the right-hand panel and select **New ➜ Folder** from the pop-up options. Give the new folder a name to suit its contents and move any relevant files to the folder by holding down the **Ctrl** key to highlight all the files, and then drag them onto the new folder.

Build a virtual filing cabinet by grouping folders together inside other folders. For example, inside your 'Holiday photos' folder you could store all the picture folders for holidays you've taken. This sort of system takes up less space in a window and makes finding your files quicker.

Stop open folders from filling up your screen. Go to **Tools ➜ Folder Options** to set the way that a folder behaves in Windows Explorer. In the **General** tab go to the Browse folders section and check **Open each folder in the same window** to avoid having your desktop fill up with new windows as you search through a set of nested folders.

Choose your views. Windows gives you several different ways to see what's in a folder. Choose an option by clicking on the **Views** Icon in the Toolbar (or right-clicking in an empty part of the folder and clicking on **View**). All folders give you the choice of **Thumbnails** – any pictures in the folder are shown in miniature; **Tiles** – files and folders appear as large icons; **Icons** – smaller icons; **List** – the most space-efficient view; and **Details** – you can see information about files and folders, such as their sizes and creation dates. Picture folders can also be viewed as a **Filmstrip** in Windows XP.

⯈ See also **Organising your Desktop**, p. 60; **Using Windows Explorer**, p. 65; and **Launching programs at startup**, p. 66.

THE MY DOCUMENTS FOLDER

The My Documents folder provides a convenient filing cabinet for your documents.

Use the My Documents folder to store all the files you create – even if a program suggests otherwise. For example, some programs offer their own folder as the default storage location when you save your files. But it's best to create and use a folder within the My Documents folder. That way, it's easier to keep track of these files and to include them in backups.

To remove the My Documents folder from the Desktop in Windows Me and 98, simply right-click on the icon and select **Remove from Desktop** from the pop-up menu.

Missing the My Documents icon on your desktop in WIndows XP? By default it isn't there, unlike in earlier versions of Windows. To show it, right-click on **My Documents** in the Start menu and choose **Show on Desktop**. You can choose to place other familiar items, such as My Computer and My Network Places, on the desktop in a similar way.

Access recent documents from the Start menu. Click on **Start ➜ My Recent Documents** to view a list of the files you have saved most recently on your PC. Often this list will include the document you want to work on and by selecting the file name, the document will open. If you can't see this list, right-click on the **Start** button, select **Properties** from the pop-up menu and in the **Start Menu** tab click on **Customize**. In the **Advanced** tab make sure that the box next to **List my most recently opened documents** is checked.

Need easy access to the Web while you work? By pressing **Ctrl+I** when My Documents is open, you can display your Internet Favorites list from Internet Explorer (or Bookmarks in Netscape) in the left-hand frame. Click on a site to log onto the Internet and visit it. Once you've finished using your Favorites list, click the **x** in the top right of the frame to close the list and return to My Documents view.

Can't find that important document?

With the My Documents window selected, press **Ctrl+F** to start a search facility in the left-hand frame. You can use it to search My Documents – or the whole of your computer – for a file or folder name. If you can't remember the name, use the **Containing text** box to search for files containing a word or phrase you can remember.

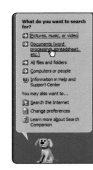

See also **Organising your Desktop**, p. 60.

HOW TO FIND FILES

Recover lost files by name, location, content or application.

Locate misplaced files or folders rapidly

with Windows' handy inbuilt Search facility. Go to the Start menu and select **Search**.

A window appears with the Search dialogue in the left-hand column. Click on **Documents**. You will be asked if you can remember when the document was last modified, and can narrow down the search by giving part of the file name. Click in the **Use advanced search options** box to target the search more exactly. Click **Search** to begin the process.

Know only part of a name?

You may have forgotten a file name but remember that it had, for example, the word 'old' somewhere in the description. To locate all file names containing that letter combination insert an asterisk (*) (known in search operations as a 'wildcard') before the word 'old' and '*.*' after. The search string then becomes '*old*.*' and will locate files with names such as 'old building' or 'manifold'.

Save time by searching one drive at a time.

If you have more than one drive installed, a search for a particular file can take ages. So, if you're confident that the file is on hard drive C, it makes sense to look through just that one first. Go to **Start ➜ Search**, click on **All files and folders** and use the **Look in** drop-down menu to select your chosen drive.

Forgotten the file name?

If you don't know where a document is and can't remember what you called it either, you can always run a search on the contents. Maybe you know it was a letter to your accountant, or a list of car expenses. Go to **Start ➜ Search ➜ All files and folders** and type what you're looking for in the **A word or phrase in the document** box. For example, to find a letter you've written to Mr. Jones, enter 'Mr. Jones'.

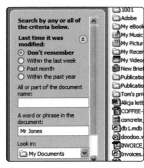

Search for files for a particular application.

This is a handy solution if you can't remember the file name or extension, but do know which program it was created in. As above, click on **All files and folders**, but this time click on **More advanced options**. Use the **Type of file** pop-up menu to select the program. The search can be refined to files in a particular range of sizes (Small, Medium or Large) but it's safest to choose **Don't remember**.

How to: Protect your files

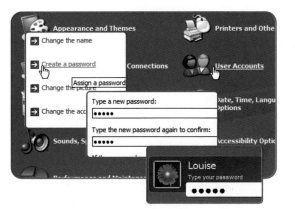

1 The simplest, but least secure, way to protect files is to change their attributes to **Read-only** or **Hidden,** or both. Right-click on a file or folder, click on **Properties,** and check **Read-only** or **Hidden** in the Properties panel that appears.

2 More security is offered by password protecting your user account. Go to **Start ➜ Control Panel ➜ User Accounts**. Click on your account then choose **Create a password**. Now enter your password twice and click **Create Password.**

3 Many programs, such as Microsoft Word and Excel, allow you to password protect particular files. In Word, click **Tools ➜ Options** and click on the **Security** tab. You can enter passwords to limit the people who can open and/or modify the file.

MOVING FILES FROM PLACE TO PLACE

Move files easily from one folder to another, or use a floppy or Zip disk to transfer them to another PC.

■ Move files using drag-and-drop.
Select the files for moving, then click and hold the mouse button as you drag them over and drop them in the appropriate folder.

■ Make haste with Cut and Paste.
Transfer files from one place on your PC to another. Right-click on the file and choose **Cut** from the menu. Release the mouse button and move the pointer to the desired location. Right-click again and choose **Paste** from the menu. The file appears in its new spot (see 'How to', p. 93).

KEYBOARD SHORTCUTS
Try these time-saving commands when you move your files around.

Ctrl+A Selects all the items in a folder.

Alt+E+I Inverts the current selection of files in a folder.

Ctrl+X Cuts a selected file or files.

Ctrl+V Pastes the files you have cut into the selected folder.

Ctrl+Z Undoes the cut and paste you performed last, or any other command you have just performed.

Windows+E Opens Windows Explorer.

Ctrl+F Starts a search if you need to find a file before you can move it.

Ctrl+S Saves any changes you've made to a document before you close and move it.

For keyboard shortcuts to carry out this operation see box, below. Select several files at once by holding down the **Ctrl** key as you click on them.

■ Make extra copies.
If you have several files to copy to the same location, highlight them all and right-click your mouse. Choose **Copy** from the menu, then open the folder and **Paste** the files. The files now exist in both locations.

■ If you want to move files to another computer,
copy them straight to a removable disk for easy transportation. Do this by highlighting and right-clicking the files, then selecting **Send To → 3½ Floppy (A:)** or **Zip** or **Removable Disk (E:)**.

■ Drag, drop and burn
Windows XP makes copying files to a CD-R very easy if your PC has a CD burner. Insert a blank CD-R in your burner, then choose **Open writable CD folder using Windows Explorer** in the dialogue box that appears. A new window will appear. Simply drag and drop the files and folders that you want to back-up onto the CD into this window. Then click on **Write these files to CD** to begin the burning process.

HOW TO COPY FILES

From time to time, you might want to copy files on your hard drive into a different folder, or transfer them to a floppy or Zip disk.

■ Use the task pane to copy and move files.
In Windows XP, every Explorer window has a task pane on its left-hand side that lists tasks that you can do with a file or folder. For example, open My Documents and select a file by clicking on it. Choose **Copy this file** in the task pane. In the box that appears, choose the folder you want to copy the file to then click on **Copy**. The **Move this file** command works similarly but deletes the original file after copying it.

■ If you want to copy the entire contents
of a folder, go to **Edit → Select All**.

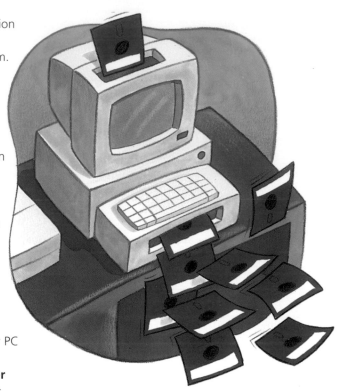

Pressing **Ctrl+A** together will also select all the files in the active window. You can now copy or move them as usual.

■ The larger the file you are copying,
the longer it takes to appear in the new folder window. In the case of very large files, or groups of files, you'll see a dialogue box detailing the progress of the task your PC is performing. With such larger files, it's always advisable to let your computer finish copying these files before attempting another operation.

▶ See also **The faithful floppy**, p. 30; and **Using Cut and Paste**, p. 115.

HOW TO DELETE FILES

Delete unwanted files regularly to free space on your hard drive.

■ Multiple files can be deleted together
by holding down the **Ctrl** key, and then clicking each file once to select it. When all the relevant files are highlighted, follow any one of the deletion procedures below.

There are three ways to delete files.
You can locate the file you want to remove, right-click it and select **Delete**. Or click on a file and, holding the mouse button down, drag it to the Recycle Bin icon. Or select the files to be removed and click on **Delete this file** on the task pane at the left-hand side of the window. Click **Yes** to confirm.

Find the confirmation message annoying?
You can eliminate this message, which asks if you're sure you want to delete the file every time you put something in the bin. Right-click the Recycle Bin and select **Properties** from the menu. Now simply uncheck **Display delete confirmation dialog** box.

After you have deleted a file,
it will be stored in the Recycle Bin. This precaution helps prevent any files from being deleted accidentally. Once you're positive you want to delete the files in there, you can empty the Recycle Bin by right-clicking it and selecting **Empty Recycle Bin**.

To delete a file without it appearing in the Recycle Bin,
right-click the file then hold down the Shift key while clicking **Delete**. Only do this if you are absolutely sure that you want to delete the file.

If there are any deleted files stored in your Recycle Bin,
the icon displayed on your Desktop will indicate this by showing that the bin is full of rubbish. To open and view the bin's contents, double-click on it and an explorer window will appear. Items can be rescued if necessary.

If you delete a file accidentally,
you can restore it by opening the Recycle Bin, selecting the file, and then going to **File → Restore**. The file will be restored to its original position on your hard drive.

When you delete a file,
you're only telling your operating system that you no longer need to use it – the file is given a name that makes it invisible, and the information stays on the disk until your operating system overwrites the space it occupies with new data. File recovery programs simply search your drive for files that have been hidden but not yet overwritten. They can unerase a file by making it visible again.

Before disposing of any removable media,
such as floppy disks, Zip disks and tape drives, make sure you have deleted any sensitive or private files from them. The best way to do this is to perform a complete reformat. Norton Utilities contains a tool called Wipe Info to perform the job. Wipe Info overwrites the data that you want to delete, so that it cannot be recovered. You can remove the data on an entire disk with the utility or choose to remove individual files.

Wipe info writes regular data
over your deleted files, to destroy any trace of the original information. For extra security, you can choose a Wipe to US Government standards – one that overwrites the data at least three times. Take care – once a file has been wiped, it is gone forever.

Delete files regularly.
You can use Windows' Maintenance Wizard or Task Scheduler to run the Disk Cleanup program regularly. As part of that process, you can ask the program to delete temporary files, which are created automatically by programs, but are sometimes left undeleted, cluttering up your hard drive.

How to: Transfer files in Windows using Copy and Paste

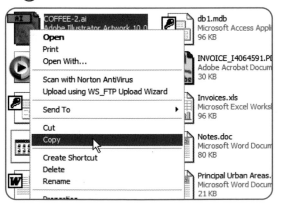

1 Locate the file you want to copy on your hard drive, right-click it, and then select **Copy** from the pop-up menu of options.

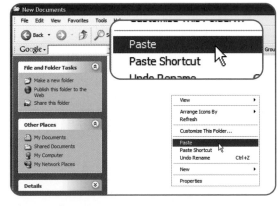

2 Now locate the folder you want to place the file into. Then right-click inside it and select **Paste** from the pop-up menu.

3 The file you have just copied should appear in the new folder window – there may be a delay if the file is large.

Accessories

Windows is normally installed with a variety of programs in the Accessories menu, covering everything from optimising your hard drive to create simple graphics. Take time getting to know all the functions these time-savers offer.

TAKE A CLOSER LOOK

Meet your Accessories. Go to **Start → All Programs → Accessories** and scroll through all the items to get an idea of what's available. Most of the program names are self-explanatory. If you want to know a bit more about something, simply launch the program and click **Help**.

🗐	Accessibility
🗐	Communications
🗐	Entertainment
🗐	Microsoft Interactive Training
🗐	System Tools
📖	Address Book
🖩	Calculator
⬛	Command Prompt
📝	Notepad
🖌	Paint

Need to zoom in on a small area of graphics or tiny fonts on a Web page? Select **All Programs → Accessories → Accessibility** and click **Magnifier**. You'll find the top eighth of your screen now displays a magnified view of the area around your cursor, making it easier to see fine detail (see 'How to', p. 62). The Windows Accessibility tools are invaluable for those who are visually impaired or have other disabilities.

You've probably taken a cursory glance at your Windows Calculator. The standard view offers basic functions – the most advanced being square root. If you require a greater choice of functions, look again. Select **View → Scientific** and suddenly a much more capable utility is presented, including statistical and trigonometric functions and computer-related hexadecimal, octal and binary figures. This makes it useful for advanced maths, computer programming, and business statistics and planning.

Make your own images. Paint is a basic program for creating graphics. You can draw and colour your own images, but if you only have a mouse to draw with, your may find your images look like the work of a three-year-old! To convert one of your creations into Desktop Wallpaper, select **File → Set As Wallpaper**.

Recently cut or copied graphics are held in an uncompressed form on the Clipboard. To know what's on the Clipboard at any given time, use the Clipboard Viewer. Go to **Start → All Programs → Accessories → System Tools → Clipboard**. Or select **Edit → Delete** to clear the Clipboard completely. If it's holding a large picture file, this can free up a lot of memory.

In Windows XP, the program is hidden away in your system files. To run it, go to **Start → Run** and type **clipbrd** in the box next to **Open**. Note that the program is now the 'Clipbook Viewer'.

How to: Use the character map

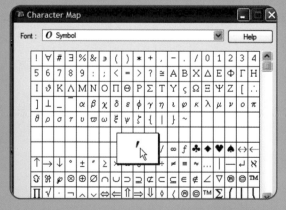

1 The Character Map shows all variations of the Western alphabet, such as é or ß. Go to **Start → All Programs → Accessories → System Tools → Character Map**. Choose your font to see the full range of characters it contains – not all fonts have the same ones.

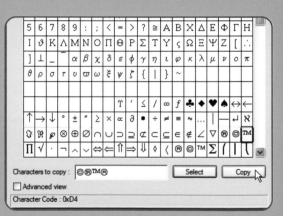

2 The Character Map uses a small font so it can be difficult to distinguish between different symbols, such as various punctuation marks, especially if you have poor eyesight. To view a magnified version, click and hold down the mouse over any one symbol.

3 Double-click on each of the characters that you want to copy, and click the **Copy** button to transfer them to the Clipboard. To paste your symbols into a document, open the file and select **Edit → Paste**.

its sheer simplicity is exactly why it's so useful. Notepad only works with plain text, it doesn't support any text formatting beyond the Tab key, and can't handle files larger than 64 KB. But it's fast to load and, if you want to view small plain text files or jot down and print out a note or reminder, there's no quicker program to do it.

Try a Notepad trick to create a daily log.
Open a new document and type **.LOG** in the very first line – note it must be in uppercase. Now close and save the file. Whenever you open it again, Notepad will add the date and time to the end. This is a simple way to keep a set of date-stamped notes, such as a diary.

Wordpad is Notepad's more sophisticated
big brother. Although still quite limited in its features, you can style and format text, so it's good for writing straight-forward letters. It can also read Rich Text files (*.rtf) and most documents in Word (.doc) format. If your word processor won't read a particular file, try Wordpad. The formatting will probably be lost, but you may well be able to recover the text.

The Entertainment category of your Accessories
is where the multimedia tools are found. In addition to Windows Media Player – which plays movies and audio CDs, and records tracks to your hard disk – it features a Sound Recorder. Providing you have a sound card, speakers and a microphone, you can use it to easily create and edit sound files.

Become a video director.
Windows Movie Maker is a powerful program able to import and edit footage from a digital video camera. You can also add titles, effects and transitions to your movie before exporting the finished work to your camera, or as a compressed video suitable for sending over the Internet.

A WAY WITH WORDS

Don't underestimate it.
Notepad is one of the most limited text editors in existence, but

TROUBLESHOOTING

To study your PC Setup,
look no further than the **System Information** program in **System Tools**. It tells you about all your hardware and software, including some things you may not have known you had. Go to **View → System History** and you'll discover the details of changes you've made to your setup – invaluable if you're trying to restore a device to working order.

Missing an Accessory?
Go to **Start → Control Panel**, then click on **Add or Remove Programs** and select **Add/Remove Windows Components**. Select a category in the Components list and then click on **Details** to see a list of individual programs within that category. Check the box next

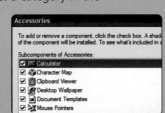

to the accessory you want to install if it isn't checked already. You may need to use your Windows CD-ROM to complete the installation.

▶ See also **Home networks,** p. 22; **Windows 95 to Me,** p. 56; **Compensating for disabilities,** p. 83; and **Optimising performance,** p. 86.

ACCESSORY SECRETS
Discover some handy little functions tucked away in Windows XP.

- **Microsoft Backup** is not installed as standard with Windows XP, but it's still available on the CD. You'll need to navigate through a few folders to install it (see p. 74).

- **The Program Compatibility Wizard** helps you to run versions of programs designed for versions of Windows before XP. Follow its steps and you may get old games and utilities going again.

- **Dr. Watson** (drwatson.exe) can help you to diagnose computer problems. Go to **Accessories → System Tools → System Information** and then **Tools → Dr Watson** to open the Utility.

- **Remote Assistance** allows someone else – perhaps a computer-savvy son or daughter – to use his or her PC to take control of your PC via the Internet and troubleshoot a problem you may be having. Don't worry – the takeover can only be done with your approval and the data that passes between the machines is scrambled for security.

Software

Discover the tricks of the trade with everything from Access to Zip files. Master mail merge, menus and macros; design newsletters and cards; create your own images, and conquer spreadsheets.

Windows software

Programs for every job

THE MULTI-PURPOSE OFFICE SUITE

Office suites are designed to fulfil most of your everyday computing needs right out of the box.

■ **An office suite is a collection of programs** that, together, meets a wide range of general needs. Besides Microsoft Office, other popular office suites include Lotus SmartSuite (www.lotus.com), Corel WordPerfect Office

(www.corel.com) and StarOffice (www.sun.com). One advantage of an office suite over a collection of programs is that its individual components are designed to be compatible.

■ **The most important part** of a software suite is its word processor; this is almost certainly the program you will use most. The next most used programs are probably contact managers, spreadsheets such as Excel and databases such as the Microsoft Works Database.

■ **Microsoft Office** comes in several different versions (see box, right), but all contain three core applications: Word (word processor), Excel (spreadsheet) and Outlook (e-mail program, calendar and contact manager). Each version caters for a specific type of user.

■ **Need to e-mail or fax a document?** Microsoft Office will allow you to e-mail or fax from within any application, provided you have the correct software installed in your PC. To do this in Word or Excel, just click **Send To** under the File Menu and choose whether you want to send the document as an e-mail or fax.

■ **Need help with a program?** Microsoft supports Office users by providing information at its Website, including detailed troubleshooting advice, program upgrades and details of new software. The site also offers downloads that add new features to existing programs or fix past problems. You can also download a variety of templates.

VERSIONS OF OFFICE XP

Choose the best suite for your needs from the following packages.

OFFICE XP STANDARD
Geared for the home-based computer user, this basic version contains Word, Excel, Outlook and PowerPoint.

OFFICE XP PROFESSIONAL
This version adds Access, a powerful database program. If you need to organise lots of information, or work regularly with outside clients, this is the best choice. This suite includes Word, Excel, Outlook, Access and PowerPoint.

OFFICE XP PROFESSIONAL SPECIAL EDITION
The Special Edition adds desktop publishing (Microsoft Publisher) and Web design software (Microsoft FrontPage) to the Professional suite. If you need to produce high-quality printed matter and good Websites, choose this version.

OFFICE XP DEVELOPER
Aimed at the 'Techie' market, this version of the productivity suite includes FrontPage, Microsoft's powerful Web page design and scripting program as well as the Office Developer Toolkit, a set of programming applications for creating complex Macros and scripts that work within the other Office component programs.

■ **If even the stripped-down Standard** version of Office provides more software than you need, Microsoft Works might be a more suitable alternative for you. It is a suite designed with home users in mind, and, like Office, it comes in several versions. Many PCs come with Works already installed.

▶ See also **Works**, p. 100; **Publisher 2000**, p. 122; **Working with Microsoft Word**, p. 124; **Excel: Microsoft's spreadsheet program**, p. 177; and **Outlook Express**, p. 320.

ADD ZEST TO YOUR PRESENTATIONS

PowerPoint lets you mix words, sounds, images and animations into a single dynamic slide show.

■ **Giving a presentation?** Microsoft's PowerPoint program offers you a range of professional features and flexibility that goes far beyond the traditional slide show and overhead projector sequence.

■ **When you first start up Power Point 2002** you will be given the option of how you want to create your presentation or slide show. In the **New Presentation** box, on the right of the window, click on **From Design Template**. Scroll through the thumbnails and click on the template that is best for your purposes to open a presentation with that design.

■ **When the template appears,** click on the area you want to work in, and type in text or place images you want to include on the slide.

■ **Add special effects** to your presentation by choosing **Preset Animation** or **Custom Animation** in the **Slide Show** menu. Highlight a piece of text or click on an image, and you can choose from a range of animation effects.

■ **When you finish a slide,** and want to move to a new one, go to the **Insert** menu and choose the **New Slide** command.

If you have a sound card in your PC, you can record a short voice-over narration for each slide using the **Slide Show → Record Narration** command. You will need to connect a microphone and speakers to use this option.

Showtime! Run a slide show by going to **Slide Show → View Show**. This steps through your slides in the sequence you have ordered them – you can choose whether or not to automate events in your slide show instead of manually clicking through them. Don't be afraid to experiment to find out what best suits your particular presentation style. To return to editing the slides at any point, simply press the **Esc** button.

UPGRADING YOUR SOFTWARE

Keep your operating system and software up-to-date with upgrades from the Internet.

Check Windows Update regularly if your PC does not check automatically. Go to **Start → All Programs → Windows Update**.

Windows XP checks for updates automatically by default. This ensures that it is always running with the latest system software. However, you may find the process annoying, especially if you have a dial-up Internet connection. To turn the feature off, go to the **Start** menu and right-click on **My Computer**. Choose **Properties** and then the **Automatic Updates** tab. Uncheck the box next to **Keep my computer up to date**. You can also use

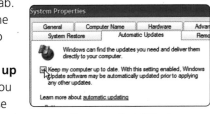

this dialogue box to set the way that Windows downloads updates when they become available.

Be wary of beta-test software. Beta-test versions are early releases of programs that have not completed testing, so they may contain potentially annoying or damaging bugs.

Check for updates regularly. If you use shareware software, it's worth checking the software Websites every few months to see if any updates are available.

You can add backgrounds to liven up your slide shows and even use your own images as a background if you wish. The quickest way to modify the design of all of your slides is by going to **View → Master → Slide Master**. Add your image to the Slide Master and it will appear on all the slides in your presentation.

How to: Add images to a PowerPoint presentation

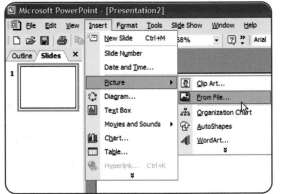

1 Choose a picture you have already downloaded from the Internet or scanned in to be placed into your presentation. Go to **Insert → Picture → From File**. You will then be asked to locate the picture you want.

2 When you have found the image you are going to use, double-click on it. To re-size an image, click on it to select it, and then move the handles or circles on the corners and edges in the desired direction. You can also apply animations to images.

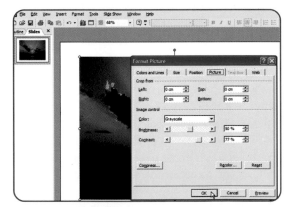

3 You can alter the contrast and brightness of the image by first selecting it and then going to **Format → Picture** and tweaking the options on the Picture tab of the Format Picture dialogue box. Click on the **Preview** button to see the results of each change.

Works

Microsoft Works is a suite of programs providing an all-in-one solution for the home PC user. It contains the essential tools for day-to-day tasks, from word processing to spreadsheets, databases and a calendar. There's also a place to store your favourite photographs and Web pages.

GETTING STARTED

There are two ways to launch Works.
If you go to **Start ➜ All Programs** you will see two entries for Microsoft Works. One is to a folder that opens to reveal direct links to each of the component programs that make up Works.

The other link (usually in the right-hand column of the list) opens the Works Task Launcher.

What is the Task Launcher? Think of it
as the control centre of Works. When you launch it, the Task Launcher Welcome Page appears. Any of the Works tasks can be started with the Launcher. You can open an existing document, check your diary, or access one of Works' range of programs or Wizards – including ones for the Web, databases and spreadsheets.

Feeling a bit lost? Take a tour. If you're
not sure where to start with Works, go to the Task Launcher and click on the **Works Quick Tour** link. Works will give you an illustrated tour of some of the main features it offers.

BASIC PROGRAMS

Use the spreadsheet program for calculations. If you need to plan your holiday
budget, work out your loan repayments, or evaluate your physical fitness, this is the program you need. While it's not as powerful as Excel, it's handy for domestic planning, and the templates can get you working a lot quicker than starting from scratch in Excel.

The database program is for making lists and keeping records. All items you want to
keep track of can be recorded under convenient categories, and you can retrieve all or just part of them whenever you want. You could record the service history of your car, with distances travelled, oil changes and repairs, so that you will

be able to provide a comprehensive history when you want to sell it. You can also cross-reference categories so that, for example, you can check details of your building insurance against your house contents insurance.

Works provides a variety of templates for spreadsheets and databases
that can be easily customised to meet your particular needs.

Use word processing for writing letters and other text-based documents, such
as CVs, formal letters and personalised stationery. You can also create typed envelopes and address labels for a professional touch. The program has all the features you need to create the perfect document, and even allows you to insert information from your Works spreadsheets, databases or calendar.

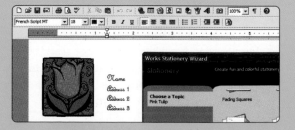

Take a look at the Letter Wizards to see ready-made formats. Open the Works Task Launcher, then click on **Tasks ➜ Letters and Labels ➜ Letters**. Click **Start this task** to display the Letter Wizard. Now follow the Wizard's onscreen instructions.

STAY IN TOUCH

Never forget another appointment

with Works' invaluable Calendar. You can organise all your events, set reminders to make sure you don't miss appointments, and even

e-mail other people your schedule from within the program. You can access the Calendar by clicking on Programs in the Works Task Launcher.

Set Works' Calendar as the default

calendar for your PC. Your computer may have various calendars available already, such as the one that comes with Outlook, and this could be a cause of confusion. Making Works your default calendar means that any appointments you make on your PC are all stored in one place, so they never get overlooked. To do this, start the Works Calendar from the Task Launcher. When a message appears to ask if you'd like to make Works your default calendar, click **OK**.

You can create your own address book in Works, as with Outlook. Use it to store all your names, addresses, anniversaries and e-mail contacts. You can even e-mail people directly from the Address Book.

To add a new contact, open the Address Book and go to **File ➜ New Contact**. Now click on the **Name** tab. Type in the contact information of the person that you're adding to the Address Book. You'll find that you don't always want to fill in every section, but it's wise to include a first and last name and an e-mail address.

Can't find a contact in the Address Book? Your Address Book may soon contain hundreds of entries, so you need to be able to

find the contact you want quickly. Go to the **List** area of the Address Book, then simply type in the first few letters of the person's name in the search box and click through the list of matches to find them.

Sort your list of contacts by last name, first name, e-mail address or any other criteria. For example, in the Address Book home page, go to **View ➜ Sort By** and click the method of your choice. Last Name will list contacts alphabetically by last names.

WORKS PORTFOLIO

The latest version of Works offers something completely new – the Portfolio. This feature provides a way to store data from a number of sources – from articles and images downloaded from the Web to simple written documents – in their own neat portfolios. Think of it as a scrapbook where you store the computerised equivalent of newspaper clippings, magazine pictures and so on.

If you don't want the Portfolio to appear every time you start your PC, you can easily turn it off. Open the Portfolio, go to **Tasks ➜ Options** and uncheck **Start the Works Portfolio every time I start Windows**. Now you can open the Portfolio only when you need it, by going to **Start ➜ Programs ➜ Task Launcher ➜ Works Portfolio**.

How to: Add a picture from a Website to a portfolio

1 Click on the Website image you want to obtain, then right-click. Select **Copy** from the pop-up menu that appears. Open the Portfolio, right-click on a blank area and select **Paste** from the pop-up menu.

2 The Item Details dialogue box should now appear. If it doesn't, go to **Tasks ➜ Options** and check the box that says 'Add comments to items when copying them into a collection'. Add any comments you want, as a label for your picture, and click **OK**.

101

Setting yourself up

If you run into problems, don't panic. Help may be easily at hand.

■ **PCs are likely to go wrong** at some point, often for small, easily rectified reasons, and only sometimes because of major faults. Windows software contains a number of troubleshooters to guide you through problem-solving tactics. By trying these first you may save yourself a lengthy and frustrating call to a customer service line.

■ **To find troubleshooters** in the program you are working in, look in the program's Help file. You'll find it in the **Help** menu. Click on the **Index** tab and type in 'Troubleshooter' or 'Troubleshooting' to display a list of options. Select the subject that suits your problem. Keep the dialogue box open while you work, so that you can refer back to any instructions it gives.

■ **For help with Windows,** go to **Start ➜ Help and Support**. Click on **Fixing a problem** then on **Troubleshooting problems**. Choose an option from the list that appears. If you want to see a list of the Troubleshooters built-in to Windows, click on **List of troubleshooters**.

List of troubleshooters
The following troubleshooters are available in Windows. You can start a troubleshooter by clicking the name in the left column of the table.

Troubleshooter	Identifies and resolves problems related to:
System setup	Installing and setting up Windows.
Startup/Shutdown	Starting and shutting down your computer.
Display	Video cards and video adapters, including your computer screen, outdated or incompatible video drivers, and incorrect settings for your video hardware.
Home networking	Setup, Internet connections, sharing files and printers.
Hardware	Disk drives (including CD-ROM and DVD drives), game controllers, input devices (such as keyboards, mice, cameras, scanners, and infrared devices), network network adapters, USB devices, modems, and sound cards. Also see the more specific hardware device troubleshooters below.
Multimedia and games	Games and other multimedia programs, DirectX drivers, USB devices, digital video discs (DVDs), sound, joysticks, and related issues.

■ **Troubleshooters work in two ways:** by simply giving you a hint or tip or by working through a gradual process of elimination. In the latter case, you will be prompted to give information about your particular problem to narrow down the solution.

■ **Having trouble with your troubleshooting?** If you can't find what you're looking for in a program's Help files, try searching with just the key words. If you need help with formulas in Excel, for example, type 'Excel' and 'Formula' rather than 'How do I create formulas in Excel?' It may help to use singular forms rather than plurals of nouns – 'formula' instead of 'formulas', for example.

▶ See also **Ask the experts,** p. 15; and **Tracking down the problem,** p. 19.

Read-me files contain information about installation, version changes and compatibility problems.

■ **Read-me files are generally found** with any files you download from the Web, or are on the installation discs for programs you buy. They contain the latest information about the product, so read them before you install.

■ **Read-me files can save wasted time.** It's always worth looking for a read-me file when you install a new program, as it will warn you of any known bugs. Most importantly, it will list the program's operating system and hardware compatibility. You may discover that it isn't worth proceeding with the installation. Some software Websites let you look at read-me files before you start a long download.

■ **Most CD-ROM software will auto-install** and offer you the option to read the read-me file after the installation is complete. These files often include sections on problems and system requirements that may differ slightly from the information published with the package.

■ **If you want to check the read-me file** before installing new software, turn off the auto insert notification feature to stop the software from auto-installing when you insert the CD. Go to **Start ➜ My Computer** and right-click on your CD-ROM drive and select **Properties**. In the **AutoPlay** tab, choose **Mixed Content** from the drop-down menu. You can now choose to have Windows open a folder containing the disc's contents instead.

■ **If your new software is compressed** into a Zip file, read the read-me file before you unzip the contents. Windows XP will unzip the file for you, or you can use a third party utility such as WinZip. When you double-click the read-me file its contents will be displayed for you to read. This avoids unzipping files unnecessarily, should information in the read-me file make you decide not to install the product.

■ **Not all read-me files are called ReadMe.txt** Look out for variations such as Readme1st.txt or ReadThisNow.txt. Any files with a .doc suffix (ReadMe.doc) need Microsoft Word or WordPad to open them. Files named file_id.diz contain short text descriptions of the shareware or freeware products to which they're linked, to help you decide if a certain program is for you.

Help files make programs easier to understand and assist you with navigation and troubleshooting.

■ **Don't waste time struggling** to make a program work. Press the F1 key and browse the program's Help file for advice. For help with Windows, go to **Start ➜ Help and Support**.

■ **Some Help files have a Favorites tab.** Once you've found the information you need, click on **Favorites** (if the program has one) and then the **Add** button so that you can quickly refer to this same information again at any time in the future. If the program does not have a Favorites tab, copy and paste the help text you need into a new Word document and save the file for quick reference.

■ **Some programs use pop-up captions** that explain what the buttons on a toolbar do, for example. To use the feature, go to the application's **Help** menu and click on **What's this?**. The cursor will turn into a question mark. Simply click on the feature you need help with.

■ **Often the text you need** will be spread across several pages within a particular Help file. Use the back and forward arrows at the top of the Help window to review the pages and locate the relevant sections quickly.

■ **Many Microsoft programs,** such as Word and Excel, have abandoned the Search tab and now provide an Answer Wizard. Here you can type in a full question, such as 'Why don't my files print properly?' and the Wizard will try to help solve the problem. Sadly, the Answer Wizard isn't always quite as helpful as you would like and you may need to resort to the basic keyword searches on some occasions.

■ **The Office Assistant** is another feature of Microsoft Help. To some, the cute animations and helpful comments add a fun element, but to others, the Assistant just gets in the way. In some Office XP programs, the Assistant is switched off by default. In other programs, right-click on the Assistant and select either **Hide** or **Options**. Under the **Options** tab, make sure **Use the**

Office assistant is not checked, then click **OK**. Watch as the Assistant reluctantly disappears from your screen! There are many other options you can choose, such as limiting the assistant to offering only high-priority tips or making it show a new tip each day.

■ **You can launch a Help file** without first running its program. Go to **Start ➜ Search ➜ All files and folders** to locate the program folder. It will probably have a .chm or .hlp extension, although a search for all files ending .chm may find many hundreds of files. Double-click on the file to display its contents. Instead, go to **Start ➜ All Programs ➜ Accessories ➜ Windows Explorer** and search that way.

■ **Use the Internet for help as well.** If you have an Internet connection, the Help facilities in many programs, such as Microsoft Office, will offer to search the Internet for answers to a query. This may be particularly useful if you are using a feature that has recently been updated, or have an obscure problem.

ALLOCATING MEMORY TO YOUR PROGRAMS

Here are some tips to help you to decide how much RAM you need to run all your programs properly.

■ **You can tell you need more memory** when your programs run slowly. Often this happens when you have several programs open. When your PC has run out of RAM, it uses virtual memory, which means it uses the free space on your hard drive to simulate extra RAM.

■ **You can increase or decrease** the amount of space Windows uses for virtual memory, but the simplest approach is to let Windows decide. Right-click on **My Computer** and select **Properties**. Select the **Advanced** tab then, in the Performance section, click **Settings**. Click on the **Advanced** tab then on the **Change** button at the bottom of the dialogue box. Click next to **System managed size** to make

How to: Install more RAM

1 Unplug your PC and disconnect the monitor and peripherals. Open up your PC by unscrewing the holding screws (usually at the back) and sliding off the outer case.

2 Locate the RAM sockets near the white PCI and green AGP slots. One or more RAM sockets will already be occupied with the PC's existing RAM, and this will look very similar to the new RAM you are installing. Spare RAM slots should be located nearby.

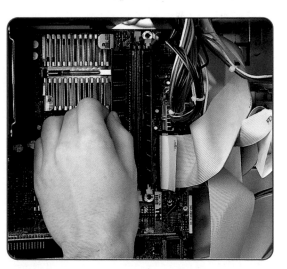

3 Holding the new RAM module by its edges, carefully slide it into the slot. The module will only go in one way, indicated by a notch at one end, which corresponds with a bump in the slot. Don't force it – it should slot in easily.

Windows choose how much disk space to use. Windows then adjusts the amount of disk space used for virtual memory based on the amount of RAM you are using. To set the values yourself (although it is not recommended), click **Custom size** and enter initial and maximum sizes (in MB).

■ Having a hard drive that is almost full
can cause problems, so clean up periodically. Empty your Recycle Bin (right-click on it and choose **Empty Recycle Bin**) and delete unnecessary programs and files. You should also delete any unwanted temporary files and activate the Disk Cleanup facility (see *Hard drive housekeeping*, p. 32).

■ When your memory resources are limited,
make sure you close programs that are not in use. Open programs take up memory even if you are not using them. Occasionally, closing a program doesn't free the RAM it was using. If your PC is still slow, save any open documents and restart it to free the space.

■ To find out how much RAM is installed
in your PC, right-click the **My Computer** icon on your Desktop and select **Properties**. Click the **General** tab. Information about your PC appears in a dialogue box, including the amount of RAM.

■ Every PC has a maximum amount of RAM
that it can contain. Older models can be upgraded and continue their active lives for years, but at some point you may reach the

maximum. All you can do then is buy a new PC or change the motherboard – although this is often not worthwhile. New PCs can use several gigabytes of RAM, and low prices mean that adding memory is now one of the most cost-effective upgrades.

■ Whenever you upgrade a program
or buy a new one, the program will inevitably require more RAM to operate than previous versions. Check the box or ask your dealer for the recommended minimum amount of RAM needed to run the program. Many games, graphics, movie and 3-D programs require large amounts of RAM. If such a program recommends, for example, a minimum of 128 MB of RAM, you will find that it runs faster and smoother with even more – perhaps as much as 256 MB or even 512 MB.

▶ See also **Hard drive housekeeping,** p. 32; and **Checking hard disk space,** p. 35.

ADAPTING PROGRAMS TO SUIT YOUR NEEDS

Customise the look and functions of your Office programs to suit your working style.

■ In most Office programs, including
Word, using the **Tools ➔ Customize** command allows you to add or remove buttons and menu items. There is a huge variety of actions you can include on your Toolbars, giving you one-click access to almost any Office function.

■ Don't go overboard –
it's easy to get carried away and add too many options to your Toolbars. Be careful to choose the functions you use most and need ready access to. Cluttering up your Toolbars with unnecessary buttons could slow you down.

■ The Tools ➔ Options command in Word
lets you set the way the program reacts in certain situations. You can set up a customised dictionary to include specialised words or phrases that repeatedly show up in your Spelling and Grammar checks. Using the View tab, you can choose which screen elements are visible – for example, highlights and hidden text.

■ In the Excel spreadsheet program,
use **Tools ➔ Options** to set preferences such as the colour of chart fills and chart lines. You can also choose whether to edit data directly on your

worksheet or whether pressing the Return key activates the next cell for editing.

■ In Outlook Express, the Tools ➔
Options command lets you choose how your e-mail is managed. Under the General tab you can choose whether to connect automatically, to be notified when new mail is received, and set how often the program checks for messages.

■ Customise your Internet Explorer.
You can choose how Internet Explorer operates with the **Tools ➔ Internet Options** command. Go to the Temporary Internet files section under the General tab to control how Windows stores files. Click the **Colors** and **Fonts** buttons to set different display options. Under the **Connections** tab choose which dial-up connection Internet Explorer will dial when the program is launched.

■ The General tab in Internet Options
gives you the option of setting your default home page. This is the page that is automatically loaded when you open Internet Explorer. Type the address in the box. Or select Internet Options when you get to the page you want, then click **Use Current**.

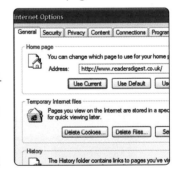

■ Content Advisor ➔ Enable. This
Internet Explorer option lets you specify (according to content) which Websites users can visit. You can also use the Security tab to set the level of safeguards your browser uses when downloading sites. This is particularly useful if you are concerned about viruses.

■ The Advanced tab in Internet Explorer's Options
is better left to the experts. Unless you really know what you're doing, tinkering with these settings can adversely affect your PC's performance. However, if you are tempted to make adjustments and create a problem, don't worry – click on the **Restore Defaults** button to return everything to normal.

PASSWORDS HELP TO PROTECT YOUR WORK

Here are some tips for keeping Word and Excel documents out of the sight of prying eyes.

■ **You can password-protect a Microsoft Excel worksheet.** After you have saved the file, go to **Tools ➜ Protection ➜ Protect Sheet**. Enter a password of your choice and click **OK**. You will then be prompted to re-enter the password to confirm the spelling. Anyone who then tries to access or modify the sheet will need to enter the password first.

■ **To protect an entire workbook in Excel,** go to **Tools ➜ Protection ➜ Protect Workbook**. In the dialogue box that appears, check the **Structure** option to prevent users from moving, deleting, hiding or renaming worksheets, inserting new worksheets, or moving or copying worksheets to another workbook. Users will also not be able to run a macro that includes a protected operation. Check the **Windows** option to prevent users from moving, resizing or closing the windows.

■ **Protect specific elements of an Excel document** by selecting any of the options offered in the Protect Sheet dialogue box. Choose which features of Excel will remain available to users of the worksheet; you can prevent them from selecting locked or unlocked cells, from formatting the worksheet's contents and from deleting columns, rows or cells.

■ **To prevent users viewing a worksheet** at all, hide it before password-protecting it. Select the sheet by clicking the relevant Sheet tab at the bottom left of the Excel window. Go to **Format ➜ Sheet ➜ Hide**. The sheet then disappears. Now password-protect the workbook and save the file. When a user opens the file, they will not be able to see the hidden sheet unless they enter the correct password to unlock the workbook and then select **Format ➜ Sheet ➜ Unhide**.

■ **Hide and protect certain rows or columns** of a sheet. Highlight the rows or columns, go to **Format ➜ Row (or Column) ➜ Hide**. Password-protect the sheet and save the file. To hide and protect an entire workbook, go to **Window ➜ Hide** and password-protect it.

■ **Hide and password-protect formulas** to prevent them from displaying in the Formula bar. To do this, first select the range of cells containing the formulas you want to hide. Go to **Format ➜ Cells** and select the **Protection** tab. Select the **Hidden** option and click **OK**. Now go to **Tools ➜ Protection ➜ Protect Sheet** and make sure that the **Protect worksheet and contents of locked cells** box is checked.

■ **You can protect some cells** in a worksheet, but leave others unprotected. This is useful if you are using the worksheet as a form, and you want to protect cells containing labels, but leave other cells unprotected so that users can place data into them. To do this, select all the cells in the form and lock them by going to **Format ➜ Cells**, selecting the **Protection** tab, checking **Locked** and clicking **OK**. Now unlock the cells that users are going to type details into by selecting them, going to **Format ➜ Cells**, unchecking **Locked**, and clicking **OK**. Finally, password-protect the sheet (see above).

■ **To remove password protection,** go to **Tools ➜ Protection ➜ Unprotect Sheet (or Unprotect Workbook)**. You will then be prompted to enter your password. If desired, opt to unprotect a workbook but leave the current sheet protected.

■ **For extra security,** mix up a word with a number to create a unique but memorable password. This method makes it especially difficult for someone to guess the password. Your password might be 'D1a2v3i4d5', which mixes up 'David' and '12345', and is still easy to remember. Passwords are case-sensitive, meaning that if you use a lower-case 'd', in this example the password will not be recognised. Don't use combinations of words or numbers that might be easy to guess, such as your name and telephone number.

■ **If you want to protect your work** so that you can't accidentally change it, but you are not worried about security, then do not enter a password. Users will be able to unprotect the sheet or workbook without entering a password.

■ **To password-protect a Word or Excel document** when you save it, go to **Tools ➜ Options** and click on the **Security** tab. In the **Password to open** box type your password and click **OK**. Retype it in the **Confirm Password** dialogue box, click **OK** and then click **Save**. If you type a password into the **Password to modify** box, users will be able to open the document but won't be able to modify it without entering the password. Go to **File ➜ Save As** and save your document (see 'How to', p. 91).

▶ See also **Passwords protect files,** p. 248.

Macros

To some people, macros – a series of actions or keystrokes saved as a sequence and run automatically – may sound intimidating, but macros can be useful to anyone, even novices. While macros usually do complex jobs, they can also perform straightforward, but repetitive tasks.

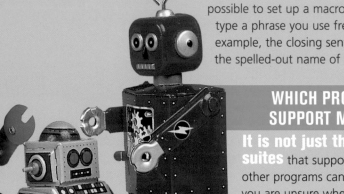

In a word processing program, it is possible to set up a macro to automatically type a phrase you use frequently; for example, the closing sentences of a letter, or the spelled-out name of your organisation.

WHICH PROGRAMS SUPPORT MACROS?

It is not just the big office suites that support macros. Many other programs can run them as well. If you are unsure whether a favourite program runs macros, check its help files or manual for this information.

When searching for macros in your software's help file, be aware that the software may not actually refer to 'macros'. Other terms you can look for are 'scripts' or even 'automated procedures' to see if macros are supported.

You can also get specialised macro programs that run macros under Windows, rather than working directly in individual programs.

Under Windows, take a look at the Task Scheduler – a program that runs maintenance macros. Go to **Start → All Programs → Accessories → System Tools** and select **Scheduled Tasks**. You can use the Scheduler to run programs automatically – for example, to perform regular back-ups or check for e-mail.

COMMON USES FOR MACROS

When do you need to make a macro?
Keep a mental note of any tasks you perform regularly, and consider whether a macro might help you be more productive. Even a simple job like formatting text in Word, or formatting a column of a spreadsheet as a currency column, can be made quicker and easier with a macro.

In a spreadsheet, macros can be used for formatting cells or performing complex operations across different workbooks.

If you use complex spreadsheet formulas a lot, but use them on different groups of cells every time, you can create a macro that has empty spaces in the formula, ready for you to insert cell ranges manually.

CREATING AND RUNNING MACROS

When you create a macro in a Microsoft program, your mouse and keyboard actions are recorded. This information is then stored in the Visual Basic programming language. To view Visual Basic in Word, go to **Tools → Macro → Macros**. Then select the macro and press **Edit**.

Test a macro first on a copy of a document before you apply it to your real document. This way, you avoid altering vital data if the macro does not perform correctly.

Add a macro to a Toolbar to make the macro easy to run. In Word 2002, click on the down arrow at the far right of the Toolbar and select **Add or Remove Buttons**. Click on **Customize** and select the **Commands** tab. Scroll

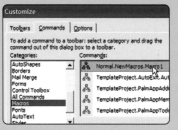

through the Categories and click on **Macros**. Choose the macro you want from the list and drag it to the Toolbar.

FINDING READY-MADE MACROS

You can share macros on the Internet. Take a look at some of the popular shareware Websites, such as Jumbo (www.jumbo.com), Tucows (www.tucows.com), ZDNet (www.zdnet.com/downloads) and CNET (www.cnet.com), and search for 'macros' to find out more about doing this.

Microsoft publishes a free collection of macros for Word 2002. You can download them from their Website (www.microsoft.com) or from CNET (www.cnet.com).

Both Corel (www.corel.com) and Lotus (www.lotus.com) provide online help on using macros with their office suites. Search their sites for more information on macros.

MACRO SECURITY

Many computer viruses are actually macros that are attached to Word or Excel documents. They run automatically on your computer, without your knowledge, when you open an infected document or disk. If you send a document with a macro virus to another user over the Internet, or pass it on to them on a disk, their PC will also become infected.

Although most macro viruses won't cause too much harm, a few are highly damaging – the Melissa virus is one infamous example – so protect yourself with good antivirus software. Make sure you update the software frequently and check the manufacturer's Website for news on the latest viruses and alerts.

Besides running antivirus software, you can avoid passing on a macro virus by sending document files as .rtf (rich text format, which keeps some formatting) or .txt (plain text) files. This way, a macro virus can't be attached.

You can set different security levels in Microsoft applications to help protect against a macro virus. In Word, Excel and PowerPoint 2002, go to **Tools ➔ Macro ➔ Security**, then select a security level. If you choose High security, the macros must have a digital identification stamp. Microsoft Office can then check and disable macros. Medium security setting prompts you to enable or disable macros each time you open a document that contains them. Low does not check macros at all.

If you want to set virus protection in Word 97 or Excel 97, go to **Tools ➔ Options**. Click on the **General** tab and make sure **Macro Virus Protection** is checked.

Download security software patches for macro-supporting applications from the Internet. Check your software supplier's Website.

Take precautions! Macros are now the most popular type of program used for spreading viruses that are specifically designed with the purpose of infecting programs such as Microsoft Word and Excel. The best way you can protect your programs is to never open documents from unknown sources. Also keep your browser current – Netscape (www.netscape .com) and Microsoft (www.microsoft.com) publish free browser updates regularly.

▶ See also **Customise your Toolbars**, p. 110; **Make the most of menus**, p. 111; and **Dealing with viruses**, p. 208.

How to: Record and run a macro in Word

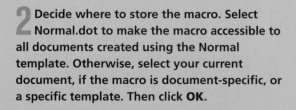

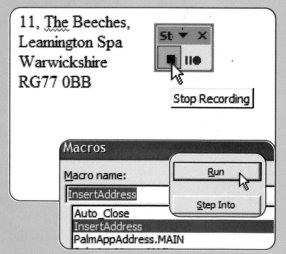

1 In Word, position the cursor at the top of the document, and go to **Tools ➔ Macro ➔ Record New Macro**. Give the macro a name, such as 'InsertAddress'. The name can contain up to 80 characters, but not spaces or non-alphanumeric symbols.

2 Decide where to store the macro. Select Normal.dot to make the macro accessible to all documents created using the Normal template. Otherwise, select your current document, if the macro is document-specific, or a specific template. Then click **OK**.

3 To record the macro, run through the entire series of actions you want performed. When you have finished, click the square button on the Stop Recording toolbar. To run the macro, go to **Tools ➔ Macro ➔ Macros**, select your macro and simply click **Run**.

Program features

SAVE TIME WITH KEYBOARD SHORTCUTS

Do you use the same menu command again and again? Often there's a faster method on the keyboard, and, if not, you can always create one.

■ **Point-and-click and drag-and-drop.** In Windows, the mouse is the operational tool. However, a keyboard shortcut is often the fastest way to perform an action. Learning a few basic commands can save you time.

■ **Many programs use the same shortcuts.** This means that once you've learned them in one program, you can use them almost anywhere. Examples include **Ctrl+O** (Open file), **Ctrl+S** (Save) and **Ctrl+P** (Print).

■ **Keyboard shortcuts are commonly** written with a plus sign (+) separator, as in Ctrl+Alt+Shift+F8, but you don't press the + when entering the shortcut. To make shortcuts like this work, you hold down the **Ctrl**, **Alt** and **Shift** keys together, and then press the final key, in this case **F8**.

■ **To assign a specific key combination** to open a folder shortcut on your Windows Desktop, right-click on it, and select **Properties**. On the Shortcut tab, click in

Start in:	"C:\My Document
Shortcut key:	Ctrl + Alt + G
Run:	Normal window
Comment:	

the **Shortcut key** box, key in the combination to be used, and click **OK**. You can now open your folder by pressing the keys you have selected.

■ **Some universally supported shortcuts** apply to clipboard operations, such as Copy and Paste. To copy the text on a Web page to the clipboard, click at the top of the page, hold down the mouse button, drag down

Save yourself some time with a few simple shortcuts.

DESKTOP

Alt+Enter	Displays the properties of the selected object.
F2	Allows you to rename the currently selected object.
F3	Displays the Search dialogue box.
Shift+F10	Displays the context (right-click) menu of the selected object.

WINDOWS EXPLORER

F4	Opens the Address box.
F6	Moves between the drive, file and the address panes.
Backspace	Moves to the parent of the currently selected folder.
Keypad +	Expands the currently selected folder to the first level only.
Keypad -	Collapses the currently selected folder.

ANYWHERE

Alt+Esc	Switches to next open window.
Alt+Space bar	Opens the Control menu for the current application.
Windows key+F	Displays the Search Files or Folders dialogue box.
Windows key+M	Minimises all open windows and displays the Desktop.
Windows key	On its own the Windows key opens the Start menu.
Windows key+E	Opens Windows Explorer.

to the bottom of the page, and then select **Edit ➔ Copy**. Alternatively, press **Ctrl+A** to highlight all the text, then **Ctrl+C** to copy it.

■ **Some programs use their own shortcuts.** Most shortcuts are usually shown next to the equivalent menu command.

■ **You can change existing shortcuts** or create new ones to suit your requirements in Microsoft Word. To do this, go to **Tools ➔ Customize**. In the Customize window, select the **Commands** tab and click on the **Keyboard** button. A dialogue box then appears that lets you assign or reassign shortcuts to keys – for example, Alt+C to create centre-aligned text.

■ **Are your other programs as simple to use as Word?** Install a keyboard macro program and you can create keyboard shortcuts to automate the most complex tasks. KeyText 2000 (www.mjmsoft.com/keytext.htm), Keyboard Express (www.keyboardexpress.com), and ShortKeys (www.shortkeys.com) are popular macro programs that you can download from the Internet. You'll find more examples in the big Internet software libraries, ZDNet (www.zdnet.com/ downloads) and Tucows (www.tucows.com).

▶ See also: **Macros**, p. 106.

USING ARROW KEYS FOR NAVIGATION

These keys can navigate you through a text file, the cells of a spreadsheet, or other document.

■ **Scroll through a document smoothly,** paragraph by paragraph. Hold down the **Ctrl** key while pressing the up or down arrow for the direction in which you want to scroll.

Highlight text easily by holding down the **Shift** key while navigating around the document with the arrow keys. If you hold down the **Ctrl** key too, you can then jump from word to word, or paragraph to paragraph, selecting passages of text even more quickly.

■ **Mouseless movement between menus!** Press the **Alt** key to take you to the first pull-down menu of an application, for example, the File menu in Word. Then use the left and right arrow keys to move back and forth between the other pull-down menus. For instance, press the right arrow key to move from File to Edit in Word. You can open the desired menu by pressing the down arrow key. Move through the opened menu using the arrow keys again then press **Return** to select an option.

■ Select multiple files in any
window, whether you are working in Windows Explorer or on the Windows Desktop. First, click on the file icon of your choice to highlight it. Now hold down the **Shift** key. Keeping it held down, use the arrow keys to move around the window until you've selected all the files you want.

▶ See also **Save time with keyboard shortcuts,** p. 108.

ARROW KEY COMBINATIONS
Navigate windows and documents using Shift and Ctrl with your arrow keys.

TO MOVE CURSOR	PRESS
One character left	**Left Arrow**
One character right	**Right Arrow**
One word left	**Ctrl+Left Arrow**
One word right	**Ctrl+Right Arrow**
One line up	**Up Arrow**
One line down	**Down Arrow**
One paragraph up	**Ctrl+Up Arrow**
One paragraph down	**Ctrl+Down Arrow**

TO SELECT TEXT	PRESS
One character left	**Shift+Left Arrow**
One character right	**Shift+Right Arrow**
To end of a word	**Ctrl+Shift+Right Arrow**
To beginning of a word	**Ctrl+Shift+Left Arrow**
One line up	**Shift+Up Arrow**
One line down	**Shift+Down Arrow**
To end of a paragraph	**Ctrl+Shift+Down Arrows**
To beginning of a paragraph	**Ctrl+Shift+Up Arrow**

DEALING WITH ERROR MESSAGES

Most error messages relate to problems that are easily resolved if you follow a few simple rules.

■ Many errors are one-time-only
problems, caused by a particular set of circumstances that are unlikely to occur again. Shut down your PC, restart it, and try to complete the process you were working on. You might be successful the second time around.

■ Don't assume you have done
something wrong when you see an error message. Every significant program in existence has plenty of bugs and idiosyncrasies, and it's possible that you have encountered one of them. As a result, you should make sure the problem really does lie in your system before taking major action. Reinstalling Windows at the first sign of trouble may cause more problems than it solves.

■ Look at what the message says.
It might seem cryptic, but working out which software or hardware the error relates to lets you consult the owner's manual for help. Refer to sections on error messages or troubleshooting.

■ The most important thing you can
do when you encounter a serious or persistent error message is to write it down. Also, make a note of exactly what you were doing at the time, such as saving a file or printing. Technical support people need all the information they can get, so the more details you can provide, the better.

■ If you have a software problem,
the chances are that someone else around the world has also had it, and they may know what you should do to fix it. Look for answers online at Google (www.google.com) or search the Microsoft Website (search.microsoft.com).

■ Some errors are caused by file
corruption. If a program can't open a document, it's usually because the file itself has corrupted, and you must recreate that file or restore it from your back-up. If the program files are corrupt, use the System Restore in Windows XP and Me or try reinstalling the program. If that doesn't work, uninstall the program using the Add or Remove Programs Control Panel.

▶ See also **Adding and removing programs,** p. 84; and **When things go wrong,** p. 102.

SCROLL BAR SHORTCUTS

Here are some shortcuts to help you use the scroll bar sliders.

■ Controlling the scrolling speed is
sometimes difficult when you're trying to navigate a large document. Often you can flash past the point you were looking for. To keep track, look at the small yellow box that appears when you click and drag the scroll box along the scroll bar in Microsoft Office programs. The current page number and heading will appear in the box.

■ Microsoft Word's scroll bar also has
viewing buttons at the bottom of the right vertical scroll bar. The top one scrolls down one line at a time. The next goes back to the previous page, and the bottom jumps to the next page. When you click the third, a round button, a menu appears that allows the defaults on the

page-scrolling buttons to be changed for another object, such as a graphic. The **Next page** and **Previous page** buttons now jump to the next or previous graphic, instead of the next or previous page.

■ **Enlarge the scroll bars** in all Windows programs by editing the scroll bar properties. Right-click on an empty area of the Desktop, select **Properties**, and click on the **Appearance** tab. Click on **Advanced** then select **Scrollbar** from the **Item** menu and increase the width in the **Size** box. Click **OK**.

■ **Avoid horizontal scrolling** – it's too difficult to read text while scrolling across a page. If necessary, you can reduce the viewing percentage or margins so the full width of the document fits easily onto the screen. If the document is a Notepad text file, go to **Edit** and check the **Word Wrap** option to fit text to the Notepad window width.

■ **Navigating long Web pages** or electronic documents is easier with a wheel mouse, such as Microsoft's Intellimouse. An additional wheel, that controls scrolling, is built in between the mouse buttons. Clicking the wheel turns on auto-scrolling, making a document move up the screen at a constant slow speed while you read it. You can move your mouse to control the speed of the auto-scrolling.

▶ See also **Making the most of your mouse**, p. 25.

See also Making the most of your mouse, p. 25.

CUSTOMISE YOUR TOOLBARS

Customise any useful shortcut tools on your Toolbars and save time and effort with your documents.

■ **Toolbars are the rows of buttons** labelled with different icons that appear along the top of your screen with your program window when it is open. They are perhaps the most used parts of any program because they offer speedy access to commands and menus. Simply clicking on a button will execute a command or take you where you need to go to do so.

KEY TO SUCCESSFUL SCROLLING
With a combination of the right keyboard and mouse combinations, you can move through a document with ease.

STANDARD MOUSE

Scroll up one line Click the up scroll arrow (at top of scroll bar).

Scroll down one line Click the down scroll arrow (at bottom of scroll bar).

Scroll up one screen Click in the scroll bar above the scroll box.

Scroll down one screen Click in the scroll bar below the scroll box.

Scroll to a specific page Click and drag the scroll box until the required page number appears in the small box that opens.

Scroll beyond the left margin Press Shift and click the left scroll arrow.

Scroll right To move across to the right in your document, click the right scroll arrow.

MICROSOFT INTELLIMOUSE

Scroll up three lines Rotate the wheel in the middle of the Intellimouse one click forward.

Scroll down three lines Rotate the mouse wheel one click back.

AutoScroll Click and hold the wheel button. Move the pointer up or down to control speed and direction.

To cancel AutoScroll Either click on the mouse button, or alternatively press any key on your keyboard.

Pan Hold the wheel button, drag the pointer left or right to move through the page.

Zoom Hold down the Ctrl key on your keyboard and rotate wheel forward or backward to zoom in or out.

■ **Each program's Toolbars** come with default settings. However, once you have used a program for a while, you may want to customise the options available – many programs allow you to alter Toolbars to suit the way you work.

■ **To find the full range of Toolbars** available for the program you are working in – for example Word, Excel or any other of the standard Office programs – go to **View ➔ Toolbars**. Alternatively, you can position the mouse pointer over an empty part of a Toolbar and right-click. The pop-up menu that appears lets you show or hide any of the Toolbars listed.

Toolbars:
- ☑ Standard
- ☑ Formatting
- ☐ 3-D Settings
- ☐ AutoText
- ☐ Control Toolbox
- ☐ Database
- ☐ Diagram
- ☐ Drawing
- ☐ Drawing Canvas
- ☐ Extended Formatting
- ☐ Forms
- ☐ Frames
- ☐ Function Key Display
- ☐ Japanese Greetings

■ **The Standard and Formatting Toolbars** in Word contain all the buttons you need to work with text, draw tables, scale and print. But there are lots of other Toolbars to choose from, such as Database, Drawing and Web. However, they are not all applicable to all programs.

To view a full list of Toolbars, go to **Tools ➔ Customize**. On the Toolbars tab select the Toolbars you want to display. Try opening a document and trying all the Toolbars in turn to see how useful they will be to you.

■ **To personalise your Toolbars,** you can simply go to **Tools ➔ Customize**. The Commands tab gives you total freedom to create and customise your own Toolbars. The dialogue box shows you different categories of commands, so you can focus on certain types of functions – for example formatting Word documents or manipulating graphics.

■ **The Options tab in the Customize window** can be a very useful feature, allowing you to set large icons on the buttons, adjust the animation for drop-down menus, and customise and display keyboard shortcuts.

■ **To add buttons to a Toolbar,** begin by scrolling through the categories on the Commands tab and looking through the lists of commands on the right. Click on a command you want to create a button for, and then drag and drop it anywhere on the Toolbar. Repeat to add as many buttons as you like, and

thus build a set of shortcuts for the commands you use most.

■ **There is no limit to the number of buttons** you can place on your Toolbars, but try to keep it simple. Too many Toolbar buttons can lead to tired eyes and even slow up your work – defeating the point of using toolbars.

■ **Too many Toolbar buttons?** Slim down your Toolbars by deleting the buttons you don't need. Select **Tools ➡ Customize**. Click on the Toolbar button you want to remove and drag it away from the Toolbar. When a box with a cross in it appears, release the mouse button. The button will not appear on the Toolbar any more.

■ **Toolbars don't have to sit at the top of the screen,** you can use them as floating palettes instead. To move a toolbar, click on the dotted mark at the left-hand end of a toolbar and hold the mouse button down. Drag the menu to where you want the palette to appear, then release the button. The toolbar icons will now be handily placed if you want to format an image, for example.

MAKE THE MOST OF MENUS

Menus provide easy access to all of the features of a software package, such as Word or Excel.

■ **Menus are usually organised** using a standardised system, which makes it easy for you to learn new applications quickly. For example, the far left menu in most applications is called **File**, and under it you find options to create new files, to save your work and to print. The next menu is called **Edit**, and provides cut and paste options. **Help** is usually found as the far right menu item and besides assistance will contain details of the program name and version.

■ **Although you can use the mouse** to make menu selections, many menus also have keyboard shortcuts. One letter of each menu option is underlined. Press the **Alt** key and that letter to access that menu item. Alternatively, you can use the keyboard arrow keys to move through the options, pressing **Enter** when the one you want to use is highlighted.

■ **By default, all Office 2000 and XP programs** show only the menu items that you use most frequently. Pass the pointer over the downward arrow at the bottom of a list of menu items and more commands appear. If you would rather see all of the options all of the time, go to **Tools ➡ Customize** and select **Options**. Check **Always show full menus** and finally click **Close**.

■ **A lot of software also offers a shortcut menu** with fast access to frequently used features that you can access by clicking the right mouse button. The range of options varies, depending on the particular context, and this feature is sometimes called a Context menu.

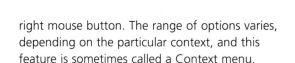

How to: Customise menus in Word

1 Adding menu commands in Word is easy. Simply go to **Tools ➡ Customize** and choose the **Commands** tab in the Customize dialogue box. Now select a category, and scroll through the Commands list that appears until you find the item you want to add.

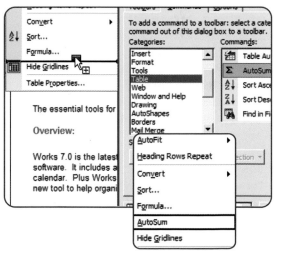

2 Drag the command to the menu that you want it to go into. The menu should drop down. Move the cursor to the command's new position, and then release the mouse button. Close the Customize window.

Templates

Templates are documents set up with a particular set of specifications. You can use a template as the pattern or model for many documents, without having to reconfigure the basic settings every time. Many popular office program suites support templates and provide some ready-made.

SPECIFIC TYPES OF TEMPLATES

If you work from home, or just need a few specific kinds of documents for personal business, templates can be especially useful. If a program supports them, you can create templates for any kind of document it produces.

TEMPLATE WEBSITES
Download templates from the Web to help to set up specific documents.

HP BIZTOWN (www.hp.ca/biztown)
Scroll down the page for links to templates for memos, calendars, fax cover sheets, letterheads, business cards, brochures and logos – all in MS Word format to download.

4TEMPLATES (www.4templates.com)
This site offers a wide range of ready-made Website templates, professionally designed, and delivered by e-mail. You have to pay, but the fees are modest.

**JOBSZOO.COM
(www.jobszoo.com/cvtemplates.html)**
Several CV templates with different layouts to try, including professional and student.

**ABOUT.COM
(businesssoft.about.com/cs/officetemplates/)**
Links to a wide range of templates for the programs in the Microsoft Office suite, most suitable for business users.

Within Word, for example, you can design templates for short documents like letters and faxes, or ones for more complex documents, such as reports or newsletters, complete with column settings and headings.

If you use Word to design a simple Web page for your club or society, set up templates to help. In fact, if you regularly produce any kind of document that involves reusing the same basic settings, a template is ideal.

Global templates are one of two types of templates used by Microsoft Word. They are the simplest kind of template and have settings used by all documents. Word opens a Global template called Normal.dot every time you start the software or open a new document.

Document templates are templates that produce a specific type of document, such as a fax form, a memo, a report or a standard letter. These have to be opened manually every time you want to use them.

Keep your options open. When using templates, three choices are available to you. You can open and use an existing template as it is, open and modify a template, saving it with a different name, or create a template from scratch.

WORKING WITH TEMPLATES

To produce a document based on an existing template in either Excel or Word, first go to **File ➜ New**. The New document panel will open on the right-hand side of the window. In the 'New from template' section you can choose from templates installed on your PC, or others available on the Net. The section also provides direct links to the templates that you have most recently used. Make sure that you remember to use **File ➜ Save As** to save the document.

You can open a new document as a template. Go to **File ➜ New**. In the right-hand panel, click **General templates**, then select the type of document you wish to create – Blank, Web Page or E-mail message. Make sure that **Template** is checked, then click **OK**.

Don't like the existing template font?
Change it by opening a new document as the template (see above). Then go to **Format ➜ Font**. Choose your preferred font, size and style settings, then click **Default**. Now click **Yes** to change the default font for the next new document created with that template.

If you modify a template in Word, documents you created using the template before it was modified will not be affected by the new changes. If you want existing documents to reflect the new template, then go to **Tools ➔ Templates and Add-Ins**. Make sure that the **Automatically update document styles** option is selected, then click **OK**.

Create a template from an existing document.
If you've designed a really good document, with special formatting and other features, save it as a template to use next time you're faced with the same situation. To do this, first make a copy of it, giving the copy a name, like 'Special Cover Letter'. Make sure the copy only has the elements in it you want to use again – delete any text that is specific to the current use, for example. When you have finished, go to **File ➔ Save As**. In the 'Save as type' box, choose **Document Template**. Word will automatically find the templates folder, and you can save the new template here or navigate to a subfolder and save it there.

COLLECTING TEMPLATES

You can download more templates
from the Internet using any Office 2002 program. Make sure you are online, then go to **Help ➔ Office on the Web**, select your country then click on **Office Templates** in the left-hand column. You can download the templates here for use with your software (see also box, p. 112, for template sites).

Office Templates

Back to: Office Templates

❖ When You're The Customer

9 Template(s), Page 1 of 1

Claiming cost of secondary repair
Provided by: Signform (UK) Ltd

Complaint about delays (Builder)
Provided by: Signform (UK) Ltd

Informing contractor of defective work
Provided by: Signform (UK) Ltd

Keep your Word templates in folders.
When you create new templates in Word, they are stored in the Templates folder, which Word locates automatically. You can create new folders within the Templates folder by clicking on the new folder icon in the 'Save As' dialogue box. Once you have saved your templates, your new folder will appear as an extra tab in the Templates dialogue box.

Use your new or downloaded templates to build a comprehensive library. Among the templates that come with Excel are invoices, purchase orders and expense statements. Word 2002 has a good range of templates, including fax cover sheets, letterheads, CVs (résumés) and some Web page designs. Many of these have instructions in them on how and where to add your own data. Follow the instructions, usually simply by clicking and typing exactly as directed, and you can easily create personalised documents from them.

How to: Create and save a fax template in Word

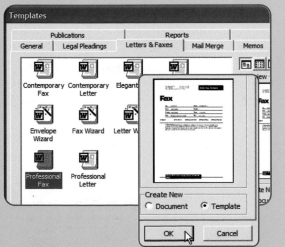

1 The easiest way to create a template is to edit an existing one. Go to **File ➔ New** and click **General Templates** in the New Document panel. In the **Letters & Faxes** tab select one of the Fax templates to open – use the previews to help you choose. Click **OK**.

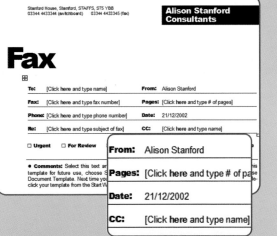

2 Now edit the template, adding your own information where required, and changing any of the data types. Insert your phone number or any other information that never changes. A macro is included to automatically insert the current date, so don't change this.

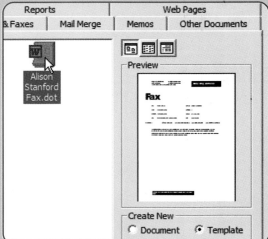

3 When you have completed your new fax template, save it with a name that will help you to remember what it is. The next time you need it, go to **File ➔ New**, and select your personalised fax template.

Commands and operations

Here are some quick ways to copy and move text, graphics, figures and other items.

■ To copy and paste between files and programs, select the item or material that you want to transfer – perhaps a picture, a passage of text or a column of figures. Then go to **Edit → Copy** to copy it to a shared area of memory called the Windows Clipboard. Switch to the target file, move the pointer to where you want the data to appear, then select **Edit → Paste** to transfer the material.

■ Keyboard shortcuts can also be useful when deciding what to copy. The quickest way to copy an entire Web page, for

example, is to press **Ctrl+A** (Select All), and then **Ctrl+C** to copy the page. Once the whole page is copied to your Clipboard, you can then paste it into another file or document using **Ctrl+V**, and then work through it to decide what information you want to keep and what to cut and throw away.

■ Sometimes you might want to perform a Copy and Paste operation in a dialogue box, perhaps like the one shown when you select **File → Open**. You may want to copy part of a filename to use for another one if you are saving a series of similar files, for example. Although there is no Edit menu in a dialogue box, you can still use the standard keyboard shortcuts instead (see above).

■ In early versions of Windows (up to 98) the Clipboard can hold only one object of a particular type. You can copy a picture to the Clipboard, for example, but if you then copy another picture, the first one is lost as it is replaced by the second. If you need to copy several pictures from one place to another, you

must copy the first, paste it to its destination, and then repeat with each subsequent image.

■ If a Paste option doesn't work, make sure the destination program can accept the type of data you're trying to transfer. For example, only text can be pasted into Notepad. If you are using a version of Windows earlier than XP, try the Clipboard Viewer, which will show you what Windows is trying to transfer. Go to **Start → Programs → Accessories → System Tools** and select **Clipboard Viewer**. The utility is also available in Windows XP, but hard to find – use Windows Explorer to go to **C: → Windows → System32** and double-click on **clipbrd.exe**.

■ Microsoft Office applications are more sophisticated. You can copy up to 24 items to the Clipboard in Office XP (up to 12 items in Office 2000). Click on the clipboard icon on the Taskbar to open the Clipboard Task Pane. You can paste items singly, or click on **Paste All** to paste everything at once.

How to: Use cut and paste to move files

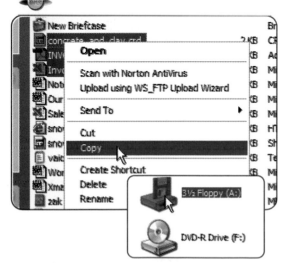

1 Select the files you want to move by holding down the **Ctrl** key and clicking on each file. Right-click on one file, and select **Cut**. Go to the new folder or disk.

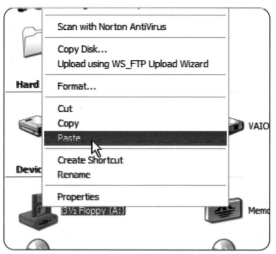

2 Right-click on your destination and select **Paste**. Windows copies the files from the Clipboard to their new location. To undo the change, select **Edit → Undo Move**.

◗ See also **Using the Clipboard**, p. 67.

USING CUT AND PASTE

Use this helpful feature to move items from one file or program to another, quickly and easily.

■ **The Cut and Paste function** lets you move text or graphics between files. To do this, just select the item and go to **Edit ➔ Cut**; this removes the selected data, and stores it on the Clipboard. Switch to the file where you want to place the data, move the cursor to the required point, and then select **Edit ➔ Paste**.

■ **You can move files or folders around** in the Windows Explorer program. The Cut and Paste options are stored in the context menu. To do this, right-click on the item and then select **Cut** from the pop-up menu. Now click on the destination folder, and select **Paste**.

HOW TO UNDO AN ACTION

This important and much used command allows you to reverse – or undo – one or more actions.

■ **We all make mistakes!** Undo them by going to **Edit** and selecting **Undo**. Alternatively, use the keyboard shortcut **Ctrl+Z**. This function undoes the last thing you did on your PC. Word, Excel and many other programs have an Undo toolbar button showing a curved arrow pointing backwards.

■ **Most actions normally performed on a PC** – such as typing, cutting, pasting, formatting, and even accidentally deleting a paragraph – can be reversed by using the **Undo** command, or by clicking the Undo button.

■ **If you click the arrow** next to the Toolbar's Undo button in Word, you will see a list of all the recent actions you can reverse. Scroll down the list until you find the one you want, and click on it to select it. Word will then cancel, or undo, that action and all the actions above it in the list. Alternatively, you can press **Ctrl+Z** several times to undo your most recent actions in the reverse order they were performed.

■ **If you decide that you didn't want to undo an action** after all, go to **Edit** and select **Redo** or press **Ctrl+Y** on the keyboard.

■ **Only some programs allow you to undo multiple actions,** and they may differ in the number of steps they will permit you to undo. Other programs allow you to undo only your most recent action.

■ **The Undo command** can be used while you are in My Computer or Windows Explorer, as well as when using a program.

CHANGING NAMES AND FORMATS WITH SAVE AS

Use the Save As option to change file names and formats.

■ **Clicking the Save icon on the Toolbar** is a fast way to save your work, but will overwrite any previous version. Instead, use **File ➔ Save As** so that you can save older drafts of your work. Add a number or date to each draft so you can tell the versions apart.

■ **Some programs – like Word and Excel –** let you add a 'Save As' button to your Standard Toolbar, so it's just as accessible as the Save button. Go to **View ➔ Toolbars** and select **Customize**. On the Commands tab, find **Save As** in the Commands panel and drag it to your **File** Toolbar. Click the **Modify Selection** button on the Commands tab, then select **Change Button Image** to assign an icon to the new button.

■ **Remember to use Save As** if your source document is read-only. All files originating from CD-ROMs will be read-only by default, as will files from a floppy disk if the write-protection tab is set. Using **Save As** lets you give your document a new name, or change the directory to which it is saved, without changing the protected original.

■ **Use Save As to change the format** of your file. This is useful if you want to convert Word or Excel files to text-only files, or to HTML files for the Web. In the Save As dialogue box, click on the **Save as type** arrow to see the formats in which your document can be saved.

File name:	Works7_fact_sheet.doc
Save as type:	Word Document (*.doc)
	Document Template (*.dot)
	Rich Text Format (*.rtf)
	Plain Text (*.txt)
	MS-DOS Text with Layout (*.asc)
	Text with Layout (*.ans)
	Word 2.x for Windows (*.doc)

SAVE TIME WITH DRAG-AND-DROP

Want to work more efficiently in Windows, Word and Excel? Try this great time-saving feature.

■ **You can drag-and-drop cells in Excel.** Click and drag the mouse to select the cells that you want to move. Then point the mouse cursor at the border of the selected cells. When the cursor changes into an arrow, you may drag-and-drop the cells to a new location.

■ **If drag-and-drop doesn't work,** it may be that it hasn't been turned on. Go to **Tools ➔ Options** and click on the **Edit** tab. Make sure **Drag-and-drop text editing** is checked then click **OK**.

Change the speed of your mouse pointer for more control when dragging and dropping. Go to **Start ➜ Control Panel ➜ Printers and Other Hardware** and click on **Mouse**. In the **Pointer Options** tab, adjust the **Pointer speed** slider in the Motion section to a slower setting. Click **OK**.

The quickest and easiest way to move files from one folder to another in Windows Explorer is by using the drag-and-drop facility. Once you have selected the files that you would like to move, left-click on one of them. Holding down the mouse button, drag the files over to their destination folder, and then release the mouse button to drop them.

When you drag-and-drop in Windows Explorer the results might seem a little unpredictable – until you know the rules. Drag-and-drop a program, and Explorer makes a shortcut, leaving the original program file where it was. Drag-and-drop files between folders on the same disk, and they move. But, if you drag-and-drop from one drive to another, files are copied.

The defaults on Explorer's drag-and-drop facility are normally the most appropriate options, but if you want to override them, drag with the right mouse button held down, rather than the left. When you drop the objects, a context menu appears showing the different operations that you can perform.

Drag-and-drop behaviour can be modified using the keyboard. In Word and Windows Explorer, holding down the Ctrl key when you perform a drag-and-drop operation, copies objects and files instead of moving them.

Drag and drop a file onto a program icon, and, if the file is one the program recognises, the program will launch and automatically open the file.

WORKING WITH DATES

Here are some tips for working with dates in documents and spreadsheets, and keeping dates updated automatically.

A quick way to insert the current date into a document in Microsoft Word is to type the first four characters of the date, such as '8 Fc' for 8 February. Word will display the full date, including the year, and then insert it if you press the **Enter** key. To ignore the offer, simply continue typing – the hint will disappear.

Word isn't completing dates for you? Go to **Insert ➜ AutoText ➜ AutoText**, and check the box for **Show AutoComplete suggestions**.

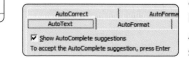

An alternative way to add dates is to select the **Insert ➜ Date and Time** menu option. You can add the current date or time – or both if you wish – in a variety of formats.

Another advantage of the Date and Time dialogue box is the **Update automatically** option. Check this, and the date

is added as a field and updated each time the document or template is opened or printed.

Excel uses a different system from Word to enter dates, but it is just as easy. Click in a cell and simply press **Ctrl+;** to insert the current date, or **Ctrl+Shift+;** to insert the current time.

The Millennium bug may have failed to cause the major predicted problems, but the confusion over dates still carries a lesson. When using dates in spreadsheets or databases, use four-digit years instead of two – for example, 2003, rather than 03 – and everything will work as expected.

If you come across a system that does use two-digit dates, there are standard Microsoft rules for applying them. The years from 00 to 29 are interpreted as 2000 to 2029 (so 17/4/04 is treated as the 17th of April 2004). Years from 30 to 99 are interpreted as 1930 to 1999. So, 24/11/35 is 24th November 1935. To change these settings, go to **Start ➜ Control Panel ➜ Date, Time, Language, and Regional Options ➜ Regional and Language Options**. Click on **Customize** and then on the **Date** tab to adjust the rules applied for two-digit dates.

When entering dates in a spreadsheet or database, remember that you can perform calculations with them. For example, with a formula that adds 28 to a date you can tell when to expect delivery of an order that will take 28 days.

HEADERS AND FOOTERS LOOK PROFESSIONAL

Use these top and bottom tag lines to give your documents and spreadsheets that extra polish.

To display the header and footer areas in Word, go to **View ➜ Header and Footer**. Click in the Header or Footer box and type the text you want to appear at the top or bottom of each page, such as a page number or title. Style the text and click **Close** on the Header and Footer Toolbar to return to your document.

■ Buttons on the Header and Footer Toolbar make it easy to format headers and footers. They offer options such as inserting the date, time, page number, file name and author, as well as previewing your document.

■ Anything you enter in a header or footer will be automatically left-aligned. Use the buttons on the Toolbar to change the alignment. To adjust spacing, go to **Format ➜ Paragraph** and click the **Indents and Spacing** tab.

■ Adjust the area taken up by the header and footer – marked by white bands on the vertical and horizontal rulers. Move your cursor over the top or bottom of the band until you see a double-headed arrow. Click and drag to adjust the size or proportions of the header or footer.

■ You can also insert a picture, clip art or graphic into the header or footer area. Click inside the Header or Footer box, go to **Insert ➜ Picture ➜ From File**. Browse to where your picture is stored, select it and click **Insert**.

■ You may not want headers or footers to appear on every page. For example, you might want to keep the first page of a report header free. To do this, go to **File ➜ Page Setup** and select the Layout tab. Here, you will find options to set a different header for the first page, omit headers on certain pages or sections, or to alternate with different ones on odd and even pages.

■ Headers and footers in Excel can help you to keep track of pages in large spreadsheets. Go to **View ➜ Header and Footer** and click the **Custom Header** or **Custom Footer** button for a selection of useful automatic options, such as the page number, the date and time, the name of the file and its location on your hard drive. Select the options you want then click **OK**.

Organise your lists and tables using the Sort tools in Word and Excel.

■ Both Word tables and Excel spreadsheets sort in similar ways. First select the entire area of information to be sorted. Then, in Word, go to **Table ➜ Sort**, or, in Excel, to **Data ➜ Sort**. Both applications provide a similar dialogue box where you can set the ascending or descending order and the columns to sort by.

■ Save your work first and select the correct information before you sort. Information can get jumbled if you don't select all the information associated with each item, and columns may end up out of order. You should get a warning about this, but it's best to be safe.

■ Any text in Word can be sorted; it doesn't need to be in a table. When sorting text Word uses the hard-return paragraph marks (¶) to separate the items to be sorted. To check that all items are properly separated, click on the **Show/Hide** Toolbar button to display the marks.

How to: Sort a list of information in Word

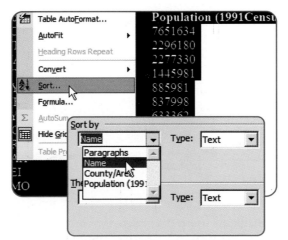

1 Create your list, making sure that a single tab is placed between items on each row. Highlight the entire table, including the category headings, to select it.

2 Click on **Table**, then choose **Sort** to access the Sort Text dialogue box. Select the **Header Row** option, and then choose the column to sort by in the **Sort by** list.

3 Click **OK** and the data in the table will be sorted according to the criteria you have set: alphabetically or in descending numerical order, for example.

To sort a list of text other than by first word, insert a comma or tab before the text you want to sort by. This identifies the next item as a new 'field', and it appears as an option in the Sort dialogue box. To sort cities by country, for example, put a comma after each one: Rome, Italy¶ Paris, France¶. Select 'Field 2' from the Sort by dialogue box.

When sorting by number, Word ignores all cell content but numbers, even if they are at the end of a cell. However, Excel sorts don't have this ability, so it might be quicker to copy an Excel table into Word for sorting. For instance, the fields Harry 5, Anne 9, and George 2 could not be quickly sorted in number order in Excel, but in Word you just need to select **Number** from the Type options in the Sort Text dialogue box.

If your table or list has headings describing the contents of each column, include these in your selected area for sorting and select the **Header row** option in the Sort Text dialogue box. This prevents the first row of your sort area from being included in the sort. Instead, the heading of each column is shown in the Sort by list instead of column or field numbers.

If a sort operation in an Excel worksheet does not work properly, check that the values are all correctly formatted; re-enter them if necessary.

SORTING DATA ALPHABETICALLY

After entering data into an application, it's often useful to be able to sort it alphabetically.

To alphabetise data in the Outlook Express Address Book, which appears in table form (with rows and columns), the most common method is to click on one of the column headers. The table is then sorted by the information in that column. An arrow tells you whether the sort is in ascending or descending order, and clicking the header again reverses this direction.

More complex, table-based applications have a Sort option in their menus. In Excel this option is in the Data menu. If you want to sort a particular column, click on its header to highlight it, select **Sort** from the menu bar, then choose **Ascending** or **Descending** in the **Sort by** section of the dialogue box.

Bring items to the top of a list by putting a space at the beginning of their names. Use this to make frequently used files or folders easily accessible. All the items with spaces will be sorted alphabetically among themselves.

If the application you are using does not allow names to begin with a space, try using an underscore (eg, '_Mary').

▶ See also **Sorting lists and tables,** p. 117.

HOW TO RESIZE AN IMAGE

Resize embedded clip art and bitmap images in Microsoft Word and Excel to make the finishing touches to your document.

Resizing an image is straight-forward. Click on your image to select it and you'll see sizing 'handles' appear at each corner and on the edges of the selection area. To resize

How to: Alphabetise a list in Microsoft Word

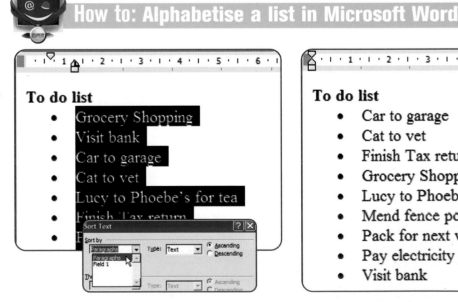

1 Begin by using the mouse to select the text you want to sort. Go to the **Table** menu and choose **Sort**. Word will display the Sort Text dialogue box. If your text is in columns, you can choose the sort field here, but for our list the default, **Paragraphs,** will do.

2 Click **OK** and the list is immediately alphabetised. If the results are not to your liking (sorting free-form text is tricky, and Word sometimes gets it wrong), click on the **Edit** menu and select **Undo Sort** to restore your document to how it was before.

the image, just click and drag a sizing handle. Release the mouse button to set the new size.

■ **To resize an image by a specific percentage,** select the image by clicking on it. Go to **Format ➔ Picture**. When the dialogue box opens, click on the **Size** tab. Enter the percentages you want in the **Height** and **Width** boxes (use the '%' sign). Click **OK**.

■ **If your image begins to become distorted as you resize it,** press the **Shift** key while dragging a corner resizing handle to resize both axes of the image together in proportion. To keep the image's current central point, press **Ctrl** while resizing.

■ **Force an image to be resized consistently** in proportion. Go to **Format ➔ Picture** and select the **Size** tab of the Format Picture dialogue box. Check the **Lock aspect ratio** box. Although you won't need to press the Shift key when resizing, you will need to uncheck the box if you want to distort the scale in the future.

■ **There are two image types in Microsoft Office:** drawing objects and pictures. Both can be resized in the standard way, but with differences. Picture formats, such as .gif and .jpg, can also be cropped. Drawing objects, such as geometric shapes, can be grouped and ungrouped for resizing separately or together.

■ **Not sure whether your image is a picture or an object?** Select it and then click on the **Format** menu. The word 'Picture' or 'AutoShape' will appear at the bottom of the list.

■ **An alternative to resizing** for pictures is cropping. Right-click on the image and select **Show Picture Toolbar**. Click on the Crop tool on the toolbar and drag the handles of the frame that appears to reduce the image size. When you release the mouse button, the area outside the crop mark will be deleted.

▶ See also **The world of graphics, p.154; Making use of clip art,** p. 190; **Drawing programs,** p. 194; and **Editing photographs,** p. 196.

AUTOCORRECT SAVES YOU TIME

Correct basic errors automatically in any one of your suite of Microsoft Office programs.

■ **Correct your most common typing errors automatically.** If you type 'teh' instead of 'the', the AutoCorrect feature will spot the problem and fix it for you. AutoCorrect has several settings like this one. If one of its rules, such as capitalising the names of the days of the week, does not fit in with how you want to work, just turn it off in **Tools ➔ AutoCorrect Options**.

| Online Collaboration |
| Letters and Mailings |
| Tools on the Web... |
| Macro |
| Templates and Add-Ins... |
| AutoCorrect Options... |
| Customize... |
| Options... |

■ **If turning off a particular rule seems too drastic,** try customising the AutoCorrect feature. For example, two capital letters at the beginning of a word is normally a

mistake, but not always – 'PCs', for example. AutoCorrect comes with some built-in exceptions to every rule, but you can add to the list by going to **Tools ➔ AutoCorrect Options** and clicking on **Exceptions** on the AutoCorrect tab.

■ **Innovation with abbreviation.** With a little thought, AutoCorrect can do much more than fix mistakes. For instance, you can use it as a time-saving device by inputting an abbreviation for a commonly used phrase, such as 'yosi' for 'Yours sincerely'. Go to **Tools ➔ AutoCorrect Options** and select the **AutoCorrect** tab. In the 'Replace' box, enter the abbreviation (eg: 'yosi') and in the 'With' box enter the phrase (eg: 'Yours sincerely'), then click **Add**. Whenever you type the abbreviation it will be immediately expanded to the full version of the phrase. Just make sure you choose an abbreviation that is not an actual word or a commonly used abbreviation, like 'etc'.

▶ See also **Working with Microsoft Word,** p. 124; **Access: Microsoft's database program,** p. 167; and **Excel: Microsoft's spreadsheet program,** p. 177.

How to: Resize an image in Word 2002

Format Picture

| Colors and Lines | Size | Layout | Picture | Text Box | Web |

Wrapping style

In line with text   Square   Tight   Behind text   In front of text

Horizontal alignment

○ Left   ○ Center   ○ Right   ● Other

Advanced...

OK   Cancel

1 Click on a picture or drawing object to see a frame around its edge. Place the mouse over one of the handles, and then click and drag the frame until it reaches your required size. Release the mouse button and the image will distort slightly to fit the new dimensions.

2 To anchor the image to its current central point on the page, select it, then go to **Format ➔ Picture**. Click on the **Layout** tab and choose **In front of text**. Click **OK**. Now, press **Ctrl** while you resize the image. The sides of the image will move as it changes size.

Don't strain your eyes – use the Zoom facility in many programs to enlarge graphics and text so you can make detailed adjustments.

■ Enlarge or reduce an area of your screen by zooming.
Enlarging a section of the screen lets you focus more clearly on the fine detail of text or graphics, while zooming out – perhaps immediately prior to printing – allows you to see how your work looks as a whole.

■ Under the View menu, Office applications include Zoom tools
for scaling your document. Microsoft Word contains preset percentages for enlarging or reducing your documents, but you can specify any zoom setting by entering a number in the Percent box on the Toolbar.

■ One way to zoom in on an Excel table
is to highlight the first row, and select **Fit Selection** from zoom options. This expands the row to take up the full width of the visible screen for maximum visibility.

■ A more efficient way to view your page layout
is to click the **Print Preview** button. Print Preview puts fully formatted pages onto the screen so that you can see exactly how they will look when printed.

■ Zoom in and out with a Microsoft IntelliMouse
or similar scrolling mouse. Zooming is made easy – simply press the Control key as you rotate the scroll wheel.

■ Most popular graphics packages –
such as Paint Shop Pro and CorelDraw – provide zoom tools so that users can even edit groups of individual pixels on a large image. Programs like Paint Shop Pro and Adobe Photoshop provide

flexible and fast zooming. Press Ctrl and the plus (+) sign on the number pad of the keyboard to zoom in or Ctrl and the minus (-) sign to zoom out. In Paint Shop Pro the mouse scroll wheel can also act as a tool for zooming in and out.

▸ See also **Scroll bar shortcuts**, p. 109.

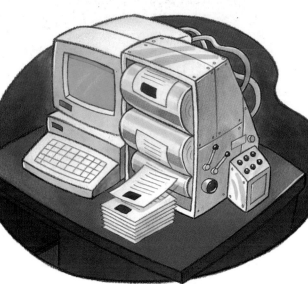

Get great results when printing your Word and Excel documents.

■ The speediest way to print out any Office document
is to click the **Print** button on the Standard Toolbar. The document will then print immediately, based on the settings you last specified in the Print box.

■ To print specific pages
or ranges of pages in a Word document, go to **File ➜ Print** and in the Page range section choose the Pages option. Then enter page numbers or page ranges you want to print, separated by commas. For example, '22,24' will print only pages 22 and 24.

■ In an Excel spreadsheet,
go to **File ➜ Print Preview** and select **Page Break Preview** to see where the page breaks are. After that, you can simply click and drag the blue lines to position page breaks where you want them.

■ Sometimes you may only want to print a small area
of a spreadsheet. To do this, select the area by clicking and dragging over it. Go to **File ➜ Print** and choose **Selection** in the 'Print what' section. Now click **OK**, and only the selected area will appear on your print-out.

■ Print several Word documents at the same time,
without even opening them. Click the **Open** button on the Standard Toolbar, and use the Open dialogue box to navigate to and open the folder containing the documents you want to print. Highlight the documents. Select **Print** from the dialogue box's Tools menu and all the documents will print out.

■ Printing a draft copy in Word.
Go to **Tools ➜ Options** and select the **Print** tab. Check the **Draft output** box and then print the document. Depending on your printer, this will give you a high-speed, but low quality print-out that you can use to check your document.

■ Select the best page orientation:
landscape or portrait. Go to **File ➜ Page Setup**, click the **Paper Size** tab, and choose the appropriate option in the Orientation section.

■ Gridlines can help guide the eye
through columns of figures in a complicated spreadsheet. To print them in Excel, go to **File ➜ Page Setup**, click the **Sheet** tab, and in the Print section select the **Gridlines** box. All the data in your sheet will now print along with the fine gridlines as displayed on screen.

■ When there is too much Excel data
to fit on a single sheet, try shrinking the printed image so that it will fit. Go to **File ➜ Page Setup** and select the **Page** tab. Either use **Adjust to** to scale the image by a percentage or use **Fit to** to specify the number of pages to fit the document into.

■ Dividing long Word documents
into sections makes reviewing and printing easier. To create a new section, go to **Insert ➜ Break**. Select the kind of section break you want then click **OK**. To print a section, go to **File ➜ Print**

and, in the Page range section of the dialogue box, select the **Pages** option. Enter 's' followed by the section number. For example, to print section five, enter 's5'.

Missing Headers and Footers?

Get them back on your printed page by checking that your page margins are wide enough. Go to **File ➜ Page Setup**, click the **Layout** tab, and in the Headers and footers section, increase the margin settings in the boxes next to **From edge**.

Row numbers and column letters

are handy on a spreadsheet printout, letting you know where you are. Go to **File ➜ Page Setup** and click the **Sheet** tab. In the Print section, check the **Row and column headings** box.

▸ See also **Printers,** p. 26.

Use Print Preview to get perfect printouts every time.

Get an instant Print Preview in Word.

Click the **Print Preview** Toolbar button or go to **File ➜ Print Preview**. In this view you can make changes, such as altering margins.

Headers and Footers are invisible

in Normal view, but will appear when you print the document. Switch to Print Layout view or use Print Preview to check them before you print.

Netscape Navigator and Internet Explorer

both have Print Preview features that let you check that Web pages will print properly.

Use Multiple Pages

in Word's Print Preview mode to check several pages at once. Click on the **Multiple Pages** icon on the Toolbar

and select the number of pages you want to see at once. Click the **One Page** icon (left) to view a single page.

Use the Magnifier tool

to zoom in on specific areas to make fine adjustments, if necessary, before printing.

To really enlarge a page element

adjust the percentage (up to 500 per cent) in the Zoom box on Word's Print Preview Toolbar.

Page breaks.

Use Print Preview to make sure they are where you want them.

Avoid printing blank pages in Word.

Click the **Show/Hide** button on the Standard Toolbar. Then delete any blank lines that appear at the end of your document.

Editing text in Word's Print Preview.

Click on the text and Word will zoom in. Click the **Magnifier** button on the Toolbar to enter edit mode then make your changes.

How to: Create printed envelopes in Word

1 Go to **Tools ➜ Letters and Mailings ➜ Envelopes and Labels**. Select the **Envelopes** tab. Type the delivery address in the top box. Check the **Omit** box if you do not want to include a return address. Click the **Options** button and select an envelope size.

2 To change the position of the address, use the up and down arrows to alter the **From left** and **From top** settings; the address will move on the Preview as the values change. Now select the **Printing Options** tab.

3 You may have to try various orientations until you manage to get your envelopes to print properly. Make sure that the correct tray is selected in the **Feed from** box and click **OK**. Then insert an envelope in your printer and click on the **Print** button.

Publisher 2002

Publisher 2002 is part of the Office 2002 suite. It is a desktop publishing program with templates and wizards that automate the creation of professional documents for print or the Web. Many templates are designed for small businesses, community groups and families.

window, you can preview the effect on your document on the right-hand side.

You will be prompted to enter information relating to your home or business. Click on an option to select the type of information required. The first time you use this function, a form will pop up for you to fill in with your details. If you decide your document doesn't need any personal information at all, just click **Update**. This will end the Wizard.

Once you have a basic document, you can customise it to suit your needs. To preview it as it will print, go to the **View** menu and make sure **Boundaries and Guides** is not checked. When the Wizard has finished, highlight the sample text and start typing your own text.

Use the task pane to change your document's design – it's the panel on the left-hand side of the Publisher window. You can choose an alternative set of fonts, or a different colour scheme. You can even choose a completely different design without losing any information.

document from the list that opens below or click on one of the graphics in the main panel.

To structure your document, create a layout grid. Go to **Arrange → Layout Guides**, and select the number of columns and rows you want in the Grid Guides section. To change the margins, enter a figure in the boxes at the top of the dialogue box. To move margins or layout guides, go to the **View** menu and make sure that **Boundaries and Guides** is checked.

For extra help use a ruler guide – a nonprinting horizontal or vertical line. To create a guide, hold down the **Shift** key, click on the horizontal or vertical ruler, and drag it to the required position. Move a ruler guide by clicking and dragging on it with the **Shift** key held down.

USING A PUBLISHER WIZARD

When you launch Publisher, the New Publication panel appears on the left of the window, displaying the categories of templates and Wizards available. A drop down list gives three ways of choosing where to start: **By Publication Type** shows you the documents that have a Wizard; **By Design Sets** groups similar styles of documents; and **By Blank Publications** is for starting by choosing a paper format, such as a folded leaflet or business card.

To start using a Wizard, select **By Publication Type** in the New Publication panel. Select a category from the list and preview the options available in the panel on the right. Browse through the designs and click on the one you want. When you select options in the left

TO CREATE A DOCUMENT

To get started, go to **File → New** and choose **By Blank Publications** in the task pane. Select the physical format for your

Every object in a Publisher document must be in a frame or box. Create a text box by clicking the **Text Box** button on the Objects Toolbar (by default on the left-hand side of the Window). You can edit text in a text frame just as you would in Word. Other tools allow you to insert pictures, clip art, WordArt elements, lines and shapes, including ovals, rectangles and more.

To add a picture, you need to create a picture frame. Select the **Picture Frame** button, click where you want one corner of the picture frame to go, and drag diagonally until the frame is the right size.

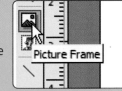

In the dialogue box that opens, browse through your hard drive for the picture that you want to use, and click **Insert**. Double-click on any existing picture to replace it with another.

To browse through a library of design 'building blocks' for your page, click **Insert ➜ Design Gallery Object**. You can add a table of contents, sidebar, or choose from boxes, borders and other decorative elements.

ABOUT TOOLBARS

When you select a text box, use the Word-style text-formatting toolbar just below the Standard Toolbar. First select the text to be modified, then click the appropriate arrows or buttons. You can opt to change the font, style, size or colour of the text, to align the text, or fill the text box with a colour.

When you select a picture box, the picture-formatting toolbar appears. Click the buttons to wrap text around the frame or picture, to select a fill or line colour. Open the Picture Frame Properties dialogue box to adjust the image's colours or to rotate it.

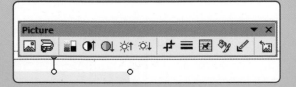

CREATING A WEB PAGE

Choose a template to start. Go to **File ➜ New** and click on **Web Sites** in the New Publication Panel. Click on one of the designs to open the template, then replace the text and images with your own material.

To change a Design Gallery element you've included, click the 'magic wand' icon below the frame. Use the thumbnails in the task pane to choose a new design.

To preview a Web page as you work, go to **File ➜ Web Page Preview**, then select **Current page**. To preview a whole site, select **Website**. Your page will appear in your default browser. If you've opted to view an entire site, you can check all the hyperlinks within it are working by clicking on them.

Using Windows XP you can publish your page to the Web in several different ways. First of all save the page to a folder such as My Documents. Next, open up the folder. To use Web space provided by Microsoft and its partners, click on the file to highlight it, then click on **Publish this file to the Web** in the left hand menu. This will launch the Web Publishing Wizard. You may need to pay a fee to use some of the services it offers. If you have Web space provided by your ISP, first set up a link to it in My Network Places. Then all you need to do is open the window for your Web server, and drag the file into it.

FUNCTIONS AND FEATURES

To zoom in on a particular element, you need to select it, click the zoom percentage window arrow, and scroll down to Selected Objects.

You can jump pages to navigate through a multi-page document by clicking on the numbered icon of the page you want to view in the bottom left of the screen.

To wrap text around a picture, right-click on the picture frame and choose **Format**

Picture. In the **Layout** tab, choose the wrapping style appropriate for your document.

To resize an object, float the cursor over one of the 'handles' located on the corners and sides of a selected object. When the pointer turns into a Resize icon, click and drag to a new size.

◗ See also **Desktop publishing,** p. 134; and **Creating a Website,** p. 228.

Tools for the job

WORKING WITH MICROSOFT WORD

Microsoft Word can be daunting for new users. Here are some general tips to make it more approachable.

■ **If you're new to Word,** adjust the Save Document settings for extra security while you're learning. Go to **Tools ➜ Options**, select the **Save** tab and check the **Always create backup copy** box. Then Word will save a copy of any file as you open it, so you can go back to the previous saved version if you run into difficulty. Only one backup is kept on file, and it is progressively replaced as you save your work.

■ **Creating a backup.** Go to **Tools ➜ Options**, select the **Save** tab, and check the **Save AutoRecover info every** box. Set it to save every five or ten minutes. This forces Word to take another backup of your work at the interval specified by you. This backup will only be available to you if Word or your PC crashes. When you exit Word in the normal manner, the AutoRecover file is deleted.

■ **To make sure that your documents are saved in the correct folder,** check the Save location settings. Go to **Tools ➜ Options** and click on the **File Locations** tab. Documents are normally saved in your My Documents folder – C:\My Documents. To choose a different default folder, click on the **Modify** button, browse to and select your preferred folder, and then click **OK**.

■ **Typing text into a Word document** is easy, but when it comes to applying formatting and making changes it can be a bit confusing at

first. Word provides three or four different ways to achieve most of its simple functions: drop-down menus at the top of the window, toolbar buttons, and mouse or keyboard commands.

■ **The drop-down menus at the top of the window** are the traditional way to get to the option you want. The most recent versions of Word hide the options it thinks you won't need and lists just those you've used recently. This makes the menus less complex, but if you're not sure where to look, finding the hidden options can be difficult. If you'd rather turn this feature off until you know your way around, go to **Tools ➜ Customize**, select the **Options** tab, and check the **Always show full menus** box.

■ **There are 19 different Toolbars** available in Word 2002. Once you're familiar with Word, you can edit these Toolbars to remove buttons you don't use and to add ones you do. To do this, go to **View ➜ Toolbars ➜ Customize**. Click on the **Commands** tab and drag and drop buttons for the commands you want to include onto the toolbars.

■ **Make accessing commands easier.** Many common commands are available to you by right-clicking the mouse button. A pop-up menu shows a combination of the most often used menu commands.

■ **If you want to move text** from one place to another in your document, you don't need to access a menu at all. Simply highlight the required text, then click on it again and, keeping the mouse button depressed, drag it to the new location. Release the mouse button to drop the text into its new position. To switch on this function if it does not work, go to **Tools ➜ Options**, click the **Edit** tab and check the **Drag-and-drop text editing** box.

■ **Taking shortcuts.** Many users prefer to use keyboard shortcuts instead of the mouse. It is quicker, for instance, to press the Ctrl and Z keys together (**Ctrl+Z**) to undo a mistake, rather than select **Undo Typing** from the Edit menu.

WORD TOOLBARS, MENUS AND KEYBOARD SHORTCUTS

Pick the best way for you to achieve common functions in Word.

TOOLBAR BUTTON	MENU SEQUENCE	SHORTCUT
	(New Blank Document) File ➜ New	Ctrl+N
	(Open) File ➜ Open	Ctrl+O
	(Save) File ➜ Save	Ctrl+S
	(Print) File ➜ Print	Ctrl+P
	(Cut) Edit ➜ Cut	Ctrl+X
	(Copy) Edit ➜ Copy	Ctrl+C
	(Paste) Edit ➜ Paste	Ctrl+V
	(Undo) Edit ➜ Undo Typing	Ctrl+Z
B	(Bold) Format ➜ Font ➜ Font style: Bold	Ctrl+B
	(Centre) Format ➜ Paragraph➜ Alignment: centered	Ctrl+E

■ **Need assistance?** There's plenty of help available from the animated Word Assistant that appears in the form of a paper clip. Go to **Help ➜ Show the Office Assistant**, and type in questions or keywords relevant to your problem. For additional support go to **Help ➜ Office on the Web**. This connects you to resources on the Internet.

Shaping the text

THE INS AND OUTS OF TYPE FONTS

Learn how to use, size, change and find all kinds of type fonts.

■ **The easiest way to change the current font** in Word is to select it from the Font box on the Formatting Toolbar. In the drop-down menu, each font name is displayed in its own typeface, so that you can see exactly what it looks like.

■ **Windows comes with a good selection of fonts** and other applications will install more, but you don't have to stop there. Internet sites have many thousands more. Try 1001 Fonts (www.1001fonts.com), Acid Fonts (www.acidfonts.com) or Font Paradise (www. fontparadise.com).

■ **The Font Size box** next to the Font box allows you to select the font size. However, you are not restricted to the sizes shown in the list – if you want to choose a specific point size, just type it into the box. To change the size of an existing block of text, highlight it first.

■ **For more control,** select **Format ➜ Font**. The Font dialogue box that appears allows you to select a range of features, such as font name, style, size and colour.

■ **To manage the fonts** on your PC go to **Start ➜ Control Panel ➜ Appearance and Themes** and click on **Fonts** in the left-hand column. Use the **View** menu to show the status bar, which tells you how many fonts you have.

■ **Whatever you do in the Fonts control panel,** leave system fonts alone (ones with a red 'A' in their icon). Windows won't work properly without them.

■ **An interesting range of special effects** is available for you to use in the Effects section of Word's Font dialogue box. For example, **Emboss** makes text appear as if it is pushed up from the page, while **Engrave** gives text that seems to sink back into the page, and **Outline** displays white letters with an outline drawn around them.

■ **Windows lets you change a font size** without the letters becoming jagged by applying 'font smoothing' to improve the font's appearance. In versions of Windows earlier than Windows 2000, this only works with TrueType fonts. For PostScript or OpenType fonts, you should download Adobe Type Manager Light, free from Adobe (www.adobe.com).

■ **If you have too many fonts** (and anything over 1,000 may cause problems) deleting some may speed up your system. Make a back-up before you delete – some programs need certain fonts to work properly.

GIVE YOUR TYPE THAT PROFESSIONAL TOUCH

Give your Word documents a professional finish by adding large initial letters.

■ **Are your documents dull,** with page after page of visually uninspiring text? Fancy formatting might be frowned on in school essays or office reports, but if you are producing something less formal, such as a newsletter, large initial letters, known as dropped caps can make your document more approachable.

■ **Dropped caps usually fit** into the body of the document, so that the text runs around them. However, if you prefer, you can position a dropped cap in the margin to the left of the main text.

How to: Add a new font

1 Go to **Start ➜ Control Panel ➜ Appearance and Themes** and click on **Fonts** in the left-hand column. The Fonts Window will open. Go to the **File** menu and choose **Install New Font.**

2 From the Add Fonts dialogue box, select the correct disk drive in the **Drives** box, select the correct folder in the **Folders** box, and then highlight your font in the **List of fonts** box. Finally, click **OK.**

■ **Your dropped cap will be in the same font** as the text of your paragraph, unless you specify a different font. If your text font is very plain, like Arial or Times New Roman, the effect may be rather uninspired. For more attractive and striking results, go to **Format ➜ Drop Cap** and select a more ornate font, such as Brush Script or Stencil.

■ **Don't overuse dropped caps.** Limit them to the beginning of each major section of a document, once per page, or at most once per story in a newsletter. Like most decorative formatting options, dropped caps quickly lose their novel appeal if you apply them too often. In the end they simply become confusing.

■ **You can also create dropped caps** in desktop publishing programs, such as Microsoft Publisher. These often give you greater flexibility and control than Word, enabling you to produce more interesting typographic effects.

▶ See also **Desktop publishing,** p. 134.

▶ See also **Desktop publishing,** p. 134.

SPECIAL SYMBOLS ADD VARIETY

Fonts can give you more than just the letters A to Z and digits 0 to 9. Symbols can add useful and fun graphics to text.

■ **Symbols come in font family sets** of graphics and special characters. Other font families, such as sans serif or decorative are made up of alternative designs of the alphabet (upper and lower case) and numbers.

To get an idea of the wide range of symbols available, select the Webdings font in your word processing application, and type hello (above).

■ **Graphic symbols are also called 'dingbats',** and there are plenty available on the Internet from commercial, shareware and freeware suppliers. Type the words 'font, 'symbol' and 'dingbat' into your search engine and it will bring up a list of Websites containing these symbols. If you need a specific subject symbol, include that word too. Symbol is a wide-ranging term, but dingbat is a useful keyword that refers specifically to graphic fonts.

■ **Unless you can remember exactly which key a symbol is mapped to,** your keyboard will be of no help to you when you are trying to add a symbol to a Word document. Instead, go to **Insert ➜ Symbol** to access the character screens for all the symbol fonts that you have installed on your computer. Select the appropriate font, locate the symbol you want to use, click on it and click on **Insert** to place it in the document.

■ **A symbol, just like any other font,** can normally be seen or used only if it is installed in the Windows font directory. This can cause problems if you want to e-mail a document to someone without the same fonts on their machine. You can get around this by embedding TrueType fonts into your document. Go to **Tools ➜ Options**, and then select the **Save** tab. Check **Embed TrueType fonts** and **Embed characters in use only** boxes. The document can now be saved normally. Note that some TrueType fonts can't be embedded in the text because of licensing restrictions.

■ **To enlarge or reduce a symbol,** simply increase or decrease its font size. First, highlight the symbol to select it, and then choose the new point size from the Font Size drop-down list on the Formatting Toolbar. If the size you want isn't there, you can type in your own point size if you wish. Most symbols can be successfully enlarged to many times their normal size.

■ **The font and the background colour of symbols** can also be changed in Word, in the same way as you would change any other character in a font. If you use a 3D text

How to: Add a dropped cap in Word

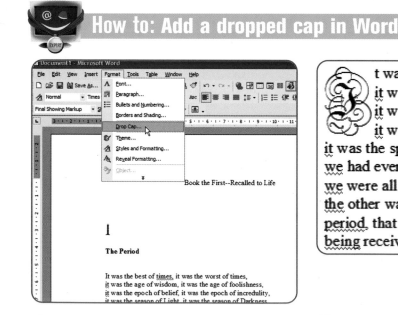

1 **A dropped cap can add an elegant touch to the beginning of a document. Click** anywhere in the paragraph where you want the dropped cap to appear and go to **Format ➜ Drop Cap.**

2 **In the Drop Cap dialogue box, click on the Dropped option. Choose a font and set the** size of the letter by adjusting the **Lines to drop** number. If the cap overlaps your text increase the **Distance from text** figure to add space between the first and second letters.

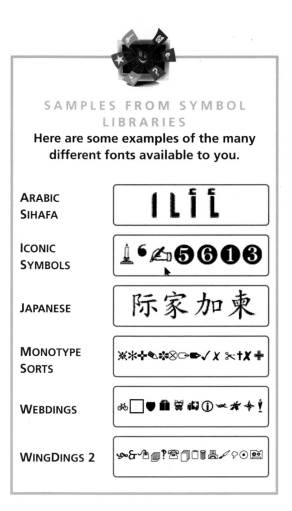

SAMPLES FROM SYMBOL LIBRARIES

Here are some examples of the many different fonts available to you.

ARABIC SIHAFA	١ﻝﻱﻝﺃ
ICONIC SYMBOLS	(symbols) ⑤⑥❶❸
JAPANESE	际家加東
MONOTYPE SORTS	❋✱✛❈✿⊗➠●✓✗✂†✗✚
WEBDINGS	(symbols)
WINGDINGS 2	(symbols)

package – like Xara3D (www.xara.com) – you can also turn your symbols into striking and attractive animated, textured 3D images.

Foreign language characters can be entered using the Symbols dialogue box. Non-Western alphabets and scripts – including Arabic, Hebrew, Hieroglyphic and Japanese – can all be installed as symbol font sets and inserted into a document. Although this is a good way to include an occasional word or expression in a foreign language, if you want to write or edit extensively in another character set, then you should use the Regional and Language Options control panel to add extra input languages. (See *Working in other languages,* p. 69 for more information.)

Any symbol that you want to use regularly – a heart or a star, for example – can be assigned its own AutoCorrect combination or shortcut key in Word. In order to do this, just go to **Insert ➜ Symbol** and click on the symbol or

character you want to assign. Click on **Shortcut key** to assign the character to a keyboard combination, or click on **AutoCorrect** to make Word substitute a symbol for a text code. For instance, pressing the **Ctrl+Alt+C** shortcut inserts the copyright symbol © into your document. Typing **(c)** initiates AutoCorrect to replace it with the copyright symbol.

◗ See also **Save time with keyboard shortcuts,** p. 108; **AutoCorrect saves you time,** p. 119; and **The ins and outs of type fonts,** p. 125.

BE CREATIVE WITH WORDART

Create decorative graphic text for your documents using Microsoft Word's WordArt feature.

In Word 2002, WordArt text is inserted by clicking on the **Insert WordArt** button that appears on the Drawing and WordArt Toolbars. If neither of these Toolbars is displayed on your screen, go to **View ➜ Toolbars** and click on the WordArt or Drawing option. While you can apply WordArt to long sentences, it is generally more effective when used with shorter pieces of text, such as headings and the text on posters or invitations.

Remember that any text included in your WordArt will not be included in your spelling or grammar checks. Either check WordArt text carefully yourself, or prepare your text as a normal Word document and run the spell check before cutting and pasting the words into your WordArt object.

If you've upgraded to Word 2002 from Word 95 or earlier, you may find that you now have two versions of WordArt – the independent applet that came with earlier versions of the program and the new integrated WordArt that Word 2002 installs. You can use either version to create objects. The main benefit of the newer version is that it creates actual drawing objects and also provides additional tools to manipulate the images it makes.

WordArt is a feature available to most Microsoft Office programs. Once you know how to insert a WordArt image into Word, you'll also be able to add WordArt to Excel worksheets and PowerPoint presentations. To insert WordArt in these programs, look for the icon on the Drawing Toolbar or click on **Insert ➜ Picture ➜ Word Art**.

Try different effects - for example you can exaggerate the 3D appearance of some WordArt styles by increasing the line weight. After creating your WordArt, click on the **Format WordArt** button on the WordArt Toolbar and experiment with the options available.

You can set any image file so it can be used as a texture for your text. Click on the **Format WordArt** button and select **Fill Effects** from the drop-down **Color** menu that appears in the Fill section. On the **Texture** tab, click **Other Texture**, select your image and click **Insert**. Select your image texture and click **OK** to apply it.

Don't overlook Word's many formatting features – they can help you to create attractive documents.

■ **Take advantage of the document templates** for preformatted letters, faxes, invoices and much more by going to **File ➜ New**, and clicking on **General Templates** in the New Document task pane on the right-hand side of the screen. Click on the different tabs in the Templates dialogue box and preview each template by clicking on its icon.

■ **If you can't find a document template** that exactly fits your needs, create your own instead. In the New Document task pane, click on **General Templates** then select the **Template** option shown in the bottom right of the box, and click **OK**. Now you can adjust the document formatting and style to suit your requirements. Choose **File ➜ Save As** to name

your file and save it as a template when you're satisfied with the result.

■ **An alternative way to format a document,** especially suitable for Web pages, is to select **Format ➜ Theme**. Choose any example you like from the list. Word customises your background colour or graphic, font, and body text and heading styles. Some themes may not be on your hard drive, so you will need to insert your Word or Office CD-ROM to access them.

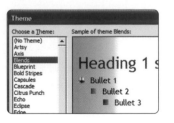

■ **If you change your mind** and decide you don't want to use a theme after all, click on **Format ➜ Theme**, and select **No Theme** from the list.

■ **Get even more themes from the Internet.** Select **Help ➜ Office on the Web** to locate and download the latest examples.

■ **Simple formatting options,** such as headings or numbered lists, can usually be left to Word to handle on its own. Go to **Tools ➜ AutoCorrect Options** and select the **AutoFormat As You Type** tab to configure precisely what you would like Word to do.

■ **Set your own specifications** by choosing **Format ➜ Autoformat**, and Word will configure lists, headings, paragraphs and other document features according to the options you select. Click on **Options** to review your options.

■ **Want to stay in control?** Go to **Format ➜ AutoFormat** and choose **AutoFormat and review each change**, and you'll get a chance to reject any modification you don't like.

■ **Don't rule out the simpler options.** Selecting **Format ➜ Borders and Shading** offers a variety of features, such as putting a box around a paragraph, or giving a page a border.

Change the spacing between lines of text to make reading easier.

■ **Access line spacing options** easily from the Format menu in Word. Go to **Format ➜ Paragraph** to open the Paragraph dialogue box. Click the **Indents and Spacing** tab to give you several line spacing options to choose from.

■ **Save time with a keyboard shortcut.** To quickly open the Paragraph dialogue box in Word, simply press **Alt+O**, followed by **P**.

■ **Need double spacing for the whole document?** You'll find it easier to compose your document using single-spaced text, then change the line spacing on completion. Press **Ctrl+A** to select all your text, then experiment with the line spacing options (see above).

■ **No need to highlight a complete paragraph** in order to alter the line spacing for

How to: Insert a WordArt heading in your document

1 Go to **View ➜ Toolbars ➜ WordArt** to open the WordArt toolbar. Click on the **Insert WordArt** button, select your preferred text style, and click **OK**. Choose a font and font size, type in your text, then click **OK**.

2 Resize, reshape and change the colours of your image using the options on the WordArt toolbar and the 'handles' on the object. You can also change and amend the chosen style here if you need to. To return to normal editing, click outside the WordArt area.

it. Simply position your flashing insert cursor anywhere within the paragraph, go to **Format ➜ Paragraph** and change the **Line spacing** setting. This will adjust the settings for that paragraph only, not the rest of your document.

MAKING YOUR TEXT TOE THE LINE

Style your text quickly and easily with Word's alignment feature.

 **With Microsoft Word,** there are four options for horizontally aligning paragraphs of text – left, centred, right and justified. Select an option by clicking one of the four Alignment buttons on the toolbar.

LINE SPACE LEXICON

Decipher all those line spacing settings to read between the lines.

Single spacing Sets the space from the largest font used in a line. Ideal where there is equal-sized type throughout a document.

1.5 Lines One and a half times single spacing. A 12-point font set at 1.5 line space gives a spacing of 18 points between the base of one line of text and the line below.

Double Twice the spacing of single, so that there is a full line space between lines.

At Least Displays the minimum line spacing that Word can adjust, so as to handle larger font sizes.

Multiple Increases or decreases the line spacing by a number set by you.

Exactly Fixes the line spacing at a preset distance throughout the paragraph.

 **To realign text** that you've already typed, highlight the relevant text, then choose your required alignment option from the toolbar. For a single paragraph, simply click anywhere in the paragraph text, select the option you want, and that paragraph will be realigned accordingly.

 **Hate reaching for the mouse each time?** Try a few keyboard shortcuts. In Microsoft Word, you can select text by holding down the Shift key as you move around with the arrow keys, then align with the relevant shortcut: Ctrl+L (left), Ctrl+E (centred), Ctrl+R (right), or Ctrl+J (justified).

 **If text doesn't align** to the left or right margin as you expect, you may have indented the paragraph. To check this, go to **Format ➜ Paragraph** and then the **Indents and Spacing** tab. If you don't want text indented, set your indents to a value of 0 cm.

 **You can also align text vertically,** either to the top or bottom of a page, or evenly between the two (justified vertical alignment). To align the text vertically in Microsoft Word, go to **File ➜ Page Setup**, click on the **Layout** tab and then use the Vertical alignment options.

PUTTING TEXT BOXES TO WORK

Want to insert some extra text material in a framed box on a letter or a report? Here's how.

 **First turn off the Drawing Canvas feature** in Word 2002 and 2000. Go to **Tools ➜ Options**, click on the **General** tab and uncheck **Automatically create drawing canvas when inserting AutoShapes**. Drawing canvases are the boxes you may have seen marked 'Create your drawing here', that can help to keep the separate parts of a graphic together, but which can irritate if you're working with text boxes.

 **To create a text box in a Word document,** go to **Insert ➜ Text Box**. The mouse pointer turns into a cross. Click where you want the top left corner of your text box to go, and Word will create a 25 mm-square box.

 **You can resize text boxes easily** by clicking on one of the small squares, or handles, on the edge of the box and dragging outward or inward. If you hold down the **Shift** key while you drag a corner handle the box resizes keeping its height and width in proportion. To resize a text box keeping its centre in the same position, hold down the **Ctrl** key as you drag.

 **Want to add a colour background to your box?** You can use the buttons on the Drawing Toolbar to modify a text box just as you would any other object. Click the arrow next to the **Fill Color** 'paint bucket' button to select a background colour for your text box.

To reposition a text box, hover the mouse pointer over any edge of the box, between the resizing squares. The pointer turns into a four-headed arrow. Click and drag the box to its new position, then release.

To rotate the text in a text box – to arrange text vertically on a poster, for example – select the text, then click the **Change Text Direction** button on the Text Box Toolbar. Don't use the Rotate and Flip commands on the Draw menu on the Drawing Toolbar – those commands rotate the box, but not the text inside it.

When you count words in a document by going to **Tools → Word Count**, Word does not include text in text boxes. To count the words in an individual text box, select the box by clicking on its border. Watch out – clicking inside the box won't work. With the box selected, go to **Tools → Word Count.**

Link text boxes in a document so that copy flows from one to the next. This is how to make text in a newsletter, for example, flow from a panel on the left page to one on the right page. Select the first box, then click the **Create Text Box Link** button on the Text Box Toolbar. The mouse pointer – which has now turned into a jug – turns into a pouring jug when it's over an empty text box. Click inside the next box that you want the copy to flow into. Repeat the procedure to link any additional boxes. When you paste text

into the first box, it will flow through all the linked boxes in turn.

To copy linked text boxes, including their text, to another document, go to **View → Print Layout**. Select the first text box in the document, then hold down the **Shift** key and select more text boxes. Then copy and paste to your new document as you would with text.

To change the size, position, and layout of a text box, as well as the colours, right-click on the box's border and select **Format Text Box** from the pop-up menu. Click on the **Colors and Lines** tab to give your box a black or coloured border and to fill it with a background colour.

Just because it's a box, a text box doesn't have to be square. You can use any of Word's AutoShapes as a text box, including geometric shapes, scrolls and stars. Select the text box that you want to reshape. On the Drawing toolbar, go to **Draw → Change AutoShape,** choose a category, and then click on the shape that you want to use.

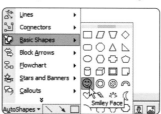

▶ See also **Desktop publishing,** p. 134; **Newsletters help create a community,** p. 161; and **Drawing programs,** p. 194.

HOW TO SHAPE TEXT AROUND PICTURES

Here are some tips to make text run neatly around pictures in Word.

To wrap text around a drawing or text box in Word, place your mouse pointer over the border. When the pointer turns into a four-sided arrow, right-click and select either **Format AutoShape** or **Format Text Box**. Select the **Layout** tab and click on the **Tight** option, then **OK**. The text will now wrap around the shape of your object.

In the Layout tab, you can specify other ways to position text and pictures. For example, if you want a square blank border around all four sides of your object, select **Square**. You can also choose to position it front of or behind text.

For greater control over how the text wraps, click the **Advanced** button on the Layout tab. Select the **Text Wrapping** tab and choose to wrap text on the left, right or both sides. You can also specify the distance between the text and image on any side by adjusting the figures in the **Distance from** text boxes option.

When you insert a picture into a narrow newspaper-style column, click the **Top and bottom** option on the Text Wrapping tab to produce complete lines of text above and below the picture. This is especially important if the picture is narrower than the column of text. If you select tight text wrapping, short words will fit raggedly around the sides of the picture.

Text may not wrap evenly around a drawing created with the Line tool (under **AutoShapes → Lines**), because the tool often produces jagged edges. For smooth curves, use the Curves tool instead. Alternatively, create a background shape with smoother edges, but make it slightly larger than your drawing and the same colour as the background. Wrap the text around this background shape for a neater look.

▶ See also **Desktop publishing,** p. 134.

COLUMNS MAKE FOR EASY READING

Make your Word documents easier to read by formatting your text into columns, newspaper style.

Columns of text work really well on a publication such as a club newsletter or magazine, giving it a professional look. To enter text in columns, click on the **Columns** button on

Word's Standard Toolbar, and scroll across to select the number of columns you need. If you can't see the **Columns** button, click the double arrows on your toolbar to call up more options.

■ Make your columns bigger or smaller.
Check the horizontal ruler at the top of the page and you'll see a marker for each column – click and drag these to adjust the column widths and/or spacing. If you can't see the ruler, select **View ➜ Ruler** and it will appear.

■ You can reformat an entire text document into columns.
Go to **Edit ➜ Select All** before clicking on the **Columns** button. To reformat only a part of a document, click and drag to highlight the text you wish to change before clicking on the **Columns** button.

■ For the maximum degree of control,
select **Format ➜ Columns**, and enter all the formatting information you require. You can also use the dialogue box to insert a line between each column.

■ To remove columns,
select the text, click the **Columns** button, and choose just one column. The text you have selected will now run on across the full page width.

These word and number aligners in Word are not as tricky to use as they sometimes seem.

■ To change the spacing between default tab stops,
select the paragraphs you want to apply the changes to. Go to **Format ➜ Tabs**. In the Default tab stops box, enter the spacing – in centimetres – that you want between tab stops. Finally, click **OK**.

■ When working with a table or spreadsheet,
clicking on the **Tab** key allows you to move from one cell to the next. It's also possible to insert a tab into a cell. Just hold down the **Ctrl** key when you click the **Tab** key.

This Toolbar appears when you create a text box with the Text Box tool on the Drawing Toolbar or by going to **Insert ➜ Text Box**.

 Use the **Create Text Box Link** tool (far left) to make text automatically flow from one text box to the next. To stop text flowing beyond a selected box, click the **Break Forward Link** button (above right). The links before and after will remain intact.

 Click the **Previous** and **Next Text Box** buttons, in Page Layout view, to move quickly between a series of linked text boxes in your document.

 Each time you press the **Change Text Direction** button, the rows of text inside the text box you have selected turn in the direction chosen.

■ Tab stops can be set with a leader,
a dotted line that draws the reader's eye from one item to another. Leaders are useful in tables of contents where items are separated by a large gap, which is hard for the eye to bridge. To create a leader, select the paragraph where you want to insert the leader, go to **Format ➜ Tabs**. In the Tab stop position box, specify how far

 across the page you want the tabbed text to appear. In the Leader section, select a dotted line style. Click **Set**, then **OK**.

■ If you have several lines that need leaders
with identical tab positions, you can format one line, and then copy and paste it as many times as you need. Change the wording for each line as necessary.

Learn how to specify exactly where you want a page break in Word.

■ When typed text exceeds
the amount that fits onto one page, Microsoft Word creates an automatic page break and a new page. In Normal View this break appears as a single dotted line across the page.

■ Force a new page
at any designated position by manually inserting a page break. Place the cursor on the line above the text that you want to appear on a new page, then go to **Insert ➜ Break**. Select **Page break** and click **OK**. In Normal view, these breaks appear as a more solid dotted line with the words 'Page Break' shown at its centre.

> s single eye in his direction, turning slowly in its turret
> ka's thick stem, positioning the cross hairs on the
> ank reared over the ridge. He had to make his shot co
> ll. He had to hit a vital spot; one not as heavily prote
>
> ·······Page Break·······
>
> e summit its gun was unable to bear down on him an
> iant salute. He picked a spot on the unprotected
> self and pressed the trigger.

If you can't see the page breaks in your document, you are probably in Web Layout view. Go to **View** and select **Normal** or **Print Layout** or click on the icons to the left-hand side of the horizontal slide bar at the bottom of the screen. In Print Layout view the breaks appear as new pages on the screen.

You can control where Microsoft Word creates page breaks. Go to **Format ➜ Paragraph**, and select the **Line and Page Breaks** tab. Use the options under **Pagination** to specify formatting. To prevent the first or last line of a paragraph appearing by itself at the top or bottom of a page, check **Widow/Orphan control**. To make sure that a page break is not created within a paragraph, first select the text, and then check the **Keep lines together** box. To lock a paragraph or heading with the text that it refers to, select the text, and then check the **Keep with next** box.

To delete a manual page break in Normal view, click anywhere on the line then press the **Delete** key on your keyboard. In Print Layout, position your cursor beneath the break, then hit the **Backspace** key. Be aware, however, that automatic page breaks cannot be deleted in this way. To remove unfortunate automatic page breaks, try adjusting your margin settings or insert a manual page break somewhere more suitable.

PREPARING ATTRACTIVE TABLES

Use Word's handy Table feature to produce interesting and useful tables quickly and easily.

Do you frequently use the same format for tables? If so, you can set that format as your default table. Go to **Table ➜ Insert ➜ Table**. In the dialogue box that appears, enter the specifications for the table in the Table size and AutoFit boxes, then check the box next to **Remember dimensions for new tables**. In the future, whenever you want to create a new table, it will have this format. To change this setting, simply alter the specifications following the above steps and check the **Remember dimensions** box once again.

To select a row in a table, place your mouse pointer to the left of the row until the pointer turns into a single small black arrow, then click. To select a column in your table, hover your pointer above the column until it turns into a downward-pointing arrow, then click. To select multiple rows or columns at once, hold down **Shift** and click on the desired rows or columns.

To move a row or column, simply cut and paste it in exactly the same way as you would treat any other piece of text. First, select the row – or column – and then press **Ctrl+X**. Now select the new location and then press **Ctrl+V**.

To move the entire table, go to **View ➜ Print Layout** and float your mouse pointer over the table until a cross-headed arrow appears at the top-left corner of the table. Now click on the table and drag it to its new position.

If you are working with figures that are not in a table but in a list separated by tabs, you can quickly convert the document to a table. Select the whole list and then go to **Table ➜ Convert ➜ Text to Table**. Enter in the specifications and click **OK**.

When you convert text to a table using AutoFit, the table is arranged to fit the width of the page. If you don't have many columns, or don't have much information in each cell, the cells will look too wide. To reduce the space, right-click in the table and select **AutoFit ➜ AutoFit to Contents** from the pop-up menu.

To resize columns manually, place the mouse pointer over the border between two columns until it changes into a double-headed arrow with two short lines across it. Click and drag the column divider to make the column wider or narrower. You can resize the outer boundaries of the table in the same way.

To see a menu for formatting a table, right-click anywhere on the table and select **Table Properties**. Select the appropriate tabs in the dialogue box to make changes.

How to: Use the AutoFormat gallery for a table

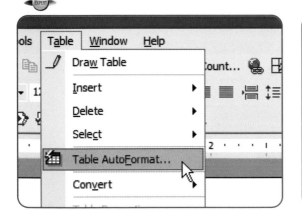

1 AutoFormat is a simple way to create tables. In Word, go to **Table ➜ Table AutoFormat**. Select a format from the list to see a sample of each one. Choose from different styles, such as Table Colorful, Table Classic, Table Contemporary or Table Web.

2 Each design can also be modified by checking or unchecking the boxes at the bottom of the dialogue box to apply special formats. Tick and untick the boxes to experiment with creating your own design.

HANDY TOOLS FOR CREATING LISTS

Microsoft Word can detect when you're creating a list, and continues adding list entries.

■ **To begin your list,** type in either '1', 'i', 'A' or 'a', followed by a full stop, dash or closing parenthesis (bracket). Now press the **Space bar** and type the text for your first entry. Press **Return** and Word will create the next number or letter in the sequence. Type the text for your second entry, press **Return** and the sequence will continue.

■ **Convert existing list entries** or paragraphs into a numbered list. Highlight the passages that are to be converted, then go to **Format ➜ Bullets and Numbering** and select the **Numbered** tab to choose a number or letter style. To create a

bullet-pointed list without numbers, click the **Bulleted** tab and choose a bullet point style.

■ **To end a list** after your last entry, hit the **Return** key twice to create a normal paragraph, returning your insertion point to the original left margin. In indented lists, you can press the **Return** key once, followed by the **Backspace** key to go back one indent level.

■ **Create a standard numbered list** by selecting the required text, then clicking the **Numbering** button on the Formatting Toolbar. To change the list to a different format, go to **Format ➜ Bullets and Numbering** and select the style you require.

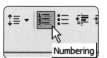

■ **You can choose your own font,** size, colour and a range of other numbering formats. Go to **Format ➜ Bullets and Numbering,** choose a style on the **Numbered** tab, then click on **Customize**. Select from the options presented and click on **Font** to change the font style.

■ **Start a list at any number or letter** you choose. Click the **Customize** button on the **Numbered** tab (see previous tip) and type your starting number or letter in the **Start at** box.

■ **For lists that don't need to be numbered,** you can use bullet points instead. Just click the **Bullets** button on the Formatting Toolbar to create your bulleted lists.

■ **Each bullet point can also be customised** in various ways. Go to **Format ➜ Bullets and Numbering,** select the **Bulleted** tab, then choose from the variety of shapes displayed in the dialogue box. Alternatively, click on **Customize**, then the **Picture** button to reveal a gallery of clip art images you can use. As another alternative, go to **Customize ➜ Character** and choose from any of the symbol fonts, such as Wingdings and Webdings.

▶ See also **Working with Microsoft Word,** p. 124.

How to: Create an outline numbered list

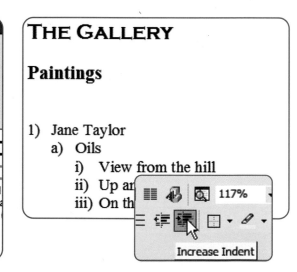

1 If your list includes sub-categories, Word can also number and indent these for you. Go to **Format ➜ Bullets and Numbering,** click on the **Outline Numbered** tab and select a style. If you wish to restyle any of your list's sub-categories, click on the **Customize** button.

2 Each sub-category has its own number style and indent position, which you can adjust. Select a Level in the top left of the dialogue box to display its description. Make any style and formatting changes you want. You can define up to nine sub-categories in this way.

3 When you've finished customising your sub-categories, return to your document. You can change the level of any paragraph of text by clicking on the **Increase Indent** or **Decrease Indent** Toolbar button. The numbering will then adjust itself automatically.

Desktop publishing

Desktop publishing used to be an expensive, highly skilled process. Laying out a page involved physically cutting up pieces of printed paper and pasting them into place. But with the advent of PCs and desktop publishing software, anyone with an interest can try it out.

GETTING STARTED

Plan your publication before you start. Eventually, you will need to copy or print and distribute your newsletter, flyer, business cards or whatever you are designing – and that's going to be your major cost. If your newsletter is going to thousands of people, consider a black and white, easy-to-photocopy design on white A4 paper. For party invitations, you might be more adventurous – lots of colours, printed on your inkjet printer on good quality card.

Set up a template. If your publication is going to be a regular feature, it's a good idea to set up a template, laying down column widths, margins, text styles and standard page elements like page numbers, dates and mastheads. That way, you will save time, and your publication will have a consistent look and feel.

Make it interesting. Don't get so carried away with how your page looks that you forget to focus on what you want to say. Everything in your publication should be aimed at making it easy and interesting to read.

SAVING IMAGES

Save photos as tiffs, using LZW compression (named after its inventors: A. Lempel, J. Ziv and T. Welch). No quality is lost during the compression process, but, because .tiff is a bitmapped image format, when you need to increase the size of the picture in your layout you will lose quality. This means that it is a good idea to start with as large an image as possible, using a high resolution like 300 dpi (dots per inch). You can also use a .jpeg format, which often reduces file sizes, but with some loss of image quality, depending on the degree of compression involved.

What's the best resolution to use? If you're printing out your work commercially, use images saved at a minimum of 250–300 dpi to avoid blurs. For most home users, images saved at 72 dpi will be good enough quality. Many home printers can be set to around 720 dpi for high-quality print results.

LAYING OUT A NEWSLETTER

Put text in columns across the page. Text is more readable in two or three narrow columns than in one wide column – although it becomes difficult when the column is only two or three words wide. Experiment with your page to find out how wide columns can be to look good while retaining readability. It's traditional to divide the page into equal columns, but sometimes it adds interest to have two wider columns containing the main text, and a narrower side column containing additional material, such as a who's who or a table of contents. Set up your columns in your template so that

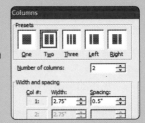

they will appear on all pages you add to the document. Don't forget to make pages that face each other into mirror images, and allow a slightly wider margin on the inner edge for binding.

Use a maximum of three fonts on any page. This helps to prevent the page looking busy and unreadable. Use a clear serif font (with fine horizontal and vertical lines at the ends of letters) such as Times, Garamond or Century, for the main text. Between 9 and 12 points is a good size, depending on your readership's age and eyesight. Find a complementary sans serif font (without lines at the ends of letters), such as Arial or Gill Sans for headlines. You might like to use a third font for captions, tables or emphasis. Set up text styles for text, headings and captions – it helps to keep pages consistent.

Use upper- and lower-case letters in your headlines. All capital letter headlines are difficult to read and take up more space than upper-and-lower-case headlines.

Limit graphics and clip art to two items per page, unless you're using a series of images for a purpose. Graphics that compete will distract the reader. It's a good idea to line up graphics with columns, and always include a caption to keep readers informed. Set text to wrap around a picture box, keeping it at least 5 points away from the image.

Line spacing can make a big difference to the readability of the main text of a document. Space between lines of text is called leading. In most desktop programs, leading

DTP PROGRAMS
Investigate these programs if you're serious about desktop publishing.

ADOBE PAGEMAKER (www.adobe.co.uk)
Combines templates, stock illustrations and digital photos with tools for page layout. With this software you can also merge text and graphics from spreadsheets and databases to create documents.

ADOBE INDESIGN (www.adobe.co.uk)
Aimed at professionals, this design software is good value when used in conjunction with other Adobe programs.

MICROSOFT PUBLISHER (www.microsoft.com)
This program has professionally designed publication templates, predefined colour schemes, Wizards and images.

QUARKXPRESS (www.quark.com)
The gold-standard desktop publishing program for design professionals.

is automatically set to 120 per cent of the font size – which would make leading for 10 point text 12 points. Vary the rule for a special effect.

Limit colours to three per page, excluding photos, to reduce the overall 'busyness' of the layout. If you cannot decide on a colour scheme then take a look at the main photograph on your page for inspiration. If you select the predominant colours in the photograph, then the whole page will blend together. Also, don't be afraid to leave plenty of white space around the words and pictures. It gives the reader's eye somewhere to rest.

PRINTING

Use a print bureau. When you have your publication printed at a print bureau your file must open on the bureau's equipment. So it's always a good idea to stick to a design using the basic fonts, which the print bureau is likely to have available. Fortunately, they will probably have the most popular fonts. However, it's an unfortunate fact of life that, while most desktop printers use TrueType fonts (look for the 'TT' icon, right), most commercial printers only have PostScript fonts. You might find it easiest to lay your publication out using TrueType fonts, but be prepared to substitute with PostScript versions of the same fonts if you decide to have the job professionally printed.

Printing at home? Always print business cards on good quality paper or card. It's also worth checking on the special papers available for inkjet printers. If you're printing flyers, you might want to use sturdy paper, whereas, for a high-volume document such as a newsletter, a lesser quality paper would be adequate.

You can't beat commercial printing, but that involves producing film and plates for the printing press, which is an expensive process and really only worthwhile for large quantities. If

you're printing in smaller numbers digital and high-end colour printers will give you a more affordable four-colour CMYK printing option. In this case, it is usually a good idea to try a high-street print bureau such as Kall Kwik.

CMYK? What does that mean? Your computer monitor uses a mixture of red, green and blue (RGB) to create the colours that you can view on your screen. However, the printing process uses a different set of colours – cyan, magenta, yellow and black (CMYK) – to create colours on paper. CMYK has a more limited range than the millions of colours displayed on your computer screen, so your printed colours won't appear exactly the way they do on your monitor.

Having a publication professionally bound can give it a really competitive, cutting-edge feel. Again, print shops offer a wide variety of binding methods. If you are having your publication professionally bound, make sure you ask your print shop how much extra margin they will need to do this.

▶ See also **How to group pictures and text,** p. 141; **The world of graphics,** p. 154; **Basic art with Paint,** p. 188; and **Creating a Website,** p. 228.

Word processing tools

Here's how to insert, link and embed one type of document into a completely different one.

■ **Need to add a table of sales figures to a report** you've produced in Word? One method is to copy your figures from a spreadsheet, then paste them into your Word document. But it's quicker to enter them directly into a spreadsheet linked to your Word document by using the **Insert → Object** command (see 'How to', below).

■ **You can create all sorts of multipurpose documents** when you go to **Insert → Object** in Word. Any application that creates an OLE (Object Linking and Embedding) item registers on the list of options. In addition to

Excel spreadsheets, you can also insert pictures, video clips, sound files and even PowerPoint presentations.

■ **Make documents richer and more interesting,** both in content and appearance, with OLE objects. Even in a simple editor, such as WordPad, you can select **Insert → Object** and add a video clip. View the document and you will see a still of the first video frame; double-click on it to play the whole clip.

■ **Whole objects may be either linked or embedded** into documents. To create a link, simply select **Insert → Object**, and then choose the **Create from File** tab. Click the **Browse** button and navigate to the file that you want to link to your document and click on **Insert**, but make sure that the **Link to File** option is checked in the Object dialogue box.

■ **Linking reduces the amount of disk space a file uses.** When you insert a link to a spreadsheet, for example, you're just

adding a reference to the spreadsheet file – a pointer to its location on your PC. The data in that spreadsheet stays in its original file.

■ **Linked objects are updated automatically** whenever the source file changes. So, if you've created a link to your personal finances spreadsheet, then you'll be able to see your latest financial information when you view the document. You can even double-click on the linked object to edit it without starting Excel.

■ **Some programs may not have** an Insert Object feature, but there is another way to do the job. To insert and link an Excel table, for example, open Excel, select the table, and then choose **Edit → Copy**. Now open the document to receive the table and click on **Edit → Paste Special**. In the resulting dialogue box, select the object to be transferred, and check the **Paste link** and **Display as icon** boxes.

■ **A linked object is inappropriate** in some cases. Maybe you want to give the document to someone else? So embed it in your document instead. Go to **Insert → Object,** and choose either a new file in the **Create New** tab or find an existing file in the **Create from File** tab. Leave the **Link to file** option unchecked. Windows embeds the object when you click **OK**.

How to: Insert a spreadsheet into a Word document

1 Open your Word document and position the cursor where you want the existing Excel spreadsheet to be inserted. Go to **Insert → Object**. Select the **Create from File** tab and check the **Link to file** box. Click on **Browse**, then locate and insert your spreadsheet.

2 The spreadsheet that appears in the Word document acts like a picture, so if you want to resize it, click on the spreadsheet and drag the sizing handles. To edit the spreadsheet, double-click on it. Your original Excel document opens so you can make changes.

An embedded object is part of the document in which it is inserted and is not a reference to another file. While this makes it easier for you to send documents to others, there is no guarantee that the recipient will be able to access it. For example, an embedded Excel spreadsheet will be viewable but impossible to edit for someone who doesn't have Excel.

STACKING OBJECTS ON A PAGE

Word's Order function enables you to change the way graphics, text and shapes are stacked.

Microsoft Word, like many other desktop publishing tools, allows you to use graphics, text and shapes on the same page. Although Word is not a sophisticated desktop publishing tool, its Order options enable you to layer graphics, text and shapes to produce leaflets, banners and bulletins, create shadow effects, position text inside a graphics box and layer multiple images.

By setting the order in which different graphics appear on the page you can achieve interesting effects. For example, you can hide part of one graphic behind another.

You can access Order through the Drawing Toolbar. If the Drawing Toolbar is not open, go to **View ➜ Toolbars** and select **Drawing** from the options. Once the toolbar opens, go to **Draw ➜ Order**. The pop-up menu gives you options for layering images.

Use Send to Back to place an item behind all other items, and **Bring to Front** to bring an item to the front. These options allow you to place items in different layers within a complex multilayered design. Use **Send Behind Text** to place graphic images behind words.

➤ See also **Desktop publishing,** p. 134; and **Drawing programs,** p. 194.

➤ See also **Desktop publishing,** p. 134; and **Drawing programs,** p. 194.

TURN TWO FILES INTO ONE

Merging is a system used in many programs to combine the contents of one file with another to create a completely new file.

Use Mail Merge in Word to create personalised copies of a letter for multiple recipients. Mail Merge can be a great time saver if you are involved in organising a club or charity, as you can easily create individually addressed letters to all the members without having to re-type each letter, or enter each address every time you want to do a mailing.

When you run Mail Merge, the software looks at your data source and, one record at a time, grabs the information it needs and inserts it into a copy of the main document. The process is automatic, so you can set the production of letters or other documents to run while you get to work on another job.

How to: Create a heading using Word's order feature

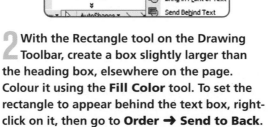

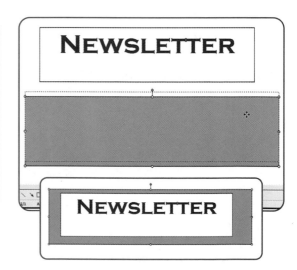

1 Open a Word document, then go to **Insert ➜ Text box**. Click in the 'Create your drawing here' box then click and drag the box within it to the desired size and location. Type in your heading and then style the font with the options on the Formatting Toolbar.

2 With the Rectangle tool on the Drawing Toolbar, create a box slightly larger than the heading box, elsewhere on the page. Colour it using the **Fill Color** tool. To set the rectangle to appear behind the text box, right-click on it, then go to **Order ➜ Send to Back**.

3 Click on the coloured box and drag and drop it into position under the text box. To enlarge or reduce the size of the box, click and drag on the corner or side handles. Adjust your text box in the same way.

To get help for setting up a data source, open Word and type 'Merge' into the **Type a question for help** box. Choose **Create a directory of names, addresses and other information** from the list of topics.

▶ See also **Take the drudgery out of mailings**, p. 162; **Building a system**, p. 164; and **Outlook Express**, p. 320.

CREATING A CONSISTENT STYLE

Standardise your Word documents by using the Style feature to format your text.

Word's styles are a powerful way to quickly and consistently apply a set of formatting characteristics to text throughout your document. Word allows you to set different styles for standard features.

You might think that you're not using styles, but whenever you open a blank Word document, you are. The Normal style

defines the default font, size, line spacing and other text characteristics before you start typing. You can see which style you're currently using in the **Style** box on the Formatting Toolbar. To see

the other standard styles available, click the arrow next to the Style box and they will be revealed in a drop-down menu.

To apply a style, click anywhere within a paragraph and then go to **Format ➔ Styles and Formatting**. A pane appears down the right-hand side of your document. To apply a style to the text in the selected paragraph click on one of the options in the 'Pick formatting to apply' box.

The Styles and Formatting pane includes the default and previously loaded styles. To access the full list click on the arrow at the side of the **Show:** box at the foot of the pane, scroll down and select **All styles**.

Turn on the View Styles feature if you're working with styles for the first time. This identifies the style applied to each paragraph on the screen. Select **Normal View**. Then, go to **Tools ➔ Options** and select the **View** tab. In the Outline and Normal options section, set the **Style area width** box to 0.75". Click **OK** to return to your document, and you will see a column down the left side of your document listing the styles used for each paragraph of text.

Create your own styles. To use an individual yet consistent style of formatting on all your work you can create your own styles, which you can then apply to different documents time and time again. To do this, go to **Format ➔ Styles and Formatting** and in the pane that appears, click on the **New Style** button. Name your new style in the dialogue box and in the Formatting section select a font type, size, colour and effect. For more advanced forms of formatting, click on the **Format** button. Once you have created a style click **OK**. It will now appear in the Styles and Formatting pane. Create a number of styles for headings, sub-headings and body text that you can regularly use.

 ## How to: Modify a Word style by adding colour

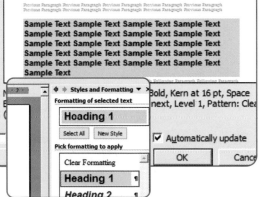

1 Go to **Format ➔ Styles and Formatting**. In the pane that appears, click on the arrow to the right of Heading 1 and select **Modify**. In the dialogue box, click on **Format** then select **Border,** then click on the **Shading** tab and select a grey fill shade. Finally, click **OK**.

2 Check the box next to **Automatically update** in the Modify Style dialogue box, and then click **OK**. Look at your Heading 1 text in the Styles and Formatting pane in your document to see the changes.

■ **To apply style changes throughout a document,** go to **Format ➔ Styles and Formatting** to bring up the Styles and Formatting pane. Then click on the part of the document you would like to change, for instance, a sub-heading or a paragraph of body text. Then, in the Styles and Formatting pane, click the **Select All** button. This will highlight all the parts of your document that have been created in the same style as the section you have chosen. By clicking on another style listed in the pane you will change all of the highlighted text at once.

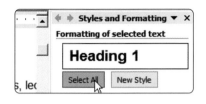

■ **If paragraphs with the same style seem to look different** in some way, it may be because some manual formatting has been applied to parts of the text within a paragraph. To remove any manual formatting, select the whole paragraph affected by triple-clicking within the affected text, then pressing **Ctrl+Spacebar**. This will reset the text to your chosen style.

▶ See also **The ins and outs of type fonts,** p. 125.

START WORK WITH AN OUTLINE

Use Outline in Word to organise the information in your documents and draw up first drafts.

■ **To access Outline in a Word document,** go to **View ➔ Outline**. A new Toolbar will appear, offering Outline features. These include formatting different headings according to their position in the Outline hierarchy. You can also use Outline features to hide or display text under particular heading levels and show some headings but not others.

■ **Do you have lots of headings and subheadings** in your document? You can use Word's Outline feature to automatically display the different levels of heading in different fonts. Indents help make these clear on screen.

■ **To see all your headings and subheadings at a glance,** click on the arrow at the side of the **Show All Levels** box on the Outlining Toolbar. Scroll down and select **Show Level 1** to display just your main headings.

Select **Show Level 2** to see your main headings and subheadings, and select other levels to reveal further subheadings. Click the **Show First Line Only** toolbar button to display headings, subheadings and the first line of paragraphs under the headings.

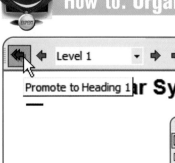

How to: Organise a Word document in Outline view

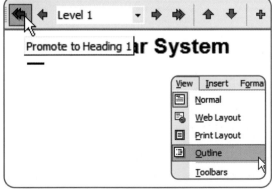

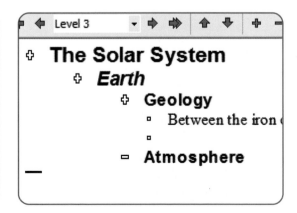

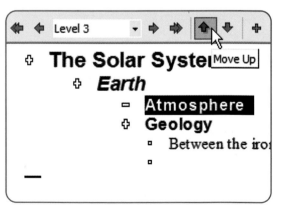

1 To display the structure of your document and the Outlining Toolbar, go to **View ➔ Outline**. Type in your main heading, then set it as Heading 1 style by clicking the green arrow at the far left on the Outlining Toolbar.

2 Continue typing your headings and subheadings. Use the **Demote** button (right arrow) to style subheadings and the **Promote** button (left arrow) to make higher-level headings. Click the double-pointing right arrow to create Normal-style body text.

3 You can move sections with the **Move Up** and **Move Down** arrows. Highlight the section you want to move. For each click of the Up arrow the section moves up one line and vice versa for the Down arrow. Change the order of your document in this way.

Customise the way your headings appear by configuring a paragraph style for each level. You can even set up different styles of headings for different kinds of documents – such as reports, business letters or job reviews – making it quick, easy and convenient to create documents for a range of purposes.

If you are writing a meeting agenda, or you want to impose structure on a long document, number the headings to make it easier to refer backward and forward through the document. To assign numbers to an existing document, go to **Edit ➔ Select All**. Then go to **Format ➔ Bullets and Numbering**. Click on the **Outline Numbered** tab and choose the style of numbering you want, then click **OK**.

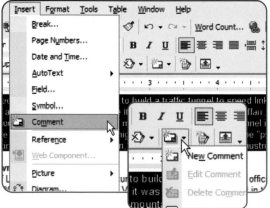

In Outline view, a plus symbol beside a heading tells you that there is subtext – body text or lower level headings – below the heading.

Double-click on the plus symbol to hide or reveal the subtext. A line appears under the heading when text has been hidden. Headings with a minus symbol have no subtext.

If outlined headings are distracting, change the view by going to **View ➔ Normal**. The heading fonts will remain in place, but the indents and the heading markers (indicated by plus signs) will no longer appear, making it easier to read the document on-screen.

▶ See also **Creating a consistent style,** p. 138; and **Attention-grabbing headings,** p. 145.

KEEPING TRACK OF COMMENTS

Use the Comments feature with a Word or Excel document to remind you of things you have to do.

You're checking a document, or perhaps reviewing one for someone else, when you spot a problem. So what do you do? Embedding a note in the document text isn't a good idea, because someone has to take it out

later on, and creating a new document for your notes will take time. The Comments feature, however, enables you to make detailed comments on any word or series of words in a document without changing the text (see 'How to', below).

As the document is revised, you may want to edit or remove comments. To do this in Normal view, ensure the Reviewing Pane is

How to: Add comments in Microsoft Word

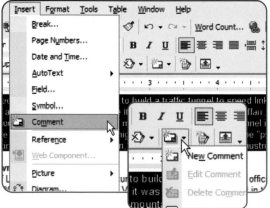

1 In your Word document, select the text you would like to comment on, then go to **Insert ➔ Comment**. You can also click on the Comment icon in the Reviewing Toolbar.

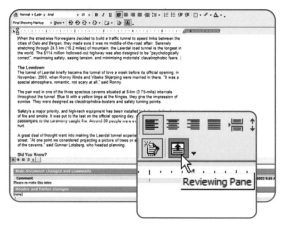

2 If your document is in Normal layout, the Reviewing Pane appears at the base of the screen. Type your comments into the pane. Click the Reviewing Pane icon in the Reviewing Toolbar to close and open the pane.

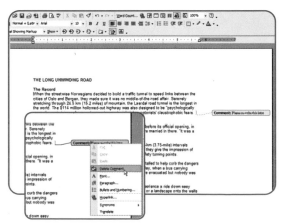

3 Commented text appears in red brackets. Go to **View ➔ Print Layout** to see comments differently – in balloons at the side of the text. Double-click a balloon to edit a comment and right-click on it to delete it.

displayed by clicking on the Reviewing Pane icon in the Reviewing Toolbar. The comments will appear in the pane at the bottom of the window. To edit, either place your cursor in the comment and type, or double-click on the red Comment bar. This will change the document view to Print Layout and balloons will be displayed containing the comment, and you can make your amendments here.

■ If you have just opened a document in Print Layout, and you cannot see any comments, go to **View →
Markup** and the comments will be displayed.

■ If your PC has a microphone, you can embed spoken comments, rather than just text, by clicking on the cassette icon in the Comments window. Keep in mind that recorded speech can take up a lot of disk space. It's probably not a good idea to use this feature on documents you intend to e-mail.

■ The Comments feature is not restricted to Word. You can also use it in Excel, where it works in the same way. Click on the cell that you want to comment on, then select **Insert → Comment**. As in Word, once you have entered your notes the cell is highlighted, this time with a small red triangle. To edit or delete your comments, right-click on the relevant cell.

■ Don't lose your comments! There's nothing more irritating than accidentally closing a document without saving your work. To avoid this happening to you, go to **File → Versions**, and select the check box next to **Automatically save a version on close**. Now, whenever you close a Word file, with or without comments added in, the latest version of the document will be saved for you.

▸ See also **Working with Microsoft Word**, p. 124.

HOW TO GROUP PICTURES AND TEXT

Use Word's Grouping feature to link objects and text together.

■ Word includes many drawing tools
on the Drawing Toolbar. They enable you to add lines, clip art and shapes to a document and to build up designs. But it's useful to group the elements so that if you move one, the others will move too. To group all the elements in a design, click on your first element to select it, then, holding down the **Shift** key, click on all the other elements in turn to select them. Then, on the Drawing Toolbar, go to **Draw → Group**. Now, if you click-and-drag a selected item, the others will move around the page with it.

■ To make the objects operate individually again, right-click on the group and choose **Grouping → Ungroup**.

▸ See also **Drawing programs**, p. 194.

WINDOWS' MINI WORD PROCESSOR

Don't overlook WordPad, a handy word processing program included with your Windows accessories.

■ WordPad might not pack in all the features of a program such as Word, but it can format text and include graphics perfectly adequately. You can also use the WordPad program to read and edit any Microsoft Word files that you might have received, even if you don't have Word available. To open the WordPad program, go to **Start → All Programs → Accessories → WordPad**.

■ Windows Notepad is your normal viewer for text files with a .txt extension. However, if you try to open a large text file, the following error message will appear on your

screen: 'This file is too large for NotePad to open. Would you like to use WordPad to read this file?'. You can safely answer 'yes' and go ahead and read the file in the WordPad program. If you make any changes to the file while you're working, make sure you save the file as a Text Document to retain the original format.

■ Many Word keyboard shortcuts also work in WordPad. The **Home** and **End** keys take you to the beginning or end of the current line. **Ctrl+Home** takes you to the start of your document and **Ctrl+End** takes you to the end.

■ WordPad normally saves files with the .doc extension, which is the Microsoft Word default. You can specify any other Windows extension (eg, .txt or .ini) when saving, but if you use an unrecognised extension, file.zzz, for example, WordPad renames the document file.zzz.doc.

■ If you want to save a WordPad file without the .doc ending, all you need to do is enclose the filename in quotes – for example, 'file.zzz'. If you save your file as a Text Document, you can then make WordPad the default application for editing files with the .zzz extension. Right-click on the icon for the file, select **Properties**, and click on the **Change** button. Now, select **WordPad** as the program you want to use, and finally click **OK**.

▸ See also **Save time with keyboard shortcuts**, p. 108.

SEEING THINGS FROM A DIFFERENT ANGLE

Spin your text and images around with Microsoft Word.

■ All the tools you need to rotate text and images in Word can be found on the Drawing Toolbar. To display it, go to

View ➔ **Toolbars** and click **Drawing**. It appears at the bottom of the screen, but you can drag it to the top or have it as a free-floating palette.

■ **You can only rotate text** that is inside tables, text boxes and AutoShapes. You can't rotate standard document text.

■ **To quickly change the direction of text,** put the text in a text box. To do this, click on the **Text Box** button on the Drawing Toolbar. Click on your document and drag to create a box, then cut and paste or type your text into the box. Go to **Format ➔ Text Direction** and choose the new alignment in the Orientation section.

■ **Use WordArt to create 'free rotating' text.** Although you can't rotate standard text in Word, you can get round the problem by creating a graphic that looks like text, and rotate that instead (see 'How to', below).

■ **To rotate an AutoShape or drawing object,** select the object by clicking on it. Hover the cursor over the small green circle that appears at the side of the object near the handles. When the cursor turns into a circular arrow, click and drag across the screen to rotate the object in the direction you want.

■ **Normally, imported pictures and graphics cannot be rotated** in Word. The only images you can rotate are drawing objects, or Clip Art that has been converted to the drawing format. However, you can import pictures and graphics into a graphics application, such as Paint Shop Pro or Paint, then rotate and save the image there, before reimporting it into the Word document.

■ **To control the amount of rotation,** use the Rotate or Flip options. Rotate turns an image through a set angle; Flip turns the whole image back to front, as in a mirror. Go to **Draw ➔ Rotate or Flip** and use the options.

▶ See also **Drawing programs,** p. 194.

▶ See also **Drawing programs,** p. 194.

Use this Word feature to eliminate inconsistencies in a document.

■ **It is easy to lose track of text** in a long document, but Microsoft Word makes it just as easy to locate it again. Go to **Edit ➔ Find**. Type the text you need in the **Find what** box, and click on **Find Next**. Keep clicking on the Find Next button to locate subsequent occurrences.

■ **One reason to find text** is that you need to change it. Go to **Edit ➔ Replace**. Type the text you want to replace in the **Find what** box and the new text in the **Replace with** box, then click **Replace All**. The changes will occur instantly throughout the document.

 How to: Rotate text using WordArt

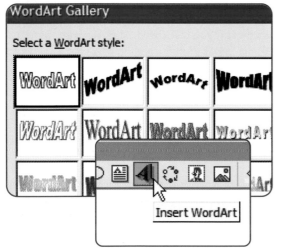

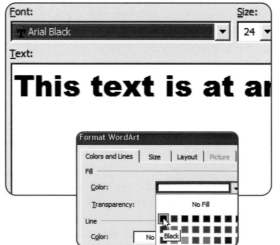

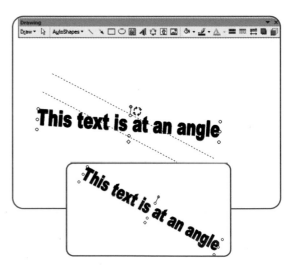

1 Open a Word document and click the WordArt button on the Drawing Toolbar (or alternatively go to **Insert ➔ Picture ➔ WordArt**). Select a suitable WordArt style then click **OK**.

2 Type in your words and set the font and font size to match the rest of your text. Click **OK**. Click on the WordArt to bring up the WordArt Toolbar. Click the **Format WordArt** button and set the **Fill Color** to black.

3 Then, select the **Layout** tab in the Format WordArt dialogue box and choose **In front of text**. Click **OK**. Hover your cursor over the green circular handle above the WordArt then click and drag the mouse to rotate the shape.

■ **Sometimes Replace All can produce unexpected effects.** Replace paint with acrylic for example, and Word might also replace painter, with acrylicer – not what you intended at all. To avoid this, click on **Find Next**, clicking **Replace** only when appropriate.

■ **You can use Replace to remove** all the occurrences of a particular piece of text throughout the document. Enter the word you want to delete, as normal, in the **Find what** box and leave the **Replace with** box blank.

■ **Use the Go To** function to quickly find a certain page or part of your document. Select **Edit ➜ Find** and click on the **Go To** tab. In the

---

FIND/REPLACE OPTIONS

For these advanced options, go to Edit ➜ Find and click More in the Find tab.

MATCH CASE
Check this option to perform a case-sensitive search. For example, if you perform a search for the word 'Fall', Word will only find 'Fall', and not 'fall' or 'FALL'.

FIND WHOLE WORDS ONLY
Check this option to locate only words that aren't part of a larger word, so you can find a word like 'personal', without getting matches like 'impersonal' or 'personality'.

FIND ALL WORD FORMS
Finds all tenses and word forms of a root verb and replaces all occurrences of that word in different tenses with another verb.

USE WILDCARDS
Use the '?' wildcard to represent any single character in a search, or use the '*' wildcard for any number of characters. For example, 'f?t' will find 'fit' or 'fat', and 'f*t' will match both 'fit' and 'fingerprint'.

Go to what box select which part of the document you would like to go to and then enter the page, section or table number and click on **Go To**. This is especially useful if you have a very long document with lots of annotations, comments and tables.

WATERMARKS IDENTIFY YOUR WORK

Adding a subtle background to your Word document is a good way of highlighting key information.

■ **Watermarks can be text or images** positioned behind the main text on printed documents. The main use of a watermark is to provide you with certain information about the status of a document with text, such as Draft, Confidential or Overdue. Alternatively, a watermark can establish the original source of the document – by watermarking it with an identifying corporate logo, for example.

■ **To create a watermark** that will be printed on every page of your document, insert it into a header or footer. To do this, go to **View ➜ Header and Footer**. Click the **Show/Hide Document Text** button on the Header and Footer Toolbar to hide the main document content. Create your watermark with the tools on the Drawing Toolbar, such as AutoShapes, Text Box, WordArt, Clip Art and drawing objects, or insert a picture. Resize and position the watermark where you want it to appear on the page, then click **Close**. If you want the watermark to show only on the current page, insert it directly into the text instead.

■ **To format your watermark** so that the main text of the document flows over it instead of wrapping around it, right-click on the object and select **Format Picture** for the object type. Click on the **Layout** tab and select **Behind**

---

text. The text in your main document will now run over the top of the watermark.

■ **If the watermark is too dark** it will distract from – and may even prevent you from reading – the main text on the page. To lighten text watermarks, select the text, click on the **Font Color** button in the Formatting Toolbar and choose another, lighter shade. To lighten an AutoShape or drawing object, double-click on it and change its line colour to a light grey and select the lightest shade of any fill colour.

■ **If you've chosen a picture file** for your watermark, you can adjust the properties to levels that won't interfere with your main text. Right-click on your picture, select **Format Picture** and click on the **Picture** tab. In the Image control section, select **Washout** from the Color drop-down menu. To adjust the image further, use the brightness and contrast slider controls.

■ **If you want to see your watermark** on a page while you type, work in Print Layout view. You can also see your watermark in Print Preview. It's a good idea to print a page with just your watermark so that you can check its quality and position before using it with documents.

If you want to know how much you've just written or got left to read, then the Word Count feature is just what you need.

Finding out the number of words in your document is straightforward. Just go to **Tools ➜ Word Count** to get an onscreen summary. The number of characters, lines, paragraphs and pages is also shown. Word Count includes symbols and numbers, and considers as a word anything that is followed by a space, so '1 + 1 = 2' will be counted as five words, while '1+1=2' will be counted as one word. Words not separated by spaces, such as Web addresses, will also be counted as single words.

Do you want to include your footnotes in your word count? You have the option to do so – just check the **Include footnotes and endnotes** box in the Word Count dialogue box. If you want to count how many words are in your footnotes, run a word count with the box checked and another with the

box unchecked. Subtract the number of words in your second count from those in your first to find out how many words are in your footnotes.

To count the words in a part of a document, highlight the area to be counted and then go to **Tools ➜ Word Count**. You can't exclude any part of the highlighted text from a word count, so count any words to be excluded separately and then deduct them from the total.

Tools	Table	Window	Help
ABC	Spelling and Grammar...		
	Language		
	Fix Broken Text...		
	Word Count...		
	AutoSummarize...		

Another way to get a word count is to go to **File ➜ Properties** and click on the **Statistics** tab. This gives you a report on count information, as well as the date and length of time the document has been worked on. If you divide the number of words written by the number of minutes the document has been edited for, you can get a quick estimate of your overall words per minute.

If you use Word Count regularly, add a button to your Toolbar or define a shortcut key so that you can quickly access this function

when you need it. Go to **Tools ➜ Customize** and click on the **Commands** tab. Select the **Tools** category on the left and scroll through the list on the right. Click on **Word Count** then drag and drop it onto your toolbar. Or you can click on the **Keyboard** button to create a keyboard shortcut for it.

Customize — Toolbars / Commands / Options
To add a command to a toolbar: select a category and command out of this dialog box to a toolbar.
Categories: File, Edit, View, Insert, Format, Tools, Table, Web, Window and Help, Drawing
Commands: Set Language..., Language, Thesaurus..., Word Count, AutoSummarize.

Want to check how many words you write, on average, in a sentence; how long your words are; or how many sentences you write in a paragraph? Word can tell you all these statistics and many more. You'll need to change your Spelling and Grammar options to enable this feature, which provides an additional report at the end of a spelling check (see 'How to', below). In addition to your word counts, this report includes an assessment of the readability of your document based on a number of built-in rules.

▶ See also **Programs to improve your grammar,** p. 152.

How to: Set up Word Count with averages and readability scores

☑ Ignore Internet and file addresses
Custom Dictionaries...

Grammar
☐ Check grammar as you type
☑ Hide grammatical errors in this document
☑ Check grammar with spelling
☑ Show readability statistics

Writing style:
Grammar Only
Settings...

Proofing Tools
Recheck Document

OK

1 In Word, go to **Tools ➜ Options** and click on the **Spelling & Grammar** tab. In the Grammar section of the dialogue box, select both the **Check grammar with spelling** and **Show readability statistics** options by clicking in the check boxes, then click **OK**.

File Edit View Insert Format Tools Table W

Normal   Times New R Spelling and Grammar
Final Showing Markup   Show ▾

Children are the new consumers, they're the new de
themselves to get to. The manufacturers and ad age
power', getting into parents' purses via their kids and
could we have let little Julie go without that expensi

2 When you're ready for a word count, word and sentence averages, or information about the reading level of your document, click on the **Spelling and Grammar** button on the Toolbar. Work your way through the spelling and grammar check of the document.

Readability Statistics

Counts	
Words	589
Characters	2766
Paragraphs	20
Sentences	36

Averages	
Sentences per Paragraph	2.5
Words per Sentence	16.0
Characters per Word	4.5

Readability	
Passive Sentences	2%
Flesch Reading Ease	69.7
Flesch-Kincaid Grade Level	7.4

3 When the spell check is complete, your document's statistics are displayed. The higher the Flesch Reading Ease score (out of 100), the easier the document is to understand.

Dressing up your work

ATTENTION-GRABBING HEADINGS

Consistently-styled headings in Word documents make the text easier to read.

■ **The next time you need to create a heading,** don't do it manually. Instead, select the text, click on the arrow beside the Style box on the Formatting Toolbar and scroll through the drop-down menu to select a heading style.

■ **If you don't see a style you want** on the Style drop-down menu, go to **Format → Styles and Formatting**, then, in the right-hand pane that appears, click on the arrow beside the **Show** box at the bottom and select **All Styles**. This displays a full list of styles available.

■ **Word can apply headings for you automatically as you type.** Although often more annoying than useful, this feature may well suit you. Go to **Tools → AutoCorrect Options** and select **AutoFormat As You Type**. In the Apply as you type section, check the box next to **Built-in Heading styles**.

■ **Text styles can make a heading stand out,** but a hanging heading, which projects beyond the left of your main text, is more eye catching. Click on the line with the heading, and select **Format → Paragraph → Indents and Spacing**. Enter a minus figure in the **Left** box in the Indentation section.

■ **To review headings in a Word document,** go to **View → Outline**. Each heading has a '+' symbol beside it, and is arranged in hierarchical order. On the Outlining Toolbar, click on a number to display only headings of that number or above.

■ **If you are preparing a contents list** for your document, sort your headings alphabetically. In Outline view, go to **Table → Sort**. Select **Paragraphs** in the **Sort by** box, **Text** in the **Type box** and check **Ascending**. Click **OK**.

▶ See also **Start work with an Outline,** p. 139.

GIVE YOUR TEXT PLENTY OF ROOM

Adjust the margins in your Word document for a variety of effects.

■ **To adjust margins in a Word document,** switch to **Print Layout** view. In this layout, a horizontal and a vertical ruler are displayed at the top and left-hand side of the document. The margin area is shaded in grey on the rulers. Rest the mouse pointer on a margin boundary (between the white and grey sections of the ruler). When the pointer changes to a double-headed arrow, click and drag the boundary to where you want it to go. The text on your page will move position to align with the margin boundary.

If you need to specify exact margin measurements, hold down the **Alt** key while dragging the margin boundary. The ruler displays the measurements while you drag. Alternatively, you can type in the measurements. To do this, go to **File → Page Setup** and select the **Margins** tab. Type in the margin sizes you want.

How to: Set up a new heading style

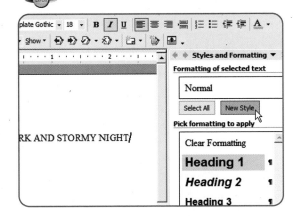

1 Type the heading in your document, highlight the text and click on **Format → Styles and Formatting**. In the pane that appears, click on the **New Style** button.

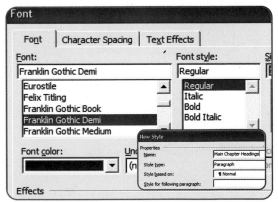

2 Name the new style and click on **Format → Font**. Choose the font, style, size, colour and any special effects and click **OK**, then **OK** again. The style will now be available in the Styles and Formatting pane. Highlight your text then click on the style to apply it.

145

■ **To change the margins for part of a document,** select the text you want to change, go to **File ➜ Page Setup** and click on the **Margins** tab. Set your margin widths. In the **Apply to** box choose **Selected text** and finally click **OK**.

■ **To change the default margin settings,** go to **File ➜ Page Setup,** click the **Margins** tab, and enter the settings you want. Click **Default**, then **Yes**. From now on, each new document you create using that template will automatically use these new margin settings.

■ **You may get an error message,** telling you your margins are set outside the printable area of the page. Click the **Fix** button to alter the margins so all the text will print.

■ **Word inserts a section break** before and after text that has been set-off by new margins. In Normal view you will see this is shown as a dotted line with the words 'Section Break'. Double-clicking on the Section Break line opens the Page Setup dialogue box.

■ **When the margins in a section have been changed,** the section may stand alone on a separate page. To change it back to normal continuous text, click in the section concerned, go to **File ➜ Page Setup** and click the **Layout** tab. Select **Continuous** in the Section start box, rather than New page, and click **OK**.

PAGE NUMBERS KEEP THINGS IN ORDER

Add page numbers to identify the sequence of multi-page documents.

■ **To number pages in Excel,** go to **View ➜ Header and Footer** and click on the **Header/Footer** tab. Select your numbering choices for the document, in either the header or footer boxes, depending on where you want your page numbers to appear – at the top or bottom of the page. Click the **Custom Footer** or **Custom Header** button to display other information alongside your page numbers – this can be text you type in or the date and time.

■ **A range of formatting options for page numbering** are available in Word. In each case, the page numbers are included within the header and footer areas.

■ **To number pages automatically in Word,** go to **View ➜ Header and Footer**, and click the **Insert AutoText** button. Select **PAGE** from the options in the drop-down menu. Word now automatically adds new page numbers to your document as you create them (see also 'How to', below left).

■ **To number each page individually in Word,** go to **View ➜ Header and Footer** and click the **Insert Page Number** button on the Header and Footer Toolbar. The page number will now appear in the header. To insert the number in the footer, first change views by clicking the **Switch Between Header and Footer** button.

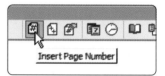

■ **Reposition page numbers** to the left, right or centre while the header and footer areas are displayed by using the alignment buttons on the Standard Toolbar.

■ **Make the page numbering more visible.** Instead of using only numbers to identify your pages, add the words 'Page' or 'Page number' to your header or footer before inserting the numbering option.

■ **To make a clean-looking cover page,** hide the first page number. Some documents, such as those that have a contents page or a decorative title of some sort, may not require a page number on the first page. If you hide the page number, it will still be counted as page 1 but the numbers will only show from page 2 on. To do this, go to **Insert ➜ Page Numbers** and uncheck **Show number on first page**.

■ **To display both the page number** and the total number of pages in a document, as in 'Page 4 of 20', for example, go to **View ➜ Header and Footer**, click the **Insert AutoText** button, and choose **Page X of Y**.

How to: Add page numbers in Word

1 Open your Word document and click **Insert ➜ Page Numbers**. In the Position box, select Top of page (Header) or Bottom of page (Footer). In the Alignment box, you can choose to place the numbers on the left, right, centre, inside or outside of your pages.

2 Click on the **Format** button to choose a style of numbering. This option allows you to select a standard number format, alphabetical increments or Roman numerals. After selecting, click **OK** twice to return to your document.

Customise the wording of a page number and total number sequence. Type the required text into the header or footer area, click the **Insert Page Number** button on the Header and Footer Toolbar, and then click the **Insert Number of Pages** button. Each numbering option appears where the cursor is positioned. You can reposition them anywhere within the area set aside for the header or footer.

▸ See also **Headers and footers look professional**, p. 116.

LIVEN UP YOUR WORK WITH COLOUR

Try spicing up boring black-and-white documents with coloured backgrounds or panels.

The Highlight button on the Word Formatting Toolbar is the quickest way to add a splash of colour to text. You can use the tool in the same way as you would a real highlighter pen. In Excel, the Fill Color button on the Formatting Toolbar performs a similar function.

It's best to use pale colours, such as yellow or sky blue, so that they don't obscure the text.

When you want to have more control over the positioning and size of a coloured background in Microsoft Word, use the text box feature (see 'How to', below). This tool will make all your documents really stand out from the crowd.

Use the WordArt feature to add special effects to words or short sentences in Word and Excel documents. Go to **Insert ➔ Picture ➔ WordArt**. You can use the tool in a number of ways: to colour, bend, stretch and distort your text, and to produce all kinds of different effects. The result is treated as a graphic object – not text – so don't forget that you won't be able to check spelling or include the text in a word count.

Coloured paper can enhance your document, with or without additional colour effects from the application. It can be expensive, but it might add a unique touch. To see what your document might look like on coloured paper, first go to **Format ➔ Background** and choose a colour, and then go to **View ➔ Web Layout** to view the document with the new background. A background colour won't print, but it can give you an idea of the overall effect.

Remember to use colour sparingly, otherwise it will detract from the message contained in your words. Use no more than two or three different colours, and avoid clashing combinations. Bold colours may look interesting, but studies show that most readers prefer black text on white paper.

Spruce up your spreadsheets. Highlight column headers or blocks of cells in Excel and colour them by using the **Fill Color** button on the Formatting Toolbar. You can also colour text by using the **Font Color** button, just to the right of the Fill Color button.

How to: Create a coloured heading in Microsoft Word

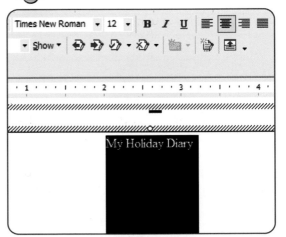

1 Go to **Insert ➔ Text Box**. Position the cursor within the 'Create your drawing here' box. Click and drag to size the box. Type in your message, and select it. Click the **Center** button on the Formatting Toolbar to centre the text in the box.

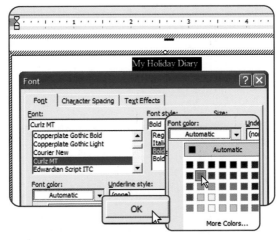

2 Right-click the highlighted area, and select **Font** from the menu. Select a font, font style, size and colour. The changes you make will be shown in the Preview window. When you're happy with the results, click **OK**.

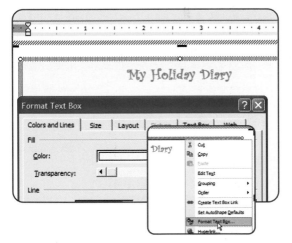

3 Right-click on the text box border and choose **Format Text Box**. You can alter background or border colours, and other features. Click the **Colors and Lines** tab. In the Fill section, choose a background colour, and in the Line section a border colour.

WORKING WITH LINES AND BORDERS

Lines and borders are an excellent way to decorate your documents, highlight areas of interest, or make a page look more organised.

■ **Make a paragraph stand out** by placing a border around it. To do this in Word, place the cursor anywhere in the paragraph, or select the paragraph by triple-clicking anywhere inside it. Go to **Format ➜ Borders and Shading**, and the Borders and Shading dialogue box will appear. Select the **Borders** tab, then choose the type of border you'd like as well as its size, colour and width. Make sure the Apply to box is set to **Paragraph**, then click **OK** to see the result (see 'How to', below).

■ **The Borders and Shading dialogue box** offers you a great deal of control over your borders. In the Setting section you can choose Box, Shadow or 3-D effects. In the Style, Color and Width sections you can choose

from a variety of line styles, colours and thicknesses. In the Preview section you can see how the border will look when it is applied, and you can choose to hide or show individual sides of the border. Just click on a side in the preview window to delete it from the border.

■ **You can set the distance separating your border** from your text. In the Borders and Shading dialogue box, click the **Options** button. You can then adjust how close the top, bottom, left and right sides of the border will be to your text by increasing or decreasing the numeric values. Check the preview of the result at the bottom of the dialogue box before clicking **OK** (see 'How to', below).

■ **Create a stylish look with page borders.** Go to **Format ➜ Borders and Shading**. Select the **Page Border** tab, then choose the type of border you'd like for your page. For special occasions use the **Art** drop-down menu to select an artistic line style – you can choose coloured symbols or festive motifs. In the **Apply to** box, select the pages you want the border applied to, then click **OK**. To see the border, view your document in Print Layout view.

■ **Frame your favourite picture.** Select the image in your document that you wish to enclose in a frame, then go to **Format ➜ Borders and Shading** and select the **Borders** tab. Choose the type of border that you would like from those that are offered, then click **OK**.

■ **Add decorative lines of separation** to your document. Place the cursor where you

How to: Place a border around a paragraph

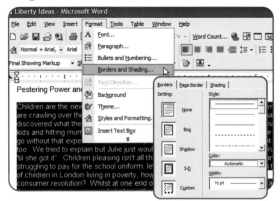

1 Open your document in Word. Select the paragraph you want to place inside a border by triple-clicking anywhere inside it. Go to **Format ➜ Borders and Shading** and select the **Borders** tab.

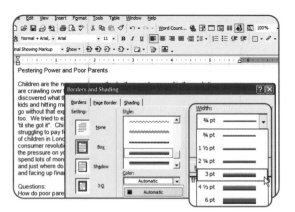

2 In the Borders tab, select the border Setting you want, together with Style, Color and Width. Check the appearance of your border in the preview window and click **OK** when you are satisfied with your choices.

3 Review the results and adjust if necessary. If you want the border closer or further away from the text, return to the Borders and Shading dialogue box and click **Options** to make the necessary adjustments.

would like the line to appear, go to **Format ➜ Borders and Shading**, then click the **Horizontal Line** button. This calls up a selection of clip art decorations that you can use to break up passages or simply enhance your text.

Activate the Borders and Shading dialogue box
instantly. Rather than going to **Format ➜ Borders and Shading** all the time, you can just press **Alt+O** and then **B**.

Use the Outside Border button
on Word's Formatting Toolbar for fast borders. This tool allows you to create borders with just a click of a button. Highlight a block of text, or click in a paragraph or picture, then click on the **Outside Border** button. Word automatically decides which type of border to add. To remove, select the text or picture, and then click the button once more.

CREATING TEXTURED BACKGROUNDS

Find, choose and add textures in Word to make backgrounds for Web pages and text boxes.

To add a textured background to a Web page
you're editing with Word, go to **Format ➜ Background ➜ Fill Effects**, and select the **Texture** tab. Click on one of the textures to select it as a background and click **OK**.

Create a textured background for a text box or AutoShape,
and it will show when you print. Select the text box or AutoShape, click the arrow next to the **Fill Color** button on the Drawing Toolbar, and click **Fill Effects**. Select the **Texture** tab, choose a texture and click **OK**.

Any scanned-in or downloaded photograph or graphic
can be used as a background for a Web page created in Word. Go to **Format ➜ Background** and select **Fill Effects**. Click the **Picture** tab, and then **Select Picture**. Browse for the desired image, select it, and click **Insert**, then **OK**. The picture will be displayed as a tiled background. You may have to lighten your image or change the colour of your text to make the words more readable.

You are not limited to the textures
that come with Word; you can use any image you like as a background texture. In the **Texture** tab, click **Other Texture** to bring up the Select Texture dialogue box. Browse to locate your texture file. Click on a file name and the image is previewed at the bottom right of the Fill Effects dialogue box. When you've made your choice, click **OK**.

Lots of free textured backgrounds
can be downloaded from the Web. Sites usually show a range of different tiles, which make up a seamless background. Save the file to your PC's hard drive. Then, from your Word document, select the background as previously described.

If you add a fancy background
to a document, you may find that the background doesn't print, even though it displays on screen. To get around this, open a new document, create a text box that is the same size as your page, and copy and paste all the text back into it. Now it will print. Remember to select **Print Preview** to see what your page looks like before you print.

▶ See also **Organising your Desktop**, p. 60; **Creating a Website**, p. 228; and **Where to find free graphics**, p. 305.

How to: Insert a line into your text

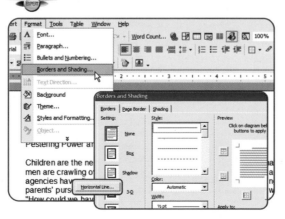

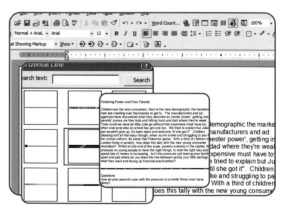

1 **Open the document you are going to work on. Place the cursor where you want the line to appear and click on Format ➜ Borders and Shading. Then click on the Horizontal Line button.**

2 **When the Horizontal Line window opens, click on the line style you want to use, and then click OK. The line then appears in your document. If the line style is not available, you may have to load it from your program disks.**

Words and images

DICTIONARIES OF EVERY TYPE

Need to spell check a medical, legal or specialised document? Buy or create the electronic dictionary you need for the job.

■ **Spell checking your documents** before sending them out ensures that they look professional – but it's not foolproof. Word, for example, comes with a limited dictionary. If you use names or technical terms, these may be flagged as errors. Prevent this by clicking the **Add** button in the Spelling and Grammar dialogue box when the spell check queries a word you often use – make sure you've spelt it correctly first! The 'suspect' word will be added to a custom dictionary and will not be flagged in future.

■ **Create a custom dictionary** for each member of your family or for a special project. Go to **Tools ➔ Options**, click on the **Spelling & Grammar** tab, then on the **Custom Dictionaries**

button. In the Custom Dictionaries dialogue box click on the **New** button. Name and save your new dictionary (see 'How to', below).

■ **To activate a custom dictionary,** go to **Tools ➔ Options**, click on the **Spelling & Grammar** tab, then on the **Custom Dictionaries**

button. Check the box beside the custom dictionary you would like to use. Spell check can refer to several dictionaries at once, so you can use more than one on a job.

■ **Editing a custom dictionary** to remove incorrect words or to add new entries is easy. In the Custom Dictionaries dialogue box, select the dictionary you want to edit and click the **Modify** button to view a list of the words it contains. Delete or modify words, then click **OK**.

■ **Need to spell check documents in other languages?** The good news is that Microsoft Office XP comes with dictionaries for

Spanish and French, along with grammar checkers and other proofing utilities. Office automatically detects the language used in a document and loads the correct tools.

■ **For enhanced proof reading of documents** in 30 different languages – everything from German and Italian to Japanese and Korean – Microsoft offers the Office XP Proofing Tools, an add-in package. Learn more about its capabilities by visiting the Microsoft Website (www.microsoft.com/uk).

■ **Online dictionaries can convert** one language to another, often free of charge. For free online translation software try YourDictionary (www.yourdictionary.com) and save yourself a fortune in professional translator's fees.

NO EXCUSE FOR POOR SPELLING

With Word's Spell Checker you don't have to look as if you were too busy talking to pay attention at school.

■ **The Spell Checker feature** checks your spelling as you type, placing a wavy red underline beneath words it thinks may be misspelt. A wavy green underline indicates possible grammatical errors. Right-click on the word and either select an alternative suggestion from the list offered or choose **Ignore All** to leave the spelling as it is. If you would like the word to be recognised in future spell checks, select **Add to Dictionary** from the menu.

■ **If you don't like the Spell Checker** querying your work while you are typing, turn it off. Go to **Tools ➔ Options** and select the **Spelling & Grammar** tab. Uncheck the **Check spelling as you type** box.

◗ See also **Programs to improve your grammar**, p. 152.

How to: Set up a custom dictionary

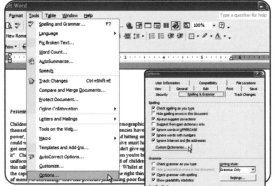

1 To create a custom dictionary, open a document and click on **Tools ➔ Options**. In the Options dialogue box select the **Spelling & Grammar** tab and click on **Custom Dictionaries.**

2 Click **New** in the Custom Dictionaries dialogue box, and name your dictionary in the Create Custom Dictionary dialogue box. Click **Save** and the name now appears in your list of dictionaries. Select it while working, and words will be added automatically.

Whatever your line of business, there's probably an online dictionary to suit your needs.

HIGH-TECH DICTIONARY
(www.computeruser.com/resources/ dictionary/dictionary.html)
Searchable online dictionary of 7,000 or more high tech terms.

EVERYBODY'S LEGAL DICTIONARY
(www.nolo.com/lawcenter/dictionary/ wordindex.cfm)
Contains plain English definitions for more than 1,000 legal terms.

CAMBRIDGE DICTIONARY
(dictionary.cambridge.org)
Search the dictionary for definitions to words and check out the word of the day.

ONLINE MEDICAL DICTIONARY
(www.cancerweb.ncl.ac.uk/omd)
A useful resource for brief definitions of medical conditions. New terms are added to the dictionary every day and all searches are logged, so that frequently requested missing terms can also be added.

YOUR DICTIONARY
(www.yourdictionary.com)
This site has over 200 different language dictionaries, from Spanish to Sinahlese. You can translate between languages and search the dictionary for word definitions. Subscribe to the word of the day or check out the 100 most often misspelled words.

INDEXES HELP YOUR READERS

Have you created a long report or a family history in Word? Adding an index is easier than you think.

■ **Although the Edit ➜ Find function makes it easy to locate topics of interest** in a Word file, once a document is printed, readers may need an index to find things. This is especially the case with a long document that is designed to be consulted. The Index and Tables command will help you to create one.

■ **To build an index as you write,** select a word or words that you want to include in the index, and press **Alt+Shift+X** (alternatively, go to **Insert**, then **Reference ➜ Index and Tables**), and click the on the **Mark Entry** button.

Now click on **Mark** to flag the selected word to be added to the index, or click on **Mark All** to index all occurrences of that word in your document, then click **Close** to finish.

■ **Wherever you mark an index entry,** Word inserts an Index Entry (XE) field, which looks something like: {XE "indexed word or phrase"}. To modify how the entry appears in the index, you simply need to change the text inside the curly brackets.

■ **When you've marked all the words you want to index,** place the cursor where you'd like the index to appear in your document and go to **Insert ➜ Reference ➜ Index and Tables**. Choose how you would like your Index to appear from the options in the dialogue box, then finally click **OK**.

■ **Take a shortcut to mark words for indexing.** First, create a concordance file – a list of words to be included in the index. Open a new Word document and create a two column table

(go to **Tables ➜ Insert Table**). In the first column, enter the exact word to be indexed as it appears in your document, and in the second column, type the index entry you want for that text, such as the page numbers where the word appears, or cross referencing information. Pressing the **Tab** key to move between the columns, repeat for all the words you want indexed. Make separate entries for plural words. Save the file. Open the document you want to index and go to **Insert ➜ Reference ➜ Index and Tables**. Select the **Index** tab, click on **AutoMark**, and choose the concordance file you have just created. Word searches through the document for each exact occurrence of text in the first column of the concordance file, and then it uses the text in the second column as the index entry. To insert the index into your document, click where you want it to appear, go to the Index and Tables dialogue box as above, select a format for your index, then click **OK**.

■ **If you add, edit or delete text after creating an index,** click anywhere in the index and press **F9**. This will rebuild the index and make sure that all the entries are still identified as being on the correct page. You will need to index again to include new words.

FOOTNOTES FOR THE STUDENT

Give your documents a professional look and feel by adding footnotes.

■ **Footnotes are a great way to show the source** of a particular piece of information in a document, or to include text that may not be of interest to every reader.

■ **Inserting a footnote is easy.** Click on your document, just after the text that you want to annotate. Go to **Insert ➜ Reference ➜ Footnote**, and the Footnote and Endnote dialogue box will appear. Choose from the options in the dialogue box then click **Insert**. You can now enter your footnote text.

■ **You can read a footnote** without scrolling to the end of the page. Hover the cursor over the footnote marker and the text pops up.

■ **You can drag and drop footnote markers** as long as you have the drag and drop option switched on. Highlight the marker you want to move, then just click and drag it to its new position on the page.

■ **Editing and deleting footnotes is easy too.** To edit a footnote, double-click the footnote marker and the text will be displayed at the bottom of the page. Place your cursor in the footnote text and start to type. To delete a footnote, highlight the footnote marker and press the **Delete** key. When you delete a footnote, Word automatically renumbers all the others.

■ **You can change the format of your footnote text.** While entering or editing a footnote, you can adjust the font size, style and alignment by using the Formatting Toolbar.

■ **You can also change the footnote separator:** the short horizontal line that separates footnotes from your main text. In Normal view, go to **View ➜ Footnotes**. In the footnotes pane, scroll down the Footnotes box, select **Footnote Separator**. You can delete the separator, use text or a Clip Art line instead.

PROGRAMS TO IMPROVE YOUR GRAMMAR

Spelling is difficult enough, but grammar can be even more problematic. Word's grammar checker is there to help.

■ **The best any computer grammar checker can do** is offer the user alternative suggestions. Grammar rules can often vary according to sentence structure and the information you are trying to convey, so they require a good grasp of language. Unfortunately, this means that you need a basic understanding of grammar to decide which suggestions are appropriate and which can be ignored.

GRAMMAR CHECKING OPTIONS IN WORD

Word can check for a host of possible problems in your documents, but what do the grammar rules actually mean?

CAPITALISATION
Checks that you have used capital letters on names and titles, such as Uncle Bruce.

COMMONLY CONFUSED WORDS
Have you used stationary (not moving) when you meant stationery (writing paper)?

CONTRACTIONS
Using contractions, like don't for do not, is not always appropriate in formal writing, and this rule highlights these cases.

MISUSED WORDS
Alerts you to such confusions as using who instead of whom.

SENTENCE STRUCTURE
Checks that your sentences are constructed properly and are not fragments or run-ons.

■ **For the least intrusive** method of checking grammar, go to **Tools ➜ Options ➜ Spelling & Grammar**. In the Grammar section select the **Check grammar as you type** box. Word checks text as you enter it, and underlines errors with a green wavy line. Right-click on the underlined text for an explanation.

■ **If Word flags text as incorrect,** even when there are no problems, postpone error-checking until the document is finished. Go to **Tools ➜ Options ➜ Spelling & Grammar**, and uncheck the **Check grammar as you type** box. Instead, select the **Check grammar with spelling** box. When you are ready, click **Tools ➜ Spelling & Grammar**.

■ **No matter which writing style you use,** the grammar checker will probably still make some suggestions that will annoy you. Before you give up on it, go to **Tools ➜ Options ➜ Spelling & Grammar**, and click on the **Settings** button. Here you can choose exactly which rules (see box, left) you want to enforce.

> Grammar and style options:
> **Require**
> Comma required before last list it
> Punctuation required with quotes
> Spaces required between senten
> **Grammar:**
> ☑ Capitalization
> ☑ Fragments and Run-ons
> ☑ Misused words
> ☑ Negation
> ☑ Noun phrases

DON'T BE LOST FOR WORDS

Struggling to think of the word? A thesaurus program can jog your memory.

■ **When the word you are looking for** is on the tip of your tongue, turn to the Internet for help – Websites and software (see box, p. 153) can help you to find the word and improve your vocabulary.

■ **Whether you are working in a document** or simply want to type a single word and find its meanings, you have a wealth of words at your disposal with a couple of clicks of your mouse. Make a start with Word's built-in thesaurus (see 'How to', p. 153) which is generally good for most day-to-day purposes.

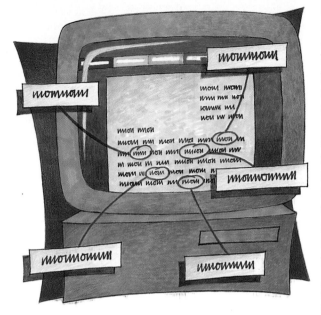

Make sure the word you want to replace is spelled correctly using the **Tools ➔ Spelling & Grammar** menu. This saves both time and anxiety by cutting out long fruitless searches. A quick way to access the Spelling and Grammar checker is by using the Spelling and Grammar button on the Standard Toolbar.

A thesaurus can help to improve a document by eliminating repetitive words. For example, if you use the word 'ridiculous' a lot in a Word letter or report, the thesaurus will provide you with at least ten alternatives. You can then ring the changes as you wish at different points of your text.

Be selective. Overusing unfamiliar words from a thesaurus can make your documents sound long-winded and pompous. Keep your language simple and use alternative words only when you really need to, to avoid excessive repetition, or to find exactly the right nuance. You could also try re-phrasing a sentence to convey the meaning without using the same word.

Make sure you check the meaning of an alternative word offered to you by the thesaurus. It may not be appropriate in the context in which you plan to use it. Also bear in mind that the thesaurus doesn't distinguish between nouns and verbs when answering queries, and this can lead to some incorrect substitutes being offered.

▶ See also **Dictionaries of every type,** p. 150.

THESAURUS SITES
Many online pages are dedicated to word searching.

WORDSMYTH (www.wordsmyth.net)
A dictionary and thesaurus in one. Free registration, 50,000 headwords, flexible searches and words of the week.

MERRIAM-WEBSTER (www.m-w.com)
This online dictionary and thesaurus includes www.wordcentral.com, an educational resource for building your own dictionary.

THESAURUS.COM (www.thesaurus.com)
Includes a variety of options to help you search this online thesaurus, plus free tools and games.

PLUMB DESIGN VISUAL THESAURUS (www.visualthesaurus.com)
This thesaurus uses spatial maps to display the alternative words to a search. Click on a word and a further map appears.

How to: Use Word's built-in thesaurus

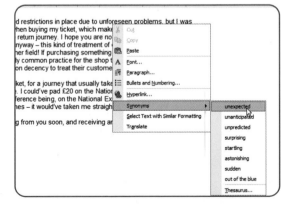

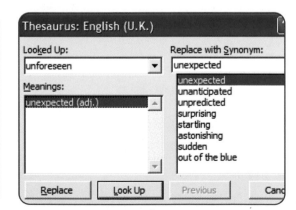

1 Place the cursor in the word for which you want a replacement. Right-click the mouse, and in the drop-down menu that appears, click on **Synonyms**.

2 A list of alternative options will appear in another drop down menu. Click on an option and it will automatically replace your original word in the text. Select **Thesaurus** to open the Thesaurus dialogue box.

3 The Thesaurus dialogue box displays the alternatives. If you are still not sure you have found the right word, click on one of the alternatives and then click on **Look Up**. This will display further possible words. Press **Replace** when you have found the right word.

The world of graphics

Graphics, with its own special language, is often baffling to those new to PCs. Despite the fact that many image-editing programs seem daunting at first, you don't actually have to be any good at drawing to create your own interesting, colourful and useful graphics.

BEFORE YOU START

What are you going to use your image for?
Is it for your Website, to go in a Word document, or to appear in the background of a newsletter? Graphics come in many shapes, sizes, formats, resolutions and colour depths, depending on what they're being used for. As a consequence, even before you start creating your design, you need to think about your ultimate goal for the graphic.

Gather your materials.
They might be Clip Art, photos, logos, fonts or various other materials. They need to be in digital format, so scan in anything

that's on paper. Use a high resolution, such as 300 dpi, and a rich colour density, like 24-bit colour. Now save all the files you need together in one folder, so that you can locate them easily.

COLOURS

Creating your own colours.
It's very easy to mix and select your own colours when you're working in a graphics program such as Paint Shop Pro. The Color Palette appears on the right-hand side of the screen. To select a new colour, either click anywhere in the Color Palette, or for more accuracy, click on the top-left coloured box and either select from the palette of basic colours or click on the colour wheel. Click the **Add Custom** button to add your selected colour to the palette and create your own precise colour scheme.

See a colour somewhere that you like?
Using Paint Shop Pro, select the Dropper tool, then left-click on the colour that you like to select it as your foreground colour, or right-click to select it as your background colour.

RESIZING IMAGES

Cropping versus resizing images.
When you resize an image, you compress the same image into a smaller area, or expand it to fill a larger area, without cutting out any of the image. In Paint Shop Pro, select **Image → Resize**, or use the shortcut keys **Shift+S**, then, in the dialogue box, select either a new size or a percentage of the original.

It's always a good idea to check the **Resize all layers** and **Maintain aspect ratio** boxes. When you crop an image, you cut off as much of the outer areas as you want to lose, focusing in on part of the image. The easiest way to crop an image in Paint Shop Pro is to select the **Crop** tool,

draw a box around the area you'd like to retain, drag the edges to adjust it, then double-click within the crop area.

It's easy to make an image smaller, but not so easy to make an image bigger. When you spread the same amount of image information over a larger area, you lose detail. So start with the image larger than you'll finally need. Before you scale down an image, switch to Millions of colours, if you're not already working in that mode. This enables the program to use a blend of different-coloured pixels to smooth the edges of the image to avoid 'jaggies' or ragged

edges. Then switch back to 256-colour mode, or whatever you were previously working in, and check that the image still looks satisfactory.

Add callouts to draw your readers' attention to hints, tips or comments. Or maybe pull an enticing idea from the main text and use it to make the reader want to read on. Word offers lots of AutoShapes that make it easy for you to create interesting graphics. Select **Insert ➜ Picture ➜ AutoShapes** to display the AutoShapes Toolbar. Click on the **Callouts** button and select a style from the drop-down menu. Click and drag to size the shape. To insert text, just click in the middle of the shape and type. Double-click on the edge to bring up the format options. On the **Colors and Lines** tab, you can select a colour to fill the shape.

Are you trying to keep the file size of your document down? You can create links to graphics saved elsewhere instead of inserting them into your document. Click at the point where you want the graphic to appear, then select **Insert ➜ Picture ➜ From File**. Select your picture file, then click the arrow to the right of the **Insert** button and select **Link to File** from the drop-down menu. You will be able to see the picture in your document, and print it, but you won't be able to edit it. Your document file size should stay small, but if you want to copy the document onto a floppy disk, you'll also need to copy the picture.

Is your document scrolling slowly? Then you may need to hide your graphics. Select **Tools ➜ Options**, then the **View** tab. To hide a picture you've imported, check the **Picture placeholders** box, and then Word will display an outline of the image instead of the whole picture.

Take care with background graphics. While a picture or AutoShape in the background of your page can look great, you must make sure it doesn't reduce the readability of the foreground text. If you've inserted a picture, double-click on the image, select the **Layout** tab, and click on

Behind text. Now click the **Picture** tab in the Image control section, scroll down the Color box and select **Washout** for a light background. For an AutoShape, double-click on it to bring up the formatting options. It's a good idea to make sure it has no line around it. Select the **Colors and Lines** tab and select **No Line** in the Line Color box. Play with the Fill colour transparency slider to make it pale enough to be unobtrusive (or dark enough, if you're running light-coloured text over it). Your image should now fade into the background. For a different effect, try blurring your image in an image-editing program before inserting it into a document.

The most important rule of Web graphics is to keep their file sizes as small as possible. A Web image should never go above 100 KB in size. The average Web viewer's modem struggles to download at a speed of anything above 3 KB per second, which means even a 50 KB image can take 20 seconds to download.

TECHNICAL TERMS
Understand the terms used for formatting images with these definitions.

COLOUR DEPTH
Colour depth tells you how many colours are used in an image. Millions of colours gives the impression of 'true colour', while 256 or 16 colours are suitable for logos, cartoons or graphics with large areas of flat colour.

FILE SIZE
The file size of an image is measured in bytes, kilobytes (KB) or megabytes (MB). It measures how much hard drive space the image takes up and gives you an idea of how long the image will take to download.

IMAGE HEIGHT AND WIDTH
You can measure the height and width of your graphics in many ways: centimetres, inches and pixels are the most common. For Web graphics, it's a good idea to use pixels, but for print, use centimetres or inches.

RESOLUTION
'Raster' images are built up from lots of tiny dots. Resolution measures the number of dots per inch (dpi) used in the image. The higher the resolution, or dpi, the more detailed and smoother your image will look.

Pick the right format for your Web image. If the picture uses lots of different colours – if it's a photo, for example, or if it has large areas of graduated colour – then it's best saved as a .jpg. If it uses only a few colours, and has large areas of flat colour – a cartoon or a line drawing, for example – then save it as a .gif.

Graphics file sizes can easily get out of hand. If you're trying to make the best possible photos for the Web, create two versions – one full-size and one much smaller. Use the smaller one on your pages and create a link to the full-size version for those visitors who want to see the photo in the best possible quality.

With .gifs, a small colour palette means a small image file size. If your image already uses only a few colours, count exactly how many in your image-editing program, then reduce its colour depth to exactly that number. To do this in Paint Shop Pro, you first need to flatten the image to one layer by going to **Layers ➜ Merge ➜ Merge Visible**. Then select **Colors ➜ Count Colors Used**. In the cartoon of a girl's head, below, the number of colours is only five, which means the palette can be reduced to five

colours. To do this, select **Colors ➜ Decrease Color Depth ➜ X Colors (4/8 bit)**. Enter '5' in the Number of colors box and select **Standard/Web-safe** and **Nearest color** for the reduction method. For an image with a lot more colours, experiment with reducing the colour depth to different numbers of colours to see how much quality you lose. You can reduce an image that uses thousands of colours down to 64 or even 32 colours without losing all that much detail.

Before you save your image as a .gif or .jpg, save it in its 'native' format first. So if you're working in Paint Shop Pro, save it in .psp format. That way you'll preserve the full colour depth, layers, effects, vector paths, masks and other features. This enables you to go back into your image and make changes to it much more easily

at a later date. Once that's done, you can start reducing the colour depth, flattening the image and carrying out any other operations necessary to get it ready for the Web. Then you can safely save it as a .gif or .jpg, knowing that you still have your original to go back to.

Never resave a .jpg. When you save an image as a .jpg, you compress it, which means the image loses a lot of detail. If you then reopen and resave the image, you compress it further, losing yet more detail. Make sure you always save a copy of your graphic in a uncompressed format such as .psp or .bmp, before saving it as a .jpg.

IMAGE-EDITING SOFTWARE
To create your own graphics, check out these popular software programs.

ADOBE PHOTOSHOP (www.adobe.com)
The professional's choice for image-editing and Website graphics creation. It's also available in a less costly Limited Edition.

CORELDRAW (www.corel.com)
This vector-based program makes it easy to create professional artwork, from logos to intricate technical illustrations.

COREL PHOTO-PAINT (www.corel.com)
Design images for print or the Web and enhance images with lenses, masks and other editing features.

PAINT SHOP PRO (www.jasc.com)
Provides you with tools to retouch, repair and redraw photos with its auto-photo enhancer feature. You can also customise images, create animations and remove red-eye effects from pictures.

PICTURE IT! (pictureitproducts.msn.com)
Discover how to enhance your photos, add templates and create Web page images with Microsoft's Picture It!

That way, if you do need to update the image, you can go to the original file, make your changes to it, and then save it as a .jpg again.

Some people still use 256-colour monitors when viewing the Web. If you use a colour on your Web page that a viewer's monitor doesn't support, then their Web browser will 'dither' your colours in an effort to reproduce a close approximation of the original. Dithering is when the browser mixes two or more colours, using small dots of each. This doesn't sound too bad, but dithering can look terrible on a large area of flat colour. So it's generally a good idea to use the Web-safe palette of colours, which all 256-colour monitors can display, no matter which Web browser is being used.

Unfortunately, the Web-safe palette only offers you 216 colours to work with. A good rule is to make sure that when you design your images, you use a Web-safe colour for any large areas of flat colour, while allowing yourself to use non-Web-safe colours for smaller areas like the edges of objects and text.

How do you know if a colour is Web-safe? Just look at its RGB values and divide by 51. The RGB value will be a number between 0 and 255 for each primary additive colour – red, green and blue. You know the colour is safe if each of these numbers is either 0, 51, 102, 153, 204, or 255 (all of which are multiples of 51). Open the colour picker by double-clicking on the colour swatches on the Color Palette, and type

some of these numbers into the Red, Green and Blue boxes. You should find something close to the colour you want by typing in various different combinations of these 'safe' numbers.

◗ See also **Tiny changes make a big difference**, p. 190; **Understanding vector graphics**, p. 193; **Drawing programs**, p. 194; **Editing photographs**, p. 196; and **Creating a Website**, p. 228.

How to: Decorate a Christmas letter with Clip Art

1 You can create an annual Christmas letter to send out to all your friends at home and abroad, telling them all your family news for the year. Start by opening a new Word document and typing the main body of the letter. Then click at the beginning of the text and select **Insert ➔ Picture ➔ Clip Art**.

2 The Insert Clip Art pane appears on the right of your document. Type 'Christmas' into the **Search For** box and click on **Search**. Select an attractive corner decoration from the variety of styles that is available. Click on the arrow at the side of the image and select **Insert** to place it in your document.

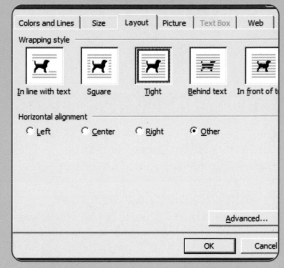

3 Double-click on the image. In the dialogue box that appears, select the **Size** tab and check the **Lock aspect ratio** box. Now click on the **Layout** tab and select both **Tight** in the Wrapping style options and **Other** in the Horizontal alignment options, then click **OK**.

4 Click on the image and drag it to the desired position. You can alter its size by placing the cursor on the corner handles and dragging the box to make it larger or smaller. To rotate the image place the cursor on the green handle and drag the mouse in the direction you want the image to turn.

5 Add a festive background by inserting more Clip Art, as in Steps 1 to 3, but choose the **Behind text** option in the Layout tab. Click on the **Picture** tab and select **Washout** from the Color menu in the Image control section. Then drag a corner handle of the image to enlarge it and position it centrally on the page.

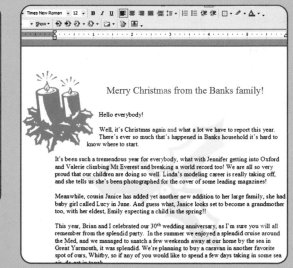

6 Now all that remains to be done is to edit your text so that it fits onto the page, then print it on a colour printer. For a more personal touch, leave the signature blank and get everyone in the family to sign each copy of the letter by hand. Then send it off to all your friends and relatives in their Christmas cards!

Creating documents

Doing that special job

DESIGNING A LETTERHEAD

Create a letterhead for your business or personal stationery.

■ **Rather than buying expensive printed stationery,** produce your own using Microsoft Word. Go to **View ➜ Header and Footer** and type your personalised letterhead into the Header box. To make a deeper header box for your letterhead, just press the Return key a few times. The more blank lines you add beneath the letterhead, the page the body text will begin. Experiment with the spacing to find a design you

like that gives your letterhead and stationery a professional feel and finish.

■ **If you run a small business,** include a brief note of the services you provide. A letterhead is an ideal opportunity to make an impression on new and existing customers, but remember to keep it short.

■ **Create the right impression.** Because your letterhead is often the first impression a client has of you, spend some time over its design. Experiment with fonts – choose something both readable and distinctive – and perhaps add an appropriate graphic of some sort.

■ **Add information at the bottom of the page.** In the Header and Footer Toolbar, click the **Switch Between Header and Footer** button. Type details such as phone, fax or e-mail in the Footer box.

▶ See also **Headers and footers look professional,** p. 116.

▶ See also **Headers and footers look professional,** p. 116.

USING THE LETTER WIZARD

Use your PC to produce business letters with a professional touch.

■ **Follow the Wizard.** Word's Letter Wizard allows you to enter certain information, such as the recipient's name, address and the current date into text windows that transfer the information to the letter. In Word, go to **Tools ➜ Letters and Mailings ➜ Letter Wizard**.

■ **Create a database of regular recipients.** Go to the **Recipient Info** tab of the Letter Wizard. Select the **Address Book** option to begin entering contacts.

■ **The Wizard can be configured** to work with preprinted stationery. For stationery with a heading created using Word's Header and Footer facility, just leave the **Pre-printed letterhead** option on the Wizard unchecked.

How to: Create a letterhead image

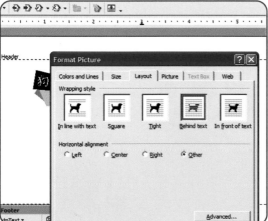

1 Open a new document. Go to **View ➜ Header and Footer**. Position your cursor in the header where you want the graphic to appear. Go to **Insert ➜ Picture** and select your graphic in the **Clip Art** or **From File** options. The graphic will be inserted.

2 Click on the image and, using the mouse pointer, drag the corners of the box to resize it. Justifying the image to the left of the screen will also justify the text, so to move your picture independently it needs to be formatted.

3 Right-click on the graphic and select **Format Picture**. Choose the **Layout** tab, choose how to arrange your graphic around the text. Experiment with this, then click **OK** to reposition the image.

Choose a style and a page design, such as Elegant, Professional or Contemporary, then click **OK** to transfer all the information to your document. The letter is now ready to accept the main body of your text.

For a one-time-only letter to a client or friend, click the **Recipient Info** tab. Insert the recipient's title and address. Add a couple of extra blank lines after the address details to create a space between the heading and the body text.

CREATE YOUR OWN BUSINESS CARD

Producing slick business cards is easier than you might think.

Make your own business cards in Word. All you need to do is buy pre-cut business card stationery and use the **Envelopes and Labels** command under **Letters and Mailings** on Word's **Tools** menu to design them to the appropriate dimensions.

Paper is important. Use good-quality card to get the best results. Avery Business Card pages are the industry standard. The Avery code number for business cards that fit ten to an A4 page is 5371 (see 'How to', right).

To give your business cards real impact, it's important to keep the main design elements simple. Do not use fancy fonts – they only make the details more difficult to read. Instead, choose a simple font, such as Arial, Avant Garde or Times New Roman, and experiment with bold, different type sizes and positioning.

Use the manual feed setting on your printer so that you can feed the pages through the machine yourself. The thicker paper will now move more easily through the printer.

Download ready-made business card templates from the Internet. Go to the Microsoft Website's Office Template Gallery (officeupdate.microsoft.com/templategallery). In the Stationery, Labels and Cards section, click on the **Business Cards** link.

Spice up your cards with Clip Art. To make your business cards stand out, you can incorporate Clip Art, WordArt or other images into your design. You may need to resize the Clip Art image to stay within the standard card size of 508 x 889 mm.

▶ See also **Making use of Clip Art,** p. 190.

MAKE YOUR CV WORK FOR YOU

Treat your curriculum vitae (CV) as a vital sales document.

Use Word's Resume Wizard to get started. Go to **File ➔ New** and click on **General Templates** in the pane that appears on the right of your document. Select the **Other Documents** tab and double-click on the **Resume Wizard**. Follow the steps onscreen to create an Elegant, Professional or Contemporary CV. The Wizard tailors the document for entry-level or other positions, and also helps you to write a suitable covering letter as well.

Keep CVs simple! For best results, resist fancy fonts and borders, and don't use a lot of colour. Don't use clip art or other graphics illustrations unless they demonstrate a skill. Avoid mixing different bullet or numbering styles, and minimise the use of bold and underline.

Don't forget that the covering letter you send out with your CV is just as important as the CV itself. It's probably the first impression the company will have of you. Don't make it too long. You can support the content of your letter by designing a letterhead for yourself.

If you want to send your CV as an e-mail attachment, check beforehand that this is OK and ask the recipient what format you should use – a Word document, for example.

▶ See also **Finding your next job on the Net,** p. 262.

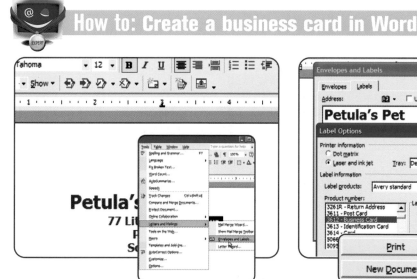

How to: Create a business card in Word

1 Enter text in a Word document as you would like it to appear on your business card. Highlight it and then go to **Tools ➔ Letters and Mailings ➔ Envelopes and Labels,** and click the **Labels** tab. Your text will now be displayed in the Address box.

2 Click **Options**. In the Label products box, select the type of label you want to use. Choose a label from the **Product number** box and click **OK**. Insert a sheet of card into the printer and click **Print** to produce a sheet of business cards, ready to be trimmed.

Stop searching for that perfect greeting card, and make your own using Word and your printer.

■ **To visualise where text and graphics will appear** on the page – and which way is up – fold a sheet of paper (in half and in half again, for example) to form the card. Mark the card 'Front', 'Back' and 'Inside' where the message will appear. Unfold the sheet and you have a layout guide.

■ **First choose the orientation of your page.** Go to **File → Page Setup** and select the **Margins** tab. Choose Portrait for top-folded cards (short and wide), or Landscape for side-folded cards (tall and thin).

■ **Because you will fold your sheet of paper** in half or into quarters, it is helpful to divide up your Word page in a similar way. To do

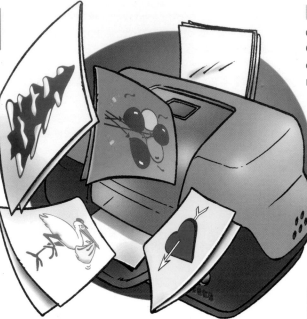

this, go to **Format → Columns**, choose **Two** and check the **Equal column width** box. Click **OK**. The horizontal ruler at the top of the page shows your new page layout. Drag each margin pointer towards the edges of the screen for more space.

■ **For more complex pages,** open a new document and go to **Table → Insert → Table**. Choose two columns and two rows, set the Fixed column width to **Auto**, and click **OK**. Word will now produce two columns that divide the page vertically. To divide it horizontally, select the table, right-click on it, then choose **Table Properties → Row**. Specify the row height you need (half your page height), and click **OK**.

■ **If you plan to paste large graphics** into your table, lock it into place to avoid the possibility of accidentally resizing it. Select the table, choose **Table → Table Properties → Table → Options**, and clear the **Automatically resize to fit contents** box.

■ **After you prepare your card layout,** select **File → Save As**, and select **Document Template** from the Save as type box. Give it a name like 'Greeting card' and it will be immediately available if you want to make other cards with the same formatting and specifications.

■ **Choose a font that is appropriate** for your message. The default Times New Roman is far too official and dull for most cards. Experiment with special effects, using either the **Format → Font** dialogue box or perhaps the WordArt option on the Drawing Toolbar.

■ **Add a graphic to your card.** If you're artistic, you can produce a graphic by using a drawing program, such as Paint, to create your own artwork. Alternatively, you can use Word's ready-made graphics. Go to **Insert → Picture → Clip Art**, and choose one of the clip art images available in Word.

■ **To reposition a clip art image,** right-click on it and go to **Format Picture → Layout**. Choose a Wrapping style other than 'In line with text' and click **OK**. You can now drag the picture to its new position on the page.

How to: Produce a greeting card in Microsoft Word

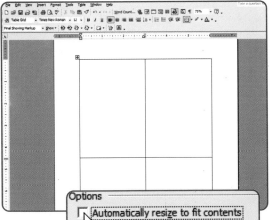

1 Go to **Table → Insert → Table**. Create a table with two rows and two columns. Drag the borders to resize the table to fill the page. Right-click on the table, select **Table Properties → Table → Options**. Uncheck the **Automatically resize to fit contents** box.

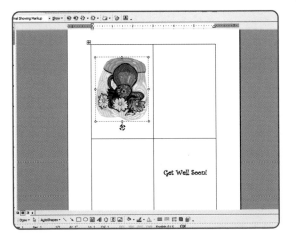

2 Type and format your message in the bottom-right corner. Insert a graphic and flip it, (see 'Seeing things from a different angle', p. 141) as the page will be folded. Paste the image into the top-left corner. Print the page and fold it to make the card.

■ **Preview your card** as you work to check its design and to avoid wasting paper on trial printouts. Go to **File ➜ Print Preview**. When you are happy with the design, print the card.

▸ See also **Drawing programs,** p. 194; and **Sending an e-greeting,** p. 318.

See also Drawing programs, p. 194; and Sending an e-greeting, p. 318.

NEWSLETTERS HELP TO CREATE A COMMUNITY

Create interesting and attractive bulletins for your community, club or church group using Word.

■ **To lay out a story in columns in Word,** go to **View ➜ Print Layout**. Then select all the text to be formatted. Click the **Columns** button on the Standard Toolbar, then click on the number of columns you want.

■ **To add visible lines between columns,** remain in Print Layout view and click in the section you want to change. Go to **Format**

➜ **Columns** and check **Line between**. Or draw lines by using the **Line** button on the Drawing Toolbar. To change the appearance, thickness or colour of the line, right-click on it, and select **Format AutoShape** from the pop-up menu. Click on the **Colors and Lines** tab and choose from the options available.

■ **To adjust column widths and spacing,** drag the column markers on the horizontal ruler. Exact column widths and spacing can be specified by going to **Format ➜ Columns** and entering your measurements in the **Widths** and **Spacing** boxes.

■ **To create a heading that spans** the columns like a newspaper, go to **Print Layout** view. Then type your heading at the beginning of the first column and press the **Enter** key. Highlight the heading text, click the **Columns** button, and select one column.

■ **'Balancing' is spreading text** in linked columns evenly between them so that the text in all the columns ends at the same point on

the page. If you are planning to insert a headline, story or picture directly below the text columns, it is important to get the columns to balance. In Print Layout view, click at the end of the columns to be balanced. Go to **Insert ➜ Break** and select **Continuous** to insert a section break at that point. Text will now be balanced equally.

■ **Download newsletter templates from the Web.** Go to the Microsoft Office, Product Updates page (officeupdate.microsoft. com/templategallery). Click on the **Template Gallery** link. Find Marketing and click on the **Newsletters** link to see a templates list. Click the Word icon next to each template for a preview. Click **Edit in Microsoft Word** to download a template and start to work with it.

■ **To get information about any new updates** and additions, click the **Get our newsletter** link on the Office Updates page.

How to: Use Word's Newsletter Wizard

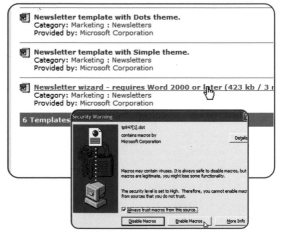

1 With the Newsletter Wizard downloaded, a security warning appears about macros. Check the **Always trust macros from this source** box, and click **Enable Macros**. The Newsletter Wizard window appears. Click the **Next** button to begin.

2 Choose a style for your newsletter by clicking, for example, **Professional**. Select Black and white or Color. Click **Next**. Enter a title, the date and the volume and issue number. Click **Next**. Choose the mailing label option you want and click **Next** again.

3 Click **Finish** to close the Wizard and view the newsletter. You can overwrite all the text, but read each section first for pointers on using the template correctly. You also have the Office Assistant to provide answers to the inevitable queries that arise as you work.

Save a created or downloaded

template file in the Templates folder so that it appears únder the General tab when you click **File ➔ New ➔ General Templates** in Word. When you save a document as a template, create a new folder for it in the Templates folder. Your folder name shows up as a new tab when you navigate to the Templates dialogue box as above.

▶ See also **Templates**, p. 112; **Publisher 2002**, p. 122; **Putting text boxes to work**, p. 129; **Columns make for easier reading**, p. 130; and **Desktop publishing**, p. 134.

TAKE THE TOIL OUT OF MAILINGS

Using Word's Mail Merge and an address database can speed up the mailing of many items.

If you already have an address

database, use it for a Word mail merge. There is no need to retype the information into a Word table if it already exists in a compatible form. You can use an existing Microsoft Word document, Excel spreadsheet, Access database or other list.

CREATING A DATABASE IN MAIL MERGE

Keep all your addresses together to use over and over again. Here's how.

1. In Step 3 of the Mail Merge Wizard, select Type a new list and click on Create to start a new address database.

2. Select **Customize** in the New Address List dialogue box, select a field and click **Delete** to remove it.

3. Add fields by clicking on **Add** and typing in a name for your field. Then click **OK**.

4. Click **Close**. The Save Address List dialogue box opens. Name and save your data file.

5. You'll now be prompted to fill in the fields on your data file. Click **Edit**. Fill in the fields and click **New Entry**.

In Windows XP the Mail Merge

Wizard gives you step-by-step instructions on how to set up a mail merge document. To use the Wizard go to **Tools ➔ Letters and Mailings ➔ Mail Merge Wizard**. A Mail Merge pane appears on the right-hand side of the window, displaying your choices for the current step of the process and a link to the next step at the bottom of the pane. Using the Wizard, you can create letters, e-mail messages, envelopes and labels.

One step at a time. At Step 1 of the

Mail Merge Wizard, select the type of document you are creating. If it's a letter or an e-mail, you can either choose to use the current document open on the screen, a template or an existing document. For a template, click the **Select template** link then choose a template from the dialogue box. Click on **Start from existing document** and the Wizard displays your existing mail merge documents. To use another document, click **Open** and locate it on your PC.

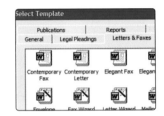

How to: Mail merge in Word

1 To send a letter, go to **Tools ➔ Letters and Mailings ➔ Mail Merge Wizard**. The Mail Merge pane appears. Select **Letters** then click **Next: Starting document**. Choose your document. Click on **Next: Select recipients**.

2 Choose from the options. If you're using your Outlook address book, select it and click on **Edit recipient list**. Check the boxes next to your chosen recipients and click **OK**. Follow the next step and write your letter.

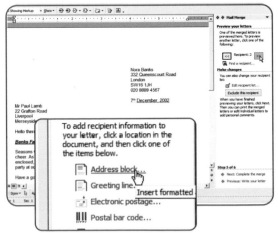

3 Place the cursor where the address will appear and select **Address block**. Make your choices in the dialogue box then click **OK**. Preview your letters in the next step, then click on **Complete the merge** then **Print**.

Preview your letters in Step 5 by clicking on the arrow boxes and scrolling through each one. Finally, complete the merge. Click **Print** to send the merge directly to the printer or **Edit individual letters** to create a new document containing all the merged letters you have created. You can review this document letter by letter and print it out as usual.

▶ See also **Building a system,** p. 164; and **Understanding how fields work,** p. 168.

A LABEL FOR EVERYTHING

With standard labels and Word, or a specialised program, you can print labels for everything, from envelopes to CDs and videotapes.

Add a finishing touch to any business letter with a professional looking printed address label. Once you've created your letter, go to **Tools ➔ Letters and Mailings ➔ Envelopes and Labels**. If the address is at the top of the letter, it will appear in the Address panel of the Labels tab.

The default print option is to print a full page of the same label. It's best to keep this option. You can always save the rest for future letters. But remember to click the **Options** button and select the correct type of labels for your print out. Otherwise, choose the **Single label** option on the Labels tab to print one copy.

Create your own labels for your CDs, DVDs and videotapes with the help of a specialised program, such as RKS Softwares' Visual Labels (www. rkssoftware.com/visual labels/overview.html), ViaPrint (www.viable software.com), or one of the numerous Avery packages (www.avery .com/software).

Need to send mail to a lot of people? Go to **Tools ➔ Letters and Mailings ➔ Mail Merge Wizard**. In Step 1, select **Labels.** In Step 2 select **Label Options** and choose your labels. In Step 3, select **Use an existing list** and click on **Browse** to locate your contacts and merge them into the labels document you have created.

If you are creating envelopes or labels at Step 2 of the Mail Merge Wizard, you can either open an existing document or change the layout of the document that is open. To do the latter, click on the **Label options** (or **Envelope options**) link. A dialogue box appears. Specify the exact size and type of envelopes or labels you are using. Click **OK** once you have made your selection and your labels or envelope will appear on screen.

The next step is to locate a list of contacts who will be receiving your letter. To create a new database of contacts see 'Create a database Mail Merge', p. 162. To use your Outlook contacts see 'How to' on p. 162. If you already have a list, select the **Use an existing list** option and click **Browse** to find the list you will be using. You can add to the list by clicking the **Edit** button. To use all the addresses in your list choose **Select All**. Alternatively, if you want to select just a few people from your list, check the boxes next to their names on the left. Click **OK**.

With your letter written, it's time to merge the letter and the addresses. Step 4 of the Mail Merge Wizard is where this occurs. Place the cursor in your document where you want the greeting line to appear and click the **Greeting line** link and scroll through the options for a style of greeting. Click the **Address block** link to insert the whole address, or choose the **More items** link to individually insert the fields of the address.

How to: Print labels in Word

1 Go to **Tools ➔ Letters and Mailings ➔ Envelopes and Labels,** and click on the **Labels** tab. Type the address in the **Address** panel. Then, in the Print section, choose either **Full page of the same label** or **Single label.**

2 Click the **Options** button and in the **Label products** drop-down menu select the make of label. In the **Product number box**, select the correct type of label. If the label isn't listed, click on **New Label** and create a label sheet to any specification. Click **OK**, then **Print.**

Building a system

Databases are specialised programs that store collections of related information. While you can use a spreadsheet program to create a table – a 'flat file' database – dedicated databases are more flexible. You can create multiple tables that let you define and extract data.

DESIGNING YOUR DATABASE

So how do you go about creating your own database – for example, if you want to organise an antique car club? You can use Microsoft Access to store membership details in table form. No matter what information you decide to add later, details specific to club members will only be held in this table. This way, you'll avoid duplication – and if details change, you only need to go to one place to modify them.

Create your first table. Start the Access program. Click on **Blank Database** under New. You'll be asked for a file name.

Type in 'Club', for example, and then click **Create**. A database window displays all the available options. Double-click on **Create table in Design view**, and you are now ready to get started on your design.

Use the table to store records. You can set up a table with each record giving details of an individual club member. A record is the electronic equivalent of a single card in an index card box. Each record in the table contains fields used to store facts about each club member. Each field has a designated data type, too.

Access supports data types such as Text, Number and Date so that information can be stored efficiently. The data type that you select also affects the kind of operations that can be performed on the data involved. For example, mathematical calculations may be carried out on data stored in Number fields, but not on data stored in Text fields.

For relational databases, Access needs to identify each data record uniquely. Because of this, you need to designate a Primary Key. If you decided to make the Primary Key the member's last name, there would be no guarantee that there wouldn't be two members with the same name. So include a field called Membership Number and select **AutoNumber** in the Data Type box. Access then generates a membership number – starting from the number 1 – for each member added to the database. Right-click on Membership Number and select **Primary Key** from the menu to set the field as the one with the unique identification of a membership record.

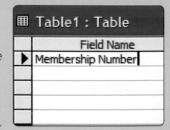

RELATIONAL DATABASES

When databases are cross-referenced, you get speedy and efficient access to information. Relationships between tables become defined when a record from one table refers to a record from another. Here's an example:

If your car club teaches classes, create three separate tables which can all be related.

Courses table lists all the courses that the club makes available to members.

Members table lists people signed up for the various classes offered throughout the year.

Attendance table lists people who have attended specific classes, plus dates.

Now define a relationship between them:

If Bruce Layman attends an engine rebuilding class on 3 August 2002, a record in the Attendance table would show the date. In the member's table there would be a reference to Bruce's record, and in the Courses table a reference to the engine rebuilding class. When a member is listed on the Attendance table, the Primary Key of a record in the Members table is referenced.

With your fields designed, Access displays your table and field headings, and you can now start entering data. From now on, the Membership Number field is automatically generated whenever you enter a record for a new member. When you have created all the fields that you need in your database, click **Done**.

DESIGNING FORMS

Forms are screens that you design to display and enter data from tables. To create a new form, go back to the Club database window, click on the **Forms** button located on the left, and then double-click **Create form by using wizard** in the dialogue box. Start by selecting all the fields that you wish to include in your form, then select a columnar format for the form.

> Create form in Design view
> Create form by using wizard
>
> The wizard asks you questions and creates a form based on your answers.

Experiment with the different options available in the Wizard and view the various

results that can be achieved. Once your form is displayed, use it to enter data and move backward and forward through the records in the table with the video-style navigation buttons.

EXTRACTING INFORMATION

One of the most powerful database features is the ability to extract information based on specific criteria – for example, you may want to pull out a list of all your members who live in a certain neighbourhood or celebrate their birthdays in February. In Access, this is known as a query. Once a query has been created, it can be redisplayed at any time to view the latest results based on current information collected and contained in the tables.

To generate a query, click on **Queries** in the main database window, then double-click the **Wizard** option. First, you'll be asked which of the fields from your table you wish to see included in the query results. In the next window, select **Modify the query design**, then

Finish. Now specify criteria for each field in your table – for example, you want to find all the members of your car club who were born after 1960. Scroll across to the date of birth field and type '>1/1/1960' into the criteria box. To see a set of matching records, click on the **!** Toolbar button.

> Create query by using wizard
> Table 1 Query

▶ See also **Access: Microsoft's database program**, p. 167 and **Creating a record**, p. 168.

How to: Import data from Excel

1 **Open Access and create a new database. Go to File → Get External Data → Import.** In the Import window, select **Microsoft Excel** from the **Files of type** menu. Select an Excel file, click **Import** and the Import Spreadsheet Wizard will start up automatically.

2 **If your spreadsheet contains column headings, they will be used as the names of** the fields in your new table. Decide if you want the new information to be used to create a new table, or if you'd like the program to insert the data into an existing table instead.

3 **You can now change the Field Name if you want to. Access also suggests you add a** column for primary keys as an identification for each row. Once you've answered all the Wizard's questions, click **Finish** and your data will now form part of your Access database.

Organising your data

Databases

WORKING WITH FILEMAKER PRO

Need a database? This powerful, but easy-to-use program has several advantages over other databases.

■ **FileMaker Pro has intuitive layout tools** and logical relational features and file lookup procedures. It offers a sophisticated database interface that a beginner will find easy to use while providing advanced functions for experienced users. You can share files with other PC users and colleagues who use Macs.

■ **If you already have a database** in Excel, Works or a text file (with tabs or commas separating the data fields), you don't have to start all over again. FileMaker Pro will make converting existing databases easy (see 'How to', below).

■ **A number of preset templates** can help you to organise your information in a variety of ways. Create and print your own business cards, an inventory of your valuables, or even a set of recipe cards. A database can also help you to keep tabs on your growing book, video or CD collection.

■ **Customise the data input panels in FileMaker** by using the Layout Assistant, which guides you through a series of options. Choose and rename the fields you want to use, but try to keep them as simple as possible and avoid any unnecessary fields.

■ **Want to scan through your records?** You don't have to scroll through the records one at a time in Form view. Choose **View → View as Table** to display all your records together in a grid.

■ **FileMaker Pro saves your work automatically** without prompting, so think twice before making any sweeping changes to your records, especially deleting. Deleting a record completely removes it from your database.

How to: Convert an Excel worksheet into a FileMaker Pro file

1 Create or open the document you wish to convert in Microsoft Excel and save it as an Excel Workbook as usual.

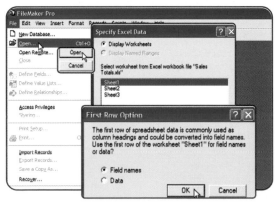

2 Launch FileMaker Pro and click **Open**. Go to the location where the Excel Workbook you previously saved is stored, highlight it, and click **Open**. Select your preferred options from the two dialogue boxes that appear, and when you are satisfied click **OK**.

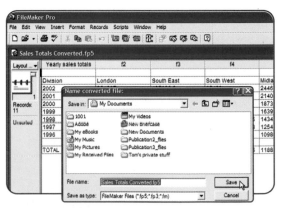

3 You will be asked to choose a name for the converted file, and to specify a file type. When you have completed this operation the document will open in FileMaker. You can re-format the cells in the new document to display the data the way you want it.

FileMaker Pro 6 has two ways to access commands: pressing buttons on the Toolbars (which can be customised) and context menus, which include only options valid for the selected item. To display a context menu, position the mouse pointer over an object or data, and press the right mouse button. The type of object and the mode you are in determines which menu appears.

▸ See also **Building a system,** p. 164.

ACCESS: MICROSOFT'S DATABASE PROGRAM

Organise and summarise information on anything from wedding lists to record collections.

Microsoft Access is a database manager. Feed it a mass of related information, such as your record collection, or details of your household bills, and it will help you to organise it in any way you want. The database enables you to easily extract the exact information you need, such as which bills haven't been paid yet this month. You can choose from a variety of printed reports to summarise your data.

Don't be put off! Beginners to Access are often frightened off by its apparent complexity, but there's no need to panic. All the information in your database appears as a grid and you can extract any data you want using the Query feature. For instance, if you have a database of your record collection, you could run a query to search for Beatles albums from the 1960s.

For simple tasks, such as finding one particular record, go to **Edit ➔ Find.** Enter the details of the required search, and Access will locate the matching records for you.

Reorganise your data. You can sort the entire contents of your database alphabetically, by any of your database's fields. For instance, in an address database, click on a last name entry, go

KEY TERMS IN ACCESS
What the keywords mean.

Record   All the information in the database for one event or person.

Datasheet   A view of the records and fields in a database displayed in a row and column format.

Query   A way of extracting a selected portion of the information in the database.

Form   A format that makes it easy to view or enter the information in an individual record.

Report   Presents some or all of the information in a database in a format that can be printed.

to **Records ➔ Sort,** then **Sort Ascending** or **Sort Descending.** To retain the new order after sorting, close the table and click **OK** when the prompt asks if you want to save the changes.

Learning how to use Queries gives you much more power, enabling you to easily group and sort data. You can speed up the way that a query runs by setting the **Indexed** property of a field to **Yes.** Open your database, go to **View ➔ Design View** and click on the field you want to index. In the Field Properties section at the bottom of the screen, click next to **Indexed** and specify the indexed property you need.

General	Lookup	
Field Size		255
Format		
Input Mask		
Caption		
Default Value		
Validation Rule		
Validation Text		
Required		No
Allow Zero Length		Yes
Indexed		Yes (Duplicates OK)
Unicode Compression		No
IME Mode		No Control

Once you've seen how much faster a Query runs on an indexed field, it's

tempting to index them all – but don't do it! Each index you create will be updated every time you alter the database, and too many can actually reduce your overall performance. Use indexes sparingly, and then only on frequently used fields where you'll see the most gain.

Automation saves time and typing. Like the other programs in the Microsoft Office suite, Access can run Macros to automate your work. They are great time savers, but beware of the potential dangers. Many viruses have been written that exploit the Macro mechanism to infect your system. If someone sends you an MDB (Microsoft Database) file, make sure you scan it with an antivirus program, just as you would any other Internet download.

It's easy to edit data in Microsoft Access. However, that's not always a good thing, especially if you're setting up a system where you want users to be able to view information, but not change it. In situations like that, one good solution is to design forms to display the information you need, and set the form's **Allow Edits** property to **No.**

A tool like the Database Splitter can be useful if you have several people who want to access the same database, such as household finances, for example. The splitter separates the data itself from the forms and

queries, meaning that each user can work with the data in their own way. Wizards and tools like the Database Splitter are not installed by default with Access, so you may need to have your Office CD handy when you want to use them.

Even if you install every option available on the Access installation disk, you will still need to update your files as Microsoft fixes errors and makes new features available. Go

to **Start ➜ All Programs ➜ Windows Update** and click on **Office Update** at the top of the screen to check if your machine needs any updates.

If you have technical problems, the
Microsoft support site (support.microsoft.com/support/access) should be your first place to look. But don't wait until things go wrong before you visit – it has lots of useful tutorials and articles.

Plenty of Websites provide advice
for users as well as tips and tricks. Try the Access FAQ site at www.mvps.org/access/, for example.

▶ See also **Building a system,** p. 164.

RECORDS KEYBOARD SHORTCUTS

Speed your progress when working with Access 2000 databases.

Ctrl + +	Adds a new record.
Ctrl + –	Deletes a record.
Ctrl + ;	Inserts today's date.
Shift + **Enter**	Saves the current record.
Ctrl + '	Inserts the data from the same field in previous record.

CREATING A RECORD

Records are one of the basic building blocks of a database program such as Microsoft Access.

What exactly is a record? It can be
compared to a file card with an address or recipe on it. It's a collection of data – called fields or cells – that have structured content. The type of entry that goes into each field or cell is clearly defined, like a date, name or postcode. When information is entered into the fields, the record can be saved into a database file.

Use record validation to protect the
integrity of the database. Validation checks that a record meets specific requirements before it is saved to the database file. This is why some data entry screens will only let you enter certain data in particular ways. For example, validation will check that you've entered a date of birth in the correct format, and that the date is consistent with other fields already in the record; for example, a date of birth cannot be later than a date of marriage.

Make sure you protect your records by only allowing authorised people to
edit and delete information. If you share your database, allow others to look at the information (read-only access), but control their access by ensuring that their log-on identity doesn't

authorise them to make changes. To set these options in Access, go to **Tools ➜ Security ➜ User and Group Permissions**.

Records are normally listed in the order in which they were entered. This order
may need to be changed, however. You might, for example, want to see all of your contacts listed together according to their last name. To do this, click on the **Lastname** field and click the **Sort Ascending** button on the Toolbar.

Want to work with a subset of your records? Perhaps only contacts who live
in Wales? To do this in Access, locate a record where the country is Wales, select the 'Wales' text and then go to **Records ➜ Filter ➜ Filter by Selection**. Access shows only the records matching the filter. To view all the records again, go to **Records ➜ Remove Filter/Sort**.

Microsoft Excel also uses database records. A table in MS Excel –
such as an address or phone number list – can be thought of as a database where the rows are

B	C	D	
First Name	Last name	House No.	Str
Julia	Lishen	34	Gru
Frank	Yedley	54A	Trir
Graham	Humpstone	Duntypin	Gro
Lemuel	Gulliver	38	Lilli
Sam	Weller	774	Pic
Miranda	Scott	Holme Lea	Cha

records and the columns are fields. The first row (or record) will generally be used for headings or labels to identify the field names.

▶ See also **Building a system,** p. 164; **Access: Microsoft's database program,** p. 167; **Presenting your data,** p. 170; and **Excel: Microsoft's spreadsheet program,** p. 177.

UNDERSTANDING FIELDS

Fields are another building block of a database, and understanding how they work is vital.

Know the difference between records and fields. At the heart of every
Access database is a collection of tables. Each row of the table is called a record, and contains all the details for a particular entry in the database, such as a single person in your Address Book. Every

row is made up of a number of boxes, or fields, each containing one aspect of that record, such as a name or a phone number.

■ **Building your own fields** gives you the most control over your database (see 'How to', below), but if you're not confident about setting up a database from scratch, Access offers the Table Wizard to guide you through the process. To

open the Wizard, open and name a new project. then click on **Tables**, then **New** and finally **Table Wizard** in the dialogue box that appears.

■ **Don't forget the field properties!** To prevent people from entering inappropriate data into your database, define a requirement for each field in the **Validation Rule** box of the General Field Properties at the bottom of the screen. Entering '>0 and <36' would limit numeric values

to between 1 and 35, while '>=#1/1/2003#' would prevent the form from accepting dates prior to 1 January 2003. You could also set up a rule to ensure e-mail addresses have the correct format, for example.

■ **Give each field a name.** Before creating your fields, it is important to spend time making sure that the labels you give clearly define the information that the field will contain. For example, in an order processing system, Date would be a poor choice for a field name, since it could refer to the date the order was taken, the scheduled delivery date or the actual delivery date of the goods.

■ **Make a field compulsory** by setting its Required property to **Yes**. This is the way to ensure that vital pieces of information aren't missed out when someone completes a form. An example would be Last

Name in a Contacts Database, or National Insurance number in a set of Employee records.

▸ See also **Building a system,** p. 164; and **Access: Microsoft's database program,** p. 167.

How to: Set up fields in Access

1 To create a contacts database, open Access and select **Blank Database**. In the task pane on the right, name your file, then select **Create table in Design view**. In the first cell, type 'ContactID'. Add the rest of your field names below.

2 In the Data Type column, click on the arrow next to **Text** to choose the option that best fits the information to be entered there. A Text field allows the greatest flexibility. To give each record a unique number, choose **AutoNumber** for the ContactID field.

3 If the field names are obvious, leave the right-hand field blank. Pick a primary key – the field used to check that a record is unique. Right-click on **ContactID** and select **Primary Key**. Save your table then go to **View ➜ Datasheet View** to enter information.

Presenting your data

Many people think spreadsheets are just for number crunching. While spreadsheets have many complex mathematical formulas built in, and can race through jobs that might take hours to do with a calculator and paper, they have potential far beyond simply manipulating figures.

SPREADSHEET BASICS

Spreadsheets arrange their information in rows and columns.

These can be sorted in any way you choose, making it easy to see the same information from different perspectives. You can employ different

WHICH SPREADSHEET?

Several spreadsheets come as part of full office suites, and it's likely one of these came with your PC.

EXCEL (www.microsoft.com/office)
Part of Microsoft Office, this is by far the most popular spreadsheet for business.

QUATTRO PRO (www.corel.com)
Comes as part of WordPerfect Office.

LOTUS 1-2-3 (www.lotus.com)
1-2-3 is part of the SmartSuite office suite.

MICROSOFT WORKS (works.msn.com)
Comes as part of the Works suite of applications. The spreadsheet component is not as capable as Excel, being aimed at home users. Works contains plenty of template spreadsheets ready for your data.

SHAREWARE
You can also find shareware spreadsheets and calculation programs on the Web. Search sites like www.tucows.com and www.jumbo.com to see what is available.

fonts and colours in a spreadsheet, and even import graphics. These kinds of features make spreadsheets ideal for jobs like keeping a family calendar, planning a garden maintenance schedule, or organising information for a holiday trip. Think creatively about your spreadsheet and it could become a vital companion.

Most spreadsheets share a set of basic conventions

when it comes to moving data around and entering it. In most cases you can move between cells using the Tab key. You will be able to align the contents of a cell or group of cells so that, for example, decimal points are centred or text is flush to the left or right of a cell. Don't forget your right mouse button either. It usually provides access to cut, copy and other frequently used features.

Working with groups of cells.

Often you need to move a group of cells, or apply formatting, such as a colour, alignment or font style change to a group. Most spreadsheets allow you to select a group by dragging the mouse cursor across your selection. Then you can make changes to all the cells at once.

Use data types.

Spreadsheets have different types of cells and can automatically format information in them as you enter it. Two useful formats are Number, which can set figures to a decimal place, and Date, which can make the look of a date consistent across your spreadsheet.

Recalculate in a second.

One of the most useful things about spreadsheets is that once you've set them up, you can easily try various alternatives. As soon as you change a number in one cell, the spreadsheet recalculates every formula that uses the cell in an instant.

MATHS MATTERS

Spreadsheets can do very complex maths

on your behalf, but you don't need to understand it. You do need to learn how to enter formulas accurately, but generally this is clearly explained in the software's Help section. The basics of how formulas work and how to input them are fairly straightforward.

In Microsoft Excel, for example,

to add the numbers from rows 2 to 7 in column C, the formula is '=SUM(C2:C7)'. The '=' sign tells the software you are using a formula. SUM indicates it is a simple adding job. The letters and numbers inside the brackets indicate the range of cells to be added up. Excel highlights these on-screen when you double-click on the formula cell so that you can check the formula. The ':' symbol indicates that you want to add up all the cells between – and including – the two you name.

SMART AND EASY TO READ

Spreadsheets are excellent for making calculations based on different scenarios. A spreadsheet will rapidly calculate repayments of loans at different interest rates, or work out how your savings will grow if you save different amounts over a set period. You can design a simple spreadsheet in which you enter one value in a cell and the calculation is completed automatically. Note that cutting and pasting formulas is much quicker and easier than constantly retyping them.

A spreadsheet can become so packed with data that it is difficult to interpret the information it contains. If this happens, try using colour in the cells to highlight sections, or try changing the font size and style to emphasise important details that you want to stand out.

Many spreadsheets include the ability to draw graphs. This can be a really useful way to create a visual representation of a set of numbers, because it is often easier for people to grasp the meaning of a graph than it is to interpret rows and columns of numbers.

Why limit your use of spreadsheets to just maths?
Because they are so good at structuring data, allow you to use colour and sort and re-sort information in different ways, spreadsheets are great for inventories such as book lists and record collections.

Sometimes spreadsheets are a nuisance to print, when one or two rows or columns spill over to a separate sheet of paper. To solve the problem, try changing the paper orientation from portrait to landscape in **Page Setup**. Many spreadsheets also have a **Fit to page** option in their printing controls, which reduces a spreadsheet so that it prints on a single page.

▶ See also **The humble cell**, p. 172; **Columns in spreadsheets**, p. 172; **Excel: Microsoft's spreadsheet program**, p. 177.

How to: Set up an Excel spreadsheet

1 Go to **Start → All Programs → Microsoft Excel**. To see how an investment grows at various interest rates over three years, click in cell A1 and type in the amount you have to invest, then enter the appropriate column headings in cells A3 to D3.

2 In cell A5, enter an interest rate. In cell B5, enter the formula to calculate the interest earned in one year =A1*(1+A5/100). In cell C5 enter the formula =(A1*(1+A5/100)^2), and in cell D5 the formula =(A1*(1+A5/100)^3).

3 Use the same formulas in subsequent rows, replacing A5 with A6, A7 and so on each time. To add a pound sign, highlight the cells and go to **Format → Cells → Number**. Select **Currency** in the Category section. Select the **£ English** symbol and 0 decimal places.

Spreadsheets

COLUMNS IN SPREADSHEETS

An appreciation of columns is important if your spreadsheet design is going to be effective.

■ **Select a column by clicking** its letter heading. For example, click on **A** to select column A, or **C** to select Column C, and so on.

■ **Beware of the AutoSum feature in the Toolbar.** Clicking the **AutoSum** button adds up all the numbers in a highlighted column, including any subtotals. This means, for example, that a sum of 2 + 2 = 4 in the column will give an AutoSum of 8 for the whole column. If you don't want subtotals included in your sums, put them into an adjacent column so they're not included in the Autosum.

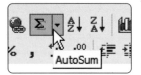

■ **To change the width of a column,** just click-and-drag the right border of the column header. You can also set the width of a column or columns to a specific number of characters. Go to **Format ➜ Column ➜ Width** and type in the number of characters you need.

■ **If your column is not wide enough** to display the entry you have input, then the quickest way to accommodate wide or narrow data cells is to double-click on the right border of that column heading. This process will expand or shrink the column so that it is just wide enough to hold exactly the required information.

■ **Select several columns at once.** Click on one column, then hold down **Shift** and click on another column. The new column and all columns in between are highlighted. Or click on one column, hold down the **Ctrl** key and click another column to add it to your selection.

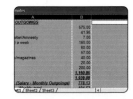

■ **You can hide a column** by dragging the right border of its column heading over the left border, effectively reducing the column width to zero. Or you can hide one or more columns by selecting it then going to **Format ➜ Column** and selecting **Hide**. To show the hidden column simply drag it out again or use the Unhide option. Select the column to the left and the column to the right of the hidden column. Then go to **Format ➜ Column ➜ Unhide**.

■ **When sorting columns,** always make a copy of the worksheet, or save it first so you can revert to the previous version if you make a

FORGOTTEN YOUR CELL FORMATS?

These options are available from the Format Cells menu when you right-click in a cell or block of cells.

Number Set the style for comma separation and decimal places, as well as styles for the appearance of currency, date, time and positive/negative numbers.

Alignment As well as centring and left/right aligning your text and numbers, you can rotate the contents of cells to any angle.

Font All the usual options for changing the font, style, size and underline colour.

Border Add thick, thin, dotted or dashed borders to your cells to highlight certain areas of your worksheet.

Patterns Add coloured or patterned backgrounds to selected cells for added impact and to help to define important elements and key cells.

Protection Decide which of the cells in your document can be changed when worksheet protection is enabled.

mistake. Highlight all the rows and columns you want to sort, excluding any header titles at the top. Accidentally omitting or including columns and rows can ruin hours of data entry work! Go to **Data ➜ Sort**, select your sort criteria and click **OK**.

▶ See also **Presenting your data,** p. 170; and **Excel: Microsoft's spreadsheet program,** p. 177.

THE HUMBLE CELL

Cells are the basic building blocks of every type of spreadsheet.

■ **Prepare a rough outline of your spreadsheet** on paper before beginning to format your cells. The Format options are important for presentation, and organising them beforehand will give you a feel for how the completed spreadsheet will look. You can use the Zoom option on the View menu to adjust the final layout of the document to suit your screen and working preferences.

■ **You can ask Excel to change the format of a cell** in particular circumstances. Highlight the cells that will be affected, go to the **Format** menu and select **Conditional Formatting**. In the dialogue box that appears, define the condition to be used to apply formatting. For example, if you wanted every value over 2,000 to be displayed in another colour, enter the condition **Cell value is** and **Greater than** and **2,000** in the boxes. Now click **Format** and set the font attributes.

■ **Make sure you format cells correctly.** Any cells intended to hold dates, numbers or currency must be properly formatted to show their values correctly. Highlight all the cells with data of the same type, right-click on the selection and select **Format Cells**. Click the **Number** tab and specify the type of data that will be entered into the cells and the format in which you want it displayed.

■ Protect the cells from accidental change.

Once you've got your worksheet looking and working the way you want it to, go to **Tools ➔ Protection ➔ Protect sheet**. Before you protect the worksheet, remember to unlock the cells you want to be able to enter data into. To do this, first highlight the cells, right-click, and then select **Format ➔ Cells Protection**. Uncheck the **Locked** box to enable data entry.

NAMING CELLS

A spreadsheet program like Excel allows you to give proper names to a cell or a range of cells to make navigation and formula calculation easier.

■ The Name Box is the drop-down box

directly under the Toolbar that shows the current cell address. On a new worksheet this will always read A1. If you want to give the cell a

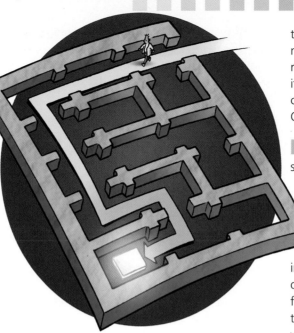

label, click in the Name Box and type the name. Press **Enter** and the name will be entered on the drop-down list so you can go back to it easily.

■ A cell name cannot include spaces,

so if you want to name a cell Total Outgoings you must enter it as TotalOutgoings. This name will then be used as the reference for

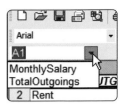

the cell on the drop-down name list. It's worth remembering this, because it's the standard naming convention for all Microsoft Office products.

■ Name your ranges.

Named ranges will simplify the look of formulas you create, and they will make your worksheets easier for other people to understand if they have to work on them as well (see also p. 180). To name a range, highlight the cells in the range and type a name into the Name Box. For instance, if you have a column of figures tracking outgoing costs, instead of an unwieldy cell-based formula such as =SUM(B12:B36), you could name the B12:B36 range 'TotalOutgoings'. Your formula would now read: =SUM(TotalOutgoings).

■ Cell names use absolute cell addresses.

This means that if you copy a formula containing a certain name into other cells on your worksheet, the name will always refer to the original, named cells. Perhaps most important of all, remember that this will affect the way your formulas work and could completely mess up all your careful calculations!

How to: Add borders to your cells

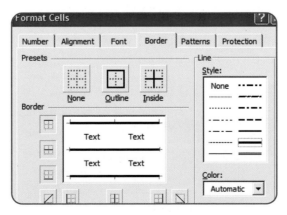

1 Open the Excel spreadsheet you wish to work on, and highlight the area that you want to enhance with a border. Right-click and select **Format Cells** from the pop-up menu that appears. Click on the **Border** tab.

2 Choose the style you want in the **Line** window, and then click on the **Border** preview panel to show where you want your lines to go. In this example, thick horizontal lines will be used to separate the text entries.

3 Click **OK** to apply the design to your worksheet. If you decide that you don't like it, simply press **Ctrl+Z** to undo the changes and go back and try another style.

Avoid confusion. Check the exact cells covered by a Cell Name. Go to **Insert → Name → Define**. A dialogue box appears listing all of the named cells in your workbook. Highlight the name that you want to investigate, then look in the box at the bottom of the window labelled 'Refers to'. The exact cell range covered by the name will be displayed there. You can now edit or even delete the range, if you want to.

▶ See also **Excel: Microsoft's spreadsheet program,** p. 177.

AUTOFILL ABOLISHES BOREDOM

Say goodbye to dull, repetitive tasks. Use AutoFill to save time when preparing your spreadsheets.

Fill a range of cells with the same value. Select the cell containing the value you want to copy. In the lower right-hand corner of the cell you will see a black square called the fill handle. Place your cursor over the fill handle and it will turn into a black cross. Drag the fill handle over the empty cells to be automatically filled and release the mouse button. The original value is then copied into all of the cells you selected.

Use AutoFill to create a series of numbers. Select the first cell in the range that you want to fill and enter the starting value for the series – 15, for example. To increment the series by a specified amount, such as 10, select the next cell in the range and enter the next item in the series – in this case 25. Now select both cells and point the cursor at the lower right corner of the second cell. Drag the fill handle over the range you want to fill. Drag down or to the right to fill in the ascending order, and up or to the left to complete the descending values.

Make a quick list of days or months. Enter the first day (e.g. Monday) or month (e.g. January) of your list into a cell, then drag the fill handle. AutoFill automatically adds

	A
1	January
2	February
3	March
4	April
5	May
6	June
7	July
8	August

consecutive days or months. It also recognises abbreviations for days and months, like Sun, Mon or Jan, Feb and so on. As well as numbers, months and days, Autofill will also generate series involving dates and quarters.

Save time with keyboard shortcuts. To quickly fill in the active cell with the contents of the cell above it, press **Ctrl+D.** To

fill it in with the contents of the cell to the left, press **Ctrl+R.** To enter the same data into several cells at once, select the cells, type the data and press **Ctrl+Enter.**

Right button drag to choose your Autofill. To specify the type of fill series, use the right mouse button to drag the fill handle over the range, release the button, then click the

How to: Create a custom fill series

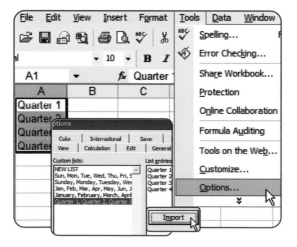

1 You can create your own AutoFill by entering the list of items you want to use as a series on a worksheet and selecting them.

2 Go to the **Tools** menu, click **Options,** and then click the **Custom Lists** tab. To use the selected list, click **Import,** then **OK.**

3 Now enter any item from your new AutoFill list and, holding the right mouse button down, drag the handle to complete the series.

appropriate command on the shortcut menu. For example, if the starting value is Jan-2003, click **Fill Months** for the series Feb-2003 and so on; or click **Fill Years** for the series Jan-2004 and so on.

■ **Can't find the fill handle?** The fill handle can disappear if you have turned off Excel's drag-and-drop editing feature. To turn it back on, go to **Tools ➜ Options** and select the **Edit** tab. Make sure the Settings box is checked for **Allow cell drag and drop**. Try AutoFill again, and the fill handle should be visible.

AUTOFORMAT FOR INSTANT TABLES

Tired of seeing everything in black and white? Create great-looking tables and charts instantly.

■ **Make your Excel tables stand out.** Select the table you want to format and click **Format ➜ AutoFormat**. Choose the style that you prefer from the list that appears – such as Colorful, or 3D Effects – and click **OK**. Excel now formats the selected table in your chosen style.

■ **Pick and choose.** You can customise the AutoFormat features to suit you. As before, go to **Format ➜ AutoFormat** and select your style, but then click **Options**. Clear the check boxes to remove any of the AutoFormat elements you don't want – such as Font, Patterns or Border. When you're satisfied with your choices, click **OK** to format the table.

■ **Quickly remove all formatting from a table.** You can use AutoFormat to remove borders, colours and other styles you have applied to a table, even if you didn't use AutoFormat in the first place. Select the range of cells you want to remove all the formatting from, and go to **Format ➜ AutoFormat**. Select **None** from the list and click **OK**. The selected cells will be stripped of all formatting, leaving a basic table.

■ **To quickly format charts with Excel,** store your favourite chart styles as user-defined AutoFormats. First, open or create a chart with the desired formatting options (see 'How to'

p. 179). Click the chart you want to save as a custom chart type. Go to the **Chart** menu and select **Chart type**. Click the **Custom Types** tab, select the **User Defined** box and click the **Add** button. In the Add Custom Chart Type dialogue box, enter a name and description for the new chart, then click **OK**. To apply the format to a chart you have just created, click on the chart, then go to **Chart ➜**

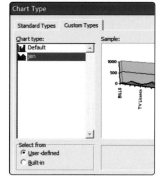

Chart Types, select the **User-defined** box, select your custom-made chart type from the list and click **OK**. Your current chart will now be formatted in the style you previously defined.

ARITHMETIC MADE EASY WITH AUTOSUM

One handy button makes tricky home finance arithmetic easy.

■ **Quickly add a row or column of figures.** Select the cell you want to insert the sum into. Try to choose a cell at the end of a row or column of data, because this will help

AUTO-ADVICE

Confused by the different Auto functions in Excel? Here's a summary.

● **AutoFill** Creates or completes a series of values in an Excel spreadsheet.

● **AutoFormat** Adds chosen attributes to your spreadsheet, such as Fonts, Borders and a range of numerical styles.

● **AutoSum** Adds up a column, row or several sets of figures in a spreadsheet.

AutoSum to guess which cells you want added together. Click the **AutoSum** button on the Toolbar, marked Σ, and AutoSum inserts =SUM, and the range address of the cells to the left of or above the selected cell. To change this selection, drag over the range you want to use, or click in the Formula bar and type in the cell range formula. Press **Enter** and Excel will then calculate the total for the selected range.

■ **Microsoft Works also has an AutoSum button,** but it doesn't work in quite the same way as it does in Excel. The instructions here are for Excel users, so if you are using Works, consult the help file for an explanation of the differences.

■ **AutoSum is not a mind reader.** Always double check the formula that Excel writes when you press the AutoSum button. Make absolutely certain that the cells included are the ones you had in mind.

■ **Use AutoSum to calculate grand totals.** If your worksheet contains several lists of figures, all in the same row or column, and you have calculated the subtotals using AutoSum or your own formulas, you can create a grand total for the values. Select all the lists together, along with a blank cell to insert the grand total into. Click on the AutoSum button and, instead of totalling the whole list, Excel will add up just the subtotals.

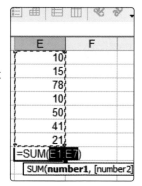

■ **Take a keyboard shortcut.** Pressing **Alt+=** will perform exactly the same function as clicking on the AutoSum button on your Toolbar.

■ **Save time creating daily or weekly totals.** Use AutoSum to add up several lists of figures simultaneously. For example, if you have a column for each day's expenditure, there's no need to add each column individually by copying and pasting the formula. Instead, you can select the row of blank cells that the totals are to be inserted into and click on **AutoSum**. Excel will add the columns automatically and insert each total in the row you've selected, so you don't have to press Enter each time.

Can't find the AutoSum button? It is
normally located on the standard Excel Toolbar. However, if you can't see it, click on **View** ➜ **Toolbars** and make sure there is a check next to **Standard** to ensure the normal Toolbar is visible. Still can't see the AutoSum button? Try clicking on **Tools** ➜ **Customize**. Select the **Commands** tab and click on the **Insert** category. Scroll down the right panel to find the AutoSum button. Now simply click and drag it to wherever you want it on the Excel Toolbar at the top of your screen, then click **Close** to close the dialogue box.

▶ See also **The humble cell**, p. 172; **Excel: Microsoft's spreadsheet program**, p. 177; and **How to write formulas**, p. 180.

LEARNING TO WORK WITH NUMBERS

How to adjust decimal places, currency, dates and other number formats in your spreadsheet.

When you are entering figures into
an Excel spreadsheet take care to format them correctly. Otherwise, amounts such as 3.45 will display correctly, but 3.40 will display as 3.4, which can cause confusion if it refers to a currency amount.

To format cells to display two decimal places, select the spreadsheet cells,
go to **Format** ➜ **Cells**, and click the **Number** tab. Select **Number** in the Category list and make sure that a '2' appears in the Decimal places box. If you want to use a comma as a marker for thousands (£1,000), check the **Use 1000 Separator** box; otherwise, leave it unchecked.

To arrange a column of figures so
the decimal points all line up, first select the column by clicking on the column header. Then go to **Format** ➜ **Cells**, click on the **Number** tab, and select **Accounting** in the list of categories.

You can add pound signs to each numeric entry (which will also be lined up) by selecting them in the Symbol window.

To display the pound sign, select the
cells to format, go to **Format** ➜ **Cells**, and select the **Number** tab. Click **Currency**. In the Symbol window, select **£ English (United Kingdom)**.

Excel allows you to display all common currency symbols (provided they are available in the font you are using). With the latest version of Excel you can also insert the Euro sign.

Apply customised number formats
by typing in a formula. To display 'Surplus' next to positive values and 'Deficit' next to negative values, for example, select the cells to be formatted, go to **Format** ➜ **Cells**, and click the **Number** tab and scroll down to select **Custom** in

FORMAT SPECIFIC AMOUNTS
Want to know when you're in the red? Here's how you do it.

1. Select the cell representing your total and go to **Format** ➜ **Conditional Formatting**.

2. In the first panel of the dialogue box select **Cell Value Is**. In the second panel select **less than or equal to**. In the third panel type '0' and click **Format**.

3. Now select **Font**, click the arrow on the **Color** box, and select the red square. Click **OK**, and in the Conditional Formatting dialogue box, click **OK** again.

4. Now, when the sum of that cell is zero or less, the cell will turn red, notifying you that the account is overdrawn.

the Category box. In the Type window, carefully type in £0.00 'Surplus' £-0.00 'Deficit'. Include a space after £0.00. Spaces typed in the formula will show up as spaces on the spreadsheet, as will characters such as $, +, -, =, /, ! and &. In the Type box, several common formats for custom numbers are shown. Experiment with some of them to discover exactly what it is they do.

Special formatting can be applied
to a single cell. For example, you might only want the total of a list to have a pound sign. To do this, right-click on the cell containing the total figure. From the pop-up menu, select **Format Cells** ➜ **Number**. Select **Currency** under Category. Click the arrow next to the Symbol box and select **£ English (United Kingdom)**.

Format cells that contain phone numbers. Excel will format some UK phone
numbers. Go to **Format** ➜ **Cells** ➜ **Number**. In the Category box choose **Special** and in the Type box select **Phone Number**. Click on the arrow at the side of the Locale (location) box and scroll down to select **English (United Kingdom)**. This will format the cell so that if you enter a phone number as a string of digits (for example, 01274783637) Excel will automatically display it as 01274 783637. However, this formatting doesn't work for longer mobile phone numbers or newer, shorter area codes.

Need to hide some confidential figures? Highlight the formatted cells that you
wish to hide, and go to **Format** ➜ **Cells** ➜ **Number**. Click the **Custom** category, select the existing numbers and press **Backspace**. Finally, type three semicolons (;;;) in the Type box. The values in your cells will now be hidden, although they will appear in the formula bar if you click in the cell. To reveal your hidden figures again, highlight them and simply click on **Number** in the Category list. The figures will reappear.

▶ See also **The humble cell**, p. 172; and **Columns in spreadsheets**, p. 172.

EXCEL: MICROSOFT'S SPREADSHEET PROGRAM

Microsoft Excel is a spreadsheet program designed to manipulate numerical information, but it is also capable of handling text and dates.

◼ Excel's standard spreadsheet

templates can help you perform a range of tasks, such as calculating expenses or producing invoices. To find the templates, go to **File → New** then click on **General Templates**, then the **Spreadsheet Solutions** tab.

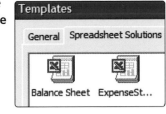

◼ Even a beginner can get a lot out

of Excel just by experimenting. Type in some figures. Select two or more by highlighting them. Excel displays the sum on the status line below

the worksheet. Right-click on this figure to calculate another value, such as the average.

◼ Learn keyboard shortcuts to reduce

the amount of time that you spend switching between your mouse and the keyboard, especially if you use Excel a lot. To select the current row or column, press **Shift+Space Bar** or **Ctrl+Space Bar**, respectively. To paste a function into a formula, press **Shift+F3**. For a complete list, search for shortcut keys in Excel's Help.

◼ Make your tables easier to

understand by turning them into charts. Excel allows you to produce impressive results with the minimum of effort. Choose from a wide range of chart styles, including pie charts and line graphs, in two and three dimensions (see p. 178).

◼ Use Microsoft's Template Gallery,

(officeupdate.microsoft.com/templategallery), where you can download a range of Excel templates for a number of different accounting tasks. The templates on offer use different

Microsoft software, but click on the **Finance and Accounting** link to download Excel templates such as a loan calculator, currency rate converter, personal budget and balance sheet.

▶ See also **Presenting your data**, p. 170; **Charts and graphs**, p. 178; **How to write formulas**, p. 180; and **Functions save time**, p. 182.

How to: Create an invoice using Excel's standard template

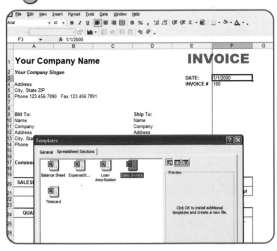

1 Launch Excel and in the New Workbook pane on the right of the window, click on **General Templates**. Select the **Spreadsheet Solutions** tab, double-click on **Sales Invoice**. Read the warning box and click **Enable Macros**. The template will now be displayed.

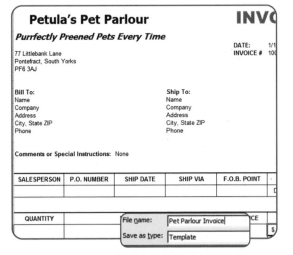

2 Click on the cells and type your name and address over the template text. Change the formatting in the currency cells to display the pound sign and adjust the VAT rate. Go to **File → Save As** and select **Template** in the Save as type box. Name it and click **Save**.

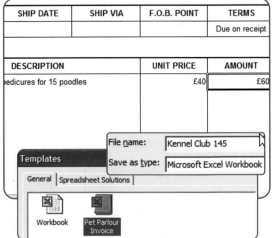

3 To open your new document, go to **File → New** and click on **General Templates** in the New Workbook pane. Click on the **General** tab to see your template. Double-click on it to open it. Fill in the billing details, then rename and save it as a Microsoft Excel Workbook.

Charts and graphs

Excel is a powerful program for analysing all sorts of data. But when it comes to getting the meaning of the figures across, a spreadsheet full of numbers can be hard to comprehend. Fortunately, Excel also has tools that let you turn dull data into colourful and clear charts and graphs.

USING EXCEL'S GRAPH FACILITY

There are two types of graphic presentation that most of us are familiar with – charts, where totals are represented as vertical columns or horizontal bars, and pie charts, where they are represented as slices of a pie. You can create both of these in Excel. You can also present your data in a variety of other chart formats. Once you've created your chart you can customise its type or colour scheme to get the precise look you want. You can also incorporate it into an Excel spreadsheet or export it to other programs like Word and, for presentations, PowerPoint.

CHART YOUR SUCCESS

The Chart Toolbar may not be visible on your Excel menu bar. To activate it, go to **View →** **Toolbars** and select **Chart**. The Chart commands will now appear as a floating Toolbar.

The quickest way to create a chart is to select the cells containing the data you want to include and then simply press the **F11** key. This instantly creates a chart on a new sheet in the default style of a column chart.

If you typically use only one kind of chart or graph, say a simple pie chart, you can speed up your chart creation by changing Excel's default column chart to the one you prefer. Just right-click a chart to call up the Chart menu, then click **Chart Type**. Select the **Custom Types** tab, choose one of the chart types offered, click **Set as default chart**, and then **Yes** and **OK**.

Get your message across with an Excel chart. To see the full range of charts available, activate the Chart Wizard by going to **Insert → Chart**, or click the **Chart Wizard** button on the Toolbar. Many of the types available have options that only specialists need, such as scatter charts, radar charts and stock charts. Most users choose column, bar, pie or line charts.

Use vertical column and horizontal bar charts to emphasise straightforward comparisons between items or their growth over time, as might be used in a sales presentation, for example. Pie charts are useful where you want to focus on the relation of parts to a whole. For example, showing how much of a telephone bill each member of a family is responsible for.

If you're unsure which type of chart is going to work best for the application you have in mind, try experimenting with the previews offered by the Chart Wizard. Simply select a sub-type, then click the **Press and Hold to View Sample** button. You'll now see your data in the selected chart format. If it doesn't quite do the job you want, you can continue to try other formats until you find the one that works best for your particular purpose.

THE MOST USEFUL GRAPH STYLES

Make sure you use the right graph for the job in hand.

 Column Ideal for showing comparative totals over specified periods of time.

 Line Good for showing key moments and fluctuations in figures over a period of time.

 Pie Best for showing the division of elements of a whole – for example, allocation of spending.

 Area Can be used to give an overall impression of the extent of change over time.

 Doughnut Useful for drawing comparisons between two pie charts with related contents, but with different totals.

Using Copy and Paste is an easy way of adding new data to a chart. Select the new cells you want to include and press **Ctrl+C** to copy them. Click in the chart itself and press **Ctrl+V** to paste the data. The updated element appears immediately in place in the appropriate style.

You can quickly and easily export charts and graphs created in Excel to other Office applications such as Word and PowerPoint using simple cut and paste techniques. Open the Excel document containing the chart and the other Office document that you want to insert it into. Select the chart and copy it using **Ctrl+C**. Now select the other Office document, click where you want to place the chart, and use **Ctrl+V** to paste it.

If an Excel graph pasted into another file is likely to change or be regularly updated, paste the chart in using the **Paste Special** command in the **Edit** menu of the importing Office program. This will keep the two diagrams constantly linked, so that any changes

made to the graph in Excel are automatically updated in the graph that has been pasted into the other Office program.

The Chart Wizard gives you plenty of options when choosing a chart style. But to get a chart just the way you want, you need to format its various elements, such as type styles and background colours. You can right-click on any element to bring up a Format menu. For example, right-click on a column, select **Format Data Series**, and click on the **Patterns** tab. You can change the colours of the columns by selecting a colour in the Area section. You can also alter the colour, style and width of the column borders in the Border section of the window. Click on the graphic background (the walls) and then right-click to alter its formatting as well.

You can also right-click on text elements to format them, changing fonts and colours from the pop-up menu. In fact, you can do so much in terms of styling

your chart that it's easy to do too much, and create something garish and confusing. Bear in mind that the chart should speak for itself; so resist the temptation to add styling just for the sake of it. The simpler the representation of data on your graph or chart, the easier it will be to understand.

▶ See also **Presenting your data,** p. 170; and **Excel: Microsoft's spreadsheet program,** p. 177.

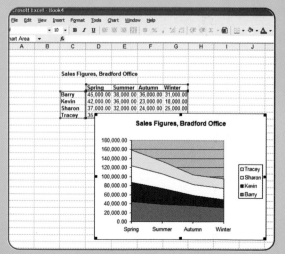

How to: Create a chart using Excel's Chart Wizard

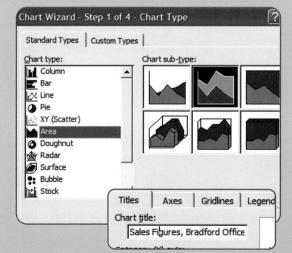

1 To produce a chart of your figures, first enter them into a spreadsheet and type explanatory labels along the top (or bottom) and side. Click and drag the mouse from one corner of the figures to the opposite corner to select them all. Go to **Insert ➜ Chart**.

2 The Chart Wizard guides you through choosing a type of chart, the precise data range, a heading and other options. Press **Next** to proceed through the stages. Don't spend too much time on this because you can edit the settings later if necessary.

3 The chart will appear when you click on **Finish**. Right-click on any part of the chart to alter its appearance. The chart is not just a picture – it is a live representation of your data. As soon as you change any of the figures, the chart updates accordingly.

CHANGING GROUPS OF CELLS

By creating a range beforehand you can quickly and easily perform an action on an entire group of cells in your spreadsheet.

■ **Create a range** by selecting an area of cells in your spreadsheet. Simply click and drag the mouse over the area you wish to select. Release the mouse and the cells remain highlighted – this is your range.

■ **Once a range has been set,** any action that you select from the Format menu – and some options from the Tools and Data menu – can be carried out on all the cells in the range. This is a quick way to standardise all the fonts, colours and borders for a worksheet.

■ **A range is denoted by the two cells** that mark both the upper left-hand and the lower right-hand corners of the selected area.

For example, a range covering those cells in columns B, C and D and rows 3, 4 and 5 is identified as B3:D5 in a formula, or as 3R x 3C in the address window, denoting a range that is three rows deep by three columns wide.

■ **To define an area of a worksheet** for printing, create a range covering the area that is to be printed. Go to the File menu, and choose **Print Area ➜ Set Print Area**. Once you've printed, you can delete the print range by going to **File ➜ Print Area ➜ Clear Print Area**.

■ **Sort the items in a range** by going to the **Data** menu and selecting **Sort**. The Sort dialogue box lets you choose which columns to sort by and whether to put your list in ascending or descending order. It also warns you if you try sorting only part of a collection of data.

■ **Think you'll need to repeat the same range?** If you need to do it more than once, then why not save and name it? Your named ranges can be quickly identified and used

in formulas and macros to simplify your worksheet design. For a step-by-step guide to naming a range in Excel see 'How to', below.

■ **Ranges don't have to be rectangular!** If you have a number of separate blocks of cells to integrate into one single range, hold down the **Ctrl** key and click on the cells you want to select. This allows you to define a range with as many cells as you need, no matter where they happen to be positioned on the worksheet.

HOW TO WRITE FORMULAS

Formulas are equations that can automatically perform a wide variety of operations on the data contained in your spreadsheet.

■ **Identify your spreadsheet formulas.** They begin with an equal sign (=), and might include individual cell references (B7, H4), cell ranges (C3:E3 represents cells C3, D3

 How to: Name a range in Excel

1 Highlight the data cells you want to include in the range. First place the cursor in the top left-hand cell (B2). Hold down the left mouse button and drag the mouse to the far right-hand cell (G3), then release the button.

2 Click in the Name Box below the main Toolbar and type the name you want to use for your range. Do not include any spaces between characters. Press **Enter** to assign the name to the range. Name as many ranges as you wish for quick reference.

3 The named ranges can now be accessed by clicking on the down arrow at the side of the Name Box. To view a named range on your worksheet, select it from the list and the cells will be highlighted automatically.

■ **Use too many names and it's easy to forget** which one belongs to which cell. If you get lost, click the drop-down arrow at the right-hand end of the Name Box, choose a cell name, and Excel will take you straight there. If there's no Name Box on your screen, choose **View ➔ Formula Bar** to display it. This also allows you to see the formula in any cell by clicking on it.

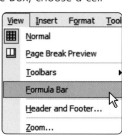

View	Insert	Format	Tool
Normal			
Page Break Preview			
Toolbars			▶
Formula Bar			
Header and Footer...			
Zoom...			

■ **Using the Formula Bar is a simple way** to build formulas. Begin by pressing the equal sign key, then select the range of cells, and Excel will insert the names or cell references for you. Add the operators or functions you need to create a working formula (see 'How to', below).

■ **For an easy way to review any formula,** click on the cell containing it, then click in the Formula Bar. Referenced cells are highlighted in different colours, providing a visual indicator of how the formula has been created.

■ **Spreadsheets are normally very dynamic;** change one of the values referred to in a formula, and Excel will recalculate everything to keep the totals up to date. This is usually a good thing, but in a really big spreadsheet the constant recalculations might slow you down. If you choose **Tools ➔ Options** and select the **Calculation** tab, and then select the **Manual** option, Excel will only recalculate when you tell it to do so by pressing **F9**.

■ **What result would you expect** from the formula = 8-2*3? The natural response is to calculate from left to right, producing 8-2 = 6, then 6*3 = 18. Excel, however, performs mathematical operations in a fixed order, and does the multiplication first, giving 2*3 = 6, then 8-6 = 2. To make this formula behave as you expect, surround the part you want to be performed first in parentheses, as in = (8-2)*3.

■ **By default, Excel stores values** to a precision of 15 digits, even if it doesn't display them. This can cause problems with financial calculations, where 157.00000025 pounds

and E3), numeric constants (17), or mathematical operators (+, -, *, /). In addition to these, a wide range of functions is available to help you perform many types of scientific, financial or statistical calculations.

■ **If a formula is particularly complicated,** click on its cell, select **Insert ➔ Comment**, and type an explanation of how it is calculated. Any cell containing a comment has a little red triangle in the top-right corner; let your

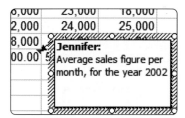

mouse hover over it, and the comment will be displayed. Right-click on the cell to edit or delete the comment.

6,000	23,000	16,000
2,000	24,000	25,000
8,000		
00.00		

Jennifer:
Average sales figure per month, for the year 2002

■ **A cryptic formula,** such as (B4/H7) * (C2+C8), may be acceptable if you're building a simple spreadsheet to do one set of calculations, but anything you intend to use regularly needs more clarity. To make formulas easier to understand, name key cells, and use the names in your formulas, such as =(TotalIncome-Taxes)/12. To give a cell a name, click on the cell and press **Ctrl+F3**. You can also name a range of cells. See the 'How to', p. 180, or select the cells and press **Ctrl+F3**, or select **Insert ➔ Name ➔ Define**.

How to: Build a formula with the formula bar

PMT	▼	X ✓ fx =
PMT		B	C
SUM			
AVERAGE		ct Office Sales
IF		
HYPERLINK		
COUNT		HYPERLINK	Jaso
MAX		COUNT
SIN		MAX
SUMIF		SIN
STDEV		SUMIF
More Functions...		STDEV
		More Functions...

January	102	121	118	93
February	107	125	142	99
March	99	131	161	129
April	133	100	138	113
May	156	106	133	140
June	144	128	102	180
July	109	122	85	201
August	96	110	104	121
September	36	158	114	140
October	88	170	122	160
November	128	164	132	143
December	105	122	165	165
Total				
Average	B5:B16)			

B I U
fx =AVERAGE(B5:B16)
C D
Office Sales Figu

1 Select a cell that you want to contain the formula and press the equals sign key. If you need to include a function, choose from the list that appears. Alternatively, you can select **More Functions** if you wish to explore a wider range of possibilities.

2 Use your mouse to select the cells you would like to use in the formula, and Excel will insert the cell references. This reduces the risk of errors made by having to type in the cell references. To make the formula active, click **OK** or press **Enter**.

makes little sense. To turn off this extreme precision select **Tools ➜ Options ➜ Calculation** and check the **Precision as displayed** box.

■ **If you experience a problem with your formula,** or the result cannot be displayed for some reason, Excel will show an error value like #DIV/0!, NAME?, #VALUE, or #####. Click on the cell and use Excel's Help function to get advice.

▶ See also **Presenting your data**, p. 170; and **Excel: Microsoft's spreadsheet program**, p. 177.

FUNCTIONS SAVE TIME

Learn how to use functions to operate your spreadsheet formulas.

■ **In spreadsheet terms, a function is a predefined formula** that performs calculations on a given set of values, or arguments. The formula = AVERAGE(A1:A10), for example, uses the Average function to produce the arithmetic mean of the first ten values in column A.

■ **Some functions work on text rather than figures.** For example, UPPER (London, England) returns LONDON, ENGLAND written in upper case letters. Other functions perform date-related arithmetic. For example, DAYS360 returns the number of days between two dates, so DAYS360 (19/7/2002, 21/3/2003, D) will calculate the number of days between 19 July 2002 and 21 March 2003.

■ **Not sure which function to use?** Select **Insert ➜ Function** to bring up the Insert Function dialogue box, where you can browse all the options available to you. For more information on a function that interests you, press **F1**.

■ **If you have an idea of what you'd like to do** but don't know how to do it, you can search for a function in the Insert Function dialogue box. Type in a keyword or words that best describe what you want to do and press **Go**. The compatible functions will be displayed below.

■ **For help on functions as you use them,** build your formulas in the Formula Bar. If the bar is not displayed, select **View ➜ Formula Bar**. You can choose from the list of Most Recently Used functions on the left side of the bar. If the function you need isn't listed, select **More Functions** to display the Insert Function dialogue box.

How to: Create a random number generator

1 In cells A3 and B3 enter the numbers between which you want to generate your set of random numbers. For example, if you want the random numbers to lie between 1 and 40 then in cell A3 enter the number 1 and in cell B3 enter the number 40.

2 In cell C3 enter the following formula: =INT(RAND()*(B3-A3+1))+A3. Excel will then return a random number between the numbers in cells A3 and B3. Press F9 each time you want to display a new random number.

3 You can get Excel to generate random numbers between any two numbers you like. Just type new numbers in cells A3 and B3 to change the range.

■ Want to know which day of the week you were born on? Use the
WEEKDAY function. Suppose you were born on 24 June 1968. Select a cell and enter the formula =WEEKDAY(24/6/68). Excel will return the number 6 (for Friday). To display the word Friday rather than the number 6, set the format of the cell to the custom format dddd. To find out which day of the week a different date fell on, just change the date at the time that you enter the formula.

■ Convert a number to a Roman numeral using the ROMAN function. To convert
the number 213, select a cell and enter the formula =ROMAN(213). Excel will return the value CCXIII. The ROMAN function will only work for whole numbers between 1 and 3999.

■ Can't find a dice to roll? Get Excel to
roll one for you. Select a cell and enter the formula =INT(RAND()*6)+1. Excel will return a random number between 1 and 6. Press **F9** each time you want to 'roll the dice' and Excel will calculate a new number for you. The RAND function returns a random number greater than or equal to 0 and less than 1, so the RAND()*6 formula returns a random number greater than or

equal to 0 and less than 6. The INT function rounds a number down to the nearest whole number, so the INT((RAND()*6)) formula returns a random whole number between 0 and 5. By adding 1 at the end we get a random number between 1 and 6. You can use a similar method

to get Excel to generate random numbers between any two numbers that you happen to choose (see 'How to', p. 182).

(see 'How to', p. 182).

PLAN YOUR FAMILY BUDGET

Keep your family finances in order with a spreadsheet program.

■ Create a budget template. In column
A, make two lists: one showing all the different parts of your monthly income, such as salary and bank interest, and the other one your monthly expenditures. These expenses could range from mortgage payments to holiday expenses and household bills. Write the months of the year as headings in columns B to N. Follow your finances by recording each piece of income or expenditure in the relevant spreadsheet cell.

■ Summarise data with subtotals and totals using Excel's AutoSum feature,
which is denoted by the Σ button on the Toolbar. Use it to add up the first monthly total for both your income and expenditure sections. Now, at the bottom of the page, subtract your expenditure total from your income total to show how much you have left. Then copy and paste the formulas across the remaining months.

■ Track your bank balance with a
running total. Create a new row below your monthly total row to keep a regular eye on the state of your account from day to day. Enter your bank balance at the start of the year in column A. Create a formula in the same row in column B to add that monthly total to your initial balance. Now you can copy that formula into the cells for all the months of the year.

■ Use Excel formatting for easy
reading of the figures on your spreadsheet. Select the table, go to **Format → AutoFormat** and choose a table style.

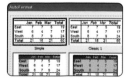

▶ See also **Presenting your data**, p. 170; and **Mastering Microsoft Money**, p. 198.

How to: Keep track of your finances

	A	B	C
		Jan	Feb	Mar
INCOME		M(B3:B5)	
Sharon's take home		1780	1780
Kevin's take home		2040	2040
Other		45	45
EXPENSES			
Mortagage		500.00	500.00
Food		160.00	160.00
Bills			
Petrol		=SUM(B7:B10)	

AVERAGE ▾ ✗ ✓ ƒx =SUM(B3:B5)

1 Key in your income and expenditure figures and then enter the following formulas for their totals: Income: =SUM(B3:B5); Expenditure: =SUM(B7:B10).

AVERAGE ▾ ✗ ✓ ƒx =B2-B6

	A	B
1		Jan
2	**INCOME**	3865
3	Sharon's take home	1780
4	Kevin's take home	2040
5	Other	45
6	**EXPENSES**	920
7	Mortagage	500
8	Food	160
9	Bills / Petrol	200
	MONTHLY BALANCE	2945

2 Enter the monthly total by subtracting expenditure from income. Type in the following formula: =B2-B6. Now enter your opening bank balance and add a formula for calculating a running total: =A12+B11.

Computer games

The PC is an extremely capable game machine, and even the most humble computer is capable of playing engaging games. Whether you prefer games that require strategic intelligence or you would rather switch off and zap aliens, there is a game that meets your needs.

WHAT DO YOU NEED?

The impression many have is that you must be young to enjoy PC games, but that isn't the case. chess, cards, war games and all types of strategic sports are available for the average PC.

WINDOWS' OWN GAMES

Your PC has several games already in the Games folder on the Accessories menu.

Freecell is a cunning card game. You have to build up the four suits in the slots on the right, in order from ace to king. The cards can be placed on top of each other at the bottom of the screen as long as they are a different colour and one rank down (a black 10 on a red jack, for example). Any of the cards can be moved up to the slots on the left. That's it – seems simple, doesn't it? Try it and you'll find that it isn't.

Minesweeper is another seemingly easy game. All you have to do is locate all the mines as quickly as possible without uncovering any of them. The number on each square tells you how many mines are immediately around its edges. If you uncover a mine, you lose the game.

Spider Solitaire is a new spin on an old favourite, which many people find therapeutic to play. If you find Minesweeper too aggressive, or want to take a break from computer work, try this relaxing game.

The kind of add-ons you need to play games depends on the kind of games you want to play. If, for example, you want to play an occasional game of cards or chess, then you probably won't have to add anything to your PC. More sophisticated action games, however, may require an upgrade such as a fast graphics card.

Generally speaking, the newer the game you want to play, the more up-to-date your computer should be. Action games, such as Unreal Tournament and Half-Life, place heavy demands on a computer, and you'll need a good graphics card, such as an nVidia GeForce 4 or later, in addition to a healthy amount of memory (preferably 512 MB of RAM) for the best possible textures and smoothest play.

If you plan on playing action games a lot, then invest in a large monitor, at least 17 inches. This not only allows you to get more immersed in the game, but it will also let you view details, such as bonus items and distant enemies, with greater clarity. Some serious gamers like to run extra monitors (through extra video cards) to have an all-encompassing view.

For simple real-time strategy games a fairly ordinary graphics card, like the ATi Rage 128Pro or nVidea GeForce 2, and about 128 MB of RAM will be enough. Before you purchase a game or download a demo version from a Website, check the system requirements to make sure that you will be able to play the game without having to buy extra equipment.

For flight simulations, you need all the processing power you can get. Many of these games, such as Microsoft's FlightSim 2002, require your PC to render vast and ever-changing landscapes with as much realism as possible, so they place heavy demands on a CPU and graphics card. Choose a top-end graphics card, such as nVidia GeForce 4 or ATi Radeon 9000 – for best performance.

The graphics card market is very competitive, which means it's possible to buy one that suits all budgets and gaming requirements. Two manufacturers make the chips found on most cards – Ati and nVidea. Watch out for bargains – cards are often heavily discounted only a few months after release.

TYPES OF GAMES

If you are not yet a game player, you may not be familiar with the various terms used to describe them. Here's a brief explanation of the most popular types.

Strategy Generally speaking, these are war games, in which you control an army and have to logically outmanoeuvre your opponent. One example is Age of Mythology from Ensemble Studios (www.ensemble.com).

Shoot-'em-ups Played from a first-person point of view, these are simple gun-'n'-run games that rely on reflex actions. They often have the facility to let you play against a friend on another computer. One very popular example is Unreal from Epic Games (www.unrealtournament.com).

Flight sims Flight simulations are available in military and civilian versions and let you fly everything from a Boeing 747 to a Mig29. An example is Microsoft Flight Simulator 2000 (www.microsoft.com/games/home).

Role playing Solve puzzles, cast spells or defeat armies of trolls. Role-playing games, commonly known as RPGs, require a great deal of strategic thinking and a sharp eye for detail. An example is Neverwinter Nights from Bioware (nwn.bioware.com).

Puzzle Card Games, strange puzzles, chess and even jigsaw puzzles have all been simulated on the PC. An example is Freecell, which comes free with all of Microsoft's operating systems (see box, p. 184).

Racing Simulators Wheel-to-wheel action comes to your computer via realistic models of cars and tracks. You can tweak engine, brake and suspension settings to achieve the perfect lap time. Try out Geoff Crammond's Grand Prix 4 (www.grandprixgames.com).

Getting the right sound card can make the whole gaming experience much better. A standard sound card will support four speakers, or more; the very best ones support a complete six-speaker surround sound set-up. These multispeaker sound cards can totally immerse you in a game, enabling you to use your ears as much as your eyes.

WHICH OPERATING SYSTEM?

Windows XP has many advantages over older operating systems. It is inherently more stable than previous home operating systems, such a Windows Me and also supports a wider range of up-to-date hardware. For maximum performance, advanced gamers recommend turning off non-essential effects that XP runs as standard, such as the 3D shadows behind windows. One school of thought recommends the Pro version of XP because it can be tweaked to an even greater extent than the cheaper Home

version. However, for most gamers XP Home is perfectly sufficient. It includes the latest version of DirectX – software routines that speed up your graphics performance even on older cards.

CONTROLLERS

Many simulation games, such as rally, CART or flight simulators, work best with the appropriate controllers. Joysticks, steering wheels and pedals add extra realism and controllability to your game play, but at a price. There are many makes available, depending on your budget and the type of game control you want. They include Logitech (www.logitech.com), Microsoft (www.microsoft.com/insider/gaming.htm), Act Labs (www.act-labs.com), and QuickShot (www.quickshot.com).

Make sure you buy the right controller for your computer. Generally, most game play controllers are compatible with recent

makes of PC. However, if your computer is very old, make sure that the controller you buy still has a joystick connector and not just the USB connector designed for more recent PCs.

When you buy a new controller, you may need to install software drivers (supplied with it) to allow your PC to understand the controller's movements and translate them into the action you experience on screen. If you don't have the appropriate drivers – for whatever reason – you can often download them for free from the manufacturer's Website. The site's address is often printed on the packaging or the directions that come with the controller.

For added realism, you can buy controllers with force feedback. These contain small motors that create resistance on the joystick or steering wheel to mimic what you would really feel if your tyres were fighting to retain grip or if you hit air turbulence in your biplane (see p. 25).

SETTING UP A GAME

So what happens if you discover, after installation, that your game is running really slowly or that it is uncontrollable? Fortunately, developers often include setup procedures in their games, which enable you to tailor the game's demands to your PC's performance. Knowing what to change, and when, can make all the difference.

Unless you have a very powerful PC (such as a Pentium 4-based machine), you probably won't be able to run a game (especially a graphics-intensive action game) at its maximum resolution. The best way to find out which resolution suits your game – whether it is 640 x 480, 800 x 600, 1024 x 768, 1152 x 864, or even 1600 x 1200 – is to start at 1024 x 768 and work your way either up or down until you get acceptable performance.

Many games have options to increase the level of detail in the game's world. Although it is always tempting to turn this setting up to full, the more detail you ask for, the more demands are placed on your graphics card and central processing unit. If you demand too much, the game will slow down. Experiment to find a balance between image quality and game speed.

It is not just the graphics settings that can affect your ability to play a game – it is also the way you play the game. For example, you may control the mouse with your left hand and find the default control settings unusable. Just as any of the control keys from the main setup

window in any game can be changed, you can also change the mouse buttons so that the primary button is the right mouse button and the secondary one is the left button.

If you find action games too hard to control, try changing the sensitivity setting of

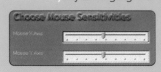

the mouse. Again, you'll find this in the game's main setup window, where it is usually depicted by a sliding scale. Choose between a sensitive mouse (better for advanced players) and one more suited to a beginner.

GAMES ON A BUDGET

Playing games on your PC doesn't need to cost you lots of money. In fact, if you act shrewdly, it's possible to play games without spending anything at all – thanks to freeware,

shareware and demo games. Check out the games you can download at GameSpot

(www.gamespot.com), Adrenaline Vault (www.avault.com), and the Gamespy Network (www. gamespy.com).

Know the difference between freeware, shareware and demos. Freeware games are titles released into the public domain by their programmers. They won't cost you a penny to buy, so just download them and start playing. Shareware is 'try before you buy'. You get a section of the fully functioning game free – usually the first stages – and if you like it, you buy the remaining parts. A demo is a truncated version of a game – often with certain functions disabled. It is designed to give you an idea of whether or not you will like the game.

Also check out popular PC magazines, which sometimes come with cover-mounted CDs. It's also worth remembering that all the big publishers have budget games labels. If you wait a year, you can pick up last year's big game for a discount price.

To play the latest games not yet in the stores, you could try being a 'beta-tester'. These are people who volunteer to try out programs and games in their late development stages to look for glitches and gremlins. You then notify the manufacturer of any problems you've encountered so they can be fixed before the product lands on the shelves of your local store. To find out more, log on to your favourite Internet search engine and type in 'beta test'. You will see hundreds of companies requesting your help. Simply read their terms and conditions and register with them.

Fancy a mental challenge? Log on to the Internet and try solving the virtual Rubik's cube (www.npac.syr.edu/projects/ java/magic). If you think the original puzzle is easy, try solving the 216-cube version!

ONLINE GAMING

Forget computer controlled opponents and artificial intelligence. The Internet lets you race, zap or challenge real people in online games.

Using the Internet, players from all over the world can join in a single game, racing each other in a simulated Grand Prix or battling in shoot-'em-ups like Unreal Tournament, Quake and Half-Life. Gaming takes on a whole new dimension when your opponents are not computer-generated, but error-prone humans just like you. It's not all about individual glory either – many games let online players join together in teams.

The faster the better
It's entirely possible to participate using a traditional dial-up Internet connection. But for the best experience you'll need a fast ADSL or cable connection. A modem and a dial-up connection may suffer from lag – when data is delayed in reaching your computer – making it hard to aim or

overtake accurately. Broadband connections are less prone to lag and are also 'always on' so your game won't be interrupted because of a dropped modem connection.

How it works
All the players in an online game will be running the same program – say Unreal Tournament – on their PCs at home. One machine coordinates all these separate versions of the game so all the participants see the same virtual 'world'. The most intense computing is still done by the player's PC – drawing 3D shapes and creating sound effects. Travelling between the computers in the game is a constant stream of data describing each player's position, stance and orientation, as well as other details such as their choice of weapon and uniform colour.

AVOIDING VIOLENCE

If you'd like to buy a game for a child or a teenager, but are worried about the adverse affects it might have on the young person in question, pay careful attention to the age rating on the box before you make your purchase. In Europe ISFE ratings have been introduced showing which age groups games are suitable for. There are five categories ranging from three and over to games suitable only for adults. Alternatively, you could visit Kids Domain (www.kidsdomain.com/games/) for links to games

suitable for younger children – and most of them are free! Other parents with children of the same age are, of course, a good source – ask for their personal endorsement.

In many cases, potentially violent games have in-game settings that allow you to tone down the more violent or frightening

aspects of the game for slightly younger children, in exactly the same way as you can change the difficulty setting. You can, for example, often turn off any mature language or remove graphics of blood and violence from the game.

Many advanced flight simulation programs are so accurate in their recreations that they can be very difficult for adults to become accustomed to, let alone children. In fact, some are so realistic that they are recommended by flight training schools to give student pilots useful experience at home. However, in most of these programs you can set certain flying options to look after themselves so that you only need to steer and control the altitude of the aircraft.

If you'd rather avoid mainstream games with violent themes entirely, there are several software houses that have a

much gentler approach to game playing on your PC. Soleau Software (www.soleau.com) make a range of educational, nonviolent, strategy, logic and arcade games. Also try Argos Gameware (www.gameware.com). For free classic arcade games for your PC, visit Arcade Games Online (www.arcadegamesonline.com).

▶ See also **How to download files,** p. 240; and **The shareware alternative,** p. 304.

How to: Download and install free games software

1 Log on to the Internet and enter the Web address for the games site – in this case it's www.liveforspeed.com. Most game sites have a Download or Demo section, so click on the appropriate link.

2 Locate the demo and click on its link to begin the download to your PC. When the file is downloaded, it may need to be unzipped, so double-click on the Desktop icon. Most programs will unzip and start the installation process automatically.

3 Click **Next** where necessary and complete any registration information required. Click the **Finish** button to complete the installation. You should be able to find the game by going to **Start ➜ All Programs.** You can then test your skills before you buy the full version.

Working with images

Art and photography

Here are some tips to help you use this handy accessory program included with Windows.

■ **Microsoft Paint may seem a little basic,** but it does contain features often found only in more comprehensive packages. The lack of confusing icons and features make it fun and very easy to use. To open Paint go to **Start → All Programs → Accessories → Paint**.

■ **The pencil is the default tool** and will produce a freehand line that is one pixel wide. To create a different type of line, choose one of the other drawing tools, such as the Brush. A selection of brush tips you can choose from are available from a pick box below the main Drawing Toolbar.

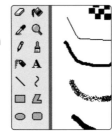

■ **The Line and Curve tools** offer a selection of line weights, from one to five pixels in width, but only a limited number of shapes can be created using the tools. The Line tool draws a straight line between your starting and finishing point; the Curve tool allows you to create a line that can be bent in any direction by left-clicking away from the line and then dragging.

■ **The Rectangle, Ellipse, and Rounded Rectangle tools** enable you to quickly produce a range of basic shapes. Select one of the tools and click-and-drag until the desired size is reached. To use the Polygon tool, left-click at several points to create an irregularly shaped polygon with numerous straight sides.

■ **Other drawing tools** include: an Airbrush with three nozzle sizes; a Fill With Color tool, which fills shapes or background with colour; an Eraser to delete mistakes; and a Color Picker to match colours exactly.

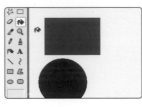

■ **Use the colours at the bottom** of the Paint window or create your own custom-made shades to fill in your design. To mix your own colours, go to **Colors → Edit Colors**. Click **Define Custom Colors**. In the colour palette that appears, mix the exact shade you want, and then click the **Add to Custom Colors** button.

■ **You can assign a different colour** to your left and right mouse buttons, which is particularly useful when filling in a large design. To do this, left-click on one colour, and right-click on another. Now both colours are available at a click of the mouse. This is a real time saver and it works with shapes, lines, brushes and fill tools.

■ **The images that you create** using Microsoft Paint can be used as a Windows Desktop background. Create your picture, save it as you would normally, and then go to **File → Set As Background (Tiled)** to repeat the image to fill your screen, or **Set As Background (Centered)** for a single image on your screen.

■ **Interesting effects** can be achieved if you go to **Image → Flip/Rotate.** You can flip an image vertically or horizontally, or rotate it through 90, 180 and 270 degrees.

■ **An image can also be stretched or skewed in Paint.** To do this, go to **Image → Stretch/Skew**. Stretching allows you to alter the height and width of an image by changing either dimension. If you change the height and width by the same amount, the picture will be resized in proportion. Skewing twists an image through either the vertical or horizontal plane in increments of one degree.

■ **The top two buttons on the Paint Toolbar** let you cut or copy a section of an image as a free-form shape or rectangle. You can remove or reposition a complete area or a detailed section around an irregular object.

■ **Paint can also be used to view** and edit other artwork files. Use the paste feature to import .jpg, .gif or .bmp files into your picture, or scan in images or photographs and alter them.

▶ See also **Drawing programs,** p. 194.

There's no need to settle for the ordinary with your photographs.

■ **Photo-editing programs provide a variety of effects** that allow you to give your photo the look of an oil painting, a pencil sketch or even abstract art. Scanners usually come with their own, basic, photo-editing programs. Top-quality software packages, such as Corel Photo-Paint (www.corel.com) or Photoshop (www.adobe.co.uk) can be expensive.

Find your own level. Unless you are a professional who needs the most advanced features, you will probably be perfectly happy with the effects offered by more affordable

programs such as Micrografx Picture Publisher (www. corel.com), or the popular program Paint Shop Pro (www.jasc.com).

Problems applying your artistic effects? Check the colour depth – the number of colours used in your image. Most photo editors will not let you apply effects to 2, 16, or 256-bit colour pictures, so you will need to convert the image to 24-bit colour. To do this in Paint Shop Pro, select **Colors ➜ Increase Color Depth** and change the colour accordingly.

You can add new editing features indefinitely, as long as the photo editor supports plug-ins. A plug-in is a program you can add to the editor, which offers new capabilities and effects. Go to Graphics Unleashed (www. unleash.com) or The Plugin Site (www.theplug insite.com) to download photo-editing plug-ins.

Less is more. Many bright and gaudy effects are overpowering when applied to an entire image. Instead, use the effect on a selected

area of the picture. For example, a 'hot neon' effect looks odd applied to a whole face, but is interesting when used on the eyes.

Create your own effects. Some software enables you to make your own effects. In Photoshop, for example, select **Filter ➜ Other ➜ Custom,** or in Paint Shop Pro select **Effects ➜ User ➜ Defined**. Just edit a number in a table and see what happens. You will need to do some experimenting to achieve results you like.

For further advice on applying effects, check the Website of your photo editor's manufacturer. Jasc (www.jasc.com/ tutorials.asp), for example, provides a number of helpful Paint Shop Pro tutorials.

▶ See also **Scanners and scanning,** p. 40; **Digital cameras,** p. 44; **The world of graphics,** p. 154; and **Editing photographs,** p. 196.

▶ See also **Scanners and scanning,** p. 40; **Digital cameras,** p. 44; **The world of graphics,** p. 154; and **Editing photographs,** p. 196.

PAINT SHOP PRO'S SPECIAL EFFECTS

Here are some of the most interesting image modifying tools to try out.

ARTISTIC EFFECTS
Instant art. How your image would look if it had been created with paint, pencil, charcoal, coloured chalk or coloured pencil.

BUTTON EFFECT
Converts your images into three-dimensional square or rectangular buttons.

CHROME EFFECT
Gives your image a metallic look.

GLOWING EDGES EFFECT
Makes your image look as if it were created from glowing neon tubes.

AGED NEWSPAPER EFFECT
Gives your image brownish tones as though it were in the pages of an old newspaper.

How to: Use artistic effects in Paint Shop Pro

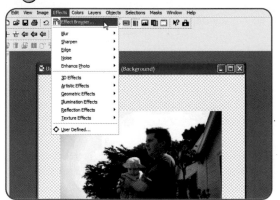

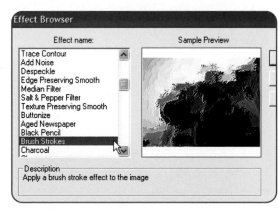

1 Open the image you want to apply effects to. Go to the **Effects** menu and select **Effect Browser** to display the list of possible effects that are available.

2 Scroll down the Effect name box and click on an effect to see what it looks like. A preview window illustrates how that effect will alter the image.

3 To customise an effect click **OK**. Adjust the options in the dialogue box to alter the effect in a number of different ways. With the Brush Strokes effect you can change the stroke length and width, and the number of bristles.

Make micro-adjustments to individual pixels to leave all your images as sharp as possible.

■ **A pixel is a single point** in a graphic image – its name comes from a meld of the words 'picture' and 'element'. Every computer image is made up of millions of black or coloured pixels arranged in rows and columns.

■ **Most graphics programs** on the PC can zoom in on an image, allowing you to edit small and delicate parts of a picture that other painting tools – such as the airbrush and fill tools – are too big to handle.

■ **You can edit pixels in Microsoft Paint,** which is usually found in the **Start** ➜ **All Programs** ➜ **Accessories** menu. It has a simple Toolbar that lets you open, navigate your way around and alter parts of an image in a few easy steps.

■ **For pixel editing in Paint,** the main tools are the Pencil and Magnifier on the Toolbar. The Magnifier tool gives you a choice of zoom levels in a drop-down box below the Toolbar itself. You can also customise the zoom in the **View** ➜ **Zoom** menu to suit your needs. Work at high magnification, and frequently return to normal view to assess progress.

■ **Clean cut.** Pixel editing is particularly useful when cleaning up the rough edges of an image part that has been cut out and moved. In Paint, you can use the Free-Form Select tool to outline and move an image element.

MAKING USE OF CLIP ART

Most clip art is free or cheap. Use these simple graphics and images to illustrate your documents.

■ **Build up your collection.** It's easy to find clip art. There are millions of images waiting to be downloaded from Websites (see box, p. 191), or you can buy CD-ROMs of clip art

images. Most collections are organised into groups. So, if you're searching the Web for clip art, decide which subjects you want to search for. Also set up folders on your hard disk to receive the images, and name them according to topic, such as people, technology or animals.

■ **Planning to collect a lot of files?** Use a clip art manager program, such as Arts & Letters Express (www.arts-letters.com). This will sort your collection into easily navigable groups. It will also provide thumbnail previews of each group to help you track down a particular image and quickly copy it into your document.

■ **Don't collect images you don't need.** It's all too easy to clutter up your hard drive with excess clip art. Instead, why not bookmark a few good clip art Websites and download images as you need them?

■ **Animated clip art** only works in Web browsers or special animation viewers. If you place a piece of animated clip art in a Word, Works or Excel document, only a static image of the animation will be displayed.

■ **Free clip art is for noncommercial use** in most cases. Make sure you check the copyright carefully when you acquire new images.

How to: Edit pixels in Microsoft Paint

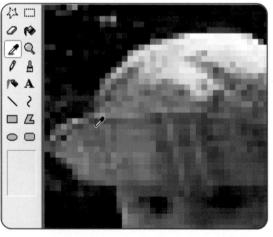

1 Once you have opened the image you want to re-touch, use the **Zoom** tool to magnify it. The Zoom tool brings up a rectangle that you place over the area you want to enlarge. Click to see a close-up of the pixels.

2 To get a perfect colour match, use the **Pick Color** tool. When you click on the image, the Picker will copy the tone it is placed over and switch to the **Pencil** tool. Then fill in the areas you want to change, pixel by pixel.

A payment may be required if you intend to use images as part of your business, even if you are not directly reselling the image itself. Even a clip art border added to your business letterhead, for example, may technically be breaching the copyright of the creator.

■ You can make your own clip art.
Clip art dates back to the time when designers and desktop publishers clipped and collected

CLIP ART SITES
Grab all sorts of great clip art from these image Websites.

ALL FREE CLIPART
(www.allfreeclipart.com)
A large collection of free images.

CLIPART GUIDE (www.clipartguide.com)
A great range, including cartoon characters.

BEST CLIPART
(www.bestclipart.com)
Links to all the best clip art sites around, most of them free.

CLIPART.COM (www.clipart.com)
Over 2.5 million downloadable images.

COREL CLIPART CENTER
(www.clipartcity.com/clipart)
One hundred thousand images are free. But if you want to get your hands on the other million, you'll have to pay up!

WEB PLACES
(www.webplaces.com/html/clipart.htm)
An enormous collection of themed links to free clip art sites.

CLIP ART CONNECTION
(www.clipartconnection.com)
This site has one of the largest collections of free clip art anywhere on the Internet.

small images that might be useful in the future. You can do the same – if you spot an interesting border or illustration, why not scan it into your PC, and add it to your collection. But remember that the copyright issue also applies to images acquired from magazines and other media.

■ Clip art comes free with Microsoft Word! To see the available images, open a Word document and go to **Insert ➤ Picture ➤ Clip Art**. The Insert Clip Art pane will appear on the right of your document. To insert art into your document, type in a search term and click the **Search** button. When you've found an image, double-click on it to insert it into your document.

■ Add more images to the Clip Gallery. Go to **Insert ➤ Picture ➤ Clip Art**. At the bottom of the Insert Clip Art pane, click on the **Clip Organizer** link. In the Clip Organizer window, go to **File ➤ Add Clips to Organizer**, then select **On My Own**. Navigate to the appropriate file on your computer and find an image you have saved. Double-click on the image to place it in the Clip Organizer. Hover your cursor over the image and a bar appears on the right. Click on the bar and select **Move to Collection**. Choose a file in which to store your image or click on **New** to create a new collection. Click **OK** to finish. You can also download clip art from the Web. To do this, just click the **Clips Online** link in the Insert Clip Art pane.

CREATING PERFECT CURVES

Do you have problems using drawing tools on your PC? Try Paint Shop Pro's Bezier curve for perfect semicircles, S-shapes and more.

■ Simply knowing that there is a Bezier curve tool won't help you to locate it. Bezier curves are a line type in Paint Shop Pro, but there is no mention of curves in the menus, or on the Toolbar. The secret is to select the Drawing

tool. Just select **Bezier Curve** from the Type drop-down menu in the Tool Options dialogue box (if this box is not visible, you can click the Toggle Tool Options Window button).

■ Bezier curves can seem confusing,
and even producing a straight line may seem difficult, so start with some simple strategies. To create a symmetrical curve, draw the initial line, then click twice on the same spot. To draw an S-shaped curve, click and drag first on one side of the line, and then the other. The secret of drawing smooth Bezier curves is practice.

■ Checking the Create as vector box
when you first draw the curve is a good idea because you can then use the Object Selector tool to select the curve again later, and resize, rotate or distort it as needed.

■ Do you need more advanced editing options? Click the **Vector Object Selection** button and then double-click on the curve. In the Vector Properties dialogue box you can change the line width, style and texture, as well as a range of other parameters.

▶ See also **Drawing programs,** p. 194.

ADDING COLOUR WITH FILL

Add colour to your Word and Excel documents with this graphic tool.

■ The Fill Color tool allows you to add colour and other visual effects to newsletters, reports or presentations. You'll find it on the Drawing Toolbar, where it is represented as a paint bucket, or go to **Format ➤ Background**. If your Drawing Toolbar isn't visible, click **View ➤ Toolbars** and check the **Drawing** option.

■ The most basic use for the Fill Color tool is to fill a shape or object on the screen with a single colour. To do this, click on the shape, then on the arrow next to the **Fill Color** button on the Toolbar, and choose the colour you want from the Colors palette that appears. Or select **More Fill Colors** for even more choice.

Clicking on the Fill Effects button

on the Colors palette gives you access to a wide range of colour effects. You can preset or design your own gradients, choose textures and patterns,

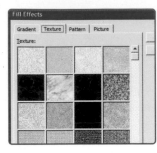

alter the colour schemes or select a picture to act as a fill. You can also combine all the effects. Practice and a little imagination will show you what is possible.

For a greater choice of standard colours, click on the **More Fill Colors** button

on the Colors palette. This allows you to mix your own custom colour, which is especially useful when you're trying to achieve an exact colour match – for a company logo, for example. If you know the colour's composition, enter its RGB (red, green and blue) values here.

▸ See also **Drawing programs**, p. 194.

▸ See also **Drawing programs**, p. 194.

WORKING WITH LAYERS

Learn how to access and use the layers tools to build up an image in Paint Shop Pro.

A layer is an individual sheet of an

image that contains part, or all, of the finished artwork. They are a feature of many graphics programs, such as Jasc Software's Paint Shop Pro. The layers in a picture are stacked one on top of the other, rather like a sandwich of photographic slides. This lets you separate the constituent parts, so that you can add and delete layers, alter their order, and edit each one in a variety of ways.

Layers are ideal for building up an

image, since they let you fine tune each component until the overall composition looks just the way you want it to. Layers offer rapid access to each constituent part and let you reposition, overlap and delete relevant parts of the picture without interfering with the rest.

To show or hide the Layer Palette,

open your image in Paint Shop Pro, go to **View ➔ Toolbars** and select the **Layer Palette** option. Like a digital artist's mixing palette, the Layer Palette lets you rearrange and blend the various components of your image.

Create a separate layer for each

addition you make instead of putting everything on the original background layer created when you started your picture. Add new layers by selecting **Layers ➔ New**. Each additional layer is transparent, so your original work remains visible.

To see a small thumbnail image of

each layer, position your pointer over a layer in the Layer Palette window. This allows you to select an individual layer and bring it to the foreground so that you can edit it.

To change the order of individual

layers click on a layer in the Layer Palette and drag it up or down the list. The item at the top of the list corresponds to the uppermost layer in the stack that makes up your image.

To delete a layer, select it in the Layer

Palette and click the small Recycle Bin button at the top of the Layer Palette.

How to: Paste an image into a window as a new layer

1 Open the new image, or create an image in a separate image window. Click on the window's title bar. Go to **Edit ➔ Copy** to copy the picture to the clipboard. Click on the title bar of the window to which you want to copy the image so that it becomes active.

2 To insert the image into the selected window, go to **Edit ➔ Paste** and select the **As New Layer** option from the menu. The picture will now appear in your new composition, and its corresponding layer button will be added to the Layer Palette.

■ **To temporarily hide a layer** while you work on others, click on the glasses button beside the layer you wish to hide. Click the button again to show the layer again.

■ **Once you are happy with your layout,** merge the layers into a single one by going to **Layers ➜ Merge All**.

▶ See also **The world of graphics,** p. 154.

UNDERSTANDING VECTOR GRAPHICS

Vector graphics could be the key to the future of fast Internet graphics.

■ **A vector graphic is a digital image** that has been created by using geometric formulas to draw lines and shapes, and fill in colours. Vector graphics are used mainly by drawing, Computer Aided Design (CAD) and animation programs, such as Adobe Illustrator, AutoDesk AutoCad, and Macromedia Flash and Freehand. A vector graphic image can be easily scaled and edited.

■ **Vector graphics have a number of advantages over bitmap formats,** which have to hold information about every pixel in the image. This information makes the file sizes of bitmaps large, and also means that any changes to the picture could result in a loss of information and quality. Bitmap files (such as .bmp, .jpg and .gif) are best used for working with photographs and scanned images in programs like Adobe PhotoShop or Jasc Paint Shop Pro. Many applications now allow you to work on both vector and bitmap formats.

■ **If you've ever tried to zoom in on a photograph** using a graphics application, you'll have noticed that the image becomes blocky. Do the same with a vector graphic, however, and the image will remain clear. This is because the drawing recalculates itself for each resolution. An image can be scaled as large or as small as you want with no loss of quality.

■ **Printers and monitors are generally raster devices** – that is, they rely on a grid (called a raster) to tell them what colour to display where. This is fine for bitmap images, but it means that vector graphics need to be rasterised before they can be displayed or printed. The software will normally handle this for you, but if you ever need to convert a vector graphic to a bitmap for printing or editing in another application, make sure you export your image at the required size. Once it is in a raster bitmap format any further resizing will probably result in a loss of quality.

■ **Many animations on the Web rely on vector graphics** to be able to appear quickly on your screen even over the slowest connections. Macromedia Flash is an animation program that takes advantage of the efficient size of vector graphics to create amazing effects that have transformed the look of many of the Internet's most popular Websites.

How to: Scale a vector image in Adobe Illustrator

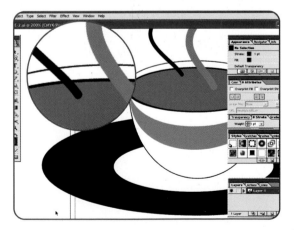

1 This image of a coffee cup was created as a vector graphic in Adobe Illustrator. To scale it, create a marquee with the direct selection tool (the white-headed arrow) and then double-click the scale tool. Enter values in the Scale dialogue box to change the size.

2 To scale the graphic manually, create the marquee as before, double-click on the scale tool, select an anchor point and drag with your mouse. Hold the Shift key down while dragging to keep the enlarged version of the image in proportion.

3 The vector image of the coffee cup will always remain sharp, no matter how much it is enlarged. Its final printed quality depends on the abilities of the printer, and a PostScript printer is required for the best results.

Drawing programs

Feel like harnessing some of your artistic impulses? Discover a wealth of creative possibilities by using drawing software on your PC. There is a program to suit all needs and capabilities, from the simplest of sketching programs to more advanced professional design packages.

GETTING STARTED

Finding a drawing program to suit your needs is often a case of trial and error, so sample as many as you can before you buy. Some of the best and most popular packages are CorelDraw, Macromedia Freehand, Microsoft PhotoDraw and Adobe Illustrator. Others are available, some concentrating on special tasks, such as preparing illustrations for Websites. You can download trial versions of most programs from the Internet.

At first, the range of tools on a drawing program can be intimidating. Begin by familiarising yourself with the toolbar. It will be somewhat different from the other toolbars you have used in Windows, and a few of the features – such as Fill and Transparency – may take time to get used to. Most programs offer basic tools, such as line and curve drawing, shape drawing, fill options, colour palette

pickers and special effects and filters. The best way to learn how to use them is to work your way through the help files and tutorials supplied with the program.

Once you've mastered the basic tools, you need to either create an image from scratch to work on, or import one from ready-made clip art. If you have an image on your PC already, use the **File ➔ Open** command to locate and open the image.

Drawing programs are easy to use because they work on a point-and-click basis. Pop-up windows control tasks such as brush or pen selection, colour picking or entering text.

Don't underestimate the Undo tool! The key to drawing artwork is to take a methodical approach. Go slowly and save your work when you have reached a point where you are happy with the result.

DRAWING SHAPES

Multiple choice. In some drawing programs – CorelDraw, for example – the freehand and polygon tools have multiple options, often denoted by a small black triangle in the bottom right of the Toolbar button. Clicking on this will reveal more available options, such as the Bezier tool, which is used for drawing curves and spiral polygons.

Almost any shape can be created on your PC. Choose from resizable rectangles, circles and polygons, or opt for freehand drawing. In CorelDraw, the shape options are found on the Toolbar under the Freehand, Rectangle, Ellipse and Polygon tools. You can also draw smooth curves using the Bezier option. Just click on the shape option you want to use, move the cursor to the desired position, and you're ready to start working on your first piece of computer art.

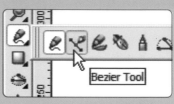

Problems creating that perfect circle or square in CorelDraw? Simply hold down the **Ctrl** key as you draw.

FILLING AND SPECIAL EFFECTS

When you first draw a shape, only the outline is shown. Adding colour and texture to

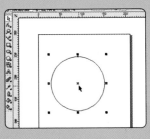

shapes is one of the most useful and rewarding elements of a drawing program. Just click on the shape with the pointer or selection tool to highlight it.

Options for filling in a drawing will vary from program to program. In general, you'll be able to use a simple colour fill, patterns (which can also be edited) and texture fills. The **Fill** tool allows you to select from an extensive array of preset or custom colours.

Filters and special effects tools make a big difference to your artwork's look. To use them well, you need to understand the difference between vector graphics and bitmaps. Vector graphics – the mode you normally work in – are shapes defined by lines and curves, which can be edited to alter the outline of the picture. Bitmap images are grids of dot-like pixels, which can also be edited. Many special effects in drawing programs will only work on bitmap images. To convert an image to bitmap in CorelDraw, go to **Bitmap → Convert to Bitmap**.

To make a shape larger or smaller in

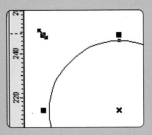

most drawing programs, click on the object with the **Item** tool (normally a black arrow). Now click and drag on any of the corner or side handles to resize the shape.

Designing an invitation, letter or poster? Experiment with the pre-prepared graphics that are installed with most of the major

graphics programs. CorelDraw comes with a set of templates useful for designing letterheads, brochures and other business stationery.

ORGANISING OBJECTS

The easiest way to move objects around is to click on them, and drag them with the mouse to a new position.

Use the Arrange tool to rotate your images. Go to **Arrange → Transformations → Rotate** in CorelDraw. Enter an angle in the transformation task pane. You might need to experiment to achieve the desired effect. If it goes wrong, use the **Undo** tool to revert to the object's previous position and try again.

Combine multiple objects with the **Group** command. Hold down the **Shift** key and click on all the objects you want to keep together. Click the **Arrange → Group** command in CorelDraw to link them. As you move one object, the other selected objects will move with it.

DRAWING FOR THE WEB

To create images that work well on Web pages, save your artwork as a .gif or .jpg file. In CorelDraw click on the drawing you want to use and go to **File → Publish to The Web**.

▶ See also **The world of graphics**, p. 154; **Tiny changes make a big difference**, p. 190; and **Understanding vector graphics**, p. 193.

How to: Use the CorelDraw interactive blend tool

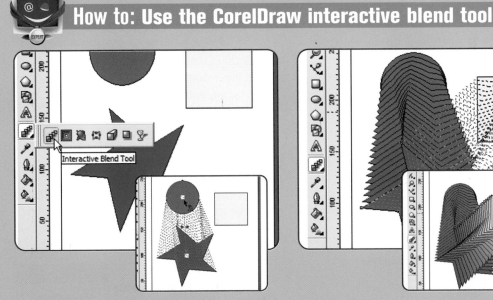

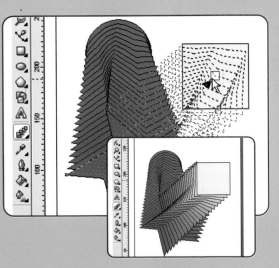

1 Open a new document in CorelDraw. Create and colour the shapes that you want to blend. Then make sure you have deselected them all before clicking on the **Interactive Blend Tool** in the vertical Toolbar.

2 Now simply click on the first shape and drag the cursor across the page to the next shape. Release the mouse button and the two shapes will create a smooth and colourful blend. Join the other shapes in the same way.

With just a PC and some photo-editing software, you can now achieve effects that used to be limited to the professionals.

■ **Products like digital cameras and scanners** make it possible for you to transfer all your photos to your PC. It's impossible to take a perfect picture every time, but you can retouch and improve less-than-perfect shots using photo editing software. You can also create collages and montages, convert colour photos to black-and-white, add tints and give photos the appearance of paintings. You can turn your favourites into calendars, postcards, greetings cards or jigsaw puzzles. All the programs listed below are capable of amazing photographic feats.

PHOTO AND IMAGE EDITING SOFTWARE

Here's a selection of available software.

ADOBE PHOTOSHOP (www.adobe.com)
The industry standard among professionals. It has a huge range of image editing tools and options, but is priced accordingly.

COREL PHOTO-PAINT (www.corel.com)
A powerful image editing and painting program loaded with tools, effects, plug-ins and options.

JASC PAINT SHOP PRO (www.jasc.com)
A versatile, mid-level image and photo editing program. One of its most useful features is the auto-photo enhancer that allows you to redraw photos.

PICTURE IT! (www.microsoft.com)
Microsoft's entry-level image editing program makes it easy for you to retouch, repair and enhance your photos.

■ **Want to display your photos at their best?** Go to **Start → Control Panel → Appearance and Themes → Display**, and click the **Settings** tab. In the Colour quality section, select **Highest (32 bit)** and click **OK**. Now your images will display in as many colours as your monitor is capable of displaying.

■ **Scanning your photos?** Wipe any dust off your photo before you start, then put it onto your scanner. If possible, make sure that it's lined up with one of the edges of the platen (the full scanning area on which your photo sits). Using your scanning software, click **Preview** and the scanner will perform a quick scan, just so that you can see exactly where the image sits on the screen. It doesn't matter if you scan your image upside-down or sideways – you can always rotate it later. Good settings for scanning photos are around 300 dpi and scaled to 100 per cent. Now simply click **Scan**, and the image will be scanned into whichever image editing program you are currently using.

■ **Save a copy of your scan** so you can return to the original version if your edits and effects don't work as well as you hoped. First rotate the image so that it's square on the screen, and crop any extraneous areas, then save your image with a name like 'wedding_original'. Once you start making major changes to the image, save the changed image under a new name, so that you've always got the original to revert to.

■ **Fix dust, scratches and blemishes.** Most photo editing software comes with photo repair tools. Many will fix scratches automatically, but this can be rather heavy-handed. You can try instead to fix each blemish manually. Zoom in on the affected area before you start working, then zoom back out at intervals to

check the overall effect. You'll be amazed by what you can achieve with a little practice.

■ **Crop in on the interesting parts of your photo** and don't feel bad about throwing away large areas of the background. Cropping is one of the skills that professionals use to create striking images. Try to crop your image so that the focus of attention is in the centre.

■ **Remove red-eye.** One of the most instantly effective improvements you can make to a photograph with editing software is to remove red-eye from pictures of people and animals taken with electronic flash. Just zoom in on the eyes, click on the red sections within the pupils, and tell your software to remove the red-eye.

■ **Get rid of date stamps on photos** by using your photo editing program to copy nearby parts of the photo and paste them over the date stamp. Zoom in so that you're working close in on the date stamp area. Keep changing the area of the image that you're copying from to make the area you're pasting to look convincing. You can get rid of unwanted elements of a photograph – even people! – in the same way. Save when you're happy with your progress and use the Undo function if you make a change that looks unsightly.

■ **Adjust brightness and contrast to lighten dark pictures,** add depth to flat pictures and darken washed-out pictures. If your image editing software offers automatic contrast/ brightness adjustment, try it to see if it

improves your image. If it doesn't, try tweaking the settings manually. In this photo of a couple by the sea, their faces are in shadow. Microsoft Picture It!'s **Touchup Painting** tool was used to increase the brightness and contrast of their faces slightly, then reduce the brightness of the white chair in the foreground, making it less distracting.

options your software has to remove fading automatically, or simply adjust the brightness and contrast to improve the image. Your software should have a tool for sharpening photos – see how much you can sharpen the image without making it look too grainy.

Which resolution and format should you save in?

If you're e-mailing it or posting a picture onto the Web, you need to get the file down to a reasonable size – preferably below 100 KB – without losing too much quality. Reduce the resolution to 72 dpi, and save as a .jpeg. Many photo editing programs offer a **Save as Web image** option, so you can gauge the effects of compression (see 'How to', p. 44).

If you're planning to print your image,

then file size is not a problem – but picture quality is. Save the picture at a resolution of at least 300 dpi. A good file format is the .tiff format, which uses LZW compression to reduce file size without losing quality. Image files saved for printing can take up a lot of disk space, so consider storing them using a removable storage medium like a Zip disk or writable CD-R.

If only!

Have you ever looked at one of your photographs of family or friends and wished that you had chosen a better background? Now you can fix the problem by combining two images into one perfect shot (see 'How to', below).

Use your images on postcards, greetings cards, calendars,

invitations or business cards. Picture It! offers a wide range of predesigned templates for your photos. On these pages, for example, a collection of photos of family and friends was given a variety of uses. The photo of a girl on a beach was made into a

calendar, the shot of a couple by the sea was made into a postcard and two photos, of a girl and some canoeists, were combined and turned into a magazine cover.

▶ See also **Scanners and scanning,** p. 40; **Cameras go digital,** p. 44; and **Artistic effects for your photos,** p. 188.

Restore old black-and-white photos.

You've got a precious photo of your grandparents' wedding, but it has not aged well. Scan the photo, then convert the image to greyscale to remove any colour cast. Try any

How to: Merge two photographs with Paint Shop Pro

1 Open both the images you are going to work on. To change the background behind the girl, first select her head and shoulders with the **Freehand** tool (the **Smart Edge** makes it easier to trace shapes). Go to **Edit ➜ Copy** to place your selection on the clipboard.

2 Open the image that you want to use as the new background. Go to **Edit ➜ Paste ➜ As New Layer** to put the image you have cut out over the new background. Use the **Mover** tool to position the new layer.

3 You can also experiment with the brightness and contrast and other aspects of the new layer to make it fit into the new background well. Once you are happy with the result, go to **Layers ➜ Merge ➜ Merge All (Flatten)** and save the file under a new name.

Working with money

Managing your finances

MASTERING MICROSOFT MONEY

Using software, such as Microsoft Money, is a convenient way to organise financial information.

■ **Every time you run Money, you will start at the Money home page.** This is an information centre displaying facts about the state of your finances. Set it up to show your main accounts, any upcoming bills and even display a graph of the day.

■ **To get the most out of Money,** you need to tell the program everything about your financial situation. This can take time, but once it's done, you will have a centralised record which will show you just where your finances stand.

■ **Microsoft Money can help you with short or long-term budgeting.** To keep track of spending, use Money to balance your chequebook on a daily basis. For greater control of your affairs, use it to monitor your investments, loans, savings and pension.

■ **In the black, or the red?** Money can analyse how you spend and produce reports based on this information, enabling you to identify areas where savings could be made or where investment opportunities may lie.

CONTROL YOUR CASH WITH QUICKEN

Take control of your finances with the complete money management program from Quicken.

■ **Seven Up.** Quicken Personal Plus (www. quicken.co.uk) is a powerful program with features that help you organise the seven key areas of your home finances: banking, taxes, investments, planning, loans, insurance and your spending and saving.

■ **Use the Accounts feature to keep track of all your expenses.** Quicken's Accounts are great for helping you manage your bank accounts and credit cards, but they're also handy for any area where you regularly exchange funds. If you've lent a friend a lot of money, why not set up an account to help you keep track of the repayments? You could also set up accounts for your children to keep a record of their pocket money, and help them save for special purchases.

■ **Get your Categories right for your needs.** Quicken includes a number of preset categories for producing reports and tracking expenditure and income, as well as watching your investments accrue. You can add and delete items from the Category & Transfer List so that the options always reflect your spending habits.

■ **Quicken lets you automate regular transactions.** If you have regular incomings and outgoings of a fixed amount – such as your monthly salary, loan repayments or annual insurance policies – you can configure Quicken to enter these sums automatically. You can also set up Quicken to prompt you to confirm whether a payment has been made or received, and to remind you of payments that need to be made.

LEARN THE LINGO
Familiarise yourself with these terms first to get the most out of your Quicken program.

● **Account** A set of common financial transactions – such as a credit card – that you want to track.

● **Category** The group label or name you attach to a Transaction. This helps with reporting.

● **File** A group of Quicken accounts kept together for easy management.

● **Memorise** Quicken can remember your transactions and reports, which is handy if you need to re-enter text and parameters.

● **Online banking** Quicken includes a powerful suite of tools to enable you to pay bills and transfer funds over the Internet by linking directly with your bank.

● **Reconcile** The act of comparing your bank statement with your Quicken record to confirm there are no irregularities.

● **Reports** Quicken's own statements, analysis graphs and tables so you can see exactly where your money has gone.

● **Summary** A screen that provides an overview of all the transactions that have taken place on a particular account.

● **Transaction** A movement of money into – or out of – an account.

■ **Quicken integrates with your online bank account.** Download transactions as they clear directly from your bank or credit card company. Note that not every bank offers this facility – ones that do include Lloyds TSB, HSBC and MBNA.

■ **Keep your receipts!** Quicken is only useful if the data you enter is accurate and complete. Going on holiday? Keep your credit and bank card receipts in a safe place so you can update Quicken on your return. Shop online? Make sure you print out your order so that you don't forget to add the transaction to Quicken next time you have a book-keeping session.

MIND YOUR OWN BUSINESS

MYOB – Mind Your Own Business – offers a complete accounting solution for everyone – from households to companies.

■ **Buying the right version.** There are four versions of MYOB – each more powerful (and complex) than the one before it – MYOB FirstAccounts, MYOB Accounting, MYOB Accounting Plus and MYOB Premier. Most individuals, families and small businesses will find that FirstAccounts caters to all their needs.

■ **Start off on the right foot.** To get the best out of MYOB (or other accounting software) take the following steps: make sure your accounts are up-to-date; make sure all the documents you need are to hand – bank statements, chequebooks etc; and give yourself enough time to get to grips with the program. Rushing the job will only result in mistakes.

■ **Timing is everything.** If you are starting off with accounting software for the first time, or are switching from a manual to a computerised method of accounting, try to make the switch at the beginning of the financial year – April 1st, for most UK taxpayers. That way, your final accounts for the previous financial year will provide you with a set of reliable opening balances to work from.

■ **Talking the same language.** If an accountant deals with your finances, it makes sense to use the same accounting package that he or she uses. However, many accounting firms can accept figures from most of the popular programs. If your accountant uses MYOB, then ask him or her to set up your accounts for you and give you a quick preliminary tutorial.

■ **Dates are very important in accounting.** It is therefore vital that you make sure that your computer has been set up to understand dates in the order of day/month/year. If MYOB thinks 7/8/01 means the eighth day of the seventh month (and not the seventh day of the eighth month), go to the **Regional and Language Options Control Panel**. Make sure that English (United Kingdom) has been selected.

WORKING OUT YOUR TAX

Calculate your income tax liability with one of the programs available on the market.

■ **For UK taxpayers** there is only a limited range of tax software intended for use by individuals and families. Business users are well catered for by a number of companies, such as

Quicken (www.quicken.co.uk), MYOB (www.myob.co.uk), Sage (www.sage.co.uk) and Sybiz (www.sybiz.co.uk), all of which offer a range of powerful tax software.

■ **Even if you have no financial programs or add-ons,** a simple database – even a list of items in a Word document, for example – can often provide an adequate means of keeping track of key financial transactions, expenses and so on.

■ **Need in-depth information on tax matters?** The Inland Revenue Website is the first place to visit (www.inlandrevenue.gov.uk). It offers advice on filing your tax return online, as well as guides to completing your return and downloadable pages that may be missing from the forms they originally sent you.

■ **Filing your tax return online is relatively easy,** although you can't decide to do it at the last minute. You first need to register online at the Government Gateway Website, www.gateway.gov.uk. You will be sent a User ID through the post, which will allow you to log on to the service. The Inland Revenue provides a program called SA Online to let you complete your tax return, although you can also use commercial packages like Intuit's TaxCalc (www.taxcalc.co.uk).

■ **Don't take risks with your personal information.** If you are storing important information on your PC, make sure that you back up your files regularly and store the copies in another location. It's also a good idea to keep your figures safe from prying eyes. In Windows XP Home edition, choose the option to keep your personal files private (right-click on the folder and choose **Sharing and Security**, then make sure the **Make this folder private** option is checked). This means that other users of your computer will not be able to access your files too easily. For even greater protection, you should encrypt your files – one reason it may be worth upgrading to XP Pro Edition.

▶ See also **Plan your family budget**, p. 183; and **Taxes in cyberspace**, p. 266.

Contact managers

A diary can quickly become unworkable as people change addresses and phone numbers. How do you separate your friends and relatives from business contacts? A contact manager program can do all this, and it has many other features to keep your life more organised.

FIELDS KEEP YOU ORGANISED

Contact manager programs store their information in fields like a database record – which gives you an extremely flexible system. A contact record typically consists of a field for first names, another for last names, individual fields for separate lines of addresses, different phone numbers and so on. If you need to include more information, however, you can easily add your own fields to suit your needs. You can sort and organise your database by fields – such as last name, street name, postcode or in any order that suits you.

Categorise your contacts. Most contact manager programs let you assign categories to contacts, which can be very useful. You could create a Christmas category for people you want to send a Christmas card to, then get the software to automatically print address labels. Or you could categorise every member of a sports team into one group, so that looking up their details is easy.

Most contact management tools can easily import data from other programs. If you want to upgrade, check the new software's Help files for instructions. Importing data is a lot faster than retyping by hand – and more accurate.

Create a card! Both Lotus Organizer and Microsoft Outlook support vCards – virtual business cards. vCards put contact information into a format that can be shared between different applications. The most common use for a vCard is to attach one to an e-mail to send your details to someone else. When you receive a vCard, Outlook and Organizer can save the details it contains into your contacts database for you. To create a vCard in Outlook, select a contact then go to **Actions ➜ Forward as vCard**.

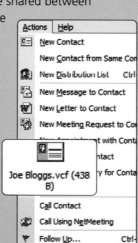

NOT JUST A CONTACT MANAGER

Microsoft Outlook and Lotus Organizer have many other features related to personal information management.

OUTLOOK COMPONENTS INCLUDE
- calendar
- to-do list manager
- phone call log
- e-mail tools
- 'today' view for organising important tasks for the day
- note pad

ORGANIZER COMPONENTS INCLUDE
- calendar
- to-do list manager
- phone call log
- management of information for Web pages you frequently visit
- year planner
- note pad
- anniversary viewer

USING OUTLOOK

Add a contact. Switch to **Contacts** view, then go to the Standard Toolbar and click on the **New Contact** button. A window appears in which you can enter information for the new contact. Use the tabs to organise all the different kinds of information. Click on the **Full Name** button to enter a complete name and use the **Address** button to enter all the address details. Click **Save and Close** when you have finished.

Lost your way? Outlook has an area on the left of the screen called the Outlook Bar that contains Shortcut icons to all the program's important elements. Single-click on the element that you wish to go to.

Manage your Outlook Shortcuts or groups on the Outlook Bar by right-clicking anywhere on the Bar and choosing from the context menu that pops up. If you want to remove an icon that you don't use, right-click on the icon and choose **Remove from Outlook Bar**.

Save typing time. If you have entered an e-mail address for a contact in Microsoft Outlook, addressing an e-mail to the person is easy. Just click on **Inbox** and then **New** on the Standard Toolbar. Then click on the **To** button, double-click the contact or contacts that you want to send an e-mail to and click **OK**. Start typing the contact's name in the Type Name box to jump to the relevant part of your contacts list. Outlook will enter the address in the To field for you.

Take a different view. You can view contacts in several different ways in Outlook. Go to **View ➔ Current View**, then select the view you want from the drop-down menu. If you want to see all your mails on the same subject grouped together, use the **By Conversation Topic** view. Likewise, to see all the mails sent by individual contacts grouped together, use the **By Sender** view. You can even create your own personalised views and choose which fields to display.

Take a shortcut. Outlook's pop-up context menus allow you to use the **Contacts** view as a starting point to initiate many different tasks. Simply right-click on any contact, and then choose from a range of different tasks relating to that contact, from printing personal details or sending an e-mail to automatically contacting the person by phone or even arranging a meeting.

EXPLORING ORGANIZER

Add a contact. In the **Contacts** view, choose the **Create** menu and click **Contact**. A window appears ready for you to add data. Use the tabs to enter more detailed information. Click **OK** when you've finished.

Organizer is easy to navigate. It takes its design from paper organisers like Filofax, with a column of tabs down the right and left-hand sides of the main window for navigating within the program. Just click the one you want to open for a new view. As with a normal book, the tab moves to the left once opened.

Never forget an important date again. Organizer has a clever built-in feature for reminding you of birthdays and anniversaries. To use it, make sure you enter birthday or anniversary details under the **General** tab of a new contact. Then you can click the **Anniversary** tab to see what is coming up this month. You can also view anniversaries for the whole year or even by Zodiac sign.

To see different views of your contacts in Organizer, first make sure you are in the Contacts area, then click the **View** menu and choose an option, such as **By First Name**. You can also change the view simply by clicking on the small icons at the bottom left of the screen. There are lots of views available, and you may find different ones useful at different times. Experiment to find out which ones you prefer.

You can edit your contacts labels if you need to by simply clicking on **View ➔ Contacts Preferences** in Contacts view and then clicking on the **Edit Labels** button.

How to: Make a phone call directly from Outlook

1 First switch to Contacts view using the Outlook Bar on the left. Click on **Contacts** to locate the person you want to call. Right-click on the name to bring up the pop-up context menu and click on **Call Contact**.

2 A new box appears. If you want to keep notes about the call, put a tick next to **Create new Journal Entry when starting new call** before you start. You will be able to make notes while the call is in progress. If you don't need a record, just click **Start Call**.

3 Pick up your handset and, when the call connects, click the **Talk** button in the Call Status dialogue and start your conversation. To finish the call click **End Call** in the New Call dialogue box.

Handy helpers

Utilities

UTILITIES KEEP THINGS RUNNING

Use Windows' utility software to keep your PC running smoothly, and to troubleshoot problems.

■ **Your PC's utilities are listed under System Tools.** To find them, go to **Start → All Programs → Accessories → System Tools**.

■ **Using extra utilities.** The utilities in Windows' System Tools folder cover the most

basic needs, but it's worth checking out add-on utilities from other companies, such as McAfee and Norton. These help to keep your PC in peak condition.

■ **If you need to free up space** on your hard drive, run Disk Cleanup. This utility scans your hard drive and lists temporary files, Internet

NORTON UTILITIES

When your PC is unwell, this software package will come to its aid.

This brand is the world leader – the best-known commercial diagnostic and repair software for PCs. Available as a software package separate from the Utilities options on your PC, it can run similar checks and organise your space, as well as repair files and recover information that has been accidentally erased (see p. 206).

---

cache files and unnecessary program files that you can delete. Access it through System Tools, or by going to **Start → My Computer**, then right-clicking the **C:** drive icon and then **Properties**. Click **Disk Cleanup** under the **General** tab. Highlight each entry in the 'Files to delete' box to see a description of the item before you delete it. Click **View Files** to see the files contained in each folder. Check the box next to the folders that you want to remove, then click **OK**.

■ **For other options with Disk Cleanup,** click the **More Options** tab and then **Clean up** to search for any unwanted Windows components or installed programs, or to reduce the amount of storage space on your disk used by System Restore.

■ **If you have an older version of Windows,** use ScanDisk to check for errors in your files and folders and automatically repair them. It also checks your hard drive for physical damage. To activate ScanDisk in versions of Windows up to Me, go to **Start → Programs → Accessories → System Tools → ScanDisk** and click on your hard drive. Under Type of test, you need to select **Standard** and click **Start**. To scan the surface of the drive for physical errors, click **Thorough** instead of **Standard**.

■ **When you save a file,** especially a large one, your PC uses whatever space it can find available on your hard drive. This means that files may be split up and located in several places, slowing your PC down when it has to search for the files all over the drive. Disk Defragmenter groups files together, which speeds up the PC's performance. To start this utility, select **Disk Defragmenter** under **System Tools**. Make sure the correct drive is highlighted at the top of the Window. Click **Analyze** if you

---

want to see how fragmented your disk is and if it needs defragmenting. Alternatively, click on **Defragment** to skip the initial check and begin the process immediately.

▶ See also **Hard drive housekeeping,** p. 32.

LEARNING WITH TASK WIZARDS

These miniprograms take you step-by-step through common computer tasks, and they can be customised.

■ **Create and send a fax** with Microsoft Word's Fax Wizard. Go to **File → New**. In the task pane on the right of the screen, click on **General Templates**, then on the **Letters and Faxes** tab and double-click on **Fax Wizard**. Follow the steps in the Fax Wizard. Under the other tabs and you'll find Wizards for CVs, memos, calendars, reports and other documents.

■ **Word's Web Page Wizard has a number of themes** that you can choose from. Each one is a distinctive design using complementary backgrounds, colours and fonts.

Not all the themes are available when you install Microsoft Word – the Office XP CD-ROM has extra ones. Click on the theme **Nature**, for example, and Word prompts you to install it. Click **Install** to start the process. You'll be prompted to insert your CD-ROM, and Word will extract the theme from it. Once it has been copied, you'll see a sample of the new theme in the right window.

Use Outlook's Import and Export Wizard

to import a list of contacts created in another program, like Word. Open Word and create your contact list, or open your existing contact file. Information (like name, address and phone number) in each individual record should be separated by tabs or cómmas. Make sure the file is saved as a .txt file, and close the document. Open Outlook and go to **File ➜ Import and Export**, and follow the instructions. Outlook Express uses a slightly different procedure with a dialogue box instead of a Wizard.

Use Word's Letter Wizard to write a letter.

Go to **File ➜ New** then click on **General Templates** in the New Document panel on the right of the window. Select the **Letters and Faxes** tab, then double-click on **Letter Wizard**. Follow the steps in the Wizard – you will be prompted to choose a design and style, select the recipient's name and address and the greeting to begin the letter. You can add standard elements such as an 'Attention:' line, and finally you will be asked to fill in your details and choose how you want to close your letter.

Excel makes number crunching easier.

Use the Chart Wizard button on the Toolbar to create bar, line and pie charts. Some Wizards help you to use two Office programs together – the Access Link Spreadsheet Wizard lets you transfer data from an Excel document into an Access database, for example.

Hide the Office Assistant.

One of the advantages of having Office XP is that the Office Assistant doesn't appear by default. If you are using an earlier version of Office and find the the animated 'help' irritating during the Letter Wizard, click the Office Assistant and click **Options** from the pop-up menu. Under the **Options** tab, uncheck **Help with Wizards**. If the Office Assistant is hidden, go to **Help ➜ Show the Office Assistant**.

You can include extra Wizards

not incorporated in a regular Word installation. Some Wizards are installed on your hard drive in compressed form. Windows extracts them the first time you double-click on their icons. There are also other Wizards on the Office CD-ROM that are not copied to your hard drive when you install Word. If you have already installed Word, add extra Wizards by going to **Start ➜ Control Panel ➜ Add or Remove Programs**, and highlight Office (or Word). Click **Change** then choose the **Add or Remove Features** option.

Even more Wizards can be downloaded

from the Net. In Word, go to **Help ➜ Office on the Web**. This takes you to the Microsoft Office Assistance Centre, where you can download any additional Wizards and templates you want.

▶ See also **How to download files,** p. 240.

CALCULATORS FOR YOUR DESKTOP

Quickly work out those tricky sums without resorting to a spreadsheet.

Windows includes two calculators in one

found by clicking on **Start ➜ All Programs ➜ Accessories ➜ Calculator**. The basic calculator is the default, with the usual standard functions. Click on the **Scientific** option in the **View** menu and the window changes to add many other functions, such as trigonometry, logarithms and statistics.

Use your memory.

You can store a displayed number for use later by clicking on **MS**.

An 'M' symbol indicates the calculator's memory is in use. Keep a running total in a series of calculations by clicking the **M+** key to add the number on the display to the one in the memory. You can press **MR** to recall the value in the memory at any time, and **MC** will clear the contents of the memory when you've finished.

Avoid typing errors.

When you've completed your calculations, you don't have to key the sum manually into your document. Use the Copy and Paste function in the Edit menu as an alternative. First, press **Ctrl+C** to copy the result from your calculator, and then click where you want the value to go in your document and press **Ctrl+V** to paste it in.

▶ See also **There's a calculator for it,** p. 301.

MP3: THE NEW FACE OF MUSIC

Discover a new musical media on your PC.

Windows Me includes an MP3 player

called the Windows Media Player. Double-click on its Desktop icon and use the File menu's Open command to select and play your MP3 files. It comes with some great 3-D visual effects that move in time with the music.

To test-drive an MP3 player,

download one for free from Download.com (www.download.com). Click the **MP3 & Audio** link, then click **Players**. There are hundreds of MP3 and CD players to choose from, and the page displays the player's name, a brief summary and the file size. Click on a program's title to see a full description and technical specifications. For more information, read the reviews and user comments. To transfer a program to your computer, click **Download Now**.

Go to the CNET Music Center

(music.cnet.com) and click **Play Music** to get all the facts on MP3 players, including reviews and user comments. You can also learn about streaming audio, MiniDiscs and even how to connect your PC to your home stereo system!

■ **Skins are add-on software** that change the look of an MP3 player. To view and download some great looking skins for your Winamp player, go to the Winamp site (www.winamp.com) and click on the **Skins** tab.

■ **Winamp has extra features.** Like most MP3 players, Winamp uses the standard buttons, such as Play and Pause, found on all CD players. But, in addition, it has features like Shuffle, Playlists and a graphic equaliser. Like Windows Media Player, Winamp can also play videos in various formats as well as sounds. For an interactive guide to Winamp's features, go to the Winamp site (www.winamp.com). Click on **Winamp** then **Walkthrough** at the top of the screen and choose a feature to explore. Roll over a button to see a description of what it does, shown in the window below.

▶ See also **Digital music players,** p. 37; and **Explore the world of MP3,** p. 285.

MAKING THE MOST OF PHONE DIALER

Use this Windows miniprogram to dial your phone for you, wherever you are in the world.

Your phone and modem must be on the same line for the program to work. To dial a number in pre-XP versions of Windows, go to **Start ➔ Program ➔ Accessories ➔ Communications ➔ Phone Dialer**. In Windows XP, Microsoft have removed the program from the Communication menu, but it's still on your hard disk. To open it, go to **Start ➔ Run** and type **dialer.exe** in the dialogue box.

Phone Dialer in Windows 98 and Me is a relatively simple program that appears like a telephone keypad on your screen. It can store a list of speed-dial numbers for people you ring often and adds prefixes to numbers – useful if

you are dialling via a switchboard, for example, or use a different telephone company for long distance and international calls.

■ **Phone Dialer under Windows XP and Windows 2000** is not simply a program for making normal telephone calls. It is also capable of using Internet telephone services, which offer great potential savings if you make lots of international calls and have a fast Internet connection. The program is also adept at handling conference calls and video conferences.

■ **If you use a calling card to make low-priced international phone calls,** use the Phone and Modem Options control panel to configure any special dialling codes or PIN numbers so that they are dialled automatically for you. Go to **Start ➔ Control Panel ➔ Network and Internet Connections** and click on **Phone and Modem Options** in the left-hand column. In the **Dialing Rules** tab, highlight a Location (a desktop machine will most likely only have one Location set up) and click on **Edit**. The three tabs in the Edit Location dialogue box offer

you a wealth of different ways to set up how your computer dials telephone numbers for you.

■ **If you have Outlook, Outlook Express or Works** on your PC, you may not need to use Phone Dialer. All three programs offer you the ability to call a selected contact from their Address book features. In the Works Address Book, for example, right-click on a contact and choose **Action ➔ Dial**. If your contact has more than one phone number, you can choose the one you want.

■ **Phone Dialer's capabilities are most appropriate for an office.** Home users will find that Microsoft's Windows Messenger can do many of the same things, such as Internet Phoning and conference calls.

SENDING A FAX

You want to send and receive faxes? No need to buy a fax machine – you may already have a basic fax program on your PC.

■ **Anyone with an old Windows 95 PC** can install Microsoft Fax directly. If you are a Windows 98 or a Windows 98SE user, you will find the same software on your Windows CD, in the **\Tools\Oldwin95\Message\Us** folder.

■ **Microsoft Fax is not provided** with Windows Me. You could try installing it from an old Windows 98 CD-ROM, but the official Microsoft position is that 'using Microsoft Fax in Windows Me may result in errors or data loss, or both', so it's best to look for another option.

■ **To fax in Windows XP** you need to install Fax Services if you have not already. A quick way to check for this is to go to the Printers and Faxes control panel and see if the 'Fax' icon appears alongside your installed printers.

If not, go to **Start ➜ Control Panel ➜ Add or Remove Programs** and click on **Add/Remove Windows Components** in the left-hand column. The Windows Component Wizard will launch. Check **Fax Services**, then click **Next**. Wait while the Wizard installs the necessary components, then finally click **Finish** to exit the Wizard. Your PC is now ready to send and receive faxes though your modem.

■ Next configure your fax settings.

Double-click on the **Fax** icon in the Printers and Faxes control panel. The Fax Configuration Wizard will launch. Click **Next**, then fill in the fields in the Sender Information page. Add any details needed in the next screens and choose whether you want to be able to receive as well as send faxes, and, if so, whether to answer calls manually or have your PC do it automatically. Bear in mind that this may interfere with an answering machine if you only have a single phone line. Once you have completed all the fields necessary,

the Fax Console will launch. This is where you will be able to view any faxes that you receive.

■ Microsoft Word also has support for sending faxes, in the form of a range of fax templates and a Fax Wizard, which walks you through the process of sending your document to its destination. For this to work, you must have a fax program loaded onto your PC.

■ Perhaps you don't use Microsoft Word? If you install Fax Services in Windows XP, you can fax any document you create in any program – drawings and pictures included. Faxing merely becomes another way of printing; to fax the document go to **File ➜ Print** and choose **Fax** in the drop-down list of printers at the top of the Print dialogue box. Click **OK** and the Send Fax Wizard will launch. If you are faxing to someone with a machine, it's a good idea to go to **Page Setup** first to make sure that your document will fit on the A4 paper that most fax machines use.

■ Symantec's WinFax Pro is an alternative to the built-in fax programs in Windows XP. It offers high-quality fax templates, a special mode for transmitting colour photographs and intelligent filters for automatically deleting junk faxes as they are received.

■ Use the Internet for sending and receiving your faxes. Sites such as j2 (www.j2.com), eFax (www.efax.com) and Onebox (www.onebox.com) offer fax and voicemail services – and what's more they're free.

▶ See also **Learning with task Wizards,** p. 202.

NOTEPAD, YOUR HANDY ELECTRONIC JOTTER

Use this accessory program to jot down notes or copy pieces of text.

■ Notepad is a simple text editor that opens and saves files in text-only format. You can't change fonts or apply any formats. To run Notepad, go to **Start ➜ All Programs ➜ Accessories ➜ Notepad**.

■ Notepad does have some limited tools for text editing. To find specific characters or words, click at the beginning of the text, then go to **Edit ➜ Find**. Type the text you want to find in **Find what**, then click **Find Next**. You can also use the **F3** key as a shortcut for Find Next.

■ Some keyboard shortcuts can be used in Notepad. You can use the standard keyboard shortcuts of **Ctrl+X**, **Ctrl+C** and **Ctrl+V** for Cut, Copy and Paste respectively.

■ New, improved Notepad – only in Windows XP. Previous incarnations of Windows came with a version of Notepad that had two major annoyances. One was that Ctrl+A did not work to select all the text in a file. The other was that the program could only open files smaller than 64 KB. Both foibles are gone with Windows XP. Its version of Notepad can cope with files as big as 1.5 MB. Anything larger can be opened with WordPad.

 How to: Send faxes from Microsoft Word

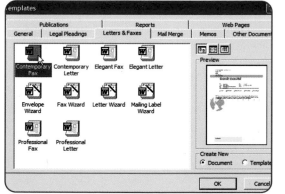

1 In Word 2002, select **File ➜ New** and click on **General Templates** in the right-hand task pane. In the **Letters & Faxes** tab, choose one of the Fax templates (the Preview window on the right shows what it will look like), and click **OK**. Type your message into the template.

2 Select **File ➜ Send To ➜ Fax Recipient**, and Word will launch the Fax Wizard. Select the document to transmit and when the Wizard asks you which fax program you're using, select **Fax**. To send your fax, click **Finish** when the Wizard has been completed.

RECORD THAT TUNE

Windows' Sound Recorder is great for capturing audio from CDs, microphones and other sources.

■ **Want to play and record from CDs** or copy audio from Internet broadcasts? Sound Recorder will do this, and more, but you need a PC with a sound card. Make sure the card has a line in socket that lets you capture sound from an external source, like your stereo or a microphone, as well as from the Net or a CD drive. To open Sound Recorder, go to **Start ➜ All Programs ➜ Accessories ➜ Entertainment**.

■ **If you have problems recording,** check that the settings are correct for the device you want to record from. Go to **Edit ➜ Audio Properties**, and then click on the **Volume** button in the Sound Recording section. The Recording Control panel will open up, and you can set the balances and inputs that Sound Recorder uses. Make sure that your input device is checked and its volume control is not set to zero. If your device

is not displayed, go to the **Options** menu, click on **Properties**, and review the checklist of audio sources.

■ **When capturing sound,** close other applications that might be working in the background and could affect the quality of the recording. Test your sound source first to check that everything is working properly before finally clicking the **Record** button. However, just note that you won't be able to check the green modulation line (which monitors the sound levels) in your dry run. This feature will not start until you have clicked Record.

■ **Edit the sound file** by moving the slider to the point in the sound clip where you want sound to stop. Make sure you save the file first, then go to **Edit**, and select either **Delete Before Current Position** or **Delete After Current Position**, depending on exactly where the section you want to remove is positioned. Play back the edited file to check that the cut has been made in the right place. To undo any edit, go to **File ➜ Revert**. If you haven't saved the file, the Revert command cannot work.

■ **Sound Recorder provides settings** that define the quality of the recording. The better the quality, the larger the file. The actual values available depend on your sound card. Typically you will be able to choose a range of recording grades between telephone quality (mono audio at a 11.025 kHz sampling rate) to CD quality (stereo at a 44.100 kHz). To set the quality, see 'How to', below.

▶ See also **Choosing a microphone,** p. 36; **MP3 music players,** p. 37; **Good loudspeakers make a difference,** p. 38; and **MP3: the new face of music,** p. 203.

KEEP YOUR PC HEALTHY WITH NORTON

Use Norton Utilities to increase your PC's performance, solve and prevent problems, and rescue your computer in case of a malfunction.

■ **Norton Utilities 2002** is several programs in one. It is a continual monitoring system that searches for problems. Any that are found are corrected automatically to prevent your PC from crashing. It will also optimise your system's performance.

■ **Don't install Norton Utilities** if you are already having problems with your PC. Make sure your PC is healthy first. If your PC can be booted up from a CD-ROM, insert the Norton disk into your PC and start – or restart – it. Run Norton Utilities from the CD. When Norton has given your PC a clean bill of health, you can then install Norton onto the hard drive.

■ **If your PC can't be booted from a CD,** make a set of emergency startup floppy disks on a friend's PC. Take your Norton Utilities CD-ROM and some blank floppies to the guest computer, insert your Norton CD-ROM, and click **Browse the CD**. Double-click the **Support** folder, then the **Edisk** folder, and double-click on **Ned.exe**. This program will create a set of emergency disks you can use to start your PC.

■ **To find and fix Windows problems,** go to **Start ➜ All Programs** and select **Norton**

How to: Set Sound Recorder quality

1 Go to **File ➜ Properties**. In the Properties dialogue box, click on **Convert Now**. Under Name, select the setting you want, such as CD, Radio or Telephone Quality. A description of the setting will appear in the Format and Attributes windows below.

2 If desired, adjust the settings and save the new format by clicking **Save As**. Click **OK**. The file will be saved in .wav format, which is best for shorter clips, such as to add audio to documents and PowerPoint presentations. By default, recording is limited to 60 seconds.

Utilities ➜ Norton WinDoctor. WinDoctor identifies and fixes problems with Windows' file-tracking registry, system files and programs, checking for problems such as lost Shortcuts, invalid registry entries or faulty programs. Click

through the WinDoctor Wizard to check your system. A list of any problems will be displayed. Click **Repair All** to automatically fix them. Alternatively you can select a specific problem and click **Repair**. However, you may not want to read all the jargon, so let WinDoctor sort it out.

■ Norton System Doctor is installed by default

and works away in the background, checking your system for problems while allowing you to continue working on your computer. It can be configured to fix many errors automatically.

■ If you haven't installed Norton Utilities yet,

and want to recover an erased file, don't install Norton – if you do, it will write to your hard drive and in the process you risk deleting the file you want to recover. Instead, insert the Norton CD-ROM and click **Launch Utilities**. At the next screen click **Norton Unerase**. When the Unerase Wizard starts, select **Find any recoverable files matching your criteria**, and click **Next**. The Wizard will scan your hard disk for files it may be able to recover and will display a list of possibilities.

■ Speed up your system

by running Norton Speed Disk. This program optimises your hard disk in a more efficient way than the Defragmenter built in to Windows. Speed disk arranges your hard drive so that all the files of one type are stored close together. Run it periodically, or whenever your system slows down. In Speed Disk, select the **C:** drive, then click **Start Optimizing**. As the disk works through its checks, it displays a map of your hard drive, with coloured squares for files. The squares line up as your hard drive is being defragmented. A legend shows what the different colours mean.

■ Run Disk Doctor to test your system files

and check for hard drive surface errors. To start it, select your **C:** drive in Norton Utilities and click **Diagnose**. You can configure Disk Doctor to repair any problems automatically in the background, so you can continue using your PC. System Doctor works in conjunction with Disk Doctor to monitor your drive for problems.

▶ See also **Hard drive housekeeping**, p. 32; **When things go wrong**, p. 102; and **Where to go for help**, p. 102.

How to: Use Norton SystemWorks One Button Checkup

1 Go to **Start ➜ All Programs ➜ Norton SystemWorks**. Click the **Begin Checkup** button. The program will launch a series of checks on your hard disk, first of all looking at the registry, part of the Windows system that can often cause trouble.

2 The checks will take a few minutes to complete. At the end you will see a summary of errors found. Click on **view details** to see more information for each category. Norton can sort out most problems – to start the process, click on **Begin Fix**.

3 Some errors aren't definite problems – in this case SystemWorks noticed that the hard drive had not been scanned for viruses recently. After a check-up with Norton Antivirus, the entire system was scanned again and passed all the tests.

TALKING TO YOUR COMPUTER

Look – no hands! How talking can be as good as typing.

■ **Voice recognition software isn't just for dictation.** Most packages let you control Windows as well. You can launch programs and open or close documents with just a quick word.

■ **All voice recognition packages** are supplied with a headset microphone, but if you are not comfortable using one of these, you can substitute it with your own headphones and a high-quality hand-held or desktop microphone.

■ **Online chat can become more like real chat** on the phone with voice recognition software. There's nothing more tedious than having to type in your side of the conversation, especially when your typing skills may not be the best. Now all you have to do is say it instead.

■ **Don't even think about using voice recognition** in a noisy open-plan office or anywhere with lots of background noise; whether it is children playing or audible traffic, the microphone will pick up surrounding noise, which will make recognition difficult.

■ **Take training seriously** if you want to get the most out of your voice recognition program. The more time you give the program to learn the peculiarities of your voice, the more accurately it will carry out your commands or reproduce spoken words as text.

■ **Check the specifications on the box** before you buy a voice recognition package. The program will work more effectively if you have a fast processor, plenty of memory and lots of available hard drive space. Think twice if your machine is not up to scratch.

■ **Speak naturally and steadily when dictating text.** Any undue emphasis will lead to mistakes. You can make dictation even more effective by buying specialised add-on vocabulary packages, such as those tailored for medicine and law. They will vastly increase the range of words the software recognises.

DEALING WITH VIRUSES

Viruses are programs that you unwittingly store on your hard disk, where they can open and cause havoc unless eradicated.

■ **Boot-sector viruses** were best known in the days of the Disk Operating System (DOS). They still exist, surviving in your hard disk's boot sector – where the files used to start up your PC are stored. A boot-sector virus becomes active each time you start up. Once active, it will copy itself onto every floppy disk inserted into your PC.

■ **Macro viruses are now more common,** with names like Concept, Nuclear and Laroux. They are written in a macro – a sequence of instructions – attached to a Word or Excel file. If you open an infected document, the macro virus writes itself into your copy of Word or Excel, and then infects all future documents created by you. Versions of Word and Excel from Office 97 onward warn you of the presence of macros in a file and offer to disable them for you.

■ **File-infecting viruses** are also known as parasitic viruses. They lurk inside a program so that when you run it, the virus starts meddling with your RAM, and then infects the other programs that you run.

■ **Viruses known as worms** spread copies of themselves over networked computers. While they can replicate themselves and use

VIRUS PROTECTION SOFTWARE
Special programs will protect your PC from vicious viruses.

PANDA ANTIVIRUS (www.pandasecurity.com)
An alternative in a market dominated by Norton and McAfee, Panda is easy to learn and has one unusual feature – when it finds a virus it talks rather than beeps!

MCAFEE VIRUSSCAN (www.mcafee.com)
The scanner component can be run from the Start menu, from Internet Explorer. Set it to run automatically at certain times or when your screensaver starts up. There's an automatic background virus checker and updates are available online or on disk.

NORTON ANTIVIRUS (www.symantec.com/nav/nav_9xnt)
A popular product with disinfection and virus-scanning components, and there are regular free updates. The Repair Wizard will guide you through removing any virus.

memory, they don't infect other programs on your PC. The Red Worm of 2001 spread to thousands of machines in a few days.

■ A multipartite virus combines boot-sector and file-infecting viruses. It is found within an executable program with the file extension .exe. When the program is run, the virus infects the hard drive's boot sector.

■ Polymorphic viruses are viruses that attempt to escape detection by changing their form each time they spread.

■ Trojan horses tend to be hidden inside programs, usually games, and they display a message, erase files or lose data. Strictly speaking they are not viruses, as they don't replicate, and you can get rid of them just by deleting them.

■ Script viruses are written in script programming languages, like Visual Basic Script and JavaScript. They can be caught by opening a .vbs or .js file, or they can be embedded into the HTML of a Web page. In theory, just opening a Web page could cause infection.

■ A floppy disk or other removable media remains a common source of infection. When someone gives you a disk, they may not realise that it contains a virus, and you can't be sure it has been effectively checked for viruses.

■ Opening an e-mail attachment could cause infection, although reading a plain text e-mail won't. Be wary – what may seem to be a .jpg file or a picture may not be harmless.

■ Downloaded software can harbour a virus. If you go to a reputable site like Download (download.cnet.com) and download a well-known program, you're unlikely to get a virus. But if someone sends you an e-mail with a new program attached, don't open it!

■ Office or home networks can spread viruses. Worms can operate over a network, and given a chance will work their way around all the PCs in an organisation within a short period of time.

TOP 10 WARNING SIGNS

Think you've got a virus? Not all these symptoms will appear, and some will conceal themselves or may be caused by other reasons – but they will provide a solid starting point for your diagnosis.

1. Your PC starts to run very slowly for no apparent reason.
2. Programs take longer to load.
3. Files disappear from your hard drive.
4. Program files expand in size.
5. You have trouble opening or saving Word documents.
6. Your PC often crashes or suddenly reboots itself.
7. Your hard drive is accessed more often.
8. Odd dialogue boxes or messages appear on screen or strange sounds come from your speakers for no obvious reason.
9. Devices that once worked, now don't, even though you haven't changed your system configuration.
10. If you are on a network, you notice that the problems affecting your computer have started occurring on other PCs in your office as well.

■ If you receive a suspect Microsoft Word file, play safe by first opening it with WordPad. This is because Word macro viruses can only infect copies of files in Word, and WordPad cannot run macros.

■ Set antivirus software to automatically scan all floppies (and other removable media,

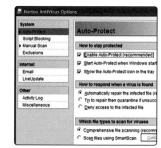

such as Zip disks) you use, even new ones. Write-protect any floppies you give to others to prevent them passing on viruses inadvertently when they return them. Hold the floppy face down, with the metal cover toward you. Slide the tab on the upper left corner up to uncover the hole to write-protect the disk.

■ Eject floppies from your disk drive before you start your PC. If the floppy has a boot-sector virus, it will infect your hard disk as soon as the PC starts. Since a boot-sector virus mimics your real boot code, it will try to start up from the floppy. The virus copies itself to your hard drive and starts doing whatever its designer intended. You can be infected whether the attempt to boot from the floppy was successful or not.

■ Create an emergency startup disk to boot up your PC if it crashes. If you have a diagnosis and repair program – like Norton Utilities – you can start up from the CD-ROM or a startup floppy that the program creates for you.

■ Use virus-protection software to safeguard your PC at all times. An effective program has two components: disinfection and scanning. First, it finds viruses on your hard drive and destroys them, then runs in the background, scanning for viruses as you open and close files, insert removable disks or surf the Internet and download files or programs.

■ Check warning sites for the latest news on viruses. Top Threats at Symantec's AntiVirus Research Center (www.symantec.com/avcenter) has stories on the latest viruses. McAfee's site contains lists of current threats as well as interesting data on how viruses affect different parts of the world. Go to www.mcafee.com. The Wild List site (www.wildlist.org), keeps a complete, updated virus listing.

Recently Discovered Viruses (Includes Viruses, Trojans, Worms, an		
Virus Name	**Date Discovered**	**Virus Type**
Downloader-BT application	01/21/2003	Program
Linux/Shinict	01/20/2003	Trojan
Linux/Exploit-Da2	01/20/2003	Trojan
PornDial-143 application	01/20/2003	Program
JS/Spth	01/16/2003	Virus
W32/Eslac.worm	01/16/2003	Virus
IRC/Backdoor.f	01/15/2003	Trojan
QDial4	01/15/2003	Trojan
Downloader-BS	01/15/2003	Trojan
MultiDropper-FE	01/14/2003	Trojan

Software for the home

An extensive range of educational and instructional programs are now widely available from computer outlets. With their help you can master everything from mathematics and music to house decoration and garden planning. You can learn at your own pace, in your own time.

FOR THE VERY YOUNG

Preschoolers can benefit from educational programs as much as school-age children. There are CD-ROMs for all ages, from the youngest to the oldest. Some are designed for parents to use with their children, and many are largely activity based. They can help children to develop good hand-eye coordination,

improve basic skills like reading and get them used to computers from an early age. Knowledge Adventure produces some excellent early learning software (www.knowledgeadventure.com).

It is important to look out for educational CDs that let parents work alongside their children. CDs that tie in with popular films are often a good idea because familiar characters can help to keep children interested. Disney (www.disney.co.uk) has a strong range of interactive CD-ROMs that are popular with children. Many parents like to use CDs with activities that can be done away from the computer. For example, some CDs contain audio tracks for you to play and sing along to and others have pictures to print and colour in. When choosing a CD, check on whether it teaches

education-based skills or life-skills. Both are valid approaches, but a CD should say clearly what it is trying to do.

SCHOOL-ORIENTED LEARNING

There are many educational CD-ROMs for school-age children. Some cover specialised school subjects and provide information, exercises and texts to supplement classroom learning. Other CD-ROMs take a more roundabout approach to learning, hiding their real subject matter within a game or other activities. For example, Physicus from Tivola (www.tivola.com) uses a game to test your understanding of physics (see 'How to', p. 211). It is best suited to users in their early teens.

SOFTWARE SOURCES

The Internet is a good place to go for more information about CD-ROMs.

GSP (www.gsp.cc)
Distributors of the highly-respected CD-ROMs created by Dorling Kindersley. Titles cover all subjects and ages from toddlers up to adults.

AMAZON (www.amazon.co.uk)
The software store has categories for Children's Fun and Learning, and Education and Reference.

BBC (www.bbcshop.com)
The BBC produces a large number of CD-ROMs aimed at schoolchildren tackling tests and exams at GCSE and other key stages.

BRODERBUND (www.broderbund.com)
US-based distributors of the wide range of educational software created by the Learning Company.

Encyclopedias are educational.
Britannica (www.britannica.com) and Microsoft's Encarta (www.encarta.com) are the most comprehensive. Both are great for school students. Encarta and Britannica are both now moving towards

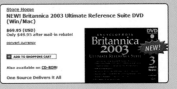

being supplied on the Web rather than on CD. Encarta, for example, is part of Microsoft's MSN 8 Web browsing and communication software.

NOT JUST FOR CHILDREN

Educational CD-ROMs are not just for children. There is a wide range of CDs that adults can use to improve their own education, learn new skills or just brush up on existing ones. Besides encyclopedias, there are CDs to help you learn everything from fancy dance steps to origami.

Some of the best educational CDs are for language learning. They use multimedia to good effect – recordings of native speakers help you to improve your accent, for example. The most advanced programs use speech recognition software to analyse your progress as you master a new tongue. As well as the main languages, such as French, you can buy programs that teach less common ones, like Welsh and even Cornish.

HOW TO CHOOSE SOFTWARE

Choosing educational CD-ROMs is very different from choosing books, because it is difficult to browse through them in a store. However, there are some ways to try to make sure you get good software. Approach your friends for advice, and if you are buying for your children, ask them what they like. If you are buying to help your children with schoolwork, remember that children like to learn in different ways, so choose software that suits them best.

Look at computer magazines both in print and on the Web. Reviewers see a lot of software and can often help you to distinguish good from bad. Try the Children's Software Review Website (www.childrenssoftware.com) for informed critiques of current and recent software titles, video games and children's Websites. Sometimes you can get a demonstration CD directly from the publisher or from their Website.

Categorising educational CDs as good or bad is a matter of personal taste – what some people find helpful and fun others might find difficult to get into or dull. But there are some general rules. A well thought-out idea with a clear explanation of the aims of the software is a good sign – check the publisher's Website and the product box and any review material you can find for this. A quick Web search can often turn up informative magazine review articles.

Look out for bargains on the Web. Educational software can cost up to forty pounds, but don't ignore less expensive software, thinking it is of poor quality. As more and more content moves onto the Internet,

publishers are selling off their CD-ROM titles more cheaply. You can often pick up extremely high-quality programs for as little as five pounds – a good place to start your search is Amazon (www.amazon.co.uk).

Is it English English? Many educational CD-ROMs were originally produced for sale in the USA, and so may contain spelling and terms that are unfamiliar to UK users.

How to: Play Tivola's Physicus

1 Physicus is an adventure game in which Earth has been hit by a meteorite and stopped rotating. Consequently, half the world is covered in ice, while the other half is too hot to inhabit. The aim is to generate enough electricity to start the Earth turning again.

2 As you move around the 3D environment in Physicus, you encounter a variety of different puzzles. You need to solve them, using your knowledge of physics, if you are to complete the rest of the game.

3 Whenever you need a little help, you can use the encyclopedia within the software to do some research. Learn what you need to know, and you can return to the game to apply your new knowledge.

WHAT CAN YOU DO?

Home design software comes in several forms.
Some programs let you work on the interior of your home, adding furniture and general design features to individual rooms. This is useful if you're planning a complete home makeover and want to experiment with several different ideas. Other software actually helps you to build your home, allowing you to configure the size and shape of rooms, add different floors and even work on the look of the roof. This is useful if you're starting a completely new home or building an extension to an existing one.

Garden design software
helps you put plants, water features and other elements into your land in the best configuration. These usually include a plant database – so you can easily fill the garden and choose plants that suit your soil and climate and meet your height, colour, fragrance and other needs. Most databases include information

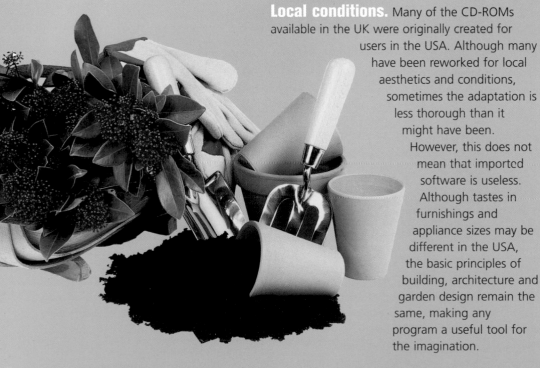

on plant care so that you can maintain your garden once it's in place.

You can buy home or garden design software,
but some does both – Punch Professional Home Design Suite, for example (www.fasttrak.co.uk). You may not need both types of program at once – many home design programs allow you to include basic landscaping and garden furniture so that you can visualise your dream home without having to go into the specifics of plant varieties.

Home or garden design software won't produce a perfect plan
on its own – it needs some help from you. You need to follow the basic principles of good design, and more often than not, the software includes a design guide to provide these. Keep your budget in mind and don't overspend. Also be realistic about the range of materials and furnishings you can buy locally, and be wary of ultra-fashionable designs that you could tire of in six months. Above all, experiment – design software lets you try as many new ideas as you want without the cost – so make the most of it.

BUYING TIPS

Local conditions.
Many of the CD-ROMs available in the UK were originally created for users in the USA. Although many have been reworked for local aesthetics and conditions, sometimes the adaptation is less thorough than it might have been. However, this does not mean that imported software is useless. Although tastes in furnishings and appliance sizes may be different in the USA, the basic principles of building, architecture and garden design remain the same, making any program a useful tool for the imagination.

Design software should be versatile and easy to use.
You'll want to tinker with your layouts – trying out many different kinds of design features – so it's important to be able to place and move items easily with just a click and drag of your mouse. Make sure you try out the program's functionality for yourself – either in a store or with a demonstration version of the software – before you part with your money.

Make it real.
You should be able to import your own scans and drawings into the software and download images from the Web. Imagine being able to add your own curtains to a room design with the touch of a button! Look out for features like creating a shopping list as you work.

MAKERS OF HOME AND GARDEN SOFTWARE
Products from these producers can be found in most large software outlets.

MINDSCAPE (www.mindscape.com)
Publisher of UK versions of Broderbund Software's successful 3D Home Architect series of titles. Extras for the programs can be obtained directly from the Broderbund Website (www.broderbund.com).

GSP (www.gsp.cc)
Publishers of 3D Home Designer and the Geoff Hamilton series of garden programs.

FOCUS MULTIMEDIA (www.focusmm.co.uk)
Visual Home Deluxe and 3D Landscape 2 are among the design programs available from this UK-based software distributor.

IMSI (www.imsisoft.com)
The producers of the professional CAD (computer aided design) program, TurboCAD, have applied their expertise to home design with FloorPlan 3D.

Stuck? Your software should offer hints on tricky tasks, provide access to online design guides and produce 3D views of your designs – this latter feature is invaluable in helping you to visualise the end result. In some software you can explore the design as if from a circling helicopter.

Garden design software generally comes with an extensive plant database that lets you add to it using scanned pictures of plants. Better still is a program that can mature your design, showing how your garden will look in years to come.

Keep an eye on your software publisher's Website. Some publishers provide extras for download that you can import into your home or garden design software. Typically, they might include new plants for your garden designer, new furniture items or a range of floor and wall coverings for interior design tools. These downloadable software extras can help you to

keep up with the current fashion trends, and they'll ultimately help you to build up a library of objects that you can use in other design projects you might undertake in the future.

For more information on plants, you can also buy separate garden encyclopedias on CD-ROM. Titles for the UK market include the RHS Plantfinder and Geoff Hamilton's Plant Encyclopedia (distributed by GSP www.gsp.cc). However, they can be difficult to find and may be out of date, so it is often better to find a public library that has CD-ROMs and use them there instead. The dedicated encyclopedias contain many more plants than your average garden design software. They are also far easier to access than regular printed guides. You can specify certain features you want, such as plant colour, height and fragrance, all in one quick search. Keep a look out for a garden encyclopedia that lets you add your own plants and allows you to annotate existing entries, making your entries as useful as possible.

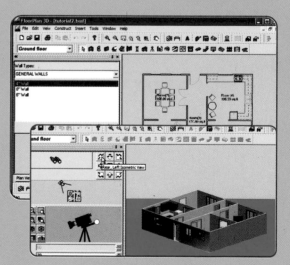

COUNTING THE COST

Home and garden design software can be excellent value. Some are very moderately priced, but even if you buy the most expensive software, it's still going to be a lot cheaper than an interior designer, and you'll be able to use the software more than once.

▶ See also **Building a CD-ROM library**, p. 34; and **How to download files**, p. 240.

How to: Download and use a trial version of IMSI FloorPlan 3D

1 First, visit the IMSI software Website (www.imsisoft.com) and click on the link to download a trial version of Floorplan 3D. You'll need to fill in your details and reply to an e-mail before you can download the program.

2 The download is a very large one – more than 60 MB, and only really suitable for a broadband connection. Once it's complete, install the program and start it up. Choose **Evaluate the product** and click **Finish**.

3 Any 3D program has a steep learning curve to get over before you can start designing well. It's best to start by opening the tutorial design that comes with FloorPlan 3D and using the extensive Help information.

The Internet

Join the information revolution and learn to surf with confidence.
Speed up your Internet access, brush up on your online etiquette,
and come to grips with the biggest data bank on the planet.

Getting online

Making it quick and easy

The Internet is a global network of millions of computers providing the largest communications system in the world.

■ What do you need to get on the Net?
You need a PC, a modem (a device that sends digital data over a phone line) and you need to sign up with an Internet Service Provider (ISP) – a company that provides Internet access.

■ Anarchy by design.
The Internet is decentralised by design. Each Internet computer, called a host, is independent of any others. Its operators can choose which services to use and which to make available to the global community.

■ There are several ways to access the Internet.
Complete online services – such as AOL, Yahoo and MSN – offer access along with their menu of special features. It is also possible to gain more direct access through a bare-bones ISP, which provides the connection service only.

■ An amazing information resource.
You can find information on every possible subject from the Web's global network. The amount of information is so vast that it's usually best to use a search engine – a powerful Website that will scan the Net for relevant sites for you. There are many popular search engines, such as

Yahoo! (uk.yahoo.com), Altavista (www.alta vista.com), AllTheWeb (www.alltheweb.com), Lycos (www.lycos.co.uk), Excite (www.excite.com) and Google (www.google.com)

■ Worldwide communication.
The Internet also enables you to send e-mail (electronic mail) to other Internet users anywhere in the world, contacting them in minutes rather than the days taken by post.

■ Interactive opportunities.
The Web also allows you to interact with others. Apart from using e-mail you can buy goods, chat online with friends or join a discussion group to meet others with similar interests to yourself.

SITES FOR LEARNING ABOUT THE INTERNET

Overwhelmed by the online world? Find out more by visiting these sites.

HOW STUFF WORKS (www.howstuffworks.com)
Type 'Internet' into the Find It window and browse a multitude of categories with information on everything from computer security to home office networking.

HOT WIRED (http://hotwired.lycos.com)
The online component of Wired magazine provides daily news in an assortment of categories, live chat guests and articles on current events and new technologies.

SQUIRREL NET (www.squirrelnet.com)
A great learning site for those wishing to use search engines effectively.

INTERNET 101 (www.internet101.org)
A beginner's guide to the Internet, created for those who want to know the basics. Sections include getting started, safe surfing, newsgroups and locating software.

REFDESK (www.refdesk.com)
A useful source for facts on the Net.

Discover how bandwidth affects the speed of your Internet access.

■ Bandwidth dictates the amount of data that's transmitted
within a fixed amount of time. For digital devices, it's usually expressed in terms of bits per second (bps). Thus, a modem that works at 56 000 bps (56K) has twice the bandwidth of a 28 000 bps modem.

■ Bandwidth obviously has a direct influence
on the amount of data that is transmitted per second. More bandwidth is needed to download a single photographic image in one second than it takes to download a whole page of text in the same amount of time. Large sound and animation files require a much larger bandwidth for fast downloading.

■ The more bandwidth you have available
via your modem, the faster you'll be able to explore the Net. But even if you have a high bandwidth connection, you can still get stuck in a data bottleneck. At peak times of day, when lots of people are online, your access speed may slow down dramatically, as the big servers and those with low bandwidth reach their full capacity.

▶ See also **Connecting to the future**, p. 47.

A Digital Subscriber Line (DSL) provides you with a fast, permanent connection to the Internet.

■ DSL is a way of transmitting digital data
on normal phone lines, which provides you with a fast, 24-hour connection. It is available in various standards, but the best for home or small business use is ADSL (Asymmetric Digital Subscriber Line). This is usually the

Thinking of joining the ADSL bandwagon? Do your research first.

ADSL Guide (www.adslguide.org.uk)
Comprehensive site with the latest UK broadband news, information on service providers and a message forum where users can exchange views and comment.

Broadband Help (www.broadband-help.com)
A helpful site complete with buyer's guide, glossary of terms, articles, news and reviews.

Broadband Map (www.broadbandmap.co.uk)
UK maps detailing the spread of broadband throughout the country.

Broadband for Britain (www.broadband4britain.co.uk)
A broadband pressure group with updates on developments in British broadband.

World of ADSL (www.world-of-adsl.com)
Information for beginners and advanced ADSL users, with ISP lists and ratings.

cheapest option and your current phone line can probably be converted with the minimum of fuss. One advantage of ADSL is that you can use your phone at the same time as using the Net.

■ Check with your phone company
to make sure that you can receive DSL. Lines can only be installed within certain distances of the telephone exchange. Speed of the connection deteriorates with distance, so phone companies impose limits on how far they will roll out a line.

■ Protect against virtual intruders.
A permanent DSL connection increases the risk of unwelcome visitors, so use firewall software to protect your system. A free application, such as ZoneAlarm from Zone Labs (www.zonelabs.com), monitors and protects your ports from attack by rendering the system invisible to roving hackers, and preventing unauthorised access to your PC.

ZoneAlarm
Basic PC Protection

Millions of users have selected ZoneAlarm as their trusted Internet security solution. The award-winning personal firewall automatically blocks dangerous Internet threats - known and unknown - guarding your PC from hackers and data thieves. ZoneAlarm provides the basic protection individuals need to secure their PC and keep their valuable information private.

Free Download

■ A special DSL modem will connect
your PC to the data line. A DSL supplier may provide this as part of the contract for the service. If you have a Windows 98, Me or XP PC, use a USB ADSL modem, or an ADSL router if you have a home network. There are varying standards so ask a supplier's advice first.

■ Choosing the right provider is always tricky!
When comparing contracts, look for guarantees that transmission rates will not drop below a certain minimum level. Ask what happens when your provider fails to meet its promises. Also ask if there are hidden charges, and whether you need to pay extra for installation or equipment rental. If, at sometime in the future, you are not satisfied with the service, how much will it cost to terminate the contract?

■ New standards of DSL include VDSL –
the V stands for video. VDSL uses new technology to transmit interactive video streams. It integrates your phone line with your TV set so that caller information can be displayed on the TV screen. The data rate is over ten times faster than that of ADSL and includes the ability to stream high-definition television signals. It might well be the next big leap forward in data transmission.

▶ See also **Choosing a modem**, p. 46; and **Connecting to the future**, p. 47.

MEASURING CONNECTION SPEEDS

Understand how the speed of your Internet connection affects your ability to surf the Web.

■ Is it baud rate or bps?
Baud rate is a measure of the amount of information that is being sent down a phone line by a modem. The term dates from the days of telegraphs, and is less exact than the more modern term bits per second (bps). Bits are the single 1s and 0s in the digital information that make up Web pages and e-mails. Modem speeds are usually quoted in bps rather than a baud rate, but some people still refer to the older term. Previously, the two terms were effectively the same, but modern modems can transmit, for example, 1200 bps at 600 baud which can lead to confusion.

■ When 56 isn't really 56.
The standard modem usually fitted in new PCs is capable of downloading information at 56 Kbps. But, in reality, the connection speed changes continually because of a number of factors. You may notice when you dial in to your ISP that the quoted connection speed can vary from 33 Kbps up to 50 Kbps. That's why a Web page can load instantly one day but take an age the next.

Don't open too many windows in your Web browser
if your connection speed is slow. Every extra Web page will put more demand on the capacity of your modem. Often, you can open a couple of new windows without too much loss of speed, but if you go beyond that the download speed will plummet.

▶ See also **Choosing a modem**, p. 46; and **Your Internet service provider**, p. 218.

Your link to the Net

Wondering where to start? These tips will help you find the best ISP.

■ What is an Internet service provider?
An ISP is a company that provides you with dial-up access to the Internet. You need to sign up with an ISP to browse the Web.

■ Ask a friend.
The best place to get information about an ISP is from someone you know. Ask around for recommendations from friends, and visit the websites of those they suggest on a friend's computer.

■ Try before you buy.
You can tell if an ISP's resources are stretched if they are always busy when you want to go online. Before joining, try dialling their connection number a few times to see if you can get through. Access them at busy times – peak hours are usually between

3 pm and 9 pm. Try several times, especially during weekdays. If you regularly hear the busy signal, try another provider.

■ E-mail an ISP and ask them a question,
such as how much they charge for technical support or if they support your Internet software. Send it to sales@[name of ISP] or info@[name of ISP], or both. You can learn a lot about an ISP from their response, and how long it takes to arrive.

■ Make sure technical support is available when you want it.
Ask what hours it is available. Phone the number and see how long it takes for the call to be answered and how helpful customer service is. For example, do they support your version of Windows software? Are they willing to help you get set up?

■ Read the ISP's terms of service.
You should be able to find the terms on the ISP Website, but if you can't, or you can't understand them, take your business elsewhere. Will they sell on your name and personal information? Are there penalties if you leave before the end of your contract? Do they mention additional, unusual charges? Are you limited by the number of hours you are allowed online?

■ Want to create your own Website?
Make sure your account includes Web space. They should offer at least a free 5–10 MB of space, and some offer an unlimited amount. Also ask your Internet service provider about Web bandwidth, that is, how much the ISP will let people download from the site each month. About 300 MB per month is a reasonable amount for most casual domestic users. Make sure you won't get charged with enormous additional fees if you go over that limit.

■ Are free ISPs worth it?
Watch out for reliability and customer service with free Internet service providers. Some have been known to cut off users (with or without notification) who haven't clicked on any of the advertisements in the last 20 minutes or so. Others limit the extent of your browsing to those sites they have agreements with. However, since the service is free, you may be willing to put up with some inconvenience in exchange for access.

ARE YOU BEING SERVED?
Evaluate your ISP or shop around for others with these Websites.

ISP REVIEW (www.ispreview.co.uk)
This site has an extensive list of free, subscriber and freecall ISPs in the UK, as well as readers' ISP reviews, complaints and an ISP top 10.

ADSL GUIDE (www.adslguide.org.uk/isp_compare.asp)
This section of the ADSL Guide Website allows you to choose up to six ISPs from a provided list. Once you've made your selection, click on **Compare** to view a graphical comparison of their performance over recent months.

UK NET GUIDE (www.ukcomputersguide.co.uk)
Click on the ISP link in the home page menu to see comment on and links to the Websites of over 100 Internet service providers.

UK BARGAINS (uk-bargains.co.uk/free-internet.html)
List of and links to free ISPs in the UK.

INTERNET SERVICE PROVIDERS' ASSOCIATION (www.ispa.org.uk)
Represents ISPs and promotes good practice in the industry. Gives advice on becoming an Internet service provider and can help consumers with a complaint against an ISP.

INTERNET MAGAZINE (www.internetmagazine.com)
Provides a guide to choosing an Internet service provider, as well as a database of 500 ISPs and an ISP news and gossip section.

EPINIONS (www.epinions.com/cmsw-ISP-All-United_Kingdom)
User reviews of a selection of Internet service providers in the UK.

MATREN (www.matren.co.uk/isp.htm)
A UK business directory for Internet service providers. Descriptions of the services are provided by the companies themselves, but the site is useful as it provides the ISPs' contact addresses and telephone numbers.

■ **One unique feature of msn.co.uk** is the Messenger Service, which lists new e-mail messages currently in the user's Hotmail Inbox, along with the names of any friends who are currently online. This is a free service, but in order to get the most use out of the Messenger Service, it makes sense to have both a Hotmail account and the Messenger software (available via a free download).

■ **Create a .net passport** to benefit from a number of services offered by MSN. With a single sign-in name and password you can access Hotmail, Messenger and other participating sites. You can also create user groups and make secure online purchases.

▶ See also **Understanding e-mail**, p. 316.

THE MICROSOFT NETWORK

The UK has its own branch of the worldwide Microsoft Network, (www.msn.co.uk).

■ **In common with other portal sites,** msn.co.uk offers users an easy way to explore the riches of the Web. It features a home page with links to areas such as cars, games and news, as well as Search, Hotmail, Shopping, Money, People and Chat. MSN's shopping area includes links to preferred stores, daily specials and a shopping search engine.

■ **MSN's most popular feature is probably Hotmail,** a Web mail account (available to all, whether you are a MSN customer or not) that allows you to send and receive

e-mail to and from any computer linked to the Internet. Hotmail is very useful when you are

travelling without a computer and want to check your e-mail at Internet cafés or via a friend's PC. However, because the Hotmail service is Web-based, it can be slow with a low bandwidth Internet connection.

PORTALS TO THE WEB

Portals are Websites that specialise in directing you to other sites on the Internet.

■ **A portal is a site designed to be your all-in-one** entry point to the Internet. Not just a search engine, it also provides you with Internet services such as e-mail, chatrooms, free personal Web pages, shopping and original content. Yahoo! UK and Ireland (uk.yahoo.com) and Virgin (www.virgin.net) are popular portals.

■ **Portals are good for helping new users** to get acquainted with what's out there and what can be done. Their downside is that they do tend to filter the sites they offer you. Portals often point you to sites that have the same kind of commercial link as themselves, rather than to the most relevant or informative site on a given topic.

■ **Different portals will suit your needs better than others.** If you can't find what you're looking for at Yahoo! or Virgin, then you could try Excite (www.excite.co.uk), MSN (www.msn.co.uk), AOL (www.AOL.co.uk) or another portal until you decide which site is the best for you.

Understanding HTML

You can quickly create a Web page using the formatting code called HyperText Mark-up Language, or HTML tags (commands). Websites use HTML to tell the browser what to display and how to display it. There are programs that create HTML code for you, but it's easy to learn the basics.

VIEW SOME HTML

To see what HTML code looks like, launch your browser, and visit any Web page. Right-click on the main part of the Web page, and select **View Source** from the pop-up menu. A page of plain HTML code will then open.

Meet the tags. All Web pages have a <HTML> tag at the top and a </HTML> tag at the bottom in either upper or lower case. The <HEAD></HEAD> tags enclose information about the page, including the title. The <BODY> </BODY> tags enclose all the words and pictures that you see on a Web page.

Working in pairs. Most HTML tags come in pairs, surrounding the information they format. For example, <B>This text is bold</B>. The opening tag switches the formatting on, and the closing tag with a forward slash switches it off.

To create a Web page, you will need a Web browser, such as Internet Explorer or Netscape Navigator, a folder on your hard drive in which to store your Web pages and a text editor, such as Notepad, to write and save your code. Avoid using Microsoft Word for writing straight code because its clever formatting tools will wreak havoc with your HTML. If you want to put pictures on your Web page, you'll also need an image-editing program, such as Paint Shop Pro (www.jasc.com) or Adobe Photoshop (www.adobe.com).

A GOOD STUDENT

Begin with a lesson. A beginner's tutorial will help you to decide what you want to do with your page. There are several useful Websites where you can learn HTML. Try Page Resource (www.pageresource.com/html/index2.htm), or a comprehensive step by step guide at HTML Goodies (www.htmlgoodies.com/tutors/). Alan's HTML Guide (www.alan.clara.net) also has advice and instructions on HTML suitable for beginners.

How to: Create a basic Web page using HTML

1 Type the following code into Notepad, with the carriage returns as illustrated above:
<html> <head> <title>Test page</title> </head> <body> This is my web page </body> </html>

2 Click on **File** and then **Save**. Name the document 'index.htm' and in the Save as type: panel select **All Files**. Save it in your Website folder on your hard drive.

3 Now view the page in your Web browser. Open Internet Explorer and go to **File**, then **Open**, then **Browse**. Find your file, select index.htm and click **Open**. You'll see a Web page with the words, 'This is my web page'. To experiment with more tags, see opposite.

MORE HANDY TAGS
Basic commands to get you started.

- **<HTML></HTML>**
Tells Web browsers that your page is written in HTML.
- **<HEAD></HEAD>**
Sits below the HTML tag. Contains information about the document.
- **<TITLE></TITLE>**
Specifies the page's title, which appears in the Web browser's title bar.
- **<BODY></BODY>**
Contains all the text and pictures that appear on the Web page, plus all the HTML that formats the page.
- **<H1></H1> to <H6></H6>**
These set your heading font sizes. <H1> is the largest; <H6> is the smallest.
- **<CENTER></CENTER>**
Centres text, images, tables, and other elements on your Web page.
- **
**
Breaks text onto a new line (leaves no space between the lines). There's no closing tag needed for this command.
- **<P></P>**
Breaks text into a new paragraph (leaves a blank line in between).
- **<I></I>**
Italicises text.
- **<B></B>**
Puts text into a bold face.
- **<IMG SRC="file name">**
Inserts an image.

Always nest your HTML tags correctly. Think of the system as first in, last out and close instructions in reverse order. For example, this is correct: <B><I><U> bold, italic, underlined text</U></I></B>, but this isn't: <B><I><U> bold, italic, underlined text </B></I></U>.

Don't type special characters, such as & or (c), straight into your HTML code because they won't appear correctly in all browsers. Always use special ASCII codes. A useful ASCII character conversion chart is available from (www.slackerhtml.com/html/ascii.html).

Organise your code neatly so that you can easily read it. Write code on separate lines, and use organisational comments to remind yourself what is where, and why. An ! with dashes inside chevrons (<>) signals a comment that stays in the source code and won't appear on your Web page. For example: <! – Navigation bar starts – > <! – Navigation bar ends – >.

Link to other sites. A good Web page can be made even better if you provide hyperlinks to other relevant Websites. This is the code you need to create a link: <A HREF="http://www.thewebsiteaddress"> Website name or any other text you want to appear as the link</A>.

Choose fonts that most people have installed on their computers. If you use a fancy font, they might not have it, and their browser will use a font that they do have instead. Safe ones to go with are sans serif fonts, which include Verdana, Arial and Helvetica. A good idea is to specify more than one font, just in case – and don't forget the Mac users out there. In the example <FONT FACE="Arial,Helvetica,sans-serif">, Arial is a Windows font, installed on almost all PCs, and Helvetica is the Mac equivalent. If the viewer has neither, the browser will look for another sans serif font.

TIPS ON COLOUR

You can specify colours in more than one way: by name or by a special code known as hex values. For example, <FONT COLOR="#FF0000"> and <FONT COLOR="Red"> both give exactly the same instruction. Although it is easier to use colour names than hex values, colour names are not recognised by all Web browsers.

If you want to choose your own range of colours for your Website but don't know the hex values for them, most HTML image-editing programs have built-in colour mixers that will work out the hex value for you.

Define your colours. The <BODY> tag is where you define the page's background colour, the colour of the text and the link colours. This means your page won't appear against a dull grey background in old browsers. It also saves you having to define font colours throughout the page. <BODY BGCOLOR="White" TEXT="Purple" LINK="Red" VLINK="Green"> sets the background colour of the page to white, the text to purple, the link colour to red, the visited link colour to green.

A FINAL ONCE-OVER

Check your code works before you go live. You could invest in a validator such as CSE's Validator (www.htmlvalidator.com) to check your HTML or do so online with ZDNet's HTML Toolbox (www.netmechanic.com/cobrands/zd_dev).

▶ See also **The world of graphics,** p. 154; **Creating a Website,** p. 228; and **Hyperlinks make browsing easy,** p. 245.

Web basics

Browsers

Get to know the ins and outs of using this popular Web browser.

■ **Customise Internet Explorer's Toolbar** to make the functions easier to access. To see the names of the Toolbar buttons, go to **View ➜ Toolbars ➜ Customize**, and select **Show text labels** in the Text options pane. To add and remove buttons on the toolbar, right-click the Toolbar and click **Customize**. Scroll

through the buttons and highlight the one you want. Click **Add** and it will move to the current Toolbar buttons menu. To remove a button, reverse the process.

■ **For basic browsing** and specific information about Internet Explorer and its features, go to **Help** and click **Contents and**

Index. To find out about, and install more components of Internet Explorer, go to **Tools ➜ Windows Update**. You will then be connected to the Internet, where you can download components that, for example, can increase the security of your Internet connection.

■ **Save time typing in addresses.** Type the URL words in the Address bar and press **Ctrl+Enter** to add http://www. and .com on either side of the word. So when searching for the

Microsoft site, enter 'microsoft', press **Ctrl+Enter**, and http://www.microsoft.com will appear.

■ **Already familiar with Netscape?** Learn about differences between Internet Explorer and Netscape Navigator by going to **Help** and clicking **For Netscape Users**. To learn more about how to use the Internet, you can go to **Help** and select **Contents and Index**.

■ **Searching is easy with Internet Explorer.** To search from the Address bar, type 'go', 'find' or '?' followed by a suitable word or phrase, then press **Enter**. To search for a word or phrase within a Web page, press **Ctrl+F** to open the Find dialogue box, type in the word or phrase, and then click **Find Next**.

■ **Learn to move quickly around the Address bar.** You can move the cursor into the Address bar by pressing **Alt+D**. To move the cursor back and forth between parts of the address, press **Ctrl+Left Arrow** or **Ctrl+Right Arrow**. To go to a new Website, press **Ctrl+O**.

■ **Learn to move quickly around a Web page.** To move to the end of a page, press the **End** key on the right-hand side of your keyboard. To move to the beginning, press the **Home** key directly above it.

■ **Move between pages faster.** Rather than clicking the Back and Forward buttons on the browser Toolbar repeatedly, use

keyboard shortcuts instead. To move back a page, press either the **Backspace** key or **Alt+Left Arrow**. To move forward a page, press **Alt+Right Arrow**. To stop a page from loading, press the **Esc** key.

■ **Get the latest version of a Website.** A good Website is updated on a regular basis, but you might not necessarily be looking at the latest version. Your PC caches (stores) Web pages on the hard disk to speed up access times. Press **F5** once your chosen Web page has loaded to ensure you download the latest version of the site.

▶ See also **Secrets of the cache**, p. 224; **Using Favorites in Explorer**, p. 225; **What the Back button does**, p. 226; **What the Forward button does**, p. 227; **How to browse efficiently**, p. 234; and **Saving Web pages**, p. 235.

Tips and tricks for using this popular Web browser.

■ **Communicator is an omnibus program** that includes the Navigator browser, the Messenger e-mail program, the Composer home page editor and Multimedia support. It can also be set to block access to objectionable Web content with NetWatch (http://home.netscape.com/comprod/products/communicator/netwatch).

■ **Bypass search engines completely** in some cases, with Navigator's Internet Keywords feature. Just type the term in your browser's Location box. There are three types of keywords. The first group includes the names of places, products or institutions, such as the 'University of Oxford', 'BMW' or 'BBC'. Navigator will often take you directly to the site of the product, place or organisation requested in the search. The second are commands that must be followed by an object, such as 'shop CDs' or 'search history'. The third combines the names of cities with specific activities and information – for example, 'Manchester movies' or 'Bristol restaurants'.

Becoming a zombie from spending too much time in cyberspace? To find out what's going on tonight in your home town, just type in www.netscape.co.uk. In the Location bar, type in the name of your town and 'entertainment' to bring up a list of relevant Websites.

Speed up your research when looking through long documents by using the Find dialogue box. Just press **Ctrl+F** and your browser will display a dialogue box for you to fill in. Enter a keyword, then click the **Find** button. The dialogue box searches the Web page until it locates the keyword. Click the **Find** button again to locate the next occurrence of the word.

Let the Web come to you by using My Sidebar in Netscape Navigator. My Sidebar displays items that you need to use all the time – the latest news and weather, your address book or Buddy List, a calendar and many other items. My Sidebar represents these items in tabs that it continually updates.

Customise My Sidebar to ensure the information it supplies suits your needs. Click on **Tabs** at the top right of My Sidebar and then select **Customize My Sidebar**. In the dialogue box that appears, double-click on the categories in the left-hand box to expand them. Highlight a tab you would like to add then click **Add**. To remove a tab, highlight it in the right-hand box and click **Remove**. Click **OK** to finish.

Add Netscape Channels to My Sidebar to have a wealth of information at your fingertips. Click on **The Netscape Channels** tabs and chose from the list of topics such as sport, movies, games, celebrity, music and business.

Experiment with different looks. You can change the appearance of your browser in Netscape Navigator by altering the font and colours, or you can apply a whole new 'theme' or complete designed look for your browser. To do so, go to **Edit ➜ Preferences➜** and double-click on **Appearance**. Click on **Themes** and choose from either Modern or Classic. For other themes click on **Get New Themes**. This takes you to the Netscape 7 Theme Park, where you can select other themes.

Take aim. When you download Netscape Communicator, you sometimes get AOL's Instant Messenger (AIM) as part of the deal. AIM's random pop-ups and memory gobbling can be annoying. To remove it, go to **Start ➜ Search ➜ All files and folders**. Type the search term 'aim' into the **All or part of the file name** box. The Find tool should turn up several AIM items, all with the Netscape logo. Right-click on these to place them in the Recycle Bin and empty the Recycle Bin to erase them completely. If you decide you want it back, go to AOL's Website (www.aol.co.uk) and download it.

SETTINGS TO MAKE SURFING EASIER

Adjust the settings in Internet Explorer to speed up and smooth out your surfing sessions.

Alter the amount of disk space assigned to temporary files by going to **Tools ➜ Internet Options.** In the Temporary Internet files section of the General tab, click on the **Settings** button. Change the amount of disk space used by moving the slide bar to the right to increase it and to the left to reduce it. If you have lots of spare hard disk space on your computer, leave the figure high to help to speed up your Internet connection.

Protect your children by screening the Websites they view. Go to **Tools ➜ Internet Options ➜ Content** and click **Enable** in the Content Advisor section. There are four different categories of content you can rate – Language, Nudity, Sex and Violence. Use the slider bar to set a rating for each category. The Description section explains each rating. Click **Apply** and **OK** when you have completed setting your ratings.

Does the sound of the modem dialling and connecting annoy you? Set your modem to dial silently to the ISP by selecting **Tools ➜ Internet Options ➜ Connections**. Select your ISP from the list and click **Settings ➜ Properties ➜ Configure**. Make sure the **Enable modem speaker** option is unchecked. Now click **OK** back through the screens.

SHORTCUTS TO USE WITH COMMUNICATOR

Tricks to make browsing easier and quicker.

Ctrl+Home	Goes to the top of a page.
Ctrl+End	Goes to the bottom of a page.
Ctrl+A	Selects all the text on a page.
Ctrl+B	Automatically opens your Manage Bookmarks page.
Ctrl+C	Copies selected text to the Clipboard.
Ctrl+D	Adds a new Bookmark to your Bookmarks file.
Ctrl+F	Opens the Find dialogue box.
Ctrl+P	Prints the current page.
Ctrl+N	Automatically opens a new browser window.

■ Turn off sounds and pictures for speedy surfing.

Go to **Tools ➔ Internet Options ➔ Advanced**. Under Multimedia, turn off **Play sounds in web pages** and **Show pictures** in order to load Websites faster. However, many sites use graphics extensively, and they may be difficult to use without them.

■ To remove underlines from hyperlinks,

go to **Tools ➔ Internet Options** and click the **Advanced** tab. In the Underline links section under Browser click **Never**.

■ Tired of the same old Web page

every time you open a new browser window? To change your home page, go to **Tools ➔ Internet Options** and type a new Web address into the Home page section on the General tab. Alternatively, to use the page currently on view, click **Use Current**. For speed, select **Use Blank**. Click **Use Default** to restore the original page.

▶ See also **Dealing with cookies**, p. 250; and **Security on the Net**, p. 254.

SECRETS OF THE CACHE

Manage your browser's cache settings to speed up your surfing.

■ When you connect to the Web,

the server stores temporary files in a folder called the cache (pronounced kaysh) in Netscape Navigator, or Temporary Internet files in Internet Explorer. If you visit the same sites regularly you'll find pages download onto your screen much faster, as your computer pulls up files it recognises from your cache instead of downloading them afresh.

■ Speed up your surfing

by increasing the amount of hard disk space allocated to cached files. Set aside around five per cent of your hard disk space for the cache. If you have a large hard disk, you can use up to ten per cent.

■ To increase your cache size in Netscape,

go to **Edit ➔ Preferences** and double-click on **Advanced**. Click on **Cache**, highlight the figure in the box next to Disk Cache, type in your new, larger figure and click **OK**. In Internet Explorer, go to **Tools ➔ Internet Options** and click **Settings** in the Temporary Internet files section. Drag the slider to the right to increase the amount of disk space and click **OK**.

■ Keep your online shopping for family presents a secret.

Open your Web browser's cache folder and locate the pages for the site you visited. Select each page and press **Delete** to erase it.

■ Remember that ISPs also cache frequently used Websites

and even if you clear your cache you may just be getting the ISP's cached page. To avoid this problem, regularly click **Refresh** or **Reload** on your Toolbar.

▶ See also **The Refresh/Reload button**, p. 227.

How to: Clear your cache in Navigator and Explorer

1 In **Netscape Navigator**, first go to the **Edit** menu and then click on **Preferences**. This opens up the Preferences dialogue box.

2 Double-click on the **Advanced** option. Click on **Cache** and select **Clear Disk Cache**. Click **OK** when warned that this will remove all files in the disk cache. Now click **Clear Memory Cache**, then **OK**. Click **OK** once more to finish.

3 In **Internet Explorer** click on the **Tools** menu and select **Internet Options**. Go to the **Temporary Internet files** section and select **Delete Files**. Click **OK** after you have viewed the warning that you're removing all temporary Internet files. Click **OK** to finish.

Navigation aids

USING BOOKMARKS IN NAVIGATOR

Access your favourite Websites easily with Netscape Navigator's handy Bookmark feature.

■ **To keep the addresses of your favourite Web pages handy** in Netscape Navigator, use the Bookmark feature. When you find a Web page you like, click on the **Bookmarks** icon on Navigator's Toolbar and choose **Bookmark This Page**. When you want to visit that site again, just click on the **Bookmark** icon and select it from the drop-down menu.

■ **Navigator can notify you when a bookmarked site changes.** To follow the latest updates on your favourite sites, go to **Bookmarks** ➜ **Manage Bookmarks**. Highlight a Bookmark from the list. Click **Properties**, then **Notify**. Select a notification option then click **OK**.

To rename a Bookmark, or alter its URL, go to **Bookmarks** ➜ **Manage Bookmarks**. Highlight a Bookmark from the list. Click **Properties** and make your amendments in the Name and Location sections of the Properties dialogue box.

■ **Remove old or incorrect Bookmarks** to keep your Bookmark list up to date. Click on the **Bookmarks** menu and select **Manage Bookmarks**. In the window that appears, highlight the Bookmark you want to remove, right-click on it and select **Delete** from the pop-up menu.

■ **You can transfer your Bookmarks** or a list of Bookmarks between Internet Explorer and Netscape Navigator. To do this, go to the PC World.com Website (www.pcworld.com/down loads) and search for the the Favtool program.

■ **Make your Bookmarks list easier to read** by inserting breaks between subjects. Go to **Bookmarks** ➜ **Manage Bookmarks**. Highlight the bookmark you want to add a visual separator before and click on **New Separator**.

▶ See also **Using Netscape Communicator**, p. 222.

USING FAVORITES IN EXPLORER

Save frequently accessed sites in your Favorites folder in Internet Explorer to make surfing the Net faster and more effective.

■ **Keep Favorites in themed folders,** like Travel or Health. This makes them easier to access and gives you a tidier list. The same applies to using Bookmarks in Netscape Navigator. If your computer has more than one user, then you may also want to organise your Bookmarks or Favorites into separate folders for each user.

■ **If you no longer use a Favorite,** delete it. It's just taking up valuable space. Right-click on the name of the site in the favorites menu and select **Delete** then click **OK**.

■ **Set aside regular time to organise your Favorites or Bookmarks.** It can be frustrating, and time consuming to search a long list of Favorites for a site you would like to return to. So make sure you move the ones that aren't in a folder to the appropriate one or create a new folder, if necessary.

■ **Organise your Favorites offline.** That way, you can take your time and consider what you want to keep and where you want to store it without running up a large telephone bill.

■ **Create a 'Temporary' Favorites folder,** in which you can store sites that don't fit easily into any of your existing categories, or that you may not eventually want to keep. It is a good idea to go through your Temporary folder periodically, and decide which Favorites to keep and where to put them, and delete those you no longer need.

How to: Organise your Bookmarks into folders

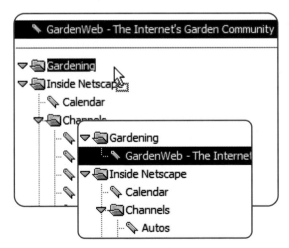

1 Click the **Bookmarks** icon, choose **Manage Bookmarks**. This opens up a window, displaying all the Bookmarks you have at present. To create a new folder, go to the **File** menu, select **New**, then **Folder**. Name the folder then click **OK**.

2 To move a bookmark into the new folder, highlight it and drag it over to the folder icon. Release the mouse to drop it into the new folder. Select View to see your bookmarks by name, location, date created, or the last time you visited them.

A site may assign a Favorite a name that won't remind you of what it is when you look at it later. User FAQ, for example, could be just about anything. In Internet Explorer, use the Rename command to give your Favorite a more meaningful title. Right-click on the Favorite (or Folder) and select **Rename** from the drop-down menu. Type a new name then press the **Enter** key.

Many Websites have a page of links to related sites. Make that page a Favorite and you'll have a ready source of reference for whatever your choice of subject.

Need to work on another computer? Take your Favorites or Bookmarks with you. Internet Explorer and Netscape let you save them as a portable HTML file, which either program can open. In Internet Explorer, go to **File → Import and Export**, and follow the Wizard's instructions. In Netscape Navigator, go to **Bookmarks → Tools → Export**. In the dialogue box scroll down the Save as type box and select HTML files. then click on **Save**.

▶ See also **Working with Internet Explorer,** p. 222.

UNDERSTANDING WEB ADDRESSES

Understanding the purpose of the names you type into your browser will help to explain why they don't always work.

Web addresses are also called URLs (Uniform Resource Locators). Every Web page has its own URL, which is made up of three parts: the protocol, such as http://, the host, or domain name, which is everything before the first forward slash and the file name, which comes after the slash.

The full domain name identifies and locates a host computer on the World Wide Web (www). It looks complex, but it

breaks down into the subdomain, domain name type and country code. For example, in www.chortle.co.uk, the subdomain is .chortle, the domain type is .co (suggesting a commercial site) and the country code .uk locates it in the UK. Most sites in the USA do not include the country code but have a .com domain type.

The http:// prefix is not the only protocol. The FTP (File Transfer Protocol) lets you download a file quickly. To use it, just type ftp:// before the domain name. If you are trying to reach ftp.bogus.com, for example, type ftp://ftp.bogus.com into your browser. To access newsgroups, use a news: opening and omit the //. For example, to reach the newsgroup alt.bogus, type in news:alt.bogus.

It is often enough to enter just a company name into your browser. Netscape and Internet Explorer will all add the http:// and www for you. For example, to reach Yahoo!, simply enter yahoo into the Address bar of the browser, and it will complete the http://www.yahoo.com for you. Explorer and Netscape also let you enter a keyword instead of a URL and will direct the query to a search engine (see *How to browse efficiently* p. 234).

Every so often, you will type in an address and get an error message. This happens because either the site has gone offline or moved – or you may have typed the address incorrectly. First try retyping the address. Then try eliminating everything after the first forward slash of the address. For example, if

www.notworking.com/computer/hassle.html did not work, try www.notworking.com. If you still have no luck, wait until later, since the site may be down for repairs or uploading. If you still can't get the site to respond, use one of the well known search engines, such as Google (www.google.com) or Yahoo (www.yahoo.com) and type in the search term 'notworking'.

WHAT THE BACK BUTTON DOES

This essential button reconnects you to Web pages that you've already visited.

If you've gone one link too far, click the **Back** button on your browser Toolbar to take you to the previous page. Finding what you need on the Internet often involves a lot of exploration, clicking on every link in an effort to locate exactly what you are looking for. Often, you'll want to retrace your steps, and the Back button is the easiest way to do this.

Jump back several pages to your starting point. The golden rule for Website design is that you're never more than two clicks away from the page you want. Not everyone sticks to this principle and some sites bury their information very deeply. To skip back several pages, click on the down arrow to the right of the Back button and choose from a menu of recently visited pages. It's much quicker than repeatedly pressing the Back button.

If the Back button is greyed out, then the last link that you followed may have opened a new browser window. Minimise your current browser window to find out where you are. Is there another window behind it? If so, you can close the new window and use the Back button on the first window to retrace your steps.

Occasionally you'll get yourself into a loop. If you visit a site that has changed its address, the page will probably redirect you to the right location. That's fine until you click on the Back button. Your browser returns to the redirect page, which then sends you forward to the page you've just left. This is where the arrow next to the Back button comes in handy again. Click on it and select a page further back up the list.

▶ See also **How to browse efficiently,** p. 234.

each page to display is just a waste of time. Instead, click on the down arrow to the right of the Forward button, and choose the page you want from the list that appears.

▶ See also **How to browse efficiently,** p. 234.

WHAT THE HISTORY BUTTON REVEALS

Use your Web browser's History button to view Websites offline, or to check back on recently visited sites.

■ **As you surf the Web, your browser lists any pages you visit** in what's known as your History. This is particularly handy if you want to download Web pages and read them later, freeing up the phone line for other members of the family to use. When you're online, just make sure you fully load each page you want to read. Then go to the **File** menu and select **Work Offline**. You can now call up the sites you've already visited by clicking on them in your History file.

■ **Worried that your children have been visiting unsuitable sites?** In order to keep their browsing in check, press the

History button on the toolbar. A list of folders for the last few days and the last week will appear in a column on the left. Double-click a folder to open it and double-click on a link to go to the site.

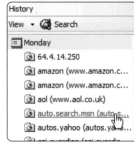

■ **To keep your surfing secret,** delete the History button from your Toolbar. Right-click on any of the Toolbar buttons and, in the pop-up menu that appears, left-click on **Customize**. You will now be able to remove the History button. While this won't fool everyone, it should be enough to keep the Net novice at bay. In turn, if you want to snoop and find that someone else has deleted the History button, you can restore it in the same way, using the Customize feature.

WHAT THE FORWARD BUTTON DOES

Use the Forward button on your Web Toolbar to navigate easily through Website pages.

■ **Your Internet browser keeps a list** of all the pages you are currently viewing on the Internet. Click on the **Back** button, and the browser will take you to the preceding page in the list. Changed your mind? Click **Forward** to move one site down the list. If the Forward button is greyed out, you're at the end of the list.

■ **It's easy to lose track of where you are,** especially after a lengthy Internet session, and you may not always know where the Forward button will take you. Internet Explorer users can regain their bearings by allowing the mouse cursor to hover over the Forward button for just a few seconds, which will cause the title of the next page to be displayed.

■ **When you've pressed the Back button several times,** clicking Forward once may not be enough. But don't click on the Forward button over and over again – waiting for

■ **Cover your tracks.** If you want to clear all current History entries, go to **Tools ➔ Internet Options** and click the **Clear History** button. Now nobody can see where you've been.

■ **Make your History as long or as short as you want.** You can set it to record just a day or a week's worth of surfing. Go to **Tools ➔ Internet Options**, select the number of days desired in the History section, then click **OK**. But be careful. If you set it to 30 days and surf often, you'll end up with an enormous list.

▶ See also **Saving Web pages,** p. 235.

THE REFRESH/RELOAD BUTTON

Called Refresh in Internet Explorer and Reload in Netscape Navigator, this button can really speed up your download times.

■ **If a Web page is loading very slowly** compared to normal load times for your computer, or you get an error of some kind on the page as it is on your screen, try reloading the page. First click the **Stop** button, and then the **Reload** or **Refresh** button on your Toolbar.

■ **Still elements to download into a page?** To check, look at the animation in the top right corner of your browser. If it's moving, the page is still loading. You may also see progress indicators in the status bar in the bottom of the browser window. If there are lots of graphics, Java applets or elements that need plug-ins, the page will load more slowly.

■ **If you think the contents of a browser's window may have changed** since the last time you viewed it, then simply click on **Reload** or **Refresh** to update the page.

■ **Sometimes, a Web page just won't fully download,** however long you wait. Perhaps you can't scroll to the end or the pictures aren't fully displayed. Clicking on **Refresh** or **Reload** instructs a new page transmission to your computer, which usually solves the problem.

Creating a Website

Whether it's to keep distant relatives up-to-date with family news or to share information about a special area of interest, a community group, or even a business enterprise, creating your own Website is a great way of communicating with people.

BEFORE YOU START

Pick up a basic understanding of how a Web page works. A Web page is actually just a simple text file that contains the information to be displayed in the page. It is marked up using a special computer language called HTML (HyperText Markup Language). Instead of a .txt extension, it is saved with a .htm or .html extension, which is how your browser knows that your document is a Web page, and not just a regular text file.

HTML code is just a simple programming language that is based on the formatting tags, or commands, that word-processing programs used to use. In its most basic format, it's merely a series of tags that you can use to format the structure and layout of a Web document (see also *HTML tag box*, page 221). To display a sentence in bold, for example, simply include the sentence in your HTML code, and put a <B> tag before it and a </B> tag after it. Other HTML tags give your browser extra information about the Web page – such as its title, a description and any keywords – which are particularly useful when your page is listed in a search engine.

Aside from formatting text, HTML can be used to create tables, which help you to control the layout of your page. You can also use HTML to display images on your page. Images are separate files that are stored alongside the Web page itself. HTML code tells your browser the image's specifications, such as where the image file is stored, what size to display it, and whether or not it should have a border. For example, the line of code: <IMG SRC="picture1.jpg" WIDTH="100" HEIGHT="150" ALIGN="Left" BORDER="1"> tells your browser to display an image called picture1.jpg, which is stored in the same folder as the HTML file itself, with a width of 100 pixels, a height of 150 pixels, and a 1-pixel-wide border, and to align it to the left of the page so that the text flows around its right side.

HTML code can create links to other pages on the World Wide Web. This is useful if you want to give your readers more information or show them an interesting site. To make a piece of text into a hyperlink, you only have to put simple HTML tags before and after the text, including the address of the Web page you want it to link to. For example, the line of code reading <AHREF="http://www.microsoft .com"> Take a look at the Microsoft site for more information!</A> turns the line of text saying 'Take a look at the Microsoft site for more information!' into a hyperlink connecting directly to the Microsoft site.

CREATING YOUR SITE ONLINE
Create your own Website online without HTML.

MOONFRUIT (www.moonfruit.com)
A Web community site that can also help you to create an interactive, animated Website. If you don't have Flash technology installed on your computer, you must download it first before you can do anything. Go to the Macromedia site (www.macromedia.com).

MSN (communities.msn.com/home)
Lets you get together with people who share your interests and helps you to set up your own Website. You can create family sites, personal pages or an online photo album.

TRIPOD (www.tripod.lycos.com)
This Website builder provides you with site building tools, photo album templates, 20 MB of storage, and plenty of bandwidth – all for free.

YAHOO! GEOCITIES (uk.geocities.yahoo.com)
A publishing community that allows you to set up your own Website for free, using File Manager, HTML Editor and Page Builder. Choose from a selection of preformatted templates, fill in the blanks, add pictures and then publish your page to the Web.

Before you even switch on your PC, think a little about the factors that affect the design of your site. What do you want it to achieve? What type of people will visit your Website? What will they be looking for? How familiar with the Internet will they be? Will they be using the latest version of Netscape Navigator or an old superceded version of Internet Explorer? Will they have a super-fast connection or a 28.8 K modem? Will they have a huge monitor, or a small 640 x 480 monitor? All of these factors will influence your site design. Try to cater as much as possible for your target viewers. Think about them now and it will save you work later.

WEB CREATION PACKAGES
Create your own site with these advanced Website creation packages.

ADOBE GOLIVE (www.adobe.com/products/golive)
Based on HTML code, Adobe GoLive lets you create and manage professional database-driven Websites. The package has been compared to Dreamweaver.

FRONTPAGE (www.microsoft.com/frontpage)
A Web-authoring package produced by Microsoft. One of the leading Website creation and management tools available, FrontPage uses HTML, Dynamic HTML, script ASP and cascading style sheets to format your Website.

MACROMEDIA (www.macromedia.com/software)
Presents the Web-authoring packages Director, Shockwave, Dreamweaver, Fireworks and Flash. Considered to be the best Web-creation packages available. Dreamweaver MX and Fireworks MX allow you to design and produce your own site by combining graphics design with Website development.

Gather your material. Pull together all the information that you want to put in your site – text, photographs and existing graphics. These elements should give you an idea about how to organise your site, and may even inspire a certain theme. You may, for example, want your site to reflect the style of your marketing materials.

Sketch out the structure of your site.
Put pencil to paper and divide your site into sections. Note what your section headings will be, what information will appear under each section, and how your users will navigate through the site. Mock up your front page and a few subpages.

SOFTWARE AND HARDWARE

You can create HTML using something as basic as Notepad, or try out a fully featured HTML editor. If you use Notepad, you'll have to code all your HTML by hand (see *Understanding HTML*, p. 220). The next step up is a HTML editor, like HomeSite, in which you still code by hand, but which offers Toolbars and buttons to make coding easier.

There are also WYSIWYG (what you see is what you get) editors, like FrontPage and Dreamweaver that hide the code from you. The editor creates all the HTML for you in the background. Microsoft Word offers a similar feature to the WYSIWYG editors – you can convert any Word document to a Web page simply by selecting **Save as Web Page**. This creates all the HTML for you. Try a few editors and see which one suits you best. Most are available to download from the Net and try free for a limited time.

If you're planning to include images of any kind on your site – photographs, logos, menu bar graphics, animations and so on – you'll need to have an image-editing program such as Paint Shop Pro or CorelDraw.

If you want to use a lot of photos on your Website, consider buying a digital camera. Save your photos in .jpeg format, which you can then easily open in Paint Shop Pro and

manipulate to the size you require. Perhaps you're not sure that you want to invest in a digital camera? If this option is too expensive, get your film developed at a lab that will also save the

photos in digital format on CD. The CD will include software for touching up your images. Check out the Kodak site (www.kodak .com) for more information.

If your images are already printed on paper or as slides, you can have them scanned at an office services outlet – although if you have a lot of images, it'll be cheaper in the long run to buy your own scanner.

CREATING YOUR SITE

An inconsistent site is confusing for a user. Try to use the same elements on each page. It's a good idea to have a consistent navigation bar or menu that appears in the same place on every page to give users an idea of where they are. A logo or heading that appears in the same place on every page reassures them that they are still at the same site. The same colour scheme – background, text and links – helps tie the pages together visually. Word's Web Page Wizard can help you to achieve this.

Put the most important information at the top of your Web page. People will only scroll down the full page if there is something of value in the information they first receive – so take care to avoid hiding the most important details at the bottom of the page.

Some people still have monitors that are only 640 pixels wide. Try not to create Web pages any wider than this. People don't mind scrolling down a page, but scrolling across it is frustrating.

Keep your images small in terms of file size. One simple way to check an image's file size is to list it in Windows Explorer, then go to **View ➔ Details**, and take a look at the figure under the Size column. For a user with a 28.8 KBps modem, each 1 KB in file size takes about a second to download, so that fancy 120 KB image you just created might not be such a good idea. Ways to cut an image's size include reducing the number of colours it uses, reducing its physical height and width and saving it in the most compressed format – .gif or .jpeg.

Use tables to reduce the width of text columns. The default in HTML is for lines of text to stretch all the way to the right side of the browser window before starting a new line. On a typical monitor, optimum line length for ease of reading is actually around 10 words, so consider putting the text for your Web page into a table, and setting the table width to 400 pixels at the most. A table is easy to create with any Web-authoring software, including Word.

Always give every page a title. When a Web page is being viewed, its title appears at the very top of the browser, and also in the status bar at the bottom of the screen. An informative title can be useful to Web surfers who come across your page in a search engine's results.

Remember that not everyone who enters your site will come in through the front door, so try to make their first impression as appealing as possible – every single page should be well designed.

PUBLISHING YOUR SITE

It's possible to turn your PC into a Web server capable of storing Web pages that anyone else in the world can access – but it is not a task for beginners, and it requires a permanent, expensive connection to the Internet.

If you already have an account with an ISP (Internet Service Provider), find out if the deal includes Web space – most offer you around 5 to 10 MB of Web space. Ask your ISP how

much it will allow other people to download from your Website – around 300 MB a month is reasonable. Also try The Free Site (www.thefreesite.com), which lists free Web hosting services. A disadvantage is that you usually have to display an advertising banner on your pages.

Transfer your site to your Web space using FTP (File Transfer Protocol). Most Internet service providers still insist that you use the FTP system for uploading Websites. This is simpler than is sounds (see p. 233). You'll need an FTP program like CuteFTP (www.cuteftp.com), which is available for download, and can be tested free.

Before you start uploading with FTP, you need to go through the folder in which you've created your site, and remove the files that

are not part of the site. You will also need to find out from your ISP the address of their FTP server, your user name and your password. Open up your

FTP program, and create a connection (see also *The secrets of FTP*, p 241). Drag and drop your Web folder onto the server and watch as it copies over.

When you've finished uploading your site, open your Web browser and type in the URL of your site (your ISP can give you this information). Check that all your pages and links work and that your images are displayed as you want them to be.

▸ See also **Understanding HTML**, p. 220; **How to promote your Website**, p. 232; **Uploading files to an ISP**, p. 233; and **The secrets of FTP**, p. 241.

U S E F U L   S I T E S   F O R   W E B
A U T H O R S

These sites can help you to develop a striking Website.

**THE FREE SITE
(www.thefreesite.com)**
A roundup of the Web's best free services for Webmasters, including site-building software and page monitoring services.

**REALLYBIG.COM
(www.reallybig.com/reallybig.shtml)**
Links to free Web resources, including clip art, sounds, and other add-ons such as guest books and hit counters.

**WEBMONKEY
(hotwired.lycos.com/webmonkey)**
A huge range of practical tips, tutorials and information, covering all the skills you need for every aspect of site-building.

How to: Create a Website in Word

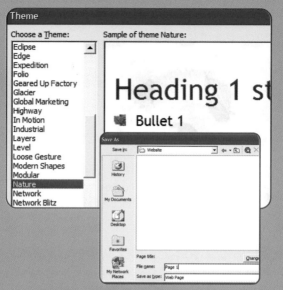

1 Firstly sketch out on paper the pages you will be creating. Open Word, select **File**, then **New**. A New Document column appears on the right. Click on **Blank Web Page** and a new document appears. In the new document, go to the **Format** menu and select **Theme**.

2 Click on your choice of visual style for your pages (here, Nature) and click **OK**. A blank Web page appears. To save it, go to the **File** menu, select **Save as Web Page** and create a new file in which to save it. Type your headline at the top of the Web page.

3 Highlight your headline, select **Format →
Font**. Choose a font style, size and colour and click **OK**. Style your body text in the same way. For neatness, place body text and photos in a table. Go to **Table → Insert → Table**, then specify the number of rows and columns.

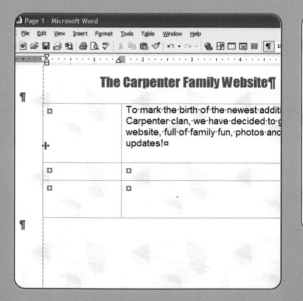

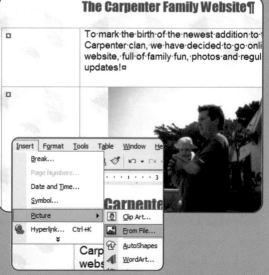

4 Adjust the width of a column by placing the mouse pointer over the column edge. When it changes to a doubled-headed arrow, press the left mouse button and drag the line to the desired width. To add body text, click in the desired row and begin typing.

5 To insert an image in the table, click in the relevant row and column. Go to **Insert →
Picture → From File**. Select your picture and click **Insert**. Make sure your images have been saved beforehand as either .jpeg or .gif files as this makes their file size much smaller.

6 Use Microsoft's Web Publishing Wizard to publish your site, if you have no Web space of your own. Go to the **Start** menu and select **My Documents**, locate your Website file and select **Publish this folder to the Web** in the File and Folder tasks, then follow the Wizard.

Your own Website

HOW TO PROMOTE YOUR WEBSITE

Once your Website is up and running, you need to let people know where to find it.

■ **It's not enough to just build a Website** and hope people will come – you have to actively promote your site to draw users. One simple way to do this is by using Web spiders, such as Submit It! (www.submitit.com), that will submit your Website to hundreds of other sites, directories and search engines.

■ **If you submit your site to search engines manually,** then you should focus on the major, or deep search engines. These use programs known as Web crawlers to roam the Web, searching for new or updated pages. But if your site isn't linked from anywhere else and you haven't registered it at all, it will be invisible to

the Web crawlers. Normally, to register your site you'll need to supply your Web address, name and e-mail, and sometimes even a description of the site and contact details. Many of the most well-known Websites are deep search engines, such as Google (www.google.com), AltaVista (www.altavista.com), Go.com (www.go.com), Excite (www.excite.com), Lycos (www.lycos.com), HotBot (www.hotbot.lycos.com), Northern Light (www.northernlight.com) and Yahoo! (www.yahoo.com).

■ **Before you register with a search engine,** you should check their advice on how to use keywords in your Web pages. For example, if your site is about teddy bear collecting, type 'teddy', 'bears', 'furry', 'stuffed' and 'toys' as keywords. Avoid using words like 'Web', 'Internet' or 'services', since they won't help to target searchers specifically to your site.

■ **If you have a large list of keywords,** your pages will be found with a broad spectrum of search strings, but they're less likely to be at the top of the results lists (this is a blanket strategy). If you use a limited number, it increases the density of those few keywords and therefore puts them high up the list (this is a targeted strategy).

■ **If any of your keywords are routinely misspelled,** include the incorrect version in your list so your site can still be found. Selling satellite TV dishes? Include both 'sattelite' and 'satallite' on your list.

■ **To help you choose the right keywords for your Website,** try the free Wordtracker trial (www.wordtracker.com). You enter keywords and the site suggests how useful these would be in the targeting of your Website by search engines.

■ **The Search Engine Watch Website,** (searchenginewatch.com/webmasters) provides handy tips for Webmasters. It covers search engine submission, placement and marketing issues. It explains how search engines find and rank Web pages and advises on what you can do to improve the search engine rankings of your site, by using better page design, for example.

■ **Another key to promoting your Website** is to build a large group of core users. There are many ways to do this. You can keep the information on your site as up-to-date as possible, or you can try to make it so complete that it effectively becomes the main resource for whatever subject your site deals with. This way people will come back to your site again and again to keep on checking the information.

■ **One way to build a community around your site** is to start a mailing list to keep people enthused about your subject. Design a subscription form and include relevant news, helpful tips and discussions. You can also include links to parts of your site. Make sure you only mail people who have asked to be put on the mailing list, and don't forget to make it easy for people to unsubscribe.

How to: Submit your site to a search engine

1 Go to one of the main search engines, such as AltaVista (www.altavista.com) or Yahoo! (www.yahoo.com). Click on the **Submit a Site** link in AltaVista, or click the **How to Suggest a Site** link in Yahoo!.

2 Simply follow the step-by-step instructions for entering your Website URL. Unless yours is a business site, you should select the free submission option. Then, once you've completed the details, your site should be included in all future searches.

UPLOADING FILES TO AN ISP

You've designed your Web pages – now it's time to put them online.

■ **What is uploading?** Uploading is the process of copying files from your computer onto another computer, via the Internet. For instance, if you have designed a Website on your computer at home, you need to upload it to an Internet server before the rest of the world can visit it. The same goes for e-mails and attachments – when you click Send, the e-mail is uploaded to the recipient's mail server until they request their e-mail program to retrieve it.

■ **First, you need some Web space.** If you have an account with a conventional ISP (Internet Service Provider), you almost certainly will have Web space to use for your site. Check the registration information or your ISP's site for details. However, if yours is a free ISP, the chances are it won't offer Web space.

■ **Test, test and test again before you upload** your new site to your Web space to ensure that it works properly. To check your Web pages with Internet Explorer or Netscape Navigator, go to the **File** menu and select **Open**, then browse your hard drive for the pages. If you

can, give a friend a copy on a disk to check that links work and that the navigation is logical.

■ **Get some help.** It's worth checking the Help section of your ISP's Website before you upload your site to make sure the details you last used, such as the server name, are still valid.

■ **Before you begin to upload your Website files,** check that you have on hand all the relevant information from your Internet Service Provider. You will need a File Transfer Protocol (FTP) log-in name and password, and you will also need to check the name of the server that you must connect to.

■ **The most common way of getting your site onto your Web space** at your ISP's Web server is to use one of the many FTP programs. Most FTP programs are easy to use,

and are freeware or shareware, so you can at least try them out for a time before you need to buy one.

■ **Use all lower case letters** for your file names and extensions when you upload, since some Web servers are case sensitive.

■ **If you use FrontPage 2002 to create your Website,** you can upload pages to your site without using FTP. Go to **File ➜ Publish Web** and type in the location of your Web space after the http:// prefix. Click on **Options** to choose to publish only changed pages. The 'all pages' option will overwrite any pages already on your site that have the same file.

■ **First time nerves?** Try uploading a test Web page if you're worried about getting things right. Create a basic HTML document in your Web editor with some text and use that to try out the procedure. When you upload your real page, you can just overwrite the test page.

■ **Test your site thoroughly** as soon as you've uploaded it. You don't want to go live and tell people about your site if it has problems. If you find any, try to rectify them quickly.

■ **Keep a copy of your site** on your PC's own hard drive. This is particularly important if you're going to update the site frequently – perhaps adding new pages or new information – because you can alter any given pages and upload only those specific ones to refresh the site.

▶ See also **Creating a Website,** p. 228; and **The secrets of FTP,** p. 241.

ADVICE AND SERVICES FOR YOUR SITE

Find out how you can promote and market your Website – often for free.

**THE ART OF BUSINESS WEB SITE PROMOTION
(www.deadlock.com/promote)**
A step-by-step guide to promoting your own commercial Website.

**BUDGETWEB.COM
(www.budgetweb.com)**
Here you'll find a listing of hundreds of different companies that offer inexpensive hosting services.

**THE SPIDER'S APPRENTICE
(www.monash.com/spidap.html)**
A useful guide to Web search engines and how they work.

PR2 (www.pr2.com)
This site provides a very useful regular e-mail newsletter packed with tips.

**SEARCH ENGINE WATCH
(www.searchenginewatch.com)**
Check the Search Engine Submission Tips for a wealth of valuable information.

**THE YELLOW PAGES SUPERHIGHWAY
(www.bestyellow.com)**
This site links to more than 1000 Websites where you can list your site for free.

Exploring the Web

Browsing

THE WORLD WIDE WEB

A vast amount of data can be found on the World Wide Web, so now the world is literally at your fingertips.

■ To use the Web, you need an application called a Web browser.
These translate the HTML code of Web designers into viewable Web pages. Wherever you go on

OFFLINE BROWSING SOFTWARE
Save time and money by trying an offline browsing program.

WEBREAPER (www.webreaper.com)
A Web crawler or spider, which works its way through a website, downloading pages, pictures and objects so that they can be viewed locally, without needing to be connected to the Internet.

COPERNIC 2001 (www.copernic.com)
Take advantage of search engine technology to speed your online searches and download relevant results for offline browsing.

SURFSAVER (www.surfsaver.com)
Download and collate Web pages with ease.

WEBCELERATOR (www.webcelerator.com)
Speeds up your online browsing as well as letting you review visited pages offline.

WEBZIP OFFLINE BROWSER (www.spidersoft.com)
Download entire Websites to your hard drive to surf the Web at leisure.

---

the Internet, your Web browser – and all its familiar controls – is there with you. Two popular browsers are Netscape Navigator and Microsoft's Internet Explorer. There are also others available.

■ Navigator and Internet Explorer offer similar features. These include Bookmarks (Navigator) or Favorites (Internet Explorer), a customisable Toolbar, built-in or linked e-mail program, and newsgroups software.

■ Your choice of browser may be dictated by which one is supplied by your Internet Service Provider (ISP) as part of its starter kit. The ISP may be preconfigured and it may even be the only browser for which they'll provide telephone support if something goes wrong.

■ Each page on the Web has a unique address, known as a URL (Uniform Resource Locater), that identifies its location on the server. To visit a Website simply type the URL in the Address bar of your browser.

■ To move through the Web quickly, connect at off-peak hours – usually in the morning or late at night. Midday and after-school are generally slowest because not only are businesses online, but that's when the next generation of Web surfers practise their skills.

HOW TO BROWSE EFFICIENTLY

Make your Web browsing as pleasant and speedy as possible!

■ Keep your browser up-to-date if you want to visit Web pages using all the latest multimedia features. Updates are freely available for Internet Explorer (www.microsoft.com) and Netscape Navigator (www.netscape.com).

■ Older PC? If the speed of your computer is less than 350 Mhz, it may work better with an older browser, such as Internet Explorer 4. Or you could try a less well known browser such as

Opera (www.opera.com), which is more compact than Navigator and Explorer.

■ Surf's up! The speed of the Net varies through the day, according to how many people are online. If you are accessing US sites, choose a time of day when most of the locals are in bed asleep. You will need to experiment to find out the best time for your particular location. Your access will also be slower if lots of people are using your ISP.

■ Choose your look. You can customise the way Web pages appear. In Internet Explorer, click on **Tools → Internet Options**. At the bottom of the General tab, there are four buttons – Colors, Fonts, Languages and Accessibility. Click on them to customise your view. Tick the **Use**

hover color box in the Colors tab to make links change color when your cursor hovers over them. In Netscape Navigator, click on **Edit → Preferences**, then double-click on **Appearance** to change your fonts or colours, or on **Navigator** to change the language.

■ **Download several Web pages all in one click.** Click on **File → New Window** and enter a Web address. Do this for as many sites as you wish to visit. Leave the windows open and click on the page you want to see.

■ **Increase your browsing speed** by regularly clearing your cache. Your cache saves recently visited Web pages. This also means that other users can't see the sites you've been to.

■ **Sophisticated graphics** and pop-up adverts can slow your download speed. Disable graphics and Java applications to make pages load faster. In Explorer, go to **Tools → Internet Options → Advanced**. Under Multimedia deselect **Show pictures**. Under Microsoft VM, uncheck the **Java logging enabled** box. In Navigator, go to **Edit → Preferences → Advanced**. Deselect the **Enable Java** box.

▶ See also **Working with Internet Explorer,** p. 222; **Using Netscape Communicator,** p. 222; **Secrets of the cache,** p. 224; and **Dealing with cookies,** p. 250.

FIRST STOP THE FAQS

Almost every Website has an FAQ page – a file of Frequently Asked Questions. Make it your first stop for information.

■ **You can pronounce it F-A-Q,** but you might lose credibility with the geeks if you do. It's more commonly pronounced 'fak'.

■ **It's only polite to read the FAQs** before you join a newsgroup, whatever the topic. That way, you run less risk of cluttering up the information exchange by asking questions to which the answers already exist.

■ **Most FAQs are relatively brief** and load instantly. So if you're new to a site, program, or a topic, it's worth taking extra time to browse the whole document. You may find the precise information you need and also discover other things that will enhance your experience.

■ **Does your Website need FAQs?** Frequently Asked Questions can be useful if you are running a business or an educational site, but if it's a personal or family site you shouldn't really need them. For detailed advice on how to prepare and publicise FAQs, go to Infinite Ink's Writing Periodic Postings site (www.ii.com/internet/faqs/writing/).

ii infinite ink
writing
WRITING PERIODIC POSTINGS (`FAQs' & `PIPs')

■ **Print out the FAQs as a handy hard copy reference.** Not only can you then read them at your leisure, you'll also avoid the need to keep an extra window open on your Desktop.

■ **FAQs can be a great way to find solutions** to computer problems when you've exhausted other possibilities. Use the advanced search facility available on most search engines to link the term 'FAQ' with the topic of interest, such as 'printers' or 'printer drivers'.

■ **Searching an archive of FAQs** can be a good way to find out whether a particular newsgroup is for you, especially if you're interested in an obscure topic. Try the searchable archive from the Internet FAQ Consortium (www.faqs.org).

▶ See also **Newsgroups,** p. 334.

SAVING WEB PAGES

You can save a complete Web page, including all the images, for later viewing offline.

■ **If you are saving just the Web page text,** one simple way to do this is to open a new Word or Notepad document then transfer the text into it using copy and paste. Just click on the page and use **Ctrl+A** to select all of the text, **Ctrl+C** to copy it, and **Ctrl+V** to paste it into your document. Of course, the text you paste into your document will have lost the formatting of the original text on the Web page.

How to: Change your home page

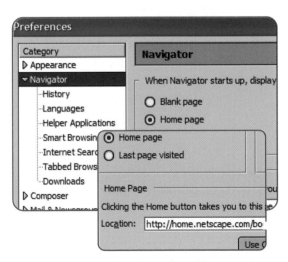

1 In **Internet Explorer** change your home page by going to **Tools,** then **Internet Options.** Click on the **General** tab to see your current home page URL. You can choose to type in a new Web address, or use the current page, the default page or a blank page.

2 If you use **Netscape Navigator,** click on the **Edit** menu and select **Preferences** then **Navigator.** Click on the **Home page** button in the 'When Navigator starts up, display' section. Now type the URL of your choice into the box for the Home Page location.

You can also save a Web page

simply by clicking on **Save As** in your browser's File menu. On some older Web browsers, however, this may save only the HTML text of the page and the graphics will be missing. You may even find that the page is hard to follow because often the headings are in graphics form on a Web page. If this happens, upgrade to the latest version of your browser.

If you use Internet Explorer 5+, you

can save a complete Web page for later browsing. When you save, choose **Web Page, complete (*.htm, *.html)** from the Save as type box. This lets you save both the HTML code and the images on the page to a Web archive on your hard drive so you can look at it later on.

There are many shareware

programs that allow you to save complete Web pages onto your hard drive, such as CatchTheWeb (www.catchtheweb.com). Search for similar shareware at ZDNet (www.zdnet.com).

See also **Working offline**, p. 243.

WORKING WITH ZIP FILES

Many files downloaded from the Internet are compressed for quick transfer, often using the Zip format.

Zip is a file compression utility:

an essential piece of software to help you manage your files. It lets you condense a large group of files into one smaller file. If you download or receive a compressed file from a friend or colleague, you'll also need to have the utility installed so you can decompress or unzip the files. The most popular Zip utility is WinZip (www.winzip.com). A trial version can be downloaded free from many shareware sites.

While many files achieve a very

high compression rate, others won't compress much at all. Graphics files, such as the .gif or .jpg, are already compressed. Zip files need to be able to reconstruct the original files exactly and cannot reduce the size of files that have already been reduced.

WinZip integrates itself with

Windows Explorer so you can easily compress your files to create a Zip file. Highlight the directory or files you want to compress, and then right-click and select **WinZip**, then choose **Add to Zip file** from the pop-up menu. WinZip generates the file, which you can give a new name in the 'Add to archive' box.

You can also unzip a file within

Windows Explorer. Right-click on it, select **WinZip**, then choose **Extract to** from the menu, and choose the folder you want WinZip to decompress the files to. Make sure the **Use folder names** box is checked so any specified folders are recreated. If it is left blank, all files will be unzipped into a single folder, making items difficult to find when you unzip the folder.

Before you unzip a compressed

file, especially one that you have downloaded from the Internet, check for viruses. Locate the file that you want to check in the virus scanner section of WinZip's program location screen. Go to **Actions** then select **Virus Scan**.

How to: Save Web images to use as a Desktop background

1 Web images can easily be made into your desktop background. Open the Web page you want to use in Internet Explorer, choose **File**, then **Save As**. Locate a folder on your hard disk to save it into, then store the file there as a Web Page.

2 Right-click on any empty space on your Desktop and select **Properties** from the pop-up menu that appears. Select the **Desktop** tab, then click on the **Browse** button to locate your image.

3 Finally, double-click on your saved file and it will appear in the preview window in the Display Properties dialogue box. To set the image as your Desktop background, click **OK**.

■ **Need to send zipped files to someone without a copy of the Zip program?** To do this, create your Zip file as normal, click the **Actions** menu, and choose the **Make.Exe File** option. This creates an executable file that can be decompressed and opened on the other person's PC without them needing to have WinZip installed.

SAVING GRAPHICS AND TEXT

You can save pictures and graphic images found on the Net onto your hard disk.

■ **To save a graphic image from the Web** for later use, just right-click on it. A list of options will appear. Choose the **Save Image As** or **Save Picture As** option, and save the file to your hard disk. Use the default name – the name used by the Web page for the file – or type in your own.

■ **When copying images or text from Web pages** don't forget to note where they came from and whether or not they were copyright free. That way, if you want to publish the text or images in your own report or Website, you will know where to seek permission. Always respect the terms of any copyrighted material.

UNDERSTANDING ERROR MESSAGES

Whenever there is a problem with connecting to a site, an error message will appear.

■ **Received the 400 Bad Request error message?** This message means there is something wrong with the Web address you typed. Either the server you are contacting does not recognise the document you're asking for, the document does not exist, or you're not authorised to access it. Check that you have typed in the address correctly. Pay special attention to the use of upper case and lower case letters, colons and slashes. Many sites put initial capital letters on

directory names but not file names. If you encounter this message repeatedly, it is possible that the source you copied the Website address from uses an incorrect mixture of upper case and lower case letters.

■ **503 Service Unavailable** has several possible causes. Your service provider's server may be down, or your own system might not be working. Wait a few minutes and try again.

■ **401 Unauthorised** signals that you are probably accessing a protected site and you're not on the host's preferred guest list. Or you may

have typed your password incorrectly. Some sites also put a block on domain types. If you're not from a .gov or .edu domain, for example, you may not be able to gain access. If you're sure you should have access, try again, but make sure you type correctly. Passwords are often case sensitive, so check that your Caps Lock is off.

■ **404 Not Found** pops up when the server that hosts the site can't find the HTML document specified at the end of the Web address you have typed in. It may be a simple case of mistyping, but

> **HTTP Error 404**
>
> 404 Not Found

it may also mean that the document doesn't exist anymore. To see if the Website is still live, try deleting the last part of the Web address to the nearest slash. If it is live, check if there are links to the document you're looking for. Failing that, delete the last slash and try typing .html instead, to see which page that gives you.

■ **Bad File Request** means that your browser is unable to work with some of the site you are trying to access. Perhaps there's an error or unsupported feature. Contact the Webmaster – the site's administrator – by e-mail (key in webmaster@[site's name]), or try accessing the site again some other day.

■ **When the Host Unknown message appears,** it usually means that either the server is down for maintenance, or you have lost the connection. It could be that your modem was disconnected from the server for some reason. First check the Website address for errors. Then click on the **Reload** or **Refresh** button, which will re-establish the connection in many cases. Otherwise, try again later.

■ **Connection refused by host.** You may not be allowed to access this document, because it is blocked to your domain or it is password-protected. If you know the password, try typing it in again. If you don't know the password, but think you might be eligible for one, e-mail the site's Webmaster and ask for it.

■ **Failed DNS lookup** means the Domain Name System can't translate the Web address you used into a valid Internet address. It is either a harmless blip or the result of a mistyped host name. Blips in DNS lookup are common, and often you can rectify this by clicking the **Refresh** or **Reload** button. If the problem persists, try again later. In the meantime, check your spelling and re-type the address if necessary.

■ **File contains no data** indicates the site you have accessed is the right one, but the Web page HTML code has errors in it. It is possible that you may have stumbled upon this site just as updated versions of pages are being uploaded. Try it again a bit later.

Search engines

The Web is home to more than a billion pages of text with a million more being added every day. So how on earth do you find anything in all that electronic noise? Search engines are the answer, but there is more to it than just typing a word into Yahoo! and seeing what pops up.

If you want to find something specific, you need to know how to use the correct search tool for the job, and how to tell it exactly what to look for. Most people just fumble around the Internet, missing out on the best material. The real art of Internet searching is knowing how to find exactly what you are looking for. Luckily, it is an easy art to master.

When you use a search engine, what you are really doing is searching the engine's database of Web pages. When someone submits a Web page to a search engine they give each page metatags – keywords which help to describe the content. The database is compiled by a Web crawler, or Web spider, which is a program that explores the Internet, looking for both new sites and

changes to sites it already has in its database. The thoroughness of a search engine depends on how much text its crawler collects and how often. While there are many different search engines, some of them use the same crawler technology, so they produce virtually identical results. GoTo and HotBot use the same crawler, while Raging Search and AltaVista share the same database.

To keep up with what's happening on your favourite search engine, check out Search Engine Watch (www.searchenginewatch.com) and Search Engine Showdown (www.searchengineshowdown.com). These sites will come up with the latest details on how different search engines work, which one currently offers the most pages, and lots more information.

Search agents are a type of search engine that gathers information, but only from a limited number of sites. The best are programs that you download. They are very useful if you want to query several different search engines at once. Copernic Agent Basic (www.copernic.com) and Search.com (www.search.com) will query hundreds of search engines, directories, e-mail archives and Usenet archives at one time.

Subject directories are search engines that will allow you to browse a range of sites under a specific topic. In a directory, the sites are arranged by subject, or by other criteria, such as entry date or rating. Directories are also compiled by people, and not by computer programmed

Web crawlers. The most popular ones are Yahoo! (www.yahoo.com), Open Directory (http://dmoz.org), About.com (www.about.com) and Suite 101 (www.suite101.com).

To find really specific information, use a specialised directory. These directories will find sites on the Internet for almost any subject or area of interest. They will collect pages that the major directories might miss. Start by searching a directory that lists such directories, such as Directory Guide (www.directoryguide.com), Earthcam (www.earthcam.com) and Go Gettem (www.gogettem.com).

POPULAR SEARCH ENGINES

Surf the Net easily and efficiently using a search engine.

ALLTHEWEB (www.alltheweb.com)
ALTAVISTA (www.altavista.com)
ANZWERS (www.anzwers.com)
ASK JEEVES (www.ask.co.uk)
DOGPILE (www.dogpile.com)
EXCITE (www.excite.com)
GALAXY (www.galaxy.com)
GOOGLE (www.google.com)
HOTBOT (www.hotbot.lycos.com)
LOOKSMART (www.looksmart.com)
LYCOS (www.lycos.com)
MAMMA (www.mamma.com)
METACRAWLER (www.metacrawler.com)
MSN (www.msn.co.uk)
NORTHERN LIGHT (www.northernlight.com)
WEBCRAWLER (www.webcrawler.com)
YAHOO! (www.yahoo.com)

Suite101.com™ 480 Topi
Real People Helping Real People 25,288 Artic
20,354 Link

HOME   DIRECTORY   UNIVERSITY

Suite University   Suite10
Welcome to Suit

NEAR and AND operators work in a similar way to retrieve documents that contain two keywords from a search. The only difference between the two is that NEAR operators limit the results of your search by requiring the keywords to be within 10 words of each other – this is useful when searching for names. For example, 'John NEAR Smith' retrieves documents containing Smith, John or John P. Smith.

documents containing the word hardware. To avoid this problem, use parentheses. The query for retrieving documents about Internet hardware and software would then be '(hardware OR software) AND Internet'.

NAVIGATING AROUND THE BROWSER

Speed up your checking by opening promising sites in new browser windows. You can do this by holding down the **Shift key** as you click on the site address that appeals to you.

If you are interrupted while searching, and have to close your browser, bring up your search results again later in Internet Explorer by opening the History panel. Under the date that you made the search, click on the relevant search engine. A list of the searches you have made using that engine appears. Hover your pointer over the entry and click on the interrupted search to carry on.

See also **How to browse efficiently**, p. 234.

BOOLEAN OPERATORS

To limit the number of hits you get from your searches, use Boolean logic, which helps you search for a subject by narrowing down the options. Go to a search engine and type in 'dog' and you will get an unmanageable number of hits. Boolean logic uses words called operators (NEAR, NOT, AND, OR) to create relationships among words and concepts. In most search engines, you can use the plus sign (+) instead of AND, a blank space instead of OR, and the minus sign (–) instead of NOT.

Type the Boolean operators (NEAR, NOT, AND, OR) in upper case letters so the search engine can recognise them. Using lower case letters makes the operators stop words – words that a search engine ignores because they are too common and will create false hits.

Most search engines use Boolean operators. For example, if you enter the query 'tom jerry', most search engines will interpret the keywords as if they contained an OR operator, as in 'tom OR jerry'. The search will contain all results for 'tom' and all results for 'jerry'.

The OR operator can be useful when searching for alternative spellings, such as 'colour OR color', or in order to broaden a query when searching for synonyms, such as 'city OR urban'.

The NOT operator excludes part of the search entry. It can also be used to help to restrict the search, as in: 'ghosts OR apparitions OR spirits NOT moonshine NOT alcohol'.

Nesting is a method of combining operators in a logical order to produce highly targeted searches. Most search engines evaluate Boolean operators in the order NEAR, NOT, AND and OR. So, if you enter the following search string: 'hardware software+internet', the results would include all documents that contain the words software and Internet, and then look for

How to: Search Altavista using Boolean operators

1 Go to AltaVista (www.altavista.com), type in two words, and click **Search**. The search returns a list of Web pages containing one or both words in small or capital letters. To search for a phrase, rather than single words, place double quotation marks around the words.

2 You can extend your search to include an alternative word or phrase by typing the word OR before it, and limit your search to sites that include a key word or phrase by typing a plus sign immediately before the word. Scroll through the resulting list of links.

FIND IT WITH YAHOO!

Yahoo! is one of the Web's foremost search engines and provides a way to search the contents of millions of Web pages simultaneously.

■ **Yahoo! differs from most of its rivals** in that searching is done by categories, although you can also do a keyword search. To search for information, just click on a category.

■ **Take a look at the Yahoo! home page** (http://uk.yahoo.com) to see a handy directory of the services that are offered – from useful cinema links to online shopping in department stores. Whatever you want, you'll almost always find a starting point here.

■ **Want to focus on what's happening locally?** Or maybe you want to visit another country or city? Look at the regional versions of Yahoo! to get a round-up of local news and events.

■ **Get personal.** Set up your own individual home page with My Yahoo!. Once you have logged on and entered some simple information, you can collect all your favourite parts of Yahoo! together in one place.

■ **Demonstrate your individuality.** Once you have established your own home page with Yahoo! you can personalise it in many ways. Not only can you change the content, but also the layout and colour scheme.

■ **Create and keep your own bit of cyberspace.** Set up a Website for free at Yahoo! GeoCities (http://uk.geocities.yahoo.com). GeoCities, the publishing community, provides you with all the necessary tools. If you're a beginner, try Yahoo! PageWizards. For more confident Web creators, there's the Yahoo! PageBuilder.

HOW TO DOWNLOAD FILES

By following a few simple guidelines, you can avoid the common problems of downloading data to your computer.

■ **Be organised.** If you don't already have one, set up a download folder on your hard drive to help you find your files after downloading – for instance, C:\Downloads. It also makes sense to keep an archive directory to store your older downloads in, such as C:\Downloads\Archive. Then, should you need the original file, you won't have to download it all over again.

■ **Checking for viruses** is always a sensible precaution, even with the most reputable

How to: Download a file using Download Accelerator Plus

1 Find an Internet site that has the file you want. The site should provide information on the size of the file and whether it is .zip, .exe, or another type of archive, as well as confirming that the program is compatible with your operating system and hardware.

2 Download Accelerator will load itself automatically. The tracking bar shows you how long the process is taking, where the file is being stored on your hard drive and whether the download can resume if the connection is lost.

3 When Download Accelerator has completed its work, you can quickly find your file by using Windows Explorer. Don't forget to scan for viruses before opening any file downloaded from the Internet.

240

of sites. Make sure your resident virus scan program is operational while you're downloading, and also make sure it is kept up to date with details of the latest viruses. Also check the downloaded file with your antivirus software before you open it.

For speed, use a download accelerator.
Programs such as Download Accelerator Plus (www.downloadaccelerator.com) can speed up your downloading by up to 300 per cent for certain file types (see 'How to', p. 240).

Use an archive program such as WinZip.
Most Websites prepare their files for downloading by compressing them with a Zip utility. This packages up multiple files into a single file and reduces its size to make it quicker to download. WinZip will unzip this package once

you have downloaded it. WinZip is available as shareware (www.winzip.com). You can download it for free and pay later if you like it.

Download files from FTP sites.
FTP stands for File Transfer Protocol – it's an old but fast method of sending files over the Internet (see p. 242). Sites that use this format tend to send files more quickly than straightforward Web pages do. If you have the program Download Accelerator Plus, it will automatically look for faster sites, including FTP ones. Large software libraries will also usually offer an FTP site.

Try using a download scheduler program.
Software like Go!Zilla (www.gozilla.

com) can manage your downloads for you, scheduling them for less busy times on the Web, when the files will copy across more

quickly. Like the Download Accelerator program, Go!zilla can also resume a broken download at some later time.

Missing files?
If you can't find a file on your computer that you're confident you've already downloaded, there's a simple procedure you can follow to locate it if you use Netscape Navigator. If Navigator is still running, click **File ➜ Save As**. When the Save As dialogue box appears, it will automatically open to the same folder you selected for the previous download. Make a note of the folder listed in the Save In field at the top of the dialogue box. Click the arrow to the right of the Save In field to identify the path to this folder. Make a note of the file path and click **Cancel**, then start tracking down your file.

RESUMING INTERRUPTED DOWNLOADS

File download gone amiss? Find out what to do next.

1. The Resume function of Download Accelerator can save time if you suffer a lost connection or have to halt a file transfer. To resume an interrupted download, just run the Download Accelerator program and double-click on the file in the entry list. The status column will indicate how much of the file has already been downloaded.

2. Some older Internet servers and some connections channelled through another networked computer may not support this function, so watch for the confirmation message on the Download Accelerator panel when you begin a transfer.

3. Download Accelerator 4 includes an AlwaysResume feature that, for files less than 10 MB, will support resume even on those connections where the standard resume is not available.

The right files?
Before you download a file, double-check to make sure it is the right type to work on your computer. Files intended for Apple Macintosh or Unix systems will not open on a Windows machine.

▶ See also **Upgrading your software,** p. 99; **Dealing with viruses,** p. 208; and **Working with Zip files,** p. 236.

THE SECRETS OF FTP

Get to know the ins and outs of this extremely useful Internet file transfer system.

Before Web pages and browsers became popular,
File Transfer Protocol (FTP) was the standard way of transferring files on the Internet. Browsing an FTP server isn't exactly user-friendly – all you see is a text-based list of file names and directories, not all of which are clear as to their content – but FTP's speed and efficiency keeps it in common use today.

One of the most common applications for FTP
is providing a means for people to upload files to their own Website.

While your browser may allow you to perform some of the functions you need, a special FTP program, or FTP client, offers the most features. Sites such as Strouds CWSApps (http://cws.internet.com/ftp.html) and WebAttack (www.webattack.com/shareware/ network/swftp. shtml) offer a wide selection.

■ All the major browsers provide some level of support for transferring FTP
files. With Internet Explorer, just type ftp://ftp.microsoft.com into the address box. Once the browser has connected to the FTP site, you'll see a list of files and folders, just as in Windows Explorer. Navigation works in a similar way too: click on a folder to open it and click on a file to display or download it.

■ There are lots of files available on FTP servers all over the Net, but you won't
necessarily find them by using one of the regular search engines such as Yahoo! or Excite. Instead, try a search engine such as Lycos that offers an

advanced FTP search facility (http://download.lycos .com/static/advanced_search.asp).

■ One specific FTP download program is WS_FTP Pro (www.ipswitch.com).
For various technical reasons, this type of program downloads files of more than 1 MB in size quicker than normal Web servers.

■ Some download programs also help with FTP file downloads. Go!Zilla
(www.gozilla.com) is ideal for all Internet downloads, but it also has a Leech feature that detects when you are trying to link to an FTP site. It automatically locates any files for download from that site. Once you've chosen a file, Go!Zilla makes sure that the download is successful – it is even able to resume a download if the connection is either deliberately or accidentally cancelled.

■ Sometimes you might be prompted to enter a user name and password before
you can log on to an FTP server. Most servers will accept anonymous FTP, which means that you can type in anonymous as the user name and enter your e-mail address as the password (most FTP clients do this automatically). If the server doesn't

How to: Download and install an FTP client

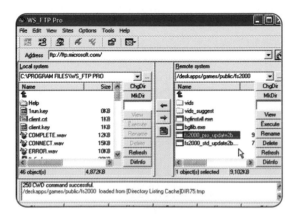

1 Connect to a shareware site and look for FTP client software. There will be many choices – we opted to try out WS_FTP Pro. Select your version of Windows and set the folder where you to save the downloaded files on your PC.

2 Once the program is downloaded to your PC, double-click on the WS_FTP Pro file to open it. Click **Next** through all the windows, choosing options for which icons you want to be displayed on your desktop and in the toolbar of Microsoft Internet Explorer.

3 Now, when you connect to an FTP site, WS_FTP Pro automatically takes over and finds all possible downloadable files. Click on **Continue Evaluation** and locate the file you want. Click on the left-facing arrow and your FTP file download will begin automatically.

allow you to do this, then you can try e-mailing webmaster@[The FTP site name] to request a real user name and password.

■ Windows comes with its own FTP client (FTP.EXE), which can be found in the Windows folder. As it is a DOS-based utility, beginners unfamiliar with the command line will not find it very user-friendly. It can be learned, however, and a knowledgeable user may find it handy to perform a simple FTP task or two on a computer that doesn't have a full FTP client. A site such as Tucows (http://html.tucows.com/webmaster/tut/dosftp.html) offers help using the Windows FTP.EXE.

■ When transferring files using an FTP client, you need to be aware of a potential snag. Files may be transferred in either ASCII (text) or binary (program) mode. If you get this wrong (in particular, transferring a .zip, .exe, or other binary file in ASCII mode), then the file will be corrupted. Most FTP clients can figure out which mode to use – most of the time – but it is not guaranteed, so check your FTP program's preferences for guidance.

■ FTP can seem quite a complex process, but there is a tutorial called Zen and the Art of FTP (www.eurekais.com/brock/ftp_tutorial) that can help you. To find others, enter 'ftp tutorial' into your favourite search engine.

WORKING OFFLINE

Connected to the Web through your phone line? Keep it free for the rest of the family by browsing offline.

Internet Explorer 6 allows offline browsing in several different ways. Found the Web page you want? Save it for viewing offline later by going to the **File** menu, selecting **Save as** and saving the page to a folder on your hard disk.

Each time you type a URL in Explorer's Address bar and press **Enter**, the page at this address is stored in the cache –

where downloaded pages from the Internet are stored. To read the last 25 pages accessed when you are offline, click the down arrow by the end of the Address bar and click on a URL.

View the Web pages you've already visited. The History button on the Explorer Toolbar lets you review pages visited within a set period of time. Set the time to suit your browsing needs by going to **Tools ➔ Internet options**. Adjust your settings in the History section of the General tab. To review a page you looked at earlier, click on **History** while you are offline and then click on the listed links. You will have to reconnect to the Net for deeper Web browsing.

■ Every Windows user needs Copernic Agent Basic. This program trawls through over 90 of the Net's top search engines to collect search results. But the true beauty of Copernic is that it lets you download all of these search results to scan through when you're offline. Download the program for free at Copernic's Website (www.copernic.com).

■ WebZIP from Spidersoft (www.spidersoft.com) lets you download Web pages while you are surfing elsewhere. You can then browse the pages offline at any time.

▶ See also **Saving Web pages,** p. 235.

How to: Browse offline with WebZIP

1 With WebZIP installed on your PC, go to **Start**, then **All Programs**, select **WebZIP** then **WebZIP** again. Type in a Website address, then go to **Profile** and select how much of the chosen site you want to download. Finally, click the **Download** button.

2 Watch the progress of the download at the bottom of the screen. When the task is complete, click the **Work Offline** button to disconnect from the Internet. Click on the **My Intranet** button and locate and open the downloaded file you want to browse.

Web page features

ANIMATIONS ON THE WEB

From commercial banners to fancy animated links on personal home pages, the Net is full of animations.

■ **Spotted a particularly good animation on somebody's Web page?** You might be able to save it to your hard disk by right-clicking on the picture and selecting **Save image as**. This only works with animations in the gif graphics format though, and you will probably only be able to view the animation by opening your browser.

■ **Why create animations** for your Web page when it's so easy to save other people's animations? Because it's a breach of copyright unless the owners have given you permission to use their work. Instead, visit a library of animated gifs, such as AnimatedGif (www.animatedgif.net), which has a vast selection of images that are freely available for all to use.

■ **Animations from a free library** won't make your site look particularly original, so why not build some of your own? Visit the MediaBuilder Website (www.mediabuilder.com) where there are a range of free online tools such as GIFworks and 3D Text Maker.

■ **More complex animations** require you to install a special animated .gif editor to produce them. But don't buy one just yet – you may already have the tools you need to do the job. Some design software, such as Paint Shop Pro 6, comes with its own animation program.

■ **So you need an animated gif editor?** You'll find a selection available at any of the big Internet shareware libraries. Start with CNet Download.com (http://download.cnet.com/

downloads), and search under Multimedia and Design, then Animation or Image Editing.

■ **Animations, by definition, contain several different pictures,** so they can potentially take a while to download – bad news if you have a slow dial-up Internet connection. So anything that reduces animation size is welcome. For advice on helpful tools, check out WebRef (www.webreference.com/dev/gifanim).

■ **While animations are fun** and look good on a personal home page, be careful if you plan to use them on a business site. Many people think animations are cute, but annoying, so business sites tend to use them sparingly, if at all.

■ **You could liven up an e-mail** by embedding an animation in it, but this only works when the recipient is using a mail program that can display HTML messages. If your recipient has old software, or checks his or her mail on a

HOW TO INSTALL MACROMEDIA SHOCKWAVE

Advanced Web animations use Macromedia Flash or Shockwave. To enjoy them, get a copy of the latest player – it's free and easy to install.

1. Visit the Shockwave download page (http://sdc.shockwave.com/shockwave/download/frameset.fhtml?), read the instructions, then click **Install Now**.

2. After a short delay, you will be asked if you want the installation to go ahead. Just click on **Yes**.

3. Your browser now downloads the Shockwave players and installs them automatically. After a few minutes the animated Shockwave logo will appear on your Desktop, which indicates the installation is complete.

Net-connected mobile phone or handheld computer, the animation won't be visible, but it will still download, taking an annoyingly long time. So send animations only to those you are certain can access them.

■ **If you find animations distracting** or if they are slowing down your surfing, Internet Explorer lets you turn them off. Click on the **Tools ➜ Internet Options**, and choose **Advanced**. Scroll down to the Multimedia section and uncheck **Play animations**.

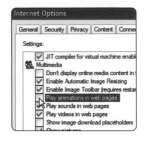

■ **Even if you think you've disabled animated effects** on Web pages, some advertisements will not be affected because there are several ways of producing them. Turning off Java will disable just about everything. In Explorer, go to **Tools ➜ Internet Options ➜ Advanced**. In the Multimedia section, deselect **Play videos in web pages**, **Play sounds in web pages** and **Show pictures**. Under Microsoft VM, deselect **Java logging enabled**.

JUST WHAT ARE APPLETS?

An applet is a small application in Java programming, usually embedded in a Web page to add features or page transition effects.

■ **To speed up browsing, turn off the applets** on your PC by disabling Java (see above). But remember that if the applet is needed for something like a chatroom on one of your favourite sites, it will no longer work, and the page may not display properly.

■ **Want to try creating your own applets?** Internet sites such as Cookie Nest (www.cookienest.com/java_manual/java_basics/5.html) and Java (http://java.sun.com) offer resources and information to help you. However, creating applets is not a job for the faint-hearted. Java can seem complex, even for people who have programming experience. But be patient, do a little at a time, and don't be discouraged.

■ To add advanced capabilities to your own Web page, you can download free Java applets from libraries such as Java Applet Collection (http://japplets.tripod.com) and The Java Boutique (http:// javaboutique.internet. com/applets). Remember, however, that visitors to your Website may have disabled Java – or their browser might not support it – so don't assume that everyone can use all your new features.

■ Diagnosing problems with Java applets can often be tricky, but if you're using Internet Explorer, there is a way to make it easier. Just go to **Tools ➜ Internet Options**. Select the **Advanced** tab, and, in the Microsoft VM section, tick the box next to **Java console enabled**. Click **OK** and restart the program. Now choose the **Java Console** option under the View menu, where you will find a window that provides status information on any applets that you might have running at the time.

HYPERLINKS MAKE BROWSING EASY

Use the hyperlink feature to make documents faster and easier to move around and access.

■ Hyperlinks, or just links, are clickable text or icons on a Web page that take you to another place on that page, or to a different Web page entirely. They contain hypertext mark-up language (HTML) – the coding that is used for producing Web pages.

■ Find a hyperlink easily. Your mouse pointer changes from an arrow to a hand when you pass it over a hyperlink. The link may also change colour or the presence of the pointer may even trigger a short animation.

■ Create hyperlinks in Word. First, highlight the text that you would like to make into a hyperlink, or place the mouse pointer at the insertion point. Now go to your Toolbar and click on **Insert ➜ Hyperlink** so that the Insert Hyperlink dialogue box appears on your screen. Enter the text you want to appear as a link in the **Text to display** window. Now, in the **Address** window, type in the URL or path name for the Web page or file that you want to link to the text. You can click on the arrow on the right-hand side of the Address window to browse through recently used files. When you are satisfied, click **OK** and the hyperlink is established.

■ To remove a hyperlink in Word, simply select the link by dragging the mouse pointer over it to highlight it. Go to the Toolbar and click on **Insert ➜ Hyperlink** and in the Edit Hyperlink dialogue box, click the **Remove Link** button and finally, click **OK**.

■ Keep activating links accidentally? You can often find yourself wanting to edit the text of a hyperlink in Word, but end up activating the link instead. To prevent this from happening, right-click the link and choose **Edit Hyperlink** from the pop-up menu. The Edit Hyperlink dialogue box now appears. Edit your hyperlink text in the **Text to display** section.

■ Create a hyperlink quickly in FrontPage Editor. Highlight, then right-click the section heading, drag it to the appropriate point on the page, and choose **Link Here** from the shortcut menu. FrontPage Editor will create a text link that duplicates the subheading's text.

■ Divide your Web pages into smaller segments. Use subheadings to create sections within a page. Then, at the top of the page, you can place hyperlinks to each subheading. By clicking one of the hyperlinks, you can go straight to the relevant section in the Web page without having to scroll all the way down the document.

■ Remember to check edited hyperlinks. If you have an edited hyperlink in a document, check that it reads correctly, then click on it to make sure that it actually does take you to the intended Website.

Click on the hyperlink to take you to the section you want to s

- Overview to the Recipe Guide
- How do I get started?
- Seasonal appetizers
- Excellent entrees
- Delicious desserts
- Glossary
- A matter of taste: herbs and CTRL + click to follow link
- Recommended site of the day

Throughout the Recipe Guide we have tried to include as man to make viewing each of the stages as easy to follow as possib

Here's what you will find on the followi

▶ See also **Working with Microsoft Word**, p. 124; **Understanding HTML**, p. 220; and **Creating a Website**, p. 228.

Children and the Web

While the Web provides vast learning opportunities for children, it can also be a worry for parents. How much time online is too much? Are your children viewing harmful information? Who are they talking to in chat rooms? However, there are ways to keep children's surfing safe.

SAFE SURFING

Consider filtering tools. If you are concerned your child may be viewing harmful or inappropriate material online there are lots of filtering tools available, but they don't all work in the same way. Some decide what is filtered, some let parents pick among preset categories, while others provide a starter list that parents can add to or remove sites from. Also, some tools allow a parent to override the filter if they consider a site appropriate for their child. For reviews of the filtering tools available – many of which have downloadable free demos – go to ZDNet (www.zdnet.com) or CNET (www.cnet .com) and search for 'children filters'.

Avoid blocking good information. Use a filter, such as CYBERsitter (www.cybersitter.com), to analyse language around keywords. For

example, if you have set a filtering tool to limit access to sites containing potentially inappropriate words such as sex or breast, you may be better off using a filter. That way, you'll avoid blocking entries such as breast cancer or chicken breast recipes.

Check out your browser. Some Web browsers have their own Internet blocking features built in. With Internet Explorer, for example, click on **Tools ➜ Internet Options**. When the Internet Options dialogue box appears, click on the **Content** tab, and in the Content Advisor section, click on the **Enable** button. You can now set four types of ratings – Language, Nudity, Sex and Violence. Click along the bar in the middle of the dialogue box to adjust the ratings for each one and click **OK**. When you have finished making settings you will be prompted to enter a password to control future access.

No filtering or blocking system is foolproof. The only way you can be positive that your child is surfing safely is to become – and stay – involved in your child's online exploration. Forbidden fruit is always attractive. Set clear rules for using the Internet and make sure your children know what the rules are. That way they will stay safe.

GET INVOLVED

Surf as a family. Before you start shopping for the children, explore fashion trends together with them, thus avoiding arguments and cries of 'Oh, Mum, that looks awful!'. Check out DailyFashion.com's Real Fashion for Real Girls (www.dailyfashion.com), GapKids.com (www.gapkids.com) and Teenmag.com's Stylin' section (www.teenmag.com).

Teach your child good financial management and money sense with the help of the Internet. Try the Kids' Money Q&A (www .kidsmoney.org/advice .htm).

SAFE SURFING GUIDELINES FOR CHILDREN

Handy hints to ensure happy times online for all members of the family.

1. Take the trip together. Make time to see what your children are doing online.

2. Teach your children never to give personal details to people they meet online, especially in public places such as chatrooms and bulletin boards.

3. Instruct your child never to plan a face-to-face meeting alone with an online acquaintance, regardless of how old they say they are.

4. Tell your child not to respond to offensive e-mail, chat or other communications. Make sure they tell you if they encounter such communication so that you can report it to the site operator.

5. Establish clear rules for Internet use for children and make sure they follow them.

6. When you are home, limit your children's non-educational surfing time by placing your computer in the family room or another open area.

Is your child an Internet zombie?

Concerned they may be spending too much time online? Perhaps you don't want them to use the Net when you're asleep or away from home? Special software, such as Net Nanny (www.netnanny.com), allows you to set limits on how much time your child spends online. Alternatively, you could set up profiles for family members so that children cannot have independent access without an adult being present (see p. 77).

INTERNET FUN FOR CHILDREN

Plan a kid's party online. There are plenty of ideas at sites such as The Complete Children's Party Survival Guide (www.kidspartysurvivalguide .com). And there are many sites that advertise the services of professional party planners and children's entertainers. You can also make a Website to invite everyone to your birthday party. Find out how to do that at The Plunge.com (www.theplunge.com).

Many browsers are created just for children's use. While they work in the same way as adult browsers, such as Internet Explorer or Netscape Navigator, they are easier to use and also filter out inappropriate words or images. Children can search from over 10,000 safe sites using ChiBrow (www.childrenbrowser.com), a free browser that lets parents decide what is appropriate first. TermiNet (www.danu.ie) is a browser that acts as a firewall, while also restricting and blocking access to sites and protocols. Or set KidDesk at Edmark (www.riverdeep.net/edmark) to start automatically when your computer starts so that your children only have access to material that you want them to see. It comes with a child-friendly browser based on Internet Explorer.

Child-oriented search engines

work just like ordinary search engines, but special features protect children from inappropriate material while helping them to locate information easily. Some of these search engines will only look within a certain group of pre-approved sites, and others search the whole Web but withhold inappropriate results. Try AOL NetFind Kids Only (www.aol.com/netfind/kids/channel) for links to child-safe sites only. Or visit Ask Jeeves for Kids (www.ajkids.com). This site allows children to ask a question and takes them to a child-safe Website for the answer.

Children love to chat with others of their own age

in chatrooms. But how can you be sure that your child is chatting about a topic that you approve of – and with another child as opposed to an adult masquerading as a child? You can rest assured that your children are chatting safely when they use a monitored chatroom, where adults keep tabs on what's being said. Headbone Zone (www.headbone.com/friends/chat) has monitored chatrooms for children and teenagers and Kid Chatters (www.kidchatters.com) has the same for children aged between nine and twelve.

▸ See also **Passwords protect files**, p. 248; and **Chatrooms**, p. 326.

HIP AND HAPPENING SITES FOR KIDS

Encourage the next generation of computer users to get online and learn more about the world around them and the potential of the Net.

CBBC (www.bbc.co.uk/cbbc)
Lots of fun and games for children, as well as information on their favourite TV shows.

GREAT SITES!
(www.ala.org/parentspage/greatsites)
This search engine provides links to more than 700 sites for fun and learning.

CARTOON NETWORK
(www.cartoonnetwork.com)
Home to favourites such as Fred Flintstone, Scooby-Doo and Space Ghost.

KIDS' CASTLE (www.kidscastle.si.edu)
The Smithsonian Institution's interactive kids site looks at many of the museum's treasures.

HEADBONE ZONE
(www.headbone.com/friends/chat)
The site offers seven chat rooms where children can interact with their peers.

THE YUCKIEST SITE ON THE INTERNET
(yucky.kids.discovery.com)
This site indulges children's fascination with all things yucky, while educating them at the same time. It's a science site full of sticky, gooey, creepy-crawly and yucky stuff.

ZOOM DINOSAURS (www.enchant-edlearning.com/subjects/dinosaurs)
An interactive online hypertext book about dinosaurs for students of all ages and levels of comprehension – great for youngsters.

Special issues

Explore the Internet without leaving behind any tracks.

■ **Your browser is probably giving personal information** to marketers, who will bombard you with product offers and ads if they are given half a chance. Once the marketers have your e-mail address, there's nothing to stop them from selling it to still more marketers. To prevent yourself from being bombarded with ads and solicitations to 'BUY NOW!! LAST CHANCE!!', you need to stay anonymous.

■ **You can maintain a low profile** while browsing the Web by using a proxy server, which forms a kind of wall between your PC and the sites you visit. Instead of capturing your information, Web servers see only the proxy's identity. If you surf the Web from your office then you're probably already protected by a proxy server or a firewall. If you connect at home, you can use one of the free public proxy servers, such as Anonymizer (www.anonymizer.com), that protect your identity by keeping your e-mail address and your surfing a secret.

■ **Take a do-it-yourself approach to becoming anonymous.** One of the most effective ways is to temporarily remove your personal information from your browser. After you have removed details such as your name and e-mail address from your browser, the only information a Website can search out is your ISP's address and geographical location.

■ **While it's tempting to use the same password** for all of the online services you join, especially if you have a poor memory, resist this urge. You don't necessarily have to use a different password for each service, but you should definitely make sure that your e-mail passwords are unique. If you were to use the same password, getting access to your private

e-mail messages is relatively easy for an unscrupulous Website owner.

■ **Forewarned is to be forearmed.** You can configure your browser to notify you if any sites that you visit could put your personal security at risk. With Internet Explorer running, click on **Tools ➜ Internet Options**, and select the **Advanced** tab. Scroll to the Security section and check the boxes beside **Check for publisher's certificate revocation**, **Warn about invalid site certificates** and **Warn if changing between secure and not secure mode**. Click **OK**, and in future you'll be warned of potentially risky sites where security might be compromised.

■ **If you share a computer,** or use a PC at work, some colleagues will probably have access to your e-mail. You can protect your e-mail privacy by collecting and sending your e-mail from a Web-based service such as Mail2Web

(www.mail2web.com) or MSN Hotmail (www.hotmail.com). Hushmail (www.hushmail.com) also offers secure storage and encrypted messaging.

■ **Digital signing is a method of protecting** the privacy of your e-mail correspondence by letting e-mail recipients confirm the identity of the sender through a third party certificate of authenticity. Download the software from VeriSign (www.verisign.com).

■ **Protect your private correspondence and surfing** from online snoopers with shareware privacy software. Pretty Good Privacy Inc.'s PGP version 8.0 (www.pgpi.org) encrypts personal items like e-mail attachments and files, allowing only those recipients with the proper key to open them. Window Washer 4.7 available from ZDNet (www.zdnet.com/downloads/internet.html) removes details from your cache, cookies, history and recent document list, allowing you to surf without the fear that anyone can find out what sites you have visited.

Protect your files by giving them a password that's known only to you.

■ **A password is a secret series of characters** that enables an authorised user to access a Website, private files, computers and programs. On multi-user systems each user must enter their own password before the computer will respond to commands. A password ensures that unauthorised users can't access your computer or private files.

■ **The password that you choose** should be a word that no one else could possibly guess, or a combination of letters and numbers. In practice, most people select something that's easy to remember, such as their name or initials. This is one reason why breaking into most computer systems is simple. For secrecy, select a word that means something to you personally, a word you haven't shared with co-workers.

■ **One common cause of security breaches** is putting passwords down on paper, especially when they're stuck to computer screens. It's always best to choose a password that you won't need to write down. Use a character substitution scheme to create one that's easy to remember, but hard to crack. For example, take your date of birth and substitute the equivalent letter in the alphabet for the numbers. For example 26/11/1959 could become BFAAAIEI.

■ **You can also devise a code to replace the letters of your name** or a phrase with letters that are a certain number of keys away on the keyboard. So if your name is Freddie, you could count two keys to the right of each letter to make the code hyTggPT (making things more difficult by choosing upper case for vowels and lower case for consonants). If you do write your password down, keep it in a safe place known only to you.

■ **For extra protection,** have a different password for every application. Within each password, combine upper and lower case and a digit or two. Passwords should be at least six characters long, but the most secure are 13 or more. You could create words that stand for the date of a big event – for example, 90wa66 could be a 6 June 1990 wedding anniversary.

■ **The most unique devices** won't make it any easier to memorise lists of lengthy character passwords, but you can always get a little extra help. Software is available to generate passwords for you and then encrypt them so that no one else will ever work them out. SafeHouse – from PC Dynamics Incorporated (www.pcdynamics.com/SafeHouse/Default.asp) is one such program. Or try shareware sites such as CNET Shareware.com (http://shareware.cnet.com).

■ **The most common way for others to gain access** to password-protected documents and accounts is when you don't log out once you've finished with your computer. If you're using a site from a public terminal, be sure to close the browser when you end the session.

COPYRIGHT AND THE WEB

Copyright laws apply to the Internet just as they do to other media. If you have your own Website, they can protect your content.

■ **Why does copyright exist?** To protect the rights of the creator. This means that the text, images, animations, video and overall design of a Website belong to the copyright owner. You can still download copyrighted text, images or music for personal use but you can't republish someone else's material on your Website or elsewhere without their permission, and you may also have to pay for the use of their work.

■ **Don't copy – link.** If there is an article or picture you particularly wish to draw to the attention of your audience, instead of copying it onto your site, provide a link to the original site to avoid legal problems. A Website address, like a telephone number, is not subject to copyright.

■ **If in doubt, ask** the originator of the material for permission to use it. Be clear about the exact use and any revenue that might be generated. Consider the options and have an alternative plan ready if the answer is no.

■ **While a copyright notice is not strictly necessary,** there's no harm in reminding visitors that this content is your creation and they should respect it! One way of doing this is to include a short statement at the foot of your home page, such as © Copyright 2002 John Smith.

■ **Need more details?** Visit the UK government's Intellectual Property Website (www.intellectual-property.gov.uk). The site offers a huge range of information on copyright, designs, patents and trade marks, and provides the latest news on copyright issues. There is also information on organisations representing intellectual property owners and links to other relevant sites. Also try the Patent Office Website (www.patent.gov.uk/copy) for more information.

How to: Password-protect your PC

1 First protect your user account with a password. Go to **Start ➜ Control Panel ➜ User Accounts,** choose your account and click **Create a password.** Enter your chosen word twice, and a hint to jog your memory, then click on **Create Password.**

2 Now right-click on the Desktop and select the **Screensaver** tab. Make sure **On resume, display Welcome screen** is selected. Now when you access your PC after the screensaver has been working, you will need to enter your password.

These tiny files are sent to your PC by Websites to personalise your surfing experience, but some people view them as snooping.

■ **On the record.** Ever wondered how a Website knows who you are before you log in? When you first visited and registered your name, the Website dropped a cookie onto your hard drive to record your details. So, the next time you visit, the site recognises your PC.

■ **Personalising pages.** Shopping sites such as Amazon (www.amazon.co.uk) use cookies to track your browsing on their sites and work out your preferences. Next time you visit, they can recommend products you might like to buy.

■ **A cookie is only a simple text file.** It isn't a program, so it can't alter or do any harm to your PC. Only the Website that sent the cookie

can retrieve it, so no other sites have direct access to the information it contains. However, the company owning the Website can pass on the information to other companies if it wants to, and it is this that concerns opponents of cookies.

■ **Some cookies are called persistent cookies.** While most cookies are deleted as soon as you finish your surfing session, others remain on your computer until their expiration date is reached. Rather like your browser's History file, persistent cookies leave a record of the sites you have previously visited.

■ **Don't like the idea of cookies?** Your browser can block or delete them. Or you can opt to be prompted whenever a site tries to put one on your hard drive – so you can choose whether to accept it or not. However, many shopping sites send cookies every few seconds. If your browser prompts you each time, surfing will be slow!

▶ See also **Keeping your interests private**, p. 248; and **Security on the Net**, p. 254.

Discover how to display foreign language characters, use translation services online and decipher foreign sites with a built-in browser.

■ **The main challenge in reading most foreign-language Websites** is getting the browser to display them accurately in the first place. You might need to install fonts containing the foreign characters you require (see *The ins and outs of type fonts,* p. 125). Internet Explorer can search for fonts at the Microsoft site (www.microsoft.com). Netscape also has online help (http://home.netscape.com/menu/intl).

■ **It's not enough to install fonts** to support a particular language – you have to tell the browser about it too. To do this in Internet Explorer, choose **Tools ➜ Internet Options** and click on the **Fonts** button on the **General** tab.

How to: Delete and block cookies

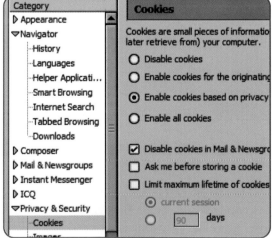

1 To delete a cookie in Internet Explorer, go to **Tools ➜ Internet Options ➜ Settings ➜ View Files**. Select the cookie you want to delete, right-click the mouse and select **Delete**. To delete all cookies, go to **Internet Options** as above and click **Delete Cookies**.

2 To block cookies in Internet Explorer, go to the **Tools** menu then **Internet Options** and select the **Privacy** tab. Move the slider bar up or down for different levels of privacy. The highest level blocks all cookies and the lowest saves all cookies. Click **Apply,** then **OK**.

3 If you use Netscape Navigator, to disable cookies, go to **Edit**, then **Preferences** and double-click on **Privacy & Security**. Select **Cookies**. Select your options from the menu. Click **View** to set your own privacy settings. Click **OK** once you have finished.

Select the language script you wish to configure and the fonts you would like to use with it.

Enabling multi-language support in a browser isn't too complicated,
but there are simpler ways of viewing foreign language Web pages. Shodouka (web.lfw.org/shodouka), for example, is a Website that accepts a Web address of any Japanese-language page and displays it as an image. Although this can slow things down, it will work in any browser.

For complex languages, including
Chinese and Korean, which contain more unusual characters, try using a completely new tool. NJStar (www.njstar.com) offers a free browser, called Asian Explorer, specially designed to work with Asian languages. TwinBridge (www.twinbridge.com) also has some useful language add-ons.

Are Websites you need in a foreign language? This can be a problem
when you don't speak the language. Before you give up, try a free online translation service, such as Free Translation (www.freetranslation.com) or Dictionary.com (dictionary.reference.com/translate/text.html. As these are automated services, don't expect perfection, but the translation should be close enough for you to work out its meaning.

Even if you have a good understanding of a foreign language,
you may still discover one or two words on the page that stump you. In situations like this, you need a good online dictionary. Sites such as Your Dictionary (www.yourdictionary.com) and Foreignword (www.foreignword.com) contain comprehensive collections of hundreds of glossary listings in every conceivable language.

Some browsers come with built-in translation facilities. Some of the best
examples of these are NeoPlanet (www.neoplanet.com), Mozilla (www.mozilla.org) and later versions of Netscape – Netscape 6 and higher (http://home.netscape.com/download). They are all much smaller downloads than Internet Explorer, so may be worth a try.

While free translation sites on the Internet might give you a general idea of what
a particular document means, they are often full of errors. If you are a serious business user, try a professional service to get the required accuracy. The Institute of Linguists (www.iol.org.uk) is an accredited awarding body and professional organisation representing translators and

interpreters. Click on their **Find-a-Linguist** link to locate a translator with the correct expertise you require. You can also find a language professional at the Languages National Training Organisation (www.languagesnto.org.uk).

If you want to read foreign language material, a more satisfying
solution might be to learn the language. Eloquence (www.elok.com) offers free courses in Spanish and French for complete beginners, while CyberItalian (www.cyberitalian.com) is a Website that takes an unusually interactive approach to learning. Travlang (http://travlang.com/languages) has lots of links to other helpful sites.

Once equipped with a knowledge of your chosen language, or a translation
tool, you can understand many more pages on the Internet. The challenge will be finding them, since foreign language sites are not highlighted at Yahoo! or Google. For a list of foreign search engines, try www.bizforms.com/search.htm.

How to: Get free online translations

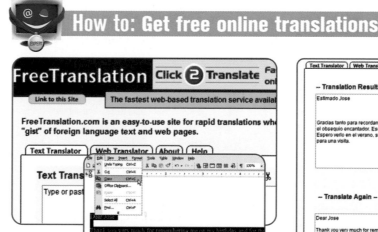

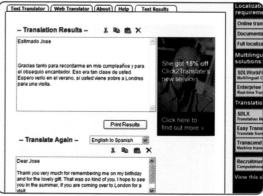

1 Highlight the text you want to translate (a few sentences at a time). Choose **Edit**, then **Copy** to copy it to the clipboard. Then, in your Web browser, go to www.freetranslation.com. Click in the **Text Translator** box, select **Edit**, then **Paste** to paste your text for translation.

2 Now choose the kind of translation you want (English to Spanish, in this case), and click on the **Translate Now!** button. The translation you requested will appear after a few seconds, ready to be copied and pasted back into your document.

PLUG-INS EXTEND YOUR CAPABILITIES

Enhance your browser to enjoy new capabilities and improve your Web experience by adding plug-ins.

■ **A plug-in is an auxiliary program** that works alongside your Internet browser. Download the free program, install it, and your browser calls on it automatically whenever it needs to. Without plug-ins, the Web would have no sound, moving images or 3-D virtual reality.

■ **The most popular plug-ins** are RealOne Player from www.real.com, which plays sound within seconds of an audio file being downloaded; QuickTime (www.apple.com/quicktime/download), which plays video in the browser window; and Macromedia's

Shockwave (sdc.shockwave.com/shockwave/download/frameset.fhtml), for playing animations.

■ **Download plug-ins before you start surfing** to save time. Have a look at the Netscape plug-in page (home.netscape.com/plugins) for a complete list of what's available.

■ **Download a plug-in as you would any other file** from the Internet. If you are using Internet Explorer, make sure you click the button marked **Save It** when the dialogue box appears. After the download is complete, exit the browser, locate the file you just downloaded, and double-click on it to install it on your hard drive.

■ **Before downloading a plug-in,** check the installation notes to make sure that your browser can use it. Many plug-ins offer several installation files for download. Read the descriptions to ensure you choose the right one.

■ **Installing too many plug-ins** may slow down your system. To remove an unwanted

plug-in, look for it in the Plug-ins subfolder in your browser's folder. Delete or move the file, and your browser will not load the plug-in.

■ **If you use Internet Explorer,** you will come across ActiveX controls – small pieces of software that run within Internet Explorer and enhance Web pages. Unlike plug-ins, they are automatically downloaded for you.

▶ See also **How to download files,** p. 240.

LIVE PICTURES OVER THE WEB

Use a webcam to create your own version of Big Brother, or just keep an eye on the baby sitter.

■ **Set up a webcam to send live pictures over the Internet.** You will need a webcam connected to your PC, a video card and a personal Website (the Website that comes with most standard ISP accounts is fine). You will

How to: Download and install a plug-in

1 Use these steps to install any plug-in (Apple QuickTime is used here). From the Apple Website (www.apple.com/quicktime/download), enter your e-mail address and name and then click the **Download QuickTime** button.

2 The Security Warning dialogue box will appear. Click on **Yes** and then the QuickTime set up will launch and you will be taken through a number of dialogue boxes. Follow the instructions and the program will begin to download.

3 A shortcut to QuickTime will appear on your Desktop, click on it and go to the File menu to load the player. When downloading appropriate files from the Internet, your computer will automatically default to your QuickTime player.

also need a software program, such as SpyCam (www.getspycam.cjb.net), to take the pictures automatically and send them by FTP (File Transfer Protocol) to your Website. You can download a range of other webcam shareware from CNET (download.cnet.com).

■ Once you have downloaded the software,

it will take you through the procedure for configuring your Website, and ask you how often you want pictures taken. Then simply leave the software running. The live updating only works while your computer is online. Programs like SpyCam will dial out, get an Internet connection, upload the image and then hang up. If you want to run a live, continuous webcam broadcast, get a fast Internet connection.

■ There are many imaginative uses for webcams.

You could broadcast your wedding, a christening or graduation to friends and relatives who couldn't attend.

■ Your webcam's frame rate

(how many new images are generated every second) is influenced by many factors, including the hardware connection, your computer's processor speed, the webcam itself, the software's video compression and decompression settings and your Internet connection. If your images are slow or freezing up, then one or more of these is probably too slow, and it's time to upgrade.

■ A webcam is like any other camcorder or camera.

To get the best picture, you need to position the camera (and yourself) correctly. Try pointing the camera so that there is a wall or screen behind you. Place a light nearby to illuminate your face and shoulders.

▶ See also **Creating a Website,** p. 228; and **The secrets of FTP,** p. 241.

UPGRADING YOUR SOFTWARE

Should you switch to the very latest version of the software you use? If you decide to do so, then the Net is the place to go for upgrades.

■ Software is constantly being improved and upgraded,

but that doesn't mean you should rush out to buy newer versions of all your programs. Look at the features being offered. Is it worth the money, considering what you will be using it for? If you do decide to upgrade, then visit the software maker's Website, where downloads of the latest versions of popular programs are often available for free or at minimum cost to registered users.

■ Newer versions of software are invariably bigger and require more memory.

Check to see if you have enough disk space to install a new version, and enough RAM to run it. You'll find this information on the product's box, or at the manufacturer's Website.

■ Provided your system can handle it, upgrading your Web browser

is always worth it because it's free! Later versions of Internet Explorer, for example, include RealOne Player plug-ins for displaying films and Flash animation. Complex graphics are common on Websites, and you won't be able to view some sites unless you have version 5 or above of Internet Explorer.

■ To find and install Windows product enhancements,

go to **Start ➜ All Programs,** then select **Windows Update** to connect to the Microsoft Website, where you can find and install product enhancements and files applicable to your own computer, including device drivers and Windows system files. The site scans your computer and displays a list of applicable components with their download times. It also informs you of components that you may have already updated. You can chose to download one item or several. After an item is downloaded, Windows installs it for you.

■ Always check the free CD-ROMs on some PC magazines.

Many contain recent versions of software like Internet Explorer, which can help to speed up download times.

▶ See also **How to download files,** p. 240; and **The shareware alternative,** p. 304.

WEBCAM SITES

Find out how to set up a webcam, or watch the action on other webcams.

EARTHCAM (www.earthcam.com)
EarthCam is a collection of all kinds of spycams from many different places.

WEBCAM CENTRAL (www.camcentral.com)
This site cross-indexes a listing of thousands of live webcams on the Internet.

WEBCAMSEARCH.COM (www.webcamsearch.com)
Want to check out Beirut's main street or the weather on Mount Everest? This site has links to webcams around the world.

Security on the net

Every day there seem to be new reports of million dollar Internet frauds or of hackers breaching the networks of Microsoft or the CIA. So it's no wonder that home shoppers are concerned about the safety of making online purchases. But you can safeguard yourself on the Net.

HOW TO TELL IF A SITE IS SAFE

Most retailers that offer value for money and treat their customers fairly at their bricks-and-mortar stores do the same online. Most companies realise that potential customers are wary of fraud, having seen the stories on TV. They therefore make an effort to reassure nervous online shoppers by creating secure locations for their customers to carry out transactions in confidence.

If you're dealing with a company for the first time, look for a real address and phone number on their site, plus at least one contact name. If you don't see these, think twice about shopping there.

Safeguard yourself against others fraudulently using your credit card. Before you type in your credit card details at an online store, make sure you're at an encrypted

site to prevent unauthorised access. In Internet Explorer, a padlock symbol appears on the status bar; in Netscape, the normally open padlock in the bottom left-hand corner turns into a closed one. Most secure sites use a URL that begins with https://, the 's' suffix standing for 'secure'.

Each site you visit using Internet Explorer can be assigned to one of four zones: Internet zone, Local intranet, Trusted sites or Restricted sites. All Websites are placed by default in the Internet zone, with a medium security level. Local intranet covers addresses on an internal server, like an office network. Trusted sites are on another server, and are Websites whose content you trust. Restricted sites are those you believe to pose a risk in their content. You can adjust the security settings for all sites under the Security tab in Internet Options (see 'How to', p. 255).

BIG BROTHER IS WATCHING

When you shop online, many companies you deal with collect your personal information and also data about the pages you have visited and purchases you have made.

Many sites have security statements giving details of their policies. You can often find a link to the legal and privacy policies on the company's home page.

Personal information is collected so that the site has a record of your name and address for shipping products. It's also used to customise the site so that, for example, it greets you by name when you log on next time. All of this information is kept strictly between you and the online store. It is not revealed to third parties.

The other information is about your purchasing preferences and favourite pages on the site. This information may be given

to third parties, such as advertisers or marketing agencies, who want to know what kind of people visit the site. The information given out won't personally identify you and will generally be used as part of the site's usage statistics.

Who are hackers? A hacker is anyone who gains access to the data within a computer system without authorisation. Their reasons vary. Sometimes it's to play a prank, or their motivation may be political or even sometimes criminal.

COOKIES

Sometimes when you go back to a site, you'll find it has remembered your name or what you bought the last time. The site can do this because of a cookie. When you give your details online, or when you make a purchase, the site you are visiting packages this information into a tiny text message called a cookie. The site then sends you the cookie and it is stored on your hard drive to be retrieved next time you visit.

You can locate and delete unwanted cookies with Internet Explorer by finding the Temporary Internet Files folder within the

Windows folder. Right-click on the cookie with the appropriate Web address and click on **Delete**.

You can choose to accept or block cookies from individual Websites. In Internet Explorer, go to **Tools ➜ Internet Options** and select the **Privacy** tab, then click the **Edit** button. In the **Address of Web site** box, type in the full URL of the site including the http://, then click **Block** or **Allow**. Finally, click **OK**.

Are cookies dangerous? No. Cookies are simply text files. They are not programs, so it is impossible for them to contain viruses, to access your hard drive or to read personal information.

Cookies contain personal information that you've provided. The open nature of the Net means that people could access this information with time and effort. Although Cookies aren't dangerous, they are an aid to gathering information about you. To learn more, visit Cookie Central (www.cookiecentral.com).

E-mails are not secure. In theory, anyone who really wants to could intercept your e-mails. There are millions of e-mails flashing around the world daily, so the risk of being intercepted is slim. But if you want to safeguard sensitive information, download the free e-mail encryption software Pretty Good Privacy (www.pgpi.org).

The International PGP Home Page

Download the latest version
Here you may download the latest freeware PGP version for your platform, whether you

PGP is a public key cryptography program. Each PGP user has a private key – a unique number known only to themselves that is never given out to e-mail recipients – and a public key that you give out freely. Each time you send an e-mail, PGP uses your private key to create an encrypted message. With PGP, the recipient uses your public key to decrypt your message and to confirm your identity and verify that the message has not been tampered with.

If your debit or credit card is used fraudulently and you can prove this to the bank or credit card lender, you should not be liable. But remember to notify the card issuer as soon as you notice an unauthorised transaction on your card statement.

Many online retailers are so confident of their security that they offer to pay a nominal sum for you in the case of fraud. So online shopping can actually be more secure than High Street shopping.

See also **Dealing with cookies**, p. 250; **Buying on the Net**, p. 306; and **Worried about credit card fraud?**, p. 308.

How to: Set security levels in Internet Explorer

1 To specify the security settings for each zone, go to **Tools ➜ Internet Options**. Select the **Security** tab, then click on the Web content zone you want to change: Internet, Local intranet, Trusted sites or Restricted sites. Click on the **Custom** level button.

2 Choose a security level from the **Reset to** drop-down menu. All the settings in the main section of the dialogue box can be customised within your chosen security level. Return a level to its default settings by clicking on the **Reset** button. Click **OK** to finish.

Using the Internet

Web services

Don't spend hours a day driving – telecommute instead! Use your PC to stay connected to the office.

■ **Depending on your job, you may need specialised technology for telecommuting.** But the basic equipment you will need is a computer, printer, phone and data lines, Zip drive and fax. Some telecommuters may also need access to their corporate LAN (Local Area Network). Try to get your company's Information Technology staff to visit your home so that you're connected up correctly from the start, and consider getting a DSL (Digital Subscriber Line) to stay connected permanently.

■ **If you work from home** as your principal place of business you may be able to claim a portion of your mortgage or rent payments as a tax deduction. Having a separate office makes the amount easier to calculate and justify to the Inland Revenue. You may also be eligible for other deductions, such as the cost

of heating and lighting. However, the rules can be complicated, so check with your accountant right from the start.

■ **Invest in some professional office furniture** to create a working environment and help you to become more productive. A properly comfortable and supportive chair is vital, as is a work surface at the correct height (see p.14).

■ **Telecommuting is a great way to add more flexibility to your life** and increase family time, but it can also create feelings of isolation. Don't forget to build socialising into your schedule. Stay in touch with co-workers and other friends. Some telecommuters form informal networks by taking coffee breaks in local cafés.

■ **Link up with other telecommuters!** The Telework Association (www.tca.org.uk) offers extensive information on telecommuting, including advice on setting yourself up and finding work. The organisation also publishes a bi-monthly magazine and has produced the Teleworking Handbook. The Cambridgeshire Travel for Work Partnership has a Web page (www.tfw.org.uk/teleworking) dedicated to teleworking, with a discussion forum and a downloadable Toolkit Guide.

■ **Let your family know not to bother you** with matters not related to work during working hours. Many people telecommute for reasons of childcare. However, keep in mind that it is very difficult to work full-time and tend to children too. Set definite family and work hours – and keep them separate.

■ **Establish clear working hours.** This will keep you on track and prevent people from calling you at odd hours. It is a good idea to get a separate phone line for work and set it to take messages after hours.

▶ See also **Fast Net access using DSL,** p. 216.

Now you can make phone calls over the Net for a fraction of the cost of using a land line.

■ **Have you got free, or fixed-price Internet access?** Internet telephony software essentially provides free computer-to-telephone calls anywhere in the world. Instead of dialling the overseas number, you just dial up your local ISP and make the call over the Net.

SOFTWARE FOR INTERNET TELEPHONING
Check out these sites for the latest telephony software.

SPEAK FREELY (www.speakfreely.org)
A free software program that allows you to use your computer as a telephone.

MICROSOFT NETMEETING (www.microsoft .com/windows/netmeeting)
Check out this service, which is free to thousands of users.

NET2PHONE (www.net2phone.com)
Place a call anywhere through the Internet.

PHONE FREE.COM (www.phonefree.com)
Free PC-to-PC calls worldwide with video and other enhanced features.

VOCALTEC (www.vocaltec.com)
One of the first programs, with the most features and a large user base.

PALTALK.COM (www.paltalk.com)
Combines instant messaging and Internet telephony, and enables live video calls and voice chat rooms.

■ **Windows users may already have the software** to make computer-to-telephone calls. To see if you have Microsoft's NetMeeting installed go to **Start → All Programs → Accessories → Communications**. If you have it, NetMeeting will appear in the drop-down menu.

■ **Phoning via the Internet does not always offer the same quality** as direct telephone connections. When you use this service, your voice is digitally encoded, then broken up into packages, and sent out across the Net. You may end up talking over each other, when you and the person you're talking to aren't properly synchronised.

■ **To make calls over the Net,** you'll need some additional basic equipment and software. CU-seeMe (www.cuseemeworld.com) and iVisit (www.ivisit.com) are good software sites for people wanting to establish communication between Macs and PCs. You will also need a 100 MHz or faster processor, a sound card (preferably a full-duplex, SoundBlaster-compatible model) plus a microphone and speakers. A

headset will give cleaner audio input and prevent feedback or echo. You also need a modem or network connection to the Net.

■ **Want to make video calls?** You'll need a webcam or video capture card and camera, like the Logitech QuickCam (www.logitech.com).

■ **For the fastest connection and fewer delays,** turn off all the other programs on your computer before making a Net phone call. Most computers come with a built-in recorder to allow you to record your Internet

phone conversation. To find your recorder, go to **Start → All Programs → Accessories → Entertainment → Sound Recorder**.

■ **ICQ (I seek you) is a pals list** to help you to find friends online and connect with them via instant messaging, e-mail and text. Go to the site (www.icq.com) to download their software for various kinds of devices.

■ **Use your phone to send e-mail** if you want to send a message but don't have access to your computer. There are many models that do this, as well as Pocket PCs and even a Palm Smartphone (www.kyocera-wireless.com) that can get you connected.

STORING FILES ON THE INTERNET

Free up space on your hard drive by storing files on the Internet.

■ **Most Internet service providers supply you with some Web storage space** of your own, but you don't have to use it just to house Web pages. Check with your ISP for site specifics. If the information you want to store is sensitive, use a utility such as WinZip (www.winzip.com) to compress the file and give it a password. Be sure to keep track of how much space you are using; if you use more space than your ISP has allocated you may incur charges.

■ **If your ISP doesn't supply Web space,** or if you need more, other companies can provide you with up to 100 MB of storage space of your own. Most do not charge for the first 25 MB, which is enough to store the equivalent of 17 high-density floppy disks, 200 word processing documents or spread-sheets, 10 PowerPoint presentations or thousands of images or MP3 files. For online storage options try Xdrive (www.xdrive.com).

■ **Access your files from anywhere in the world** with Internet storage space. Do you have an important business meeting in France but you want to travel light? If you store your files on the Internet, you can retrieve them from any computer with an Internet connection, or from a WAP (wireless access protocol) phone. An entire presentation can be sent to a business contact without you having to be there yourself – just store it online and send your contact the Web address and password.

■ **Want to send some very large files?** Don't e-mail them – store them on the Internet instead. Large e-mails can take a long time to download, and attachments do not always travel well. Create a collaborative workspace with Web-based storage. Some services will allow you to create a folder and type in the e-mail address of people you want to share it with. It will then send an e-mail on your behalf granting people access to the folder.

■ **Use Internet storage to create a photo album.** Upload your digital photos to your Web storage space and send friends and family the Web address. They can then visit the site for themselves, in their own time, eliminating the need to e-mail them the photos.

■ **If you're a teacher,** create online storage space for your class. Students who cannot attend class can pick up their assignments or hand them in online. Students can also access documents at school or home without the need to carry around easily lost or damaged disks.

READ YOUR NEWSPAPER ONLINE

Save a tree by reading your favourite paper on the Internet.

■ **Newspapers rarely put entire editions online.** But online editions let you find related stories and past articles, as well as in-depth background on current events.

■ **Are you looking for a particular story?** Try a news directory such as News Directory.com (www.newsdirectory.com) or Newslink (newslink.org). Or, you can look in a multiple news archive (for a fee) such as eLibrary (ask.elibrary.com). For a particular paper, try Newspapers.com (www.newspapers.com). PaperBoy (www.thepaperboy.com) offers links to thousands of newspapers worldwide.

HAVE THE NEWS SENT TO YOU

Have regularly updated news reports sent to your Desktop.

■ **Searching through the daunting array of online newspapers** for stories on particular topics can be a time-consuming exercise. Instead, get news headlines and reports

NEWS ONLINE
Go online to get an international perspective on the news.

CNN (www.cnn.com)
BBC (news.bbc.co.uk)
ANANOVA (www.ananova.com)
ASSOCIATED PRESS (http://wire.ap.org)
EL PAIS (www.elpais.es)
THE JERUSALEM POST (www.jpost.com)
LE MONDE (www.lemonde.fr)
NEW YORK TIMES (www.nytimes.com)
ABC NEWS (abcnews.go.com)

on subjects of interest to you sent directly to your e-mail inbox every day. News services like CNN (www.cnn.com) and Guardian Unlimited (www.guardian.co.uk) will send news reports to

you by e-mail. On the Guardian Website you can choose from daily AM and PM updates, sports media and political news. At CNN, sign up for categories like Politics, Law, Space Update and more.

■ **Get up-to-the-minute news reports** by installing a news ticker tape on your desktop. News Index (www.newsindex.com), DesktopNews (www.desktopnews.com) and the BBC's news site (news.bbc.co.uk) all offer personalised news ticker tapes. The sites all have their own downloadable software.

■ **A useful Website that lists headlines and links** to news stories is 1stHeadlines (www.1stheadlines.com). Click on

the links to rapidly search the content of hundreds of newspapers and news Websites for the stories that you find most interesting. You can search for a story by region or by topic.

■ **Create a custom news page online,** featuring stories on only the topic you want, drawn from many different news sources. Both Crayon (www.crayon.net) and Infobeat (www.infobeat.com) offer this service. Crayon will also deliver your news by e-mail. Both of these sites provide detailed instructions on how to go about setting up your news page.

The latest news stories straight to your mobile phone.
There are many services that text the latest news headlines direct to your mobile phone. Ananova (www.ananova.com) also offers this service, but for certain networks only. The BBC Website (news.bbc.co.uk) also offers text and WAP services for mobile phones and PDAs.

■ **Watch and listen to the news over the Net.** Let streaming technology bring up-to-the-minute news clips to your computer. You will need the RealOne Player program (uk.real.com). Many major news sites now have streaming video but some, such as CNN (www.cnn.com) and The Feed Room (www.thefeedroom.com), require users to subscribe before they can view the streaming video footage.

■ **The major UK TV news services** have an Internet presence. Try the Sky News site (www.sky.com/skynews/video) for video clips of all the latest news stories. ITV (www.itv.com/news) and the BBC (news.bbc.co.uk) also stream video reports on some of their top stories.

■ **Portals can also provide news.** Yahoo! Broadcast (broadcast.yahoo.com) offers television news broadcasts on the Web, plus regular entertainment and sports updates.

■ **Want to know first-hand what's happening** in the world's most powerful nation? C-Span's (www.cspan.org) live video and audio feeds come to you direct from cameras in the US Capitol's corridors of power.

■ **If you're looking for an alternative to mainstream online news reports** take a look at the Obscure Store and Reading Room (www.obscurestore.com), which offers offbeat daily news selections and links to a variety of weird sources. Also try the Opinion Pages (www.opinion-pages.org), which allows you to search editorials, opinions, commentaries and columnists from English-language newspapers and magazines. This service includes a letters to the editor database, which is indexed twice daily.

■ **Gone but not forgotten.** Television news may seem ephemeral, but there is one organisation dedicated to preserving it for posterity. The Television News Archive at Vanderbilt University (tvnews.vanderbilt.edu) is the world's most extensive archive of television news, dating back to the 1980s.

▶ See also **Plug-ins extend your abilities**, p. 252; and **Online video expands your horizons**, p. 285.

THE WORLD OF ONLINE RADIO

Embark on an audio voyage around the world and listen to hundreds of radio stations on your computer. Log-on and let your new discoveries provide a musical accompaniment when you're at work on your PC.

■ In order to listen to radio online,
all you need is a computer with a sound card (in other words, any recent PC), free software such as RealOne Player (uk.real.com) or Windows Media Player (www.windowsmedia.com), and a station to listen to. Once you're set up, it's as easy to turn your dial to BBC Radio 2 as to Studio 1 in Chelyabinsk, Russia.

■ Online radio stations can only transfer data (sound) as fast as your
connection will allow. So a fast connection doesn't necessarily translate into better sound. Sound files are usually encoded at a low enough rate for the average connection speed. While you can't expect perfect fidelity over the Net, sound quality should be between that of AM and FM.

■ There are two types of online radio:
live broadcasts and pre-recordings. The live broadcasts are just like radio, except that you can listen to thousands of stations across the world, broadcasting everything from speeches to concerts (and, of course, recorded music). With on-demand audio, the material is prerecorded, so no matter when you decide to log on to a broadcast, you will always start at the beginning.

■ Overwhelmed by all the radio content online?
In fact, there is so much choice available these days that your main concern will be to narrow down what you want to listen to. To get started, you may want to use an Internet radio directory to help you find a site playing something that appeals to you. Try tuning in to any of the following radio directories: Radio Tower (www.radiotower.com), Penguin Radio (www.penguinradio.com) and Radio Locator (www.radio-locator.com).

■ You can access online radio in XP through Windows Media Player.
Go to **Start ➜ All Programs ➜ Accessories ➜ Entertainment ➜ Windows Media Player**. Click on **Media Guide** then select **Radio** to see the Editor's Picks, featured radio stations and to search for a station by music genre. Alternatively, click on **Radio Tuner** to browse the featured stations. You can create a list of your preferred stations by clicking on **Add to My Stations** once you have selected a station you like.

■ Start up your own online radio station.
Unlike traditional radio, no special licenses are needed to set up an online radio station. For more information on do-it-yourself broadcasting, or to listen to the attempts of others, visit the following sites:

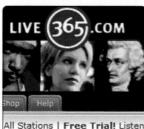

Icecast (www.icecast.org), Shoutcast (www.shoutcast.com), or Live365 (www.live365.com).

■ Pick up speech radio and listen to drama and comedy online.
There's more to Internet radio than music – BBC Radio 4 (www.bbc.co.uk/radio 4), BBC 7 (www.bbc.co.uk/bbc7) and One Word (www.oneword.co.uk) all have drama, speech and comedy output online.

■ Listen in on real-life drama on your Desktop.
Reality TV is enjoying huge popularity, but you don't have to resort to the box for your daily fix. Try American police scanner live emergency feeds, which are available from Police and Scanning Info (policescanner.8m.com) and Strong Signals (www.strongsignals.net).

GREAT RADIO SITES
Live concerts, broadcasts and interviews with your favourite artists all online.

RADIO FEEDS (www.radiofeeds.co.uk)
An up-to-date list of UK radio stations simultaneously broadcasting on the Web.

RADIO NOW (www.radio-now.co.uk)
Provides over 300 audio listening links for UK radio stations live on the Internet. There is also radio industry news, features and a feedback section where users can e-mail queries and questions.

BBC LOCAL RADIO (www.bbc.co.uk/england/radindex)
A region-by-region guide to local BBC radio stations throughout England. Find your local station's Web page and browse presenter profiles, the programme schedule and listen to the latest news bulletin online.

YAHOO! BROADCAST (broadcast.yahoo.com/home.html)
A wide range of on-demand audio and video, ranging from music to news and film.

WINDOWS MEDIA RADIO GUIDE (www.windowsmedia.com/radio)
Links to hundreds of radio stations worldwide. You can also download free player software from this site.

RADIO AUTHORITY (www.radioauthority.org.uk)
The UK's official radio licensing body.

Internet banking

Why spend your lunch hour standing in long bank queues, or manually updating your chequebook, when you can track your finances online? Paying bills, transferring money and viewing transactions electronically is what online banking is all about, and it has never been easier.

GETTING STARTED

First, visit your current bank's Website and find out whether it offers online banking. The chances are that a variety of features are already provided. Think about the type of banking you do most frequently – business, personal, loan management or investments – and select a service that suits your needs best. Most banks will let you check your account balance for free, but you may need to pay for other services.

To find your bank's site try searching via a search engine such as Yahoo! (uk.yahoo.com). Type in the name, and to make your search easier, remember to tick the box next to **UK only**.

In addition to your PC, all you need to get started is a modem and Web access. In a few cases, you'll also need bank-specific software, but your bank will provide this, if necessary.

Millions of people worldwide already bank online. In the UK the sector is growing rapidly. As well as online versions of most major high street banks and building societies, there are now many Internet-only banks operating exclusively on the Web. Before signing up, make sure your bank offers all the services you need. The best banking Websites go beyond bill-paying and balance updates to let you transfer funds to individuals at other banks, view share prices and even make tax payments.

SAFETY AND SERVICE

Is Web banking safe? The general consensus is 'yes'. All banks use the industry standard Secure Socket Layer (SSL) encryption in the interactive sections of their sites. For even

tighter security, use either Navigator or Explorer 4.0 or later versions, which are capable of 128-bit encryption. Check the padlock symbol on your Taskbar. If you get a message saying the browser can't communicate with the site, don't do business there. Be sure to quiz banks on customer service. How quickly do they respond to e-mail? How do you reach a live person? If you find that your bills have not been paid, how will the bank respond to your query?

The biggest security breaches come after setting up super-secure encrypted and password-protected banking accounts, when people then enter their security information into the computer and walk away from the

desk to have lunch or run an errand. To keep your banking details safe, make sure you always log off whenever you are away from your PC.

Make sure your bank has enough live support. Accidentally sent someone the wrong amount, or discovered that payments have not been going out? You need to be confident that your bank will fix it quickly.

Back up, back up, back up! While this may seem obvious, make sure that you keep back-ups of all your banking information. Filing paper copies away doesn't hurt either.

BILL PAYING

Most banks allow bill payment online. And increasingly, utility companies, local councils and credit card companies are providing

INTERNET BANKING
Want to find out more? Check these sites for additional information and help.

THIS IS MONEY (www.thisismoney.com /advice/banking)
A useful site that offers advice on choosing a wide range of financial services, including Internet banking.

UK 250 (www.uk250.co.uk/bank)
Part of the UK250 Web guide featuring thousands of quality UK Websites in 250 categories. Has a Bank Website of the Day and links to other related financial sites.

E-BANKING (www.e-banking.co.uk)
This site provides comparisons between high street and Internet banks and provides links to sites offering various financial services.

online bill-paying facilities through secure servers on their own Websites. Contact your utility companies to see if they provide this service, or surf the Net to find their Websites and check out the online services they have to offer. You may have to register with the site to make regular payments, and in some cases you will also be able to access information about your account.

Bill paying online is much more efficient than using written cheques and the mail. The first time you make a regular payment, you enter in the name and bank account details of the recipient. After that, all you have to do is enter in the amount and select the date you want the payment sent. The bank then credits the account of the payee.

You can easily schedule recurring payments via an Internet bank account. Most allow you to set up either standing orders or direct debits, by the month, week or quarter. This is useful for your personal loan or mortgage bills. If you make a mistake in an online payment, you can usually stop it, provided you catch the error at least five working days before the payment was scheduled to be made.

Making one-off payments is also easy online and most Internet current accounts allow you to do this, instead of writing a cheque or using cash.

BANKING SOFTWARE

Ready to turn your computer into a chequebook? The first thing you must do is to

visit your bank's own Website. Most online banking services use Net-based software, which means that you can use the same browser you use for other Internet access, and you don't have to download any extra programs to use the banking service. The programs tests your browser to see whether it is suitable whenever you try to use the service. If you have an old browser you may have to update.

Some services also let you export data to popular money management software.

Quicken is banking software that includes an array of alerts that let you know, for example, when the balance on one of your accounts slips below a specified amount, as well as more advanced online banking and bill payment functions. It also has several extras that have been created with more experienced computer users in mind.

SMALL-BUSINESS CONCERNS

Setting up your own business? Dread the thought of spending days driving from bank to bank, filling out applications and waiting for loan officers to pass judgment? Head for an online broker instead. You log on, give an overview of your company and detailed financial information, and request the type of loan you want. The site then sends out online information to a network of lenders. Within an hour or two, several institutions will bid on your loan. Use a search engine to find brokers, using terms such as 'online loan', and limiting the search to the UK – which is something you can do with a search engine like Google (www.google.co.uk).

Some online companies help budding entrepreneurs to manage their money better, earn interest on their hard earned cash, pay bills, write cheques, make payments, process their payroll and manage taxes online. Of course, businesses usually have to pay for the convenience of online banking facilities, but in general these fees can ultimately prove to be lower than the corresponding high street bank charges. Again, conduct an online search for institutions that offer the precise services you are looking for.

▶ See also **How to pay bills online,** p. 263.

ONLINE BANKS

Most of the major banks now offer banking and bill-payment services. Visit their sites, and those of the Internet-only banks to see what's on offer.

CAHOOT (www.cahoot.co.uk)
An Internet-only bank from the Abbey National Building Society.

HSBC (www.hsbc.co.uk)
The UK Internet banking site of one of the largest financial services organisations in the world.

VIRGIN ONE (www.virginone.com)
This service puts your mortgage, loans and current account into one single account.

BARCLAYS (www.barclays.co.uk)
From one of the 'big four' high street banks, this site offers a full range of personal and business banking services.

SMILE (www.smile.co.uk)
Online-only service from the Co-operative Bank, which has an ethical investment policy.

NATIONWIDE (www.nationwide.co.uk)
This building society also offers a full Internet banking service with competitive rates.

By subscribing to a site, you can get the browser to automatically check for new content whenever you log on.

■ **When you subscribe to a site,** your Web browser copies that Website to your hard drive so that you can view it offline. During the setup procedure for your subscription, you can specify how often you want your browser to update the site, so that it will do it automatically. This means that you don't have to worry about viewing out-of-date content, even though you are reading the site offline. To find out how to subscribe, see the 'How to', below.

■ **Want to unsubscribe from a site?**
In Internet Explorer, go to **Favorites ➔ Organize Favorites**. Right-click on your chosen site and select **Properties**. Make sure that the **Make this page available offline** option is checked in the Web Document tab. Click the **Schedule** tab and tick **Only when I choose Synchronize from the Tools menu**. Click **OK**. Explorer will only update your Website subscription when you ask it to.

■ **Keep track of the headlines!** Use the Windows Active Desktop feature to put Web pages directly on your Desktop, and they will automatically refresh their content. But don't set up too many, since they will slow your PC down.

▶ See also **Bringing the Web to your Desktop,** p. 78; **Using Favorites in Explorer,** p. 225; and **Saving Web pages,** p. 235.

FINDING YOUR NEXT JOB ON THE NET

Use the Internet to speed up your search for a new career.

■ **The extreme CV drop technique** is the e-mail equivalent of blindly sending your CV to every company you can think of. While mass mailing is ineffective ninety-nine times out of hundred, there is always that hundredth time. Also, the technique is so quick and easy that your details can reach many companies inexpensively and efficiently. Companies who are hiring usually publish an e-mail address in their newspaper ads, and you can also try to find e-mail addresses in trade directories or by calling companies directly.

■ **Are you a student looking for work** and want to sound more experienced? Your university campus e-mail address – with an .edu extension on the end – advertises your student status. Consider signing on with a general-access ISP for the duration of your job search. Serious searching online is best done with a .com or .net account.

■ **Create an online CV with easily searchable keywords.** If you have Web space, you could put your CV on the Web. Remember, however, that most employers search for nouns, not verbs, so your CV needs to emphasise these. Nouns act as buzzwords that employers look for in potential candidates. If the keywords describing your strengths – team player,

How to: Subscribe to a site using Internet Explorer

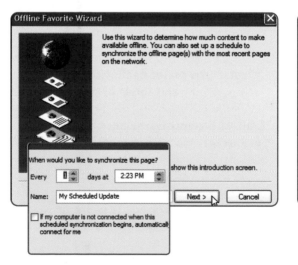

1 Visit a site and click **Favorites ➔ Add to Favorites.** In the dialogue box, check **Make available offline** and click **Customize** to launch the Offline Favorite Wizard.

2 Work through the Wizard. Select **I would like to create a new schedule** in the third window and click **Next.** Choose how often to update the page and click **Next** again.

3 If you need to log in to the site, type in your user name and password in the next window. Click **Finish,** then **OK.** Your browser will now copy the site to your hard drive.

Excel, Word, Express – are not already in your CV, redesign it so that it includes them in a separate keyword section.

■ **There are active and passive Net CV postings.** With an active posting you chase particular employers and jobs, while with a passive posting you wait for employers to find you. The key to getting responses is the subject line – include as many keywords in it as possible.

■ **Active posting** involves surfing individual employer postings or job postings and responding directly with an e-mailed CV. This can be a very productive method, since it is more direct and personal. It also gives you the opportunity to add comments about yourself that are relevant to a specific employer, as well as your contact details.

HOW TO PAY BILLS ONLINE

Take control of your finances – pay your bills online.

■ **Many utility companies, local councils and other companies** now offer online bill-paying facilities through secure servers on their Websites, where you can make regular payments and check the details of your account with them. However, paying all your bills this way means you will have to register with various different sites to make and monitor your payments. You may want to consider using your current bank account online or an Internet bill paying service so you can have all the information about your bills in one place.

■ **Set up regular payments online** for your fixed bills. These could include mortgage, rent, personal loan repayments and utility bills. If you use Internet banking facilities already, you can quickly and easily set up direct debits and standing orders, just by logging into your current account and following the on-screen instructions. One-off bills and expenses are also easy to pay using your online current account. And you can cancel direct debits and standing orders at the click of a mouse, which is much quicker than writing to your bank instructing them to do so!

■ **Girobank's online bill paying method** (www.billpayment.co.uk) allows business or personal customers of any UK bank or building society who has a debit card to pay bills over the Internet. You will need to register with the site, but before you do, check the list of companies and organisations that use the service, to ensure your payees are listed.

■ **MSN also provides a secure online bill paying service** (msn.clear.co.uk). It allows you to keep all your bills in one place and notifies you by e-mail of incoming bills.

■ **Protect your personal details.** Before becoming a customer of a bill payment site check that it has a clear privacy policy. It is vital that your personal information is sufficiently protected. Also make sure that your financial status won't be passed on to other companies – or you may find yourself deluged with advertising.

■ **Faster payment means faster debits.** Bill payments are received faster online than by post, and your payment may be debited sooner than you expect. Factor this into your calculations to ensure you don't go into the red!

■ **Check your bill payment system uses a Secure Sockets Layer** (SSL) to stop anyone reading the data transferred between its Website and your computer. Get the latest Web browser software for increased protection.

▶ See also **Security on the Net**, p. 254; and **Internet banking**, p. 260.

PRICING AND PAYING BILLS
Save yourself time and money by looking online.

GIROBANK (www.billpayment.co.uk)
Holders of major debit cards can make online bill payments to a number of local councils and utility companies.

TXU ENERGI (www.txuenergi.co.uk)
On the Website of this electricity and gas supplier you can enter meter readings, view your bills and make payments online.

DIRECT DEBIT (www.directdebit.co.uk)
Online information for individuals and businesses on setting up direct debits, and advice on budget management.

MSN'S MANAGE BILLS (msn.clear.co.uk)
A complete online bill management service from MSN and Clear. You can pay bills with debit or credit cards or set up direct debits. This service also sends you e-mails informing you of incoming bills.

UK POWER (www.ukpower.co.uk)
If the bills you are paying are too high, try this site for price comparisons between the gas and electricity suppliers in your area.

BRITISH GAS (www.house.co.uk)
Manage your gas bill account online.

PLAN YOUR NEXT TRIP ON THE WEB

The Internet has become a popular destination for people planning their family holidays, business trips or romantic weekends away.

■ Go paperless by buying e-tickets

for flights online – it's one less thing to leave behind on the sideboard! Most airlines now offer this facility with e-mail booking confirmation. Some even give you a discount for booking online. All you need for check-in is proof of identity, such as your driver's licence or, if you're travelling abroad, your passport.

■ Research your destination before you go.

There are thousands of online travel guides and magazines. The award winning Rough Guides Website (www.roughguides.com) contains

a vast resource of detailed information on more than 14,000 destinations around the world, and it has a weekly Spotlight feature focusing on one specific location. Lonely Planet (www.lonely planet.com) is a less comprehensive site, but it's a great place for first-hand advice and inspiration, where you can check out the opinions and experiences of other travellers.

■ There are hundreds of travel Websites

and many are online versions of popular magazines. For adventurous tales, visit *Outside* magazine (www.outsidemag.com) or *Travelmag* (www.travelmag.co.uk). If you prefer less challenging travel options, take a look at *Condé Nast Traveler* (www.concierge.com) or *Travel and Leisure* (www.travelandleisure.com).

■ For an in-depth profile of foreign lands,

head for individual government Websites. Alternatively, the CIA World Factbook (www.cia.gov/cia/publications/factbook) is unbeatable for global facts and statistics. Or, if you don't mind facing the fact that you're going

to be a tourist, try Tourism Offices Worldwide (www.towd.com).

■ Look up an online city guide

to discover the festivals, fairs and exciting cultural events taking place in the destination of your choice. TimeOut (www.timeout.com) has guides to more than 30 cities, with restaurant, club, bar, and hotel reviews. Another city guide site is WCities (einstein.wcities.com). You can also investigate UK cities with CityNetGuide (www.citynetguide.co.uk).

■ Picture this.

You need to plan a conference call with Beijing, but you're in Belgrade and your boss is in Bogota. If you have a Java-enabled browser you can use the International Java Clock at the BioTactics Clock page (www.biotactics.com/clockjava.htm) where times are simultaneously posted for a dozen cities

around the world. The page also lists other time references, including the CIA's World Time Zone map, and hyperlinks to sites that can help you calculate time differences.

■ Before travelling to a foreign country,

it's best to brush up on a few basic phrases. Travlang (travlang.com/languages) offers tutorials in more than 70 languages. With a little practice, you should be able to make just about anyone understand you!

■ Want to get off the beaten track?

One of the great features of Web travel is that it allows you to plan exciting holidays in little visited corners of the globe. Perhaps you'd like to go diving, take a dog sledge trip across Alaska, climb Mount Everest or take a flight in a modern combat aircraft. You can do all of these and more. Check out Travelbag Adventures

SNAP UP A BARGAIN

Ticket prices can determine whether you set off on that big great adventure or decide it's out of your reach. Keep the following resources in mind when hunting down a deal.

CURRENT SALES

Depending on the number of tickets sold up to the point of sale, ticket prices are often adjusted up or down. To get the best deals, plan your trip as far in advance as possible. Many Websites have an e-mail support service, which will let you know when the price to a particular destination reaches the amount you're willing to pay.

INTERNET SPECIALS

Look out for special deals that are only available through the Internet.

LAST MINUTE BARGAINS

Internet-only deals are offered through airline, hotel and travel operators. Try Bargain Holidays.com (www.bargainholidays. com), Ebookers.com (www.ebookers.com) or Expedia.co.uk (www.expedia.co.uk).

TRAVEL AUCTIONS

Several auction sites specialise in airline tickets, while others sell unwanted holidays as well. Get the thrill of an auction, and the chance for a bargain holiday in one fell swoop! To go online and place your bid, try Holiday Auctions (www.holidayauctions.net) or Auctionair (www.auction-air.com). Ebay, (www.ebay.co.uk) the popular auction site, has a section offering tickets and travel. Here you can also bid for accessories and guides.

NAME YOUR PRICE

Some Websites allow you to bid on a destination, then wait for a matching price. Because you must commit to buying the ticket if your price is reached, these sites work best when you're certain of your destination, travel dates and how much you want to pay.

(www.travelbag-adventures.co.uk) or Where in the World Travel (www.whereintheworld.co.uk).

■ Avoid Montezuma's Revenge and

other illnesses on your adventure holiday. Before you go, look up a medical site. The Department of Health (www.doh.gov.uk/traveladvice) has online advice available for travellers, with a comprehensive chart of immunisations needed for travel in many countries of the world. There's also

advice on taking medicines and first aid treatments. The World Health Organisation (www.who.int/ith) also gives health travel advice. For

the really careful traveller, the Center for Disease Control's Website (www.cdc.gov/travel) has news on outbreaks and diseases around the world.

■ Don't struggle with complex maths for currency conversion. Use

Oanda.com (www.oanda.com/convert/cheatsheet) or The Universal Currency Converter (www.xe.com/ucc). Oanda will create and print a currency converter table. Select the language, date and currencies you need, and the rate you believe is

most relevant to your needs. For an at-a-glance list of the exchange rate for Sterling, try Ananova (www.ananova.com/business/touristrates). This site also has a currency converter.

■ Play it safe. The Internet may be a great

place to plan and book your holiday, but there can be pitfalls. On the Web, you are often dealing with people you know nothing about except their e-mail address. They may promise the world, but what happens when you have handed over your hard earned cash and arrive at your destination only to find the hotel you booked has never heard of you? Take a few simple precautions with Web operators. Only deal with organisations who are affiliated to professional travel bodies such as ABTA (The Association of British Travel Agents). Always ask for brochures and information, and read the literature carefully. Be sure to ask lots of questions. Don't be afraid to enquire about how long an operator has been in business, who their clients are and where their business comes from. Try to check the validity of any claims through an independent source.

■ Travel on the cheap. Fancy being paid

to travel? Well, you can almost manage the dream by becoming an international courier. Air couriers ferry valuable documents to their destination and then generally spend a few days there while waiting for another job. You don't get paid for the work, but you do get cheap airfares. Try the International Association of Air Travel Couriers (www.courier.org).

■ Planning a trip to the US? If you are

going to use public transport while you are there (and who can afford anything else these days?) you will find the American Public Transportation Association's United States Transit site (www.apta.com/sites/transus) invaluable. With its help you can access timetables all over the country.

■ If time is no object, why not consider

travelling to your destination by ship? The golden age of sea transport may be over, but freighters still ply the world's oceans, often calling at exotic destinations off the general tourist routes. As one of a small number of passengers, you will get the run of the ship, dining with the captain

and officers. Freighter World Cruises (www.freighterworld.com) will give you the lowdown.

▶ See also **Don't be caught out by the weather**, p. 303; and **Book your flight online**, p. 308.

TAX SURVIVAL SITES
Explore the sites below to find your way through the tax jungle.

**INLAND REVENUE
(www.inlandrevenue.gov.uk)**
This site has news and information on tax and national insurance matters in the UK, with help and advice for individuals and businesses. Fill in your tax return and calculate your payments online.

TAXAID (www.taxaid.org.uk)
A charity Website offering free tax advice to people in financial need. The organisation also promotes public understanding of tax and campaigns for a simpler tax system.

IETAXGUARD (www.ietaxguard.co.uk)
A UK tax return service whose site offers tax tips, a tax database and a calculator to work out your payments and benefits.

TAXCENTRAL (www.taxcentral.co.uk)
An online tax service offering a choice of ways to complete your UK tax return. You can either order software, complete an online tax return or find a tax advisor to help you. There is also tax news, an archive of useful questions, calculators and a tax guide.

**MONEYEXTRA
(www.moneyworld.co.uk/tax)**
Tax advice and budget information, a tax calculator and tax tables. There's also a helpline for assistance with your tax return.

TAX CAFE (www.taxcafe.co.uk)
This site offers tax advice and users can submit specific tax questions online. However, there is a charge for this service.

File your tax return online to reduce the stress of paying the taxman.

■ **If you are thinking of filing your tax return online,** visit the Inland Revenue's Website (www.inlandrevenue.gov.uk) and navigate to the relevant area. Have a look at all the information and read the Frequently Asked Questions to get an overview of what is involved. The whole process is very easy. Even if you don't want to file your return electronically, you can still use the Website to download extra pages for your return, or guides on how to complete it.

■ **Just follow the steps.** First you need to register at the Government Gateway website (www.gateway.gov.uk). You will be sent a user ID that lets you log on to the service, although you will need an activation code that is sent to you through the post. This means that you can't decide to submit your tax return online at the last minute – it can take up to 8 days for the code to

How to: Register for the Internet Self Assessment service

1 First visit the Government Gateway site (gateway.gov.uk). This is where you can register for Government Services online. Click on **Enter the Gateway**. On the next screen choose **register as an individual**.

2 You can either register with a User ID (the usual choice) or with a digital certificate (a digital document you must pay for that verifies your identity). Some people already have digital certificates for another purpose, such as sending secure or encrypted e-mail.

3 Now fill in the details required to issue your User ID. Supply an e-mail address so that that the Inland Revenue can contact you, and a password to use when you activate your User ID. Keep your Unique Taxpayers Reference handy – it's at the top of your Tax Return.

reach you. When you receive it, log on at the Inland Revenue website and start downloading the software you need to complete your return.

■ Worried about government snooping?
The Inland Revenue has a privacy statement on its Website that explains how it uses the information that you provide when you submit your return online. The Website uses encryption to ensure that all data you submit to it cannot be intercepted.

■ Software can soften the blow
of preparing your tax return and avoid mistakes that could cost you a fine from the Inland Revenue. Programs such as TaxCalc (www.taxcalc.com) calculate how much tax you should pay or rebate you should claim. Many programs also integrate with the Inland Revenue's online submission facility, and may be easier to use than the software the Revenue provides for free.

■ If you're worried about filing your own tax return,
you can get an accountant to do the job for you. Most accountants now submit returns to the Inland Revenue electronically, but this usually involves at least one visit to their office. If you really want to save yourself the trip, you could try an accountant with an online service.

▶ See also **Working out your tax,** p. 199.

YOUR BUSINESS AND THE NET

The Internet can be a real boon to small businesses searching for software, help and inspiration.

■ Small businesses can get a great deal of help from the Internet.
It allows them to compete in the free market, with access to a worldwide customer base, while keep running costs low.

■ Keep all your business accounts up to date
with software like MYOB (www.myob.co.uk) or Quicken (www.intuit.co.uk/quicken). These programs will help you with all aspects of business accounting.

■ Not quite sure how to do that job?
There is a wealth of business software to help you deal with almost every conceivable task. Apart from the big players, such as Microsoft, there are plenty of other companies producing useful products. Try AptiView (www.aptiview.co.uk) for business contact, sales and marketing software or Palo Alto (www.paloalto.co.uk) for business planning software. Otherwise, check out shareware sites such as Tucows (www.tucows.com) or CNET Shareware.com (shareware.cnet.com).

■ Smarten up your professional image
by printing custom stationery and business cards from your computer. Programs such as Microsoft Office or Microsoft Works provide a set of basic templates for most stationery, from letterheads and invoices to business cards. All of them can be customised.

▶ See also **Internet banking,** p. 260.

SITES FOR SMALL BUSINESSES
Keep your business affairs in order and your stress levels down.

BUSINESS LINK (www.businesslink.org)
This is the Website of the national business advice service, with information on starting and funding a business, grants, EU funding and employment related regulations.

DEPARTMENT OF TRADE AND INDUSTRY (www.dti.gov.uk/for_business.html)
A government site offering business information and advice. This site provides links to other useful sites about a range of business subjects, from training and development to employment law.

UK ONLINE FOR BUSINESS (www.ukonlineforbusiness.gov.uk)
Help and information specifically for businesses operating online. Register with the site to access a wealth of information.

BBC BUSINESS (www.bbc.co.uk/business)
Visit the BBC's business pages for business news, features, handy tips and listings for all the BBC's TV and radio business programmes.

COMPANIES HOUSE (www.companies-house.gov.uk)
The site of the official office where companies are registered and must legally file certain documents. The site offers a subscription-based service to those wishing to access company information.

BUSINESS EUROPE (www.businesseurope.com)
More advice and information for small businesses. This site features news, resources, case studies, a company directory and user forums for exchanging ideas.

The Internet is a powerful tool for the investor. Use it simply for research or take the plunge and try share trading online.

▪ There's no excuse for being under-informed if you use the Internet.
Whatever the type of investment you have in mind – from simple savings accounts to share dealing and complex spread bets – you'll find huge amounts of information and data online.

▪ A wealth of websites offer basic investment know-how. Some sites are free,

but can only offer generalised advice that may not be entirely up-to-date. Others charge subscription fees, but give much more detailed information. A good place to start for level-headed advice is The Motley Fool

(www.fool.co.uk), whose advice covers all forms of investment. The Website of Moneywise Magazine (www.moneywise.co.uk) has monthly articles and news, as well as guides you can download on personal finance issues.

▪ For more detailed financial information, try the Investors Chronicle site
(www.investorschronicle.co.uk). The Website is thorough – it covers every company listed on the UK stock market – but you will have to pay a subscription to read most of its content.

▪ News sites are good sources of investment intelligence. The BBC
Website has information and advice in several places. Its News pages (news.bbc.co.uk) have an extensive business section with market data covering all UK share prices. Elsewhere, the Business and Money section has information on all forms of investments and savings. Go to www.bbc.co.uk/business.

▪ If you use Microsoft Money, you will
benefit from its close integration with MSN Money (money.msn.co.uk). The Website carries stock alerts, share tips and advice on the full

range of investment devices. Microsoft Money is a powerful tool for helping you to plan your savings and for working out what funds you have available for investment.

▪ Track your savings using online banking. Choose a savings account that you
can keep an eye on via the Internet. Use the transfer facilities to ensure that you maximise your

How to: Track share prices online

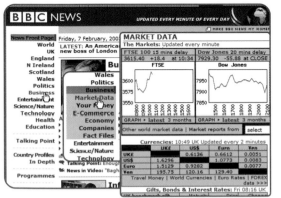

1 Go to the BBC News Website (news.bbc.co.uk) and click on **Business** then **Market Data**. The page shows the day's movements in the principal stock markets, as well as key exchange rates and bond prices. The data is regularly updated.

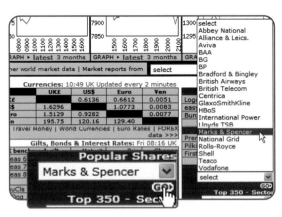

2 To find out more about a particular share, go to the right of the page and select the company you are interested in. Some of the most popular shares have direct links, but it's easy to search for other companies by market sector or by alphabetical order.

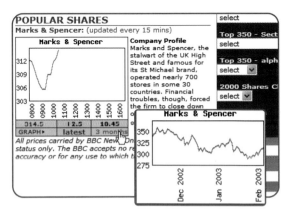

3 A page will open with a brief description of the company and its recent performance. A graph shows the share's price movements during the day. Click on **3 months** to see the movements over a longer time frame.

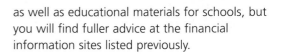
interest and avoid unnecessary bank charges by transferring funds between your current and savings accounts.

Many sites offer share price quotes. Be aware that the prices shown on these sites are delayed by 15 minutes – which can be a long time in the world of finance. If you want to see share prices in real-time, you will have to pay for the privilege.

Before you start investing online, make sure you have got your priorities right. It's always wise to make sure that you have a rainy-day fund of instantly accessible savings (most advisors recommend keeping the equivalent of 3-6 months' salary in this form). And often the best way of saving money is to reduce debt. You are very unlikely to make more from your investments than you pay in interest on your borrowings. Mortgages are a slightly different case, but some advisors recommend paying down your mortgage as a wise investment step.

Need to talk to an expert? Use the Internet to find an Independent Financial Advisor (IFA). A large number of sites will list local IFAs for you, but it's a good idea to visit the Financial Services Authority Website (www.fsa.gov.uk) – the FSA regulates IFAs in the UK – and download their guide to financial advice first.

Share dealing is not for the faint-hearted. Anyone going into it needs to be aware of the risks involved, and should also take time to work out what the true costs of share transactions can be.

There is a very wide choice of online brokers, with accounts that vary according to how actively you will be trading, and the size of transaction that you will be undertaking. Many of the personal finance

Websites have pages comparing the services of the different brokers as well as guides pointing out what you should look for.

Although buying online does not eliminate the commission that you must pay to a broker, it is considerably reduced. Most online brokers charge flat fees, irrespective of the size of your trade, which can be a money saver on larger deals.

Don't forget stamp duty. This is currently charged at 0.5 per cent of the price of any shares that you buy. Taken together with commission, this can render any profits you might make smaller than you hoped. Any gains that you make from selling shares could also be liable for capital gains tax.

Online brokers must meet the same requirements as traditional firms. All investment activity in the UK is regulated by the Financial Services Authority (www.fsa.gov.uk). You should also look for a dealer that is a participant in the Financial Services

Compensation Scheme. The FSA website has some useful information for the consumer, especially on the subject of pensions, as well as educational materials for schools, but you will find fuller advice at the financial information sites listed previously.

You are not limited to shares when you deal online. You can also buy units in funds such as Stock Market trackers. It's even possible to get into complex devices such as options, but this is only something to try if you are truly knowledgeable about the markets and are prepared to take on a high risk.

UK investors don't have to invest only in UK markets. Many of the online brokers allow you to buy and sell shares listed on the main American and European exchanges as well, such as the New York Stock Exchange and the NASDAQ technology stock market.

Be wary of what you read in chatrooms and forums. Most of the financial information sites have forums where users can swap information about quoted companies. However, all may not be what it seems. A contributor may have less than altruistic reasons for talking up – or down – the company under discussion. Take any tips or information you read with a large grain of salt.

ONLINE SHARE DEALING BASICS
Here's what you need to know to make your investments count.

1. Make sure you choose your broker carefully – search through the major financial information sites to compare commissions and account types.

2. To avoid losing large sums – should the market suddenly shift – always use limit orders for trading online.

3. Take advantage of the free services offered by some online brokers that allow you to receive automatic e-mail messages whenever there is news about your shares.

4. Professional traders don't buy and sell on whim, nor should you – do research.

5. Keep a careful watch on where you get your information. Take advice from reliable sources, not anonymous experts you come across in chatrooms.

6. As with betting or buying, decide first how much money you can afford to spend and do not exceed that limit. As a beginner, you may want to stick to lower-risk investments such as mutual funds.

Stay fit and healthy

We all want to stay healthy and have access to the latest medical information. The Net allows you to do all this, and more. When surfing for information, select sites backed by accredited organisations – but remember, nothing can replace a consultation with a real live doctor!

FEELING A BIT BELOW PAR?

Can't get out to see a doctor? Have one come to you instead via the Net. There are several Internet 'doctors' surgeries' available but often there is a charge for the online consultation and some services require you to pay a subscription fee to register with the site. Try Askamedic (www.askamedic.com) or E-med (www.emed.co.uk). Both sites offer online consultations with qualified practitioners. However, bear in mind that it may be more reassuring to have a face-to-face consultation with your own GP.

Check out your medication's compatibility with other drugs at Drugs.com (www.drugs.com). The site has information on over 24,000 different drugs and medicines, as well as a drug interaction checker. Also check RxList (www.rxlist.com), where you can find out the actions and side effects of prescription medication. These sites are American and, while many drugs are international, there may be differences in the range of drugs available and their commercial names. Pharmacy2U (www.pharmacy2U.co.uk) is a UK online chemists with an e-mail service for advice on drugs and medication.

Do some serious research. Search the medical journals to learn more about your condition. Access the US National Library of Medicine's database (www.nlm.nih.gov) with over 3500 medical journals and archives dating back to 1966. Or you can look for links at Martindale's Health Science Guide (www-sci.lib.uci.edu/HSG/HSGuide.html) or PubMed (www.ncbi.nlm.nih.gov/PubMed).

Need advice on workplace health and safety? The government's Health & Safety Executive is responsible for the regulation of almost all the risks to health and safety arising from work in Britain. The executive has its own Website (www.hse.gov.uk) where you can find out more about the health and safety system in Great Britain.

Organise your medical records and manage health information You can purchase Health-Minder Software from www.health-minder.com. The manager can also store your pet's medical records, file insurance claims, help you budget for medical expenses and keep track of your children's vaccinations. Clinnix Health Manager (www.clinnix.net) is similar software that also provides a health encyclopaedia, the latest health information delivered to your PC daily, illustrations and instructional videos.

LINK UP WITH OTHERS

If you or a loved one has a medical condition or disease, or is in need of an operation, staying well informed and talking to others who have had similar experiences is vital. You can do this via the Net. Many health sites have chatrooms. Or try typing the name of the condition into a search engine like Yahoo! and see what comes up. There's a Website and chatroom for almost every ailment.

Never been able to afford that tummy tuck? Now you can explore the possibilities online by visiting a site such as Cosmetic Surgery

YOUR VERY GOOD HEALTH!
Enhance your well-being – log on to thousands of topics, Q&As and more.

NHS DIRECT ONLINE (www.nhsdirect.nhs.uk)
The NHS's national Internet health resource with an online encyclopaedia, a self-help guide, advice on reducing the risk of major diseases and local services search facility.

ACHOO (www.achoo.com)
Links to thousands of health-related sites, e-zines, headlines, and a unique Human Health and Disease directory.

INTERNET MENTAL HEALTH (www.mentalhealth.com)
This site's goal is to improve understanding, diagnosis and treatment of mental illness.

MAYOCLINIC.COM (www.mayoclinic.com)
A to Z listings of diseases and conditions, with treatment and self care advice.

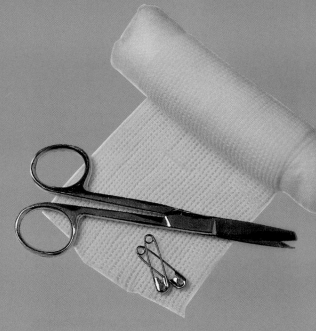

Avoid quackery. While many Websites offer reputable advice and treatment, others only want your money. Check them out first at Quackwatch (www.quackwatch.com) or Internet ScamBusters (www.scambusters.com); the latter site specialises in more general information on fraudulent practices. Otherwise, log on to the National Fraud Information Center (www.fraud.org), which tracks complaints of inappropriate practices. You can report a fraud to the Serious Fraud Office (www.sfo.gov.uk), or check out the Office of Fair Trading's Website (www.oft.gov.uk).

How's your health? Get an online assessment. HealthStatus (www.healthstatus .com) offers personalised calculations for body mass, body fat, target heart rate, blood alcohol levels, daily energy expenditure and more. You First (www.youfirst.com) has various assessments to work out your individual risk of early death or disease. But take any results not based on an actual physical examination with a pinch of salt.

Planning a trip overseas? Check out the World Health Organization's site (www.who.int). It has an extensive list of countries with health and disease information about each. There is also a comprehensive list of health topics to surf. The Department of Health provides advice for travellers (www.doh.gov.uk/traveladvice), whilst Healthfinder (www.healthfinder.gov) and the US National Library of Medicine (www.nlm.nih.gov) are also good sources of information.

Ever wondered about the inside of your body? Satisfy your curiosity (or get information for school projects) by visiting The Inner Learning Online Website (www.innerbody .com), the Virtual Body at MEDtropolis (www.medtropolis.com/vbody) or the BBC Website (www.bbc.co.uk/science/humanbody).

▶ See also **Unhappy with traditional medicine?** p. 272.

UK (www.cosmetic-surgery-uk.co.uk). This online directory has links to many types and sources of cosmetic surgery available in the UK and users can subscribe to a regular newsletter. You can also research other people's first-hand experiences of plastic surgery. Check out Cindy Jackson's Website (www.cindy jackson.com). Cindy holds the world record for having the most cosmetic surgery procedures so her site is full of useful information.

GET THE SCOOP ON GOOD HEALTH

Can't get to a pharmacist? Bring the pharmacist to you instead. National Co-operative Chemists (www.co-oppharmacy.co.uk), Garden .co.uk (www.garden.co.uk/pharmacy) and Pharmacy2U (www.pharmacy2u.co.uk) are all online chemists stores. Pharmacy2U has a free prescription delivery service.

Beware of sites selling prescription-only medicines. Many of these sites specialise in offering Viagra online. As much as you might want to try miracle treatments that are on offer, you should always visit your GP instead of attempting to obtain drugs online.

FLEX YOUR FINGERTIPS

Tap into the latest health trends, find out more about nutrition and improve your overall fitness levels with the help of the Web.

BBC HEALTH (www.bbc.co.uk/health)
This site is packed full of information and has an interactive area where you can take online tests, quizzes and courses.

WOMEN'S HEALTH (www.womenshealthlondon.org.uk)
An independent voluntary organisation, Women's Health provides information on gynaecological health issues.

NEWCENTURYNUTRITION.COM (www.newcenturynutrition.com)
Fascinating articles on nutrition and health, as well as an extensive list of everything to do with herbal cures and remedies.

BRITSH NUTRITION FOUNDATION (www.nutrition.org.uk)
This site offers a wide range of information about diet, health, energy and nutrients.

REALAGE (www.realage.com)
Find out how old your body feels – as opposed to how old it really is – and use this information to create your own age-reduction plan. This health assessment program also evaluates how genetics, nutrition, fitness and stress affect your wellbeing.

HEALTH & FITNESS (www.hfonline.co.uk)
Online version of popular health magazine.

House and home

UNHAPPY WITH TRADITIONAL MEDICINE?

Get healthy and stay healthy with complementary advice from online sites. But always consult your GP about any serious conditions.

■ **Check out online newsletters** for the latest in alternative health developments. Alternative Health News Online (altmedicine.com) is prepared by journalists for the public, and aims to separate the hogwash from the effective. Updated daily, it offers a free, weekly e-mail newsletter, plus bulletins and alerts on health matters. eHealthy News (www.mercola.com), which is free to subscribers, offers articles on a wide range of health-related issues.

■ **Learn how to give a massage** and buy massage equipment from online sources. Start your search with Massage Therapy UK (www.massagetherapy.co.uk), The British Massage Therapy Council (www.bmtc.co.uk) and The Academy of On-Site Massage (www.aosm.co.uk). For equipment, try The Back Shop (www.thebackshop.co.uk/massage.htm).

■ **Learn how to use herbs and plants** to keep you healthy. Medicinal Herbs Online (www.egregore.com) offers a useful list of herbs and herbal preparations. Algy's Herb Page (www.algy.com) is a forum with an extensive collection of links to sites concerned with the using and growing of herbs.

■ **Thousands of complementary medicine Websites** are available online. Speed up your search by finding a directory

devoted to the subject, such as The Alternative Health Directory (www.alternativehealthuk.co.uk), Alternative Medicine.com (www.alternativemedicine.com) or About Alternative Medicine (altmedicine.about.com).

■ **Homeopathy is widely accepted** as a complementary therapy, gaining in popularity and often used with traditional medicine. Head for Homeopathy Home (www.homeopathyhome.com), which is the most extensive homeopathic portal on the Web, or browse the information at the Homeopathic Website (simillibus.com).

■ **Herbal medicine has a long tradition, especially in China.** NewCenturyNutrition (www.newcenturynutrition.com) has a Chinese herbal database and more. The Chinese Herb Academy (www.chineseherbacademy.org) is a voluntary body of licensed healthcare practitioners specialising in Chinese herbal medicine. Chinese

Herb Garden (healther.stormloader.com) has scientific articles on Chinese medicines and recipes.

▶ See also **Stay fit and healthy,** p. 270.

SITES SPECIALISING IN COMPLEMENTARY HEALTH MATTERS
Use natural remedies to ease your aches and pains.

BE YOU (www.be-you.com)
Articles, information and resources on a whole range of complementary health and lifestyle topics and issues. You can find local practitioners of a large number of therapies and treatments.

BIORHYTHM GENERATOR (the.sitefoundry.com/biorhythms)
Prepare for your ups and downs in advance with this Biorhythm Generator. Fill in the onscreen form and check out your best days.

THE OFFICIAL DEEPAK CHOPRA WEBSITE (www.chopra.com)
Deepak Chopra's site. Meditation and mindfulness tips from the master.

QUACKWATCH (www.quackwatch.org)
Before you buy that potion or follow the latest offbeat health fad, check it out first.

YAHOO!HEALTH (uk.dir.yahoo.com/health)
Links to thousands of different sites, from apitherapy to yoga.

THE WORLD'S BIGGEST COOKBOOK

Use the Internet to look up new and unusual recipes, put together a personal cookbook or collate your own recipe collection.

■ **There's no need to clutter up your kitchen** with collections of bulky cookbooks. The Internet gives you access to tens of thousands of recipes from all around the world. You can even create your own customised digital cookbook by putting together a unique database of delicious downloaded recipes.

■ **Cooking Christmas dinner,** but can't remember Aunty Vi's cranberry sauce recipe? Just look it up in an online recipe book. Sites such as Delia Online (see box, right) contain hundreds of recipes that you can access anywhere, any time you wish.

■ **Read your favourite cooking magazines online.** Epicurious' cooking site (www.epicurious.com) offers recipes, techniques, cooking tips, guides and glossaries. Other gourmet magazines include Fine Cooking Online (www.taunton.com/finecooking). Helen's British Cooking Site (www.hwatson.force9.co.uk) has a regular magazine feature, and, for a more famous

British cook, try Delia Online (www.delia online.com) It's also worth taking a look at Cuisine magazine's site (www.cuisine magazine.com), with its step-by-step recipes and tips.

■ **Take a cooking course over the Internet.** Today's video streaming technology enables you to view video clips of cooking techniques in your own home. You'll have to pay for some of the courses on offer, but there are also plenty of free ones. Learn basic techniques or try your hand at gourmet cuisine. You'll find a whole catalogue of online cooking courses at World Wide Learn (www.worldwidelearn.com).

RECIPE WEBSITES

Catch the word on the culinary scene and cook up something special for dinner!

COOKING BY NUMBERS (www.cookingbynumbers.com)
Basic cooking tips and suggestions for meals using what you already have in the fridge.

DELIA ONLINE (www.deliaonline.com)
Techniques, tips and recipes from Delia Smith.

DELICIOUS GLOBE (www.deliciousglobe.com)
Links to sites with recipes from every corner of the world, from Lithuanian baked potato pudding to Burmese squid and dandelions.

FOODWEB (www.foodweb.com)
In addition to readers' recipes and recipe cards, this site offers links to food and drink sites, and handy measure conversion charts.

HEALTHY-COOKING.CO.UK (www.healthy-cooking.co.uk)
Low fat recipes for better health.

BBC FOOD (www.bbc.co.uk/food)
An archive of recipes from all your favourite TV cooking shows. Select your favourite small screen chef for a list of his or her top dishes.

■ **Ever wondered what the Vikings ate** when they set off to explore the New World? Or who invented crisps, and why? Taking an historical approach, the Food Timeline (www.gti.net/mocolib1/kid/food.html) tracks the development of food from 17,000 BC to the present day and offers recipes from the various eras. Or would you like to take a virtual culinary tour of the world?
Delicious Globe (www.deliciousglobe .com) provides links to a vast array of Websites with recipes from all over the world. But prepare for some of the links to be out of date!

■ **Can't find yams and want to know what to substitute?** Consult the Cook's Thesaurus (www.foodsubs.com), an encyclopedia covering thousands of ingredients and kitchen tools. As well as the suggested ingredient substitutions, the entries on this useful site include pictures, descriptions and synonyms. There are other online cooking dictionaries that may be useful; try the Good Cooking Website (www.goodcooking.com/diction.htm).

KEEP YOUR HOME UP TO SCRATCH

Do it yourself or find someone else to do it for you on the Web.

■ **The Internet is an enormous how-to manual.** Access a huge range of tips and instructions for just about any home improvement project, from unclogging a drain to roofing a house. Good sites include DIYonline (www.diy online.com), DIY Doctor (www.diydoctor.org.uk), DIYFixIt (www.diyfixit.co.uk), DIY.co.uk (www.diy .co.uk) and Changing Rooms (www.bbc.co.uk /homes/changingrooms). Print out the information and create your own manual for a project.
You can also check out the tips and hints in the At Home section of the Reader's Digest Website (www.readers digest.co.uk/athome/ DIY_intro.htm).

■ **Start looking for the best trades-person** for your home improvement job with the help of the Internet. Good tradespeople can be hard to come by and often word of mouth

is the best way to find a plumber or builder you can trust. However, the Web is a good starting place. Try Tradesmen Online (www.tradesmen-online.net) for trade-by-trade listings of services in different areas of the UK. The site is far from exhaustive, but you may get lucky and find just what you are looking for. The Yellow Pages Website (www.yell.com) is also a useful resource for finding just about any product or service. The Guild of Builders & Contractors also has a Website with listings of tradespeople in different areas (www.buildersguild.co.uk).

HOME IMPROVEMENT INFORMATION SITES
Sites to help you keep your house in tiptop condition.

NATIONAL HOME IMPROVEMENT COUNCIL (www.nhic.org.uk)
Online advice and information for those wishing to undertake DIY and make home improvements.

TOOL UP (www.tool-up.co.uk)
Suppliers of DIY tools and materials online, with over 100,000 items to choose from.

DIY DOCTOR (www.diydoctor.org.uk)
A useful and informative site with DIY tricks and tips and even a 'Cowboy Control' page in association with QuoteCheckers. Become a member and you can have your queries answered by the DIY doctor online.

HOME IMPROVEMENT ENCYCLOPEDIA (www.bhg.com/bhg/category.jhtml? catref=cat10002)
A comprehensive site covering topics such as carpentry and bricklaying, with handy calculators to estimate materials.

HOME IDEAS (www.homeideas.com)
Research that project before you start tearing the house down.

■ **Visit the who's who of glue.** People have a need to glue things to other things, and, as long as they do, they'll find Thistothat (www.thistothat.com) indispensable. This site tells you exactly what glue you need to use to attach

just about any two things together. Manufacturers' specifications on hundreds of glue products are given, as is helpful advice on gluing.

■ **Buy your materials and tools online.** Many major DIY stores can be found on the Internet and you can buy your DIY supplies without leaving home. Try Homebase.co.uk (www.homebase.co.uk), Screwfix.com (www.screwfix.com), B&Q (www.diy.com) or Plumb World (www.plumbworld.co.uk).

■ **Never be stuck for a decorating idea again.** You can look up home decorating ideas from your favourite TV shows online. The BBC Website (www.bbc.co.uk/homes) has pages on its DIY programmes with factsheets and advice, and you can even apply to appear on the shows! The Channel 4 Website also has a section dedicated to its home improvement shows (www.channel4.com/4homes).

■ **See others do it for themselves.** If all that home repair is wearing you out, why not watch someone else doing the hard work for a change? Drop in on a home improvement project on the This Old House Webcam (www.this oldhouse.com). You can check on the progress 24 hours a day and maybe get some inspiration while you're there. There is also a time lapse archive so you can see how the project developed over the course of a previous day's work.

■ **Do-it-yourself feng shui.** Feng shui is the Chinese art of designing your living and working spaces to allow for the harmonious flow of energy, and it has become very popular in the West. To find out more, visit The Ultimate Feng Shui Resource (www.qi-whiz.com) and World of Feng Shui Online (www.wofs.com).

■ **Search for a super sofa.** Once you've finished refurbishing your home, why not fill it with new furniture? Have that new sofa delivered to your door with shops like Furniture Busters (www.furniturebusters.com). Alternatively, order it direct from your favourite store's Website.

■ **Make your own furniture.** Are you reasonably handy with the chisel and plane? You can do it yourself with furniture too – just download plans from design Websites such as Absolutely Free Plans (www.absolutelyfreeplans .com). Also visit a useful page of links to furniture plan Websites provided by Vicnet (home.vicnet.net.au/~woodlink/plans.htm).

▶ See also **Software for the home,** p. 210.

LOOKING AFTER THE GARDEN

Use the Net to design landscaping, order plants and help you to look after your garden.

■ **Don't leave your plants out in the cold.** Make sure your local climate is right for the plants in your garden and always check what the weather has in store before you do any gardening. The Met Office (www. met-office.gov.uk) has regional forecasts for all parts of the UK. On the BBC's weather pages (www.bbc.co.uk/weather) you can even find the weather forecast for your town. Pick the best time to plant spring bulbs or sow the seeds of summer annuals by keeping up to date with the changes in the weather, as well as frost and flooding predictions.

■ **Choose the best plants for home or garden** with a plant finder. You'll find one at the BBC's Gardening site (www.bbc.co.uk/ gardening/plants/plant_finder). It's a database of 1,000 plants with advice on the best time to plant and the ideal light and soil conditions.

People love their pets! Many of the most popular online sites are about keeping pets happy and healthy.

■ **Looking for a pet?** The most humane option is to adopt one from a shelter. Millions of pets worldwide are put down every year due to overpopulation. Start with your local branch of the Royal Society for the Prevention of Cruelty to Animals (www.rspca.org.uk) or check on other shelters that are sometimes run by local authorities or charitable organisations.

■ **There's nothing quite as heartbreaking as losing a pet.** After you have called the local shelters, put signs up around your neighbourhood and placed an advertisement in the local newspaper, you could try the Internet for sites that help locate lost pets. Help Lost Pets (www.helplostpets.com) and Petsearch UK (www.ukpetsearch.freeuk.com) both seek to do this. Also try looking up the Website of your local council – many local authority sites have pages with information and advice on searching for lost pets.

■ **When your pet is sick,** there is help and advice available online. Link2vets (www.link2vets.co.uk) is an online vet search where you can locate a practice in your area. You can consult with an Internet vet at the Online Veterinary Practice (www.onlineveterinarypractice.com) for a fee or post a question on the vet billboard on the Pet Planet site (www.petplanet.co.uk).

■ **A landscape design program** will help you to plan large gardens, letting you try different layouts, suggesting plants and allowing you to model your garden in three dimensions. Landscape designers work best when you have a large area and a lot of plants to organise, and it may not pay to invest in a landscape designer if you only need a few plants. Software can be bought on DVD from 3D Garden Composer (www.gardencomposer.com), or check out the range of gardening software available at Amazon.co.uk (www.amazon.co.uk).

■ **Information on city gardening topics,** such as home composting, wormeries, rooftop gardening and sprouting on your kitchen worktop – can be found on the Internet. One good source of inspiration is the City Farmer's Urban Agriculture Notes Website (www.cityfarmer.org), a nonprofit organic gardening collective that encourages the growth of greenery within our concrete jungles.

■ **Knowledge for experts.** Keen gardeners often develop their interest to become expert botanists with a wide knowledge of plants. The Web has a wealth of information for budding specialists, such as Botany.com's Encyclopedia of Plants (www.botany.com).

GARDENING SITES

Everything's sure to come up roses when you visit these sites.

LET'S GO GARDENING (www.letsgogardening.co.uk)
A packed site with links to other sites selling plants, seeds, garden accessories and furniture. There's also a wealth of information on all aspects of gardening, from planting vegetables to growing exotic palms.

BBC GARDENING (www.bbc.co.uk/gardening)
This site has advice, tips, competitions, message boards and a regular gardening newsletter. There are also links to the home pages of all your favourite BBC gardening TV and radio shows.

ROYAL HORTICULTURAL SOCIETY (www.rhs.org.uk)
Founded in 1804, the Royal Horticultural Society is now one of the world's leading horticultural organisations. Their site has gardening advice and event listings.

GARDENLINKS (www.gardenlinks.ndo.co.uk)
An online directory providing hundreds of categorised links to UK gardening online. Find sites that offer gardening advice, gardening products, celebrity gardeners, horticultural courses and gardens to visit.

CARRY ON GARDENING (www.carryongardening.org.uk)
This site aims to offer easy ways of gardening, especially for those who may find it difficult because of accident, illness, disability or the problems associated with growing older.

HDRA (www.hdra.org.uk)
The Henry Doubleday Research Association is dedicated to researching and promoting organic gardening, farming and food. The site has advice and information on tending to an organic garden, ecological pest control and garden waste recycling.

There's no need to leave your pet behind when you go on holiday! Travel Pets (www.travelpets.com) lists over 20,000 pet-friendly bed and breakfasts, inns, hotels, motels and resorts throughout the world, with many listings for the UK. For local accommodation that will accept pets, try typing phrases like 'dogs welcome' or 'pets welcome' into your favourite search engine. Some search engines, such as Google (www.google.co.uk), allow you to limit your search to sites from the UK only.

TAKING THE STRESS OUT OF WEDDINGS

Weddings can be anxious times. But don't fret if you're about to walk up the aisle – help is at hand.

The best day of your life means getting hitched, not hitting a hitch! Online services (see panel, right) can help you with the planning. Have a look at Smart Wedding Planner Software for Windows (www.smartwedding.com) with its guest list manager and expense tracker, among other useful utilities.

Send e-mail invitations. Cheaper than using the post, this high-tech method can also be more fun. Look for free e-mail software that allows you to send cartoons or other graphics together with the message. Alternatively, you can simply attach a photo file of the happy couple.

Design your own wedding album in Word. Style your pages using words and fonts of your choice, then go to **Insert ➔ Picture ➔ From File** and pull in the photos. Use scanned pictures or download shots from a digital camera. You can also crop and change your photos using Windows' built-in accessory program Paint.

Find your perfect wedding music on the Web. There are plenty of sites with suggestions and helpful tips. The Wedding Music Company (www.weddingmusic.co.uk) provides professional musicians and wedding music CDs. For more ideas, check out the top-selling wedding music CDs at Quality Books.co.uk (www.qualitybooks.co.uk/music/wedding/htm) or the favourite songs at Wedding Tips Online (www.weddingtips.com/wtfavori.html).

If friends and family are scattered far and wide, beam the ceremony live across the Net. Using a webcam and a laptop running Windows 98 or higher, send the video to a Website that will host it. Most ISPs offer a Web hosting service, although you may have to pay a little bit extra for it.

Your wedding video is only a mouse-click away. Windows XP has its own video-editing application, called Windows Movie Maker. It is a fairly basic editor that captures video (as well as still images and audio), slices footage into segments so you can rearrange them in any order you want, and then can convert the finished video to a highly compressed format so you can e-mail it as an attachment, or post it on the Web.

▶ See also **Scanners and scanning,** p. 40; **Cameras join the digital revolution,** p. 44; **Live pictures over the Web,** p. 252; and **Understanding e-mail,** p. 316.

GOD MOVES IN MYSTERIOUS WAYS

Gather information about the world's religions, study scripture or find a place to worship near you.

Search classic scripture texts online. The Internet is a powerful resource for comparing and researching texts. Whether you're a serious student, or just curious to know more about a certain religion, try the Academic Info Website (www.academicinfo.net/religindex.html). It has a comprehensive guide to the study of many different religions.

WEDDING SITES
Make it a day to remember when you organise your wedding on the Web.

HITCHED.CO.UK (www.hitched.co.uk)
Provides information and advice on every aspect of getting married, from the engagement through to the honeymoon. There is also a diary planning wizard that timetables the preparations for the big day.

WEDDING SERVICE UK (www.wedding-service.co.uk)
An online directory to wedding services throughout the UK. Search by location or click on a subject link for listings of services available in different parts of the country.

WEDDINGS.CO.UK (www.weddings.co.uk)
On this site there's wedding information and articles, online bridal collections, a discussion forum, links to products and services and free wedding planner software.

ALTERNATIVE WEDDINGS (www.alternative-weddings.com)
If you're looking for a unique, exclusive or unusual venue for the big day, or fancy a themed wedding, then check out this site.

■ **When using a search engine to find religious links,** it makes sense to enter the name of the religion you want. If you're unsure about the religious base of an enquiry, or are looking for something more general, some of the best metasites are sponsored by academic institutions. Try Duke University Department of Religion (www.duke.edu/religion) and Syracuse University (www.syr.edu/index.html).

■ **Check the date of all the major religious holidays** so you can wish your friends and business associates a happy Diwali or Rosh Hoshanah on the right day each year. Whatever your friends' religion, the Calendar Zone (www.calendarzone.com/Religious) can provide an online list of holidays. Or try the Interfaith Calendar (www.interfaithcalendar.org).

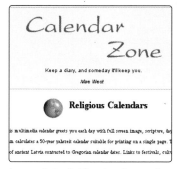

Calendar Zone

Keep a diary, and someday it'll keep you.
Mae West

● **Religious Calendars**

This multimedia calendar greets you each day with full screen image, scripture, day
It calculates a 50-year yahrzeit calendar suitable for printing on a single page. T
of ancient Latvia contrasted to Gregorian calendar dates. Links to festivals, cult

■ **Find a retreat or meditation centre** geared to your interest, location or spiritual path. Metta.org.uk (www.metta.org.uk/retreats.asp) lists Buddhist meditation and other retreat centres in the UK. The Circle of Light Website (www.circleoflight.co.uk) offers a number of different retreat weekends in the UK and abroad. Search The Retreat Company's site (www.retreat-co.co.uk) for the type of retreat you're interested in and the location of where you would like to go. Alternatively, learn how to meditate online at the Breathing Space (www.bspace.co.uk).

■ **Need to know the answer to questions** like 'How many Pentacostalists were there living in the UK in 1996?' or 'What percentage of the world is Zoroastrian?'? Visit Adherents.com (www.adherents.com), a research organisation offering over 40,000 different statistics and geography citations. You will find references to published membership/adherent statistics, and also the congregation statistics for over 4,200 religions, churches, denominations and religious bodies.

■ **Pray online.** Get a live view of the Western Wall in Jerusalem at Aish Ha Torah's Window on the Wall (aish.com/wallcam). The site also offers an Internet service for people who are

not in Jerusalem who wish to place a note in the Wall. Just enter your prayer in the specified box on the site. It will be printed out and placed in the Wall for you.

■ **Interested in exploring Islam?** The Web offers huge resources for anyone interested in the Islamic faith. Visit Islam World (www.islamworld.net), Al-Islam (www.al-islam.com) or IslamiCity (www.islamicity.com) and explore the immense resources offered by these sites, with links to many more.

■ **If you aren't quite sure which way to face for Mecca,** or exactly which time to pray, log onto Salam Iran (www.salamiran.org/Religion/Praytime). All you have to do is enter your location and the Website will point you in the direction of Mecca and also give you the times for daily prayers.

■ **The world of the Buddha.** Begin your voyage along the path to inner peace at DharmaNet International (www.dharmanet.org), one of the largest Buddhist Websites on the Net. Those with interests in particular branches of Buddhism can also pursue their studies online. Tibetan Buddhists, for example, can find links at The World Wide Web Virtual Library (home.it.net.au/~murrayk/tib-centers.html). For local links, try Buddhanet (buddhanet.net/euro_dir/eur_uki1.htm) or The Network of Buddhist Organisations (UK) (www.nbo.org.uk).

SCRIPTURE WEBSITES
Practice your faith from wherever you are in the world.

THE BIBLE GATEWAY (bible.gospelcom.net)
A Biblical scripture site with nine different versions of the Bible.

HUMANITIES TEXT INITIATIVE (www.hti.umich.edu)
Peruse the Book of Mormon at the University of Michigan's Website.

ISKCON (www.iskcon.org)
A chapter-by-chapter translation of the Bhagavad-Gita at ISKCON, the Krishna site.

ISLAMICITY (www.islamicity.com)
Search the Koran in Arabic or English or hear any sura (passage) recited on audiofile.

JEWISH TORAH AUDIO (www.613.org)
Study the Torah in Hebrew or English, or view the collection of Torah audio and video files.

FIND A CHURCH (www.findachurch.co.uk)
Travelling around the country? Use this Website to find a local Christian church.

▋Researching your family tree

The Web makes researching your family tree so much easier. A lot of information is available online, from church records to census data. There are also online genealogical societies and libraries offering all sorts of data and tips. So here is some advice to help your research bear fruit.

GETTING STARTED

Begin with yourself. Write down your name, birth date, place of birth and parents' names. If you are married, record your spouse's name, and the date and place of your wedding. Note your children's names and their dates of birth. Do the same for all the other relatives you know of. Before you know it, you'll have the makings of a tree.

Quiz any living relatives for first-hand accounts and recollections. All those stories your grandparents told you when you were a child could come in handy now! When you've found out as much as you can about your family history, it's time to begin following up your leads online.

Your genealogical information can be broken down into individual family groups: your family, your mother's family, your father's family and so on. To help you organise all this mass of information, keep a group sheet and a pedigree chart for each family in your line. Several companies produce ready-made pedigree charts that you can just fill in.

Start with a simple search. As a first step, enter the names that interest you into one of the genealogy search engines to see what turns up. Ancestry.com (www.ancestry.com) is a US site, but its content is global. The Ancestry World Tree contains over 84 million names! To begin searching in the UK and Ireland, try UK Genealogy (www.ukgenealogy.co.uk) or GenUKI (www.genuki.org.uk).

Keep print-outs of your research information for further study offline – the more involved you get in your hobby, the more you'll find yourself travelling in the pursuit of knowledge! Even if you keep records on a handheld PC or laptop, it's worth having print-outs available.

ONLINE DETECTIVE WORK

Find out if anyone else has already researched your surname or family history. For links to sites and Usenet groups (see also *Newsgroups*, p. 334) to help with a particular name, check out RootsWeb (www.rootsweb.com).

Many of the Websites and Usenet groups covered have message boards and you can follow the **Message Boards** link on the site to find postings made in different areas of the UK and the world.

If you're researching an unusual surname, try typing it into one of the regular search engines such as Yahoo! or Anzwers. You may be lucky enough to find a long lost family member out there with a Website or home page all of their own.

Cut down on search engine time. Many genealogical Websites have done the donkey work for you by gathering together

GENEALOGY PROGRAMS
Give your research a kickstart with this handy software.

ANCESTRAL QUEST (www.ancestralquest.com)
Family tree software designed for Windows.

BROTHER'S KEEPER (www.bkwin.net)
Shareware for the novice genealogist.

CLOOZ (www.clooz.com)
An electronic filing cabinet to help organise your genealogical records.

FAMILY REUNION (www.famware.com)
A download from the Web (there is a fee) that collates all your family data for you.

FAMILY TREE MAKER (www.genealogy.com/soft_ftm.html)
A very popular family tree program.

THE MASTER GENEALOGIST (www.whollygenes.com)
Comprehensive genealogy software.

collections of useful links. One such site is Genealogylinks.net (www.genealogylinks.net). It has links to over 7,000 sites, giving you access to everything from cemetery records and parish registers to censuses. Genealogy-Links.co.uk (www.genealogy-links.co.uk) also provides links to hundreds of useful sites in the United Kingdom. For those of Scottish, Irish or Welsh descent, try the Scottish Family Research site (www. lineages.co.uk), Irish Insight (www.irish-insight.com/a2z-genealogy) or GenDocs (www.gendocs.demon .co.uk/wales.html).

OVERCOME OBSTACLES

Remember that place names change over time. Knowing the exact town or city your ancestor was living in can make the difference between finding a record and coming up with a blank. Try searching a site such as the Gazetteer of British Places Names (www.gazetteer. co.uk). It has over 50,000 entries with commonly accepted alternative spellings, as well as Welsh and Gaelic versions.

USE GOVERNMENT RESOURCES

Start with your local library. Such is the interest in genealogical research, that most libraries in the UK provide some resources for family history research, often with useful advice and guidance for beginners. Start with the British Library (www.bl.uk). After that, move on to local or regional libraries. The UK Public Libraries Page (dspace.dial.pipex.com/town/square/ac940/ ukpublib.html) has links to hundreds of UK public libraries on the Web. Libraries Online (www. libraries-online.com) also has useful links to UK and international libraries.

Archives offices are invaluable resources for tracking down historical information. The national archive of England, Wales and the UK is the Public Records Office (www.pro.gov.uk). Not all of the records are available online but some can be downloaded.

MAKE THE MOST OF YOUR PC

Your computer could be your most valuable tool! As well as using it for group and pedigree sheets, you can also download programs to create your own family tree or

ancestral and descendancy charts. Try Legacy (www.legacyfamilytree.com), which has a range of comprehensive and easy-to-use family history software free to download (see p. 278 for other useful sites). Alternatively, you could try using Ancestry.com's online family tree organiser (www.ancestry.com) which incorporates several specialist search engines and useful historic document retrieval facilities.

Scan in any first-hand data you can, such as photographs, birth, marriage and death certificates, and even correspondence. It's a handy way to keep a record of what you have, without constantly having to shuffle through files.

You could even create your own Website of results and queries – who knows what contacts you could make through an online presence. Maybe some unknown third cousin twice removed will suddenly drop you an e-mail.

See also **Building a system**, p. 164; **Creating a Website**, p. 228; and **Share your interests with others**, p. 329.

TOP TEN RESEARCH TIPS
Handy hints to help you trace your roots.

1. Contact living relatives for assistance.
2. Get to know the history of the area in which you are conducting research.
3. Use period-appropriate maps of the area where your ancestors were living.
4. Use family group sheets and pedigree charts or group sheet software to help organise your data.
5. Don't gather information on everyone with the surname you are researching, unless it is an uncommon name.
6. Don't forget that the spelling of surnames can evolve over time.
7. Use common sense when reading family histories. If a source for information is not listed, be cautious about accepting it – it could be hearsay.
8. Use primary sources, such as land, probate, church and county records, and rely on printed histories.
9. Keep a master copy of your data somewhere safe in case you lose anything. When you're travelling for research purposes, take a duplicate copy of your information.
10. Persevere – it's worth it in the end!

Arts, entertainment and recreation

WHAT YOU NEED IS A HOBBY

Bored? Watching too much TV? You need an interest, and the Internet is there to help you find one.

■ **The first place to look is in a directory.** DMOZ (dmoz.com) and About.com (www.about.com) are two of the best for listing hobby resources, newsgroups and information about almost every recreation imaginable.

■ **Don't be alone, join a sports club.** Head to the UK Sports Directory (www.sportslinks. info) to discover listings of hundreds of clubs all around the UK devoted to every kind of activity, from badminton to powerboat racing. Or check out BritishSports.com (www.britishsports.com). Select the sport you're interested in and this site will not only display links to clubs around the UK, but also links to associations and governing bodies for the sport, as well as information sites.

■ **Get outside and into action even faster.** Search the metasites. GORP (www.gorp.com) offers over 100,000 pages on everything outdoors, from exotic international destinations, ranging from Antarctica to Tibet, to more accessible outdoor environments, such as Italian hill towns or national parks. If you really want a challenge, try one of the adventure travel sites, such as Wild Dog (www.wild-dog.com). There you can sign yourself up to do almost anything, from climbing, canoeing, mountain biking and caving to dog sledding, camel trekking and elephant-back safari.

■ **Feeling arty?** There are thousands of sites worldwide devoted to just about every form of creative art known, from the International Guild of Glass Artists (www.igga.org) to Ceramic Art (karaart.com/ceramic/index.html).

■ **Are you a coin collector?** You can use the Web to find out more about your treasures. To see if that ancient coin you purchased in an alley in Damascus is real or a clever fake, check with the Coin Shop (emporium.turnpike .net/M/mikec/index.htm) or Numismatica (www.limunltd.com/numismatica).

■ **Become an expert.** Turn your casual hobby into a serious interest by using resources on the Net. Visit the British Wildlife Guide (www.tiscali.co.uk/ reference/encyclopaedia/wildlife/ invertebrates_contents.html) to discover what that sea creature was that you spotted in a tidal pool. Find out about sea shells at Conchology (www.conchology. uunethost.be).

■ **Simply out of this world!** You can collect lumps of outer space from the Meteorite Shop (www .meteoriteshop.com) and Meteorite Central

(www.meteoritecentral. com). Want to know more? Find out which planet you've bought a piece of at New England Meteoritical Services (www.meteorlab.com/homepage.htm).

■ **Pieces of eight...** You won't find pirate maps with X marking the spot, but there are lots of treasure hunting tips to be gleaned from the

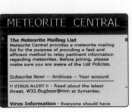

ARTS AND CRAFTS
Get in touch with your creative side.

UK ARTS AND CRAFTS (www.ukartsncrafts.com)
Read the articles and use the directory to find other art and craft related Websites.

CRAFTS BEAUTIFUL (www.crafts-beautiful.com)
Online version of popular craft magazine. The site has stories, practical articles and a monthly news archive.

CRAFT GALLERY (www.craftgallery.co.uk)
An online collection of contemporary arts and crafts. Exhibit your creations on the site or browse the gallery to search for items you would like to buy.

ALL ABOUT CRAFTS (www.allaboutcrafts.co.uk)
Buy your art, craft and hobby supplies online at this site.

TOP 100 CRAFT SITES REPORT (www.artcraftmarketing.com/topsites /index.htm)
This site claims to update the top 100 report every 30 minutes and reset it every seven days. It lists sites selling craft supplies and products, offering free patterns and downloadable projects.

Web. Check out Lost Treasure Online (www.losttreasure.com) or Shipwreck Internet Resources (main.blclinks.net/~sshort/shipwrecked/swlinks.htm) for likely locations to start. For newsgroups, go to Treasure Net (www.treasurenet.com).

Go out with a bang!

If your hobby involves countdowns and complex discussions on the merits of various flammable propellants, look up Rocketry.Org (www.rocketry.org) for information on amateur and experimental rocketry. To get technical, try Rocket Equations (www.execpc.com/~culp/rockets/rckt_eqn.html).

Hot to try firewalking?

Firewalk with John Shango (shangofire.com) takes you through the steps required. Or consult Tolly Burkan, the father of firewalking (www.firewalking.com). Learn all about the psychology and preparation required before you take your first steps. You can even order instructional videos.

Are you a rail enthusiast

who can't get enough of snorting steam locomotives and elegant wooden carriages? There are plenty of sites out there to spur on your interest. Try Historic Steam Models (www.steammodels.co.uk) or Steam Dreams (www.steamdreams.co.uk). You can sign up to join the Vintage Trains Society at www.vintagetrains.co.uk or offer to do some volunteer work maintaining and restoring trains, fundraising or helping out at a visitors centre.

PARADISE FOR THE MOVIE FAN

Movie reviews, show times in your area, information on your favourite film celebrities, and made-for-PC movies – it's all at your fingertips.

Coming soon from a PC near you.

The major film studios have their own Websites listing current and upcoming movie releases, as well as news and information on casting and pre-production on yet-to-be-made movies. Visit 20th Century Fox (www.fox.co.uk), Paramount (www.paramount.com), Universal Pictures (www.universalpictures.com), Warner Bros (www2.warnerbros.com) or MGM (www.mgm.com) to see what's due for release. Also try the MovieWeb site (www.movieweb.com/movie/links.html) for links to the sites of these and other major Hollywood film studios.

Want to know what's on and where to see it?

Try Firstmovies (www.firstmovies.com). Or visit the Scoot Cinema finder (www.scoot.co.uk/cinemafinder), input the name of the movie you want to see and the town you're in and the site lists the local cinemas where the film is showing. Alternatively, try the Websites of the major cinema chains, such as Odeon (www.odeon.co.uk) and Warner Village Cinemas (www.warnervillage.co.uk) for film listings and online ticket booking.

Watch the trailers of upcoming movies

at the Coming Soon site (www.comingsoon.net). The release dates are listed for the US, which usually means the UK release date will be some time later, so you really do have the chance to see the trailers well in advance.

Get all the latest movie gossip

at a famous and influential fan sight. Ain't It Cool News site (www.aintitcool.com) has all the latest news, movie reviews and discussion forums.

Want to know more about local films?

Try the Britfilms site (www.britfilms.com), which has an online database of British films made from 1998. Also check out the British Film Institute's top 100 British films of the 20th Century (www.bfi.org.uk/features/bfi100).

MOVIE MAGIC

Check out the latest movie news, reviews and celebrity gossip.

E! ONLINE (www.eonline.com)
Packed with movie news, gossip and features on big screen stars past and present, as well as coverage of all the major award ceremonies and prize-winner predictions.

EMPIRE ONLINE (www.empireonline.co.uk)
The online version of the popular UK movie magazine offers news, competitions, reviews, features and an online store.

THE FLYING INKPOT'S INCREDIBLE MOVIE LINKS PAGE (inkpot.com/movielinks)
Hundreds of links to movie-related sites, offering magazine and newspaper reviews, screenwriting resources, film festival information and cult movie facts.

INTERNET MOVIE DATABASE (www.imdb.com)
A searchable database of information on thousands of movies. Great for film facts.

Many small studios are making short films with original and innovative content just for the Web. Download a short film to take a break during a stressful day or just broaden your horizons and see something different. Atomfilms (www.atomfilms.com), ifilm (www.ifilm.com), iMovies (www.imovies.com) and Mediatrip (www.mediatrip.com) are just some of the sites that allow you to download original movies to your PC for free.

The Internet Movie Database (www.imdb.com) is the online movie reference site. Started back in 1990 on the rec.arts.movies newsgroup, the site catalogues information on more than 200,000 different movie and TV shows, as well as 400,000 actors, 40,000 directors, and hundreds of thousands of production people.

Use it to settle a family argument about a movie, or track down that half-forgotten film that you now want to watch so badly.

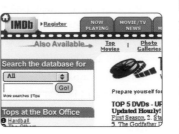

MUSIC TO SUIT EVERY TASTE

Find a score of the music that's been going around in your head, check out next weekend's gigs or simply listen to the latest single.

Sample CDs before you buy from online stores, listen to online concerts, and tune in to live and archived radio broadcasts from around the world with an audio player. You will need to download RealOne Player (www.real.com) or Media Player (www.microsoft.com/windows /windowsmedia/players.asp). To run an auxiliary MP3 player, download Winamp (www.winamp. com). For music shareware, head straight to Hitsquad at www.hitsquad.com/smm.

Feel the urge to go to a concert? Find out who's playing where at Bigmouth (www.bigmouth.co.uk). The site lists all the major tours and artists currently gigging in the UK. Search by town at the Aloud Website (www.aloud.com) for listings of concerts in your local area. Alternatively, search the Net for a guide to your town or city to see the concerts happening locally.

To purchase CDs locally, try CD Wow (www3.cd-wow.com), 101cd.com (www. 101cd.com), Amazon (www.amazon.co.uk), Ebay (www.ebay.co.uk), Tower Records (uk.towerrecords.com) or CD Zone (www. cdzone.co.uk). To buy overseas (provided that the exchange rate is favourable) try Best Music Buys (www.bestwebbuys.com/music),

Virgin Megastore (www.virginmega.com), CD Universe (www.cduniverse.com) or Fun Records (funrec.de/shop).

Use a search engine to answer all your musical questions. The MusicSearch site (www.musicsearch.com) is one of the most comprehensive guides on the Web. Along with a search engine wholly dedicated to music, there are extensive lists categorised by artist, genre, instrument and events.

Having trouble remembering who sang Louie Louie? Never fear, several Websites are available to help you. Among the best is Songfile (www.songfile.com) which can also help you to track down recordings and sheet music.

Rock fans are not the only music lovers on the Internet. There are many sites exclusively devoted to classical music. Classical Music UK (www.classicalmusic.co.uk) is one such site, with features, articles and listings of classical music concerts throughout the UK. Classical Net (www.classical.net) features thousands of CD reviews and links to other classical music Websites. The All Classics site (www.pmclassical. iicinternet.com) has a large range of musical masterpieces in MP3 file format to transform your desktop into a concert hall.

MUSIC SITES
Hit the right note with these sites.

DOT MUSIC (www.dotmusic.com)
Music news, reviews, chart information and upcoming release dates, streaming videos and music downloads.

CLASSICAL MUSIC UK (www.classicalmusic.co.uk)
Features, giveaways and a classical music listings calendar with dates of concerts around the UK.

NME.COM (www.nme.com)
The Website of the best-known music weekly. The site has an artists index, news, interviews, features and reviews, as well as bulletin boards and a chat room.

ROYAL ACADEMY OF MUSIC (www.ram.ac.uk)
Find out about courses and how to apply to this prestigious music school. There's also a calendar of events, festivals and concerts at the Academy.

COMPUTER MUSIC (www.computermusic.co.uk)
Guide to making music on PCs and Macs.

Opera buffs can indulge their passion on the Net too. To find out about performances, go to the Website of the Royal Opera House (www.royalopera.org) or by using the events calendar on the English National Opera's site (www.eno.org). You can even plan your holidays around live performances by using The Worldwide Opera & Concert Information Service (www.wocis.com), which will take care of your bookings and travel arrangements. The transcripts for hundreds of operas – in original languages and translation – can be found at Bob's Opera World (www.castle.net/~rfrone/operas/operas.htm) and at E-libretti (www.geocities.com/voyerju/libretti.html).

▶ See also **Digital music players**, p. 37; **MP3: the new face of music,** p. 203; **Explore the world of MP3,** p 285; and **The shareware alternative,** p. 304.

WELCOME TO TV ON THE WEB

Enjoy TV? Of course you do, and you can also discover all kinds of useful information about it on that other global medium – the Net.

Want to know when your favourite TV show is on air? Don't have a TV guide? There are lots of listings sites. Try the Radio Times (www.radiotimes.co.uk), for example, or Ananova (www.ananova.com/tv). Yahoo! also has a TV guide (uk.tv.yahoo.com) with listings for terrestrial and major cable channels. Or go to the Websites of the major television channels where you'll find full programme listings: BBC (www.bbc.co.uk/whatson), ITV (www.itv.com), Channel 4 (www.channel4.com), Five (www.channel5.co.uk) and Sky (www.skynow.co.uk)

Want to relive your favourite Seinfeld episodes, yet again? Several sites offer episode guides to popular TV shows. Most cover American TV but with so many US imports popular in the UK, you're bound to find plenty of information on one of your favourite series. Try Epguides.com (epguides.com), EpisodeGuides (www.episodeguides.com) and Television Without Pity (www.televisionwithoutpity.com).

Go game show crazy. UK Game Shows.com (www.ukgameshows.com) has an A to Z listing of TV game shows past and present. Indulge in a little nostalgia by looking up your favourite game shows from the past or try to get on TV by looking at the contestant calls page.

Watch live TV on your computer with Live TV (www.comfm.com/live/tv). Live TV lets you watch live video feeds that come direct from hundreds of different TV stations.

Switch to the digital age. Get the facts about digital television hot off the Net. The government's digital television Website (www.digitaltv.culture.gov.uk) has information about the government's policies for digital television. The BBC now offers a number of digital services which you can look up at their site: www.bbc.co.uk/digital. The What Satellite and Digital TV site (www.wotsat.com) provides the latest news on digital and satellite TV services in the UK.

Get out of the house to watch the box and visit a TV museum. If you want to find out more about TV production and the history of television, check out what's on offer at the The National Museum of Photography by visiting their Website (www.nmpft.org.uk).

TRIVIA IS JUST FOR FUN

Useless knowledge fascinates us all, and where better than the Internet to seek a treasure trove of trivia questions and answers?

Did you know elephants can't jump? For more unusual information about animals, people and just about anything else you can think of, try one of the many trivia sites on the Net. Pick up a few nuggets at the Fun Facts site (www.funfacts.co.uk) to impress and entertain your friends and colleagues. Also try the custom made insults – it's just for fun but not

---

NEWS OF THE TV WORLD
Can't get enough TV? Track down your favourite shows and stars on the Web.

TV CREAM (www.tv.cream.org)
Re-discover long-dead TV programmes, enjoy your favourite TV theme tunes and see the old BBC and ITV channel logos.

EASTENDERS (www.bbc.co.uk/eastenders)
CORONATION STREET (www.coronationstreet.co.uk)
Catch up on the latest dramas on the Street and in the Square at these soap-opera sites.

E!ONLINE (www.eonline.com)
Packed full of celebrity news and gossip.

THE FRIENDS PLACE (www.friendsplace.com)
This Website allows you to read every script of every episode of the extremely popular TV series, *Friends*. A site for serious fans.

SIT.COM (www.mgnet.karoo.net)
Test your sitcom knowledge with an online quiz and search the archives for your favourite sitcoms and comedy characters.

GONNA (www.gonna.co.uk)
Catch up on the latest celebrity gossip and visit the television page for small screen news.

recommended for children. Test your knowledge at the Fun Trivia site (www.funtrivia.com) with hundreds of quizzes on different subjects.

■ **Beef up your movie knowledge** with the help of the inexhaustible reference source that is the Internet Movie Database (www.imdb.com). If you want to know who was in what movie and when, or just about any fact related to the movies, this is the best place to start your search.

If you don't find what you're looking for, just try entering the terms 'film' or 'movies' in one of the search engines.

■ **Test your movie knowledge** once you've done your research, by trying the quizzes at the Cool Quiz Website (www.coolquiz.com/quizzes). There's a movie trivia quiz, a movie poster quiz and a sound clip quiz that plays snippets of dialogue which you have to match to the correct movie. This site has a mass of other trivia, quizzes and fun facts too.

ONLINE VIDEO EXPANDS YOUR HORIZONS

Get the most out of your PC's multimedia capabilities by watching video clips online.

■ **Streaming is the process** by which your PC downloads digitised video from the Web and plays it back without waiting for the whole file to download. The data streams almost directly from the Internet onto your computer screen. This means that the waiting time before you see the video is reduced and that you don't need to store large files on your hard drive.

■ **To watch video on your PC,** you need to download the appropriate player from one of the main video format software companies. In fact, you should install all three of the main players – RealOne Player (see 'How to', below), Microsoft Windows Media Player and Apple Quicktime – because video content on the Web generally needs a specific player.

How to: Download RealOne and play a video clip

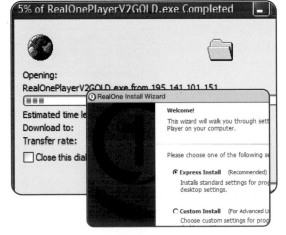

1 Go to uk.real.com and click on the **Free RealOne Player** link. Click on the **Download Now** button for the basic player. Select a location option and click to start the download. In the next dialogue box click **Save** and find a place to save it on your PC.

2 Once the download is complete click **Open** in the dialogue box to install, then follow the Wizard, choosing the **Express Install** option. Restart your computer to complete the process. Then go to **Start ➜ All Programs ➜ RealOne Player** to launch the player.

3 RealOne Player includes a list of Channels that you can access for the latest video news, music and entertainment channels. Click on a link and enjoy the show!

■ **Install the players** and you'll be ready to start watching online video. The free players plug into your standard Web browser and they will automatically activate themselves whenever you click on a compatible video clip. They'll manage the process of streaming the data file to your computer and showing it on your monitor.

■ **There is a host of free material available for you to watch online,** thanks to competition between the three main suppliers of streaming video. The most popular of these are music videos, movie trailers and TV news channels. The Website of each video software company provides lots of links to video content. You can also use your players to listen to online radio stations. RealOne Player has hundreds of online radio stations around the world that you can tune into.

■ **To work effectively,** streaming audio and video requires a consistently good quality connection to the Internet. If the servers are busy or if there are problems with your line quality, the content may occasionally pause or get blocky. These blocks are called artifacts because they are the remains of previous images that haven't been updated because of the data delay. Turn off any background browsing or downloading that might be 'stealing' bandwidth from the streaming content.

EXPLORE THE WORLD OF MP3

MP3 is a digital music format that compresses large audio files into smaller, near CD quality, files.

■ **With minimal effort, you can track down your favourite songs** on MP3 sites and download them to your computer or portable MP3 player. MP3s also make it extremely easy to transport music around. For example, the classic Beach Boys song 'God Only Knows' would fill up 29 MB of hard drive space as a standard CD file and take almost two hours to download with a 56 Kbps modem. When converted to MP3 format,

this same file is just over 3 MB, one-tenth the size. The music still remains high quality – the compression process is extremely clever, and, to most people, a high-quality MP3 is very hard to distinguish from an uncompressed CD track.

■ **We usually associate MP3 with music,** but there are also popular spoken-word selections, such as Audible.com (www.audible.com). Audio books, newspapers and jokes are also easily available.

■ **While MP3s are surrounded by controversy,** they are in no way illegal. In the same way that you can make a tape of a music CD, you can make an MP3 copy of any CD you own, so long as it's for your own use. Distributing MP3s, though, is illegal, unless you own the copyright or the songs are in the public domain. There are numerous file-sharing sites, such as Audio Galaxy (www.audiogalaxy.com) and they come and go with great frequency. You could also try downloading LimeWire file sharing software (www.limewire.com).

■ **To play MP3 files,** you'll need at least a 75 MHz Pentium processor computer with 16 MB of RAM, a 16-byte sound card, a CD-ROM drive and speakers or headphones. Creating MP3 files requires a 133 Mhz Pentium processor, or better,

MP3s ON THE INTERNET
Music used to be hard to find on the Web. Now, MP3s are everywhere.

MP3.com (www.mp3.com)
Hitsquad (www.hitsquad.com)
Liquid Audio (www.liquidaudio.com)
Look4MP3 (www.look4mp3.com)
SoundClick (www.soundclick.com)
Peoplesound (www.peoplesound.com)
Audiogalaxy (www.audiogalaxy.com)
MP3s4free (www.mp3s4free.net)
Easy Music Download (www.easymusicdownload.com)

with 32 MB of RAM. You'll also need a lot of hard drive space to store MP3 files – they may be small, but even at 3–5 MB per file, you can fill up a hard disk very quickly. It is reasonable to budget a couple of gigabytes of hard disk space for your MP3s or plan to store them on Zip disks or CD-ROMs.

■ **Windows XP has its own MP3 software,** called Media Player. You can launch Media Player by going to **Start** ➜ **All Programs** ➜ **Windows Media Player**. If you use it often, the program will automatically appear in the Start menu. If you use an older version of  Windows you can download the most up-to-date Media Player software at the Microsoft Website (www.microsoft.com/windowsmedia). Or there are other MP3 players such as Winamp (www.winamp.com) or MusicMatch Jukebox (www.musicmatch.com) available as free downloads from the Web.

■ **Once you start to accumulate** a collection of MP3s, you'll need more than just a player; in fact, you'll need a whole jukebox. Luckily, jukeboxes are easy to download and some are available for free (although, you may find that it's worth paying a small amount of money to get more features). MP3 jukeboxes organise your collection and playlist, look up track listings, search your hard drive for media files and more. Download RealJukebox from Real (www.real.com), Musicmatch jukebox from Musicmatch (www.musicmatch.com) or check other players at www.mp3machine.com/win/PLAYERS.

■ **Perhaps even more popular than downloading** the actual files is listening to streaming MP3 online radio stations. Windows Media Player has a Radio Tuner built-in. You can select the category of music you want to hear, and the program automatically seeks out the stations playing that type of music. You can also do keyword searches for stations and add them to a handy My Stations page.

If you're planning a Karaoke night, there are shareware plug-ins available that try to remove the vocals from your MP3 files so that you can sing along instead. Vocal Remover (www.analogx.com/contents/download/audio.htm) is

available in Winamp format – you need Winamp 2.0 or higher, a stereo system and high byte rate. It can also remove some of the instrumentals.

You may find that you want to edit your MP3s. Most songs that you download have a few seconds of silence on either end. These sounds of silence can not only spoil a party for an aspiring DJ, but they also take up valuable hard drive space. Although MP3s have a small file size, multiply those silences by a hundred and the amount of wasted space is quite noticeable. Trim the fat with MP3Trim – available from Rocket Download (www.rocketdownload.com) and Logiccell.com (www.logiccell.com/~mp3trim). This is a free program that lets you remove unwanted sound and silence from the start and end of an

MP3 file. It has features such as auto detect silence and preview so you can hear your new edited version before saving.

When encoding MP3 files, be sure to use a high enough byte rate to produce good quality music. For most people, this means using a byte rate of 128 Kbps or higher. Anything below that and the treble tends to sound thin. Byte rates above 128 Kbps give higher quality, but of course, the file sizes are correspondingly larger. If you're not getting decent music at 160 Kbps, you need a better encoder. Encoding programs, such as RealJukebox and iCast, are available on the Net at Websites such as MP3.com (www.mp3.com).

▶ See also **Digital music players,** p. 37; **MP3: the new face of music,** p. 203; **The world of online radio,** p. 259; and **Music to suit every taste,** p. 282.

GREAT MUSEUMS OF THE WORLD

Tour the world's most interesting exhibits and collections, and shop from a museum store – all from your living room.

Take a virtual tour of the world's museums. Even if you don't have the time or money to travel, you can still visit thousands of museums without leaving home. Virtual museums let you research and experience art, collections and exhibits from all over the world. For links to online museums, visit MuseumStuff.com (www.museumstuff.com) or ICOM (www.icom.org). MuseumStuff also has an one of the most complete lists of museum links, all organised by subject.

Visit some of the great British Museums, and the smaller ones too. To find museums in the UK check out Museum Net (www.museums.co.uk) and search for a museum by key word, postcode or town. Or try the Museum Documentation Association's online list of UK Museums (www.mda.org.uk/vlmp).

If you want pictures of celebrated works of art, the National Gallery's Website (www.nationalgallery.org.uk) has hundreds of famous paintings for you to peruse. Copies of the artworks can be made for non-commercial personal use and you can download the images as a desktop pattern or to print out for your own enjoyment. Check out past, current and future exhibitions or browse by artist. You can also buy art posters and prints at Artcyclopedia Online (www.artcyclopedia.com).

MUSEUM SITES
Broaden your horizons when you take a virtual museum tour.

NATURAL HISTORY MUSEUM (www.nhm.ac.uk)
Get the latest news from Britain's biggest museum of the natural world. Browse the site by gallery and check out the fun stuff on the interactive pages.

NATIONAL MUSEUM OF PHOTOGRAPHY, FILM & TELEVISION (www.nmpft.org.uk)
Get the background on all things media-related, including news, animation, TV, advertising and photography. There's also a 'Magic Factory' sub-site with fun learning games for children.

SCIENCE MUSEUM (www.sciencemuseum.org.uk)
Browse the numerous online exhibitions covering a range of subjects from space exploration to alcoholism.

NATIONAL RAILWAY MUSEUM (www.nrm.org.uk)
Take a virtual tour of the museum online or visit one of the site's digital 'exhiblets'.

TATE (www.tate.org.uk)
A comprehensive site with information on the four Tate art galleries in the UK.

■ **Take a real tour of a museum.** Find out what shows and exhibits are on view all around the world. Travelling to Paris, Singapore or Birmingham and want to take in some art? You can look at what's on offer and when at the Virtual Library museums pages (www.icom.org/vlmp).

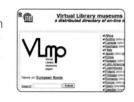

■ **Shopping for unusual gifts and educational items?** There's nothing as special as a museum shop. On the Net, you can shop at hundreds of museum shops, specialising in everything from dinosaur memorabilia to replicas of ancient Egyptian art and collector Dinky toys. You will find a comprehensive list of online museum stores and catalogues at MuseumStuff.com (www.museumstuff.com).

▶ See also **Education on the Net,** p. 298.

CELEBRITY SITE OF THE DAY (www.csotd.com)
Exactly what it says on the package – a new celebrity site every single day of the year.

ENTERTAINMENT TONIGHT ONLINE (www.etonline.com)
The latest gossip on Hollywood, TV and music industry stars, updated daily.

REAL NAMES OF CELEBRITIES (celebrityalmanac.com/real.shtml)
The true identity of dozens of stars revealed. For example, Doris Day is Doris Kappelhof!

BIOGRAPHICAL DICTIONARY (www.s9.com/biography)
The Biographical Dictionary contains a searchable database of 28,000 celebrities, old and new.

PEOPLE.COM (people.aol.com/people)
News, features and interviews on the perennial celebrity theme.

CELEBRITY EMAIL (www.celebrityemail.com)
Send e-mails to your favourite celebrities (sadly not to their personal addresses!).

ZINES: THE FUTURE OF PUBLISHING?

A zine is an online magazine that is published on the Web and contains news, feature articles, tips and advice.

■ **Like a Website,** in its purest form a zine is an electronic publication that Net users can access. They range from 1099 (1099.com), an award-winning zine with expert advice essential to independent professionals, to Failure Magazine (www.failuremag.com), an offbeat zine dedicated to glorious failures through the ages, in fields ranging from the arts to entertainment and science, from technology to history.

■ **To start reading online zines,** simply type in the words 'zine' or 'ezine' in a search engine and see what you come up with!

■ **Don't believe everything you read in zines,** some of them are just for fun. Never be tempted to pass on personal information through them and always double-check any financial or health advice with an expert before you act upon it.

■ **One of the longest established zines** on the Net is The Onion (www.theonion.com). When the real news gets you down, try The Onion's spoof take on the world. For British satire, try the online version of Private Eye (www.private-eye.co.uk), with cartoons and text from the current edition. A popular (and controversial at times) zine is Pop Bitch (www.popbitch.com). Published in the UK, Pop Bitch has a weekly lowdown on all the latest celebrity gossip.

■ **Want to keep an eye on the latest fitness news?** The LentilHealth Website (www.lentilhealth.com/fitness.html) puts fitness first. FitRec (www.fitrec.com) helps you achieve your personal goals. It includes sports training guides, from baseball to skiing, and a section specifically on sports events for the disabled. Also worth a look is GolfWeb (www.golfweb.com), which is devoted to international aspects of the royal and ancient game, with articles on players and tournaments, and even video highlights.

■ **For the latest in travel news,** visit Travelmag (www.travelmag.com) the online magazine for independent travellers, or Babylon Travel Mag (www.babylontravel.net) for travel writing from around the world.

FIVE MINUTES OF FAME

Keep up with all the latest news on your favourite stars.

■ **Try typing your favourite star's name** as a Web address, between www and .com – such as, www.britneyspears.com. You'll probably go straight to their site with one click.

■ **You can expand your collection** of celebrity memorabilia by buying photographs and books online. To get you started, try Celebrity Books.com (www.celebritybooks.com) or Celebrity CD (www.celebritycd.com).

■ **Find out all the latest news** and rumours about the rich and famous. Sites such as E!Online (www.eonline.com), Ain't It Cool News (www.aint-it-cool-news.com) or Entertainment Tonight Online (www.etonline.com) will help you to keep track of all the stars. For local gossip, Gonna (www.gonna.co.uk) will keep you up to date with what's happening in the UK; just click the links for music, TV and film.

▶ See also **Welcome to TV on the Web,** p. 283.

■ A feast for sports fans

The Internet has enough live coverage and information to keep all sports fans happy. In addition to cricket and football statistics, the Internet can tell you where to go skydiving and how to hit a better backhand. So get your sports kit on and get ready for a wild Web workout.

Follow the career and off-field antics of your favourite sports stars. ESPN is a well-known US sports Website (espn.go.com). But for news from home try BBC Sport (www.bbc.co.uk/sport) or Sky Sports (msn.skysports.com). For sports of all kind, try Sportal (www.sportal.co.uk).

WATCH THE WEB

If you're a sports couch potato, why not watch on the Net? You can find sports not usually broadcast on TV, as well as more complete coverage of sports that are. Japanese baseball, golf competitions, tennis matches – watch them all online.

Some Websites offer video streaming, using the plug-ins QuickTime or RealOne Player. As long as you have an up-to-date Web browser, you won't need to download any extra software to view the video. Visit sites such as Camvista (www.camvista.com/sports/index.php3), which has feeds from three of Britain's biggest football clubs.

Buy a ticket to see cricket, football, rugby or any other sport in the UK or abroad with Ticketfinders International (www.ticket-finders.com). Try the tickets pages of the UK Net Guide (www.ukticketsguide.co.uk) for a list of links to other sites supplying tickets to a range of sporting events. For travel to tournaments overseas, try Indigo Sports Tours (62.172.71.34/indigo/sports).

If you're a member of a football team, try Sports Tours (www.sports-tours.co.uk) who specialise in organising team trips and tournaments.

LESSONS AND OTHER INFO

If you want to learn how to bend it like Beckham, take some online football coaching with TopLeague (www.topleague.co.uk) and follow the animated demonstrations to learn a number of passing, dribbling and free kick techniques. You can even buy football coaching software on the Internet. Mastersport Multimedia's Soccer Academy (www.mastersport.co.uk/sa.html) has illustrations, tackle demonstrations and training exercises to help football coaches.

FOOTBALL CRAZY
Follow the beautiful game online.

THE FA (www.the-fa.org)
There's news, information, games and an online store. Check out the Sven Tracker to see what the England manager's been up to and watch streaming video footage of your favourite England players.

FOOTBALL365 (www.football365.com)
This comprehensive site has news, opinion, features, pundits pages, polls, and transfer gossip. If you want to place a bet on your team, the site also has all the odds on all the games.

BANANA TV (www.bananatv.com)
Watch Premiership Bizarrio on 'TV' on your computer, presented by footie fans Nige and Fergy. Keep up to date with the latest news, and for anything you may have missed, you can watch previous episodes from earlier weeks of the Premiership.

SOCCERLINKS (www.soccerlinks.co.uk)
Thousands of links to football clubs all over the world, from major teams to Sunday leagues. There are also links to players pages, merchandise, tickets, online football games and stadium sites.

EXTREME SPORTS

If extreme is your scene, or you just love vicarious thrills, start here.

EXPN EXTREME SPORTS (expn.go.com)
Headline news from the adventure sports scene. Chat with sporting legends and read features on exotic destinations.

MOUNTAINZONE (www.mountainzone.com)
All types of extreme sports activities and reports for anyone with a head for heights.

EXTREME SPORTS (www.extremesports.com)
Links to water sports, skateboard and motocross sites, among many others.

GRAVITY GAMES (www.gravitygames.com)
A youth-oriented Website that features extreme sports pictures, news of upcoming events and lifestyle topics.

AJ HACKETT BUNGY (www.ajhackett.com)
Make a pilgrimage to the home of bungy.

ADVENTURE TIME (www.adventuretime.com)
Online magazine covering inline skating, BMX biking and mountain biking.

Place your bets! If you fancy a wager on a sporting event, there are plenty of people on the Net who are more than willing to take your money. The major high-street bookmakers now have online betting. Try Ladbrokes (www.ladbrokes.com) or William Hill (www.willhill.com). There are many others too: UKbetting (www.ukbetting.co.uk), Bet365 (www.bet365.com), Tote UK (www.tote.co.uk) and SportingOdds (www.sportingodds.com) all take bets on numerous sporting events.

Skiing is unpredictable. You can plan your trip months in advance, but the snow still falls only when it wants to. So get the scoop on where to find the best powder and keep track of the latest conditions with on-mountain snow cams. If you want to ski in North America, check out the snow reports on Ski Central (www.skicentral.com). For Europe try Pistoff.com (www.pistoff.com). At the On The Snow site (www.onthesnow.com) there are snow reports for regions worldwide.

GET IN ON THE ACTION

Follow your favourite game while you're on the move by arranging for the scores to be sent to your mobile phone. Try the Yahoo! Alert Service (uk.sports.yahoo.com). You can be notified when the game starts, get instant updates or find out the final score. Sky Sports also offers an alert service (www1.sky.com/mobile/sms.html). However, services like these are often only available to users of certain networks.

Learn from the amazing experiences of others. Read about the exciting and inspirational adventures of adrenaline junkies and explorers at Global Online Adventure Learning (www.goals.com/homebody.asp). Expedition 360, for instance, is circling the world by human power. Bill and Helen Thayer have been to the Arctic, the Amazon and the Sahara, whilst Chris Duff has paddled around New Zealand's South Island. Another adventurer, Mick Bird, is hoping to become the first man to row around the world.

New in town? Use the Internet to find a sports team or event near your new home. One of the best sites is DMOZ (www.dmoz.org). Type in the sport you're interested in and the search engine will come up with hundreds of teams around the world. For example, for cricket teams, try www.dmoz.org/Sports/Cricket/Clubs. ID03 (www.1do3.com/uk) has an athletics club finder for the UK. You could also try the site for your local authority, which will give details of local sports centres and leisure activities in the area.

Calling all armchair sports lovers! Do you long to own a cricket bat autographed by the greats of English Cricket, or perhaps a Rugby League World Cup England jersey, autographed by the entire team? To find your very own treasure, log onto Bid4Sport (www.bid4sport.com), which offers memorabilia and books signed by sports stars. Formula One fans can find memorabilia at www.f1-memorabilia.co.uk and for rugby fans, try www.rugbyrelics.com.

See also **What you need is a hobby**, p. 280.

Community issues

Women may be from Venus and men from Mars, but the Internet has done a lot to bring women's concerns down to Earth.

■ **Search for sites** with relevance to women's issues at Women.com (www.women .com). The site screens every link submission for its appropriateness to women's interests and excludes offensive links.

■ **Many general interest and gateway sites** are geared for women. The sites contain chat and content focused on parenting, health, fitness and beauty, sex, jobs, relationships, money and other topics of interest

to women. For the biggest variety of women-centred topics, try iVillage (www.ivillage .co.uk), Handbag (www.handbag.com) or Femail (www .femail.co.uk).

■ **Get politically active on women's issues.** Pay a visit to the Equal Opportunities Commission (www.eoc.org.uk) or the Women's National Commission (www.thewnc.org.uk). This is an independent advisory body representing the views of women to the government. The European Women's Lobby (www.womenlobby .org/home-en.asp?LangName=english) also campaigns for female equality and strives to serve as a link between political decision makers and women's organisations at European Union level.

■ **The official line.** Learn what the government has to say about women's issues. Start with the Women and Equality unit (www. cabinet-office.gov.uk/womens-unit) for reports and findings on a number of issues including domestic violence and women in the workplace.

■ **Explore international women's rights.** Learn what Amnesty International (www.amnesty.org) is doing to increase the human rights of women. WomenWatch (www. un.org/womenwatch) is a gateway for United Nations research and information on women's issues worldwide.

■ **When it comes to health,** it's good to talk. There are a growing number of places on the Web where women can get health information and discuss issues with others who know what they are going through. Go to the NHS Website (www.nhsdirect.nhs.uk) and type 'women's health' into the search box. This will bring up a number of results on different topics. Women's Health (www.womens-health.co.uk) has information for women regarding pregnancy and common gynaecological conditions. The BBC also has Women's Health pages with advice and information (www.bbc.co.uk/health/womens).

■ **Mums to be and new mums** can find a wealth of information, advice and support over the Internet. Sites such as Baby Parenting (www.baby-parenting.co.uk) and Motherbliss (www.motherbliss.co.uk) have pregnancy and baby information. BirthChoice UK (www.birth choiceuk.com) helps women choose where to have their babies and Babyworld (www. babyworld.co.uk) has discussions and diaries.

■ **Balancing work and children is no mean feat.** Get some advice from sites dedicated to making this juggling act easier. Advancing Women (www.advancingwomen .com) is devoted to women who balance work and family and provides workplace strategies, parenting information, articles and tips.

■ **Whether you want to employ a nanny** or an au pair for help with the children, you can use the Internet to find out who is available. There are numerous agencies online. Try Job Match for Au Pairs (www.aupairs.co.uk), Au Pairs by Avalon (www.aupairsbyavalon.com), Star Nannies (www.starnannies.co.uk), Nannies Incorporated (www.baby-nurse.co.uk) and Eden Nannies (www.eden-nannies.co.uk).

■ **Tired of being treated like a second-class citizen** at the car dealer or garage? The best defence is a strong offence. Get all the knowledge you need at automotive sites geared just for women. The Woman Motorist (www.womanmotorist.com) is an American site, but much of the advice and help is useful.

■ **Keep track of your own financial health** with sites designed just for women. MsMoney (www.msmoney.com) is focused on providing women with the tools and resources necessary for learning about and managing their finances. Moneylife (www.ivillage.com/money) is a personalised and practical online guide to saving, investing, borrowing and spending your cash. For a sympathetic financial planner, try Find an Independent Financial Adviser (www.ifap.org.uk).

■ **Women in the workplace.** Women who run their own businesses will be interested in what the Every Woman site has to offer (www. everywoman.co.uk). It is an online network and resource provider for women business owners, offering bulletin boards for exchanging information and expert advice on finance and marketing.

Good role models are important in building self-esteem. Find female role models at Distinguished Women of Past and Present (www.distinguishedwomen.com). This site offers a comprehensive list of notable women.

For all you toastmasters, gain inspiration from Gifts of Speech: Women's Speeches from Around the World (gos.sbc.edu).

The site contains speeches by influential or 'modern' women, such as Christiane Amanpour, Gloria Steinem and Maya Angelou.

Women are telling their stories, discussing issues that affect them, and sharing hard-won wisdom online. Voices of Women (www.voiceofwomen.com) offers articles, topics, links and a marketplace of woman-friendly businesses to empower you on your journey. She-Net (www.she-net.com) is a virtual community where women share feelings and views.

If you're an independent traveller try Journeywoman (www.journeywoman.com), which is an online magazine for women who love to travel.

All kinds of adventurous urges are catered to on the Web. If you like cold climates, Arctic Ladies Adventure Traveling for Women (www.arcticladies.com) provides travel for women to Alaska. Las Olas Surf Adventures (www.surflasolas.com), on the other hand, offers all-female adventures in Mexico.

Have kids but love to travel? Why not take them with you? For family adventure holidays check out Walks Worldwide (www.walksworldwide.com/familyholidays.htm).

Find a like-minded friend. Love the opera, art galleries, fine wine? Or are you more at home singing along to popular show tunes? Simply type your interest into a search engine and join an online discussion group.

Ever thought of trying women's football? Find out all about it at She Kicks (www.shekicks.net) with news, fixtures and results, and links to football clubs in the UK. If rugby's your thing go to the women's page on the Rugby Football Union site (www.rfu.com/index.cfm/fuseaction/RFUHome.Womens_Home), with all the latest match news.

▶ See also **Plan your next trip on the Web,** p. 264; **Stay fit and healthy,** p. 270; **Taking the stress out of weddings,** p. 276; and p. 306.

SITES FOR AND ABOUT WOMEN

Here are a few of the many women's interest sites worth visiting on the Web.

THE WOMEN'S LIBRARY (www.thewomenslibrary.ac.uk)
The womens' library has the most extensive collection of women's history in the UK, with a searchable online archive.

WWWOMEN (www.wwwomen.com)
An extensive site that promotes itself as the premier search directory for women online.

FOR WOMEN ONLY (www.cyberparent.com/women)
Delves deeply into the topics of work, relationships, health and sex.

HERSPACE.COM (www.herspace.com)
An online community for creative women, centred around music, art and writing.

ALL THAT WOMEN WANT (www.allthatwomenwant.com)
Fun, resources and best of the Web picks.

MAKING THE MOST OF YOUR GOVERNMENT

Take an interest in how the country is governed and find out what the politicians have been doing for you all these years.

Go straight to the top. Visit our head of state and see what she's been up to lately at Her Majesty's informative home page (www.royal.gov.uk). You can also visit 10 Downing Street on the Net (www.number-10.gov.uk), where you can download full transcripts of the Prime Minister's press conferences and post your opinions on the discussion forums. There is also an informative History section with information about previous Prime Ministers.

Visit the Houses of Parliament online at www.parliament.uk. Here you can read reports of all parliamentary debates; follow the status and text of bills before parliament; access the directory of MPs and peers; and find out about the role and work of the parliamentary select committees. There's also information on visiting parliament in person.

Start your search for anything concerning the UK government at www.online.gov.uk. The A to Z of central government provides links to more than 1,000 government and public service Websites. Similarly, the A to Z of local government provides links to local authority Websites for information about council and community services, local government and public service Websites.

Want to lobby your local member? The good news is that many politicians now have their own Websites. Go to www.parliament.uk/commons/lib/alms.htm for alphabetical listings of all MPs. There are links to their Websites and biogs, and you can also send them e-mails via the site.

■ If regional affairs are your concern, visit the online office of the Deputy Prime Minister and his Government Offices for the English Regions (www.rcu.gov.uk/GO) and keep track of what your regional government office is doing for you. The Local Government Information Unit Online (www.lgiu.gov.uk) has links to local government Websites, as does the Oultwood site (www.oultwood.com/localgov/england.htm). Richard Kimber's Political Science Resources site (www.psr.keele.ac.uk/local.htm) links to the sites of Metropolitan, Unitary, County, District, Town and Parish councils throughout the UK.

■ The great feature of a democracy is that if you don't like the government you can always sack them! Plan your revenge by becoming an expert on the electoral process at The Electoral Commission (www.electoral commission.gov.uk).

■ Want to make your mark in politics? Find out what the existing parties stand for at www.conservatives.com, www.labour.org.uk, and www.libdems.org.uk. If you're looking for an alternative to the the main politcal parties, browse the links at the Political Science Resources site (www.psr.keele.ac.uk/parties.htm).

■ Not the official line. The Internet has provided a forum for anyone who has a point of view, and almost everyone has something to say about politics. To explore the full spectrum of ideas and opinions, just type a search term like 'politics' into your search engine and explore the sites that appear. If you achieve nothing else, you can whip yourself into an indignant frenzy!

STAY UP TO DATE ON GLOBAL POLITICS

Stay informed, get active and keep up with politics around the world.

■ There are elections happening all the time, all around the world. To follow election news worldwide, Klipsan Press (www.klipsan.com/elecnews.htm) provides concise coverage, including links to detailed election results. Elections Around The World (www.electionworld.org) is an international database with the latest results of elections worldwide.

■ Stay informed about political news. You can find out who's in and who's out, and what they've been getting up to on the BBC's politics pages. It has news, interviews, political links and streaming online video coverage of debates in the Houses of Parliament. The Guardian Unlimited Website (politics.guardian.co.uk) also has extensive coverage.

■ Far-flung activists can now work together. Use the Net to get active: visit the Independent Media Centre (www.indymedia.org). This site reports on important issues worldwide, and claims to be 'a collective of independent media organisations and hundreds of journalists offering grassroots, non-corporate coverage'. Visit CorpWatch (www.corpwatch.org) for views on issues ranging from globalisation to third-world sweatshops. Numerous organisations have Websites devoted to issues of interest, such as DRCNet (www.drcnet.org), which is concerned with drug reform, or NukeNet (www.ejnet.org/nukenet), which campaigns against nuclear weapons and nuclear power.

■ Many political issues now have global as well as local dimensions. If you want to change the world, then the Internet is the place to find others who will help. In an area such as human rights, for example, there are

How to: Find foreign government information

1 As a jumping-off point, use diplomatic links. These concentrate on up-to-date information designed for a general audience. Try Embassy World (www.embassyworld.com).

2 The WWW Virtual Library (www.vlib.org) has links to government information. For geographically arranged links to government sites, visit the Worldwide Governments pages (www.gksoft.com/govt/en/world.html).

thousands of Websites that deal with particular concerns. At a local level you might want to see what the human rights group Liberty is up to (www.liberty-human-rights.org.uk). For a global perspective, try Amnesty International (www.amnesty.org) and get a briefing on current issues of concern. Amnesty's brilliant Links page demonstrates the extent of interest in this issue worldwide. Among sites worth checking out are the International Crisis Group (www.intl-crisis-group.org), a private multinational organisation, and the Carnegie Council on Ethics and International Affairs (www.cceia.org/themes/humanrights.html).

■ **Fed up with dull local politics?** Visit a country that really knows how to conduct its public affairs. For fascinating facts on the famous, access American FBI documents that have been released as part of the US Federal Freedom of Information Act. The FBI has a freedom of information reading-room site (http://foia.fbi.gov), which includes intriguing, declassified information on Marilyn Monroe, Elvis Presley and the British Royal family, as well as other, less famous, people. To use the reading room, you'll need Adobe Acrobat Reader, which you can download for free at www.adobe.com.

GETTING LEGAL ADVICE ONLINE

The Internet can't argue for you in court, but it can help you to find the right lawyer or advice.

■ **Want to talk to a lawyer, but feel intimidated?** Why not start out with an online consultation? Online legal advice is becoming more popular and allows you to get a rough idea of what is on offer before you commit yourself. Take a look at the LegalServicesShop (www.freelawyer.co.uk), Community Legal Services (www.justask.org.uk) and Legalpulse (www.legalpulse.com).

■ **For a multitude of legal links** visit Legal Sites on the Web (www.ih2000.net/ira/legal.htm). Here you will find worldwide law sites, glossaries of legal jargon, regional listings of

lawyers, advice and forums, and even sites about Internet related legal issues. And while you're there, why not pay a visit to US CourtTV.

■ **Find a qualified lawyer.** The Lawyer Locator site (www.lawyerlocator.co.uk) has a search facility listing solicitors and barristers in different areas of the UK and with different legal expertise. Law 4 Today (www.law4today.com/findalawyer/findalawyer.htm) has a similar service.

ONLINE LEGAL TIPS
AND TACTICS
These hints can help guide you safely through the legal jungle.

● Evaluate your legal needs carefully before you try to solve them online. As a general rule, the more specialised your needs, the harder you will have to search to find Web information relevant to your situation.

● Make sure you know the source of information before you act on it, especially if it's from a newsgroup.

● If a site is advertising itself as offering legal advice, especially if it is charging you, check their credentials with the relevant professional body in your area.

● What is the date of the information? Last year's rulings may not be relevant today. And advice that is accurate in one country may be inapplicable in another.

● Don't be too quick to use legal forms downloaded from the Web or copied from a CD-ROM. Your local system may require something different or more specific.

● Find out if you need a barrister. Some cases legally require that a member of the Bar represent you whether you actually need them or not.

STAYING CLEAN AND GREEN

The Internet has ideas to help you do your bit to preserve the planet for future generations.

■ **What is your government doing about environmental issues?** Find out by visiting the Website of the Department for Environment, Food and Rural Affairs (www.defra.gov/uk). Check out the latest news and current issues, and browse the online publications. There are also links to the department's government agencies and non-departmental public bodies.

■ **Many environmental issues have become global concerns.** Discover what you can do to help at the Greenpeace Website (www.greenpeace.org). For a global perspective on environmental issues check out the Organisation for Economic Cooperation and Development (www.oecd.org/env), where sections are devoted to issues including sustainable consumption, globalisation and climate change.

■ **Renewable energy is a hot topic.** See what the government thinks at the Department of Trade and Industry (www.dti.gov.uk/renewable). For a European perspective on the issue, go to EuroREX (www.eurorex.com).

NEVER TOO OLD FOR THE NET

It's never too late to enter the electronic age, and the Internet isn't just for younger generations.

■ There's no need to travel alone.

Use the Internet to find like-minded travellers. Try Saga Holidays (www.saga.co.uk/travel), Laterlife (www.laterlife.co.uk) and UK SilverSurfers (www.silversurfers.net/traveladvice.html) for tours that are specifically for the over 50s.

■ Begin your Web surfing at a portal for the over 50s.

Just as the World Wide Web caters for the needs and interests of children, teenagers, mothers and fathers there are sites, portals, links, chat rooms and discussion forums for people of advancing years. 50Connect (www.50connect.co.uk) is a portal designed with the interests of the over 50s in mind. The site provides links and information on finance and pensions, as well as numerous lifestyle channels. CenNet (www.cennet.co.uk) is another site with links to health, travel, shopping and money sites.

■ If you want to get politically active,

and raise your awareness of political issues for pensioners, try the Better Government for Older People Website (www.bettergovernmentforolderpeople.gov.uk). Or if you would like to campaign on pensioners issues, it's worth looking at the Website of the National Pensioners Convention (www.natpencon.org.uk) or Age Concern (www.ace.org.uk/ageconcern).

■ While many chatrooms focus on the 20-somethings,

there are plenty of sites for senior citizens looking to make new friends. The Baby Boomer Bistro (www.babyboomerbistro.org.uk) claims to be the first chat cafe in the UK developed for the over 50s, with discussion forums where you can post messages. For live chat, try Overfifties.com (www.overfifties.com).

■ It's never too late to learn.

Use the Internet as the launch pad in your quest for knowledge. The University of the Third Age (www.U3a.org.uk) can put you in touch with a group in your area that offers courses by and for older people. If there is no group near you, then you could always start one.

■ If you just fancy a good read

there are several sites you might want to try. *The Oldie* magazine, established in the 1990s as the antidote to a media obsessed with 'yoof', has an online version (www.theoldie.co.uk) with some of the content of the magazine. For some irreverent humour, as well as serious issues, try the Hells Geriatrics site (www.hellsgeriatrics.co.uk). And *Quicksilver* magazine (www.quicksilver.co.uk) has features, interviews, competitions and regular sections on travel, health and money.

■ Help for the doting grandparent.

Did you know that grandparents spend more than £1 billion a year on their grandchildren? For ideas on how to spend on your grandchildren and help them to make the best of their childhood try See How They Grow (www.seehowtheygrow.com), an online grandparent's guide, with news, story–telling tips, ideas for days out and theatre listings.

■ To make Web pages easier to read,

you can increase the size of the type displayed. In Internet Explorer, go to **View** ➜ **Text Size** and select **Largest**. In Netscape, go to **Edit** ➜ **Preferences**, select **Appearance** ➜ **Fonts**, and choose a larger point size.

■ For even better legibility,

change the typeface that a Website displays. Sometimes fonts are ornate, but it's easier to read a plain typeface, such as Arial, Helvetica or Verdana. To change the typeface in Internet Explorer, go to **Tools** ➜ **Internet Options**, and from the **General** tab, select **Fonts**. In Netscape, go to **Edit** ➜ **Preferences**, and select **Appearance** ➜ **Fonts**. Make sure the **Allow documents to use other fonts** box is checked, as some Web pages may look odd using your choice all the time.

SITES FOR OVER 50s

Whatever your age, there's no excuse not to get online!

SILVER SURFERS (www.silversurfers.net)
An over 50s portal with links to hundreds of other sites. Try the Alphabetic Site Index and check out the star site of the week.

ABLE TO GO.COM (www.abletogo.com)
This Website brings hotels, guest houses, self catering and caravanning holidays to those with mobility difficulties. To get the best of the site you will have to register and become member.

I DON'T FEEL 50 (www.idf50.co.uk)
For the over 50s who are young at heart! Post your poetry or photos on the site, join the discussion forums or visit Dr Mac's Computer Clinic for PC troubleshooting.

BOOMERS INTERNATIONAL (www.boomersint.org)
'The worldwide community for the baby boomer generation', this site is packed with information with everything from online counselling to music downloads.

UK ONLINE: A NATION ON THE NET

The Internet provides a perfect opportunity for every UK citizen to express and exchange their views, thoughts and culture.

■ **Start your exploration of national culture and issues** in the United Kingdom  with the official government bodies. Make virtual visits to 10 Downing Street (www.number-10.gov.uk), and the British (www.parliament.uk) and Scottish Parliaments (www.scottish.parliament.uk), and find out about their roles, history and procedures. You can also visit the official sites of the Northern Irish Executive (www.nics.gov.uk) and Assembly (www.ni-assembly.gov.uk) and the Welsh Assembly (www.wales.gov.uk).

■ **Northern Irish, Scottish and Welsh politics in Britain** are hotly debated topics with long and complex histories. The Guardian's Devolved Politics site (politics.guardian.co.uk/devolvedpolitics) has many features and links on issues surrounding Scottish Parliament and the Irish and Welsh Assemblies. There's an interactive guide to Northern Ireland (www.guardian.co.uk/Northern_Ireland), and the BBC site (www.bbc.co.uk/history/war/troubles) has a history of the origin of conflicts in Northern Ireland. For a southern perspective, visit the Irish goverment's Department of Foreign Affairs (www.irlgov.ie/iveagh/default.htm). Electric Scotland (www.electricscotland.com/spolitics.htm) has a guide and list of links to official and not-so-official Scottish politics, but for a comprehensive analysis of Welsh political issues visit GJW Wales (www.gjwwales.co.uk), a public affairs consultancy, and The Institute of Welsh Affairs (www.iwa.org.uk), an independent think-tank.

■ **You're history!** Get the historical low-down on Britain's chequered past from a range of online sources. Brittania (www.brittania.com) has narrative histories of England, Scotland and Wales, and at SCRAN (www.scran.ac.uk), the award winning history and culture website, you can find over one million records from museums, galleries and archives. You'll also find Scottish histories at Electric Scotland  (www.electricscotland.com/history) and the BBC site (www.bbc.co.uk/history/scottishhistory), Irish histories at Ireland.org (www.ireland.org/irl_hist/default.htm) and CELT (www.ucc.ie/celt) and Welsh histories at Data Wales (www.data-wales.co.uk) and the BBC site (www.bbc.co.uk/wales/history/davies/index.shtml), which includes a version of Welsh history written by a leading historian especially for the web.

■ **Ever wondered who the British are?** What it means to be British, and what are the origins of British culture? Learn.co.uk (www.learn.co.uk/citizenship/subjects/english/activity4.asp) has activities, ideal for teachers and students, that explore what it means to different people to be British. At Historic UK (www.historic-uk.com/CultureUK/index.htm), you can read about the origin of such great British inventions as fish 'n' chips, afternoon tea and wellies!

■ **Celtic culture online.** The Celts are hugely influential upon Scottish and Irish histories, and there's lots to discover about Celtic culture on the Net. At the soc.culture.scottish newsgroup page (www.siliconglen.com/scotfaq) you can browse frequently asked questions to learn hundreds of facts about Scottish culture, whilst Rampant Scotland (www.rampantscotland.com) contains many links to all things Scottish.

THE NATION'S PAST ONLINE
Start your exploration of UK histories with these resources.

BBC HISTORY (www.bbc.co.uk/history)
The BBC's History zone has dozens of links to information about many excellent programmes, including A History of Britain, Great Britons and What the Romans, Tudors, Stuarts and Victorians Did For Us!

THE BRITISH LIBRARY (www.bl.uk)
This virtual bookshelf of the world's knowledge is the national library of the United Kingdom.

QUESTIA (www.questia.com)
Research UK history and locate information at the world's largest online library.

HISTORY.UK.COM (www.history.uk.com)
Hundreds of British history links, articles and timelines for tourists, teachers, educators, and history enthusiasts.

BRITAIN EXPRESS (www.britainexpress.com)
A heritage guide to British history and culture, with some great features on the folktales, myths and legends of Britain.

SUITE101.COM (www.suite101.com/welcome.cfm/british_history)
A well-resourced site with many articles and links that cover modern British histories.

BRITANNIA (www.britannia.com/history)
Although a US site, Britannia's Britain is great for researching the chequered histories of Scotland, Wales and England.

BBC YOUR HISTORY (www.bbc.co.uk/history/your_history)
The BBC's Your History site enables you to explore the history of your family, home and community.

Irish Culture and Customs (www.irishcultureand-customs.com) has insights into the Celtic influence on Irish life, and Irelandseye (www.irelandseye.com) has many features on Irish history and culture. All About Irish (www.allaboutirish.com) is a site about the Irish diaspora, with some revealing facts about Irish words in English sayings! You can also read an informative and well-linked article on The History and Status of the Welsh Language (users.comlab.ox.ac.uk/geraint.jones/about.welsh) and the importance of Celtic culture to Wales.

■ Discovering multicultural Britain.

The people of Britain are made up of a wide mix of migrant cultures that have influenced and

enriched every part of British life. The Independent Race and Refugee Network has a history of Afro-Caribbeans and Asians in Britain (www.irr.org.uk/history/index.html), and the BBC's site

features a Multicultural History (www.bbc.co.uk/history/society_culture/multicultural/index.shtml), tracing the experiences of communities worldwide in Britain. Channel 4's site (www.channel4.com/history/microsites/B/blackhistorymap) has a gateway to websites about black and Asian history across the British Isles. The British Library's site (www.bl.uk/collections/britasian/britasia.html) has an excellent array of articles and learning from their Oriental and Indian Offices on Asians and their contributions to the culture of Britain. BBC's Radio 4 site (www.bbc.co.uk/radio4/news/asiandiasporas.shtml) also has features and links relating to their Asian Diasporas series.

■ Flags and their symbols are bold statements of nationality and identity.

Discover the history of the dragon and other Welsh symbols at Data Wales (www.data-wales.co.uk/flag.htm) and at Scottish History Online (www.scotshistoryonline.co.uk/saltire/saltire.html) you can read up on the origins of the St Andrew's Cross. Meanwhile, at CAIN, learn about the many flags used in the region of Northern Island (cain.ulst.ac.uk/images/symbols/flags.htm). There's a comprehensive history of the Union Jack at the Official Website of the British Monarchy (www.royal.gov.uk/output/page398.asp), and at The History of the Union Flag (home.12move.nl/~sh829487/historyflag.htm) you'll find concise histories of the Union flag, the Ulster flag, the St Andrew's Cross flag and the Welsh flag.

■ Dealing with racism.

In a multi-racial society, it is a sorry fact that racist attitudes still exist. However, there are lots of online resources that aim to help combat racism, and join and empower individuals and minorities. The Love Music Hate Racism Website (www.lmhr.org.uk), organised by the Anti-Nazi League, promotes the

positive energy of the music scene to fight against racism. Crosspoint (www.magenta.nl/crosspoint/uk.html) is an anti-racist resource site, with many links to UK organisations, groups and communities working against prejudice. Childline (www.childline.org.uk/Racism.asp) dedicates part of its site to countering racism and encouraging tolerance, with excellent practical advice addressed particularly to children.

EASING THE BURDEN OF DISABILITY

People with disabilities face formidable obstacles, but the Net enables individuals to overcome some of these difficulties.

■ Disability is more than a national issue,

and this is reflected in the vast number of sites around the world that offer help and advice, both of a general nature and for those with specific problems. The Disability Network (www.disabilitynetwork.com) is a global network offering chatrooms, children's pages and links. Further resources are available from The World Association for Persons with Disabilities (www.wapd.org), whose site has chatrooms, bulletin boards and hundreds of Internet links.

■ Closer to home, a vast amount of help can be found at the Websites of organisations set up to help the disabled, both generally and within particular organisations. The Disabled Living Foundation (www.dlf.org.uk) provides a huge amount of help and resources for independent living and is well organised. Also very useful is DIAL (www.dialuk.org.uk), which serves the Disability Advice Network Group, and has details of local services for disabled people, while EQUIP (www.equip.nhs.uk/groups/

disability.html) is a NHS gateway of disability information and has links to many services.

■ Know your rights. If you are interested in civil rights, check out The Disability Rights Commission (www.drc-gb.org/drc/) and The Disability Rights Task Force site (www.disability. gov.uk/drtf/), part of the Disability Unit.

■ Look out for Bobby. You may have noticed that some Websites carry the 'Bobby Approved' logo, a friendly policeman with a wheelchair logo on his helmet. This is Bobby (bobby.watchfire.com/bobby/html/en/about.jsp), a web accessibility tool used by Website creators to help to identify changes that their pages need so people can use them more easily.

■ While computers and the Internet can be liberating for many, they can also be a further source of frustration to some. AbilityNet (www.abilitynet.org.uk) is a national charity and a leading provider of expertise on computing and disability, and addresses a number of problems concerned with disability access. Ability (www.ability.org.uk) is a similar site, dedicated to equality and quality of life through computing technology. For information on the problems faced by the visually impaired, try Visugate (www.visugate.org) a site of helpful online resources.

■ Express yourself. Art is a fantastic means of self-expression, and there are many organisations online to put disabled people in

touch with community groups, artists and galleries. Anweb (www.anweb.co.uk/ l_04_e2/e2a25.htm) is a resource for artists, which features links to organisations working to increase and promote access to the arts for disabled people. The National Disability Arts Forum (www.ndaf.org), funded by the Arts Council of England, is also a good site, with links to information, news, projects, organisations and an arts events calendar.

■ Sport for the disabled is enjoying increasing worldwide support. Disabled athletes with their sights set on fame should check out the sites of the British Paralympic Association (www.paralympics.org.uk) and the International Paralympic Committee (www .paralympic.org), both of which have lots of information on individual sports, international services and links to other organisations. Organisations also exist to promote the sporting aims and ambitions of those with particular disabilities, such as Blind Sport (www.british-blindsport.org.uk). The Website offers advice, support and information on a wide range of sports (including archery, martial arts, athletics, 10-pin bowling and judo) played by blind and partially-sighted people.

■ Travel can be a great problem for many with disabilities. Tripscope (www.tripscope.org.uk) is a nationwide service offering travelling advice and information for the disabled and those who are concerned about travelling. The BBC Website (www.bbc.co.uk/ holiday/disabled_traveller/index.shtml) provides excellent advice on holidays and getting about, with essential links and resources for the disabled traveller. Also worth checking out is Disability View Online (www.disabilityview.co.uk), an Internet version of the lifestyle magazine with features and news, including travel and holidays.

■ There is a wealth of online support for people with specific disabilities. Scope (www.scope.org.uk) focuses on people with cerebral palsy but is also an excellent source of general disability support and information. Mencap (www.mencap.org.uk) is for people with learning disabilities, their families and their carers, and provides easy-to-use pages specially designed to be clear and understandable by people with a learning disability.

Education on the net

In the Internet age, education isn't just about how many facts you know, but knowing where to look for them in the first place. The Net has sites to help you learn, sites where you can find schools and universities and sites to teach you fun – or more serious – subjects.

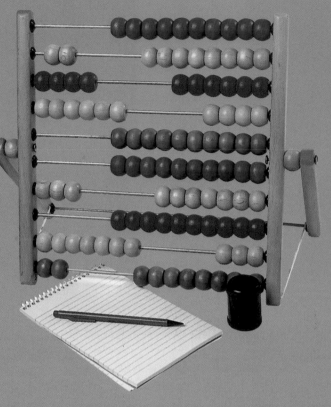

ONLINE LEARNING OPTIONS

Start your search for knowledge with an education-oriented metasearch.
Education World (www.education-world.com) is a database of 100,000-plus educational Websites. Search by keyword, use advanced search options

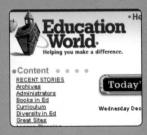

such as Boolean (see p. 239), or you can search by region, event calendar and many other categories. You can also search with Yahoo! (http://uk. yahoo.com), which will come up with thousands of sites in numerous categories dealing with education.

Going to university is one of life's major steps and finding the right one for you can be hard. You can speed up your search by looking on the Internet. Start with the University of Wolverhampton's Higher Education Map (www.scit.wlv.ac.uk/ukinfo/uk. map.html). It locates colleges, universities postgraduate and foreign institutions throughout the UK. The site also has an Alphabetical list of links to UK universities and HE colleges, as well as links to other important sites for education and university funding. If you know what you'd like to study, you can search for the universities that teach your subject at the UCAS site (www.ucas.ac.uk). It is designed to help students, teachers and higher education staff. There's advice for students and useful statistics.

The demands of the Internet age now require that you know more than ever before. With so many options for online learning, you don't need to go back to university

to acquire new skills. World Wide Learn (www. worldwidelearn .com) offers a directory of online courses and learning resources available from around the world on almost every topic, from classical animation and cartoon development to an accelerated online MBA program. You can also find distance education resources, links and contacts at the University of Plymouth's Website: www.fae.plym.ac.uk/tele/ resources.html#Europe).

Want to study while working? The Open University has an extensive Website (www.open.ac.uk) with a list of courses that can

CHILDREN'S EDUCATION

Covering preschool through to sixth form, here are some Websites where your child can have fun and learn.

ARTY THE PART TIME ASTRONAUT (www.artyastro.com)
This site uses exciting animations and games to explain how the Solar System works.

BBC SCHOOLS (www.bbc.co.uk/schools)
There's help and learning information for children of all ages, from preschool to A-level students. There are games, activities and stories for the very young and revision guides and message boards for older children. You can also access TV listings for the BBC's educational programmes.

BONUS.COM (www.beakman.com)
Learning can be fun, and this site offers a scientific twist. Find out the answers to such vitally important questions as Why do feet smell? and Why does the TV reception get worse when the vacuum cleaner is on?

NATIONAL GEOGRAPHIC (www.nationalgeographic.com/kids)
Check out the creature features, amazing facts and weird plants here. Or play the GeoBee Challenge and share favourite books at the Bookworm Corner forum board.

be studied at graduate and postgraduate level at your own pace to fit around working hours. The

university also runs computer courses so students can learn some essential basics for home study.

Most colleges and universities now have Websites
with up-to-date information about the courses they provide and the facilities they offer. In most cases it is fairly easy to guess the Website address, which will be prefixed by a www. and suffixed by .ac instead of .co before .uk. Most institutions usually also have a Web page devoted to links to other universities or colleges in the area.

It's not only universities that are online.
An increasing number of schools have their own Websites. To find out which schools are online, go to Schoolsnet.com (www.schoolsnet .com). This lists schools by region, and then by town, and gives some basic information about each school, as well as providing a Website address if they have one. The site also offers online lessons and revision help.

Secondary school students
can find a wealth of useful material on the Net. Take a look at the BBC schools site (www.bbc.co.uk/schools) and click either the **Ages 11-16** or **16+** links.

With the 'bitesize' revision guides you can read up on a subject and then test yourself to see what you have learned. There are also useful Web links.

Check the accreditation.
With many institutions now offering online learning it is easy to find an institution or program to suit your needs. However, if you or your child intends to take an online course, pay close attention to whether the school is accredited or not. While this may not matter for some courses, if you need to have a recognised qualification, the school needs to be accredited by an official body.

LEARNING CAN BE FUN

When your learning needs are less academic and more growth or hobby oriented,
visit one of the many lifestyle learning sites on the Net. Worth a look is the BBC Learning site (www.bbc.co.uk/learning/courses) where you can take part in online courses such as Get Confident, First Aid Action and Build-A-Bot Techlab. The BBC also offers online language courses in French, German, Italian and Spanish. For free online tutorials, log on to WannaLearn .com (www.wannalearn.com) where they boast 'Over 300 categories of free, first-rate, family-safe online tutorials'.

SITES FOR UNIVERSITY EDUCATION AND BEYOND
Look on the Net for educational and learning resources.

THE OPEN UNIVERSITY (www.open.ac.uk)
The Website of the best-known home study university in the UK, with many degree and postgraduate courses on offer.

BBC LEARNING (www.bbc.co.uk/learning/adults)
There's help with literacy, numeracy and Web skills, as well as online courses and links to other sites for learners.

THE ASSOCIATION OF BUSINESS SCHOOLS (www.the-abs.org.uk)
The ABS Represents more than 100 of the leading business schools of UK universities, higher education institutions and independent management colleges.

LEARN DIRECT (www.learndirect.co.uk)
A site designed to help you advance in your chosen career, or start in a new one. There are details of a large number of training and career devlopment courses, as well as online education and training resources.

There's more to education than the three R's!
These days, children use the Internet to explore all kinds of subjects. Mix education with fun at the Yuckiest Site On The Internet (http://yucky.kids.discovery.com). This site indulges children's fascination with yucky stuff to help them learn about science. Or try StarChild (http://starchild.gsfc.nasa.gov) NASA's educational site about the solar system and outer space.

INTRODUCE THE NET EARLY

Education begins as soon as a child is born
and Internet education starts once a child has learned how to use the computer. You can speed up this process by introducing your children to computers at an early age. The BBC schools site has a preschool section with fun and games for youngsters (www.bbc.co.uk/schools). Jamboree (www. jamboreetv.com) also has activities and educational games for very young children.

Home schooling is increasingly popular
and there are online resources and advice available for parents who wish to educate their children at home. Try Home Education UK (www.home-education.org.uk) as a starting point.

◊ See also **Software for the home**, p. 210.

Education and science

Online or CD-ROM encyclopedias give quick access to information.

■ **Get access** to the contents of one of the world's most respected information sources – Encyclopaedia Britannica (www.britannica.com). You can see a limited amount of information for free, but for in-depth research on a subject you will have to pay a subscription fee.

■ **Got a DVD-ROM drive in your PC?** The DVD edition of Britannica 2003 (http://britannicashop.britannica.co.uk) includes a world atlas, dictionaries, timelines and a collection of images, videos, audio clips and animated maps.

■ **Need a specialised encyclopedia?** Just add the topic to your Internet search term. For example, use "encyclopedia wine" (both words between double quotes) and the search engine will look for the two words as a phrase.

■ **Stumped by that trivia quiz question?** Try The Encyclopedic Fun Trivia Website (www.funtrivia.com/trivia.html). It has a searchable database with thousands of categorised trivia entries.

▶ See also **Education on the Net,** p. 298.

A MAP FOR EVERY TRIP

Need to find the fastest route to John O'Groats? Plan your next adventure with maps from the Net.

■ **For maps of the UK** and Europe, try Multimap.com (www.multimap.com). You can search for a street by postcode or simply click on a country or town and continue clicking for further detail. You can also buy aerial photos of many parts of the UK. Mapquest (www.mapquest.co.uk) provides driving directions, simply type in the house number, street name town and postcode of your starting point and your destination, choose how you'd like your instructions displayed, and the site provides a guide to get you where you want to go, with the total distance and an estimated driving time.

■ **For maps of the world,** no publication is more trusted than National Geographic. Their Website (www.nationalgeographic.com) includes a detailed map section, providing maps from all over the world, a name finder for locating

hard-to-find places and information on cartography. Mapquest (www.mapquest.co.uk) also has a world atlas, with key geographic and social information about each country.

■ **Want to see the future of maps?** Visit Microsoft's TerraServer (www.terraserver.microsoft.com), where the US Geological Survey provides free online access to USGS digital aerial photos, known as digital orthophoto quadrangles,

and access to digital topographic maps, known as digital raster graphics. Starting from a continent-wide view, you can zoom in on any part of the US, right down to the level of streets and houses. Unfortunately, this service is only available for areas within the continental USA.

■ **Do satellite views interest you?** Several sites offer a range of images of the UK and other parts of the world from space. The Dundee Satellite Receiving Station (www.sat.dundee.ac.uk) maintains an up-to-date archive of images from several orbiting satellites. The Met Office

(www.met-office.gov.uk/satpics/latest_IR.html) also has up-to-date views of the UK from a fixed satellite. Also worth a visit for space views is the Visible Earth site (www.visibleearth.nasa.gov).

■ **The Geography and Map Division of the Library of Congress** (http://lcweb2.loc.gov/ammem/gmdhtml) holds more than 4.5 million items. Although only a fraction have been digitised, the Map Collection is still an amazingly extensive catalogue of maps from around the world dating back to 1544. It is organised according to seven major categories, including towns and cities, military campaigns and cultural landscapes. The indexes for all categories are searched simultaneously, and maps can be downloaded if necessary.

■ **If you need to print or e-mail topographic maps,** orthographic maps, aerial charts and nautical charts, head over to Maptech's MapServer (www.maptech.com). The site gives free access to the online database of National Oceanic and Atmospheric Administration (NOAA) digital charts and USGS maps.

■ **For links to more map sites than you ever thought existed,** go to the University of Iowa's Center for Global & Regional Environmental Research (www.cgrer.uiowa.edu/servers/servers_references). This extensive selection of links to map sites includes

EarthRise: a Map Index to Space Shuttle Imagery; Xerox PARC Interactive World Map Viewer and the BigBook Yellow Pages and Map Locator.

NEED HELP WITH YOUR HOMEWORK?

Stumped by your studies? There's online help for students of all ages.

■ Search the Web for the answers.

There are plenty of sites providing homework help, try Channel 4's Homework High (www. 4learning.co.uk/apps/homework/index.jsp). The site has live advice sessions at scheduled times and you can e-mail in questions or search the archive to see if your question has been answered previously. Links4Kids.co.uk (www.links4kids.co .uk/homeworkhelp.htm) provides to links to numerous education, information and reference sites that can help with study. Many local authorities also have homework help pages on their Websites.

■ Ask an expert. Stuck on a tough

question? Sometimes it helps to seek expert advice. Several sites provide real people who will answer almost any question you can think of. Ask an Expert (www.askanexpert.com) is a directory of links to people who volunteer their time to answer questions, and to Web pages that provide information. Alternatively, try asking What Is? (http://whatis.techtarget.com) for help. Sites like these are especially useful for questions that are complex or that require in-depth knowledge to answer. Bear in mind, though, that the experts will usually take a few days to respond.

■ For a complete listing on homework subjects visit the About.com

Homework Help Website (www.about.com/ homework). It has an extensive list of topics divided into subject areas such as art, history, languages and sciences. Click on a suitable link, to see advice and titles of articles written by lecturers, teachers and education specialists.

■ No time to read the whole book?

Read the notes instead. Several Websites such as SparkNotes (www.sparknotes.com) provide free notes and test preparation aids on a wide variety of scholarly and literary works. Mantex (www. mantex.co.uk) has writing and study guides, as well as literary tutorials covering the works of some of the world's great writers. At the Novel Guide Website (www.novelguide.com) you can access chapter-by-chapter summaries of many classic works of fiction. The site also provides character profiles, metaphor analysis, theme analysis, the top ten quotes from each work and author biographies.

▶ See also **Software for the home,** p. 210; and **Education on the Net,** p. 298.

HOMEWORK HELPERS
These sites are great for giving your homework an added edge.

HOMEWORK ELEPHANT (www.homeworkelephant.co.uk)
There's a wealth of information on this site, with over 5,000 resources to help with homework, as well as reference materials and links to other useful sites.

HOWSTUFFWORKS (www.howstuffworks.com)
Next time your child asks why exercise makes you healthy or how the refrigerator works, find the answers right here.

MATHS HELP (www.maths-help.co.uk)
For help with all those tricky equations and calculations at secondary school level, try this site. It also offers a chat facility so you can talk on-line to other students.

RESEARCHPAPER (www.researchpaper.com)
This site offers an abundance of ideas for essay topics and sources.

THERE'S A CALCULATOR FOR IT

There's a free online calculator for almost every job you can think of, from working out loan repayments to solving complex equations.

■ Work out whether you can afford that new house, and how long it will take

you to repay the loan, using an online mortgage repayment calculator. These are available on sites such as BBC Business (www.bbc.co.uk/business /money/calc.shtml), MSN Money (http://money .co.uk/mortgages) and YourMortgage .co.uk (www.your mortgage.co.uk). All you need to provide is the rate of interest and the loan period.

■ Solve that tricky maths or statistical problem with a little bit of help

from the Calculators On-Line Center (www.sci .lib.uci.edu/HSG/ RefCalculators.html). There are over 11,000 specialist calculators online here, covering everything from basic maths to linear equations and fluid mechanics.

■ Planning a big trip across several countries? Get to grips with all that foreign

money by using a currency conversion calculator, such as those to be found at The Universal Currency Converter (www.xe.com/ucc) or Oanda.com (www.oanda.com). With minimal mental gymnastics, you will soon be confident at converting your pounds into a foreign currency, or vice versa, when you want to work out what all those souvenirs cost.

■ Fine-tune your fitness programme and balance food intake. Calculate the

number of carbohydrates you need to meet your energy needs (www.ivillage.com/diet/tools/ healthcalc) or how much energy different activites consume (www.primusweb.com/fitnesspartner).

▶ See also **Calculators for your Desktop,** p. 203.

KEEPING INFORMED ABOUT SCIENCE

There's a wealth of scientific information on the Internet to keep you up to date and help you to understand the world better.

■ **Interested in space?** The Web's the place to be. Head to NASA (www.nasa.gov) for updates and program information. You can find out about each of the missions that NASA runs, from the position of space probes as they explore the solar system to the longitude, latitude, and altitude of the International Space Station as it orbits the Earth. Special sections of the site cater for children and educators.

■ **Find out where ET went!** Help the search for extraterrestrial life by configuring your PC to analyse data downloaded from the Arecibo Radio Telescope as part of the SETI (Search for Extra-Terrestrial Intelligence) project. The program works as a screen saver, analysing data

when you're not using your computer, and sending it back to SETI whenever you connect to the Internet. One of the largest combined computing efforts ever attempted, SETI at Home now involves hundreds of thousands of PCs. Join them at setiathome.ssl.berkeley.edu.

■ **Ever come across a science word you haven't seen before?** Wondering what it is? Head for the Net, where you'll find hundreds of scientific dictionaries. The Enchanted Learning site (www.enchantedlearning.com /science/dictionary) has illustrated dictionaries for astronomy, geography, botany, palaeontology, wildlife and more. For more specialist information, budding genetic researchers can try The Genome Database at (www.gdb.org), while biologists can use The Dictionary of Cell and Molecular Biology (www.mblab.gla.ac.uk/dictionary). And you can find definitions for space terms at the NASA Jet Propulsion Laboratory (www.jpl.nasa.gov).

■ **Thousands of science journals and magazines exist online** to help you research and keep up to date with the latest breakthroughs and experiments in your area of interest. For a readable

international perspective on all aspects of science, visit New Scientist (www.newscientist.com). Keep up with new medical research at The Lancet (www.thelancet.com); explore the wonders of the world with National Geographic (www.national-geographic.com); and delve deep into hard science with Scientific American (www.scientific-american.com) and Technology Review (www.techreview.com).

■ **Get regular updates on scientific news** at the BBC Science site (www.bbc.co.uk /science). Read the top science stories and explore the hot topics. You can subscribe to a regular newsletter and there are links to the homepages of all the BBC's science programmes. Or subscribe to Netsurfer Science (www.netsurf.com/nss) and receive bulletins on subjects that interest you. There are dozens of other popular science sites, among them Discover (www.discover.com), Discovery (www.discovery.com), Popular Science (www.popsci.com) and Nature (www.nature.com), all of which offer news and articles.

■ **Have your questions answered on the Internet.** Ever wondered how a fridge keeps food cold, or why a bridge stays up? Get the answers at HowStuffWorks (www.howstuff works.com). Or select a site where scientists will personally answer all your questions.

Try Mad Sci Network (www.madsci.org) when you absolutely must know at 4 am why the sky is blue. Dr. Science (www.ducksbreath.com), Dr. Universe (www.wsu.edu/druniverse), and Pitsco's Ask an Expert (www.askanexpert.com) are also available to answer your questions.

■ **Conduct your own scientific experiments with help from the Web.** There are many sites with fun, easy experiments that demonstrate scientific principles. You can try them out at home, and in many cases you only require a few basic household items to aid you in your research. Try Reeko's Mad Scientist Lab (www.spartechsoftware.com/reeko). Begin with an easy experiment that demonstrates the principles of flotation and work up towards the more advanced task of building your own volcano. Or try The Science Explorer (www. exploratorium.edu.science_explorer) for more simple home science. The Fun Science Gallery (www.funsci.com) has more advanced activities for the amateur scientist, such as building your own microscope or telescope.

DON'T BE CAUGHT OUT BY THE WEATHER

Should you take the umbrella to work? Use the Internet to get the latest weather information.

■ **Wondering what to wear?** Get regular weather updates by text to your mobile phone when you sign on at one of the popular Web portals. Providers like Yahoo! (http://uk.yahoo.com) will deliver regular updates

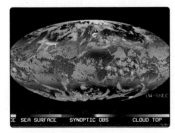

■ **Going on a trip and want to know what the weather will be like?** Try the Met Office Website (www.metoffice.com) or the BBC Weather Centre (www.bbc.co.uk/weather) for weather maps, forecasts, warnings and satellite images for the entire country. Numerous other Websites also supply weather details, such as The Weather Channel (www.weather.co.uk) and ITV Weather (www.itv.com). On most of the major weather sites, you can see a five-day forecast for your particular location in the UK. There are also worldwide weather reports for those planning to go abroad.

■ **Get an astronaut's view of the weather** with the scenes beamed back to earth from weather satellites. Start with the big picture – an updated view of the entire world's weather (www.ssec.wisc.edu/data/comp/latest_cmoll.gif). Then move in for a closer view. Most of the major weather Websites (mentioned above) all have links to satellite imagery covering the UK, Europe and the rest of the world.

■ **Watch the weather on a webcam.** To see the weather in some of the furthest reaches of Scotland, check out the webcams at The Met Office site (www.metoffice.com). At the

BBC Weather Centre (www.bbc.co.uk/weather) there are hourly slideshows featuring a snapshot taken every four minutes of the view from a camera mounted on the roof of the BBC TV Centre in London. The camera is often positioned by a weather forecaster to view a particular event of interest. For weather webcams at other locations in the UK try the Douglas Weather Webcam (www.manx.net/weather/Douglas.asp), The Snowdon Weather Stations Project (www.fhc.co.uk/weather/live) and the Sheffield weather webcam site (www.instantinfo.co.uk).

■ **Be prepared for severe weather** by getting up-to-date storm warnings. The Met Office (www.metoffice.com) and the BBC Weather Centre (www.bbc.co.uk/weather) both issue regular bulletins on any severe weather events that may cause loss of life or damage to property. Weather Wise (www.weather-wise.com) provides news reports and explanations of various weather phenomena around the world.

■ **Learn more about meteorology.** The Met Office (www.met-office.gov.uk/education/index.html) provides information and resources for learning about the weather. The BUBL Link/5:15 Catalogue of Internet Resources (www.bubl.ac.uk/link/m/meteorology.htm) provides links to many sites explaining various meterological phenomena such as rainbows, hurricanes and snow crystals. Many university Websites also have pages dedicated meteorology. Try the University of Reading (www.met.rdg.ac.uk) or The University of Edinburgh (www.met.ed.ac.uk).

■ **Storm chasing** isn't as popular in the UK as the USA, but try SevereWx.co.uk (www.severewx.co.uk.chasing.htm) to learn more about it.

WEATHER REPORT SITES
Here are some helpful sites for more information on local and global weather.

WEATHER ONLINE (www.weatheronline.co.uk)
This site has an abundance of weather information. There are UK and world weather summaries, snow reports, water temperatures and humidity levels.

ENVIRONMENT AGENCY (www.environment-agency.gov.uk)
For the latest flood warnings in force throughout the UK, and local news on flood prevention schemes.

THE MET OFFICE (www.metoffice.com)
UK and world weather forecasts and news, satellite pictures, webcams and severe weather warnings.

LANDINGS: EVERY WEATHER LINK KNOWN (www.landings.com/_landings/pages/weather.html)
A fantastic collection of weather links. No matter what it is, if it is related to world weather you will find a link to it here.

Software and resources

THE SHAREWARE ALTERNATIVE

Inexpensive software programs, distributed on the honour system, can be downloaded and purchased.

■ **Is it the program for you?** Before buying expensive software, check to see if there is a low price shareware program available that performs exactly the same task. You can sample shareware for free before deciding to buy.

■ **Shareware is often offered free to nonprofit or educational institutions.** If you are a student, teacher, or work for a charity, you may be able to get a program for nothing.

■ **Although most shareware is free of charge,** the author usually requests that you pay a small fee if you like the program and use it regularly. By sending the fee, you become registered with the producer so that you can

receive service and updates. You can copy shareware and pass it to friends, but they too are expected to pay a fee if they decide to use it.

■ **Shareware differs from public domain software** in that it is copyright protected. This means that the copyright holder retains the right to choose how his or her creation can be used.

■ **Trying to choose between several different software programs** that do the same thing? Many shareware sites list how many other people have downloaded the program. If it is very popular, the chances are that the program will be good. Other shareware sites, such as ZDNet (www.zdnet.com), let users give programs ratings

■ **To avoid contracting a virus,** download your shareware from a dependable site on the Net, such as Tucows (www.tucows.com) or CNET (http://download.cnet.com).

■ **Remember, shareware is a means of distribution,** not a statement of quality. There are a lot of great shareware products out

there, and a few duds. That's why it's best to try out the program first before you pay for it, which is the beauty of shareware. But if you do keep the program, don't forget to pay.

■ **If you have problems downloading** or using a shareware program, you can always contact the author directly. Most problems can be easily cleared up this way. If the author is a member of the Association of Shareware Professionals, and you are unable to resolve a dispute, then try contacting the ASP ombudsman by filling in a Web form at www.asp-shareware .com/info/asp-ombudsman.asp.

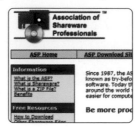

■ **Shareware organisations can also help with PC problems** and questions. Try the Website of The Association of Shareware Professionals (www.asp-shareware com). CNET Shareware.com (shareware.cnet.com) has an extensive range of problem-solving guides.

■ **If you have written a program and would like to distribute it** on the Internet as shareware, upload your program to one of the top Shareware sites by FTP (File Transfer Protocol). Uploading instructions can be obtained from DotNet (www.dotnet.com/wsftp.html), and Simtel.net (www.simtel.net/upload.php).

◗ See also **How to download files,** p. 240.

SOFTWARE FOR NOTHING

Who said there is no such thing as a free lunch? A mass of freeware is available from Internet libraries.

■ **Different people define freeware in different ways.** It is quite common for applications to be free only for home use, while business users have to pay. Other freeware libraries may contain restricted demo versions of a software package or programs that are only free because they force you to watch advertisements.

SHAREWARE AND SHAREWARE INFO SITES
Your guide to free or inexpensive Internet downloads.

CNET DOWNLOAD.COM
(http://download.cnet.com)
Offers a large selection of shareware.

CNET SHAREWARE.COM
(http://shareware.cnet.com)
This service lets users browse and download freeware, shareware, demos and upgrades.

SHAREWARE FAQ
(www.faqs.org/faqs/shareware-faq)
A frequently-asked-questions site.

NERD'S HEAVEN
(http://boole.stanford.edu/nerds heaven.html)
Links to a wide range of software directories where you can find almost anything.

JUMBO.COM
(www.jumbo.com)
A large library of shareware, including games, business software, multimedia programs, desktop publishing, screensavers and MP3 players.

Make sure you read all the details before you download a program – it is time well spent.

■ **Do be wary of free software.** Make sure you consider the consequences when you download files from an unknown source. Also, some hackers create apparently useful freeware programs, which have a hidden, malicious function, such as installing a virus on your computer (these are called Trojans). Wherever your freeware comes from, make sure you check it with a recent antivirus program before using it.

■ **Where can you find freeware?** All the best libraries on the Internet have a few freeware programs at least, and a wide selection of sites specialise in freeware and nothing else. Just type 'freeware' into a search engine to find them, or try the freeware sites listed above.

■ **Searching the Internet for freeware can be a time-consuming exercise,** so why not let someone else do all the work for you? The Lockergnome Website

(www.lockergnome.com) produces a free daily newsletter, sent to you by e-mail, with lots of pointers to useful freeware.

▸ See also **How to download files,** p. 240.

WHERE TO FIND FREE GRAPHICS

Whether you are interested in photographs, clip art or graphics, you can get them on the Internet.

■ **Found an image you like?** Just right-click on it, select **Save Image As**, and it's on your hard disk for you to access whenever you wish. Bear in mind, however, that although copying for personal use is not a crime, reusing material in a newsletter or on a Website without the owner's permission means you are breaching copyright.

■ **Want some special graphics for a birthday or Christmas?** Claire Amundsen Schaeffer's Free Graphics site (www.freegraphics .com) has links to 130 sites in her holiday section alone. The site provides an excellent directory of other graphics sites as well.

■ **A larger directory, covering everything on the Internet that's free,** is the FreeSite (www.thefreesite.com). Its biggest sections cover such topics as Web space and software, but it also has a useful list of free graphics resources. To get a regular e-mail, register for the weekly newsletter.

■ **Quantity doesn't always guarantee quality,** so don't restrict yourself to the biggest sites. Much useful software can be found at smaller sites, often run by individuals. How do you set about finding these 'boutique' sites? Try visiting the Graphics Ring (www.graphicsring .com), where you can find hundreds of such sites.

■ **Still haven't found a site that provides what you need?** Visit your favourite search engine. Enter the phrase 'free graphics' at Google (www.google.com) and you will probably get over 100,000 hits.

■ **You can get photographs from the Web as well.** It's not just graphics that are available free of charge on the Internet. Although they're harder to find, there are some great Websites, such as Free Images (www.freeimages .co.uk), that provide free photos to download.

▸ See also **The world of graphics,** p. 154; and **Copyright and the Web,** p. 249.

Buying on the net

There are thousands of online shopping sites, selling everything imaginable, and giving you access to a wider range of goods and services than ever before – often at lower prices. You can shop for bargains, find unusual or rare items, or just buy your groceries.

KEEPING A SENSE OF PROPORTION

Weighing the pros and cons. Internet shopping is growing in the UK and there are more and more online stores based in this country. However, some of the online stores you turn up in an Internet search will be in the USA. It is, of course, possible to buy from overseas, but you will need to calculate the full cost of your goods in UK currency to see if it is worthwhile or not. You will also need to take into account the length of time it will take to receive your purchase, and whether you will have to pay taxes on arrival.

SHOP SAFELY ONLINE

Armed with the following advice, you're ready to shop till you drop!

- Make sure that amazing discount item really is a bargain.
- Comparison shop before you buy, if possible.
- Look for bargains at online auctions.
- Beware of hidden costs and don't forget to account for shipping and handling.
- Be sure to weed out unreliable vendors and individuals.
- Avoid illegal or questionable products and services.
- Make sure sites are secure before giving them your credit card number (see p. 308).
- Protect your privacy – avoid the Internet curse of spam (see p. 323).
- Always pay by credit card.
- Keep paper copies of all your records.

If you've just gotta have it ... It is often the case, particularly if you are interested in a specialised area, such as classic science fiction films on video, or rare maps, that what you want is simply not available in the UK. In that case, buying on the Net may be your best option. But, before you go mad in the virtual shopping centre check the price of the product plus delivery and convert it into sterling. Most large shopping sites provide handy currency converters for you to make the calculation.

Save time and effort by using a search engine that allows you to limit your search for online shops to UK sites only. You can do this with Yahoo! (uk.yahoo.com), Google's UK site (www.google.co.uk), Lycos (www.lycos.co.uk) and Excite (www.excite.co.uk).

IS THE PRICE RIGHT?

Many Websites claim to offer huge discounts, but to know if they are accurate, you need to know what the standard retail price is in the first place. Before making your purchase online, compare the prices with those in high street stores.

Find the best prices. Comparison shop at price clearing houses. Sites such as The Price Guide UK (www.priceguideuk.com), Kelkoo (www.kelkoo.co.uk), and abcaz (www.abcaz.com) list prices from hundreds of vendors on thousands of products. Others, like CNET Shopper

(http://shopper.cnet.com), specialise in one kind of item – in this case, computer equipment – but from dozens of vendors. Some of these services allow you to make comparisons across the entire Web, but sorting out the vast numbers of vendors to find one near you can be tedious.

Don't forget the hidden costs of the shipping and handling of any items you purchase. Additional costs can sometimes be added off-screen and the true total purchase price is only sent to you at a later date in the e-mail order confirmation. If you cannot get specific charges in writing or printed from the Website, shop elsewhere. It may not be that the company is hiding costs, but it is always best to be cautious. Many e-retailers, particularly computer and peripheral sellers, will also charge you when you return unsatisfactory merchandise.

Buy in bulk. If shipping and handling fees seem set to cancel out the discount of shopping online, consider the possibility of spreading the costs. Talk to friends and family about bulk buying, especially around Christmas time.

TIME TO HIT THE SHOPS

Shopping with a conscience. Want to make sure workers get a fair wage for their labours? You can buy great things at fair trade sites and feel virtuous about it as well. Try One Village (www.onevillage.co.uk/fairtrade.htm) or Oxfam (www.oxfam.org.uk/shop).

Do your weekly shop online and get your food delivered to your door. Most of the major supermarkets now have online services with home delivery. Try Tesco (www.tesco.com), Sainsburys (www. sainsburys.co.uk) or Asda (www. asda.com).

So many shopping sites, so little time. How do you find what you want? Some stores are linked together into 'virtual malls', but nowadays many have their own domain name. To find your favourite chain store, try typing in the name, sandwiched between www and .co.uk or .com. If that doesn't work, or if you're looking for a smaller store, check one of the shopping directories. Take a look at UK Shop Online (www.uk-shop-online.co.uk), Shop and Save (www.shopandsave .co.uk) or Shop Safe (www.shopsafe.co.uk). This site lists the top UK online shops that have been quality checked for security, range, delivery of goods and prices.

FOREARMED IS FOREWARNED

To prevent fraud, shop by credit card. Some card companies will cover your entire loss if you do get caught out. Consider getting a separate card for e-commerce to keep track of your spending.

To avoid schemes and scams, always look for a physical mailing address and phone number – a PO box number is not enough. If the company refuses to hand out this information, be suspicious. Legitimate retailers will always have these details clearly stated. Never trust a vendor who asks for highly personal information.

Do your research first. Fraud-alert Websites, such as Internet ScamBusters (www. scambusters.org), list reports of shady characters and scams. Or post a message in a newsgroup or chatroom to see if anybody knows of a particular e-tailer. Still concerned? Try another site.

You can get arrested for seemingly innocent transactions. For instance, beware of buying a new credit identity, which often uses fake identification documents. A number of agencies around the world are turning extra attention toward dubious Internet offers.

You may be shopping electronically, but you still need to keep paper records. If the company site has any guarantee regarding the item you are buying, print it out – Web pages can change very quickly. Print out a copy of the order confirmation as well and save any paperwork shipped to you, such as acknowledgments

receipts and even business letters. Most Internet fraud centres around small print that was never there and subscriptions that won't or can't be cancelled. A paper trail will help you fight these.

To avoid floods of junk mail, unwanted phone calls and spam, make sure you shop only at sites that post a privacy policy. Otherwise, the owners of the site are perfectly within their rights to sell your name and information onto unknown third parties.

See also **Worried about credit card fraud?** p. 308; **Home buying the easy way,** p. 309; **Finding the ideal car,** p. 310; **Becoming a global collector,** p. 311; **Amazon: the Internet success story,** p. 312; **Auction it though eBay,** p. 312; and **Auction sites,** p. 314.

MAJOR SHOPPING SITES

Millions of sites are devoted to online shopping, so have your credit card at the ready!

DIY
Many of the major DIY stores are now online.
Homebase (www.homebase.co.uk)
Screwfix.com (www.screwfix.com)
B&Q (www.diy.com)
Plumb World (www.plumbworld.co.uk)

BOOKS
There are thousands of online bookstores.
Amazon UK (www.amazon.co.uk)
Bol.com (www.bol.com)
WH Smith (www.whsmithonline.co.uk)
Reader's Digest (www.readersdigest.co.uk)

HOME ELECTRONICS
The big names in electrical goods are online.
Comet (www.comet.co.uk)
Dixons (www.dixons.co.uk)
Currys (www.currys.co.uk)
Dabs.com (www.dabs.com)

TOYS
Find a gift for the child who has everything.
Early Learning Centre (www.elc.co.uk)
John Lewis (www.johnlewis.com)
Adventure Toys (www.adventuretoys.co.uk)
Popcorn (www.popcornlive.co.uk)

Shopping online

WORRIED ABOUT FRAUD?

Concern about Internet crime stops many people from buying online. However, you just have to exercise a little caution, and online shopping can be safe and fun.

■ **Keep your standards.** Apply the same rules to purchasing online as you do when buying from a store or over the telephone. Make sure you are satisfied that the company you're dealing with is trustworthy. Are they an established business or are you responding to an unsolicited e-mail promising goods at too-good-to-be-true

prices? Is there a telephone helpline and a street address? If the Website does not inspire confidence, then shop elsewhere.

■ **Can your browser use Secure Sockets Layer?** SSL is a data encryption system used by Websites to ensure that your personal details are transmitted in a secure format. Version 2 and later of Netscape Navigator and Microsoft Internet Explorer support SSL. To see whether a Website is operating the Secure Sockets Layer before submitting your details, look out for a small locked padlock symbol or key at the bottom of your Web browser window.

■ **Look for a Digital Authentication Certificate.** This guarantees that the site you're looking at is what it purports to be, and not a front set up to

deceive you into releasing your financial details. Click the key or padlock icon to view the certificate.

■ **If your debit or credit card is used fraudulently** and you can prove this to the bank or credit card lender, you should not be liable. But remember to notify the card issuer as soon as you notice any unauthorised transactions. Many online retailers are so confident of their security that they offer to pay a

AIR TRAVEL SITES

Want to make a quick getaway? Check out the following sites.

EASY JET (www.easyjet.com)
OPODO (www.opodo.co.uk)
**CHEAP FLIGHTS 123
(www.cheap-flights-123.co.uk)**
These flight sites offer similar services. These generally include a flight finder and booking form, together with details of discount or Internet-only specials.

AIRLINE GUIDE (http://the-travel-guide.com/airlines.htm)
A listing of all the world's best and most reliable airlines with links to their Websites.

ABOUT.COM (http://airtravel.about.com)
This portal offers guides to various online reservation Websites, aviation security sites and a host of other travel ideas.

---

nominal sum to you in the case of fraud. So online shopping can actually be more secure than High Street shopping.

▶ See also **Security on the Net,** p. 254; **Internet banking,** p. 260; and **Buying on the Net,** p. 306.

BOOK YOUR FLIGHT ONLINE

The Internet makes it easy to book flights, shop around for the best deals or grab that last-minute bargain holiday of your dreams.

■ **Airline ticket Websites all plug in to** one of the four global computerised airline reservation systems for their information. When you're looking for the best flight deal, always check\out at least two – and preferably three or four – agencies to make sure you cover all the the options and get the best possible deal.

■ **Try specialised airline ticket and travel sites** for that spur-of-the-moment trip. The well-known Lastminute.com (www.lastminute .com) is geared toward all sorts of last-minute travel deals, while Opodo (www.opodo. co.uk) has regularly updated lists of special offers.

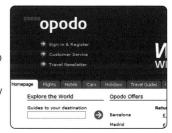

■ **There's more to air travel than just buying a ticket.** A little extra information on aircraft and airports can make the whole experience much more enjoyable. Try About's air travel area (http://airtravel.about.com) for a wealth of information and sensible advice.

■ **Lost baggage, delayed flights, rude staff?** These are all things that can happen to anyone. When you want to let the world know about it – and have your complaint forwarded to the offending airline – go to the Civil Aviation Authority's Website (www.caa .co.uk). The site offers advice on how to lodge a complaint against an airline or tour operator.

■ **For cheap long-haul flights** try being a courier. Get big discounts for delivering a package. Try The International Association of Air Travel Couriers (www.aircourier.co.uk) for details.

▶ See also **Plan your next trip on the Web,** p. 264.

HOME BUYING THE EASY WAY

It is now possible to locate a home, apply for a loan and even complete the deal all on the Internet.

■ **Find your ideal home,** without traipsing around open houses every weekend. Look on the Net – there are many sites that can locate estate agents and properties all over the country. Fish4 (jobs.fish4.co.uk/homes/estate/index.jsp) has an estate agent directory, as well as a 'Find a Home' service which allows you to search for a property specifying the type, price, range, location and number of bedrooms. AllTheAgents.com (www.alltheagents.com) has a list of estate agents in many major UK towns and cities. Websites, such as Your Move (www.your-move.co.uk) and Prime Location.com (www.primelocation .com) also offer similar property search services.

■ **Skip the middleman** and sell your home directly on the Internet. Sites such as Homes On Sale (www.homesonsale.co.uk), Capital Residence (www.capital-residence.co.uk) and Private Houses for Sale (www.privatehousesforsale.co.uk) let you list your home yourself on their site, and you can also supply a photograph in many cases. Selling privately means there is no estate agent and no commission to pay, although you do have to spend more time filtering offers.

■ **Get all the facts.** The prospect of buying a house can be a bit daunting. Fortunately there is a wealth of advice available on the Web. Read widely to get a balanced view of the what's involved. Many sites have a particular point of view to push, which is why they put the information on the Net in the first place. Start with a visit to all the major banks, where you can read their online home buying advice, even if you don't plan to approach them for a loan. For advice supplied by organisations other than mortgage lenders, try Websites such as Channel 4's 4homes (www.channel4.com/4homes) and the BBC (www.bbc.co.uk/homes/property).

■ **Apply for a mortgage online.** Shopping on the Web may work for buying gifts and airline tickets, but a mortgage? Most banks and building societies now offer mortgage services online, and these sites also offer other useful tools, such as checklists and mortgage  calculators. The best sites will ask questions then recommend the most appropriate product. Begin your search for a mortgage lender by checking out some mortgage guide sites, such as UKMortgagesOnline.com (www.ukmortgages online.com), or Mortgages Advice (www. mortgages-advice.co.uk) The UK Mortgages Guide (www.ukmortgagesguide.co.uk) lists banks, building societies and mortgage brokers.

■ **Don't forget the government.** There is a range of government help available to home buyers, including financial assistance to first home buyers in some cases. If you are in the market for

---

HOME-BUYING HELP
Seek some useful online advice for buying or selling your property.

**BBC HOMES
(www.bbc.co.uk/homes/property)**
Advice on buying, selling and moving house, as well as tips on how to add value to your property and de-clutter your home. There's also a mortgage calculator and price guide.

YOUR MOVE (www.your-move.co.uk)
An online estate agent, with property search facilities, buying, selling and moving guides, and conveyancing services.

**THE MORTGAGE CODE
(www.mortgagecode.co.uk)**
The mortgage code sets the standards of good practice for mortgage lenders.

EASIER2MOVE (www.easier2move.co.uk)
An online conveyancing service. You can monitor your move on the Web and receive text message or e-mail alerts to let you know when progress has been made.

**OVERSEAS REAL ESTATE
(www.overseasrealestate.co.uk)**
If you're looking to move abroad or buy a second home for holidays, this site has property listings from around the world.

**ALLTHEAGENTS.COM
(www.alltheagents.com)**
Find a local estate agent by searching the A to Z list of major UK cities and towns.

a house or land, check out your local authority Website to see what's on offer. Also have a look at the Website of the Office of the Deputy Prime Minister (www.housing.odpm.gov.uk).

Once you've bought your house, there's the small matter of moving in. Head for a Website with help and advice on the moving process. Help I Am Moving.com (www.helpiam moving.com) has useful links, a moving guide and checklist. There are even downloadable change of address cards.

Looking for something a bit larger? Purchase a castle, chateau or vineyard through French Castles (www.french-castles.com), Best Properties (www.best-properties.com) or Castles for Sale (www.castles-for-sale.com).

Islands in the stream. If you're looking for a gift for the person who has everything, how about buying them an island? For listings of islands for sale, take a trip to Vladi Private Islands (www.vladi-private-islands.de) and The Property Organisation (www.property.org.uk/unique/ islands.html). Some islands, notably those off the coast of Canada's Maritime provinces, are very cheap. If you do decide to buy an island, remember to make sure it has a source of fresh water.

▶ See also **Getting legal advice online**, p. 293.

FINDING THE IDEAL CAR

Research, compare and purchase the car of your dreams.

OK, so you can't test drive a car online, but it's the perfect place to begin your initial research. Visit the sites of all the main manufacturers, such as Ford (www.ford.co.uk), Peugeot (www.peugeot.co.uk), Volkswagen (www.volkswagen.co.uk) and Toyota (www. toyota.co.uk). A typical site will have brochures and specifications for current models and links to dealers in your area.

Search for local dealers. When you feel it's the right time to start looking for a new car, visit the Websites of local dealers to see what they are offering. There are many sites that can point you in the direction of local dealers and

CAR SITES
Put yourself firmly in the driver's seat by browsing online before you buy.

ONE STOP CAR ADVICE (www.onestopcaradvice.co.uk)
This site has everything for the prospective car buyer and more. There are links to car dealerships, as well as valeting, repairs and insurance services.

RAC (www.rac.co.uk/carbuying)
Advice on car buying and ownership from one of the UK's leading breakdown services.

AUTO TRADER (www.autotrader.co.uk)
The online version of the well-known second-hand car magazine, with more than 200,000 vehicles available.

AUTOBYTEL (www.autobytel.co.uk)
There are new and used cars for sale on this site that also offers finance and insurance.

those specialising in certain makes of car. At One Stop Car Advice (www.onestopcaradvice.co.uk) there are extensive listings of new and used car dealers. On the Carworld's dealers page (www. carworld.co.uk/dealers/index.htm) you can search for a dealer according to geographic location in the UK. Fish4 also has a dealer directory (www .fish4.co.uk/cars/dealer/index.jsp).

Get quotes from several different sites before you buy. Information is power, especially when haggling over the price of your new car. Obtain quotes from some of the bigger sites such as CD Bramall (www.cdbramall.co.uk) and Modern Autos (www.modernautos.co.uk). Not all Internet quotes are reliable, so if one seems to be much better than the others, then it probably is too good to be true.

You can find real bargains on auction sites such as eBay (http:// pages.ebay.co.uk/ebaymotors), but there are plenty of overvalued cars, too. Take note of eBay's warning that the seller assumes all responsibility for listing this item. You should contact the seller to resolve any questions before bidding. Buying at auction is always a gamble, but you can bag a bargain by taking a risk.

Need financing for your car? Remember, there's no need to take out a loan with the same dealer who is selling you your car – unless they can offer a really competitive rate of interest. Visit several dealers and banks to compare repayments.

After buying a car, search for the history of that make using a search engine like Google (www.google.co.uk). Unless your choice of car is very rare, you will probably find several examples. Discover owners clubs, too. These are sites where people who own the same car share information, such as news, recommendations and servicing advice.

Own a classic car? There's a vast online community out there, where you can swap everything from advice to car parts and news. To link up with other classic car owners, or browse the classifieds for your dream machine, check out Old Classic Car UK (www.oldclassiccar.co.uk) or Classic Cars.com (www.uk-classic-cars.com).

▶ See also **Buying on the Net,** p. 306; and **Auction sites,** p. 314.

BECOME A GLOBAL COLLECTOR

The world's largest marketplace, the World Wide Web, puts you just a few clicks away from millions of individual buyers, sellers and merchants of collectable goods.

Come together. Wanted or For Sale notices on collectibles sites bring buyers and sellers together, and posting a request on a site's message board is likely to bring you many offers. The more message boards you try, the more chance you have of finding what you want.

More than a garage sale. Collectibles sites are a great resource for learning as well as trading. You can often swap information with other collectors, or get the benefit of expert advice and background on a particular item.

If you're a beginner in the world of collectibles, start with a community guide, such as About.com's (http://collectibles.about .com). You'll find sensible advice from the more experienced enthusiasts on how to start building collections. You can also use the message boards to ask for advice, check on the availability of items and compare prices. Collectors love to share their enthusiasm and knowledge.

> **In The Spotlight**
> Wed, Feb 12, 2003
> **Pixieware Cookie Jar**
> The vintage Pixie kitchen accessories produced the one thing that's been missing from the line is Howards has remedied that.
> **More:** Barb's Cookies - & Crumbs -- Not Always
> **Contest:** Enter - The Monthly Drawing!
>
> **New Collectible Stuff This Month:**
> Cute Baby Boyds Plush, Thomas Blackshear's T
> **Special:** Matchbox 2003 - New Releases Show
>
> **Mike's Card Corner**

Narrow down your choice of sites when searching. Instead of typing in a request for collectibles, which will bring up hundreds of Websites, try, for example, cricket collectibles. To find precisely what you're looking for, you can define the search even further, by typing, for example, 'Muhammad Ali boxing collectibles'.

Attend sales at online auction sites. Vendors post their goods with a reserve price – the minimum they're prepared to accept. The item then remains on the site for a fixed period, typically 10–14 days. The highest bidder at the end of that period gets the goods.

Broaden your horizons. Visit a Website where collectors from all over the world meet to trade and chat. Sites such as World Collectors Net (www.worldcollectorsnet.com) can open up different sources, especially in Europe.

Find out what your collectibles are worth. Use an online price guide, such as Kovels (www.kovels.com). Registration is free and you will find price guidelines for thousands of antiques and collectibles. Alternatively, get an online appraisal for items you suspect may be valuable. Some of the major auction houses, such as Sotheby's (www .sothebys.com), provide online valuation forms.

A picture is worth a thousand words when it comes to selling a collectible. It's a lot easier for buyers to make a decision if they can see what the object looks like. Use a digital camera, or scan in a conventional photograph, then upload the image from your computer to the Website where you wish to sell the item.

▶ See also **Buying on the Net,** p. 306; **Auction it through eBay,** p. 312; and **Auction sites,** p. 314.

COLLECTIBLES SITES
Whether you're buying, selling or just browsing, try these sites.

**ANTIQUES UK
(www.antiques-uk.co.uk)**
This site has listings of UK and international antique dealers and auctions, as well as clubs and trading associations.

**WORLD COLLECTORS NET
(www.worldcollectorsnet.com)**
The online meeting point for collectors. There's information and features on dozens of popular collectibles.

BOOKFINDER (www.bookfinder.com)
Absolutely the best site for book collectors. Type in a title or author and see what is on offer around the world, arranged by price. You will be amazed by the range of books that appear when you enter a query.

EBAY COLLECTIBLES (http://pages.ebay. co.uk/collectibles-index.html)
With thousands of items up for grabs, there's something here for everyone.

The world's largest online book shop, with no checkout queues.

■ **Amazon (www.amazon.co.uk) is so big** that it has encouraged other retailers to join in cooperative ventures, selling their products alongside those that are offered by Amazon itself.

Next time you're at the Amazon site, check out the range of zShops, where you can buy anything from toys to lighting.

■ **You'll need to set up an account** before you can buy anything from Amazon, but you can still add items to your shopping basket. Buying from Amazon for the first time? Shop first, then click **Proceed to Checkout** and the sign-in page appears. If you don't have an account, select **I am a new customer** and follow the prompts.

■ **Once you've entered the checkout and account pages** the address should change to 'https://' or a closed lock should appear on the bottom bar. If this doesn't happen, don't buy anything – it means your browser doesn't support secure shopping.

■ **Buying several items?** Pay close attention to the shipping instructions. Remember, there is a minimum shipping cost. If the items are not all in stock, Amazon may ship them one at a time, thus increasing your shipping fees. If you don't mind waiting, it will be much cheaper to have everything shipped at once.

■ **If you purchase items regularly from Amazon** you will notice personalised recommendations whenever you sign in. This is because the site remembers the items you buy and suggests other similar items you may be interested in purchasing.

■ **At the Amazon marketplace** you can sell your unwanted books, CDs and electrical goods. To become a marketplace trader you must

first register, and agree to abide by the code of practice. Marketplace traders are rated by the Amazon customers who buy from them, so if you sell goods regularly this way, prospective buyers can get an idea of how reliable you are at dispatching your goods and how accurately they fit your description. The Marketplace means you can also buy items you want cheaper than the listed Amazon price. When you make a selection, look for the box entitled More Buying Choices. New, used and collectable versions of your choice will be listed here, if there are any.

▶ See also **Buying on the Net,** p. 306.

The auction Website at eBay is a great way to buy and sell just about anything, from CDs to cars.

■ **Don't dive in and start bidding immediately.** Take time to research the item and the seller – eBay (www.ebay.co.uk) provides plenty of help. Most pages include lists of frequently asked questions (FAQs). There are also Online tutorials and community forums for help.

■ **Check the feedback and add your own.** Sellers will often ask buyers to comment on the service being provided. Regular sellers quickly build up a profile, which should reassure you about their honesty and ability to honour any agreement you make with them. Whenever you complete a buying or selling transaction on eBay, it's always a good idea to contribute your feedback, whether it is positive or negative. This will help future bidders to make an informed judgment when dealing with the same seller.

■ **Look for sellers who are ID verified.** All sellers have to start somewhere, so not everyone is going to have dozens of positive feedback reports. If a new seller has an ID Verify logo in their Feedback Profile, it means that they have satisfied an independent agency, acting for eBay, that they are who they say they are and that they reside at the address they have supplied. So at least you know who you are dealing with.

How to: Buy a book or record from Amazon

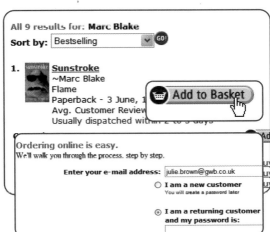

1 Connect to amazon.co.uk. Click on the appropriate tab for the type of item you want. Amazon has extensive search facilities for tracking down goods. If you are browsing for books or records, read the reviews and comments posted by other buyers.

2 If you want to buy an item, place it in your shopping basket. When you have finished browsing, go to the checkout. New customers will need to register and receive a password. Existing customers must confirm their address, payment details and shipping method.

■ **Check where the item you want is located.** Since eBay is now a worldwide service, items listed in eBay's search engine may be drawn from Europe, Japan or America, and you may incur additional shipping fees and import duties when you buy. For mainly local content, use the local eBay site (www.ebay.co.uk). If you're considering an international purchase, make sure that the seller will send the item abroad before you make your bid.

■ **Bids move up in even, incremental amounts,** but these are just a minimum and you can sometimes get an edge by increasing your bid slightly above the minimum amount. For example, in a £5.00 increment auction, you can increase each of your bids by £5.01.

■ **If you plan to sell an item,** consider the situation from the buyer's perspective. Would you bid for the item you are selling? Reassure potential customers with as much information about yourself and your items as possible. Set up an About Me page with relevant information, and get ID Verified in the rules and safety section if you do not have positive feedback yet.

■ **Think visually – scan in a photo of your item.** People like to see what they're buying. A picture reassures buyers that the item exists and gives them at least some idea of its condition. Keep the image file size small:

potential buyers might lose interest if they have to wait a long time for it to load onto their screens. Instructions on uploading a picture to the eBay server are given on the eBay site.

■ **Set a reserve price.** Unless you want to risk selling for much less than you expected, set a minimum acceptable final bid. Then, if the auction fails to reach the reserve, you do not have to sell. The reserve price is not the same as your starting price, which can be very low to tempt buyers to start bidding.

■ **Post a link to your auction** in relevant newsgroups and forums to draw potential buyers. If you plan to be a regular seller, create a Web page and advertise your upcoming sales to attract the maximum amount of interest.

■ **If your item doesn't sell,** you can try again for free, but it's a good idea to change the formula to make the item look fresh. You could swap the image, change the lot title, and lower the minimum and reserve prices.

▶ See also **Become a global collector,** p. 311; and **Auction sites,** p. 314.

How to: Bid for an item in an eBay auction

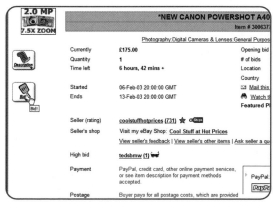

1 When you see an item you're interested in, click on the description to find out more about it. The item line tells you the current highest bid, how many bids have been made and how long the auction has to run.

2 The next screen gives you access to information about the item and the seller. The icons next to the seller name indicate how many previous auctions the seller has run and whether the seller has a personal information page. To place a bid, click on the bid icon.

3 At the bidding screen, enter your maximum bid. eBay acts as a proxy bidder on your behalf, bidding in the stated increment until your maximum bid is reached. If you are successful, the seller should contact you within three days to make arrangements.

Auction sites

Buying through auction Websites can be addictive; you suddenly realise that you can't live without that string-art kit, like the one you had in the 1970s. Whether you make the occasional bid, or are serious about buying and selling, there's no denying that Net auctions are good fun.

GETTING STARTED

A large part of the appeal of online auctions is that you can tap into global markets. You are not restricted to buying only what is available locally. Bear in mind, however,

that buying overseas does have its pitfalls. Make sure you know the relevant exchange rate, the cost of delivery (and how long it will take) and whether or not you will need to pay import duty. Many of the online auction houses on the Web are in the USA, but if you don't want to buy globally, restrict yourself to local ones.

Take advantage of interactive auction sites that generate automatic bid alerts, send auction schedules to your Inbox, and deliver a running commentary during the action. Or eliminate days of hassle and nail-biting by waiting until the last minute to bid. eSnipe (www.esnipe.com) will help you get a better price at eBay (www.ebay.co.uk) by monitoring an auction for you and bidding on your behalf at the last possible minute.

There are two types of online auction sites: commercial and person-to-person. At a commercial site, buyers compete with one another to buy goods owned and stored by a company conducting the auction. A person-to-person auction site such as eBay, on the other hand, acts as a go-between for both the buyer and the seller. After the bidding, the site notifies the winning bidder and the seller, who must then make their own arrangements to complete the transaction privately.

SPECIALITY SITES

Looking for that missing album to complete your collection of Grateful Dead memorabilia? Try one of the many specialist auction sites.

DABSXCHANGE.COM (www.dabsxchange.com)
Printers, cameras, camcorders, speakers and hard drives – buy and sell electrical and computer goods on this site.

LOT WATCH (www.auctionlotwatch.com)
Search several auction sites at once. Type in the item you want to buy and Lot Watch will locate it in different online auctions.

EROCK (www.erock.net)
Everything concerned with rock 'n' roll

memorabilia. Auction categories include The Beatles, Kiss Memorabilia and Vinyl Albums.

GOLDCAST JEWELLERY AUCTION (www.gold-cast.co.uk)
Gold, silver, fashion, antique and modern jewellery items are auctioned at this site.

NEW LINE CINEMA AUCTIONS (www.auction.newline.com)
Can't live any longer without owning Jackie Chan's camouflage suit from *Rush Hour 2*? This is the site for you!

BEFORE YOU BID

One way that person-to-person sites try to prevent fraud is by posting buyer and seller feedback. On eBay, for example, other buyers and sellers can attach their positive, negative or neutral comments to your account, depending on how they rated your reliability and honesty. If your feedback rating falls to minus four, your account is terminated and you will no longer be allowed to participate. Always check a seller's feedback rating before you make a bid.

All bidding is not the same. Some auction sites will allow you to state just how much you want to pay and will let you know if anyone accepts your bid. In reverse auctions, the prices go down until someone buys. Other auction sites work by searching merchants for the price that you specify. Collaborative sites pool buyers and seek the best deal from merchants.

Some commercial auction sites have live bidding forms. With these you can make bids

BIDDING DOS AND DON'TS

Enjoy the thrill of bidding but keep it safe, armed with these tips.

- Do use credit cards to make purchases. They protect you against fraud.

- Don't ever send cash. If someone demands cash, it's a sure sign of fraud.

- Don't deal with people who won't provide their name, street address and telephone number. Several auction sites supply information about how long a seller has been a member and whether they have had previous sales. Others require a valid credit card number from anyone who wants to buy or sell via their site.

- Don't be afraid to ask the seller lots of questions. If a seller will not answer a question, perhaps they have something to hide about the item for sale.

- Do check out what similar items have sold for in previous auctions. Several auction sites, including eBay, let you look at the history of items sold in the past 30 days.

- Do try to get help if you are a victim of fraud. Auction sites will often reimburse you to maintain their reputation. Check the site's terms and conditions.

in real time, so you don't have to sit there waiting for your e-mail to eventually show up. However, you'll find that you get hooked on auctions much faster this way.

Auctions usually run for three to seven days. The last hour of a multi-day auction is a study in consumer psychology. It often features such players as the Must-Make-A-Deal beginner, who indiscriminately fires bids in at the upper price range; the Stealth Bidder, who sneaks in just at the bell to grab your find; and the Shopping-Is-Hell Veteran, who has invested too much time over the last five days to walk away now. The final few minutes can be agonising – and expensive if you don't watch out.

Want to know the value of a family heirloom or just find out more about its history? Visit the auction house Sotheby's (www.sothebys.com) for possibly the most extensive database of antiques, collectibles and memorabilia on the Internet. Alternatively, Christie's (www.christies .co.uk), which has sales rooms in London, New York and Los Angeles, lets you see upcoming auctions and locates specific lots for sale.

SECRETS OF SUCCESS

Before you make your first bid, check out the shipping costs at the auction house's FAQ page. Shipping fees vary from site to site, even though all auction houses use standard courier services. These costs can easily run up the price of your fabulous find to an unacceptable level.

Done your research? Set your top price and don't falter. Put in a low bid first, and if you receive notice that your bid was trumped, you can move higher. If you fear that you might weaken under pressure, submit your price and don't ask for updates.

Buying high-priced items? Consider an escrow service, like Auctionpix.co.uk (www.auctionpix.co.uk/escrow.html). This

company, and others like it charge a percentage of the price to act as a go-between. You mail payment to the escrow service, they verify it, alert the seller when

everything checks out, and the goods are shipped. After an examination period, you notify the service, which prepares a cheque and mails it to the seller. Escrow services often accept credit cards, so buyers get extra protection.

If you crave quick action, jump into one of the short-term auctions. These lightning rounds always start at crazy low prices, but the bids don't stay there long.

Buying and selling online for profit? You may have to pay taxes. The Inland Revenue expects you to report profits when you complete your tax return. Buying from overseas? You may need to pay import duties. Check out the HM Customs and Excise site (www.hmce.gov.uk).

See also **Buying on the Net**, p. 306; and **Auction it through eBay**, p. 312.

E-mail

Before there were e-companies, e-business, eBay and e-commerce, there was e-mail.

■ **What can you do if you want to send** someone an e-mail, but you don't know what their e-mail address is? Normally, you would go to the From field of the last e-mail the person sent you to obtain the return address. But what if the person has never e-mailed you? Well, the first solution – and the simplest one – is to phone the person and ask for the address. Alternatively, you could try accessing an online directory of e-mail addresses. You can find a list of directories at www.emailaddresses.com/email_find.htm.

■ **What if the name you need isn't in an e-mail directory,** or you can't decide which John Smith is the one you want to get hold of? Many people give their e-mail address when they contribute to online discussion groups, or place information on the Internet. If you know that the person you are looking for has an interest in some subject, then you can use a search engine to look for their name, coupled with a keyword. With luck, you may find a page featuring the person's e-mail address. For example, if your friend Beth Jones is an avid gardener, you can try typing 'Beth Jones' and 'garden' into a search engine.

■ **It was only a matter of time** before someone turned faxes into e-mails. In fact, there

are numerous services that enable you to use your e-mail account as a fax. Some supply you with a personal fax number and when anyone faxes that number, the fax is converted into an e-mail attachment and sent to the e-mail address you

specified. Most suppliers charge a fee, although some, such as NKmessage (www.nkmessage. co.uk) and eFax (www.efax.com) are free.

■ **If fax to e-mail works,** then e-mail to fax must also be possible. And it is: you can send a message or document via e-mail to the fax

service's site and then have it forwarded via fax to the number you specify. Fax.co.uk (www.fax.co.uk) and eFax (www.efax.com) offer this service, as does j2 Global Communications (www.j2.com). Most of these companies charge on a per-fax and per minute basis.

■ **Want to send a phone message** to someone who doesn't have computer access, but you don't want to speak to them directly? Or maybe you'd like to send yourself a wake-up call? Then try the Nortel Networks Website (www. nortelnetworks.com). The site takes your e-mail message, converts it into a voice message through a speech synthesiser, then delivers it to a phone number at a time you choose. This is ideal for communicating between different time zones.

■ **Travelling light with just a mobile phone?** There are now a number of services that will let you access e-mails from a telephone. You can also check to see if you have received any new messages. Check out the services offered by Philips (www.philipsspeechprocessing.com /t/pages/t_frameset.htm?t_222.htm).

■ **Want to keep using your regular e-mail address** with your ISP while you're on a business trip or holiday? Use an e-mail gateway site to access the account and read and send messages. All you need when travelling is access to a PC with a Web browser, so you'll be able to use any cybercafé or a friend's Internet-connected computer. One such gateway is Mail2Web

WEB-BASED E-MAIL SERVICES
Check out these special sites for help with your e-mailing needs.

ANONYMIZER (www.anonymizer.com)
Mask your ISP address by sending e-mail through this third party re-mailer.

HOTMAIL (www.hotmail.com)
Microsoft's very popular, free e-mail service.

EXCITE (www.excite.com)
The site offers free e-mail accounts.

YAHOO! (www.uk.yahoo.com)
A free, web-based e-mail service including spam protection and many other features.

DISNEYSITES (www.mickeyfan.com)
Host your e-mail on Disney's Website, and have a mickeyfan.com address.

SPAM FREE (WWW.SPAMFREE.ORG)
Learn how to deal with (and ditch) junk e-mail that finds its way into your inbox.

(www.mail2web .com). You will need to give the name of your e-mail server (this is usually the part after the @ symbol in your e-mail address), your user name (usually the part before @), and your e-mail password. When you reply to mail, your reply will look as though it has come from your usual account even though you've accessed it elsewhere. These services are usually free, but there's often a catch – you may have to view a short advertising message.

Pick Up Your Email

■ Ever wonder how people manage

to get e-mail addresses like trueblue@woopwoop .com? They use a forwarding service. These services let you choose almost any address. Anything mailed to that address is re-routed to your real e-mail service provider. Forwarding services also let you keep one e-mail address, no matter how many times you switch ISPs. Both Mail.com (www.mail.com) and V3 (www.v3.com) offer an e-mail forwarding service, where you can choose your address.

■ Few people realise that it's sometimes possible to recall and delete an

e-mail message before it reaches its destination. To do so from Outlook, open the message from your Sent folder and click on **Actions**. Now select **Recall this message**. If the message still resides on your company's or ISP's mail server, it will be deleted and you'll be informed that the process of deletion has taken place. But remember you will need to react almost immediately to recall the message in time.

■ Concerned about e-mail privacy?

The person most likely to be reading your e-mail is probably your boss. Don't assume that anything you send from your personal office e-mail is private. To keep your e-mails to yourself, send them from a third party account, such as Hushmail

(www.hushmail.com), which offers secure and encrypted mail, or Hotmail (www.hotmail.com).

■ Do you receive a lot of regular

mail from the same few people? Set up an e-mail filter. E-mail filters look for names, words or phrases within the messages, and transfer any that match your filter settings straight to a designated folder as soon as you receive them. Automatic sorting makes your mail easier to keep track of (or ignore), and can be indispensable if you are on a number of mailing lists or receive a lot of junk mail. In Outlook Express,

> 1. Select the Conditions for your rule:
> ☐ Where the From line contains peop
> ☐ Where the Subject line contains sp
> ☐ Where the message body contains
> ☐ Where the To line contains people
> 2. Select the Actions for your rule:
> ☐ Move it to the specified folder

filters are stored under **Message Rules** in the **Tools** menu. To activate the filters, check the relevant boxes. In Netscape, you will find **Message Filters** in the **Edit** menu.

■ Setting up an e-mail to exchange

files? There's no guarantee that attachments will arrive intact. The best idea is for both parties to enable the MIME (Multipurpose Internet Mail Extensions) standard in their e-mail software. Eudora, Outlook, Outlook Express and Messenger all support MIME. Even with MIME engaged, expect some quirks. For example, the only way to reliably transmit from Eudora to Lotus Notes is by stuffing files in Zip archives before sending them.

■ Internet e-mail addresses typically

have two main parts, separated by an 'at' symbol (@): brian@bigbusiness.co.uk, for example. The user name (brian) refers to the recipient's mailbox. The host name (bigbusiness), also called the domain name, refers to the mail server – the computer where the recipient has an electronic mailbox. The host name is usually the name of a company or organisation. Then there's a dot followed by two letters (.co), indicating the type of domain (commercial) and finally the country code (.uk), which is United Kingdom. US E-mail addresses don't contain a country code (.com, .org and .edu are examples), but most others do. Many country codes are easy to guess, such as .nz for New Zealand and .jp for Japan.

■ An address containing .com or .co

typically means that the host is a business or commercial enterprise, or an online service. Most companies use this extension. A host name ending with .edu indicates a university or educational facility, .org shows the host is a non-commercial organisation and .gov is used by government agencies. Other extensions include .mil for military and .net for network.

■ If you know where someone

works, you can usually guess the domain name part of their work e-mail address. But what about the user name? The recipient's name may be their last name, their first initial and last name, or their first and last name separated by a full stop, dash or underscore – it's worth experimenting.

HOW TO GET A PORTABLE E-MAIL ADDRESS

Get an e-mail address that you can take with you wherever you go.

■ Keep up with your e-mail while

you're on the road or away from home on holiday. Subscribe to a Web-based provider, such as Hotmail (www.hotmail.com) or Yahoo! Mail (www.mail.yahoo.com). These services let you check mail from any computer that is connected to the Net. You can set them up to retrieve mail from your other e-mail accounts.

■ Don't forget to delete mail you've

read from an account mailbox. If you exceed the fixed amount of storage space allocated to you, the provider may delete messages for you.

■ When your first-choice name is

already taken on one Web-based e-mail provider – and you don't want to be janesmith98 – try another site. One of them may have your name available. For an extensive list of Web-mail providers, visit the Free Email Address Directory (www.emailaddresses.com).

■ Get a free e-mail address for life.

Sign up with a mail-forwarding organisation such as Bigfoot (www.bigfoot.com). You get one e-mail address to give out, and the mail will be forwarded to any account you want.

■ Check Web-mail accounts regularly. Some services terminate your account if it is not used for a given period – typically, 90 days.

■ About to change your ISP, job or city? Fear you'll lose touch by having a new e-mail address? To avoid this, you can register your details with an online service such as ContactDetails (www.contactdetails.com). All you do is list the site ID on e-mails, business cards, and so on, so that others can have access. If you change your e-mail address, the updated details will always be available at the ContactDetails site.

SEND AN E-GREETING

Snail mail greetings cards may go the way of the horse and cart now that e-cards come with sound and animation.

■ The easiest way to send an e-greeting is to log on to one of the many

Websites offering themed e-cards such as Hallmark (www.hallmark.com), the BBC (www.bbc.co.uk/e-cards/), Excite (www.excite.co.uk/ecards) or Reader's Digest (www.readersdigest.co.uk/ecards). Just select the image, type in a message and the address of the recipient, and off it goes.

■ Before you send an e-greeting, use the site's preview facility to see the card as the recipient will. Some sites also let you choose a time and date to send the greeting.

■ The same e-card can be sent to many different people by simply clicking the site's **Add Recipient** button. This is an ideal way to send out party invitations, for example.

■ If a simple photograph or cartoon doesn't seem exciting enough, send an animation instead. You will need the Flash plug-in to view most animated cards, as will your recipient. You can download the latest version of Flash for free from the Macromedia site (www.macromedia.com/downloads).

■ Want to make sure an e-greeting card got there? Ask for e-mail confirmation to be sent to your own mailbox. When your recipient checks their mail, you'll know they've seen your card.

■ Some sites allow you to add a voice message to your e-greetings. To hear the message, your recipient needs the RealPlayer plug-in (downloadable from www.real.com).

■ Use your favourite e-greetings Website's address book to store e-mail addresses and important dates so all the information you need is gathered in one place.

▸ See also **Understanding e-mail**, p. 316.

MANAGING YOUR ADDRESS BOOK

Outlook Express has an Address Book to store e-mail addresses, but it can do much more.

■ Use a keyboard shortcut to open the Address Book quickly by pressing **Ctrl+Shift+B** while Outlook Express is open. Alternatively, click on the **Address Book** button on the Toolbar.

How to: Create an e-greeting in Outlook Express

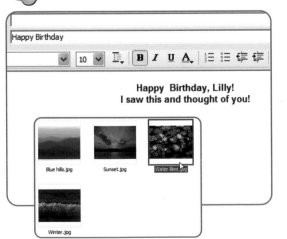

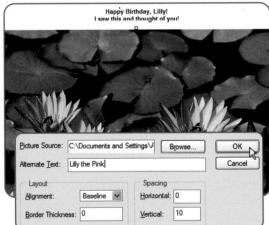

1 Open a new message in Outlook Express. Type in your greeting and format it the way you want. Centring short phrases can add impact. Go to **Insert → Picture**. Click **Browse** in the dialogue box and navigate to where the picture is stored. Select it and click **Open**.

2 Then click **OK** in the Picture dialogue box. The picture appears beneath your message. If the picture is too large or too small, you can resize it by grabbing the handles at the edges and corners. Now you can save the message and e-mail it to your friend.

Sharing a PC with others? Make sure each user sets up a separate identity, so each member of your family or work group has their own Address Book. In Outlook Express, go to **File ➔ Switch Identity** and click on **Manage Identities**. In the pop-up dialogue box that appears, click **New** and enter the name and password for a new identity.

To add a new contact to the Address Book manually, open the Address Book and click on **New ➔ New contact**. In the Properties box, enter the details you want to record under each of the tabs, then click **OK** when you have completed all the necessary information.

The Address Book can store much more than just e-mail addresses. Use it to record home and business telephone numbers and addresses, as well as personal information and notes about your contacts.

Add new contacts to your Address Book as soon as you receive an e-mail. When you open the message, right-click on the person's name, then click **Add to Address Book**. To add from your Inbox or another folder, right-click on a message in the message list, then click **Add Sender to Address Book**.

Add e-mail addresses to your Address Book every time you reply to a message – useful if you reply to a group e-mail. Go to **Tools ➔ Options ➔ Send** tab, and check **Automatically put people I reply to in my Address Book**.

The Address Book can be used without running Outlook Express, so you can update details independently. To access the Address Book from the Windows Desktop, go to **Start ➔ All Programs ➔ Accessories** and select Address Book.

Transfer contacts from another program, such as Netscape Messenger to Outlook Express. To import the data directly into your new Address Book, go to **File ➔ Import ➔ Other Address Book**. Choose the program you've been using and click on the Import button. If your old program is not there, try exporting the addresses from it as a file and then importing the file into Outlook Express.

Your Outlook Express Address Book is a database that gives you powerful methods for organising and viewing your contact details. You can sort the contacts alphabetically by first name, last name or by e-mail address and choose to see them in ascending or descending order. In the Address Book, go to **View ➔ Sort By**, and select the desired option from the drop-down menu.

Often you may want to send messages to a group of people. With the Address Book, you can organise your contacts into mailing groups for different purposes, so that you can send e-mail to everyone in the group (see 'How To', below). You can have any number of different groups, and contacts can belong to as many of the groups as you wish.

How to: Set up a mailing group in Outlook Express

1 In the Address Book, highlight the folder from which you want to create your mailing group. Select **New Group** from the File menu. The Properties dialogue box appears. Enter a name for your group in the Group Name box and click on **Select Members**.

2 Your main contacts list appears on the left hand side. Highlight a name and click **Select** to add that person to the list of group members in the box on the right. Continue until you have selected all the members of your group, then click the **OK** button.

3 To add a person who isn't in your Address Book, enter a name and e-mail address in the boxes at the bottom of the Properties dialogue box and click **Add**. To send a group message, type the group name in the To box, write your message, and click **Send**.

Outlook Express

Outlook Express is the ideal e-mail and newsgroup program for home and small business users. You can store your friends' and colleagues' e-mail addresses and other details, set up folders in which to store messages, and work offline or online.

SENDING & RECEIVING E-MAILS

Outlook Express checks for new messages every 30 minutes by default, as long as you are online. To change this, go to **Tools ➜ Options**, select the **General** tab, and enter the new time interval in Send/Receive Messages.

Send a file as an e-mail attachment. You can transmit almost any type of file – a photo of your new baby or a newsletter, for example –

but avoid attachments larger than 1 MB. Write your e-mail, click the **Attach** icon on the Toolbar, select the file, and send the message as usual.

Accessing attachments. E-mails with attached files have a small paperclip icon beside them in the message list. When viewing the message, click on the large paperclip to open the attachment or save it to your hard drive. Save several attachments at once by going to **File ➜ Save Attachments**.

OUTLOOK EXPRESS TOOLBAR BUTTONS
Here are the tools of the trade for an express ride with e-mail.

 Addresses Opens your address book, where you can store and retrieve e-mail addresses, phone numbers, home addresses and much more.

 Find Lets you search e-mails by word, topic or name. Click the arrow next to the button for more options, such as online directory searches.

 Create Mail Opens a new message. Click on the arrow to the right of the button to choose from a range of stationery options.

 Forward Opens the selected e-mail so you can send it on to another person. Any attachments received in the original e-mail remain attached and are sent to the new addressee.

 Reply Opens a new message window in which to type a reply to the sender of the selected e-mail.

 Reply All Opens an e-mail for replying to everyone to whom the selected e-mail was first sent. Use with great care, particularly if your reply is at all sensitive to some of those concerned!

 Send/Recv Tells Outlook Express to connect to the server, send any outgoing e-mails waiting in your Outbox and download incoming e-mails.

Print Allows you to print out the e-mail you have selected, to keep a paper copy of it for your records or perhaps to read later at your leisure when you're away from your computer.

Forgotten your friend's birthday? Send them an e-greeting card on the day. Click on the arrow next to New Mail and select a design from the drop-down menu. Or, click **Select Stationery** to see more designs. Choose one, type your message, and click **Send**.

Deleted an e-mail containing vital instructions? Take a look in the Deleted Items folder. It might be there if you haven't emptied the folder. To empty the Deleted Items folder select **Edit ➜ Empty Deleted Items Folder**. If you are certain that you will never want to look at any deleted e-mails again, set Outlook to empty the folder each time you exit the program. Go to **Tools ➜ Options**, select the **Maintenance** tab, and check the top box.

MULTIPLE USERS AND ACCOUNTS

Separate personal mail from hobby newsletters. Set up two different e-mail accounts (see 'How to', p. 321), each one with a different address. You can monitor them both at the same time by clicking the **Send/Recv** button, or check just one of your accounts at a time by clicking the arrow beside the Send/Recv button and selecting the account that you want.

Set up Inboxes and Address Books for each family member. Go to **File → Identities → Add New Identity**. Type in a name and password, if required. To switch identities, go to **File → Switch Identity**, and select a new name. There's no need to close Outlook Express or treminate your Internet connection.

THE ADDRESS BOOK

Add your new neighbour's e-mail address. Click the **Addresses** button on the Toolbar. Click **New → New Contact**. Select the **Name** tab and type the name. Add the e-mail address and other information. Click **OK** to create the contact.

Do you regularly e-mail a group of people? Create a Mailing Group so you can send the same e-mail to several people at once. Open the address book, select **New → New Group** and name your group. Click on **Select Members** and choose all the people you want to include by highlighting them and clicking the

Select button. Next time you e-mail your group, click the small **Addresses** button next to 'To:' at the top of your message, and select your group from the pop-up menu (see 'How to', p. 319).

NEWSGROUPS

Use Outlook Express as a newsgroup reader. A newsgroup is a discussion forum, where users air their views on a particular topic. In order to join one, set up a news account. Contact your Internet service provider (ISP) and ask them for their News server (NNTP) address. Go to **Tools → Accounts**, and select the **News** tab. Go to **Add → News**, and enter your ISP's NNTP server information.

There are millions of newsgroups worldwide, covering everything from local news to knitting. But how do you find them? Go to **Tools → Newsgroups** and type in a word or topic. All the newsgroups on that topic will appear. Click the most likely group, press **Subscribe**, then **OK**. To unsubscribe, right-click

the group and click **Unsubscribe**. You can't view newsgroup listings until you've completed all the steps to set up a news account.

WORKING MORE EFFICIENTLY

Inbox out of control? Create folders for storing different types of messages. Click on the **Local folders** icon. Go to **File → Folder → New** and type in a name. Click **OK**. Now simply drag and drop messages into the appropriate folder.

See also **Your Internet service provider**, p. 218.

How to: Set up an e-mail account

rdplus.net
Welcome to Online Signup

The Internet Made Easy

Congratulations! You're just a few minutes away from full Internet access!

...plus.net bring you the very latest in Internet software, which you have just installed, and now an unbeatable offe ...ternet access - exclusively available to rdplus.net customers in the UK.

...he pages that follow allow you to sign up with rdplus.net and then start using the Internet straight away. It should ...ore than 5 minutes to complete the re... ...ly set ...ou full free Internet access.

...couldn't be easier to register with rdpl... ...and ...me brief contact details. Then choos... ...e au...

User Name	
Pick a suggested User Name	○ joanne.smith2@rdplus.net ○ j.smith4@rdplus.net ○ joanne.s2@rdplus.net
- or	
Choose your own User Name	joanne_smith @rdplus.n...

User Name and Email Address

The User Name you choose has two functions. Firstly it's the nam... ...also your Email Address. So, if you chose the User Name of ismi...

Done

1 **Sign up with an Internet service provider, such as rdplus (www.rdplus.net), that includes e-mail addresses and newsgroup access. Your ISP will give you the details you need to set up an e-mail account: your account name, password, e-mail and server addresses.**

Tools | Message | Help

Send and Receive ▶
Synchronize All
Synchronize Folder
Mark for Offline ▶

Address Book...   Ctrl+Shift+B
Add Sender to Address Book

Message Rules ▶

Windows Messenger ▶
My Online Status

Accounts...
Options...

Add ▶	Mail...
Remove	News... Directory Service...

Joanne Smith
Find a

Read Mail

E-mail address: joanne.smith2@rdplus.net

For example: someone@microsoft.com

2 **Open Outlook Express and go to Tools → Accounts and click on the Mail tab. Click on Add → Mail. Now start entering the details for your account. You'll need to give the account a name (you may add further accounts later) and fill in your e-mail address.**

My incoming mail server is a   POP3 ▼   server.
    POP3
    IMAP
    HTTP

Incoming mail (POP3, IMAP or HTTP) server:
pop3.rdplus.net

An SMTP server is the server that is used for your outgoing e-mail.

Outgoing mail (SMTP) server:
smtp.rdplus.net

Password: ●●●●●●
    ☑ Remember password

Congratulations

You have successfully entered all of the information required to set up your account.
To save these settings, click Finish.

3 **On the next screen fill in the addresses of the incoming and outgoing mail servers at your ISP (try the Help section on your ISP's website if you don't know them). Finally add your e-mail password and your new account is set up and ready to use.**

USE FILTERS TO SORT YOUR MAIL

When the sheer volume of incoming e-mail gets overwhelming, filtering functions let you file and store messages in a manageable way.

■ **Set up folders and filters** for the main categories of e-mail you receive, such as work, finance and family. As mail is received, any that can be categorised is stored in the relevant folder.

■ **Filters are a great way to organise newsgroup messages**, which can arrive in overwhelming numbers. You can create newsgroup filters the same way as e-mail filters.

■ **Are you being bombarded by junk e-mail** from specific addresses? Use filters in Outlook Express to keep unwanted messages out of your Inbox. Go to **Tools → Message Rules → Blocked Senders List**, and add the address or addresses. Now all e-mails from that source will go straight to the Deleted Items folder.

■ **Reorganise that bulging Inbox** in Outlook Express by applying a newly created filter (or filters) to messages that have already been downloaded. Go to **Tools → Message Rules → Mail**. In the Message Rules dialogue box, click on the **Apply Now** button. Select a rule or rules then press the **Browse** button and choose the folder to which you wish to apply the rules. Click on **Apply Now** and the rules will take effect.

▶ See also **Understanding e-mail,** p. 316; and **Outlook Express,** p. 320.

JUST A FRIENDLY REMINDER

Arrange an e-mail to remind you of anniversaries, birthdays or those jobs that always slip your mind.

■ **There are hundreds of reminder services** on the Internet that will help you keep track of minor events, such as when to take your car in for its regular service, or major events, such as a wedding anniversary or business meeting.

■ **Need help getting your day organised?** RememberIt.com (www.rememberit.com) is a free e-mail reminder service. Enter any important dates and the service will send you reminders via e-mail to your computer or phone. Alternatively, you can use a scheduling service that lets you perform a wide range of helpful tasks. ScheduleOnline (www.scheduleonline.com/login.php) helps you to schedule meetings and tasks, create to-do lists, e-mail invitations and send e-mail reminders.

■ **Use an online personal organiser.** A free virtual notepad that stores phone numbers, addresses, e-mail addresses, Web bookmarks and notes is available from Jungle Mate (www.junglemate .com). Or organise your daily activities with shareware such as RedBox Organizer, which you can download from Pass the Shareware's Website (www.passtheshareware .com/software_downloads.htm).

How to: Set up filters in Outlook Express

1 Go to **Tools → Message Rules → Mail**. Click **New** and in the top section of the dialogue box set the conditions for the rule (Outlook Express's name for a filter). Scroll through the options and check how you want incoming e-mail filtered.

2 In section 2 select the actions for your rule. You may select more than one. You can place messages in a folder, for example, or choose not to download a message from the server. Click on the underlined text in section 3 to define the rule further.

3 Follow the instructions in the dialogue box. In the top line of the Select People dialogue box, type the text you want the rule to search for, click **Add**, and then **OK**. Finally, give the rule a name and click **OK**. The new rule is now listed in the Message Rules window.

Get your life organised by using a free calendar service. Yahoo! Calendar (www.calendar.yahoo.com) is accessible from any Internet-connected computer and allows you to automatically send yourself reminders of appointments, birthdays, job deadlines and other important dates.

Set different reminder applets to appear on your screen at different times of the day. Reminder (www.geocities.com/ SiliconValley/Lakes/5365/reminder.html) provides a free applet that acts as a reminder note. Once launched, it runs in the background as a small and unobtrusive window on your PC's Desktop.

Create coloured notes to display on your Desktop. There are lots of shareware sticky note programs available on the Internet. You can use virtual notes to write messages to yourself and 'stick' them on your computer Desktop. Try Stickynotes (www.cs.utexas.edu/users /tbone/stickynotes.html) or StickyNote (www.tenebril.com/products/stickynote).

Problems keeping those New Year's resolutions? Resolutions Reminders (www.hiaspire.com) is an award-winning site that offers a free e-mail reminder service. It includes goal-tracking tools, and lots of information on keeping resolutions of all kinds, from losing weight to quitting smoking.

KEEP YOUR RESOLUTIONS THIS YEAR!! Sign up for a **FREE** monthly **Resolution Reminder** e-mail th

USING SIGNATURE FILES

End your e-mails with a signature, joke or your contact information.

To create a signature file in Outlook Express, go to **Tools ➜ Options**. Outlook Express will display a dialogue box. Click the **Signatures** tab to create a simple text signature or configure the program to use a specific file for your signature. You can also configure Outlook Express to include the

signature in every message. To add a signature on a message-by-message basis, open a New Message window, then go to Insert and select **Signature**.

In Netscape Messenger, first create a separate text file that includes your signature information. You can use any text editor – for example, NotePad, WordPad or Word (so long as the file is saved as text only). Save the text file to your hard drive in your e-mail program folder. After you create the text file, use **Edit ➜ Preferences ➜ Identity ➜ Choose** to tell your e-mail program where to find the file so that it can attach copies to your e-mail messages.

DEALING WITH INTERNET JUNK MAIL

Spam is the Internet version of junk mail – unwanted and unsolicited e-mail that clogs up ISPs and slows down the Net.

Think twice before you allow your name to appear in member directories or other places listing e-mail addresses. Spammers (people who send spam) use programs called Web crawlers, which trawl the Internet looking for Web addresses.

Use an Internet service provider that takes a hard line with spammers. Since there is no law targeting spam, it's up to ISPs to stem the junk mail tide. The more conscientious ISPs fine any spammers they catch abusing their service, while others won't allow members to send a message to more than 50 people at the same time.

Never respond to spam. Don't buy anything from spammers and don't ask to be removed from their list – any sort of response from your email address confirms you as a 'live' address. The best solution is to delete any spam that arrives in your inbox as soon as you receive it.

Retaliation almost never hurts spammers, but you could end up hurting yourself. One of their favourite tactics is to forge the e-mail address of the last ISP administrator to boot them off. When people retaliate – by sending the spammers back 50 copies of what they sent, for example – the ISP administrator receives your retaliation instead of the spammer. The ISP then complains to your ISP, and you risk being the one to lose service for harassment.

You can try to throw Web crawler programs off their track by placing a set of invalid characters in your e-mail address. For example, if your address is john@ihug.com, you can put john@NOSPAMihug.com in your return address field. Include a note in any e-mails you send explaining that, to respond to you, they'll need to remove 'NOSPAM' from your address.

If you can't beat it, filter it. One of the most effective ways to deal with incoming spam is to filter it. Most e-mail programs offer filtering features (see p. 322). You can get all your incoming messages screened as they download for specific words and known spammer e-mail addresses. Your e-mail account will automatically reroute the suspect spam to a designated folder. Then you can delete the spam without having to waste time reading it.

The Internet community

JOINING A MAILING LIST

A mailing list brings together people who share a common interest or hobby and lets them communicate by e-mail.

■ **There are thousands of mailing lists,** covering wide-ranging, and often bizarre topics, from flower arranging to conservation. So if you're a Rolling Stones fan, you might like to find out about Rolling Stones mailing lists, where you can chat via e-mail with many other like-minded enthusiasts.

■ **How does it work?** Most mailing lists are just collections of addresses of people – from as few as 10 to 100 or more – who are interested in the same topic. Every message that is written is copied automatically to all the other people on the list, and everyone is free to reply. Individuals list members can also e-mail each other in private if they wish to.

■ **There is another type of mailing list,** however, in which one person is responsible for gathering material from subscribers and other sources. This material is then compiled into a newsletter which is sent out at regular intervals to subscribers. Subscribers e-mail the administrator of the list only, not each other. Many newsletters carry advertising to help cover costs, and some can be little more than vehicles for advertising.

■ **Mailing lists can be very useful professionally,** quite apart from their entertainment value. If you work as a researcher or a programmer, for example, a mailing list can put you in touch with a community of other professionals around the world who are working in the same field. If you strike a particular problem, a quick e-mail to the list will reach the people most likely to be able to offer you useful

suggestions and help. What's more, you can reach your community of virtual friends often within a matter of minutes.

■ **Some lists generate too many messages.** Avoid the e-mail avalanche by subscribing to a list's digest mode if it is offered. This sends you all the messages to the group each day in a single e-mail that is easier to manage. .

■ **How do you find a mailing list?** There are several directories of mailing lists on the Web (see box, p. 325). Otherwise, use a search engine such as Google (www.google.com). For example, entering 'Rolling Stones' and 'mailing list' into a search engine should bring up a few Rolling Stones mailing lists.

■ **Check your favourite Websites.** Another way to find mailing lists is to scour Websites about the topic you're interested in. The sites might include links to relevant mailing lists.

■ **If you can't find a list you like** on a specific subject, host your own. You can set one

up for free at sites like Yahoo! Groups (uk.groups.yahoo.com), MSN (groups.msn.com) or CoolList (www.coollist.com).

■ **How do you subscribe,** now that you've found a mailing list that interests you? Wherever the mailing list is shown – such as on a Website – you should also find instructions on how to subscribe. This will generally involve sending an e-mail to the mailing list administration address provided, along with a special command, such as 'subscribe' followed by your e-mail address.

■ **When you send your subscription e-mail,** open up a new, blank e-mail, type the address into the To: field, leave the Subject field blank, and type any subscription commands in the body of the e-mail, right at the top. Usually you don't need to type anything else. If you have a signature file with your name and address, disable it.

■ **Keep the welcome note!** Once you have subscribed to a mailing list, you'll receive a welcome e-mail, giving you more information about rules and etiquette, how to post to the list and how to unsubscribe. Save this e-mail somewhere safe for later reference. It's a good idea to create a folder in your e-mail program for keeping all these registration details.

■ **Having problems subscribing?** Even if you've used slightly incorrect terminology for the mailing list software, it can usually recognise that you're trying to subscribe and will send you a Help file containing a detailed explanation. If you still can't work it out, you can take a look at the Mailing List Gurus'

advice (www.gurus.com/lists/subbing.html).

■ **Lurk for a while.** Don't send off your opinions, questions and comments straight away. Spend some time just reading through the e-mails that come through, to get a feel for the list. If the list has an FAQ document, read that.

■ **Turn off the delivery confirmation option** if your e-mail program has one. These confirmations – known as receipts or confirm delivery options – are a big annoyance to list administrators. If you fail to disable them, every time you receive a message from your mailing list your mail account will automatically send a confirmation reply, which will go to the administrator and everyone on the list. Not the best way to make yourself popular!

■ Don't use Rich Text Formatting (RTF) or HTML formatting
in the e-mails you post to the list. A mailing list will have people using all kinds of e-mail programs, some of which have problems dealing with RTF or HTML e-mails. Check through your e-mail software to see if there's an option to turn either of them off. Rootsweb (helpdesk.rootsweb.com/listadmins/plaintext.html) has instructions for various e-mail programs. In Outlook Express, for example, go to **Tools ➔ Options**, click the **Send** tab, and select Plain Text, not HTML, for both settings.

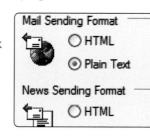

■ Stick to the topic.
If you've joined a list about the Rolling Stones, the other list members would love to read snippets of news, stories, song lyrics, opinions or anything else about the band. They probably don't want to read the joke your friend just sent you, no matter how hilarious it is, or receive virus warnings – most of which are hoaxes anyway.

■ Make your e-mails easy for others to read.
Remember, your e-mails could be reaching hundreds or thousands of people. Use short, informative subject lines. Don't type in capitals. Don't use acronyms, unless you are sure that everyone else on the list will instantly know what you are talking about. Leave lines between paragraphs, use punctuation and re-read and spellcheck your e-mails before hitting Send.

■ When replying,
include enough of the original e-mail to give the context for readers. Not everyone will have read the original e-mail. On the other hand, don't quote absolutely everything in your reply. Feel free to delete earlier, irrelevant threads of replies in the e-mail you receive. If you're replying to someone who wrote at length before actually posing their question, delete everything but the question you're replying to.

■ Don't send file attachments.
If you have a file you'd like to share with the list, post a note asking if anyone wants it. They can then e-mail you separately to request the file.

■ Consider replying privately
instead of to the whole list. Think about whether everyone is really interested in a lengthy discussion you and one other person are having. The same goes for arguments. If you want to get heated, take it offline for a while. Most people don't want to read other people's e-mail wars.

■ Be considerate.
A mailing list is a community and its tone is set by the e-mails you and other users send. Always try to be polite and friendly. The other people on the list could come from anywhere in the world and may have very different beliefs and humour from yours. Think carefully about how you'd present yourself in person and try to do the same online.

■ Aaargh! How do I unsubscribe?
Remember that e-mail you received on subscribing? Now's the time to dig it out and search it for instructions on unsubscribing. Alternatively, next time you receive an e-mail from the list, look carefully at the beginning and the end. There may be instructions on how to unsubscribe. If you still can't work out how, or if the information isn't clear, visit the Publicly Accessible Mailing Lists Website (paml.alastra.com), where you will find links to a detailed guide on the best way to unsubscribe.

■ Changing e-mail address?
When changing your e-mail address, unsubscribe from all mailing lists first. Otherwise, any e-mails sent to your old address will bounce back to the mailing list. The unfortunate list owner will be avalanched with lost mail and will have to delete you from the list.

■ Off on holiday?
If you're planning to set up an 'I'm on holiday' autoreply message, unsubscribe from all mailing lists to avoid bouncing messages and autoreplies. Mailing list administrators hate it when mail bounces back.

▶ See also **Understanding e-mail,** p. 316; **Outlook Express,** p. 320; **Use filters to sort your mail,** p. 322; **Using signature files,** p. 323 and **The rules of netiquette,** p. 331.

LISTS OF LISTS
Want to know more about mailing lists? Visit these sites of directories.

TOPICA (www.topica.com)
This directory of over 63,000 mailing lists is not only organised into subject categories, but it's also searchable. It covers the major lists as well as independently managed ones.

GOOGLE WEB DIRECTORIES (directory.google.com/Top/Computers/Internet/Mailing_Lists/Directories)
Google's compilation of mailing directories gives thousands of lists by category.

YAHOO! (uk.groups.yahoo.com)
Yahoo!'s searchable list arranged by category.

TILE.NET (www.tile.net/lists)
Search or view by name, description or host country. Only includes Listserv mailing lists.

PUBLICLY ACCESSIBLE MAILING LISTS (paml.alastra.com)
One of the original directories of lists.

PRODIGY (www.goodstuff.prodigy.com/Mailing_Lists/index.html)
An index of this ISP's own up-to-date mailing lists, searchable by name or subject.

Chatrooms

One of the most popular uses of the Internet is as a forum for people all over the world to communicate in real time. This is done using IRC (Internet Relay Chat), which consists of various separate networks of servers that allow you to chat online with anyone at anytime.

WHAT IS A CHATROOM?

A chatroom is an online discussion group where you can converse with your friends and colleagues in real time. This means that instead of having to wait for a reply, as happens with ordinary e-mails, your message is sent simultaneously to all the other people in the chatroom and appears on their screens at the same time as well. Similarly, any reply or new message that they type will appear on your screen and those of the rest of the group.

What about my children? As with the rest of the Internet, children should be supervised at all times when using chatrooms. Some rooms have a 'Host', who watches the conversation and warns users if they break the rules, and excludes repeat offenders. While most rooms, even if they do not have a host, follow a code of conduct that means they are likely to be polite and friendly, some are certainly not suitable for children. Your Internet Service Provider should be able to block access to chatrooms if you want them to.

GET CONNECTED

The IRC networks vary a lot in size. The largest are probably Undernet, IRCnet, DALnet, NewNet and EFnet. The original IRC net, EFnet, is still extremely popular, and often has more than 32,000 people online at any one time.

To connect to an IRC server, you need to run a program known as a client. Go to mIRC

(www.mirc.com) to download a free client. This site will guide you through the download process, which takes just a few minutes. Once connected to a server, you can join one or more channels, devoted to topics ranging from movies to the weather.

You don't have to connect to IRC to have a chat. Many Internet sites, such as Yahoo! (uk.chat.yahoo.com) and Lycos (chat.lycos.co.uk) have chatrooms of their own. There are also Web-based chat sites with hundreds of rooms, like Talk City (www.talkcity.com) and Chat House (www.chathouse .com). None of these alternative chat facilities requires special software. In order to find a list of popular Web chat channels, check out the list at the 100hot site (www.100hot.com/chat).

Conversations may be public (where everyone in a channel can see what you type) or private (messages between just two

people, who may or may not be on the same channel). There are hundreds of IRC servers worldwide. To find a list of them, go to the IRC Help site (www.irchelp.org/irchelp/networks).

Once you have downloaded your IRC client software and logged on to one of the servers, see what channels are available on that server by typing '/list'. You can view thousands of listed channels. To narrow the list down, type '/list-min 10' for example, to view channels that currently have a minimum of 10 users.

FAVOURITE EMOTICONS AND ABBREVIATIONS

Chatrooms often use abbreviations and combinations of keyboard characters that create face symbols called 'emoticons'.

:-)	Λ smiley face (on its side)
:-(	A frown
;-)	A wink
:-P	Someone sticking their tongue out
X=	Fingers crossed
{}	Hugging
$-)	Greedy
0:-)	Angelic
}:>]	Devilish
brb	Be right back
bbiaf	Be back in a flash
bbl	Be back later
ttfn	Ta ta for now
np	No problem
imho	In my humble opinion
lol	Laughing out loud
jk	Just kidding
wb	Welcome back
rotfl	Rolling on the floor laughing

To navigate the IRC, you need to use commands. All commands start with a forward slash symbol (/). If you omit the /, anything you type will be transmitted to the channel as a message. Although there are hundreds of commands, you can get by most of the time with just 20 or 30 of the basic ones (see box, right). For a complete list of commands, check either the help file of the server or NewIRCusers.com (www.newircusers.com/ircmds.html).

CREATING A CHANNEL

A channel is a chat forum. Begin by picking a name that is not already in use. For example, to start a channel called 'film real', type '/join #film real'. A window pops up showing you as the only person on 'film real'. Promote yourself to the channel operator by typing '/op', followed by your nickname (see below). Your nickname will now appear with an @ in front of it. Now that you're the operator, you can change the topic by typing '/topic', followed by the channel name and the new topic. Type '/quit' when you want to leave the IRC.

Every user on the IRC is known by a nickname of

their own choosing, such as Rad Lad, Sparky or Monkey. To avoid conflicts with other users, it's best to use a nickname that is not too common.

Some programs let you have a second nickname to use if your main one has been taken. The nickname for a nickname is 'nick', as in 'what's your nick?'. For a full list of the addresses and nicknames of all the people present on a channel, type '/who *'.

Channels are run by channel operators,

abbreviated to ops, who control the channel by choosing who may join, banning mischievous users and moderating the channel (in other words, choosing who may speak at any particular time). Ops have complete control over their channel, and their decisions are final. If you

BASIC IRC COMMANDS

Start your online chatting with the help of these handy IRC shortcut commands. Channel names usually begin with a hash symbol (#).

- To join a channel, type the channel name after the # symbol as follows: **/join#<name of channel>**
- To clear the contents of the window: **/clear**
- To find out who else is on the channel that you might want to chat to: **/who #<channel>**
- To show the others on the channel that you are away or not paying attention: **/away**
- To leave the channel: **/leave #<channel>**
- To get some information about someone: **/whois <nickname>**
- To change your nickname to 'hitchcock', for example: **/nick hitchcock**

- To evict someone from the channel: **/kick #<channel><nickname>**
- To ignore a nickname of another IRC user: **/ignore <nickname>**
- To find out the delay between you and others on the channel: **/ping <#channel>**
- To start a private conversation with a specific nickname: **/query <nickname>**
- To send a private message to a nickname: **/msg <nickname><message>**
- To view a list of available channels on a particular server: **/list**
- To view a list of available commands for online chatting: **/help**

are banned from a channel, you can only type '/msg' to the operator and ask nicely to be allowed back in. If that doesn't work, you will have to try another channel.

NET SPLITS AND OTHER PROBLEMS

You may occasionally find yourself disconnected from a channel by a net split. Net splits occur when networks become divided, separating you from other participants. Splits are often relatively short, but quite common on busy days. When one occurs, wait a while, then try to connect again.

A frequent IRC problem is lag, the noticeable delay between the time you type and the time someone else gets to read it. One way to reduce lag is to choose a nearby server. You can measure how bad the lag is by typing '/ping' – this tells you the current length of delay. On most clients, typing '/links' shows a list of servers on your current net. Use this command sparingly, or you may be mistaken for a link-looking troublemaker. To avoid lag, type '/dcc chat' to establish one-on-one connections, which won't be broken by a net split.

In most client software (see p. 326), you can set up a DCC chat connection by typing '/dcc chat' then the nickname of the other person. To talk through that connection, just type '/msg =nick' (note the = sign). In mIRC, you can also start a DCC chat session by selecting **DCC** and then **Chat** from the Menu. Now enter the nickname of the user with whom you wish to chat. A new window will open for that session.

Whenever you leave a chatroom, remember your netiquette and say goodbye, especially if you've participated. To quit completely, and so others can see that you're leaving, type '/quit goodbye'.

It's easy to change IRC servers. To leave one server and try another, simply type '/server' followed by the server name. It's worthwhile trying different IRC servers to see what the service is like and which one will suit your needs.

▶ See also **The rules of netiquette**, p. 331.

POST IT ON A BULLETIN BOARD

Swap information and gossip at the wired world's oldest meeting posts.

■ **A Bulletin Board Service** (BBS) is an online community, like a miniature Internet. People use Bulletin Boards both to post messages and to exchange files. Like newsgroups, they cover a wealth of subjects, from stamp collecting to bodybuilding. Depending on your interests, you can choose to access a local Bulletin Board, or one hosted in another country.

■ **No, not everyone uses the Internet!** More than 20,000 Bulletin Boards are inaccessible from the Net. Instead, you have to connect directly to the computer that hosts the BBS service using special dial-up software.

■ **You can download shareware dial-up software,** if you need it, from BBS Corner (www.dmine.com/bbscorner/). Click on the BBS Software link to see a list of programs, both freeware

and shareware, each with a brief description. Download any programs that sound promising and try them out.

■ **Many Bulletin Boards** can also be accessed from your Web browser. All you need is Telnet software, which comes free with Windows. Double-clicking on an Internet BBS link in your Web browser will bring up a Telnet window, which displays the text-based home page of the BBS. If this doesn't happen, you will need to show your browser the telnet.exe file, which you'll find in the Windows folder. Refer to your browser's Help file for details on how to do this.

■ **Beware of costs.** When dialling a BBS directly, you're charged as if you were making a normal voice call. If the BBS is on the other side of the globe, it could cost you a small fortune! To keep it cheap, choose a BBS that's local to your area. You'll also be talking to your neighbours, enhancing the community feel.

■ **Read your BBS messages offline** with an offline mail reader program. If you do want to use a foreign BBS this will help to keep your costs down. The mail reader software downloads messages to a virtual mailbox on your computer, where you can read and answer them at your leisure. When you're ready to send your replies, the application creates a new mailbox, which you can upload by redialling the BBS. This system means that fewer users are connected at any one time, keeping the service speedy and easily accessible for everyone who wishes to use it. You can download an offline mail reader from BBS Archives (www.archives.thebbs.org).

SUPPORT GROUPS KEEP YOU SANE

When you need to seek advice or just talk to someone, get online support from others in similar situations.

■ **Online support groups exist** for just about every ailment, disease, condition or state of mind you can think of. For disability-related resources, Family Village (www.familyvillage.wisc.edu) is a good place to start. Otherwise, try typing the name of your concern into your favourite search engine. You'll find plenty of links that you can explore.

■ **The most private type of support group** is a mailing list (a discussion conducted via e-mail). Write to the list and everyone else sees your message as an e-mail in their Inbox. To find a mailing list on any topic, go to Publicly Accessible Mailing Lists (paml.alastra.com).

■ **To set up a mailing list support group** of your own, contact someone in charge at your ISP, such as a system administrator or customer service representative. They will assist you in setting up and running it.

■ **Discussion groups** are another type of online support group. They work in a similar way to chatrooms. For lists of thousands of Web-based discussion groups, visit Tile.Net (www.tile.net/lists).

■ **Get 12 Step help online.** Online meetings, lists of meetings around the world, and lists of newsgroup and bulletin board support groups are all available on the Internet. Take a quick trip to the 12 Step Cyber Café (www.12steps.org) or the Twelve Step Homepage (www.twelvestep.com).

▶ See also **Joining a mailing list**, p. 324; **Chatrooms,** p. 326; and **Newsgroups,** p. 334.

SHARE YOUR INTERESTS

Web rings are collections of linked sites on the same topic that allow Web users to share interests and hobbies and to pool information.

■ **Web rings are one of the most popular ways** to organise Websites on the Internet. People like them because they often have non-commercial information and don't rely too much on intrusive banner ads.

■ **Use a Web ring as a refined search engine,** limited to a single subject or hobby. Once you've found a Web ring that interests you, find more information within it. Search within a ring on a topic and save trawling

through irrelevant sites on a search engine. Yahoo! (www.yahoo.com) lets you search individual rings or its entire network of rings.

■ **Use navigation buttons at the end** of a Web ring page to work through sites. After you visit one site, a mouse click takes you on to the next and so on until you complete the ring by returning to the first site. You can also view sites at random or in lists of five.

■ **Look out for structures** similar to Web rings, such as The Rail (www.therail.com), which takes you straight through the sites without looping you back to the beginning.

■ **Can't find a Web ring that suits your interest?** Start one of your own. Some rings have just a handful of sites; others have hundreds. By logging onto and joining WebRing (dir.webring.com/rw), you can create your own ring in simple steps. When you have finished, your new Web ring appears on the side of your home page.

■ **Web rings make very effective promotional tools,** if only for your own site or home page. In fact, the Web ring was created because of the explosion in personal home pages. You could start a Web ring to celebrate birthdays on a certain day, perhaps, or to sell memorabilia.

ALT NEWSGROUPS: THE WILD SIDE OF THE WEB

Accessed in the same way as regular newsgroups, alt newsgroups can turn up some weird news and views.

■ **You can find alt newsgroups** by using the list of groups available at Google (www.groups.google.com), including a search engine to unearth the more obscure topics.

■ **Read the newsgroup's FAQs** before you dive in; they will tell you what to expect. Check out lists of FAQs by newgroups in the FAQ section at www.landfield.com.

■ **Don't be baited into an argument** that could make you look foolish. Some people – on alt newsgroups, in particular – post trolls (outrageous messages) to provoke arguments.

■ **Not everyone wants to reveal** his or her true identity in an alt newsgroup. To remain anonymous, open another account with your ISP

 How to: Find a Web ring in Yahoo!

1 Log onto the Internet and type the WebRing Website address (www.webring .com) in your browser's Address box.

2 Search for a Web ring on your desired topic by typing a subject into the Search box and clicking on **Search**. Alternatively, select a category in the WebRing directory.

3 A list of Web rings will now appear, with the number of sites in each ring. Simply click on one you like to begin navigating your way through the Web rings.

using a nickname, or use an alternative screen name if you're an AOL user. Alternatively, open a new account with another ISP, or use a Web-based e-mail service, such as Hotmail (www.hotmail.com).

■ **Exercise extreme caution** if your children want to participate in alt newsgroups. While most are safe – if sometimes eccentric – others are objectionable. Try using blocking software (see Security on the Net, p. 254).

■ **Want to start up your own newsgroup?** It's much easier to do so under the alt hierarchy than under the traditional hierarchies. Check out Landfield's creation guide (www.landfield.com) for further details.

■ **Conspiracies,** from Area 51 to the assassination of JFK, are among the liveliest topics on alt newsgroups. Scan them all at Topica (www.topica.com/lists/Conspiracy_News).

▶ See also **Newsgroups,** p. 334.

INTERACTIVE GAMES

Join in the fun online by playing interactive games with thousands of others.

■ **You will need a fast connection,** such as an ADSL or cable line, to play 3D games online, as well as a fast processor, lots of RAM and 3D video acceleration. Avoid wasting time by making sure that your video card and operating system are supported before you start downloading a large game file.

■ **There are two types of online games:** those on private networks and those on commercial networks. If you are just starting out, you may want to begin with a private network. The best games on the commercial networks – called premium games – are either pay-to-play or require a subscription to connect to the network. For private network games, download GameSpy Arcade (www.gamespy .com/software) or Kali (www.kali.net). These will enable you to connect to games, a few of which are text-based play-by-e-mail (PbeM) games.

■ **Commercial networks** provide Internet-accessible game servers. GameSpy Arcade (www.gamespyarcade.com), GameHost (www.xoanan.com/gamehost/default.htm) and MSN Gaming Zone (uk.zone.msn.com) all give priority to games. The networks are fast, but they do charge. This is where you will find the team games, called MMORPGs (Massively Multiplayer Online Role-Playing Games), that allow hundreds of players to join in.

■ **Never played a role-playing game before?** Get experience by lurking in a play-by-e-mail (PbeM) game. The PbeM and private network games are all about creating a fantasy persona and immersing yourself in that character during the game. This can take some practice. Many e-mail games allow lurkers – people who follow the game but don't participate – to read the same game e-mail messages as the players do. Alternatively, check out the newsgroups, alt.mud (MUD is an acronym for multiuser dungeon), and rec.games.mud, or the site www.godlike.com/muds, for tips on how you take part in a role-playing game.

■ **Chat with your teammates or opponents** while you play a MMORPG, using Roger Wilco (rogerwilco.gamespy.com). Roger Wilco is a free voice chat application that allows players in an online game to talk to each other, thus eliminating text messaging – a slower means of communication. The program allows hundreds of players to chat by mixing their voices with the game's audio in real time. As well as the program you'll also need a sound card with an audio input and a headset to plug in – free-standing microphones are not a good idea because they tend to pick up noise from the game.

■ **If you are looking for a new game,** try buying specialist gaming magazines, such as PC Power Play and PC Gamer, rather than downloading demos from the Web.

■ **Before playing a PbeM game,** make sure you are familiar with your e-mail program. Many players are overwhelmed by the amount of e-mail they receive once they start playing. Setting up aliases and filters will make your game-playing smoother. Also make sure you know how to organise your e-mail using folders.

■ **Looking for professional chess or poker players** to match your skills against? Then you may well be better off in a pay-to-play or fee-based gaming site. These sites are able to attract the more serious-minded and tournament-quality players.

■ **Play premium online role-playing games** for free by participating in the beta-testing stage. Many game designers let people play for free in order to establish characters before the game is released to the public. Online magazines such as Zdnet and manufacturers' game sites will sometimes carry ads for recruiting beta-testers.

■ **Play your favourite Shockwave games** without a Web connection. Once you've played a Shockwave game on the Internet, you will find it stored in your browser's cache directory. Look for a file with *.dcr in the name. Move this file to a different folder, so it doesn't get deleted when your browser empties its cache. Now, whenever you want to play the game, fire up your browser (there is no need to actually connect to the Internet), select **File → Open File**, and open the .dcr file. Because Shockwave games are cross-platform, you can take this file to any computer with the Shockwave plug-in installed in its Web browser and play the game.

■ **You don't have to be an adolescent** to find interesting games on the Internet. If you are a crossword puzzle fan, head to your favourite newspaper site and print out the puzzle.

Many newspapers have interactive versions of their puzzles that you can complete – and check – on screen. Also try Yahoo! (uk.dir.yahoo.com/recreation/games/puzzles/word_puzzles) or 4Anything (www.4crosswords.4anything.com) for a large selection of word puzzles and crosswords.

▶ See also **Computer games,** p. 184.

THE RULES OF NETIQUETTE

Learn the basics of good Internet behaviour and how to use the Net politely and responsibly.

■ **The first rule of netiquette** is always try to give people you meet – and converse with – online the same respect that you would give someone in person. Get the full story on netiquette hints and tips from the online book Netiquette by Virginia Shea, which you can read at www.albion.com/netiquette.

■ **Flame on/flame off.** Flame is personal abuse or strident language. When Internet conversation degenerates into name-calling, it's known as a flame war. Every newsgroup has its own FAQs, describing the group rules – reading it first may save you from a flame war and help you to make friends, not enemies!

■ **Watch those capitals!** Be extremely careful about the excessive use of capital letters. The chatroom version of yelling is to write in capitals. If you do it too much, others will quickly scold you for it.

■ **Don't get taken in by e-hoaxes.** If it sounds too strange to be true, then it probably is. To learn the truth about an e-hoax, urban myth, chain e-mail or any of the pervasive flotsam and jetsam floating around on the Internet, check it out at CNET's E-Hoax Central (www.cnet.com/techtrends/0-7311128-8-7150827-1.html).

■ **Be nice to newbies.** Everybody has to begin their chatroom life at some point, so if there is someone in your chatroom who is obviously new to the medium, show them patience. If someone has a problem and you can help, do so. They may repay the favour some day.

■ **Mailing out jokes and video clips?** Make sure the people who receive them actually want them. When you spend 15 minutes downloading a huge e-mail from somebody, and then discover that it's just a video joke file that you've already seen, it's not so funny.

■ **When attaching files to an e-mail,** make sure you send virus-free files and inform the recipient of the size and type of file.

■ **Don't spam.** Spam is that dreaded unsolicited e-mail with screaming banner headlines. It's irritating and congests the Net.

▶ See also **Security on the Net,** p. 254; **Dealing with Internet junk mail,** p. 323 and **Chatrooms,** p. 326.

KEEP IN TOUCH WITH INSTANT MESSAGING

Instant messaging lets you know when friends are online so that you can chat with them privately.

■ **Instant messaging is a system of communications** that allows you to create a private online chat room with another person. There are various competing systems, but each can only connect you with other people using the same system.

■ The major instant messaging systems include AOL Instant Messenger (www.aim.com), Windows Messenger or MSN Messenger (messenger.msn.com), ICQ (web.icq.com) and Yahoo! Messenger (uk.messenger.yahoo.com). Windows Messenger is built into Windows XP and is compatible with MSN Messenger. Like many of the other systems, it allows you to send pictures or files to the people you are chatting with.

■ If you are using Netscape Communicator with Windows and the AOL Instant Messenger keeps popping up when you don't want it to, there is a fix. Go to the **Setup** button on the Instant Messenger sign-on screen, select the **Misc** tab, and uncheck **Start Instant Messenger when Windows starts**. Now the program will only load if you request it to do so.

■ ICQ (I-seek-you) is a most popular online instant messaging system. It is similar to AOL's Instant Messenger program. Once you have downloaded and installed ICQ on your PC, you can create a list of friends, family, business associates and others who also have ICQ installed on their PCs. ICQ uses this list to find your friends

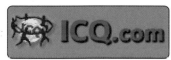

for you and tells you when they are signed onto the Net.

■ Don't forget to apply the usual security precautions when using instant messaging. Never run files sent to you by strangers, and for extra protection operate behind a firewall. You can download a free firewall from ZoneAlarm (www.zonealarm.com).

HOW TO TRACK PEOPLE DOWN

Wherever they are, you can often find clues to a person's location with the help of the Internet.

■ Despite all the hype, it's not that easy to find people on the Internet, especially if they don't want to be found. There's no problem with people active in business or the community. In

those cases a simple search using an engine such as Yahoo! or Google will generally turn up enough leads to enable you to track them down. E-mail address search sites have a similar problem. Most rely on participants posting their addresses, so again the directories can only put you in touch with those who want to be found.

■ There are many sites to help you track down individuals and businesses, and some of them are free. BT's online directory (www.www.bt.com/directory-enquiries) will find UK home phone numbers and addresses and Yell (www.yell.com) will find business and consumer contact details.

■ For a fee, information look-up services and online investigators will dig out personal details on almost anyone. Such services are not cheap, but this is probably the best solution if you don't have time to do all the leg work yourself. Just type 'missing persons', 'investigations' or 'private detective' into your favourite search engine.

■ When things get serious, and you really do need the service of a private enquiry agent, go to a site where you might expect some guarantee of integrity and reliability. Try the UK Investigation Group (www.ukig.co.uk), or the UK Research Bureau (www.private-investigator-uk.co.uk) both of which offer private and corporate investigation services.

■ Searching for phone numbers overseas? Try Infobel (www.infobel.com /teldir/) or WorldPages International Directories (www.worldpages.com) for global listings. For the USA, trace phone numbers and addresses with 411 (www.411.com), 411 Locate (www .411locate.com). Another alternative is Switchboard.com (www.switchboard.com).

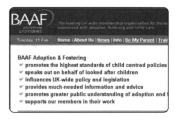

■ If it's Internet or e-mail addresses you're looking for, try one of the numerous search sites that offer help in tracking people down. Try

Email Addresses, a site listing e-mail directories (www.emailaddresses.com/email_find.htm), also, Yahoo! People Search (uk.people.yahoo.com) and WhoWhere? (www.whowhere.lycos.com).

■ If you're an adopted child who is searching for your birth parents, or if you want to find a child that you gave up for adoption, then the British Agencies for Adoption and Fostering (www.baaf.co.uk) is an ideal first port of call. The Department of Health adoption pages (www.doh. gov.uk/adoption), Family Records (www.familyrecords.gov.uk/topics/adoption.htm) and the Adoption Register for England and Wales (www.adoptionregister.net) are all also good information and resource sites.

■ If you'd like to track down your long-lost friends, the hugely popular Friends Renunited (www.friendsreunited.co.uk), with over 8 million registered members, is a great place to begin. Register with Friends Renunited to find old friends from primary and secondary schools, college, university, work, sports teams or clubs. If you pay a modest fee the site allows you to send your old friends e-mail messages.

■ **Learn the tricks** and techniques of the detective trade to make your search professional at How To Investigate (www.howtoinvestigate.com) and Investigate Anyone Online (www.investigateanyoneonline.com/basics.shtml).

■ **If you're concerned about global issues,** pester the politicians to take action! The easiest way to find goverment information and services online is at www.open.gov.uk. Tagish (www.tagish.co.uk/links) gives links to central and local government agencies and offices.

START YOUR OWN SEARCH
Use online resources to get your investigation off the ground. You'll soon be able to find almost anyone.

INVESTIGATE ANYONE ONLINE (www.investigateanyoneonline.com/basics.shtml)
A source of concepts, techniques and procedures for those involved in investigation and people tracing.

INFOBEL (www.infobel.com/teldir)
The Internet's most complete index of online international phone books.

INTERNET ADDRESS FINDER (www.iaf.net)
Claims to have nearly seven million listings. Search in languages other than English.

SHERLOCK@ (www.sherlockat.com)
Enlist the help of the world's greatest sleuth! The latest tips, tricks, and resources.

PEOPLESITE (www.peoplesite.com)
Alert thousands of pairs of eyes to help you look for your first love or a lost relative.

WHOWHERE? (www.whowhere.lycos.com)
Trace people and businesses worldwide by e-mail, phone (in the US) or Web presence.

■ **Search for servicemen and women** through Forces Reunited (www.forcesreunited.org.uk), a large database of UK forces and ex-forces personnel. Armed Forces Friends (www.armedforcesfriends.co.uk) offers a similar service, while Comrades and Colleagues (www.comradesandcolleagues.com) is an international database of servicemen and women. Service Pals (www.servicepals.com), endorsed by the Royal British Legion, is similarly dedicated to bringing service people together and has lots of useful links for finding military friends. It's also worth checking the Ministry of Defence site (www.mod.uk); look under their Freedom of Information link that connects to archives of personnel who served in the Army, Navy and Royal Air Force. The Commonwealth War Graves Commission (www.cwgc.org) is another resource.

■ **Are you worried about a missing friend?** Contact the National Missing Persons Helpline (www.missingpersons.org), the UK charity dedicated to helping missing persons and their family and friends. To conduct a search worldwide, register their name, details and a photograph at Missing Persons Throughout the World (www.mispers.com).

SHARE YOUR PHOTOS WITH FRIENDS

Put your photo gallery on the Net, share photos with friends and relatives and send prints without going through a photo developer.

■ **Sending photos by e-mail can be slow,** and large attachments can take ages to download. The alternative is an  Internet photo gallery, like Photofun (www.photofun.com), that lets you share your photos with anyone.

■ **Before you can share your photos** via the Web, you must have a digital image. Don't have a digital camera? You can still put your photos on the Internet. Many photo labs will scan images and transfer them onto a CD-ROM.

■ **The fastest way to upload images** from a PC to the Website is by client application. This is a program that runs on the PC and manages the uploading process for you. Many Web photo sharing and photofinishing sites provide free client application software.

■ **Don't be tempted to speed up** your upload time by reducing the resolution or applying more compression to the pictures. To get photo-quality prints from the images you display on the Web, upload the largest image file size you have. A large .jpg file only takes a few minutes to upload with a 56 Kbps modem.

■ **Another advantage of Web photo-sharing** is access to top-quality prints without a trip to the developer. At most photo-sharing sites, you can have hard copies made on the same photographic paper used for normal prints.

■ **Windows XP has a built-in Print Ordering Wizard.** Click on Order prints online in the left-hand column of My Pictures. The Online Print Ordering Wizard will start and offer you a choice of printing services to use.

▶ See also **Cameras join the digital revolution,** p. 44 and **Editing photographs,** p. 196.

Newsgroups

Despite the name, newsgroups are not essentially concerned with the latest events happening around the globe. Newsgroups are part of Usenet, the Internet's primary discussion area, where you can talk openly with experts in almost every field.

ACCESSING USENET

To access Usenet, you will need an Internet connection, a newsreader program, access to a news server, and an e-mail account that supports the protocol POP3. This means Web-based accounts like Hotmail, Juno or Excite won't work unless you've upgraded them to allow POP3 access. Netscape and Internet Explorer come with newsreaders already installed, and most ISPs (Internet service providers) maintain a news server as part of their access package. Call your ISP's support line or check their home page to find your news server address.

If you are using Outlook for your e-mail, then you will have to download a newsreader. There are a very large number of different programs available – try searching at

Tucows (www.tucows.com) for something suitable for your version of Windows. You can also access Usenet through one of the Web interfaces such as

Google Groups (groups.google. com) or Supernews (www. supernews.com).

Newsgroups are divided into topics according to a naming system known as a hierarchy. Hierarchies include alt., for alternative topics; biz., for business topics; soc., for social, cultural and religious topics, and many more. Newsgroup names are structured with the main topic first, down to the specific subject area. For example, the group rec.sport.baseball.info takes you to information all about baseball.

When you get a list of newsgroups from your news server, some of the names may contain a wildcard character (*). You might, for example, see alt.football.*. All this means is that there are several groups under the alt.football discussion hierarchy. To see them, just double-click the name (or click the plus sign to the left) and the list of groups will expand.

Finding newsgroups is no problem at all, but finding the ones that contain the information that you really want is not an easy task. If you want to access a particular discussion, there are search services that target newsgroups. Try Google Groups (groups.google.com/advanced_group_search). Tile.net (www.tile.net/news) also offers excellent newsgroup search engines.

If you use Outlook Express to subscribe to and use newsgroups, by default

it only downloads the header – or subject line – of the new messages. It does this to save time, so that you can browse through the headers. To see the message itself, you must click on the message header and press the spacebar. Within a few moments the message will be downloaded to your PC and displayed in the bottom panel of the Outlook Express window.

NEWSGROUP MESSAGING

Most newsgroups receive hundreds of new messages every day. When you are downloading them automatically that can quickly add up to thousands of messages. For this reason, Netscape Communicator allows you to

THE BIG EIGHT

Here are the eight main categories of newsgroups, known as the Big Eight.

Comp Lists computer science, technology and development newsgroups.

Humanities Discusses fine arts, literature, music, philosophy and the classics.

News Network news and Usenet itself.

Rec Shows a list of recreational pastimes, hobbies and arts newsgroups.

Sci Records and discusses scientific research and applied computer science.

Soc Covers social issues, such as history, culture, religion and lifestyle.

Talk Online live group conversation.

Misc Carries topics that don't fit into any of the above categories.

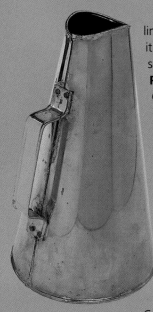

limit the number of messages it downloads automatically. To set this option, select **Edit ➔ Preferences** from the Communicator menu, which opens the Preferences dialogue box. From the Category menu, select **Mail & Groups ➔ Groups Server**, which opens the Groups Server window. Now check the **Ask Me Before Downloading More Than** option, then enter a number for the message limit. Before downloading any messages, Communicator will inform you when the amount of messages on the server exceeds the limit you've set and that way you can override your limit if you wish. To save your settings and close the Preferences box, click **OK**.

You can also download messages to read offline at a later time. To do this in Outlook Express, click on the **File** menu and

choose **Work Offline** before you connect to the Internet. Select a newsgroup that you have subscribed to in the left-hand column, right-click on it and go to **Properties**. In the **Synchronize** tab, check the **When synchronizing this newsgroup, download** box and then select the **New messages (headers and bodies)** option. Click **OK** and then go to **Tools ➔ Synchronize Newsgroup**. Outlook Express will connect to the Internet and collect all the new messages for the newsgroup. You can then disconnect and read the messages at your leisure.

In a newsgroup, raising a new topic is known as starting a thread. Any

replies to the initial message are then added to that thread. Many newsreaders will at first display a thread as a single line showing the subject of the original message. Clicking on a '+' or arrow next to the thread will reveal the rest of the messages that have been posted in it.

CREATING A USENET NEWSGROUP

Setting up a newsgroup is a little complicated, especially for beginners, because each Internet service provider decides for itself whether to carry any new newsgroup. Starting a newsgroup in one of the big eight hierarchies (comp., humanities., misc., news., rec., sci., soc., and talk.), as opposed to an alternate (alt.) group, requires that you adhere to some very specific rules in your application. Here's a simplified version of the procedure:

The discussion

1 Submit your initial outline to group-mentors @acpub.duke.edu for advice.
2 Post a request for discussion to news. announce.newsgroups, news.groups and any other newsgroups hosted by your server other than those related to the topic.
3 Put your proposal in the proper format. You can find this format on How to Format and Submit a New Group Proposal, which is posted regularly to the news.announce.newsgroups and news.groups hierarchies.

The vote

1 Usenet Volunteer Votetakers (UV.) take the request and post a call for votes in newsgroups related to the subject or type of group that you want to set up.
2 Voting occurs over a 21 to 31-day period, and only votes sent directly to the votetaker are counted. These include mass acknowledgments (a list of all names who are opposed to or in favour of the group) and are strictly nontransferable.

The result

1 There is a 5-day waiting period after voting ends. To be approved, there must be no serious objections to your newsgroup. There should be at least 100 more 'yes' votes than 'no' votes, and at least two-thirds of voters must be in favour of the new group.
2 If all the above requirements are met, news.announce.newsgroups send out a message to announce your new newsgroup.

For more on creating a newsgroup, read So You Want to Create an Alt Newsgroup at www.faqs.org/faqs/alt-creation-guide.

NEWSGROUP SITES
A useful selection of newsgroup resources, advice and software to set your mouse pointer in the right direction.

USENET REFERENCES (www.faqs.org/usenet)
A range of links to articles that will provide answers to many Usenet questions.

HOTBOT (www.hotbot.com)
Hotbot lets you search newsgroup postings for articles of interest.

NETIZENS: AN ANTHOLOGY (www.columbia.edu/~rh120)
A comprehensive history of Usenet, plus descriptions of what Usenet is, and speculations about its future.

TILE.NET NEWSGROUP (www.tile.net/news)
The place to view the latest newsgroups.

USENET HELP (www.ibiblio.org/ usenet-i/usenet-help.html)
An extensive collection of helpful guides to aspects of Usenet, including Netiquette, Usenet writing tips and instructions for creating your own newsgroup.

BINARY BOY (www.binaryboy.com)
Binary Boy is just one of many software packages designed to make searching and accessing newsgroups easier.

Glossary

A

A: The floppy disk drive on a PC. In speech, it is referred to as the A drive.
▶ See also **Floppy disk**.

Accessories Mini-programs, such as Calculator or Notepad, built into the Windows operating system to perform simple tasks.

Active window The window you are working in. To activate a window, click on it, and it will jump to the front of your screen, in front of any other open windows.
▶ See also **Window**.

ADSL Asymetric Digital Subscriber Line. A technology that allows you to access a high speed broadband internet connection on a normal telephone line.
▶ See also **Broadband**.

Alt key A key that gives commands when pressed in combination with other keys.

Application A program that performs specific kinds of tasks. For example, Microsoft Word is a word-processing application that is used to create text-based documents.

Archive To transfer files to a separate storage system, such as a Zip disk.

Arrow keys The four keys usually at the bottom right of the keyboard that move the cursor up, down, left and right.

Attachment A file, such as a picture or spreadsheet, sent with an e-mail message.

Audio file A file containing a digital recording of a sound. In Windows, audio files usually have the suffix .wav after their file name.
▶ See also **Digital**.

B

Back-up A duplicate copy of a file, made in case of loss or damage to the original file.

BIOS Basic Input/Output System. Instructions that control the computer's hardware at the most basic level. The BIOS tells the operating system which hardware to expect to come into operation, and how it is arranged.

Bit The smallest unit of computer memory. Bit is a contraction of binary digit. Its value can be only 1 or 0. All digital computers use the binary system to process data.

Bitmap An on-screen image made up of tiny dots or pixels.
▶ See also **Pixel**.

Bits per second (bps) A measurement of the speed at which data can be sent to or from a computer via a modem.

Boot or boot up To switch on the computer.

Broadband A term used for high speed internet connections capable of carrying data at a rates of more than 500 Mb/s.

Bug An accidental error or fault in a computer program. Bugs may cause programs to crash, which can lead to data loss.

Button An on-screen image that can be clicked on using the mouse. Clicking on a button performs a function, such as opening a dialogue box or confirming an action.

Byte A unit of computer memory, made up of eight bits. It takes one byte of memory to store a single character, such as a letter of the alphabet.
▶ See also **Bit**.

C

C: The hard disk of a PC, on which all programs and documents are stored. In speech, it is referred to as the C drive.

Cable modem A device that allows you to have a broadband internet connection delivered along the same wires used for a cable TV service.

Cache A section of high-speed memory that stores data recently used by the PC's processor, thereby increasing the speed at which that data can be accessed again.

Cell A small rectangular section of a spreadsheet or database, into which text or figures are entered. Click on a cell to make it active, ready for entering data.
▶ See also **Spreadsheet**.

CD-ROM Compact Disk Read Only Memory. A CD containing up to 650 Mb of data. Most software programs now come on CD-ROMs.

CD-R Compact Disc, Recordable. A CD that can have data permanently recorded onto it via a CD writer or 'burner'. CD-RW (Compact Disc,

Rewriteable) discs are similar but can be erased and rewritten to many times over.
▶ See also **Drive**.

Chip An electronic device that processes information at the most basic level within a computer. A processor chip carries out calculations and a memory chip stores data.

Click To press and release a mouse button once. This is how menu and dialogue box options and Toolbar buttons are selected.

Clip art Graphic images that can be inserted into text-based documents and then resized and manipulated in various ways.

Clipboard When text or an image is cut or copied from a document, it is stored on the Clipboard. The main Windows Clipboard stores only one piece of data at a time, regardless of its size – anything from a comma to this whole glossary. Each new Cut or Copy operation automatically overwrites the previous material on the Clipboard. Some programs, such as the Microsoft Office Suite, have their own clipboards that can hold more than one clipping at a time. These special clipboards can only be used within the program or suite that they belong to.
▶ See also **Cut**, **Copy** and **Paste**.

Close A command, usually found on the File menu, that shuts the active document, but not the program. A document can also be closed by clicking the close button, usually found in the top right-hand corner of its window.

CMOS Complementary Metal Oxide Semiconductor. An electronic memory chip that stores the computer's configuration settings, as well as the date and time.
▶ See also **Configuration**.

Compressed files Files that have been temporarily condensed to occupy less storage space and can be copied or downloaded in a fraction of the time it would otherwise take.
▶ See also **Zip file**.

Configuration The settings used to make sure that hardware or software runs as desired.

Control Panel Any adjustments made to your system or its settings are made through the Control Panel. For example, you can change the way your Desktop looks, add new hardware or alter your PC's sound output. To access the Control Panel in Windows XP, go to **Start ➜ Control Panel**.

Copy To make a duplicate of a file, image or section of text.

CPU Central Processing Unit. The electronic 'brain' at the heart of a PC, which carries out millions of arithmetic and control functions every second. The power of a CPU is usually defined by its speed in GigaHertz (GHz) or MegaHertz (MHz), which is the number of times it 'thinks' per second. For example, a 3 GHz CPU carries out 3000 million calculations per second.

Crash Your PC has crashed if it has stopped working, the screen has frozen, and there is no response to keyboard or mouse commands. A crash usually requires you to restart.

Cursor A marker, usually a flashing vertical line, that indicates where the next letter or digit to be typed will appear in the document.

Cursor keys ▶ See **Arrow keys**.

Cut To remove selected text and/or images to the Clipboard, where they are stored for later use.

D

Data Any information processed by, or stored on, a computer.

Database A program used for storing, organising, and sorting information. Each entry in a database is called a record, and each category in a record is called a field.

Default Settings and preferences automatically adopted by your PC for any program when no other settings are specified by the user.

Defragmenter A program that tidies files stored on the hard disk. When a file is saved to the hard disk, Windows may not be able to save all parts of it in the same place, so the elements of the file become fragmented. This makes the retrieval of the file much slower. The Disk Defragmenter program solves this problem by regrouping all related data in the same place.

Delete To remove a selected file, folder, image or piece of text completely. If you delete text or another item from a document, you can immediately undelete it using the **Edit ➜ Undo** function or the Undo Toolbar button.

Desktop When Windows has finished starting up, it presents you with a set of icons on screen.

The icons represent the items you would normally find in an office, such as files, folders and a waste basket. These icons, together with the Taskbar and Start button are known collectively as the Desktop.

▶ See also **Icon** and **Taskbar**.

Dialogue box A window that appears on the screen displaying a message of some sort from the program currently in use. The message usually asks for preferences or other information to be typed in by the user.

▶ See also **Prompt**.

Dial-up connection The process of accessing an ISP or another computer along a phone line.

▶ See also **Modem**.

Digital Data that exists in the form of binary numbers – a string of zeros and ones. Digital computers process only digital data.

Digital image An image stored in the form of digital data – zeros and ones – which can be transferred to hard disks or removable storage disks, displayed on screen or printed.

Disk A device for storing digital information. A hard disk is composed of a stack of rigid disks; a floppy disk has just one flexible disk.

Disk tools Programs that manage and maintain the hard disk. They can make sure that data is stored efficiently and that the hard disk runs at optimum speed.

Document A single piece of work created in a program. Also referred to as a file.

DOS Disk Operating System. The standard operating system for PCs before Windows.

▶ See also **Operating system**.

Dots per inch (dpi) The number of dots that a printer can print on one square inch of paper. The more dots, the greater the detail and the better the quality of the printout.

Double-click To press and release the left mouse button twice in quick succession.

Download To copy a file or program from another computer to your own. For example, when you collect e-mail from an Internet Service Provider, you are downloading it.

Drag A mouse action used to highlight text, reshape objects, or move an object or file. To move an object with the mouse pointer, for instance, click on it and keep the left mouse button held down. Move the mouse pointer and the object moves with it.

Drive A device that holds a disk. The drive has a motor that spins the disk, and a head that reads it – like the needle on a record player.

▶ See also **CD-ROM, Floppy Disk**.

Driver Software that translates instructions from Windows into a form that can be understood by a hardware device such as a printer.

DVD Digital Versatile Disc or Digital Video Disc. A CD-like disk that can store 4.7 Gb or more of information – several times more data than a CD-ROM. It can store an entire movie. Recordable DVD discs are available in a number of different formats. DVD-R and DVD+R can be written to only once. DVD-RAM, DVD-RW and DVD+RW can all be erased and rewritten to many times over.

DVI Digital Video Interface. A type of connector between a flatscreen LCD monitor and a computer that uses digital information to draw the picture, making for more accurate images than those from analogue monitor connections.

E

E-mail Electronic Mail. Messages sent from one computer to another through the Internet.

Error message A small window that appears on screen warning the user that a fault has occurred and, where appropriate, suggesting courses of action to remedy it.

Ethernet The type of connection used for most home and office networks. Depending on your network equipment, ethernet can transmit data at 10Mb/s, 100Mb/s (megabit ethernet) or 1000Mb/s (gigabit ethernet).

▶ See also **Network**.

Expansion card An add-on piece of hardware that fits into a PC and expands its functions – for example, a soundcard.

▶ See also **PCI slot**.

External hardware Additional computer equipment – such as a printer or scanner – that is attached by a cable to a PC.

▶ See also **Peripheral**.

F

Field A category of information in a database, such as name, address or telephone number.

File Any item stored on a computer, for example a program, a document or an image.

File extension A code that appears at the end of a file name to indicate what type of file it is. Extensions are usually three letters, but can be more or less (see list below).

File format The way in which files created by different programs are saved. This differs from program to program, so that one program may have difficulty reading files created by another. Common file format extensions are:

Text	.asc .doc .html .msg .txt .wpd
Image	.bmp .eps .gif .jpg .pict .psp .tif
Sound	.au .mid .ra .snd .wav
Video	.avi .mov .mpg .qt
Compressed	.arc .arj .gz .hqx .sit .tar .z .zip
Program	.bat .com .exe

FireWire Apple Computer's name for a high-speed type of connection with the technical name IEEE 1394. A digital video camera can connect to a PC via a FireWire cable. Sony's name for the same standard is iLink.

Find A command in a program that searches a file for specified information, such as a phrase.
▶ See also **Search**.

Floppy disk A portable data storage device. Each disk can hold up to 1.44 MB of information. Often used to back up data from the hard disk.
▶ See also **Hard disk**.

Folder An electronic storage compartment used to keep related files and documents – such as a collection of images – in one place on a disk.

Font A specific point size, style and set of characters for a typeface (e.g. 12 point Arial Bold). A typeface is a particular type design.

Format To establish the appearance of a document – for example, its typography, layout, shape and so on.

Freeware Programs, usually produced by hobby programmers, for which users do not pay a fee. Freeware can be downloaded from the Internet.
▶ See also **Shareware**.

Function keys Keys (labelled F1, F2 etc, up to generally F12 or F15) found at the top of the keyboard. They perform special tasks, depending on which program is being used. For instance, Shift+F7 in Word will call up the Thesaurus.

G

Gigabyte (GB) A unit of memory capacity. A single gigabyte is 1000 megabytes which is equivalent to almost 200 copies of the Bible.

Graphics Pictures, photographs, illustrations, clip art and any other type of image.

GIF Graphics Interchange Format. A common file format (.gif extension), used for storing images and bitmapped colour graphics, especially those found on the Internet.

H

Hard disk A computer's high-speed storage device. It contains the operating system, the programs and all created files. The hard disk is referred to as the C drive or hard drive.

Hardware The physical parts of a computer (as opposed to its software), including the CPU, monitor, keyboard and mouse.

Header The area at the top of a page in a document. Text entered in the header appears on every page of the document. The same area at the bottom of a page is called a Footer.

Help key Usually the F1 key. It is pressed to access advice and information on how to perform the task the user is currently engaged in.

Highlight To select a word, a section of text or a group of cells in a spreadsheet by clicking the mouse and dragging the cursor over them.

I

Icon A graphic representation of a file or a function, which is designed to be easily recognisable as the item it represents. For example, the printer icon on the Toolbar accesses the print function.

Import To bring in and use an element, such as text, a picture or clip art image, from another file into the active document.

Inkjet printer A printer that works by squirting tiny drops of ink onto the surface of the paper. Inkjets are by far the most common type of printer used in homes or small offices.

Install To copy a program onto the hard disk and then set it up so it is ready for use. Programs are usually installed from CD-ROMs, but can be downloaded from the Internet.

Internet Millions of computers throughout the world linked together by telephone and cable lines. Computer users can communicate with each other and exchange information over the Internet with a phone connection to their Internet Service Provider.

ISP Internet Service Provider. A company that provides customers with their connection to the Internet (compare OSP).

J

JavaScript A programming language that allows designers to create websites with greatly enhanced interactivity.

JPEG Joint Photographic Experts Group. A file format (.jpg or .jpeg extension) used for storing images that have been compressed.
▶ See also **Compressed files**.

K

Keyboard shortcut A method of issuing a command with a combination of keystrokes. For expert users, this is quicker than using a mouse.

Kilobyte (KB) A unit of memory capacity. A single kilobyte is equivalent to 1000 bytes. A short letter created in Word uses about 20 Kb.
▶ See also **Gigabyte, Megabyte**.

L

Landscape ▶ See **Orientation**.

Laptop A portable computer.

Laser printer A printer that uses a laser beam to etch images onto a drum and then transfers the image to paper. The reproduction quality is usually higher than with an inkjet printer.
▶ See also **Inkjet printer**.

Launcher A window in some software suites, such as Microsoft Works, through which the suite's various programs are opened.

Logging on The process of accessing computers, files or Websites using a password or other instructions or procedures.

M

Maximise To increase the size of a window so that it fills the entire screen. The Maximize button is the middle button in the set of three in the top right-hand corner of a window. Once it has been used, it becomes a Restore button. Click on it to restore the window to its original size again.

Megabyte (MB) A unit of memory capacity. A single megabyte is 1000 kilobytes, which is equivalent to a 400-page novel.

Memory A computer's capacity for storing information (not a reference to its disk space).
▶ See also **RAM** and **ROM**.

Menu bar The line of menu options that runs along the top of a window. When a menu is selected, its entire list of options (often a drop-down menu) is displayed.

MIDI Musical Instrument Digital Interface. A universal standard language that allows specially adapted musical instruments to communicate with computers. MIDI cables are required to connect the instrument to the computer.

Minimise To reduce a window to a button on the Taskbar. The Minimize button is the left button in the set of three in the top right-hand corner of a window. To restore the window to the screen, click on its button on the Taskbar.

Modem A device that converts digital signals from a computer into analogue signals that can be transmitted by phone, then reconverted by another modem into the original digital data.

Monitor The viewing screen on which you see your computer's files. Images are made up of thousands of tiny dots.
▶ See also **DVI**.

Motherboard The circuit board that houses a PC's central processing unit (see CPU), some memory, and slots into which expansion cards can be installed.
▶ See also **Chip, Memory** and **Expansion card**.

Mouse pointer A small arrow on screen that moves when the mouse is moved. Other representations of the pointer – depending on the program being used and the type of action being carried out – include a pointing hand, a pen and a cross. When you click in a text document, the cursor will appear.
▶ See also **Cursor**.

Multimedia Sound, images, animated graphics, text and video are all different types of media – means of communicating. A single document using more than one of these can be said to be a multimedia document. A computer able to provide and handle different media is generally referred to as a multimedia computer.

My Computer An icon found on any PC Desktop running Windows. Click on the icon to open a window that gives access to all the computer hardware present in the system. These might include the hard drive (C:), floppy drive (A:), CD-ROM drive (usually D:), printer, and tools for monitoring and adjusting the system set-up.
▶ See also **Icon**.

My Documents A folder icon located on the Desktop (or in the Start Menu in Windows XP) of any PC running the Windows operating system. It represents a storage location for files that users have created themselves. Click on the icon to open the folder.

N

Network Several computers and printers connected to one another so that they can share files and messages.
▶ See also **Ethernet, WiFi**.

O

Online The status of a computer that is actively connected to the Internet. Sometimes also used as a general term for people who are able to connect to the Internet.
▶ See also **Internet**.

Open To look inside a file or folder so that you can view its contents. To open a file or folder, either double-click on its icon, right-click on it and select Open from the pop-up menu, or select it and go to **File ➜ Open**.

Operating system The software that controls the running of a computer, allowing, for example, programs to communicate with hardware devices such as printers. Windows is the most popular operating system for PCs.
▶ See also **DOS, Windows**.

Orientation An option available when creating a document. Users can choose to set up a page as either landscape (of greater width than height) or portrait (of greater height than width), depending on how they want the final version of the document to appear.

OSP Online service provider. A company that provides not only Internet access (see ISP), but also additional content, such as shopping, entertainment and leisure channels, chatrooms, and newsgroups. The biggest and best known OSP is AOL (America OnLine).

P

Page break The point at which one page ends and another begins. In Microsoft Word, a page break can be inserted by pressing the Ctrl and Enter keys at the same time.

Parallel port A socket at the rear of a computer that allows you to connect a printer.

Paste The insertion into a document of text or other data that has been cut or copied.

PC-compatible Software or hardware that will work on a standard PC.

PCI slot A spare space inside a PC for installing extra expansion cards, such as a soundcard or graphics card.

Peripheral A device, such as a scanner or CD burner, that can be connected to a PC but is not vital to its function.

Pixel An individual dot on a computer screen. The number of pixels horizontally and vertically on the screen determines the level of detail and the quality of the image that can be displayed. This can be set and altered by the user.

Plug-ins Programs that are needed to open and run certain files, such as video clips or sound files, for example. Websites often provide plug-ins for visitors to download, so that they are able to view everything the site has to offer.
▶ See also **Download**.

Point size Measurement used for typefaces. For example, the type on this page is 9.5 point; newspaper headlines are usually between 36 and 72 point.

Port A socket at the rear of a computer that allows users to connect a monitor, printer or a peripheral device, such as a scanner.

Portrait ▶ See **Orientation**.

Primary key In a database this is the main category by which you generally sort your database entries.

Printer driver A piece of software that enables Windows to communicate with the printer connected to your PC.
▶ See also **Driver**.

Print Preview An on-screen display that shows users exactly how the active document will look when it is printed.

Processor The central processing unit (CPU) at the heart of every computer.
▶ See also **Chip, CPU**.

Program Software that allows the user to interact with the computer's hardware to perform a specific type of task. For instance, a word-processing program allows the user to direct the computer in all aspects of handling and presenting text.

Prompt A window that appears to remind users that additional information is required.
▶ See also **Dialogue box**.

Properties The attributes of a file or folder, such as its creation date and format. To access the Properties window, right-click on an item and select Properties from the menu that appears.

R

RAM Random Access Memory. Memory chips used for the temporary storage of information, such as the currently active file.

Record An individual entry in a database comprising several categories of information. For example, an address book database comprises entries – or records – each of which has a name, address and telephone number.

Recycle Bin A Desktop feature that allows you to delete files. To delete a file completely, drag it onto the Recycle Bin, right-click, and select Empty Recycle Bin from the menu.

Registry This is Windows' own database of instructions and settings that is the operating system's main reference for the effective running of the computer.

Reset button A button on a PC that allows users to restart if the computer freezes and refuses to respond to any commands. The Reset button should only be used as a last resort.

Resolution The degree of detail on a screen or a printed document. It is measured in dots per inch (dpi). The more dots per square inch, the greater the level of detail.

Right-click To press and release the right mouse button once. Most commonly used to display a pop-up context menu.

ROM Read Only Memory. Memory chips used by the computer for storing basic details about the PC, such as BIOS.

Router A device that allows you to share a single internet connection (usually broadband) between two or more computers.
▶ See also **Broadband**.

Run command A Windows feature that allows you to type in the name of the program you want to use, or the DOS command you want to execute. To use, go to **Start ➜ Run**.

S

Save To copy a document to the computer's hard disk for future use. To do this, press Ctrl+S on the keyboard, click on the Save Toolbar button, or go to **File ➜ Save**.

Save As A way of saving a file under a different name or format. If the file was previously saved under a different name or format, that version will remain unchanged. This is useful for saving an edited file, while still keeping the original.

Scanner A device for converting images on paper or film into electronic images that can then be manipulated and reproduced by a PC.
▶ See also **Digital, Digital image**.

Screensaver A picture or animation that appears on screen when a PC is left idle for a specified period of time.

Scroll To move through the contents of a window or menu vertically or horizontally.

Search A utility built in to Windows that looks for files on your computer that match your chosen criteria. You can search for files by name, size, creation date or type. In early versions of Windows the utility was called 'Find'.
▶ See also **Find**.

Search engines Huge databases on the Internet that are used to locate Websites relevant to specified search criteria. Users can look for either key words or phrases or for categories, then subcategories.

Select To choose a file, folder, image, text or other item, by clicking on it or highlighting it, before manipulating it. For example, you must select some text before you can style it.

Serial port A socket at the rear of a computer that allows one of a number of peripheral devices, including a modem, to be connected. Most PCs have two serial ports, identified as COM1 and COM2.
▶ See also **Parallel port**.

Shareware Programs, or reduced versions of programs, that can be sampled free for a limited period of time. Users must then purchase the program if they are going to continue using it.

Shortcut An icon on the Desktop that links to a file, folder, or program stored on the hard disk. It is created to provide quicker access to the file, and looks identical to the icon of the linked item, except that it has a small arrow in the bottom left-hand corner.

Software Programs that allow users to perform specific functions, such as to write letters. Jasc Paint Shop Pro and Microsoft Word are examples of popular software.

Software suite A collection of programs that come in a single package, often supplied when a PC is bought. For example, Microsoft Office is a software suite that includes word processing, database and spreadsheet programs.

Soundcard A device that lets users record, play and edit sound files. It fits into an expansion slot on the motherboard.
▶ See also **Sound file**.

Sound file A file containing audio data. To hear the sound, double-click on the file (you will need loudspeakers and a soundcard).

Spreadsheet A document for storing and calculating numerical data. Spreadsheets are used mainly in businesses for financial planning and accounting purposes.

Start button The button on the far left of the Taskbar, through which users can access the Start menu and its options, which include Programs and Help. The Start button is sometimes referred to as the Windows button.

Status bar A bar along the bottom of program windows, that gives users information about the document being worked on. In Internet Explorer, the Status bar shows the program's progress as it downloads a Webpage.

Styling Establishing the appearance of the contents of a file. For example, by making the text bold (heavier-looking and more distinct) or italic (slanting to the right), or by changing its colour and size.
▶ See also **Format**.

System software The software that operates the PC, managing its hardware and programs. DOS was the original system software for PCs, but Windows is now the most popular.
▶ See also **Operating system**.

System unit The box-shaped part of the PC that contains the hard disk, the CPU, memory and sockets for connections to peripheral devices.

T

Tab A function used for setting and presetting the position of text. Also a panel of related information within a dialogue box.

Tab key A key on the keyboard (next to the Q key) used to tabulate text, to move between cells in spreadsheets, or to move from one database field to the next.

Taskbar A bar usually situated along the bottom of the screen in Windows that displays the Start button and buttons for all the programs and documents that are currently open. The Taskbar can be moved to any of the four edges of the screen, as required, by clicking on it and dragging it to a new location.

Task Wizard ▶ See **Wizard**.

TIFF Tagged Image File Format. A file format (.tif or .tiff extension) used for storing bitmapped graphic images, such as scans.
▶ See also **Bitmap**.

Template A format for saving a document, such as a letterhead, the basic elements of which you want to use in future documents. When you open a template, a copy of it appears for you to work on, but the template itself remains unaltered for further use.

Tile To reduce in size a group of open windows and then arrange them so that they can all be seen on screen together at once.

Toolbar A bar or window containing clickable buttons used to issue commands or access functions. For example, spreadsheet programs have a Toolbar containing buttons that are clicked on to perform calculations or add decimal places. Other Toolbars let you make changes to pictures or drawings.
▶ See also **Taskbar**.

Typeface ▶ See **Font**.

U

Undo A function provided in some programs that allows you to reverse the task most recently carried out. Some programs allow you to undo a a number of tasks, one after the other. Go to **Edit** → **Undo** or click on the Undo Toolbar button.

Uninstall To remove programs from the PC's hard disk. It is always best to use an uninstaller program to remove a piece of software from your PC, to ensure that hidden program files and settings are properly deleted. Software is available for uninstalling programs that do not contain their own in-built uninstall option.

Upgrade To improve the performance or specification of a PC by adding new hardware components such as a higher capacity disk drive, a faster graphics card or more RAM chips.

URL Uniform Resource Locater. A standard style used for all Website addresses. The first part of the URL, such as 'www.yahoo.com', indicates the location of a computer on the Internet. Anything that follows – such as '/myhome/mypage.htm' – gives the location of a particular file on the computer's storage disks.

USB Universal Serial Bus. A hardware connector that allows users to add devices such as mouse, modems and keyboards to a computer without having to close down and restart. USB 2.0 is a version of the standard capable of very fast data transfer rates – up to 480Mb/s.
▶ See also **Hardware**.

Utilities Software that assists in housekeeping or troubleshooting computer functions, such as uninstalling and virus checking. Popular suites of utilities are sold by companies such as Norton.

V

View Options provided in many programs through which users can change the way a file is displayed on the screen. For example, users can choose to see a Word document in Normal, Web Layout, Print Layout or Outline View.

Virus A program designed to damage or interfere with a computer system. Viruses can be spread through floppy disks or through programs downloaded from the Internet.

W

Wallpaper An image or pattern used as the background on the Desktop. One of the features to help users personalise their machines.

WiFi Popular name for IEEE 802.11, the standard used for linking computers together in wireless networks in homes and offices. Data is transferred via radio waves at speeds of up to 54Mb/s.

Window Each program or file on your PC can be viewed and worked on in its own self-contained area of screen called a window. Several windows can be open at once on the Desktop.

Windows Microsoft's very popular operating system for PCs, which allows users to run many programs at once and open files on screen enclosed by frames called windows.
▶ See also **Operating system**.

Windows Explorer A program that allows users to view the contents of a PC's hard disk – and other disks – in a single window.
▶ See also **Hard disk**.

Wizard A tool within a program that guides users through an unfamiliar procedure.

WordArt A graphic text image that can be imported into a document for decorative effect.

Word processing Text based operations on the PC, such as letter writing.

World Wide Web A part of the Internet which is composed of millions of linked Web pages, that can be viewed using browser programs such as Netscape Navigator or Microsoft Internet Explorer.
▶ See also **Internet**.

Z

Zip disk A portable storage device that is capable of storing up to 750 MB of information. Zip disks require a special Zip drive.

Zip file A file that has been compressed for transfer or storage with WinZip or another compression program. The term is not related to Zip drives or disks.

Zoom To enlarge or reduce an area of a document for ease of viewing.

Index

Acknowledgments

1001 Computer Hints & Tips
was originated by Planet Three Publishing
Network, Northburgh House, 10 Northburgh
Street, London EC1V 0AT for
The Reader's Digest Association of Pleasantville,
New York, USA

**This edition adapted by Purpleman
Publishing (www.purpleman.co.uk)**
from the Australian and New Zealand edition,
prepared for Reader's Digest (Australia) Pty Ltd
by Capricorn Press Pty Ltd, 11 Smail Street,
Ultimo, NSW 2007, Australia

Project Editor Tom Ruppel
Art Editor Paul Cooper
Editor Jennifer Banks
Proofreader Tim Gow
Design Assistant Kim Devlin
Contributors Mark Roberts, Tim Gow

For the Reader's Digest, London
Editor Alison Candlin
Art Editor Louise Turpin
Technical Consultant Tony Rilett
Editorial Assistant Rachel Weaver
Pre-press Accounts Manager Penny Grose

Reader's Digest General Books, London
Editorial Director Cortina Butler
Art Director Nick Clark
Executive Editor Julian Browne
Managing Editor Alastair Holmes
Picture Resource Manager Martin Smith
Style Editor Ron Pankhurst
Book Production Manager Fiona McIntosh
Pre-press Manager Howard Reynolds

Origination Colour Systems Limited, London
Printing and Binding Mateu Cromo, Madrid

1001 Computer Hints & Tips
was published by Reader's Digest Association
Limited, London

First edition Copyright © 2003
The Reader's Digest Association Limited,
11 Westferry Circus,
Canary Wharf,
London E14 4HE

We are committed to both the quality of our
products and the service we provide to our
customers. We value your comments, so
please feel free to contact us on 08705
113366 or via our Website at:
www.readersdigest.co.uk
If you have any comments or suggestions
about the content of our books, email us at:
gbeditorial@readersdigest.co.uk

Copyright © 2003 Reader's Digest Association
Far East Limited
Philippines Copyright © 2003 Reader's Digest
Association Far East Limited

Every effort has been made to establish
ownership of copyright material depicted in
this book. All queries regarding copyright
issues should be directed to Martin Smith at:
martin_smith@readersdigest.co.uk

We would like to thank the following
organisations for their assistance in producing
this book:
Adobe, Agfa, Casio, Corel, Epson, Filemaker,
Fuji, Hewlett Packard, IBM, Logitech,
Microsoft, Microtech, Sony, Superhire,
Symantec, Texas Instruments, Twinhead, Yepp

Oracle code	250005345H
Concept code	UK1381/IC-AU
Book code	400-091-01
ISBN	0 276 42790 4